DOS:

POWER USER'S GUIDE

DOS:
POWER USER'S GUIDE

Kris Jamsa

Osborne **McGraw-Hill**
Berkeley, California

Osborne **McGraw-Hill**
2600 Tenth Street
Berkeley, California 94710
U.S.A.

For information on translations and book distributors outside of the U.S.A., write to
Osborne **McGraw-Hill** at the above address.

A complete list of trademarks appears on page 909.

DOS: POWER USER'S GUIDE

   34567890 DODO 898

ISBN 0-07-881310-7

To Debbie

For the places we've been,
    feelings we've shared,
and the lifetime we'll spend together.

Contents

Preface   xiii

1:   **Developing the Power User Mindset**   **1**
The History of DOS   3
Learning to Ask Questions   4
Understanding the Role of Microsoft Windows   6
Developing the Concurrent Mindset   7
Resource Management   9
Sharing the CPU   10
Memory Management   16
Real Versus Protected Mode Processing   22
OS/2 and DOS   23
How to Prepare   23

2:   **Exploiting Batch Procedures**   **25**
Rationale   25
Sequential Batch Processing   29
Terminating a Batch Procedure   34
Basic Batch Commands   37
Conditional Batch Processing   47
Iterative Processing   55
Passing Parameters to DOS Batch Procedures   58
Removing the Batch File Diskette   63
Changing Directories   64
Invoking Nested Batch Procedures   65
Recursive Batch Functions   66
AUTOEXEC.BAT   67
Batch File Processing under OS/2   68
AUTOEXEC.BAT Versus STARTUP.CMD   71
CMD File Extensions   72
Named Parameters   72
DETACH (Running Background Commands)   73

3: DOS Redirection and Pipe Operators　　　　77

I/O Redirection　　77
The DOS Pipe　　85
Using I/O Redirection to Improve User Interface　　89
File Handles　　91
Programming DOS I/O Redirection　　92
OS/2 I/O Redirection　　100

4: DOS System Configuration　　　　105

System Configuration　　105
DOS 3.3 Parameters　　126
OS/2 System Configuration Parameters　　134

5: Managing DOS Directories　　　　155

Getting Started with DOS Subdirectories　　155
Accessing Subdirectory Files　　172
Locating Files by Using TREE　　175
Defining an Execution Path　　177
Defining a Data File Path by Using APPEND　　180
Improving System Performance　　182
Substituting Long Path Names with a Drive Letter　　183
Joining a Drive to Your Directory Structure　　185
Rules of Thumb　　187
Manipulating Directories from Within Applications　　188
OS/2 Directory Manipulation　　189

6: DOS System Services　　　　191

8088 Registers　　192
INT 21H　　194
ASCIIZ　　199
Other High-Level Languages　　272
OS/2 System Services　　278

7: DOS Programming Concerns　　　　313

Critical Error Handling　　314
Available Disk Space　　318
Volume Labels　　320
Exit-Status Processing　　322
Creating Unique Files　　326
Video Display　　328

File Attributes   330
CTRL-BREAK Processing   335
Available Memory   336
Spawn   337
Spooled Printing   340
Object Code Libraries   342

8: Addressing the PC   349
Physical Memory   350
Memory Mapping   367
OS/2 Memory Addressing   377

9: Maximizing Command-Line Processing   387
Command-Line Basics   388
Command-Line Processing from C   390
Command-Line Processing from Turbo Pascal   393
DOS Command-Line Processing   399
Supporting Command-Line Parameters and I/O Redirection   407

10: Disk Structure   413
Disk Structure   414
Sectors, Tracks, and Sides   419
Once Around the Track   421
Disk Space Allocation   428
File Allocation Table (FAT)   433
Directory Entries   442
File Deletion   447
Sure-Kill Deletions   460
Reading a Directory File   461
Extra Features   471
How Fixed Disks Differ   476
Fixed-Disk Architecture   480
What Happens at Boot Time   482

11: How the DOS FORMAT Command Really Works   485
Hard Disk Concerns   501

12: Utilizing the DOS Environment   503
Examining the Environment   508
Utilizing Environment Entries   517
OS/2 Environment Issues   519

13: Breaking Apart DOS Data Structures   **525**

DOS Memory Map   525
OS/2 Memory Map   532
Mapping the Boot Record   535
Program-Segment Prefix   540
Media Descriptor Information   543
File Date and Time Stamps   546

14: DOS File Operations   **549**

File Control Blocks   551
File Handles   552
Random-Access Files   569
Advanced File Manipulation Routines   602
DOS Wild-Card Characters   606
OS/2 Directions   624

15: Memory-Resident Programs   **643**

DOS Memory-Resident Programs   649
Extending the Type-Ahead Buffer   651
Capturing the Print-Screen Interrupt   655
Memory-Resident Alarm Clock   658
Subliminal-Message Processing   659
Screen Save   665
Word of Warning   669
OS/2 Impacts   669

16: OS/2 Overview   **673**

The Need   673
Multitasking   675
Real Versus Protected Mode   678
Virtual Memory   679
Device Virtualization   686
System Requirements   687
System Structure   689
Interprocess Communication   692
Scheduling   697
Threads   698
Networking Future   700
Presentation Manager   701

17: OS/2 Programming Considerations   705
   A Simple Example   705
   BIND   710
   EXE Structure   712
   Module-Definition File (DEF)   719
   BIND Processing Capabilities   724
   MAKE   725
   OS/2 Applications   728

18: OS/2 Command Summary   743
   OS/2 Sessions   743
   CMD.EXE versus COMMAND.COM   747
   OS/2 Commands   749
   Batch Processing   792
   OS/2 I/O Redirection Operators   793

19: OS/2 Questions and Answers   797
   Identifying the Need   798
   Getting Started   801
   Philosophy   804
   Specifics   807
   General Questions   846

A: ASCII Codes   851

B: DOS Commands   855

   Index   911

Preface

Thousands of people every day start using DOS for the first time. Today, over 10 million people use DOS, making it quite possibly the most influential software package ever.

Many books have been written about DOS. These books have taught us the syntax of DOS commands and have given us hints of the inner workings of DOS. Although these books have been critical to our success with DOS, they have taken us only so far. Unlike the other books before it, *DOS: Power User's Guide* takes you beyond the basics, past the advanced commands, to the secrets of the inner workings of DOS. In this book you will implement the majority of DOS commands, enhance the functionality of many, learn tricks the "masters" use to write memory-resident pop-up programs, learn to use the DOS system services from high-level languages, and even develop file recovery programs. For the first time, you will perform tasks that you have only heard about in the past. Upon completion of this book, you will truly qualify as a "DOS power user."

OS/2 AND DOS

OS/2 is the new multitasking operating system for the 80286 and 80386. Unlike DOS, which executes only one program at a time, OS/2 allows you to execute several programs simultaneously. As a DOS power user, you will be at the forefront of OS/2 use and application development. This text gives you a detailed description of OS/2 and its capabilities and implementation. The end of each chapter briefly examines the impact of OS/2 on the topic discussed in that chapter. In essence, this is also a complete guide to OS/2.

WHAT'S INSIDE

Each chapter discusses a unique DOS topic from the "power user's" perspective. In many cases, the discussion is accompanied by C or Pascal routines that utilize or implement the specific topic. Unlike other texts that only discuss a concept's implementation, this book gives you complete source code.

The chapters are organized as follows:

Chapter 1 presents the power user mindset. It discusses the goals of the text and introduces OS/2.

Chapter 2 discusses DOS batch processing considerations. In this chapter you will learn how to use batch parameters, named parameters, each of the DOS and OS/2 batch processing commands, and how to create recursive batch procedures.

Chapter 3 introduces I/O redirection via the DOS pipe and I/O redirection operators. You will learn how to write C and Pascal programs that support I/O redirection. In addition, you will learn how OS/2 increases your command-line processing capabilities.

Chapter 4 discusses the impact of each DOS CONFIG.SYS entry and the subtleties of disk buffering and file handles. Each of the OS/2 CONFIG.SYS entries are examined in detail. By the end of this chapter you should have a strong grasp of OS/2 multitasking.

Chapter 5 examines the DOS directory structure and its manipulation, capabilities, and rationale. You will learn how to perform each of the DOS directory manipulation commands from within your high-level language programs.

Chapter 6 discusses the DOS system services. DOS provides a very powerful built-in set of procedures called *system services* that you can access from within your application programs. Each service is presented with a high-level language implementation. The chapter concludes by examining OS/2 system services.

Chapter 7 discusses programming considerations that can directly improve the quality of your applications.

Chapter 8 examines memory addressing under DOS and OS/2. In this chapter you will learn how to peek and poke values to and from specific memory locations. This chapter discusses OS/2 virtual memory in detail.

Chapter 9 looks at DOS command-line processing. The chapter discusses how command-line arguments increase the generic nature of your programs, how to access command-line arguments from C and Pascal, and finally, where DOS stores the command line. If you program in FORTRAN, this chapter teaches you how to develop a powerful command-line parser that allows you to access command-line arguments from within your FORTRAN programs.

Chapter 10 looks at the DOS disk layout. You will examine sectors, tracks, and cylinders. In addition, you will learn how to read directories, the FAT, and the system boot sector. This chapter shows you how to undelete files.

Chapter 11 examines the DOS FORMAT command and its capabilities and implementation. You will look at several low-level ROM-BIOS services that allow you to format tracks on a disk.

Chapter 12 examines the DOS environment. The chapter teaches you how to access environment entries and discusses the advantages that the DOS environment provides to your programs.

Chapter 13 looks at DOS data structures. You will learn how to decode the DOS date and time formats and the boot sector while examining the DOS and OS/2 memory maps.

Chapter 14 discusses files — everything that you could ever want to do with files. You will write programs that modify file attributes, perform complex directory listings, and expand the processing capabilities of each DOS file manipulation command. This chapter also teaches you how to use low-level services to write a complete ISAM database management system.

Chapter 15 is for fun! In this chapter you will learn how to write memory-resident programs. The chapter shows how to capture DOS and timer interrupts in order to develop sophisticated programs. Among the Chapter 15 routines is a program that displays subliminal messages to the user.

Chapter 16 begins a four-chapter discussion on OS/2. This chapter presents an overall description of OS/2's capabilities.

Chapter 17 examines OS/2 from a programmer's perspective. In this chapter you will create protected-mode programs and migrate them to DOS via compatibility-mode executables. This chapter examines the OS/2 API in great detail, implementing several complete programs.

Chapter 18 is an OS/2 command reference. Complete examples accompany each command.

Chapter 19 concludes the OS/2 discussion by presenting a series of questions and answers. This chapter provides a detailed look at OS/2, laying the foundation for your "OS/2 mindset."

Appendix A provides an ASCII chart.

Appendix B provides a complete DOS command reference.

DISKETTE PACKAGE

The programming examples in *DOS: Power User's Guide* are available on disk. The diskette package is shipped in a solid container that is ideal for carrying your diskettes to school or the office. In addition to the routines presented in the text, the diskette package contains TECH-HELP, an on-line technical reference for each DOS system service, data structure, and parameters. TECHHELP eliminates the need for technical reference manuals.

DOS: Power User's Guide
Diskette Order Form

Enclosed is my check or money order for $32.45 ($29.95 plus $2.50 shipping and handling). (Foreign orders, send $7.50 for airmail shipping and handling.)

Name _____

Address _____

City _____ State _____ ZIP _____

Make checks payable to Kris Jamsa Software, Inc.

Kris Jamsa Software, Inc.
P.O. Box 26031
Las Vegas, Nevada 89126

Osborne **McGraw-Hill** assumes NO responsibility for this offer. This is solely an offer of Kris Jamsa Software, Inc., and not of Osborne **McGraw-Hill**.

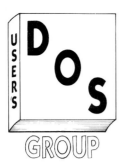

DOS USER'S GROUP
P.O. Box 26601
Las Vegas, Nevada 89126
(702) 363-3419

U.S. Members $25.00 annual fee
Canada, Mexico, and Europe $35.00 annual fee

Quarterly newsletter which includes:

DOS Command Tutorials
— Basic overview
— Tips, tricks, and traps
— Source code for implementation

DOS Customization Hints
— Thorough examination of CONFIG.SYS entries
— Tips, tricks, and traps

Question and Answer Forum
— Large user base of experience

Third Party Software Reviews and Discounts
— Indepth reviews of major software packages
— Discounts to user group members

Turbo Pascal Secrets
— Low level DOS programming techniques from Turbo Pascal

Programming Hints
— Linker and Librarian commands
— Tips, tricks, and traps

MS Windows
— User perspective
— Programmer prospective

OS/2
— General overview
— Programmer information
— Advanced concepts

Batch Processing
— DOS batch commands
— Tips, tricks, and traps

The DOS User's Group is an international user group consisting of members who are:

Novice Users, Programmers, Buyers, Manufacturers, Developers, Authors, MIS Directors

each of whom want to maximize their knowledge of DOS, MS Windows, and OS/2.

$25.00 Annual Membership Fee (U.S.)
$35.00 Annual Membership Fee (Canada - Europe)

☐ Money Order
☐ Personal Check

Name_____

Address_____

City_____ State_____ Zip_____

1: Developing
the Power User
Mindset

DOS power users are a unique breed. Having conquered the elementary concepts of DOS, they desire a mastery of the software that provides them with the interface to their computer system and application software (see Figure 1 - 1). DOS power users are inquisitive. They want to know exactly what makes DOS tick and, in most cases, how to make it tick faster. Most DOS power users are programmers, but that is not a requirement. Many successful consultants have risen to the top of their fields simply by understanding the flow of DOS well enough to integrate third-party software and hardware packages. Whether they are in it for wealth, conquest, knowledge, or just for fun, DOS power users share a common goal: the most thorough understanding of DOS that they can achieve.

This chapter begins by laying the foundation to build upon to become a DOS power user. Next, the chapter examines the development of DOS since its introduction in 1981: the reasons behind the revisions and the lessons that can be learned from them.

The chapter then prepares you for your first steps under OS/2. As DOS power users, you will be at the forefront of an exciting era in

1

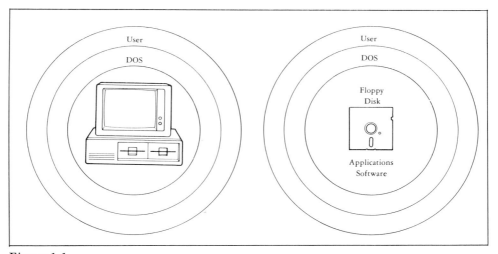

Figure 1-1.

Interface between power user and
applications

microcomputer history. Although still in its infancy, OS/2 represents
the first step toward taking the microcomputer from a home computer
to a fully functional, multiuser office workstation. This discussion will
introduce you to OS/2 development goals, implementation, and ramifications. Remember, you mastered DOS through extra effort and a desire
to fully understand its inner workings. Now is the best time to do the
same with OS/2.

The chapter concludes with a look at the future of DOS. What will
happen to DOS? What impacts will OS/2 have on users, developers,
programmers, and data processing management? Where should you go
next, and how should you prepare for the microcomputing future?

As you read this chapter, formulate questions. Remember, even the
most sophisticated power user was once a novice. Only by taking the
time to ask how and why does the power user become an expert.

THE HISTORY OF DOS

In 1981, with the introduction of the IBM PC, IBM and Microsoft each introduced DOS version 1.0 (PC-DOS and MS-DOS, respectively). This original DOS version provided several basic commands for the user. More important, it laid the foundation for the DOS file-management system that DOS and OS/2 use today. By utilizing this solid file-management subsystem, which is based around the file allocation table (FAT), all DOS versions since 1.0 have maintained file compatibility. This means that DOS 3.x and OS/2 can still read data files created with DOS 1.0. Although the command set provided with DOS 1.0 appears restrictive in light of today's operating systems, the foresight of the DOS 1.0 developers has been unparalleled.

In 1982, Microsoft enhanced DOS by providing support for the double-sided diskette. "Mature" PC users may recall that early versions of the PC came with single-sided diskettes capable of storing 160K of files.

In 1983, IBM and Microsoft each released DOS 2.0. At this time, DOS made the decision to follow UNIX in terms of functional aspects, breaking free from the CP/M mindset. DOS 2.0 fully supported DOS subdirectories, the DOS pipe, and an enhanced command set. In addition, DOS 2.0 provided the ability to migrate from file control blocks (FCBs) to file handles, which allowed the implementation of I/O redirection.

Throughout 1983, both IBM and Microsoft released minor enhancements to DOS, mainly for fixing system bugs. For those of you not fully conversant with DOS version numbers, here is a quick review. Each DOS version number comprises two parts, a major and a minor version number. In DOS 3.2, for example, 3 is the major version number, and 2 is the minor.

Most software developers follow this convention when they upgrade software: if the upgrade is a major enhancement to the software package, they increment the major version number (2.0 becomes 3.0). If the changes are minor (such as fixing a bug), they increment the minor version number (2.0 becomes 2.1). DOS versions 2.0, 2.01, 2.10, 2.11, and 2.25 were released in 1983.

In 1984, with the advent of the IBM PC AT, Microsoft and IBM each released DOS 3.0. DOS 3.0 provided support for 1.2MB floppy drives and larger fixed disks. The same year, both companies released DOS 3.1, which provided local area network support. Although overall functional changes were minor, DOS 3.1 greatly changed the face of DOS and established the groundwork for multiuser servers and workstations. Having started out only three years earlier as a basic single-user system, DOS was already beginning to challenge UNIX and XENIX in the multiuser environment.

An onslaught of laptop computers occurred in 1986. To maximize storage space while minimizing consumption of disk drive space, laptop systems used 3.5-inch disks. IBM and Microsoft each introduced DOS 3.2 to support the 3.5-inch microfloppy diskette.

In April 1987, IBM announced the Personal System/2 (PS/2) series of computers. This line of computers provided new technology enhancements for the 8088, 80286, and 80386 line of microprocessors. At the same time, IBM released DOS 3.3, which the PS/2 series requires, and Microsoft and IBM each announced OS/2, a multiprogramming environment for the 80286 and 80386 line of microprocessors. This book examines OS/2 in detail in this and later chapters.

Tables 1-1 and 1-2 summarize the growth of DOS since 1981.

LEARNING TO ASK QUESTIONS

It is extremely important that you continually ask questions. For example, while you read the DOS chronology, you might have formulated questions as follows:

Statement:	The 1983 DOS 2.0 introduced file handles.
Question:	Does DOS use file handles to implement I/O redirection? If so, how?
Question:	What was wrong with file control blocks?
Question:	Are file handles associated with the HANDLES= entry in the CONFIG.SYS file?
Question:	How do my applications access file handles?

Table 1-1.

Versions of DOS

Version	Date	Functionality
1.0	1981	Original disk operating system
1.25	1982	Support for double-sided disks
2.0	1983	Support for subdirectories
2.01	1983	Support for international symbols
2.11	1983	Bug fixes
2.25	1983	Extended character set support
3.0	1984	Support for 1.2MB floppy disk
		Support for larger hard disk
3.1	1984	Support for PC networks
3.2	1986	Support for microfloppies
3.3	1987	Support for IBM Personal System/2 line computers
OS/2	1987	Fully functional multiprogramming environment

From *Advanced MS-DOS*. Reprinted by permission of Microsoft Press. Copyright 1986 by Ray Duncan. All rights reserved.

Table 1-2.

IBM Versions of DOS

Version	Date	Functionality
1.0	1981	Original disk operating system
2.0	1983	Support for subdirectories
2.10	1983	Bug fixes
3.0	1984	Support for 1.2MB floppy disk
		Support for larger hard disk
3.1	1984	Support for PC networks
3.2	1986	Support for microfloppies
3.3	1987	Support for IBM Personal System/2 line of computers
OS/2	1987	Fully functional multiprogramming environment

From *Advanced MS-DOS*. Reprinted by permission of Microsoft Press. Copyright 1986 by Ray Duncan. All rights reserved.

The list could continue endlessly. You may even want to record your questions in a notebook.

This text should answer many of your questions. More important, however, it should stimulate many more. Only through questioning can you achieve understanding. This is the power user's secret.

UNDERSTANDING THE ROLE OF MICROSOFT WINDOWS

If DOS is the most influential software package of the 1980s, Microsoft Windows is very likely second. If you have not yet used Windows, try it. If you have used Windows and don't like it, reevaluate your decision. OS/2 provides a software interface called the Presentation Manager. In essence, this program manages the manner in which OS/2 presents itself to the user. The OS/2 Presentation Manager is based on Windows, its interface, and its resource control. In the future, most PCs running OS/2 will use this interface. Like it or not, that's the way it is. But the Presentation Manager has many advantages.

At the highest levels, the Presentation Manager provides a consistent user interface for *all* applications, eliminating the need to memorize nebulous DOS commands. Old-time command line users shouldn't fret, though, because OS/2 still allows you to access the command line. However, since most end users will be using the Presentation Manager, you should become fully conversant with its interface. The best way to do that is to start using Windows.

For the software developer, programming OS/2 is similar to programming Windows applications. If you are serious about developing applications well into the 1990s, you should acquire the Windows Software Development Kit and begin learning how to develop applications for the Presentation Manager. A good reference guide is *Windows Programming Secrets*, by Kris Jamsa (Berkeley, Calif., Osborne/McGraw-Hill, 1987).

DEVELOPING THE CONCURRENT MINDSET

By now, most of you are comfortable with issuing commands at the DOS prompt. After booting, DOS displays its prompt for a command. You type in the command, DOS executes it, and the process repeats until you turn off the computer. This serial command execution (one command after another) is the only way most users have ever issued DOS commands. They are used to the computer performing one task at a time. How then does the DOS PRINT command work? When a file is placed in the print queue, how can DOS continue to print while executing other commands?

The personal computer has only one CPU. By its very nature, it can perform only one task at a time. The goal of a multiprogramming operating system is to give the appearance of several things happening simultaneously. This is done through time-sharing of the CPU.

For example, imagine you are typing a letter on your word processor. The CPU is so fast it spends most of its time waiting for you to press the next key. This waiting time, or CPU idle time, can be a considerable percentage of your CPU utilization (see Figure 1-2).

To fully utilize the CPU, a multiprogramming operating system

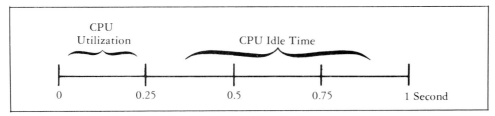

Figure 1-2.

CPU processing time

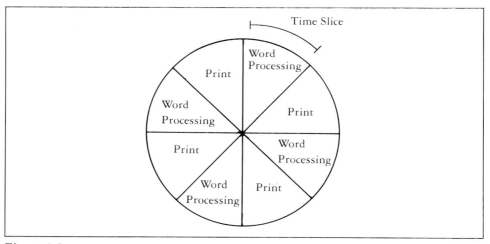

Figure 1-3.

CPU processing time example

divides CPU processing time into small pieces known as *time slices*. The CPU gives a slice to each active program. For example, if you were word processing while the DOS PRINT command printed the contents of a file, the operating system would divide the CPU time as shown in Figure 1-3.

Each program gets control of the CPU for a short period of time (time slice) to perform its processing. The operating system then switches control of the CPU to the next program. In this case, the word processing program has initial control of the CPU. Next, the PRINT command gets its time slice. The process repeats as the word processing application regains control of the CPU. The transition occurs so fast that both programs appear to be executing simultaneously. As OS/2 begins to execute more programs, each gets a time slice (see Figure 1-4). In this fashion, the operating system appears to be executing multiple programs concurrently.

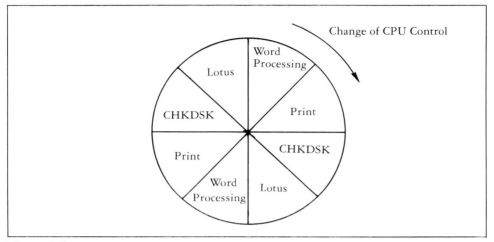

Figure 1-4.

CPU time-sharing

RESOURCE MANAGEMENT

One of the operating system's primary functions in a multiprogramming environment is *resource management*. Resource management controls which programs can access specific hardware devices and when. For example, if two programs are executing concurrently and one is displaying its results to the screen, the operating system must not allow the second program to display its output at the same time. Otherwise the screen would display a garbled combination of the output of both programs. Similarly, imagine what would happen if several programs attempted to write to the disk simultaneously.

> ### RESOURCE MANAGEMENT
>
> Resource Management is the process of controlling and distributing access of hardware devices to programs to ensure fairness and protection in a multiprogramming environment.

When multiple programs execute in the same environment, they must cooperate. OS/2 has several subsystems, each responsible for ensuring fair distribution of resources. The logical grouping of these subsystems forms the OS/2 Resource Manager. Of course, resource management is not unique to OS/2. Any multiprogramming environment (such as Windows, TopView, or OS/2) must have a complete resource management facility.

SHARING THE CPU

As a time-sharing operating system, OS/2 distributes CPU processing time to each program in the system. In so doing, OS/2 gives the appearance of executing multiple programs simultaneously. In most cases, OS/2 delegates CPU time in round-robin fashion.

However, as the number of concurrent programs increases, the amount of time a program must wait before it receives a time slice also increases.

This is one reason all the programs in the system appear to grind to a halt when you load several programs under Windows. The sharing of memory (and file swapping) is a second reason for slow response. Although the round-robin distribution of CPU time is the fairest method available, a program often needs to be able to access the CPU whenever it has data available to it.

Consider the following scenario. Your multiprogramming system is executing three programs. The first is an attendance program that logs employee schedules, absences, and tardiness. The second is a word

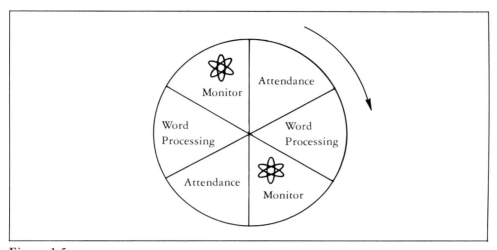

Figure 1-5.

Distribution of CPU time slices

processor that creates weekly reports. The third is a meltdown monitor for a nuclear reactor (see Figure 1-5).

At time *n,* the monitor receives the following:

```
Time       Message
----       -------
n          Possible problem in sector eight.
```

The monitor program requests additional information from the reactor system. In the meantime, the operating system switches control to the attendance program, which performs its processing (see Figure 1-6). Next, the word processing program becomes active (see Figure 1-7). Finally, the monitor program again regains control of the CPU (see Figure 1-8).

At this time it receives the following message:

```
Time       Message
----       -------
n+3        Please advise.
```

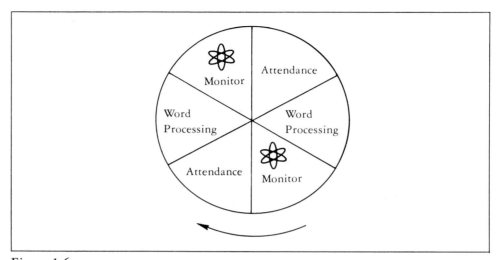

Figure 1-6.

Attendance program gaining CPU
control

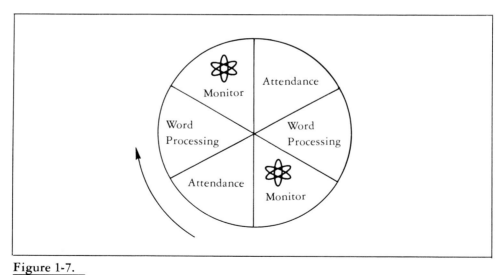

Figure 1-7.

Word processing program gaining
CPU control

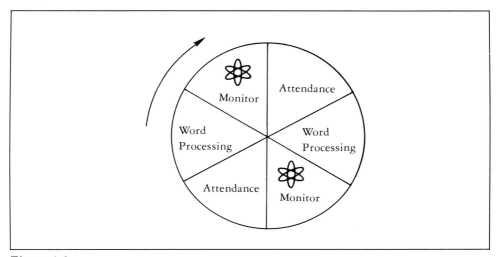

Figure 1-8.

Monitor program regaining CPU
control

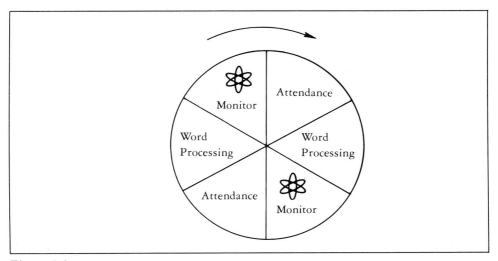

Figure 1-9.

Monitor program relinquishing
CPU control

Advise on what? What was the message? Unfortunately, when the warning messages arrived from the reactor system, the monitor program was not active, so the messages were discarded! The monitor program again requests additional information. However, it must again relinquish control of the CPU (see Figure 1-9). The next time the monitor program becomes active, it receives the following message:

```
Time        Message
----        -------
n+6         Perform reactor shutdown? (Default: No).
```

Before it can respond, however, it has used up its time slice. When the monitor program becomes active again, it receives the following message:

```
Time        Message
----        -------
n+9         Meltdown complete.  No messages to follow.
```

An enhancement to round-robin scheduling is clearly required. OS/2 enhances its scheduling algorithm by assigning a priority to each program in the system. The time-critical applications (such as a data communications or a nuclear reactor monitor) have higher priority than standard applications (such as word processors).

PROGRAM SCHEDULING

In most cases, OS/2 uses round-robin scheduling to distribute CPU processing time to each of the programs in the system. In situations where time-critical applications exist, OS/2 allows you to assign priorities to each program, thus ensuring that time-critical applications have first access to the CPU.

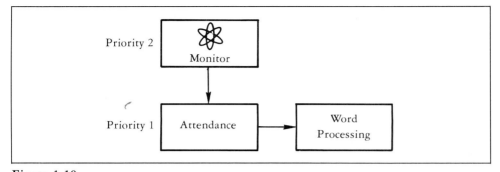

Figure 1-10.

Priority assignment under OS/2

Each time OS/2 completes a time slice, it checks its list of high-priority programs to see if any are ready to execute. If so, those programs gain control of the CPU. If not, OS/2 moves to the next priority level and begins its search there. In the previous example, you might assign the monitor program a priority of 2, while the other two applications receive a priority of 1 (see Figure 1-10).

When a time slice is completed, OS/2 first checks the monitor program. If the program is ready to execute, OS/2 assigns it control of the CPU. Otherwise, OS/2 performs round-robin scheduling among the lower-priority programs. The flowchart in Figure 1-11 illustrates the scheduling algorithm.

In this manner, a time-critical program gains control of the CPU whenever it needs it. The rest of the time OS/2 uses round-robin scheduling to delegate CPU time to lower-priority programs. As shown in Figure 1-12, OS/2 allows you to have several priority levels.

You may be wondering whether this scheduling algorithm could prevent a program from ever executing. Indeed it can. In some cases, this is simply a fact of life. The higher-priority programs are so important that it doesn't matter if OS/2 can execute anything else. In Chapter 4 you will learn about OS/2's optional dynamic scheduling algorithm, which ensures that every program eventually gains control of the CPU.

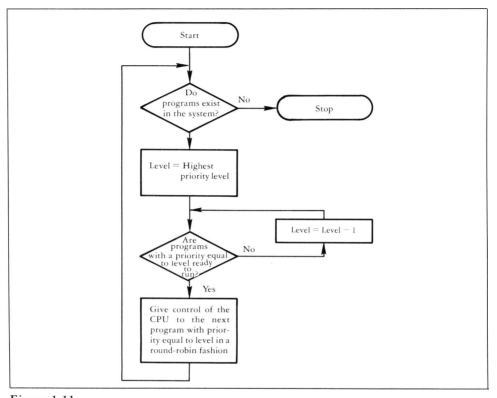

Figure 1-11.

Scheduling algorithm of OS/2

MEMORY MANAGEMENT

To execute multiple programs simultaneously, OS/2 must be able to place several programs into memory at one time and prevent them from interfering with one another. In the previous example, OS/2 had three programs executing concurrently. The OS/2 memory requirements are shown in Figure 1-13.

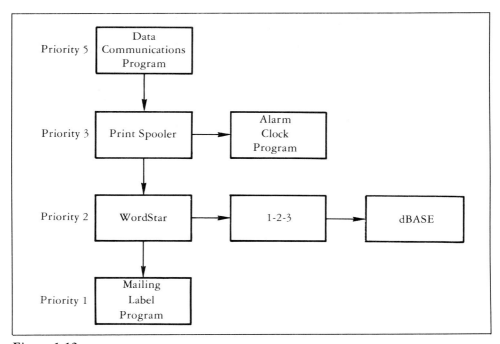

Figure 1-12.

Priority levels of OS/2

When OS/2 attempts to load a fourth program, it must ensure that ample memory is available. If memory is not available OS/2 must make space by temporarily moving one of the first three programs from memory to disk while the fourth executes. This process is known as *swapping* (see Figure 1-14).

The more applications to be executed concurrently, the higher the likelihood of swapping. One disadvantage of swapping is that it produces significant system overhead. This is due to the large number of disk I/O operations OS/2 must perform each time it swaps a program to disk.

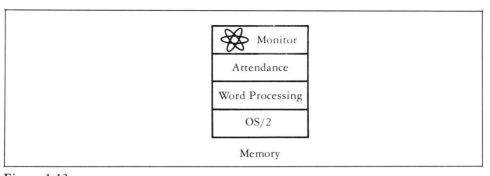

Figure 1-13.

OS/2 memory requirements

Preventing one program from affecting the code or data of another is a major operating system concern in a multiprogramming environment. The OS/2 memory management subsystem must provide the flexibility to execute multiple programs simultaneously, while maintaining the strictest levels of security. OS/2 performs memory management by using a technique known as *virtual memory*. Although the actual OS/2 implementation of virtual memory is not simple to understand, the general idea is relatively straightforward.

In order for a program to execute, it must reside in the computer's physical memory. Each location in physical memory has a physical memory address (see Figure 1-15).

Under OS/2, however, applications do not address physical memory as they did under DOS 3.x. Instead, every application maps to its own *virtual memory address* space (see Figure 1-16). The large virtual address space available to applications means that programs are no longer restricted to 640K, as they were under DOS 3.x. OS/2 applications, therefore, can be virtually any size, regardless of the amount of physical memory you may have in your system.

OS/2 is responsible for mapping virtual addresses to physical memory locations when each program executes (see Figure 1-17). If multiple programs are executing, each has its own virtual address space, and OS/2 maps each to the available physical memory (see Figure 1-18).

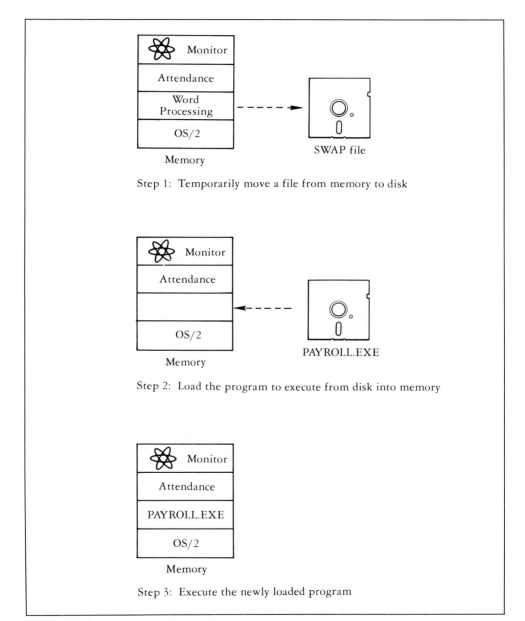

Figure 1-14.

OS/2 swapping process

DOS: Power
User's Guide

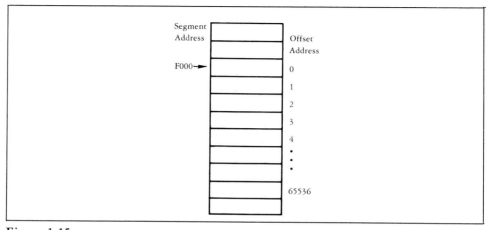

Figure 1-15.

Computer physical memory address

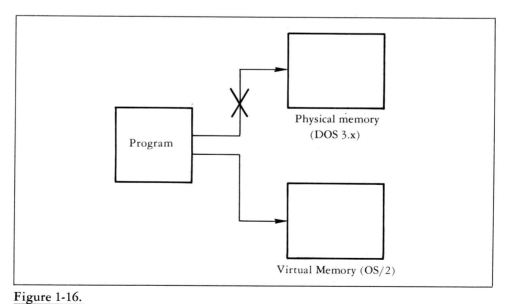

Figure 1-16.

Computer mapping of virtual
memory

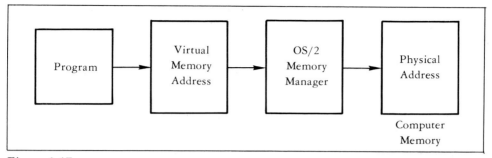

Figure 1-17.

Mapping of virtual memory
addresses to physical memory

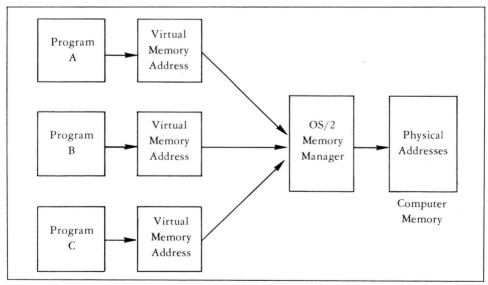

Figure 1-18.

Mapping multiple programs to
physical memory

By mapping virtual addresses to physical memory, OS/2 can prevent applications from accessing each other's code or data. OS/2 virtual memory, therefore, provides several advantages. First, OS/2 applications are no longer restricted to 640K. Second, multiple OS/2 applications can reside in memory simultaneously without posing a threat to security. Third, OS/2 can maximize memory utilization and ensure that no wasted physical memory locations exist. Later chapters examine OS/2 virtual memory implementation in more detail.

REAL VERSUS PROTECTED MODE PROCESSING

To ensure compatibility with all DOS software packages, OS/2 runs in two modes, real and protected. In real mode, applications can directly access hardware, perform low-level I/O operations, and map directly to the video memory. This is the mode of execution with which most of us are familiar. Unfortunately, a multiprogramming environment requires cooperation among executing programs. Programs running in this manner execute in protected mode.

Unlike real mode programs, protected mode programs cannot directly access hardware, perform low-level I/O, or gain exclusive use of the machine. The OS/2 Resource Manager, Scheduler, and I/O subsystems maintain control. Rather than performing low-level I/O by using a **printf** or **writeln** statement, most programs in this mode use OS/2 application program interface (API) services. In this way, OS/2 always controls the state of the system.

Probably the easiest way to make the distinction between real and protected mode applications is to compare your DOS applications to those that execute under Windows. Windows is a multiprogramming environment similar to OS/2. In this environment, all programs must cooperate, obtaining resources through the Windows' resource manager. This is in direct contrast to programs such as Lotus 1-2-3, which assume complete control of the machine.

To allow you to execute any DOS software package and take advantage of multiprogramming, OS/2 supports both real and protected modes.

OS/2 AND DOS

More than 10 million people currently use DOS. Most of these users are running 8088 machines. Since OS/2 runs only on the 80286 and 80386 series of microprocessors, DOS will remain the PC operating system standard for years to come. And because OS/2 is geared toward the office workstation environment, upgrading to OS/2 is of little benefit to most home computer enthusiasts. (OS/2 is of most use where multiple programs must coexist in memory.) Although most users will eventually migrate to OS/2, that transition may take many years. In the meantime, DOS will thrive, fully supported by Microsoft and IBM.

A word of advice to data processing or information systems managers: Don't fall behind. Get your staff conversant with Windows as soon as possible. Consider having them devote an hour a day to researching OS/2 and Windows. When it comes time to train your users, you will find it was time well spent.

HOW TO PREPARE

OS/2 was built upon the Windows foundation. Start familiarizing yourself with Windows now. If you are a programmer, use the Windows Software Development Kit to develop Windows applications. You will find these applications quite similar to OS/2 Presentation Manager applications. This is an exciting period in microcomputer history. The success of OS/2 will weigh heavily on the applications available for it. If you are a serious programmer, you should start preparing today.

2: Exploiting Batch Procedures

Most users are familiar with DOS batch processing concepts. This chapter reviews batch processing, its advantages, and each of the DOS batch commands. For those of you already familiar with DOS batch processing, this chapter presents several advanced batch processing concepts and introduces OS/2 batch processing considerations along with the OS/2 DETACH command.

RATIONALE

From your first DOS command onward, the majority of commands you have entered at the DOS prompt have been interactive. DOS receives the command from your keyboard entry, processes the command, and redisplays its prompt indicating that it is ready for another command (see Figure 2-1).

Throughout this processing, you are forced to wait for DOS to
execute the command before you can issue subsequent commands.
Processing of this type, wherein the user is in constant interaction with
the computer, is called *interactive processing.* Most personal computer
processing today occurs in this manner. However, it is often more
convenient to issue a series of DOS commands at one time via DOS
batch files than interactively issuing keyboard commands. A DOS batch
file is a text file that you create with an editor or word processor, or by
copying the file contents from the keyboard with the command

```
A> COPY CON TEST.BAT
```

The batch file contains one or more DOS commands that you want
to execute. Most of the time you will want DOS to execute these
commands sequentially. You can "program" DOS batch files by using the

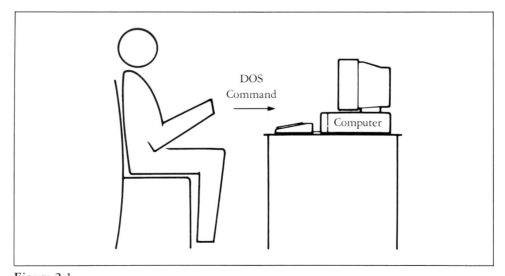

Figure 2-1.

Interactive processing

DOS IF command to perform one or more commands based upon a specific condition *(conditional processing),* and the DOS FOR command to repeat a DOS command in a simple manner *(iterative processing).*

Many seasoned DOS users are unaware of the time savings that batch files provide. For example, consider a mailing-list application that generates a list of mailing labels for a specific ZIP code region, sorts the list by name, and prints the mailing labels. In this case, the following three DOS commands execute

GENLABEL   Creates the mailing labels for the ZIP code region
SRTLABEL   Sorts the mailing labels by name
PRTLABEL   Prints the mailing labels

In most cases, a user will first issue the GENLABEL command at the DOS prompt.

```
A> GENLABEL
```

When that command completes, the user enters

```
A> SRTLABEL
```

The user then issues the command to print the mailing labels.

```
A> PRTLABEL
```

Although none of the programs require user intervention once execution begins, the user has to remain near the computer to start the next program. Rather than acting as a servant, the computer makes the user subservient.

DOS batch files solve this problem. The user places the commands into a text file, as shown here:

```
GENLABEL
SRTLABEL
PRTLABEL
```

Assuming that the name of the file is MAILLIST.BAT, the user simply enters the following command at the DOS prompt:

```
A> MAILLIST
```

DOS will execute the series of commands in the batch file without further user intervention. The batch file MAILLIST.BAT contains all of the commands that DOS is to execute for this application, so the user is free to perform tasks away from the computer. As a result, DOS batch processing saves time.

Many users feel they can complete tasks faster without a computer. This is because they are slow typists. DOS batch files allow you to abbreviate a long command or series of commands that you use on a regular basis. For example, consider the following DOS command that compiles the C program GENLABEL.C:

```
A> cl -d -c -AS -Gsw -Oas -Zpe -FPa -FoGENLABEL.OBJ GENLABEL.C
```

Rather than typing the command line every time you want to compile the program, you can create a DOS batch file to perform the task. Instead of typing the entire command, you simply enter the DOS batch file name—a significant savings in keystrokes.

The following list summarizes the advantages of DOS batch files over interactive processing:

- Batch files eliminate keystrokes by allowing you to abbreviate a command or series of commands.

- DOS batch files save time by reducing the amount of typing you must perform.

- Batch files allow you to group logically related commands into one file that you can execute unattended.

- DOS batch files are programmable.

SEQUENTIAL BATCH PROCESSING

Most of your DOS batch processing will be sequential in nature. In other words, the batch file contains a list of commands that DOS executes one after another. For example, enter the following to create a file called TEST.BAT:

```
A> COPY CON TEST.BAT
CLS
DATE
TIME
^Z
         1 File(s) copied
```

DOS uses the CTRL-Z keyboard combination to signify the end of a file. When you are creating a file by copying it from the keyboard in this fashion, you can enter CTRL-Z in one of two ways. Press either the F6 function key or the Z key while depressing the CTRL key.

> CTRL-Z (^Z) END-OF-FILE-MARKER
>
> When you are copying a file from the console device
>
> A> COPY CON TEST.BAT
>
> you can signify the end of file by pressing either the F6 function key, or the Z key while the CTRL key is depressed.

Use the DOS TYPE command to display your newly created batch file.

```
A> TYPE TEST.BAT
CLS
DATE
TIME

A>
```

This file is a sequential batch file. DOS will first execute the CLS command, clearing the screen contents.

```
A>
```

Next, DOS issues the DATE command.

```
A> DATE
Current date is Sun  7-05-1987
Enter new date (mm-dd-yy):
```

Last, DOS executes the TIME command.

```
A> DATE
Current date is Sun  7-05-1987
Enter new date (mm-dd-yy):
A> TIME
Current time is 22:28:29.75
Enter new time:
```

Now create a DOS batch file that performs the following tasks:

- Clear the screen

- Display the disk volume label

- Display the current directory

```
CLS
VOL
CD
```

Upon invocation, the batch procedure displays

```
A> VOL
 Volume in drive A is DOSDISK

A> CD
A:\

A>
```

By now, the creation and execution of sequential batch files should be clear to you. Rather than obtaining the commands from the user (as done in interactive processing), DOS reads a command from the batch file, executes it, reads the next command, and repeats this process until it encounters the end of the batch file.

The following are valid sequential batch files:

```
DATE
TIME
VER
```

or

```
CLS
VOL
CHKDSK
```

or

```
CD  C:\
C:
DIR
```

It is important to note that you can also create DOS batch files with the EDLIN text editor provided with DOS, as shown here:

```
A> EDLIN TEST.BAT
New File
*I
        1:* CLS
        2:* DATE
        3:* TIME
        4:*^C
*E

A>
```

To create and execute a batch file, complete the following steps:

1. Using a text editor, create a file with the extension BAT.

2. Place the DOS commands that you want to execute into the file.

3. At the DOS prompt, enter the file name of the batch file. DOS will begin execution of the file's commands.

The flowchart in Figure 2-2 gives a summary of sequential batch processing.

What happens when one of the batch file commands is invalid or does not exist? Consider the following batch file:

```
CLS
VAL
CD
```

This batch file is almost identical to the batch file examined previously. In this case, however, the user has mistyped the command VOL as VAL. When the user later executes the batch procedure, DOS will display

```
A> VAL
Invalid command

A> CD
A:\

A>
```

If an error exists in your batch file, DOS skips the command and processes the next command in the file. In essence, the error has the same effect as entering

```
A> VAL
Invalid command

A>
```

at the DOS prompt. DOS, therefore, treats batch and interactive commands in an identical fashion.

INVALID OR NONEXISTENT BATCH COMMANDS

When DOS encounters an invalid command within a batch file, it simply displays the message

Invalid command

and processes the next command in the file.

TERMINATING A BATCH PROCEDURE

Once DOS begins executing the commands in a batch file, it continues until it encounters the end of the file. If you need to terminate batch file processing for any reason, press the CTRL-C keyboard combination.

BATCH FILE TERMINATION

To terminate a batch procedure from the keyboard, use the CTRL-C or CTRL-BREAK keyboard combination. DOS will respond with the prompt

Terminate batch job (Y/N)?

To terminate the batch job, press the Y key; otherwise, press N to allow the job to complete.

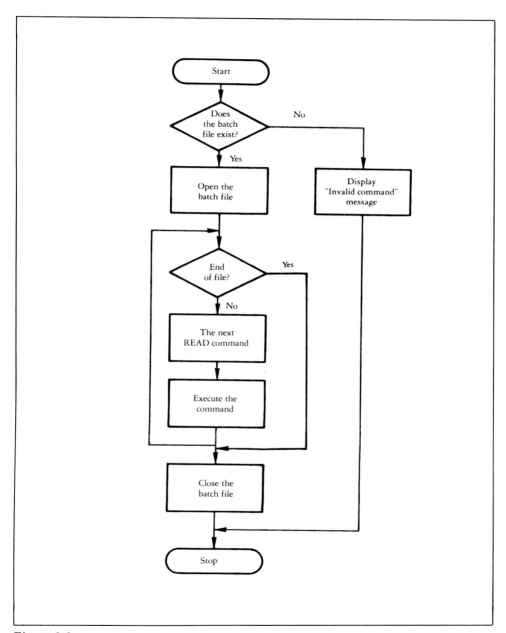

Figure 2-2.

Sequential batch processing

When you terminate a batch job in this fashion, DOS will respond with

```
Terminate batch job (Y/N)?
```

If you do want to terminate the batch file, press Y; otherwise, press N, and DOS will continue processing.

Consider the following example:

```
DATE
TIME
```

Invoke the procedure and press the CTRL-C combination at the DOS prompt for the system date.

```
A> DATE
Current date is Sun  7-05-1987
Enter new date (mm-dd-yy):
```

DOS will respond with

```
Terminate batch job (Y/N)?
```

In this case, press Y, and DOS will terminate the batch file processing.

```
A> DATE
Current date is Sun  7-05-1987
Enter new date (mm-dd-yy):
Terminate batch job (Y/N)? Y

A>
```

Repeat the process, this time responding with the N key at the terminate prompt. DOS will continue the batch file processing.

```
A> DATE
Current date is Sun  7-05-1987
Enter new date (mm-dd-yy):
Terminate batch job (Y/N)? N

A> TIME
Current time is 22:50:34.00
Enter new time:
```

BASIC BATCH COMMANDS

Now that you are familiar with the basics of DOS batch file processing, you can begin to use some DOS commands that will enhance your batch files. The REM command allows you to display remarks during the execution of DOS batch files. These remarks inform the user about the state of the batch processing. For example, to enhance the mailing-list application, you might include the following remarks:

```
REM Generating mailing labels for ZIP code 89126
GENLABEL
REM Sorting mailing labels by name
SRTLABEL
REM Printing mailing labels
PRTLABEL
```

These messages provide the user who is unfamiliar with the function of GENLABEL, SRTLABEL, and PRTLABEL with a better understanding of the processing. So if you take the time to include remarks, make them as meaningful as possible.

The format of the DOS REM command is

REM [*message*]

where *message* is an optional string of up to 123 characters.

The following are valid uses of REM within a batch procedure:

```
REM Message to the user
REM REM is used for remarks within a batch file
REM REM doesn't require a message as shown next
REM
```

Upon invocation the batch procedure will display

```
A> REM Message to the user

A> REM REM is used for remarks within a batch file

A> REM REM doesn't require a message as shown next

A> REM

A>
```

Note how the use of REM with no message displays a blank line.

The second common use of REM within batch files is to increase readability of programming code. For example, consider the following batch file:

```
CLS
DATE
TIME
VER
DEL *.BAK
DIR *.DAT
GENLABEL
SRTLABEL
PRTLABEL
PRINT LOG.DAT
DEL LOG.DAT
```

Watch how REM can increase its readability.

```
REM
REM Clear the screen and set the system date and time
REM
CLS
DATE
TIME

REM
REM Display the DOS version to the user
REM
VER

REM
REM Clean up yesterday's files
DEL *.BAK
DIR *.DAT

REM
REM Perform the mailing label series of commands
REM
GENLABEL
SRTLABEL
PRTLABEL

REM
REM Print today's appointment log, delete yesterday's
REM
PRINT LOG.DAT
DEL LOG.OLD
```

Consider the following C program that implements REM:

```
main (argc, argv)
  int argc;
  char *argv[];
 {
  printf ("REM ");
  while (*++argv)
    printf ("%s ", *argv);

 }
```

The program simply displays the command line arguments it receives. The following Turbo Pascal program performs the same function:

```
program REMTEST;

var
  i: integer;

begin
  write ('REM ');

  for i := 1 to ParamCount do
    write (ParamStr(i), ' ');
end.
```

A convenient and often under-utilized batch processing command is PAUSE. The format of PAUSE is

PAUSE [*message*]

where *message* is an optional string of up to 123 characters.

Upon invocation PAUSE displays the optional message the user provides, and then pauses to display the prompt

```
Strike a key when ready . . .
```

At this point, the user can press any key to continue the execution of the batch procedure, or press the CTRL-C combination to terminate the processing.

RESPONDING TO THE PAUSE PROMPT

When PAUSE displays the prompt

Strike a key when ready. . .

pressing any key results in DOS continuing the processing of a batch procedure. To terminate the procedure, press the CTRL-C or CTRL-BREAK keyboard combination.

The following are valid uses of PAUSE:

```
PAUSE READY TO GENERATE MAILING LABELS
GENLABEL
PAUSE PLACE BLANK DISKETTE IN DRIVE A FOR SORT
SRTLABEL
PAUSE DONE WITH SORT READY TO PRINT
PRTLABEL
```

Upon invocation the procedure will display

```
A> PAUSE READY TO GENERATE MAILING LABELS
Strike a key when ready . . .

A> GENLABEL

A> PAUSE PLACE BLANK DISKETTE IN DRIVE A FOR SORT
Strike a key when ready . . .

A> SRTLABEL

A> PAUSE DONE WITH SORT READY TO PRINT
Strike a key when ready . . .

A> PRTLABEL

A>
```

Assume that the mailing label program requires a blank diskette in drive A prior to processing. Use PAUSE as shown here:

```
PAUSE PLACE A BLANK DISKETTE IN DRIVE A
GENLABEL
SRTLABEL
PRTLABEL
```

Now, upon invocation the batch file displays

```
A> PAUSE PLACE A BLANK DISKETTE IN DRIVE A
Strike a key when ready . . .

A> GENLABEL

A> SRTLABEL

A> PRTLABEL

A>
```

Once the user presses any key to continue, the batch file processes in the manner previously shown.

You will find the DOS PAUSE command very convenient in most batch applications. The following C program implements PAUSE:

```
#include <conio.h>

main (argc, argv)
  int argc;
  char *argv[];
  {
  while (*++argv)
    printf ("%s ", *argv);

  printf ("\nStrike any key when ready . . .");

  getch();
  }
```

Likewise, the following Turbo Pascal program provides the functionality of PAUSE:

```
program PauseTest;

var
  i: integer;
  c: char;

begin
  for i := 1 to ParamCount do
    write (ParamStr(i), ' ');
  write (chr(13), chr(10), 'Strike any key when ready . . .');
  read (kbd, c);
```

Each of the batch files examined has displayed on the screen the names of each program DOS was executing. For example, the batch procedure

```
GENLABEL
SRTLABEL
PRTLABEL
```

displays

```
A> GENLABEL

A> SRTLABEL

A> PRTLABEL

A>
```

It is often desirable, however, to suppress the command names or messages normally displayed by REM. The DOS ECHO command allows you to do this. The format of the ECHO command is

ECHO [ON ¦ OFF ¦ *message*]

The bar (¦) between ON, OFF, and *message* means that you must select one of those three options.

ON   Directs DOS to display the command names and messages produced by REM

OFF   Directs DOS to suppress the command names and message produced by REM

message   An optional string of up to 123 characters

If you invoke ECHO from the DOS prompt without any parameters, ECHO displays its current state (either ON or OFF), as shown here:

```
A> ECHO
ECHO is on
```

Consider the following batch file:

```
GENLABEL
SRTLABEL
PRTLABEL
```

Upon invocation the file displays

```
A> GENLABEL

A> SRTLABEL

A> PRTLABEL

A>
```

ECHO OFF suppresses messages and command names. Make ECHO OFF the first line of the batch procedure, as shown here:

```
ECHO OFF
GENLABEL
SRTLABEL
PRTLABEL
```

Upon invocation the procedure displays

```
A> ECHO OFF

A>
```

Many programmers use ECHO during application installation procedures. Consider the following batch file:

```
ECHO OFF

ECHO ================================================
ECHO ==    DOS POWER USER SERIES DISKETTE PACKAGE  ==
ECHO ==                                            ==
ECHO ==         KRIS JAMSA SOFTWARE, INC.          ==
ECHO ==                                            ==
ECHO ==              P.O. BOX 26031                ==
ECHO ==          LAS VEGAS, NEVADA 89126           ==
ECHO ==                                            ==
ECHO ================================================
```

Upon invocation the procedure displays

```
A> ECHO OFF

================================================
==    DOS POWER USER SERIES DISKETTE PACKAGE  ==
==                                            ==
==         KRIS JAMSA SOFTWARE, INC.          ==
==                                            ==
==              P.O. BOX 26031                ==
==          LAS VEGAS, NEVADA 89126           ==
==                                            ==
================================================
```

CONDITIONAL BATCH PROCESSING

All of the batch procedures examined in this chapter have been sequential in nature; they exhibit no decision-making capabilities. The IF command allows your DOS batch files to perform simple decision making. The format of the IF command is

IF [NOT] *condition* DOS__COMMAND

where the following is true:

NOT directs DOS to perform a Boolean NOT of the result of condition. For example, if condition is TRUE, NOT condition results in FALSE, and vice versa.

condition must be one of the following:

    ERRORLEVEL *number*
    EXIST *file__specification*
    STRING1 == STRING2

DOS__COMMAND is the command you want to execute when the condition is TRUE.

The first condition, ERRORLEVEL *number,* works as follows. Many programs return a status value to DOS when they terminate. The DOS ERRORLEVEL condition tests this status value. For example, the following batch procedure executes the program GENLABEL. If GENLABEL exits with a status value *greater than or equal to 1,* the batch file executes the program SRTLABEL. If GENLABEL's exit status is less than 1, the batch file terminates.

```
GENLABEL
IF ERRORLEVEL 1 GOTO SORT
GOTO DONE
:SORT
SRTLABEL
:DONE
```

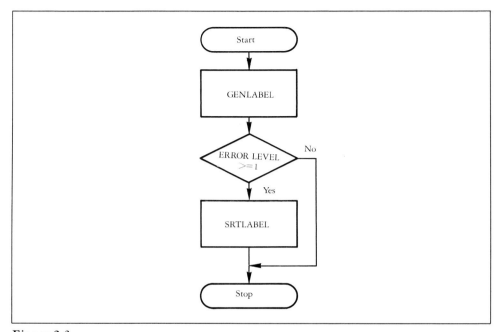

Figure 2-3.

Execution of GENLABEL

Figure 2-3 illustrates this processing.

The second condition, EXIST *file—specification,* evaluates to TRUE when the file referenced by *file—specification* exists as specified. For example, the following are valid expressions using EXIST:

IF EXIST C:CONFIG.SYS COPY C:CONFIG.SYS B:
IF EXIST B:AUTOEXEC.BAT B:AUTOEXEC
IF EXIST B:\DOS\UTIL\MATH.DAT TYPE B:\DOS\UTIL\MATH.DAT

The following batch procedure searches the root directory for the files AUTOEXEC.BAT and CONFIG.SYS. If the files are found, the procedure displays a message stating so:

```
ECHO OFF
IF EXIST \AUTOEXEC.BAT ECHO AUTOEXEC.BAT EXISTS
IF EXIST \CONFIG.SYS ECHO CONFIG.SYS EXISTS
```

Assuming that both files exist in the root directory, the output of the batch procedure is

```
A> ECHO OFF
AUTOEXEC.BAT EXISTS
CONFIG.SYS EXISTS

A>
```

You can modify the previous batch procedure slightly to illustrate the use of the Boolean NOT. In this case, if either file does not exist, the batch procedure displays a message stating such.

```
ECHO OFF
IF NOT EXIST \AUTOEXEC.BAT ECHO AUTOEXEC.BAT MISSING
IF NOT EXIST \CONFIG.SYS ECHO CONFIG.SYS MISSING
```

The flowchart in Figure 2-4 illustrates the processing of the batch file.

The STRING1 == STRING2 condition evaluates as TRUE when the characters contained in the first character string (STRING1) are identical to those in the second (STRING2). Here is an example:

IF "TEST"=="TEST" ECHO EQUAL

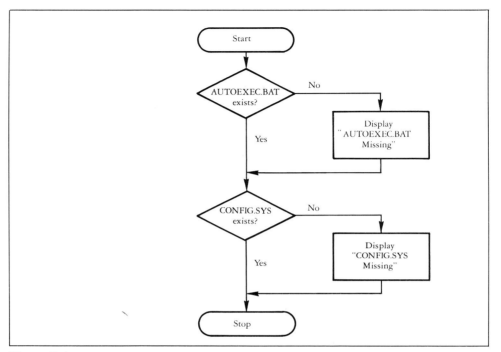

Figure 2-4.

Batch file processing

Since the strings are identical, DOS displays the message

EQUAL

Note that the characters in the two strings must match identically. DOS does not consider

PC-DOS == Pc-DOS

to contain equivalent strings. The reasons for this condition will become clear as you examine batch file parameters later in this chapter.

BATCH CONDITIONS

DOS batch file processing supports the following conditions:

ERRORLEVEL *number*   If the program preceding this condition exits with an error status greater than or equal to number, the condition is TRUE.

EXIST *file specification*   If the file exists on disk as specified, the condition is TRUE.

STRING1=STRING2   If the characters in both strings are identical, the condition is TRUE.

The DOS GOTO command gives DOS batch files a large degree of programmability. The format of the GOTO command is

GOTO *label__name*

where the following is true:

label__ name is a unique sequence of characters that defines a location within the batch file. DOS distinguishes labels from commands in that the first character of a label must be a colon (:DOS__label). DOS uses only the first eight characters of a label name, although the names can be virtually any length. Keep in mind that this means DOS will consider labels such as LABEL__NAME1 and LABEL__NAME2 identical.

Consider the following DOS batch file that loops (repeats) forever, displaying the message "LOOPING":

```
ECHO OFF
:LOOP
ECHO LOOPING
GOTO LOOP
```

Upon invocation the procedure displays

```
LOOPING
LOOPING
LOOPING
LOOPING
LOOPING
LOOPING
LOOPING
LOOPING
LOOPING
LOOPING
LOOPING
LOOPING
LOOPING
LOOPING
```

The only way to terminate this procedure is to press the CTRL-C combination. Note that the actual label has a colon before it. When DOS reads this line, it knows that the line contains a label. In this way, DOS will not attempt to execute a label as a command.

The following batch file checks for the existence of the file CONFIG. SYS in the root directory. If the file does not exist, the batch file terminates. Otherwise, it displays configuration information as shown here:

```
IF NOT EXIST \CONFIG.SYS GOTO DONE
TYPE \CONFIG.SYS
:DONE
```

The flowchart in Figure 2-5 illustrates this processing.

The following C and Turbo Pascal programs demonstrate the DOS ERRORLEVEL condition. The first program, ONE.C, exits with a status of 1:

```
main ()
{
  exit (1);
}
```

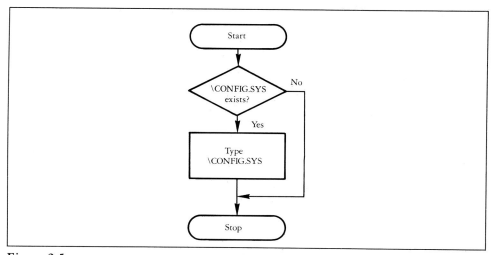

Figure 2-5.

Processing of batch file for checking CONFIG.SYS

Likewise, TWO.PAS exits with a status of 2:

```
Program Two;
begin
 Halt (2);
end.
```

The following batch procedure displays a message according to the error status generated by each program:

```
ECHO OFF
REM
REM put program to execute here
REM
IF ERRORLEVEL 2 GOTO TWO
IF ERRORLEVEL 1 GOTO ONE
GOTO DONE
:TWO
ECHO T W O
GOTO DONE
:ONE
ECHO O N E
:DONE
```

If a DOS GOTO command specifies a nonexistent label, DOS terminates the batch processing, as shown here:

```
GOTO DONE
:D
:DO
:DON
:DONT
```

```
A> TEST
A> GOTO DONE
Label not found
```

This chapter examines conditional processing in further detail in the discussion of DOS batch file parameters.

ITERATIVE PROCESSING

An *iterative process* is a process that repeats itself for a specific period of time. In programming, iterative processing allows programs to repeat a series of instructions for a specific duration. You have already seen one form of iterative DOS batch processing: the use of the DOS GOTO command. The following batch file, for example, displays a directory listing forever (or until the user presses the CTRL-C combination to terminate processing):

```
:LOOP
DIR
GOTO LOOP
```

DOS also provides the FOR command to execute a specific DOS command for a given set (collection) of files. The format of the FOR command is

FOR *%%variable* IN (*set*) DO DOS__COMMAND

where the following is true:

%%variable is the name of a memory location in which DOS stores the name of a file during each iteration of the loop.

set is a collection of DOS file names separated by commas. DOS wildcard characters are valid names. The following are valid set entries:

AUTOEXEC.BAT, CONFIG.SYS

*.DAT, *.BAT

.

DOS__COMMAND is the name of the DOS command that FOR is to execute with each iteration of the loop. Note that the FOR command is not a valid command for execution here. In other words, DOS does not support nested FOR commands.

DOS executes the FOR command as follows. On the first iteration, DOS places the first file name contained in the set into the variable referenced by *%%variable*. DOS then issues the command associated with DOS_COMMAND. For example, consider the following FOR command:

FOR %%F IN (AUTOEXEC.BAT, CONFIG.SYS) DO TYPE %%F

DOS assigns %%F the value AUTOEXEC.BAT during the first iteration and then issues the TYPE command with

TYPE AUTOEXEC.BAT

Once the TYPE command completes, DOS assigns %%F the value CONFIG.SYS and repeats this process. On the third iteration, DOS does not find another file in the set to assign to %%F so the FOR command terminates.

The flowchart in Figure 2-6 illustrates the processing FOR performs.

The following batch file command line displays the contents of each batch file in the current directory:

FOR %%F IN (*.BAT) DO TYPE %%F

Likewise, this batch file command line displays the contents of three specific files:

FOR %%F IN (AUTOEXEC.BAT, CONFIG.SYS, TEST.BAT) DO TYPE %%F

When batch file parameters are examined later in this chapter, you will see how the flexibility of the FOR command can increase.

Many users are aware that they can use the DOS FOR command within DOS batch files. However, DOS also allows you to issue the FOR

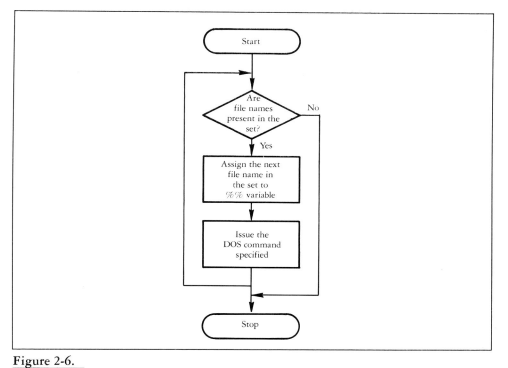

Figure 2-6.

Processing of FOR command

command from the DOS prompt. In this case, however, use a single percent sign (%) in front of variable names.

FOR %F IN (*.BAT) DO TYPE %F

Issuing a **FOR** command from the DOS prompt in the presence of your peers will bring you instant recognition as a DOS power user.

Consider the following FOR command, which searches all files with the extension TXT for the string "DOS":

```
A> FOR %F IN (*.*) DO TYPE %F | FIND "DOS"
```

PASSING PARAMETERS TO DOS BATCH PROCEDURES

DOS batch files provide you with tremendous flexibility and time savings. You have seen how to abbreviate the C compilation command line for the program TEST.C. This section shows you how to increase the number of applications that a batch file will support by using DOS batch file parameters. In essence, you will make your batch files more generic and increase their processing capabilities. In this way, many applications (instead of just one) can use the same series of commands.

A *batch parameter* is a value that you place in the command line when you invoke the batch procedure from the DOS prompt. For example, consider the following:

```
A> CP A.DAT B.DAT
```

In this case, CP is assumed to be an existing DOS batch file. A.DAT and B.DAT are the batch file parameters (or values) that you want the command procedure to utilize.

You access DOS batch parameters within a batch file by using the variables %0 to %9. In this case, upon invocation of the command

```
A> CP A.DAT B.DAT
```

the parameters will contain

%0 CP
%1 A.DAT
%2 B.DAT
%3 NULL
.

.

.

%9 NULL

Note that DOS assigns the NULL value to batch parameters that do not have a corresponding command line argument.

The following procedure T.BAT allows you to abbreviate the DOS TYPE command. It displays the contents of the file specified on the command line.

TYPE %1

If, for example, you invoke T.BAT with the file AUTOEXEC.BAT

```
A> T AUTOEXEC.BAT
```

the batch file will display the contents of the file on the screen. Similarly, if you invoke the procedure with the file CONFIG.SYS

```
A> T CONFIG.SYS
```

the batch procedure displays the contents of that file on the screen. In this way, DOS batch file parameters allow one command to work successfully for an unlimited number of files.

Notice how batch parameters increase the functional capabilities of the FOR loop in the following procedure:

FOR %%F IN (%1) DO TYPE %%F

The following is a summary of the processing performed for each command listed:

T *.*	Displays the contents of all files
T *.DAT	Displays the contents of all files with the DAT extension
T AUTOEXEC.BAT	Displays the contents of AUTOEXEC.BAT
T	Displays no files

You may already have noticed the special function of the %0 batch parameter. The %0 parameter always contains the name of the batch procedure that is currently executing. For example, the following batch file simply displays its own contents:

TYPE %0.BAT

You can also use batch parameters with the DOS IF command. For example, the following batch file tests the value of %1 and performs either a fixed disk or floppy disk installation of a software package:

```
IF %1 == HARDDISK GOTO HARDDISK
IF %1 == FLOPPY GOTO FLOPPY
```

The user invokes the procedure as

```
A> INSTALL HARDDISK
```

or

```
A> INSTALL FLOPPY
```

If the user fails to specify either hard or floppy disk, the procedure simply displays a message and terminates.

You may be wondering what happens if you need more than nine (%1 to %9) parameters. The DOS SHIFT command provides you with a solution. The format of the SHIFT command is

SHIFT

SHIFT rotates (to the left) the values of each batch parameter. For example, consider the following command line:

```
A> TEST A B C
```

The batch command line parameters will contain

%0 TEST.BAT
%1 A
%2 B
%3 C
%4 NULL
.
.
.
%9 NULL

Executing SHIFT within the batch procedure results in each parameter containing

%0 A
%1 B
%2 C
%3 NULL
.
.
.
%9 NULL

The next invocation of SHIFT produces

%0 B
%1 C
%2 NULL
.
.
.
%9 NULL

If you have more than nine parameters on the line,

A> TEST 1 2 3 4 5 6 7 8 9 10 11 12 13

SHIFT will rotate a new parameter into %9 with each invocation (see Figure 2-7). When no new parameters exist, DOS replaces %9 with the NULL value.

To utilize batch parameters fully, you must be able to test for a NULL (nonexistent) value. Consider the following IF command:

IF '%1' == '' GOTO NULL

In this case, if %1 does not have a value (i.e., it is NULL), the string replacement results in

IF '' == '' GOTO NULL

which DOS equates as TRUE.

```
%0    %1    %2    %3    %4    %5    %6    %7    %8    %9
TEST  1     2     3     4     5     6     7     8     9
After SHIFT
%0    %1    %2    %3    %4    %5    %6    %7    %8    %9
1     2     3     4     5     6     7     8     9     10
After SHIFT
%0    %1    %2    %3    %4    %5    %6    %7    %8    %9
2     3     4     5     6     7     8     9     10    11
```

Figure 2-7.

Rotation involved with SHIFT
command

The following batch procedure illustrates parameter shifting and testing for a NULL parameter:

```
ECHO OFF
:LOOP
IF '%1' == '' GOTO DONE
ECHO %1
SHIFT
GOTO LOOP
:DONE
```

This procedure allows you to display all of the parameters on the batch command line by using the SHIFT command. As you can see, the test for the NULL value in %1 allows you to terminate processing.

REMOVING THE BATCH FILE DISKETTE

Often during the course of executing several commands from a batch file you must temporarily remove the diskette that contains the batch file commands. When this occurs, DOS will display an error message stating that the disk containing the batch file is missing, as shown here.

```
Batch file missing
```

Insert the diskette and DOS will continue processing.

CHANGING DIRECTORIES

DOS allows you to change directories throughout the execution of the batch procedure. For example, consider the following batch file:

```
CD \UTIL
GETFILE
CLS
VER
```

DOS will first change directories to \UTIL and then execute the command GETFILE. Next, DOS executes the CLS and VER commands. Upon completion of the batch file, your current working directory remains \UTIL.

CHANGING DIRECTIVES
WITHIN A DOS BATCH
FILE

DOS allows you to execute the CHDIR command within your batch files without affecting its processing. It does not change the default directory back to its original setting. The last directory for which you issue the CHDIR command remains in effect.

INVOKING NESTED BATCH PROCEDURES

Many batch applications require you to invoke additional batch files from within your batch procedure. If the secondary batch file is the last command in your file

```
CLS
VER
BATFILE
```

you should have no problem. However, to invoke a second batch procedure from within the middle of a batch file

```
CLS
BATFILE
VER
```

requires the use of COMMAND, as shown here:

```
CLS
COMMAND /C BATFILE
VER
```

DOS requires you to use COMMAND in this fashion since previous commands may have overwritten the contents of the transient portion

of the DOS command processor. By invoking the secondary batch file
with COMMAND in this fashion, DOS loads a new command processor
that exists for the duration of the nested batch procedure.

NESTED BATCH PROCEDURES

DOS allows you to invoke other batch files from within a batch file. If the
invocation occurs within the middle of the batch procedure, you must use
COMMAND as shown here:

CLS
COMMAND /C BATFILE
VER

RECURSIVE BATCH FUNCTIONS

A *recursive function* within a program is a function that repeatedly
invokes itself to complete a specific task. If you are not familiar with
recursion, you may want to skip this section. The following batch file
repeatedly invokes itself to complete a specific task. Once the task is
complete, each invocation of the batch procedure terminates.

```
ECHO OFF
ECHO %1 %2 %3 %4 %5 %6 %7 %8 %9
SHIFT
IF NOT '%1'=='' RECBATCH %1 %2 %3 %4 %5 %6 %7 %8 %9
```

In this case, the batch file displays the batch parameters %1 to %9.
Once it has displayed the parameters, the procedure uses the SHIFT
command to rotate the parameters one position to the left. Next, the
procedure checks to see if additional parameters exist (%1 is not equal

to NULL). If parameters exist, the procedure invokes itself to repeat the process. Otherwise, the procedure terminates.

```
A>  RECBATCH  1  2  3  4  5  6  7  8  9
A>  ECHO  OFF
1  2  3  4  5  6  7  8  9
2  3  4  5  6  7  8  9
3  4  5  6  7  8  9
4  5  6  7  8  9
5  6  7  8  9
6  7  8  9
7  8  9
8  9
9
```

Few actual batch processing applications require recursive processing.

AUTOEXEC.BAT

By now you should be fully conversant with the ins and outs of DOS batch file processing. All DOS batch files have the BAT extension. DOS batch file names follow the same convention as all DOS file names (that is, up to eight characters). DOS reserves one batch file name, however, for a specific use. Each time DOS boots, it searches the root directory on the boot drive for the file AUTOEXEC.BAT. If DOS finds AUTOEXEC. BAT, it reads and executes the contents of the the file in the fashion just discussed. If the file does not exist in the root directory, DOS invokes the familiar DATE and TIME commands.

AUTOEXEC.BAT is functionally equivalent to the batch files examined thus far. AUTOEXEC.BAT fully supports all the batch file commands that have been examined in this chapter. DOS allows you to perform conditional and iterative processing within AUTOEXEC.BAT as you would with any batch file.

Do not confuse AUTOEXEC.BAT with CONFIG.SYS. These files have completely different functions. AUTOEXEC.BAT is simply a DOS

start-up command procedure into which you can place the commands
you want DOS to execute each time it boots. CONFIG.SYS, on the other
hand, contains the DOS system configuration parameters that DOS uses
to generate an operating system specific to your needs. Chapter 4
examines CONFIG.SYS and its entries in detail.

AUTOEXEC.BAT

Each time DOS boots, it searches the root directory for the file AUTOEXEC.BAT.
If DOS finds this file, it executes its contents in the same fashion as all standard
DOS batch files. If the file AUTOEXEC.BAT does not exist, DOS displays the
DATE and TIME commands.

BATCH FILE PROCESSING UNDER OS/2

Although OS/2 has significant advantages over DOS 3.x, DOS batch file
processing remains basically unchanged under OS/2. OS/2 fully supports all of the following batch processing commands:

COMMAND
ECHO
FOR
IF
PAUSE [*message*]
REM [*message*]
SHIFT

In addition, OS/2 adds the following commands:

CALL BATCH__FILE [*arguments*]
EXTPROC *batch__processor__name* [*arguments*]
ENDLOCAL
SETLOCAL

The first command, CALL, allows you to execute batch files nested within another batch file. Using CALL is similar to using COMMAND /C. For example, the following OS/2 batch procedure performs the recursive batch processing presented previously:

```
ECHO OFF
ECHO %1 %2 %3 %4 %5 %6 %7 %8 %9
SHIFT
IF '%1'=='' GOTO DONE
CALL RECBATCH %1 %2 %3 %4 %5 %6 %7 %8 %9
:DONE
```

Upon invocation, the procedure displays

```
A> RECBATCH 1 2 3 4 5 6 7 8 9
A> ECHO OFF
1 2 3 4 5 6 7 8 9
2 3 4 5 6 7 8 9
3 4 5 6 7 8 9
4 5 6 7 8 9
5 6 7 8 9
6 7 8 9
7 8 9
8 9
9
```

THE CALL COMMAND

The OS/2 CALL command allows you to invoke nested batch procedures, as shown here:

CLS

CALL BATCHJOB

VER

CALL is functionally equivalent to COMMAND/C in DOS 3.x.

The OS/2 EXTPROC command allows you to specify a batch command processor for an OS/2 batch file. The EXTPROC command must be the first command in the batch file, as shown here:

```
EXTPROC COMSHELL.EXE
MYPROG
YOURPROG
```

In this case, OS/2 uses the program COMSHELL.EXE as the batch command processor. COMSHELL.EXE is simply a user-defined executable program. Most users will never require this batch command.

THE EXTPROC COMMAND

The OS/2 EXTPROC command allows you to specify an alternate command processor for your batch file. EXTPROC must be the *first* command in the batch file.

OS/2 batch files use the SETLOCAL and ENDLOCAL commands in conjunction within a batch file. As discussed previously in this chapter, DOS allows you to change directories during the execution of batch procedures. When the batch procedure completes, your current directory remains the same as the last directory to which you issued a change-directory command. With OS/2 you can use the SETLOCAL and ENDLOCAL commands rather than requiring your batch procedures to determine the current directory prior to processing commands and then restoring the directory before terminating.

SETLOCAL saves the current drive, directory, and environment variables. ENDLOCAL restores them to the saved values. For example, although the following batch procedure changes the default drive and directory during its command processing, the use of OS/2 SETLOCAL and ENDLOCAL commands ensures that the changes exist only for the lifetime of the batch procedure.

```
SETLOCAL
MYPROG
CD \UTIL
PROMPT >>>
YOURPROG
ENDLOCAL
```

When the batch file processing completes, your default drive, directory, and environment settings will be unchanged.

THE SETLOCAL AND ENDLOCAL
COMMANDS

The OS/2 SETLOCAL and ENDLOCAL commands work in conjunction to ensure that upon completion of a batch file, the current disk, directory, and environment variables maintain their values prior to the batch file invocation.

AUTOEXEC.BAT VERSUS STARTUP.CMD

OS/2 runs in either protected or real mode. In real mode, OS/2 executes the file AUTOEXEC.BAT as the start-up procedure. In protected mode, however, OS/2 uses STARTUP.CMD. Both files serve the same function—specifying a list of commands the operating system is to execute each time it boots. Place commands in STARTUP.CMD as you would in AUTOEXEC.BAT.

> ### AUTOEXEC.BAT VERSUS
> ### STARTUP.CMD
>
> OS/2 executes in either real or protected mode. Under real mode, OS/2 executes AUTOEXEC.BAT. In protected mode, OS/2 executes STARTUP.CMD. Both files serve the same function — providing you with DOS start-up commands.

CMD FILE EXTENSIONS

Under OS/2, batch file extensions change from BAT to CMD. You have already seen an example of this with the file STARTUP.CMD. Thus OS/2 supports three types of executable files: EXE, COM, and CMD. As you migrate to OS/2, you will have to change your file extensions.

NAMED PARAMETERS

Earlier you examined the replaceable batch parameters %0 to %9. OS/2's expanded functional capabilities provide complete support for named parameters. You create an OS/2 named parameter by using the SET command, as shown here:

SET PARAM=VALUE

For example, the following batch file defines a named parameter called FILE and then displays its contents:

```
SET FILE=TEST.DAT
TYPE %FILE%
```

Note the use of the percent sign around the named parameter. In this case, the batch file defined the named parameter. However, the user could have easily defined the parameter from the OS/2 prompt and then invoked the batch file.

```
A> SET FILE=TEST.DAT

A> BATFILE

A> TYPE TEST.DAT

TEST TEST TEST TES
T TEST TEST TE
ST TEST TEST

A>
```

DETACH (RUNNING BACKGROUND COMMANDS)

Batch file processing is a user convenience. OS/2 takes this convenience one step further, allowing you to execute programs in a background mode while you perform interactive tasks at the keyboard. The DOS print spooler is a good example of a background task. The print spooler shares CPU time with your interactive commands, making the computer appear to be performing two tasks simultaneously. In actuality, the operating system switches control of the CPU back and forth between the PRINT command and your commands in round-robin fashion (see Figure 2-8).

The OS/2 DETACH command allows you to (in the background) run any command that does not require user intervention, while you perform (in the foreground) tasks at the keyboard. The format of the DETACH command is

DETACH DOS__COMMAND__LINE

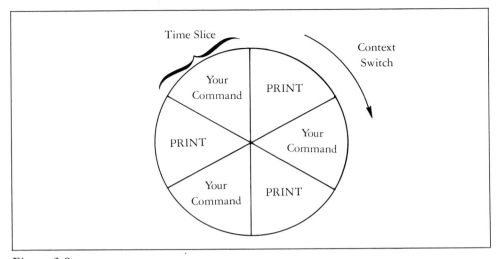

Figure 2-8.

Round-Robin CPU scheduling

For example, the following command line performs the DOS CHKDSK
command and writes the results to the file DISK.STS:

```
A> DETACH CHKDSK > DISK.STS
```

Since this command does not require user intervention once it begins,
OS/2 allows you to run it in the background. This means that the
command will execute and complete concurrently with other commands
issuing from the keyboard (or invoked as background commands via
DETACH).

The command line

```
A> DETACH CHKDSK > DISK.STS
```

directs OS/2 to perform the CHKDSK command in the background. Upon invocation, OS/2 displays the process identification for the background application, as shown here:

```
The Process Identification Number is 134
```

For now, think of this identification as the way OS/2 keeps track of the executing applications. Once you invoke this command, OS/2 begins alternating CPU time between the foreground and background in round-robin fashion.

If you print a file by using PRINT, OS/2 will divide CPU time as shown in Figure 2-9. Because the CPU is so fast, all three programs appear to functioning simultaneously. In reality, OS/2 is executing one at a time and switching rapidly between them. In so doing, OS/2

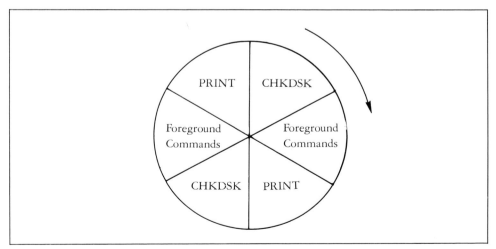

Figure 2-9.

PRINT and CHKDSK sharing
CPU under OS/2

minimizes CPU idle time and ensures that your CPU is utilized to its fullest.

THE DETACH COMMAND

The OS/2 DETACH command allows you to execute in the background programs that do not require user intervention, while you continue to execute commands in the foreground. In so doing, OS/2 helps maximize CPU initialization.

This chapter traversed the entire spectrum of DOS batch processing. By now you should have learned to create sequential, conditional, and iterative batch files. You should also be conversant with the following batch file commands:

COMMAND
ECHO
FOR
IF
PAUSE [*message*]
REM [*message*]
SHIFT

In addition, you should be able to use the DOS replaceable batch parameters %0 to %9 to enhance the functional capabilities of your batch files. You should know how to invoke nested batch procedures and how to define the file AUTOEXEC.BAT. Finally, you should understand the changes to batch file processing under OS/2.

3: DOS Redirection and Pipe Operators

$\blacksquare$ost DOS power users are conversant with DOS input/output (I/O) redirection through use of redirection operators and pipe operators. For those who are not, this chapter provides a quick review of DOS I/O redirection. The chapter then covers the creation of programs that utilize the DOS I/O redirection and pipe operators from Turbo Pascal and C. The chapter concludes with a discussion of changes to I/O redirection under OS/2.

I/O REDIRECTION

By default, each time you issue a command, DOS obtains its input from the keyboard and displays its output to the screen (see Figure 3-1).

Issue the command

```
A> DIR
```

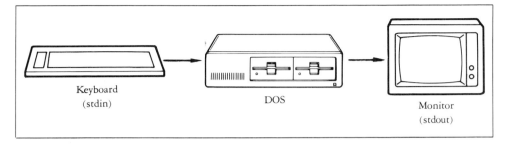

Figure 3-1.

Input from keyboard; output to
screen

DOS displays the directory listing to the screen. For this command, DOS
uses the screen as its standard output (stdout) device. For most programs, you will want DOS to display the output to screen. But DOS also
allows you to redirect its standard output device to a system printer, a
communications port, or a file by using the output redirection operator
($>$), and to other programs by using the DOS pipe operator ($|$).

Issue the command

```
A> DIR > DIR.DAT
```

In this case, DOS did not display the command output to the screen.
Instead, the DOS redirection operator $>$ directed DOS to write the
program output to the file DIR.DAT. Figure 3-2 illustrates the I/O
redirection. The DOS redirection operator $>$ redirected the standard
output (stdout) destination to the file DIR.DAT instead of to the screen.

Now turn on your system printer and issue the command

```
A> DIR > PRN:
```

This time, DOS redirects the command output from the screen to the
system printer (see Figure 3-3). The DOS redirection operator $>$ allows
you to conveniently redirect output to files and devices.

THE DOS OUTPUT REDIRECTION
OPERATOR (>)

The DOS output redirection operator (>) directs DOS to redirect output from the default standard output device (the screen) to a file, the printer, or a communications port. If you redirect output to a file, DOS creates a new file or overwrites existing files with the same name.

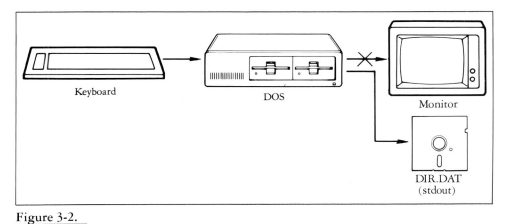

Figure 3-2.

I/O redirection to DIR.DAT

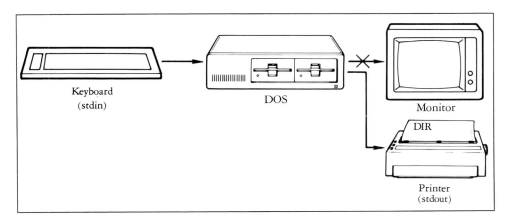

Figure 3-3.

I/O redirection from screen to
printer

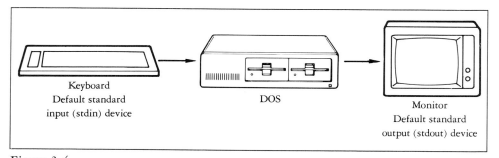

Keyboard
Default standard
input (stdin) device

DOS

Monitor
Default standard
output (stdout) device

Figure 3-4.

Flow of DOS standard input and
output

By default, each time you issue a DOS command, DOS uses the keyboard as its standard input (stdin) source. The general flow of DOS standard input and output is shown in Figure 3-4.

The DOS input redirection operator ($<$) works essentially the same way as the DOS output redirection operator ($>$), in that it redefines the standard input source. However, the number of programs that support redirected input is fewer than the number that support redirected output. To get a better feel for input redirection, create the file LETTER.DAT as follows:

```
A> COPY CON LETTER.DAT
A
B
E
D
F
C
^Z

        1 File(s) copied
```

Next, issue the following DOS SORT command:

```
A> SORT < LETTER.DAT
```

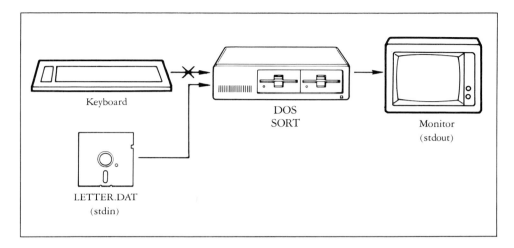

Figure 3-5.

I/O redirection from LETTER.DAT

In this case, the DOS input redirection operator (<) directs DOS to obtain the input for the SORT command from the file LETTER.DAT instead of the keyboard (the default stdin), as shown in Figure 3-5. Try sorting other text files in this fashion.

```
A> SORT < AUTOEXEC.BAT
```

If you invoke SORT without the DOS redirection operator <,

```
A> SORT
```

DOS does not redirect the standard input source from the keyboard. SORT waits for you to type in the data to sort from the keyboard.

```
A> SORT
A
B
E
D
F
G
^Z
```

Remember, DOS uses the CTRL-Z combination to represent the end of a file. Since the command line did not redirect SORT's input to a file, you must specify the end of input by pressing CTRL-Z. Upon end-of-file, SORT sorts the data you input and displays the result, as shown here:

```
A> SORT
A
B
E
D
F
G
^Z
A
B
D
E
F
G

A>
```

THE DOS INPUT REDIRECTION
OPERATOR (<)

The DOS input redirection operator (<) directs DOS to obtain the input for a command from a file rather than from the default standard input device (the keyboard).

DOS allows you to place multiple redirection operators on your command line. For example, the following SORT command uses the file

LETTER.DAT as its input source, and then writes the sorted data to the file LETTER.SRT:

```
A> SORT < LETTER.DAT > LETTER.SRT
```

Figure 3-6 shows this operation.

DOS provides a third I/O redirection operator ($>>$) to append the result of a command to a DOS file. For example, the command

```
A> DIR >> DIR.DAT
```

directs DOS to append the output of the directory listing to the file DIR.DAT. In this case, if the file DIR.DAT already exists, DOS will append the result of the directory command to it. If the file does not exist, DOS will create it. Again issue the command, and then display the result (see Figure 3-7).

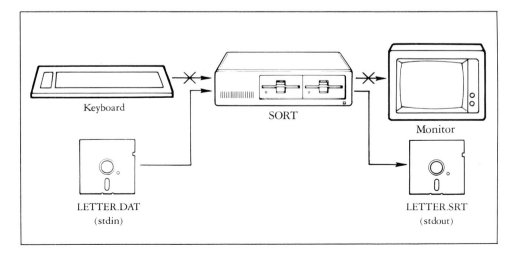

Figure 3-6.

Input from LETTER.DAT with
output to LETTER.SRT

```
A> TYPE DIR.DAT

   Volume in drive A is DOSDISK
   Directory of   A:\

   DIR      DAT         0    7-06-87    9:56p
   WS       COM     45056    1-01-80   12:08a
   WSMSGS   OVR     29056    1-01-80   12:26a
   WSOVLY1  OVR     41216    1-01-80   12:26a
   SOLUTION DAT      2395    7-06-87    7:29p
   X                   18    7-06-87    9:41p
   TWO      PAS        44    7-06-87    7:18p
   LETTER   DAT        18    7-06-87    9:38p
         8 File(s)         9216 bytes free

   Volume in drive A is DOSDISK
   Directory of   A:\

   DIR      DAT       427    7-06-87    9:57p
   WS       COM     45056    1-01-80   12:08a
   WSMSGS   OVR     29056    1-01-80   12:26a
   WSOVLY1  OVR     41216    1-01-80   12:26a
   SOLUTION DAT      2395    7-06-87    7:29p
   X                   18    7-06-87    9:41p
   TWO      PAS        44    7-06-87    7:18p
   LETTER   DAT        18    7-06-87    9:38p
         8 File(s)         8704 bytes free
```

Figure 3-7.

Contents of DIR.DAT

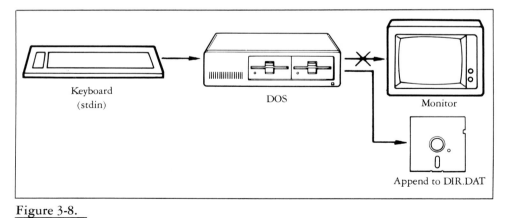

Keyboard
(stdin)

DOS

Monitor

Append to DIR.DAT

Figure 3-8.

Output of TYPE appended to
DIR.DAT

Invoke the TYPE command again, this time appending the result to the existing DIR.DAT file.

```
A> TYPE DIR.DAT >> DIR.DAT
```

In this case, rather than creating a new file named DIR.DAT, DOS appends the output of the TYPE command to the existing file (see Figure 3-8). The file contents will now appear as shown in Figure 3-9.

> ### THE DOS APPEND REDIRECTION OPERATOR (>>)
>
> The DOS append redirection operator (>>) directs DOS to append the data written to the standard output device to the file you specify. If the file does not exist, DOS creates it.

THE DOS PIPE

Many DOS users fail to exploit DOS I/O redirection with the most powerful DOS redirection operator — the DOS pipe (¦). Rather than directing I/O to or from a DOS file, the pipe redirects the output of the first program on the command line to become the input for the second program on the same command line. Consider the following SORT command:

```
A> DIR ¦ SORT
```

In this case, DOS redirects the output of the DIR command to become the input of the SORT command (see Figure 3-10). DOS pipes the output of the directory command (stdout) to become the input of the SORT command (stdin).

```
A> TYPE DIR.DAT

   Volume in drive A is DOSDISK
   Directory of  A:\

DIR        DAT          0   7-06-87    9:56p
WS         COM      45056   1-01-80   12:08a
WSMSGS     OVR      29056   1-01-80   12:26a
WSOVLY1    OVR      41216   1-01-80   12:26a
SOLUTION   DAT       2395   7-06-87    7:29p
X                      18   7-06-87    9:41p
TWO        PAS         44   7-06-87    7:18p
LETTER     DAT         18   7-06-87    9:38p
        8 File(s)          9216 bytes free

   Volume in drive A is DOSDISK
   Directory of  A:\

DIR        DAT        427   7-06-87    9:57p
WS         COM      45056   1-01-80   12:08a
WSMSGS     OVR      29056   1-01-80   12:26a
WSOVLY1    OVR      41216   1-01-80   12:26a
SOLUTION   DAT       2395   7-06-87    7:29p
X                      18   7-06-87    9:41p
TWO        PAS         44   7-06-87    7:18p
LETTER     DAT         18   7-06-87    9:38p
        8 File(s)          8704 bytes free

   Volume in drive A is DOSDISK
   Directory of  A:\

DIR        DAT        427   7-06-87    9:57p
WS         COM      45056   1-01-80   12:08a
WSMSGS     OVR      29056   1-01-80   12:26a
WSOVLY1    OVR      41216   1-01-80   12:26a
SOLUTION   DAT       2395   7-06-87    7:29p
X                      18   7-06-87    9:41p
TWO        PAS         44   7-06-87    7:18p
LETTER     DAT         18   7-06-87    9:38p
        8 File(s)          8704 bytes free

   Volume in drive A is DOSDISK
   Directory of  A:\

DIR        DAT        427   7-06-87    9:57p
WS         COM      45056   1-01-80   12:08a
WSMSGS     OVR      29056   1-01-80   12:26a
WSOVLY1    OVR      41216   1-01-80   12:26a
SOLUTION   DAT       2395   7-06-87    7:29p
X                      18   7-06-87    9:41p
TWO        PAS         44   7-06-87    7:18p
LETTER     DAT         18   7-06-87    9:38p
        8 File(s)          8704 bytes free
```

Figure 3-9.

New contents of DIR.DAT

Issue the following command:

```
A> DIR | MORE
```

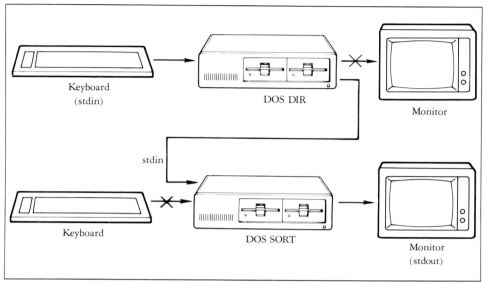

Figure 3-10.

Redirection of output of DIR to
input of SORT

When the DIR command completes, DOS sends an end-of-file (CTRL-Z) character to the MORE command, which terminates it. As with DOS redirection operators, you can place several pipe operators on the same command line:

```
A> DIR ¦ SORT ¦ MORE
```

In this case, DOS redirects the standard input (stdin) and standard output (stdout) for each command (see Figure 3-11).

THE DOS PIPE OPERATOR (¦)

The DOS pipe operator (¦) directs DOS to make the output of one program (stdout) the input of the next program (stdin).

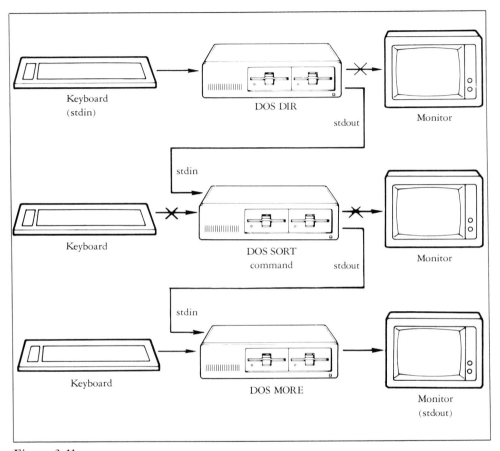

Figure 3-11.

Redirection of stdin and stdout

DOS does not restrict you to placing only one type of redirection or pipe operators on the same command line. For example, the following command writes a sorted directory listing to the file DIR.SRT:

```
A> DIR | SORT > DIR.SRT
```

In this case, DOS redirects the output of the DIR command to become the input of the SORT command.

Rather than displaying its results on the screen, DOS redirects the output of SORT to the file DIR.SRT (see Figure 3-12).

USING I/O REDIRECTION TO IMPROVE USER INTERFACE

For some applications it may be desirable to hide confusing prompts from the end user. For example, the first time you issue a DOS PRINT

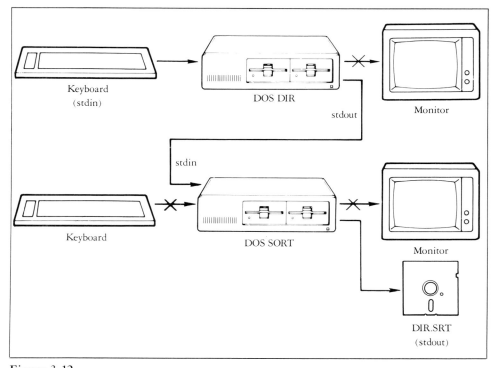

Figure 3-12.

Redirection of SORT output to
DIR.SRT

command, PRINT prompts you for the device information, as shown here:

```
A> PRINT
Name of list device [PRN]:
```

Some end users may not understand this prompt. Normally you just press the ENTER key to use the DOS defaults.

DOS I/O redirection allows you to use files to remove this requirement. Create the following file by entering

```
A> COPY CON RETURN.DAT
^Z
        1 File(s) copied
```

The file contains a carriage return, which is equivalent to pressing the ENTER key. Next, create a BAT file by entering

```
A> COPY CON PRNINIT.BAT
PRINT < RETURN.DAT
^Z
        1 File(s) copied
```

When DOS executes the PRINT command, rather than prompting the user for the device information, the carriage return redirected from the file RETURN.DAT directs PRINT to use its default value. In this case, you can place the PRINT command in the user's AUTOEXEC.BAT file to ensure that it always behaves in the same manner.

In a similar fashion, I/O redirection allows you to suppress messages. Consider the following messages:

```
A> PRINT
Name of list device [PRN]:
Resident part of PRINT installed
PRINT queue is empty
```

DOS provides a NUL (nonexistent) device to which you can essentially
route data that you want discarded. The name of the device is NUL:.
Consider the following command:

```
A> PRINT < RETURN.DAT > NUL:
```

Rather than displaying the message on the screen, DOS routes the
message to the "bit bucket," where it is essentially thrown away.

FILE HANDLES

A key to your understanding of I/O redirection is DOS file handles. A
file handle is a value that DOS uses for file and device I/O. The FILES=
entry in CONFIG.SYS defines the number of file handles that DOS
supports each time the operating system boots. By default, DOS supports eight file handles. However, DOS defines the first five handles as
shown in Table 3-1. This means that your application programs are
restricted to opening three files, as shown here:

8	file handles supported
−5	predefined file handles
3	available file handles

Table 3-1.

DOS File Handles and Applications

File Handle	Default Device	Name	Operations
0	con:	stdin	keyboard
1	con:	stdout	screen
2	con:	stderr	screen
3	aux:	stdaux	aux:device
4	prn:	stdprn	printer

Most users, therefore, place the following entry in CONFIG.SYS to ensure that ample file handles are available for their application programs:

FILES = 20

Each time you redirect an application's input or output, DOS redirects the file handle associated with a handle listed previously.

PROGRAMMING DOS I/O REDIRECTION

The following applications fully utilize the DOS pipe and I/O redirection operators. Each program is presented in C and Turbo Pascal. All the programs obtain their input from the DOS standard input (stdin) and direct their output to the standard output (stdout) file handle. For example, the following program displays each line of input it receives, followed by the number of characters in the line. For example, if the file TEST.DAT contains

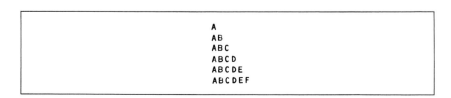

```
A
A B
A B C
A B C D
A B C D E
A B C D E F
```

the command

```
A> CHARCNT < TEST.DAT
```

will display

```
1 A
2 AB
3 ABC
4 ABCD
5 ABCDE
6 ABCDEF
```

The following C program presents CHARCNT.C:

```
#include <string.h>
#include <stdio.h>

#define MAX_STRING 255

main ()
 {
  char string[MAX_STRING];

  while (fgets(string, MAX_STRING, stdin))
    printf ("%d %s", strlen (string)-1, string); /* length
                                              includes \n */

 }
```

Remember that in C, the **printf** function directs its output to stdout. To redirect input or output from a Turbo Pascal program you must place the following compiler directive at the top of program:

($P256,G256)

The directive ensures that Turbo Pascal uses the stdin and stdout file handles for input and output.

The following program implements CHARCNT.PAS:

```
{$p256,g256}

Program CharCnt;

var
 str : string[255];
 line_number : integer;

begin
 while (not EOF)
   begin
     readln (str);
     writeln (Ord(str[0]):4,' ', str);
   end;
end.
```

This program simply writes its output to the screen, as do most Turbo Pascal programs. The difference is that the compiler directive {$P256, $G256} gives your program added flexibility in that it now supports I/O redirection.

In a similar manner, the following program displays a count of the characters, lines, and pages contained in the input it receives. For example, the command line

```
A> STATS < TEST.DAT
```

results in

```
Summary
Characters 21
Lines 6
Pages 0
```

The following C program implements STATS.C:

```c
#include <string.h>
#include <stdio.h>

#define MAX_STRING 255
#define LINES_PER_PAGE 25

main ()
 {
  int lines = 0;
  int characters = 0;

  char string[MAX_STRING];

  while (fgets(string, MAX_STRING, stdin))
    {
     characters += printf ("%s", string) -1;
     lines++;
    }

  printf ("SUMMARY\nCharacters %d\nLines %d\nPages %d",
          characters, lines, lines / LINES_PER_PAGE);
 }
```

Likewise, this Turbo Pascal program implements STATS.PAS:

```pascal
{$p256,g256}

Program Stats;

const
  LINES_PER_PAGE = 25;

var
  characters: integer;
  lines : integer;
  str : string[255];

begin
  characters := 0;
  lines := 0;

  while (not EOF)
    begin
      readln (str);
      characters := characters + ord (str[0]);
      lines := lines + 1;
    end;

  writeln ('Summary');
  writeln ('Characters ', characters);
  writeln ('Lines ', lines);
  writeln ('Pages ', lines div LINES_PER_PAGE);

end.
```

Next, the program FINDWORD displays the line and line number of each line of the input stream that contains the specified word. For example,

```
A> DIR | FINDWORD DIR
```

results in the display shown in Figure 3-13. Note that the program matches the word regardless of the mixture of uppercase and lowercase. The command

```
A> DIR | FINDWORD dir
```

is equivalent to the previous command line.

```
 3   DIRECTORY OF  C:\
 7  DOS        <DIR>     4-30-85     8:30P
 8  POWER      <DIR>     6-29-87     6:19P
12  DOSBOOK    <DIR>     9-14-86     8:44P
13  UTIL       <DIR>     5-02-85     7:30P
14  WS         <DIR>    10-12-86    12:11P
17  PTOOLS     <DIR>     7-12-86     5:43A
18  MACRO      <DIR>     7-15-85     5:45P
19  BIN        <DIR>     3-16-87    11:10A
21  LIB        <DIR>     3-16-87    11:10A
22  DOSUSER    <DIR>     2-16-87    10:21A
23  INCLUDE    <DIR>     3-16-87    11:10A
24  B3         <DIR>     8-10-85     8:17A
25  SPRINT     <DIR>     5-04-87     7:40P
26  TEMP       <DIR>     3-16-87    11:19A
28  WINDOWS2   <DIR>    11-23-86     8:15P
```

Figure 3-13.

Redirected output of FINDWORD
directory

The following program implements FINDWORD.C:

```c
#include <stdio.h>
#include <string.h>

#define MAX_STRING 255

main (argc, argv)
  int argc;
  char *argv[];
  {
  int line_number = 0;

  char string[MAX_STRING];

  if (argc >= 2)
    {
    strupr (argv[1]);
    while (fgets(string, MAX_STRING, stdin))
      {
      strupr (string);
      line_number++;
      if (index (argv[1], string) != -1)
        printf ("%d %s", line_number, string);
      }
    }
  else
    printf ("Invalid usage: FINDWORD STRING\n");
  }

index (s1, s2)
  char s1[], s2[];
  {
  int i, j, k;

  for (i = 0; s2[i] != NULL; i++)
    for (j = i, k = 0; s1[k] == s2[j]; k++, j++)
      if (s1[k+1] == NULL)
        return (i);

  return -1;
  }
```

Likewise, this Turbo Pascal program implements FINDWORD.PAS:

```
{$p256,g256}

Program FINDWORD;

Type
    string79 = string[79];

procedure Str_to_Uppercase (var STR: string79);

var
    I:  integer;                         {counter for loops}

begin

{call UpCase each character in the string}
    for I := 1 to Length (STR) do
       STR[I] := UpCase (STR[I]);

end;


var
  str : string79;
  word: string79;
  line: integer;

begin
  line := 0;

 if (ParamCount >= 1) then
    begin
       word := ParamStr(1);
       str_to_uppercase (word);

       while (not EOF)
          begin
          readln (str);
          str_to_uppercase (str);
          line := line + 1;
          if (Pos(word, str) > 0) then
             writeln (line:4, ' ', str);
          end;
       end
   else
      writeln ('Invalid Usage: FINDWORD STRING');
end.
```

It is important to be able to bypass the I/O redirection when an error
occurs. To prevent I/O redirection of error messages, you must direct
the error message to the stderr file handle. For example, the following

program numbers each line of text in the input stream. Each time a blank line occurs, however, the program displays the message

```
Skipping Blank Line
```

to the standard error file handle.

Note the use of the stderr file handle in the following C program:

```c
#include <string.h>
#include <stdio.h>

#define MAX_STRING 255

main ()
 {
  int line = 0;

  char string[MAX_STRING];

  while (fgets(string, MAX_STRING, stdin))
    {
     if (strlen(string) -1 == 0)
       fprintf (stderr, "Skipping Blank Line\n");
     else
       printf ("%d %s", ++line, string);
    }

 }
```

The following Turbo Pascal program performs the same task in a similar manner. Note the use of the file pointer Con:, which directs Turbo to write the string to the stderr device.

```
{$p256,g256}

Program Line;

var
  lines: integer;
  str: string[255];

begin
 lines := 0;

 while (not EOF)
   begin
     readln (str);
     lines := lines + 1;
     if (ord(str[0]) <> 0) then
       writeln (str)
     else
       writeln (con, 'Skipping Blank Line');

   end;

end.
```

Try to develop your application programs in a manner that supports DOS I/O redirection. The little extra effort I/O redirection requires within your programs is well worth the effort in terms of functional capabilities.

OS/2 I/O REDIRECTION

Under OS/2, your DOS command lines maintain the same degree of flexibility with the standard DOS redirection operators ($>, >>, <$, and ¦). OS/2 enhances command-line processing by adding several new command-line operators.

The first OS/2 command-line operator is the double ampersand (&&). Consider the following command line:

```
A> DIR TEST.DAT && TYPE TEST.DAT
```

If OS/2 successfully executes the first command (DIR TEST.DAT), it then executes the second command (TYPE TEST.DAT). If the first command fails (the file does not exist), OS/2 does not execute the second command. In this example, if the file TEST.DAT exists, OS/2 types its contents. If the file does not exist, OS/2 ignores the TYPE command. OS/2 considers any program that exits with a status of 0 to be successful.

THE OS/2 AND COMMAND-LINE OPERATOR (&&)

The OS/2 AND command-line operator (&&) directs OS/2 to first execute the command to the left of the double ampersand. If the command completes successfully, OS/2 executes the command to the right of the ampersand. If the first command fails, OS/2 ignores the second command.

OS/2 provides a similar operator which uses the symbol that was previously used for the DOS pipe twice (| |). The OS/2 OR command-line operator works as follows. If the first command on the command line fails, OS/2 executes the second. If the first command is successful, OS/2 ignores the second.

Consider the following command:

```
A> DIR A:CONFIG.SYS || COPY B:CONFIG.SYS A:
```

OS/2 checks to see if the file CONFIG.SYS exists on drive A. If so, the DIR command completes successfully, and OS/2 ignores the second command. By ignoring the second command, OS/2 does not overwrite an existing CONFIG.SYS file. If the file CONFIG.SYS does not exist on drive A, OS/2 copies the file from drive B to drive A.

THE OS/2 OR COMMAND-LINE
OPERATOR (||)

The OS/2 OR command-line operator (||) directs OS/2 to first execute the command to the left of the OR operator. If the command successfully completes, OS/2 ignores the second command. If the command fails, OS/2 executes the second command.

OS/2 uses the single ampersand (&) command-line operator to separate multiple commands on a single line. For example, consider the following command line:

```
A> PROG1 & PROG2 & PROG3
```

OS/2 executes PROG1 first. If the program exists, OS/2 executes it. Otherwise, OS/2 continues with the next command on the line. OS/2 executes the commands it finds in a sequential fashion, from left to right.

THE OS/2 COMMAND SEPARATOR (&)

The OS/2 command separator (&) allows you to place multiple commands on one command line. OS/2 executes these commands from left to right. If a command fails or is invalid, OS/2 continues with the next command on the line.

OS/2 uses the caret (^) as its escape symbol. When placed on a command line before any other DOS I/O redirection operator, the escape symbol directs DOS to suppress the operator's function. For example, the command line

```
A> DIR ¦ FINDWORD ^<DIR^>
```

contains two DOS I/O redirection operators ($<$ and $>$). The escape operator prevents OS/2 from attempting the redirection. To search for the string $<$DIR$>$ and redirect the output of FINDWORD to a file, you would enter

```
A> DIR ¦ FINDWORD ^<DIR^> > RESULT.DAT
```

Since the final redirection operator is not preceded by an OS/2 escape symbol, redirection of output occurs.

THE OS/2 REDIRECTION SUPPRESSION
OPERATOR (^)

The OS/2 redirection suppression operator (^) directs OS/2 not to perform I/O redirection based upon the I/O operator it precedes. This allows you to pass redirection operators as command line parameters.

DOS I/O redirection operators are a powerful tool. By now you should be able to redirect input or output to or from a program or file.

Table 3-2.

Redirection Operators

>	Output redirection operator	Modifies an application's standard output device (stdout) to a file or device
<	Input redirection operator	Modifies an application's standard input device (stdin) from a file
>>	Append redirection operator	Directs DOS to append data written to stdout to the file or specified device
¦	Pipe operator	Directs the output of one program (stdout) to become the input of a second (stdin)
&&	OS/2 AND operator	Directs OS/2 to perform the command to the right of the operator first. If the command is successful, OS/2 executes the second command
¦¦	OS/2 OR operator	Directs OS/2 to execute the command to the left of the OR operator. If the command fails, OS/2 executes the second command. If the first command is successful, OS/2 ignores the second command
&	OS/2 command separator	Allows you to place multiple commands on one line. OS/2 executes the commands from left to right
^	OS/2 redirection suppression operator	Allows redirection operators to be passed as command-line parameters

You have seen that developing applications that support the DOS pipe is relatively straightforward and leads to very functional programs. Finally, you have gained an appreciation of the expanded command-line operators provided under OS/2. Table 3-2 summarizes the DOS and OS/2 command-line operators.

4: DOS System Configuration

M ost DOS users are always interested in improving their system performance, making their computers run faster, and using their computing time more effectively. This chapter takes a detailed look at the DOS system configuration parameters, and discusses how each affects your overall system performance. If you are already conversant with the DOS file CONFIG.SYS and its entries, this chapter also provides the DOS 3.3 and OS/2 configuration parameters. Examining these system parameters should help you to better understand OS/2 and its complexities.

SYSTEM CONFIGURATION

Each time DOS starts, it searches the root directory on the boot drive for the file CONFIG.SYS. If DOS finds this file, it opens and reads it to configure the operating system characteristics in memory. If DOS does not find this file, it uses its default values to configure the operating system. The flowchart in Figure 4-1 illustrates the processing involved.

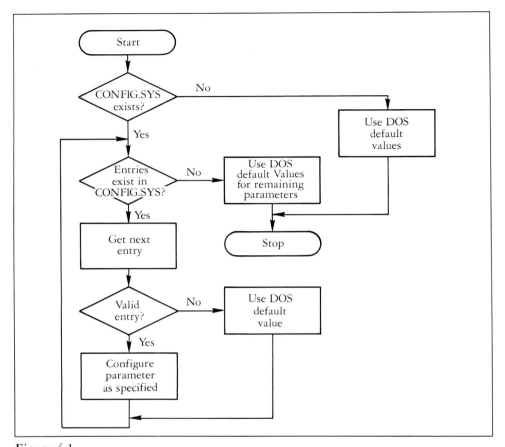

Figure 4-1.

Flowchart depicting system
configuration

CONFIG.SYS is an ASCII text file that you can create with a text
editor or by copying it from the console device, as shown here:

```
A> COPY CON \CONFIG.SYS
```

The file contains entries that DOS uses to define specific operating system attributes. The following is a list of the entries DOS supports through version 3.2:

BREAK
BUFFERS
COUNTRY
DEVICE
DRIVEPARM
FCBS
FILES
LASTDRIVE
SHELL

Be careful when you place entries into CONFIG.SYS. Each entry directly affects a specific portion of DOS; therefore, incorrect entries can degrade your system performance significantly. Once you modify an entry in CONFIG.SYS, you must reboot the operating system to make the changes take effect. This is because DOS has already configured itself in memory. The only time system configuration occurs is during system startup. To modify DOS system parameters, follow these steps:

1. Edit or create the file CONFIG.SYS in the root directory.

2. Place the desired entries in the file.

3. Reboot the operating system.

Familiarize yourself with each of the system generation parameters.

BREAK (Default: BREAK=OFF)

By now, you know that you can terminate an application by pressing the CTRL-BREAK or the CTRL-C key combination. This is often your only means to terminate a runaway program other than by rebooting. By default, each time DOS writes to the screen or printer, or reads from the keyboard, it checks to see if the user has pressed the CTRL-BREAK key combination. If so, DOS issues an interrupt to the CTRL-BREAK interrupt handler, which normally terminates your program's execution.

Programmers should note that it is possible to capture the CTRL-BREAK interrupt by directing DOS not to terminate applications when the user enters CTRL-BREAK at the keyboard. For example, the Turbo Pascal compiler directive {$C—} disallows CTRL-BREAK processing, as shown here:

```
{$C-}

Program TEST;

begin
  while (true) do
    writeln ('Looping');
end.
```

This directive must be the first line in your program. This restricts the user from exiting applications by alternate means.

By using the BREAK=ON entry in CONFIG.SYS, you can increase the number of functions that DOS will check for a CTRL-BREAK when it completes them. When BREAK=ON, DOS not only checks for CTRL-BREAK after screen and keyboard I/O operations, but also upon completing disk I/O. BREAK=ON, therefore, increases system overhead since DOS must now check for CTRL-BREAK after each disk operation. This in turn makes your applications run slower. You may want to set BREAK= ON only during program development and debugging.

BREAK

The DOS BREAK configuration parameter allows you to increase the number of
DOS services that DOS will check for a user-entered CTRL-BREAK key combination upon completing. This additional testing increases system overhead.

To turn CTRL-BREAK checking on, place the following entry in
CONFIG.SYS and reboot:

BREAK=ON

BUFFERS (PC Default: BUFFERS=2
PC AT Default: BUFFERS=3)

Each time DOS reads or writes data to or from disk, it uses storage
locations in memory to hold the transferred data. These storage locations are disk buffers. A buffer is 528 bytes long (see Figure 4-2).

When your application program reads or writes a record of data that
is not equivalent to the disk sector size (a *sector* is normally 512 bytes),
DOS buffers the record. A sector defines the smallest unit DOS disk
operations will transfer. If your application uses 64-byte records, a single
DOS sector can store 8 of them (see Figure 4-3).

For example, if your program requests record 1, DOS will read the
entire sector that contains record 1 from disk into a buffer, as shown in
Figure 4-4. This means that records 2 through 8 are also available in

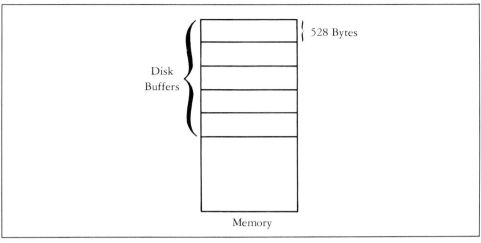

Figure 4-2.

Disk buffers

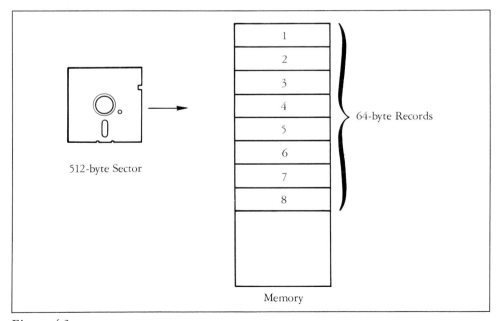

Figure 4-3.

Disk sectors

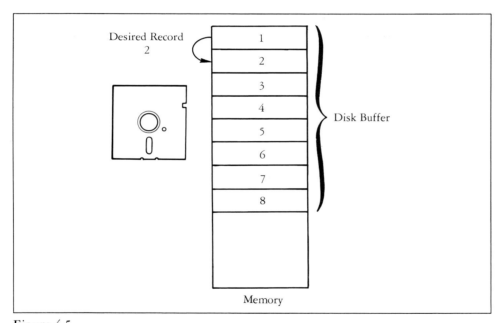

Figure 4-4.

Records within an application

Figure 4-5.

Searching memory buffers for a
record

memory. When your program later requests record 2, DOS first searches
its memory buffers for the record (see Figure 4-5).

If DOS finds the record, it does not have to read a new sector from
disk (a slow process). Therefore, DOS satisfies your I/O request much
faster. If you increase the number of file buffers that DOS supports,

applications that perform random access file I/O (such as database and word processing applications) will show considerable performance improvements. Conversely, making the number of buffers too large

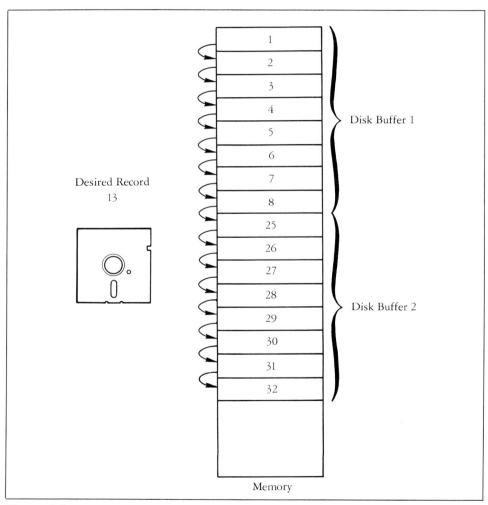

Figure 4-6.

Effect of too many buffers on system
overhead

induces system overhead, since DOS must now spend considerable time searching each buffer for the desired record (see Figure 4-6).

The following list may prove helpful in determining the proper number of buffers to allocate for your applications.

Database	10-25
Word processing	10-20
Large number of subdirectories	10-25
Fixed disk	3 minimum

Note that file I/O buffering affects disk output. If your application writes records to disk that are smaller than a sector, DOS will buffer each record. Once the buffer is full, DOS writes (or flushes) the buffer to disk.

Consider the following C program that writes 128-byte records to the file TEST.DAT:

```
/*
   Program to demonstrate disk buffering.  Note that the program
   writes a 128 byte record with each iteration.  However, DOS
   buffers 4 records in memory prior to writing them to disk.
*/
#include <stdio.h>

#define RECORD_SIZE 128

char string[RECORD_SIZE] =
"123456789012345678901234567890123456789012\
123456789012345678901234567890123456789012\
123456789012345678901234567890123456789012\
123456789012345678901234567890123456789011";

main ()
 {
  FILE *fopen(), *fp;

  if ((fp = fopen ("TEST.DAT", "w")) == NULL)
    printf ("Error opening TEST.DAT\n");
  else
    do {
      fputs (string, fp);
      printf ("Press Enter to display the next record, ^Z to
              terminate\n");
      }
    while (getchar() != EOF);

  fclose (fp);
 }
```

Each time the program writes a record, it prompts you to press the ENTER key. It repeats this process until you press CTRL-Z. Note, however, that although the program writes a record with each iteration, your disk access light only illuminates on every fourth record. This is because DOS is buffering the records until a complete sector is available (see Figure 4-7).

Most C compilers provide a routine that you can invoke to flush disk buffers after each disk output operation. This prevents DOS from buffering your disk output and forcing each record immediately to disk.

Assume that the previous C program was a database program. Again the record size you are using is 128 bytes. You invoke the program and update two records. The program issues the I/O operations and returns a successful status, informing you that the database has been updated. But DOS has buffered the records in memory, waiting for a full sector. Prior to DOS writing the buffer to disk, your computer experienced a power flux. You are not concerned, however, because your application reported that it had successfully updated the database. In reality, your last two updates are lost, and your database is corrupted.

COUNTRY (Default: COUNTRY=1)

The DOS COUNTRY configuration parameter allows you to define DOS international country characteristics. By default, DOS configures itself for the United States symbol set shown here:

```
Country Code 1 United States

Date format mm dd yy
Currency symbol $
Thousands separator ,
Decimal separator -
Time separator :
Decimal significant digits 2
Currency format 0
12 hour time format (1-12)
Data list separator ,
```

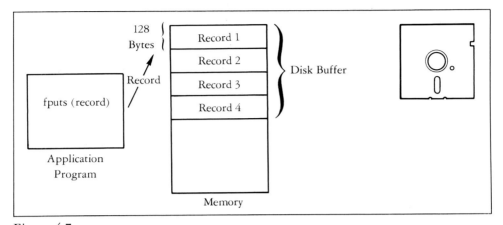

Figure 4-7.

Buffering records until a complete
sector is available

To support the ever-increasing foreign market, DOS provides support
for the countries listed in Table 4-1. To select the United Kingdom
symbol set, for example, the CONFIG.SYS entry is

COUNTRY=44

Rather than directly modifying the CONFIG.SYS file in this fashion,
most users issue the DOS SELECT command, which defines the country
code and keyboard configuration.

COUNTRY

The DOS COUNTRY configuration parameter allows you to define an international symbol set for your system. Most users allow the DOS SELECT command
to perform this processing.

Table 4-1.

Symbols Used by Each Country

Country Code	Country	Date Format	Currency Symbol	Thousands Separator	Decimal Separator	Date Separator	Time Separator	Decimal Significant Digits	Currency Format	Hour Format*	Data List Separator
1	United States	mm dd yy	$	,	.	-	:	2	0	1-12	,
31	Netherlands	dd mm yy	-	.	,	-	:	2	0	0-23	;
32	Belgium	dd mm yy	F		,	/	:	2	0	0-23	;
33	France	dd mm yy	F		,	/	:	2	0	0-23	;
34	Spain	dd mm yy	π	.	,	/	:	2	0	0-23	;
39	Italy	dd mm yy	Lit.	.	,	/	:	2	0	0-23	;
41	Switzerland	dd mm yy	Fr.	,	.	.	.	2	0	0-23	,
44	United Kingdom	dd mm yy	£	,	.	-	:	2	0	0-23	,
45	Denmark	dd mm yy	DKR	.	,	/	.	2	0	0-23	;
46	Sweden	yy mm dd	SEK	.	,	-	.	2	0	0-23	;
47	Norway	dd mm yy	KR	.	,	/	.	2	0	0-23	;
49	Germany	dd mm yy	DM	.	,	.	.	2	0	0-23	;
61	Australia	dd mm yy	$	,	.	-	:	2	0	0-23	,
358	Finland	dd mm yy	MK	,	.	-	:	2	0	0-23	;
972	Israel	dd mm yy	-	,	.	/	:	2	0	0-23	,

*1-12 is 12-hour format; 0-23 is 24-hour format.

DEVICE

Every hardware device on your system (such as disk drive, keyboard, or mouse) has a *device driver* associated with it. By default, DOS provides support for the standard devices such as the disk drive, keyboard, and system clock. Each time it boots, DOS loads into memory the software (device drivers) required to communicate with these devices. When your programs later need to access these devices, the device driver provides the interface.

Many users have added devices such as a mouse or a plotter to their systems. These "nonstandard" devices often require additional software support. Normally, the device manufacturer provides you with the device driver software on floppy disk when you purchase the device.

Once you add the new hardware to your system, you must inform DOS of its existence by installing the device driver. To do so, place the following entry in CONFIG.SYS:

DEVICE=*file__specification*

file__specification is the complete DOS path name for the file containing the device driver.

For example, to install a driver for a Brand X mouse, you may need to place the following entry in CONFIG.SYS:

DEVICE=XMOUSE.SYS

As you will find, most developers use the extension SYS to signify a device driver. The documentation that accompanies your hardware device normally includes the required CONFIG.SYS entry.

Depending upon your version of DOS, your disk may contain several device drivers. The two most common are ANSI.SYS and VDISK.SYS.

The first, ANSI.SYS, allows you to enhance your keyboard and video output processing. The ANSI driver is simply a piece of software that captures keyboard and screen data. In so doing, the driver can replace or enhance one sequence of characters with another.

For example, the ANSI driver uses the following Pascal character sequence to clear the screen and place the cursor in the upper-left corner:

writeln (Chr(27),'[H', Chr(27), '[J');

As you will see, the ANSI driver provides escape sequences to set character colors and attributes, clear lines of text on the screen, and position the cursor. Table 4-2 summarizes many of these commands.

To use the ANSI driver capabilities from Turbo Pascal, you must place the compiler directive {$p256} at the top of your program, as shown here:

```
{$p256}

Program Test;
```

The following Clear—Screen routine uses the ANSI driver from C, Pascal, and FORTRAN to clear the screen contents.

```
Clear_Screen ()
  {
   printf ("%c[H%c[J", 27, 27);
  }


procedure Clear_Screen ;
begin
   writeln (chr(27), '[H', chr(27), '[J');
end;


        subroutine Clear_Screen

        write (6, 1) 27, 27
   1    format (x, a1, '[H', a1, '[J')
        end
```

To use the ANSI driver from within your applications, place the following entry in CONFIG.SYS:

DEVICE=ANSI.SYS

Remember, you must reboot the operating system for the change to take effect.

The DOS device driver VDISK.SYS allows you to define a virtual, or RAM, disk in your computer's random access memory (RAM). If you have never used a RAM drive, here is how they work.

Table 4-2.

Character Codes Supported by ANSI

ANSI Function	ANSI Code
Set cursor position	Esc[Row;COLH
Clear screen	Esc[HEsc[J
Cursor up *n* rows	Esc[nA
Cursor down *n* rows	Esc[nB
Cursor right *n* columns	Esc[nC
Cursor left *n* columns	Esc[nD
Save cursor position	Esc[s
Restore cursor position	Esc[u
Erase to end of line	Esc[K
Erase to bottom of screen	Exc[2J
Device status report	Esc[6n
Report cursor position	Esc[n;nR
Redefine a keyboard character (the ASCII character defined by ascii1 is redefined to the ASCII character defined by ascii2)	Esc[ascii1;ascii2p
Redefine a function key key is defined as follows: F1 = 59...F10 = 68 F1...F10 = 59...68	Esc[0;key;"string"; 13p

The DOS VDISK device driver allows you to emulate the existence of a DOS disk in your computer's memory. This disk can store files or directories, and is treated by DOS in the same manner as any other disk. The one exception to this rule is that when you turn off your computer's power, the contents of the RAM disk are lost. Remember that the computer's main memory is volatile, which means it loses its contents when power is lost. Since the RAM disk resides here, its contents are also destroyed.

The main advantage of a RAM disk is speed. Floppy and fixed disks are mechanical, which means that by their very nature they are slower than the computer's electronic counterparts. RAM disks, on the other hand, are electronic, so they are not constrained by the slowness of mechanical arms.

You may use RAM drives by saving your files to fixed or floppy drives periodically to avoid loss of data. The format to install the VDISK device driver is

DEVICE=VDISK.SYS [*disk_space* [[*sector_size*] [*file_limit*]]] [/E]

where the following is true:

disk_space specifies the number of kilobytes of memory DOS is to allocate for the RAM drive. The default size is 64K.

sector_size defines the size of each RAM disk sector in bytes. The default sector size is 128 bytes.

file_limit is the maximum number of files that the RAM disk will support. The default is 64 files.

/E directs DOS to place the RAM disk in extended memory for the IBM PC AT.

Each of the following entries is valid for VDISK.SYS:

DEVICE=VDISK.SYS 128 512 32
DEVICE=VDISK.SYS 256 512 128
DEVICE=VDISK.SYS 64 128 4

In the following case, VDISK is installed with its default values:

DEVICE=VDISK.SYS

This entry installs a RAM disk with space for 360K of files, 512-byte sectors, and a maximum of 128 files.

When DOS boots, it displays the following to notify you that it has installed the RAM drive:

```
VDISK Version 1.0 virtual disk D:
    Directory entries adjusted
    Buffer size:       128 KB
    Sector size:       512
    Directory entries:  16
```

Each RAM disk requires an additional 768 bytes of memory for DOS data structures. Also, DOS requires a minimum of 64K of available memory after the installation of a RAM drive. Once DOS installs the RAM disk, you access it just as you would any standard drive:

drive__id:

For example, if your RAM disk installation results in drive D, you would use D:. Use the DOS CHKDSK command to note the amount of free memory on your system:

```
Volume DOSDISK      created Jan 16, 1987 7:25p

 21309440 bytes total disk space
   116736 bytes in 7 hidden files
   147456 bytes in 56 directories
 11249664 bytes in 1230 user files
    20480 bytes in bad sectors
  9723904 bytes available on disk

   655360 bytes total memory
   616336 bytes free
```

Next, install a RAM drive with the default values

DEVICE=VDISK.SYS

Again invoke CHKDSK to note the amount of memory DOS consumed
to create the RAM drive:

```
    Volume DOSDISK       created Jan 16, 1987 7:25p

   21309440 bytes total disk space
     116736 bytes in 7 hidden files
     147456 bytes in 56 directories
   11247616 bytes in 1229 user files
      20480 bytes in bad sectors
    9725952 bytes available on disk

     655360 bytes total memory
     550032 bytes free
```

DRIVPARM

DOS version 3.2 allows you to define the characteristics of block devices
at system boot time. A block device differs from a character device (such
as a printer) in the manner in which DOS transfers data. *Character
devices* are serial in nature — one character follows another. Character
devices do not support random access I/O; each character must be dealt
with sequentially. *Block devices* transfer data in large sections (such as a
sector) and allow you to access data in any order (random access I/O).
The CONFIG.SYS DRIVPARM entry, which allows you to define attributes of block devices to DOS at boot time, is

DRIVPARM *drive__number* [*/CHECKDOOR*] [*/F:formfactor*]
  [*/M:max__head__number*] [*/NONREMOVEABLE*]
  [*/S:sectors__per__track*] [*/T:tracks__per__side*]

where the following is true:

drive__number is the number associated with the logical drive of which you are setting
attributes (A=0, B=1, and so forth). This value must be in the range 0-16.
/CHECKDOOR directs DOS to perform door-lock checking.

/F:formfactor specifies the form factor for the device, as follows:

Form Factor	Characteristic
0	320/360K
1	1.2Mb
2	720K
3	8-inch single-density
4	8-inch double-density
5	Fixed disk
6	Tape drive
7	Other device

/M:max_head_number specifies the maximum head number for the device (1-99).

/NONREMOVEABLE informs DOS that the device is nonremoveable.

/S:sector_per_track defines the number of sectors on each track of the disk.

/T:tracks_per_side specifies the number of concentric tracks on each side of a disk.

Most users will never require this configuration parameter.

FCBS (Default: FCBS=4,0)

Early versions of DOS used file control blocks (FCBs) to track each open file. A *file control block* contains the state and structure of a specific file. If you are not running older application programs (pre-DOS version 2.0), you should never have to specify this parameter in CONFIG.SYS. However, if you experience a problem with older programs as you migrate to newer versions of DOS, you may need to modify this entry. The format is

FCBS=*max_files, protected_files*

where the following is true:

max_files specifies the maximum number of files that DOS can open concurrently by using file control blocks. This value must be in the range 1-255.

protected_files specifies the minimum number of files that DOS must leave open when it needs to open other files. This value must be in the range 0-255.

As mentioned, DOS 2.0 replaced file control blocks with file handles. Most users, therefore, will never require this parameter. The following example allows DOS to open 16 files concurrently with the FCBS, ensuring that at least 4 are protected.

FCBS=16,4

FILES (Default: FILES=8)

DOS version 2.0 introduced the concept of file handles for file I/O operations. Prior to file handles, all DOS file I/O used file control blocks. Unfortunately, many programmers found that they could bypass the DOS file I/O services by directly manipulating the fields of the file control block. This practice led to nonportable programs that did not work under new releases of DOS. File handles enforce good programming practices while providing DOS with the ability to perform I/O redirection using predefined file handles. Table 4-3 shows common file handles and applications.

The format of the FILES entry is

FILES=*num__handles*

where *num__handles* specifies the maximum number of file handles DOS will support.

By default, DOS allocates memory to support up to eight file handles. DOS predefines five of these handles at boot time, leaving your application with the ability to open three files. Most users, therefore, will want to place the following entry in CONFIG.SYS:

HANDLES=20

The entry ensures that DOS can open sufficient files for each application. The memory overhead for each entry is 48 bytes per handle over the default number of 8.

Table 4-3.

DOS File Handles and Applications

File Handle	Default Device	Name	Operations
0	con:	stdin	keyboard
1	con:	stdout	screen
2	con:	stderr	screen
3	aux:	stdaux	aux:device
4	prn:	stdprn	printer

LASTDRIVE (Default: E)

The CONFIG.SYS LASTDRIVE entry allows you to specify the last disk drive identification that DOS can access. The format of the entry is

LASTDRIVE=*drive_letter*

where *drive_letter* is the letter (A-Z) associated with the disk drive letter of the last drive DOS can refer to. Few applications require modification of this entry.

SHELL (Default: SHELL=COMMAND.COM)

The SHELL entry in CONFIG.SYS allows you to invoke a command processor other than COMMAND.COM. The format for this entry is

SHELL=*file_specification*

where *file_specification* is the complete DOS path name of the file DOS is to use as the command interpreter.

Most users will never modify this entry. However, to understand its use fully, format a bootable floppy diskette and modify CONFIG.SYS on the floppy as shown here:

SHELL=SHELL.COM

Next, create the executable program (SHELL.PAS in Figure 4-8) that you want to serve as the command processor. This program understands three commands: CLS, VER, and VOL. Compile this program, place the file SHELL.COM on the floppy disk, and boot it. In this case, the system will respond with

SHELL>

DOS 3.3 PARAMETERS

DOS 3.3 supports each of the configuration parameters previously discussed. In addition, DOS 3.3 adds the STACKS entry along with the device drivers DISPLAY.SYS, DRIVER.SYS, KEYBOARD.SYS, and PRINTER.SYS. DOS 3.3 is strongly tied to the IBM Personal Series/2 (PS/2) line of computers. Most of the device drivers added to DOS 3.3 address the international PC market.

STACKS (PC, XT, and Portable Default: STACKS=0,0
PC AT Default: STACKS=9,128)

Each time a hardware interrupt occurs in the system, DOS must store the current system context (register values) in its stack pool before servicing the interrupt. This allows DOS to restore the system later to its original state as if it had never been interrupted. If your system incurs too many hardware interrupts too quickly, DOS will eventually use up all of its available stack space. If this occurs, DOS will experience a fatal error and your system will hang up. To avoid this problem, you can increase the stack space available to DOS by using the STACKS entry in CONFIG.SYS. The format is

STACKS=*number_of_frames, frame_size*

where the following is true:

number_of_frames defines how many stack frames are available to DOS. This value must be in the range 0-64.
frame_size specifies the size of each frame in bytes. This value must be in the range 0-512 bytes.

When an interrupt occurs, DOS allocates one stack frame. When the interrupt processing is complete, DOS releases the frame. If you are not experiencing stack problems, you will probably never need to modify this parameter.

Remember that increasing the size of any DOS system configuration parameter requires memory consumption, which may degrade overall system performance.

PRINTER.SYS

The PRINTER.SYS device driver expands the capabilities of the IBM Proprinter models 4201 and 5202, along with the Quietwriter III. Although this is an IBM-specific configuration entry, the concepts it supports merit discussion here.

Each piece of data the computer stores is a numeric value. When the computer displays the value on the screen or prints the value, DOS first converts the numeric value to a specific character set. This is done by mapping the value to a code page. For example, Figure 4-9 represents the code page for the United States.

The character "A" is represented in ASCII by the hex value 41. If you move from left to right to the column labeled 4 and then down to the row labeled 1, you will find the character "A". DOS 3.3 defines code sets as shown in Figure 4-10.

```
{$C-}

Program SHELL;

const
  forever : boolean = false;

Type
  DOS_command = string[8];
  REGISTERS = record
                 AX, BX, CX, DX, BP, SI, DI, DS, ES, FLAGS: INTEGER
              end;

procedure Display_Version;

var
   REGS: REGISTERS;   {AX, BX, CX, DX, BP, SI, DI, DS, ES, FLAGS}
   MAJOR, MINOR: integer;

begin
     with REGS do
       begin

{set AX to request the DOS version number}
       AX := $3000;      {DOS function code}

{invoke the DOS interrupt which returns the current DOS version}
       MSDos (REGS);

{return the major and minor version numbers}
       MAJOR := Lo(AX);
       MINOR := Hi(AX);
      end;

   writeln ('DOS Version ', MAJOR, '.', MINOR);

end;

procedure Display_Volume;

var
     VOLUME_LABEL: string[11];
     REGS: REGISTERS;
     SEARCH_SPEC: string[11];
     DTA_SEG,
     DTA_OFS : integer;  {address of disk transfer area}
     I       : integer;  {counter for loops}

begin
     with REGS do
       begin

{convert the search specification to asciiz and set the registers

to find the volume label}
       AX := $4E00;                           {DOS function code}
       SEARCH_SPEC := '*.*';
       DS := Seg(SEARCH_SPEC[1]);
       DX := Ofs(SEARCH_SPEC[1]);
       CX := 8;                               {attribute of label}
```

Figure 4-8.

SHELL.PAS program

```
      {invoke the DOS interrupt which finds the volume label}
            MSDos (REGS);

      {set AX to request the disk transfer area}
            AX := $2F00;

      {invoke the DOS interrupt which returns the disk transfer area}
            MSDos (REGS);

      {return the segment and offset addresses}
            DTA_SEG := ES;
            DTA_OFS := BX;

            I := 0;
            while ((I < 11) and (Mem[DTA_SEG:DTA_OFS+30+I] <> 0)) do
              begin
                VOLUME_LABEL[I + 1] := Chr(Mem[DTA_SEG:DTA_OFS+30+I]);
                I := I + 1;
              end;

              VOLUME_LABEL[0] := Chr(I);
          end;           {with REGS}

      if (I <> 0) then
        writeln ('Volume label ', VOLUME_LABEL)
      else
        writeln ('Volume is unlabeled');

  end;

  procedure to_uppercase (var command: DOS_command);
  var
   i: integer;

  begin
   for i := 1 to Length(command) do
     command[i] := UpCase(command[i]);
  end;

  var
    command: DOS_command;


  begin

      repeat
        write ('SHELL> ');
        readln (command);
        to_uppercase (command);

        if command = 'VER' then
          Display_Version
        else if command = 'VOL' then
          Display_Volume
        else if command = 'CLS'then
          ClrScr
        else
          Writeln ('Invalid command');
      until (forever);

  end.
```

Figure 4-8.

SHELL.PAS program (*continued*)

Code page 437 (United States)

Hex Digits 1st→ 2nd↓	0-	1-	2-	3-	4-	5-	6-	7-	8-	9-	A-	B-	C-	D-	E-	F-
-0		►		0	@	P	`	p	Ç	É	á	░	└	╨	α	≡
-1	☺	◄	!	1	A	Q	a	q	ü	æ	í	▒	┴	╤	β	±
-2	☻	↕	"	2	B	R	b	r	é	Æ	ó	▓	┬	╥	Γ	≥
-3	♥	‼	#	3	C	S	c	s	â	ô	ú	│	├	╙	π	≤
-4	♦	¶	$	4	D	T	d	t	ä	ö	ñ	┤	─	╘	Σ	⌠
-5	♣	§	%	5	E	U	e	u	à	ò	Ñ	╡	┼	╒	σ	⌡
-6	♠	▬	&	6	F	V	f	v	å	û	ª	╢	╞	╓	µ	÷
-7	•	↨	'	7	G	W	g	w	ç	ù	º	╖	╟	╫	τ	≈
-8	◘	↑	(	8	H	X	h	x	ê	ÿ	¿	╕	╚	╪	Φ	°
-9	○	↓	)	9	I	Y	i	y	ë	Ö	⌐	╣	╔	┘	Θ	∙
-A	◎	→	*	:	J	Z	j	z	è	Ü	¬	║	╩	┌	Ω	·
-B	♂	←	+	;	K	[	k	{	ï	¢	½	╗	╦	█	δ	√
-C	♀	∟	,	<	L	\	l	|	î	£	¼	╝	╠	▄	∞	ⁿ
-D	♪	↔	-	=	M	]	m	}	ì	¥	¡	╜	═	▌	φ	²
-E	♫	▲	.	>	N	^	n	~	Ä	Pt	«	╛	╬	▐	ε	■
-F	☼	▼	/	?	O	_	o	⌂	Å	ƒ	»	┐	╧	▀	∩	

Reprinted, by permission, from *Disk Operating System Version 3.30 Reference* (International Business Machines Corporation, 1987), C-3.

Figure 4-9.

Code page for United States

DOS users in the United States should never have to specify alternate code pages. However, if you live in any of the countries shown, specify the CONFIG.SYS entry. The format is

DEVICE=PRINTER.SYS *LPT*#[:]=(*type*[,[*control_page*]
[,*additional_pages*]])

where the following is true:

LPT# is the device identification of the desired printer.

type specifies the printer type (4201, 5202).

control__page defines the specific code page as shown previously.

additional__pages defines the number of additional code pages that can be prepared (up to 12).

Consider the following example:

DEVICE=PRINTER.SYS LPT1:=(5202,437,0)

This entry works in conjunction with the NLSFUNC, CHCP, and MODE commands, which perform the actual code-page switching.

DISPLAY.SYS

The DISPLAY.SYS device driver allows you to use code-page switching on the PC convertible LCD screen as well as on EGA and IBM PS/2 display screens. The format of this device driver entry is

DEVICE=DISPLAY.SYS CON[:]=(*type*[,[*control__page*]
     [*additional__pages*]])

where the following is true:

type specifies the display type (mono, cga, ega, lcd).

control__page defines the specific code page as shown previously.

additional__pages defines the number of additional code pages that can be prepared (up to 12).

Consider the following example:

DEVICE=DISPLAY.SYS CON:=(CGA, 437,0)

Code page 850 (Multilingual)

Hex Digits 1st→ 2nd↓	0-	1-	2-	3-	4-	5-	6-	7-	8-	9-	A-	B-	C-	D-	E-	F-
-0		►		0	@	P	`	p	Ç	É	á	▓	└	ð	Ó	-
-1	☺	◄	!	1	A	Q	a	q	ü	æ	í	▒	┴	Ð	β	±
-2	☻	↕	"	2	B	R	b	r	é	Æ	ó	▓	┬	Ê	Ô	=
-3	♥	‼	#	3	C	S	c	s	â	ô	ú	│	├	Ë	Ò	¾
-4	♦	¶	$	4	D	T	d	t	ä	ö	ñ	┤	─	È	õ	¶
-5	♣	§	%	5	E	U	e	u	à	ò	Ñ	Á	┼	ı	Õ	§
-6	♠	▬	&	6	F	V	f	v	å	û	ª	Â	ã	Í	µ	÷
-7	•	↕	'	7	G	W	g	w	ç	ù	º	À	Ã	Î	þ	
-8	◘	↑	(	8	H	X	h	x	ê	ÿ	¿	©	╚	Ï	Þ	°
-9	○	↓	)	9	I	Y	i	y	ë	Ö	®	╣	╔	┘	Ú	¨
-A	◙	→	*	:	J	Z	j	z	è	Ü	¬	║	╩	┌	Û	·
-B	♂	←	+	;	K	[	k	{	ï	ø	½	╗	╦	█	Ù	¹
-C	♀	∟	,	<	L	\	l	|	î	£	¼	╝	╠	▄	ý	³
-D	♪	↔	-	=	M	]	m	}	ì	Ø	¡	¢	=	¦	Ý	²
-E	♫	▲	.	>	N	^	n	~	Ä	×	«	¥	╬	Ì	¯	■
-F	☼	▼	/	?	O	_	o	⌂	Å	ƒ	»	┐	¤	▀	´	

Code page 860 (Portugal)

Hex Digits 1st→ 2nd↓	0-	1-	2-	3-	4-	5-	6-	7-	8-	9-	A-	B-	C-	D-	E-	F-
-0		►		0	@	P	`	p	Ç	É	á	▓	└	┴	α	≡
-1	☺	◄	!	1	A	Q	a	q	ü	À	í	▒	┴	┬	β	±
-2	☻	↕	"	2	B	R	b	r	é	È	ó	▓	┬	┬	Γ	≥
-3	♥	‼	#	3	C	S	c	s	â	ô	ú	│	├	└	π	≤
-4	♦	¶	$	4	D	T	d	t	ã	õ	ñ	┤	─	├	Σ	⌠
-5	♣	§	%	5	E	U	e	u	à	ò	Ñ	┤	┼	┌	σ	⌡
-6	♠	▬	&	6	F	V	f	v	Á	Ú	ª	┤	├	┤	µ	÷
-7	•	↕	'	7	G	W	g	w	ç	ù	º	┐	╟	┼	τ	≈
-8	◘	↑	(	8	H	X	h	x	ê	Ì	¿	┐	╚	╩	Φ	°
-9	○	↓	)	9	I	Y	i	y	Ê	Õ	Ò	╣	╔	┘	Θ	∙
-A	◙	→	*	:	J	Z	j	z	è	Ü	¬	║	╩	┌	Ω	·
-B	♂	←	+	;	K	[	k	{	Ì	¢	½	╗	╦	█	δ	√
-C	♀	∟	,	<	L	\	l	|	Õ	£	¼	╝	╠	▄	∞	ⁿ
-D	♪	↔	-	=	M	]	m	}	ì	Ù	¡	┘	=	█	φ	²
-E	♫	▲	.	>	N	^	n	~	Ã	Pt	«	╬	Ì	■	ε	■
-F	☼	▼	/	?	O	_	o	⌂	Â	Ó	»	┐	┴	▀	∩	

Reprinted, by permission, from *Disk Operating System Version 3.30 Reference* (International Business Machines Corporation, 1987), C-5 and C-4.

Figure 4-10.

Code sets for DOS 3.3

Code page 865 (Norway)

Hex Digits 1st→ 2nd↓	0-	1-	2-	3-	4-	5-	6-	7-	8-	9-	A-	B-	C-	D-	E-	F-
-0		►		0	@	P	`	p	Ç	É	á	▓	└	╨	α	≡
-1	☺	◄	!	1	A	Q	a	q	ü	æ	í	▒	┴	╤	β	±
-2	☻	↕	"	2	B	R	b	r	é	Æ	ó	▓	┬	╥	Γ	≥
-3	♥	‼	#	3	C	S	c	s	â	ô	ú	│	├	╙	π	≤
-4	♦	¶	$	4	D	T	d	t	ä	ö	ñ	┤	─	╘	Σ	⌠
-5	♣	§	%	5	E	U	e	u	à	ò	Ñ	╡	┼	╒	σ	⌡
-6	♠	▬	&	6	F	V	f	v	å	û	ª	╢	╞	╓	μ	÷
-7	•	↨	'	7	G	W	g	w	ç	ú	º	╖	╟	╫	τ	≈
-8	◘	↑	(	8	H	X	h	x	ê	ÿ	¿	╕	╚	╪	Φ	°
-9	○	↓	)	9	I	Y	i	y	ë	Ö	⌐	╣	╔	┘	Θ	•
-A	◙	→	*	:	J	Z	j	z	è	Ü	¬	║	╩	┌	Ω	·
-B	♂	←	+	;	K	[	k	{	ï	ø	½	╗	╦	█	δ	√
-C	♀	∟	,	<	L	\	l			î	£	¼	╝	╠	▄	∞	ⁿ
-D	♪	↔	-	=	M	]	m	}	ì	Ø	¡	╜	═	▌	φ	²
-E	♫	▲	.	>	N	^	n	~	Ä	Pt	«	╛	╬	▐	ε	■
-F	☼	▼	/	?	O	_	o	⌂	Å	ƒ	¤	┐	╧	▬	∩	

Code page 863 (Canada-French)

Hex Digits 1st→ 2nd↓	0-	1-	2-	3-	4-	5-	6-	7-	8-	9-	A-	B-	C-	D-	E-	F-
-0		►		0	@	P	`	p	Ç	É	¦	▓	└	╨	α	≡
-1	☺	◄	!	1	A	Q	a	q	ü	È	´	▒	┴	╤	β	±
-2	☻	↕	"	2	B	R	b	r	é	Ê	ó	▓	┬	╥	Γ	≥
-3	♥	‼	#	3	C	S	c	s	â	ô	ú	│	├	╙	π	≤
-4	♦	¶	$	4	D	T	d	t	Â	Ë	¨	┤	─	╘	Σ	⌠
-5	♣	§	%	5	E	U	e	u	à	Ï	¸	╡	┼	╒	σ	⌡
-6	♠	▬	&	6	F	V	f	v	¶	û	³	╢	╞	╓	μ	÷
-7	•	↨	'	7	G	W	g	w	ç	ú	¯	╖	╟	╫	τ	≈
-8	◘	↑	(	8	H	X	h	x	ê	¤	Î	╕	╚	╪	Φ	°
-9	○	↓	)	9	I	Y	i	y	ë	Ô	⌐	╣	╔	┘	Θ	•
-A	◙	→	*	:	J	Z	j	z	è	Ü	¬	║	╩	┌	Ω	·
-B	♂	←	+	;	K	[	k	{	ï	¢	½	╗	╦	█	δ	√
-C	♀	∟	,	<	L	\	l			î	£	¼	╝	╠	▄	∞	ⁿ
-D	♪	↔	-	=	M	]	m	}	=	Ù	¾	╜	═	▌	φ	²
-E	♫	▲	.	>	N	^	n	~	À	Û	«	╛	╬	▐	ε	■
-F	☼	▼	/	?	O	_	o	⌂	§	ƒ	»	┐	╧	▬	∩	

Reprinted, by permission, from *Disk Operating System Version 3.30 Reference* (International Business Machines Corporation, 1987), C-7 and C-6.

Figure 4-10.

Code sets for DOS 3.3 *(continued)*

DRIVER.SYS

The DOS DRIVER.SYS device driver helps you configure external disk drives into your system. For DOS to recognize external devices, you must place the proper entry in CONFIG.SYS. The format for this entry is

DEVICE=DRIVER.SYS /D:*drive__number* [/T:*tracks__per__side*]
[/S:*sectors__per__track*] [/H:*max__head*]
[/C] [/F:*form__factor*] [/N]

where the following is true:

drive__number is the logical drive number (0-255).

tracks__per__side defines the number of tracks on one side of the disk (1-999).

sectors__per__track defines the number of sectors for each track (1-99).

max__heads defines the maximum number of heads (1-99).

/C states that the IBM PC AT changeline support is required.

/N states that the device is nonremoveable.

form__factor specifies the device type as follows:

Factor	Device
0	160/180K
0	320/360K
1	1.2MB
2	720K
7	1.44MB

OS/2 SYSTEM CONFIGURATION PARAMETERS

OS/2 supports each of the system configuration parameters presented in this chapter for DOS version 3.x:

BREAK
BUFFERS
COUNTRY

DEVICE
FCBS
HANDLES
SHELL

Because OS/2 is a multitasking system, its system configuration parameters are much more complex than those found under DOS 3.x. Most beginning OS/2 users will very likely choose simply to allow OS/2 to configure itself in memory by using the system default values. As you will see, most of the additional OS/2 configuration parameters relate directly to the execution of multiple programs simultaneously under one computer system.

CODEPAGE (Default: CODEPAGE=437)

As mentioned, a code page is the table that DOS uses to define a character set. Figures 4-9 and 4-10 illustrate the code pages DOS supports. Most users will never use a code page other than the system default. If, however, you are using a foreign character set, you may need to specify the alternate code page in CONFIG.SYS as follows:

437	United States
850	Multilingual
860	Portuguese
863	French/Canadian
865	Nordic

For example, the following entry selects the Nordic code page at system start-up:

CODEPAGE=865

OS/2 also allows you to define a secondary code page as shown here:

CODEPAGE=865,863

In this case, Nordic is the primary code page, while French/Canadian is secondary. For each device that is to use the code page, you must include a DEVINFO entry.

DEVINFO (Default: none)

The OS/2 DEVINFO configuration entry informs DOS that code-page switching is in use for the specified device. The format for the entry is

DEVINFO=*device__name, subtype, file__specification,*
          [*ROM*=[(code__page1[,code__page2)]]

where the following is true:

device__name is the name of the device using code-page switching (KBD$, LPT#, PRN, SCREEN$).

subtype specifies the physical device type (such as EGA).

file__specification is the complete DOS path name of the file containing the desired code-page tables for output devices or the keyboard translation tables.

ROM optionally specifies the primary and secondary code pages for output devices.

The following example defines a code page for the screen device:

DEVINFO=SCREEN$,CGA,COLOR.TBL

IOPL (Default: IOPL=NO)

Since OS/2 is a multitasking operating system, it must strictly control which programs can perform I/O operations at specific times. For example, if you are executing a calculator program on the screen, a second program that is also executing should not be allowed to randomly overwrite the current screen contents. To enforce this, OS/2 strictly controls I/O operations, granting only the most privileged applications the ability to perform low-level I/O by defining rings of I/O protection levels.

The input/output protection level (IOPL) defines the minimum ring level of protection an application must possess before it can perform low-level I/O operations. If an application outside of this ring attempts a low-level I/O, OS/2 generates a general protection fault and the operation fails. OS/2 does not prevent programs from performing I/O. It simply requires that the applications running in a multiprogramming environment cooperate. Program I/O operations therefore normally go through predefined OS/2 services defined in the application program interface (API).

If you set IOPL to YES, OS/2 allows applications to perform low-level I/O operations. Most users, however, want the programs running in a concurrent environment to cooperate, so they leave IOPL set to NO.

LIBPATH (Default: boot_device: \)

OS/2 and Microsoft Windows allow programmers to link modules in one of two ways. The first (and most familiar) is simply to link OBJ and LIB files with the DOS LINK command. In this case, OS/2 combines files from disk to produce an executable file (see Figure 4-11).

The second (and most powerful) method of combining modules is by using dynamic link libraries (DLLs). Unlike *static modules* (which the DOS linker resolves prior to execution of your code), *dynamic link libraries* are not combined with the program code until program execution. This means that the OS/2 program loader not only loads the program to execute into memory, but that it also resolves any external references to dynamic link modules. The libraries (often referred to as *dynlink libraries*) can reside in memory or on disk prior to the execution of the program that references them. If the libraries are on disk, the OS/2 loader must load the library file into memory from disk.

Consider the following flowchart shown in Figure 4-12. Dynamic link libraries provide your applications programs with several advantages. First, since the code contained in the dynamic link library is not linked to an executable file, the file size for your programs is much smaller. Second, the code in dynamic link libraries is can be shared. If you

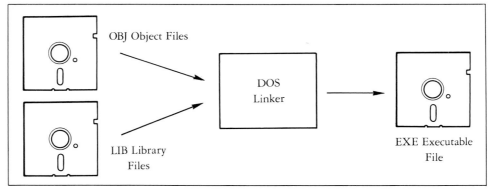

Figure 4-11.

Static linking

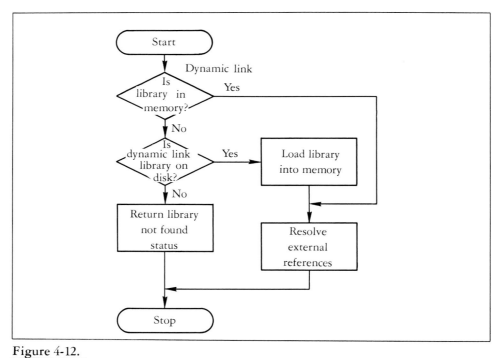

Figure 4-12.

Flowchart depicting linking of OBJ
and LIB files

have several programs executing in memory simultaneously, each application can share one copy of the dynamic link library (see Figure 4-13).

This indirectly makes program updates easier. Since programmers can create their own DLLs, they can have several programs refer to a DLL. If the code in the DLL later needs to be modified, the programmer simply modifies the DLL, compiles it, and reloads it into memory. None of the applications that use the library are affected—no relinking is required.

The OS/2 LIBPATH system configuration entry specifies where OS/2 places dynamic link libraries by default. The OS/2 loader searches this location each time it must load a DLL from disk into memory. If you place all of your DLL files into the DOS subdirectory file \DYNAMIC,

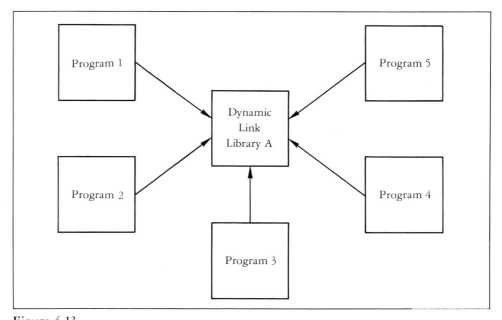

Figure 4-13.

Shared dynamic link libraries

your CONFIG.SYS entry will be

LIBPATH= \DYNAMIC

By default, OS/2 searches the root directory on the boot device.

MAXWAIT (Default: MAXWAIT=3)

Because OS/2 is a multitasking environment, it must have facilities to determine which applications should execute when. Under OS/2, these facilities are contained in the scheduler. The OS/2 scheduler is responsible for examining the list of programs available for execution and selecting the specific application to receive control of the CPU.

OS/2 determines which process to execute by assigning a priority to each program in the system. For example, assume that you have three programs that execute simultaneously. The first, CALCULATE__PAYROLL, generates your company payroll. The second, STOCKS, monitors the stock market by way of a modem, notifying you of significant trends. The third, PAY__CHECKS, prints the company payroll checks.

Since OS/2 is multitasking, each of these applications appears to be running simultaneously. Because it has a direct influence on whether the company makes money, the stock market monitor (STOCKS) is the most critical program. Whenever data is available for this program, it should get control of the CPU. Therefore, this program has a priority of three.

If no data exists on the modem for the monitor program, OS/2 should give the CPU to the program CALCULATE__PAYROLL to ensure that payroll is complete. Therefore, this program is given a priority 2.

Lastly, if neither the stock monitor nor the payroll program has processing to perform (each may be waiting for a disk I/O to complete), OS/2 should execute the PAY__CHECKS program, which has a priority of 1. The flowchart in Figure 4-14 illustrates how OS/2 will select the program to execute.

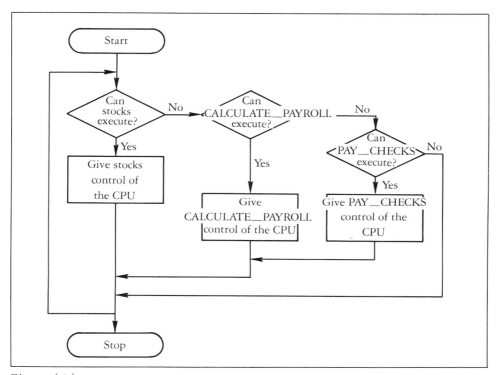

Figure 4-14.

Flowchart depicting how OS/2
selects a program to execute

There may be many times, however, when several programs with high priorities exist (see Figure 4-15). In this case, OS/2 will first check the first program at priority 3 to see if it can execute. If it can, OS/2 executes it.

After a period of time (a time slice) OS/2 gives the processor to the next available program at a higher-than or equal-to priority. In this case, OS/2 continues distributing the CPU in this manner until no programs exist with a priority equal to or greater than the previous program's priority. Then OS/2 moves to the next lower priority and begins distribution of the CPU among the programs at that level in a round-robin fashion.

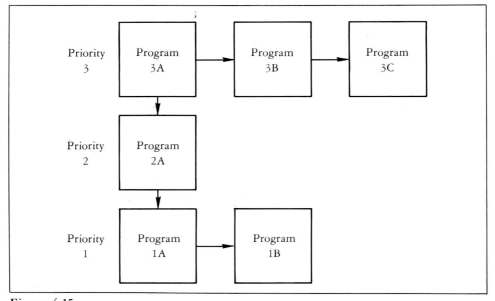

Figure 4-15.

Several programs with high priority
levels

It is possible, however, that processes with low priorities never would execute. To prevent this, OS/2 provides dynamic priorities. This means that although a process may have an initial priority level of 1, OS/2 may periodically increment this priority if it appears to OS/2 that the process is never getting the CPU. Once the process gets the CPU for a time slice, OS/2 reassigns its initial priority, and the process begins its climb up the lower priorities again.

The OS/2 MAXWAIT system configuration parameter defines the maximum amount of time a process must wait before it gets the CPU. By default, OS/2 uses

MAXWAIT=3

This means that every three seconds, OS/2 increments the priority for the processes waiting for the CPU. Most users will find this default value satisfactory. This parameter is dependent upon the CONFIG.SYS PRIORITY entry examined later in this chapter.

MEMMAN (Floppy Default: MEMMAN=NOSWAP,MOVE Fixed Default: MEMMAN=SWAP,MOVE)

With the flexibility of a multitasking environment come significant memory management considerations. *Memory management* refers to the steps OS/2 takes to determine how much memory a program can use; whether OS/2 can move programs temporarily to disk to make room for other programs (swapping); and whether OS/2 can perform memory compaction (moving segments of code) to prevent memory fragmentation and thrashing. By temporarily swapping a program from memory to disk, OS/2 can allow more programs than actually fit into memory to execute (see Figure 4-16).

Each time the OS/2 scheduler selects a process for execution, OS/2 must check to see if the process resides in memory. If it does, OS/2 executes it. If it does not, OS/2 must bring the program from disk into memory, as shown in Figure 4-17. If insufficient space exists in memory

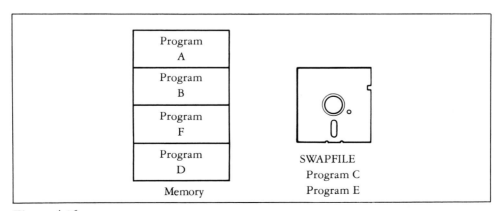

Figure 4-16.

OS/2 allowing more than one
program into memory

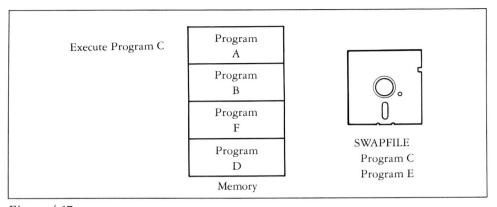

Figure 4-17.

OS/2 bringing program from disk
into memory

for the program, OS/2 must swap another program temporarily to disk (see Figure 4-18).

As you might expect, the greater the number of currently executing programs, the more swapping OS/2 must perform. Since swapping requires many disk I/O operations, it produces significant system overhead. OS/2, therefore, allows you to disable swapping. In so doing, you also limit the number of programs that OS/2 can execute concurrently.

A major memory management concern in all multitasking environments is the prevention of memory fragmentation. Consider the following scenario. OS/2 has three programs to execute: A, B, and C. OS/2 loads each into memory as shown in Figure 4-19. Later, program A completes, and OS/2 removes it from memory (see Figure 4-20).

Next, OS/2 needs to load program D. Unfortunately, OS/2 does not have enough contiguous memory to load the program. However, by shifting the other two applications downward in memory, OS/2 gains sufficient space, as shown in Figure 4-21.

The OS/2 virtual memory model makes such memory compaction moves, and they are relatively easy for the operating system to perform. OS/2 performs the entire memory compaction transparently to the executing programs.

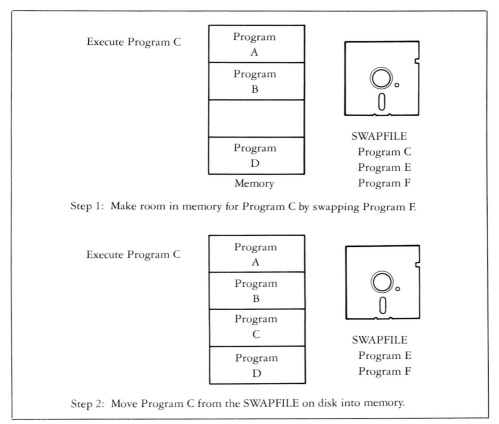

Step 1: Make room in memory for Program C by swapping Program F.

Step 2: Move Program C from the SWAPFILE on disk into memory.

Figure 4-18.

OS/2 swapping program
temporarily to disk

The OS/2 MEMMAN entry allows you to disable movement of memory sections in the fashion previously discussed by specifying NOMOVE. Users in an office environment who concurrently run several programs should normally never set NOSWAP and NOMOVE. In so doing, they greatly restrict their own capabilities. Indeed restricting each option reduces system overhead (swapping and moving are expensive in terms of CPU and disk I/O time), but flexibility outweighs performance considerations in most multiprogramming environments.

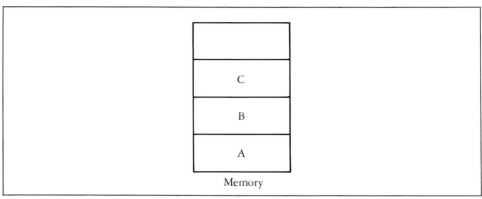

Figure 4-19.

OS/2 loading three programs into
memory

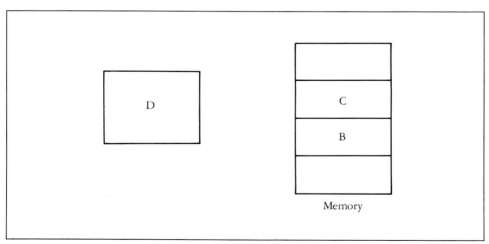

Figure 4-20.

Program A removed from memory

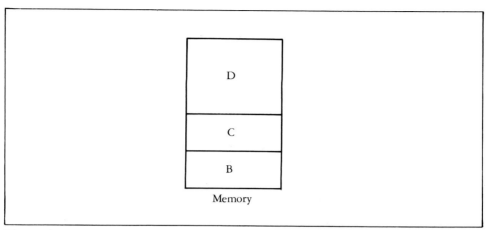

Figure 4-21.

OS/2 shifting programs down in
memory

The syntax for the MEMMAN entry is

MEMMAN=NOSWAP,NOMOVE

or

MEMMAN=SWAP,MOVE

or

MEMMAN=NOSWAP,MOVE

PRIORITY (Default: PRIORITY=DYNAMIC)

As discussed in the section on the MAXWAIT system configuration
parameter, OS/2 is a priority-driven operating system. By default, OS/2

grants control of the processor to the process with the highest priority and periodically increments the priority of processes waiting for the CPU. This priority scheme is *dynamic priority*. OS/2 can change program priority "on the fly" (dynamically) as it sees fit to ensure fairness of execution. The need may rarely arise for a system to ensure that OS/2 always executes the highest priority programs without incrementing the priority of programs waiting on the CPU. In this fashion it is possible to starve a process of CPU time. Most users, therefore, will always use the default PRIORITY setting of DYNAMIC to ensure fairness. If, however, your application requires that you prevent dynamic priority boost (a real-time monitor program, for example), specify

PRIORITY=ABSOLUTE

in CONFIG.SYS and reboot. In so doing, OS/2 ensures that the priority for every program in the system remains constant.

PROTECTONLY (Default: PROTECTONLY=NO)

OS/2 executes programs in two modes: real and protected. In real mode (typically 8088 programs), applications can directly access memory, hardware, ports, and the video display. Although this mode of program execution has been the mainstay of microcomputer processing for the past ten years, it is unacceptable in a multitasking environment such as OS/2. When multiple programs execute simultaneously, each must cooperate in terms of hardware access and control.

OS/2 meets the requirement of upward compatibility — the ability to execute DOS 3.x programs by switching from real to protected mode as program needs require. As you might suspect, this mode switching induces extra system overhead. If you anticipate never running DOS 3.x applications (Lotus, WordStar, or dBASE), you can specify the following in CONFIG.SYS:

PROTECTONLY=YES

In this mode, OS/2 will only support OS/2 applications. For most users this mode is unacceptable. Therefore, the default value of

PROTECTONLY=NO

is used.

RMSIZE (Default: System Dependent)

In real mode, OS/2 can execute DOS 3.x applications. Unlike OS/2 virtual memory applications, real mode programs cannot exceed 640K. The OS/2 RMSIZE configuration parameter allows you to specify the number of kilobytes of memory you want OS/2 to reserve for your real mode applications. The format for the entry is

RMSIZE=KBYTES

where *KBYTES* specifies the number of kilobytes OS/2 is to reserve for real mode applications. This value must be in the range 0-640.

The actual memory available to real mode applications is the value of *KBYTES* minus the space required for DOS. Most users will set this value at 512-640 as shown here:

RMSIZE=512

If you anticipate never running real mode applications, you can set this value to 0, giving OS/2 more memory for protected mode programs.

RUN (Default: None)

The OS/2 RUN system configuration parameter allows you to execute an application in background mode during system start-up. The format of the entry is

RUN *file__specification* [*command__line__arguments*]

where the following is true:

file__specification is the complete DOS path name of the command to execute.
command__line__arguments specifies each command line argument the program uses
to execute.

The following entry starts a background program called
CHKSPACE that records available disk space for each drive:

RUN CHKSPACE A: B: C:

Starting an application in this mode differs from running the
application from STARTUP.CMD in that the program will run in the
background as system start-up completes. Programs in STARTUP.CMD
run in the foreground unless you invoke them using the DETACH
command.

SWAPPATH (Default: boot__device: \)

When OS/2 concurrently executes multiple programs, it must periodically swap one program from memory to disk to make space for others.
When OS/2 swaps a program it places the program's code and data into
a swap file. The OS/2 SWAPPATH system configuration entry allows
you to specify the location of the swap file. The format of the entry is

SWAPPATH=*drive:*[*file__specification*]

where the following is true:

drive specifies the disk drive identification OS/2 uses for the swap device.

file_specification is the DOS path name for the file OS/2 is to use as the swap file.

For example, the following entry directs OS/2 to use the file SWAP-FILE.DAT in the root directory on drive C:

SWAPPATH=C: \SWAPFILE.DAT

To minimize the system overhead associated with swapping, always be sure that your target disk is a fixed disk.

THREADS (Default: THREADS=48)

This chapter has made the simplification that OS/2 schedules processes for execution. In actuality, however, OS/2 schedules an entity called a *thread.* OS/2 applications are composed of one or more threads that OS/2 treats as individual items to be scheduled. Therefore, OS/2 can concurrently execute multiple portions of the same program. Each part of the program is a thread (path of execution) to which the scheduler grants the CPU.

View the THREADS entry in CONFIG.SYS in a manner similar to the FILES entry. The FILES entry specifies the maximum number of file handles DOS and OS/2 will support. Likewise, THREADS specifies the maximum number of threads (paths of execution) that can exist in the system. For most users, the default value of 48 is sufficient. However, if you are concurrently running many applications, each of which has multiple threads, you may wish to increase this parameter. The format for the entry is

THREADS=max—threads

where *max—threads* defines the maximum number of threads OS/2 will support in the system. This value must be in the range 48-255.

The following entry sets the maximum number of threads to 128:

THREADS=128

TIMESLICE (Default: None)

OS/2 shares the processor with each program executing in the system by dividing processor time into time slices. The OS/2 system configuration parameter TIMESLICE allows you to specify the minimum and maximum amount of time that OS/2 can grant the CPU to a process. The format for the entry is

TIMESLICE=*minimum*[*,maximum*]

where the following is true:

minimum specifies the minimum number of milliseconds that OS/2 can use for the CPU time slice. This value must be greater than 31.

maximum specifies the maximum number of milliseconds that OS/2 can grant as a time slice. This value must exceed the value specified for *minimum*.

If you specify only one value,

TIMESLICE=64

OS/2 uses the value for both the *maximum* and *minimum* time slice.

This chapter has presented a considerable amount of technical material. Most users will never have to use many of the system generation parameters discussed, but it is critical that you have a general understanding of each parameter. The best way to learn about the system configuration parameters is to select one parameter a week that you strive to understand fully. Spend a week learning all of the ramifications of setting each parameter. After a few months, you will be fully conversant with the DOS start-up process and the CONFIG.SYS entries.

5: Managing DOS Directories

Many DOS power users fail to utilize DOS directories and directory commands to enhance system performance. This chapter discusses DOS subdirectories in detail, examines the DOS subdirectory commands, looks at directory manipulation from C and Turbo Pascal, experiments with the DOS pretender commands, and looks at directories under OS/2. Before learning the details of directory manipulation, you should have a solid foundation of DOS directory basics.

GETTING STARTED WITH DOS SUBDIRECTORIES

When you started with DOS, you had very few files spread out over one or two floppy diskettes. If you were lucky enough to have a hard disk, you were probably in awe of its enormous storage capacity. In those days you did not have to worry about file management since you had relatively few files. Times have changed. The tremendous storage capabilities offered by today's computers have turned users into file packrats. By the very nature of DOS, the only way that you truly become a "power user" is to examine the works of your predecessors. This means you have to collect and experiment with files. Unfortunately, most users are guilty of not maintaining organized files.

Most directory listings contain numerous files. If you have a hard disk, many file names probably clutter your screen with each directory listing that you perform. This makes locating a specific file difficult. If this is indeed the case with your diskettes or fixed disk, DOS subdirectories are a likely solution.

DOS subdirectories exist for one purpose: file management. Indeed, subdirectories provide you with several advantages, such as increased file organization, faster file access, and increased flexibility of DOS commands by using the PATH, APPEND, JOIN, and SUBST commands. When you think about it, each of these advantages is a direct result of increased file organization.

If you have never worked with DOS subdirectories, consider the following scenario. You are a manager of a restaurant and lounge, and you must track sales and inventory separately for both the restaurant and the lounge. As you lay out your disk structure, you have two choices. First, you can simply use the disk as it is, combining the receipts, purchases, sales, and inventory of the restaurant and the lounge into one location.

Although at first glance this appears to be the easiest solution, it has several disadvantages. The combined files result in a cluttered, disorganized collection of files that makes retrieval of a specific file nearly impossible. Second, if you do not use DOS subdirectories, regardless of the amount of free disk space you have, you are still restricted to a limited number of files, as shown in Table 5-1. Later chapters that discuss the DOS disk and directory layout explain why these restrictions exist.

Your second choice for your disk layout is to use DOS subdirectories. View DOS subdirectories in the same manner as you would the drawers in a filing cabinet. As Figure 5-1 shows, the filing cabinet has three drawers labeled REST, BAR, and MISC. This compares to the three DOS subdirectories shown in Figure 5-2.

Table 5-1.

Subdirectories Supported by Root
Directory

Disk Space	Maximum Number of Subdirectories in the Root Directory
160K	64
180K	
320K	112
360K	
1.2MB	224
Fixed disk	Based upon partition size

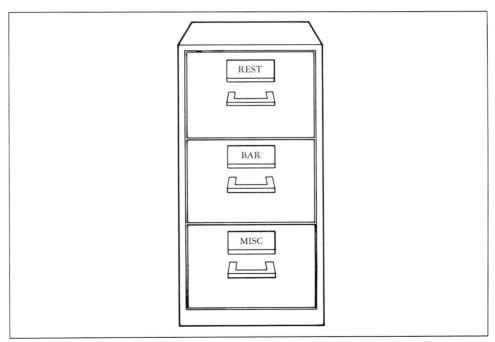

Figure 5-1.

Filing cabinet example

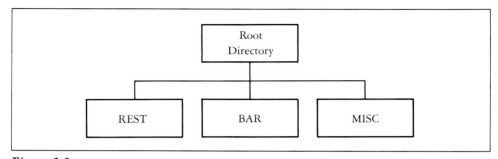

Figure 5-2.

Three DOS subdirectories

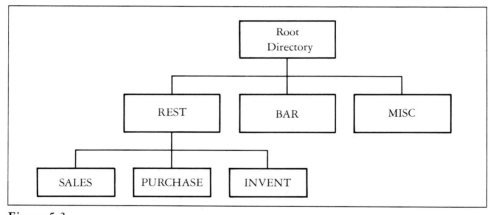

Figure 5-3.

Subdirectories within REST

Each DOS disk has a *root directory* from which all other directories grow. Although the number of subdirectories is virtually limitless, each disk has only one root directory. In the previous example, each subdirectory branching off of the root directory is a *child* of the root.

You can see that it is possible to further break down your file organization into an even stricter organization, as shown in Figure 5-3. This is equivalent to placing dividers into the drawers of your filing cabinet, as shown in Figure 5-4. In this case, the subdirectories SALES, PURCHASE, and INVENT are each children of the subdirectory REST. They are (as are all subdirectories) also *descendants* of the root directory.

By always placing your files into the correct subdirectory you will increase diskette organization tremendously. You should always know the exact location of specific files. Taking these concepts one step further, your subdirectory structure becomes that shown in Figure 5-5.

Now that you know the background of DOS subdirectories, consider how you create them. The DOS MKDIR (or MD) command creates the subdirectory that you specify. The format of the command is

MKDIR [*drive:*]*path__name*

or

MD [*drive:*]*path__name*

where the following is true:

drive is the disk drive identification (A, B, or C) on which you create the subdirectory.

path__name is the complete DOS path name for the subdirectory that you are creating.

Examine the following directory listing:

```
Volume in drive A has no label
Directory of   A:\

File not found
```

As mentioned, each DOS disk has a root directory from which all subdirectories grow. DOS identifies the root directory with the backslash (\ ). In this directory listing, DOS is displaying the listing for the root directory on drive A (A: \ ).

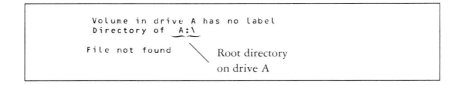

```
Volume in drive A has no label
Directory of  A:\

File not found
```

Root directory
on drive A

If you issue the command

```
A> MKDIR REST
```

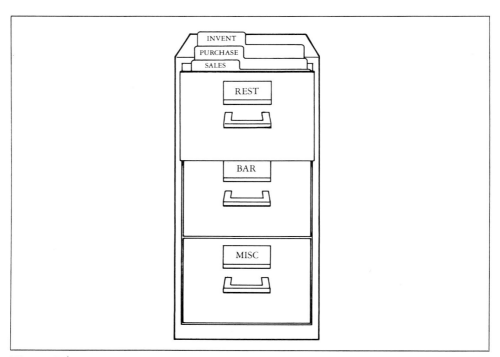

Figure 5-4.

Filing cabinet with "subdirectories"

DOS creates the specified subdirectory as follows:

```
Volume in drive A has no label
Directory of   A:\

REST            <DIR>       7-10-87    7:28p
          1 File(s)     361472 bytes free
```

The disk now contains the directory structure shown in Figure 5-6.
Likewise, the commands

```
A> MKDIR BAR
A> MKDIR MISC
```

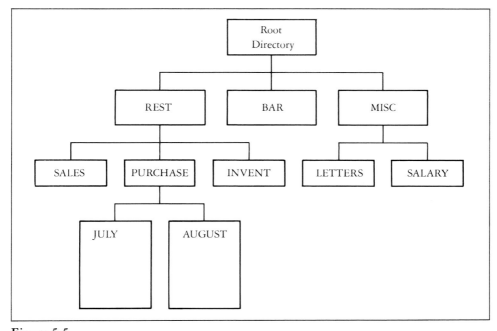

Figure 5-5.

Subdirectories within subdirectories

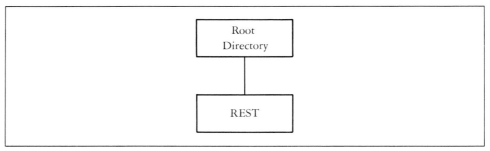

Figure 5-6.

Basic disk structure with root and
subdirectory

produce

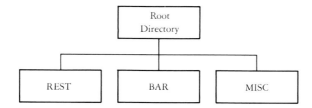

```
Volume in drive A has no label
Directory of  A:\

REST           <DIR>        7-10-87    7:28p
BAR            <DIR>        7-10-87    7:32p
MISC           <DIR>        7-10-87    7:32p
          3 File(s)     359424 bytes free
```

This directory structure is as follows:

DOS supports the concept of the *current directory*. By default, DOS uses the current directory to find commands or data files, unless you override the default with a complete DOS file specification. For example, when you issue the DOS DIR command, the current directory is the root:

```
Volume in drive A has no label
Directory of  A:\

REST         <DIR>        7-10-87    7:28p
BAR          <DIR>        7-10-87    7:32p
MISC         <DIR>        7-10-87    7:32p
         3 File(s)     359424 bytes free
```

By default, the DOS directory command only displays files contained in the current directory.

A complete DOS file specification starts at the root directory (\ ) and continues through a series of directory names. For example, the complete path name for the subdirectory BAR is \BAR. This is because BAR is a subdirectory of the root. If your directory structure is as follows, the complete path name for the subdirectory SALES in the BAR subdirectory is \BAR \SALES:

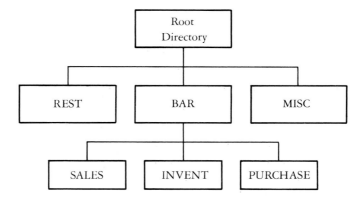

Note how the path name begins at the root and traverses the BAR subdirectory, finally reaching the subdirectory SALES. DOS uses the backslash (\ ) to separate subdirectory names. Assuming the SALES subdirectory contains the files JULY.DAT, AUG.DAT, and SEPT.DAT

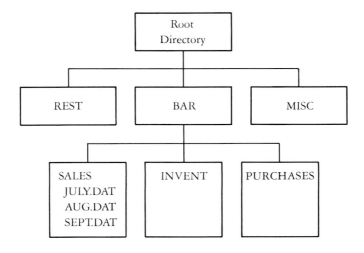

the complete path name for each file is

\BAR \SALES \JULY.DAT
\BAR \SALES \AUG.DAT
\BAR \SALES \SEPT.DAT

Given the directory structure shown in Figure 5-7, the complete path
name for each file is

\REST \SALES \JUL.4
\REST \SALES \JUL.5
\BAR \SALES \JULY.DAT
\BAR \SALES \AUG.DAT
\BAR \SALES \SEPT.DAT
\BAR \INVENT \BEER.DAT
\BAR \INVENT \LIQUOR.DAT
\MISC \LETTERS \DEBBIE.RES

Likewise, given the following directory structure,

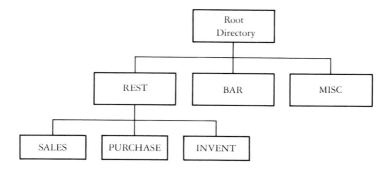

each of the following is a valid **MKDIR** command:

```
A> MKDIR BAR
A> MKDIR \MISC
A> MKDIR \REST\SALES
A> MKDIR REST\INVENT
```

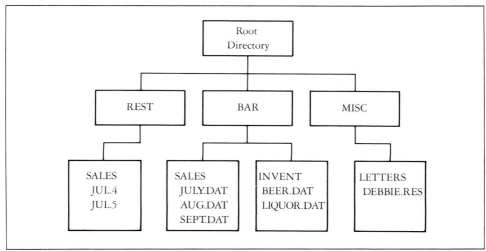

Figure 5-7.

Disk structure showing
subdirectories within subdirectories

When you use the MKDIR command to create a DOS subdirectory, DOS can do one of two things. First, if the target directory name has a complete DOS path name starting at the root

```
A> MKDIR \REST\SALES
```

DOS creates the subdirectory at the specified location. However, if you simply specify a subdirectory name

```
A> MKDIR INVENT
```

DOS will create the subdirectory in the current directory, regardless of your intentions.

Although DOS allows you to create virtually unlimited subdirectories

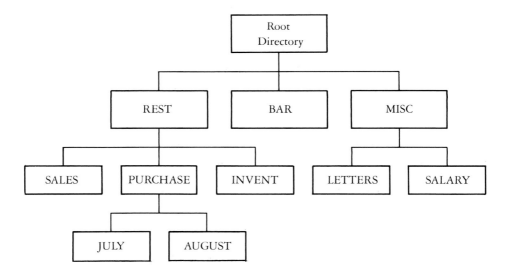

the longest path name that DOS will process is 63 characters.

\DEB\NEVADA\REST\SALES\1987\JULY\MONDAY\MORNING\BREAKFAS\JULY31

If the following subdirectories do not exist on your diskette, create them now by using MKDIR:

```
Volume in drive A has no label
Directory of   A:\

REST          <DIR>       7-10-87    7:28p
BAR           <DIR>       7-10-87    7:32p
MISC          <DIR>       7-10-87    7:32p
       3 File(s)      359424 bytes free
```

Your directory structure should now be as follows:

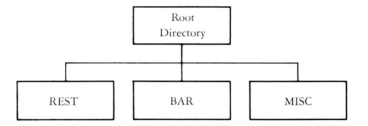

DOS treats the current directory in the same fashion it treats the default disk drive. This is the location DOS searches for files and commands, unless you specify otherwise. Each time you boot your computer, DOS selects the root directory of the boot device as the current default directory. Just as you can change the default drive, DOS allows you to select the current directory.

How do you access the files contained in each directory? The DOS CHDIR command allows you to traverse DOS subdirectories. The format of the command is

CHDIR [*drive:*]*path_name*

or

CD [*drive:*]*path_name*

where the following is true:

drive is the disk drive identification (A, B, or C) on which to set the current subdirectory.
path__name is the complete DOS path name for the subdirectory that you are selecting as the current default.

When you issue the CHDIR command, DOS does one of two things. If the target directory name is a complete DOS path name, DOS sets the current default directory to the specified subdirectory name.

```
A> CHDIR \REST\SALES
```

If the target directory is just a subdirectory name, DOS searches for the subdirectory in the current directory. Therefore, assuming that the root directory is the current default and given the directory structure shown in Figure 5-7, the command

```
A> CHDIR SALES
```

fails since SALES is a subdirectory of \BAR, which requires you to perform one of the following sequences of commands:

```
A> CHDIR \BAR\SALES
```

or

```
A> CHDIR \BAR
A> CHDIR SALES
```

If you do not specify a complete path name, the target directory is dependent upon the current default directory. Given the directory structure shown in Figure 5-7, the following CHDIR commands are valid:

```
A> CHDIR \REST
A> CHDIR \BAR\SALES
A> CHDIR \MISC
A> CHDIR \MISC\LETTERS
```

Change your current default directory to the subdirectory \BAR. Issue DOS directory command

```
A> DIR
```

Note the directories . and .. in the directory listing.

```
Volume in drive A has no label
Directory of   A:\BAR

.                <DIR>        7-10-87     7:32p
..               <DIR>        7-10-87     7:32p
        2 File(s)     359424 bytes free
```

DOS predefines each of these as follows:

.   DOS defines the single period as the *current* directory

..   DOS defines the double periods as the *parent* directory of the current default

Issue the following command:

```
A> DIR .
```

DOS displays the contents of the current directory. Likewise, if you issue the command

```
A> DIR ..
```

DOS displays the contents of the parent directory, in this case the root. DOS also allows you to use these directory names in other DOS commands, as shown here:

```
A> DIR ..
A> TYPE ..\CONFIG.SYS
A> CHDIR ..
A> DIR ..\REST\SALES
```

In a manner similar to MKDIR and CHDIR, the DOS remove directory command (RMDIR) allows you to delete DOS subdirectories when you no longer require them. The format of the RMDIR command is

RMDIR [*drive:*]*path___name*

or

RD [*drive:*]*path___name*

where the following is true:

drive is the disk drive identification (A, B, or C) from which to remove the subdirectory.
path___name is the complete DOS path name for the subdirectory that you are deleting.

Assume that you have the following directory structure:

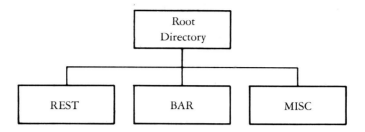

If you issue the command

```
A> RMDIR \MISC\LETTERS
```

the directory structure becomes as follows:

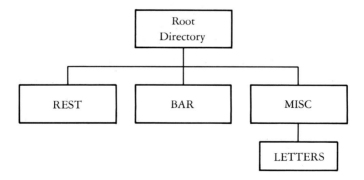

Likewise, assuming the directory MISC contains no files the command

```
A> RMDIR \MISC
```

results in the following directory structure:

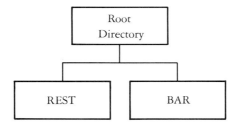

DOS does not allow you to remove directories that contain files. This prevents you from accidentally deleting files contained in a directory. If you attempt to do so, DOS will display the following message:

```
Invalid path, not directory,
or directory not empty
```

If you no longer require the files contained in the directory, you must use the DOS DEL command to delete the files and then use RMDIR to remove the subdirectory. The DOS DEL and ERASE commands do not remove subdirectories.

ACCESSING SUBDIRECTORY FILES

You can access data files contained in DOS subdirectories other than the current default directory by specifying complete DOS path names. For example, if you have the following directory structure,

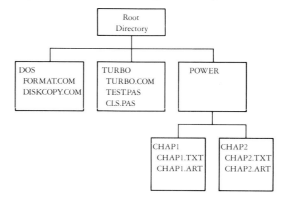

the complete path names for each file are

```
\DOS\FORMAT.COM
\DOS\DISKCOPY.COM
\TURBO\TURBO.COM
\TURBO\TEST.PAS
\TURBO\CLS.PAS
\POWER\CHAP1\CHAP1.TXT
\POWER\CHAP1\CHAP1.ART
\POWER\CHAP2\CHAP2.TXT
\POWER\CHAP2\CHAP2.ART
```

Therefore, you can issue the following commands:

```
A> TYPE \POWER\CHAP1\CHAP1.ART
A> DIR \TURBO\TURBO.COM
A> DEL \TURBO\TEST.PAS
A> COPY \TURBO\CLS.PAS \POWER\CHAP1\CHAP1.MSC
A> REN \POWER\CHAP2\CHAP2.ART *.OLD
```

Issue the following command:

```
A> COPY CON \BAR\SALES\NOTES.DAT
BAR SALES UP 23% FOR
JULY.  CONTACT JVE.
^Z
```

In this case, you have just created the file called NOTES.DAT in the subdirectory \BAR\SALES. You can copy this file to subdirectory \MISC by issuing the following command:

```
A> COPY \BAR\SALES\NOTES.DAT \MISC\NOTES.DAT
```

To compare the contents of each file, issue the following command:

```
A> COMP \BAR\SALES\NOTES.DAT \MISC\NOTES.DAT
```

Change your default directory to \MISC and examine the file's contents.

```
A> CD \MISC
A> TYPE NOTES.DAT
```

As you can see, accessing data files contained in DOS subdirectories is straightforward.

If you also have executable files contained in the following subdirectories

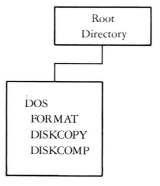

you execute them by specifying complete path names to the commands at the DOS prompts, as shown here:

```
A> \DOS\DISKCOMP A: B:
A> \DOS\FORMAT B:
```

You will see shortly how the DOS PATH and APPEND commands make file manipulation under DOS subdirectories even easier, often transparent, to the user.

LOCATING FILES BY USING TREE

The DOS TREE command allows you to display the directory structure of a disk. The command lists all of the subdirectories (and, optionally, their files) to the standard output device.

The format of the TREE command is

[*drive:*][*path__name*]TREE [*source__drive:*] [/*F*]

where the following is true:

drive is the disk drive identification (A, B, or C) containing the file TREE.COM.

path__name is the complete DOS path name of the subdirectory containing the file TREE.COM.

source__drive is the disk drive identification (A, B, or C) of the drive TREE is to display the structure of. If you omit the drive, TREE uses the current default.

/*F* directs TREE to display the names of all files in each subdirectory.

Assuming that your directory structure is that shown here

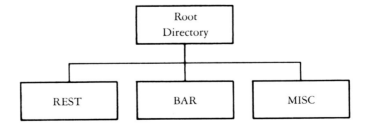

invoking the DOS TREE command results in

```
DIRECTORY PATH LISTING
Path: \REST
Sub-directories:   None


Path: \BAR
Sub-directories:   None


Path: \MISC
Sub-directories:   None
```

Likewise, if you want to display all of the files, issue the following command:

```
A> TREE /F
```

TREE is useful when you use it in conjunction with the DOS pipe. For example, the following command lists all of the files and the directory structure to your printer.

```
A> TREE /F > PRN:
```

Likewise, the following command allows you to determine if a specific file is on your disk:

```
A> TREE /F | FIND "FILENAME"
```

DEFINING AN EXECUTION PATH

The DOS PATH command provides you with a method of directing DOS where to look for commands not contained in the current directory. Each time you execute a command, DOS first checks its list of internal commands (such as CLS, MKDIR, RMDIR, and so forth). If DOS finds the command name is an internal command, it executes it. If DOS does not find the command, it first searches the current directory for the file. If DOS finds either an EXE, COM, or BAT file that matches the command name, it executes it. If DOS has still not located the command, it checks to see if you have defined a path of other subdirectories it should examine in search of the command. The flowchart in Figure 5-8 summarizes this processing.

The format of the PATH command is

PATH [*drive:*][*path__name*][;[*drive*][*path__name*]...]

or

PATH ;

where the following is true:

drive defines a disk drive identification (A, B, or C) where the subdirectory DOS is to examine resides.

path__name specifies a complete DOS path name of a subdirectory that DOS is to search for executable commands.

... indicates that the process can repeat indefinitely.

Consider the following command:

```
A> PATH C:\
```

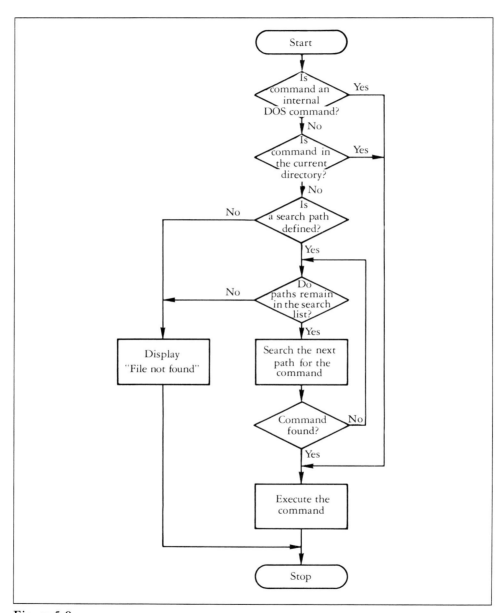

Figure 5-8.

Flowchart summarizing PATH
command processing

If DOS does not find the command name as an internal command or a
file within the current directory, it will search the root directory on drive
C for a matching file name. Likewise, the PATH command

```
A> PATH C:\;B:\;A:\
```

directs DOS to search the root directories on drives C, B, and, A (in that
order) for commands it cannot locate. This process is shown in Figure
5-9. Upon exhausting all of the specified paths, DOS will display the
message

```
A> DISKCOPP
Bad command or file name

A>
```

If you invoke the DOS PATH command without any parameters,
DOS displays the currently defined command search path.

```
A> PATH
PATH=C:\
```

Also, if you invoke PATH with a semicolon,

```
A> PATH ;
```

DOS deletes the current command search path.

```
A> PATH ;
A> PATH
No Path
```

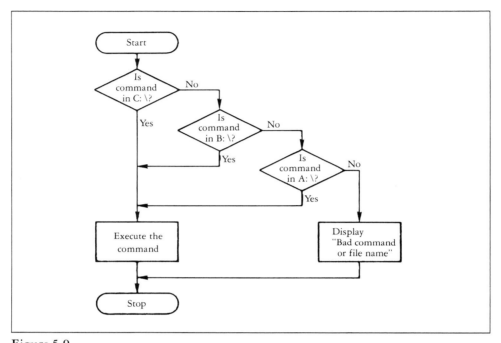

Figure 5-9.

Flowchart showing PATH searching
root directories for files

When this occurs, DOS again only searches the current directory or the
path name that you specify for commands.

DEFINING A DATA FILE PATH
BY USING APPEND

In a manner similar to the DOS PATH command, starting with DOS 3.2
you are allowed to specify a search path that DOS examines when it does
not find the data file that you specify in the current directory. The format

of the APPEND command is

APPEND [*drive:*][*path_name*][;[*drive:*][*path_name*]...]

or

APPEND ;

where the following is true:

drive defines a disk drive identification (A, B, or C) where the subdirectory that DOS is to examine resides.

path_name specifies a complete DOS path name of a subdirectory that DOS is to search for data files.

...indicates that the process can repeat indefinitely.

Consider the following example:

```
APPEND C:\;B:\;A:\
```

In this case, if DOS cannot locate the data file that you specify in the current directory, it searches the root directories on drives C, B, and A (in that order).

As with the DOS PATH command, if you invoke APPEND without any parameters

```
A> APPEND
```

DOS displays the current data file search path, as follows:

```
APPEND = C:\;B:\;A:\
```

Likewise, if you invoke APPEND with a semicolon as an argument, DOS deletes the current data file search path

IMPROVING SYSTEM PERFORMANCE

Both the DOS PATH and APPEND commands are meant to be conveniences. If you do not fully evaluate your search path layout, however, you could greatly reduce system performance. Consider the directory structure shown in Figure 5 - 10. In this case, the subdirectory MISC has a very large number of files. Likewise, the subdirectory DATA contains many files. The subdirectory UTIL, however, only contains your more commonly used utility programs.

Consider the following DOS PATH command:

```
A> PATH=\MISC;\DATA;\UTIL
```

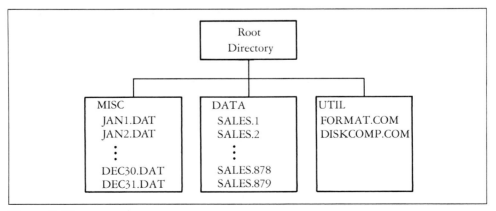

Figure 5-10.

Subdirectory with numerous files
versus subdirectory with few files

If DOS does not find the command you entered as an internal command, or in the current directory, it begins its search of the command path. In this case, DOS must examine every file in the subdirectories MISC and DATA before it arrives at the subdirectory UTIL. The overhead in this search can be considerable. Simply by rearranging your PATH command as follows

```
A> PATH=\UTIL;\DATA;\MISC
```

you greatly improve system response time. Likewise, if you further divide the files contained in the DATA and MISC directories into additional subdirectories, you can reduce search overhead even more. This is how DOS subdirectories improve system performance.

SUBSTITUTING LONG PATH NAMES WITH A DRIVE LETTER

If you utilize DOS subdirectories to their fullest extent, you can create a directory structure that is several layers deep. If you name subdirectories in a meaningful fashion, your DOS path names can become quite large, as shown here:

```
A> DIR \REST\SALES\JULY\MORNING\SPECIAL
```

You can abbreviate the command as

```
A> SUBST D: \REST\SALES\JULY\MORNING\SPECIAL
```

The following command is now identical to the previous DIR command:

```
A> DIR D:
```

The DOS SUBST command allows you to abbreviate a DOS path name with a DOS disk drive identification. The format for the SUBST command is

SUBST [*drive:*][*path_name*][/D]

where

drive is the disk drive identification (D, E, or F) with which you are abbreviating the DOS path name.
path_name is the complete DOS path name that you want to abbreviate.
/D directs DOS to delete a previously defined substitution.

Consider the following example:

```
A> SUBST D: \BAR\SALES\JUNE
```

In this case, rather than repeatedly typing \BAR \SALES \JUNE, you can simply refer to drive D. If you issue the command

```
A> DIR D:
```

DOS will display a directory listing of the subdirectory

\BAR \SALES \JUNE.

If you invoke SUBST without any parameters

```
A> SUBST
```

DOS will display the current substitutions.

```
D: => A:\BAR\SALES\JUNE
```

Likewise, to remove a substitution, simply enter

```
A> SUBST D:/D
```

Again, SUBST will only allow you to abbreviate path names up to 63 characters long.

JOINING A DRIVE TO YOUR DIRECTORY STRUCTURE

The DOS JOIN command (DOS 3.1 or greater) allows you to join another disk drive to your current directory structure by using DOS subdirectories. The format of the DOS JOIN command is

JOIN [*drive:*][*path_name*][/D]

where the following is true:

drive specifies the disk drive identification (A, B, or C) that you want to join to your current directory structure.

path_name is the complete path name for an empty DOS subdirectory with which you want to refer to the disk drive.

/D directs DOS to remove the JOIN.

Before you can issue the JOIN command, you must have an empty directory.

```
A> MKDIR \JOINDIR
```

Next, invoke JOIN with the disk drive identification that you want to place in your directory structure.

```
A> JOIN B: \JOINDIR
```

Now, when you issue commands against the directory JOINDIR, you will see the disk access light for drive B illuminate. JOIN allows you to access all of the files contained in drive B as if they were files in the subdirectory JOINDIR on your current device. Once you have joined a disk to a directory, DOS does not care if you change the diskettes in the joined drive.

If you invoke JOIN without any parameters

```
A> JOIN
B: => A:\JOINDIR
```

DOS will display any current joins.

To remove a join, simply use the /D qualifier, as shown here:

```
A> JOIN B:/D
```

Most users will never require the DOS JOIN command. It is presented here to complete the discussion of DOS directory manipulation commands.

RULES OF THUMB

Use the following list as a guideline when you create your DOS subdirectories.

- DOS directory names must conform to the same format as DOS file names, with up to eight characters for a file name followed by an optional three-character extension. The following are valid DOS directory names: BAR.SLS, BAR.INV, and BAR.MSC.

- If you do not specify a complete path name for a target directory, DOS assumes that you are referencing a file in the current directory.

- Use the disk drive specifier B:SUBDIR to manipulate directories contained on disks other than the current default.

- Do not create subdirectory names identical to file names in the same directory.

- Do not create a directory called \DEV. DOS uses a hidden directory called \DEV to perform device I/O. For example, to print the file NOTES.TXT, issue the command

```
A> COPY NOTES.TXT \DEV\PRN
```

- DOS path names cannot exceed 63 characters in length.

- The root directory on every disk is restricted to a specific number of files. DOS subdirectories, however, can store as many files as you have disk space for.

- Logically group all of your files into subdirectories.

MANIPULATING DIRECTORIES
FROM WITHIN APPLICATIONS

One of the most convenient methods of hiding data from end users is to allow your software programs to use DOS subdirectories. In so doing, the programs themselves can traverse your directory structure, adding and deleting directories as they require. This prevents the end user from having to understand directories and their manipulation.

Turbo Pascal provides four predefined procedures that perform the following:

ChDir (directory);	Sets the current directory
MkDir (directory);	Creates the directory specified
RmDir (directory);	Removes the directory specified
GetDir (drive, directory);	Returns the current directory

Each routine is fairly straightforward to use. If for any reason one of the procedures fails, each sets the IoResult flag to a value other than 0. For example, the following Turbo Pascal program sets the current directory to 'TEST':

```
Program Change_Dir;

begin
{$I-}                        {capture I/O errors}
  ChDir ('\TEST');
{$I+}                        {allow Turbo to process errors}
  if IoResult <> 0 then
      writeln ('Invalid directory');
end.
```

Likewise, if you are using Microsoft C, the run-time library contains the routines

chdir (string);	Sets the current directory
mkdir (string);	Creates the directory specified
getcwd (string, len);	Returns the current directory
rmdir (string);	Removes the directory specified

Each routine returns a status of 0 if it was successful and −1 if an error occurred. The following C program displays the current working directory:

```
#define MAX_STR 255

main ()
 {
  char directory[MAX_STR];

  if (getcwd(directory, MAX_STR) == 0)
    printf ("Invalid command\n");
  else
    printf ("%s\n", directory);
 }
```

If you are not using Microsoft C, most C compilers should provide similar routines. If they do not, or if you are using FORTRAN, the C-to-DOS Interface and FORTRAN-to-DOS Interface diskette packages developed by this author provide complete directory manipulation control, along with access to each of the DOS services.

OS/2 DIRECTORY MANIPULATION

Quite possibly the area of DOS least affected by OS/2 is file and directory management. This ensures upward compatibility of disks and files that you have created under previous versions of DOS. OS/2 fully supports each of the commands examined throughout this chapter. It does not add new, significant capabilities to them, however.

DOS subdirectories provide a major benefit to your computer productivity by allowing you to organize your files, to reduce system overhead, and to place an unlimited number of files on your disk. The importance of file management cannot be stressed enough. Take time today to clean up your disks. You will reap the benefits every day thereafter.

6: DOS System Services

$\mathbf{C}$hapter 1 discussed how the operating system serves as the interface between the user and the machine. The operating system, therefore, must perform the user interface, provide complete support for file-manipulation operations, and allow the user to use each of the devices connected to the computer, as well as provide facilities for program invocation and execution. Developing an operating system is indeed a tremendous programming effort. To facilitate their software development, the DOS developers used modular coding, and broke down each function into small manageable code fragments called system services (see Figure 6-1).

Each time DOS boots, it loads these services into specific memory locations that it later accesses to perform such operations as

- Open, read, write, close a file

- Get keyboard input

- Terminate a program

- Create, rename, delete a file

- Allocate, free, modify a memory region

- Get, set current disk drive

- Make, change, delete a directory

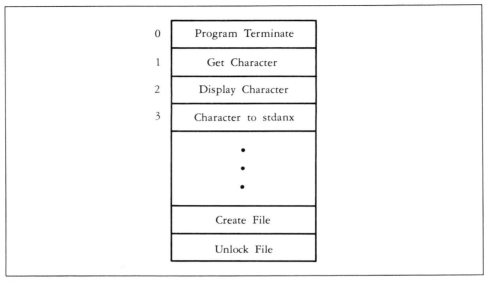

Figure 6-1.

DOS system services

Because these services are already present in memory, and because of their tremendous capabilities, the DOS developers have made each of these services readily available to your application programs. Before examining each of the DOS services, first consider the interface that DOS requires your applications to use to access the services.

8088 REGISTERS

The IBM PC and compatibles are based on a processor chip called the 8088. Within this chip are a set of storage locations known as *registers*. Since the registers are contained in the CPU itself, the 8088 can manipulate values contained in these registers very quickly. The 8088 has 14 registers, each capable of storing 16 bits of data. Visualize the 8088 registers as follows:

General-Purpose Registers

	AH	AL			CH	CL
AX				CX		

	BH	BL			DH	DL
BX				DX		

Base and Index Registers

SP [ ]   SI [ ]
Stack Pointer   Source Index

BP [ ]   DI [ ]
Base Pointer   Destination Index

Special-Purpose Registers

[ ]   IP [ ]
Flags Register   Instruction Pointer

Segment Registers

CS [ ]   SS [ ]
Code Segment   Stack Segment

DS [ ]   ES [ ]
Data Segment   Extended Segment

Your programs communicate with the DOS services through the registers. For example, if you want to determine the DOS version that you are using, place the following value into the register AH and invoke the DOS interrupt 21H:

AH   30H DOS Get Version Status

Upon completion of the Get DOS Version Number service, DOS will place its major and minor version numbers into the register AX as follows:

AH   Minor version number

AL   Major version number

INT 21H

An *interrupt* is a signal to the CPU from a program or hardware device to suspend the function that it is performing temporarily and instead to execute a specific task. For example, each time you press the SHIFT and PRTSC keys together, DOS temporarily suspends what it is doing to print the screen's contents. DOS uses interrupt 21H as its interface to the DOS system services. Each time DOS encounters an interrupt 21H, it examines the contents of each of the 8088 registers to determine the specific DOS service to perform, along with the required parameters for the service. In most cases, DOS obtains the service number from register AH.

For example, the DOS service 02H directs DOS to display the character contained in register DL to the standard output device.

Register	Entry Contents
AH	02H DOS Display Character Service
DL	Character to display

To invoke this routine, place corresponding values into the correct registers and invoke INT 21H as shown in the following assembly language code fragment:

```
MOV AH, 02   ; display character service
MOV DL, 65   ; character A
INT 21H      ; DOS interface
```

Most DOS users probably use high-level languages such as C or Turbo Pascal. If you are using C, most compilers provide you with a run-time library of routines that provide your programs with access to the DOS system services. In the case of Microsoft C, this routine is called **intdos**. To use this routine, you must include the header file **dos.h** at the start of your program, as shown here:

```
#include <dos.h>
```

The file contains a structure definition that allows your C program to emulate the 8088 registers. As previously stated, the DOS services use the contents of the 8088 registers to determine the desired interrupt service along with its parameters.

```
struct WORDREGS {
        unsigned int ax;
        unsigned int bx;
        unsigned int cx;
        unsigned int dx;
        unsigned int si;
        unsigned int di;
        unsigned int cflag;
        };

struct BYTEREGS {
        unsigned char al, ah;
        unsigned char bl, bh;
        unsigned char cl, ch;
        unsigned char dl, dh;
        };

union REGS {
        struct WORDREGS x;
        struct BYTEREGS h;
        };


struct SREGS {
        unsigned int es;
        unsigned int cs;
        unsigned int ss;
        unsigned int ds;
        };
```

Your C program simply assigns the appropriate register values to each member of the structure. When you invoke **intdos**, that routine maps the structure values to the appropriate registers, as shown in Figure 6-2. Similarly, the service maps the register values back to the structure members, as shown in Figure 6-3. This C program displays a character on the screen by using the DOS service 02H:

```
#include <dos.h>

main ()
  {
  union REGS inregs, outregs;

  inregs.h.ah = 0x02;
  inregs.h.dl = 65;
  intdos (&inregs, &outregs);
  }
```

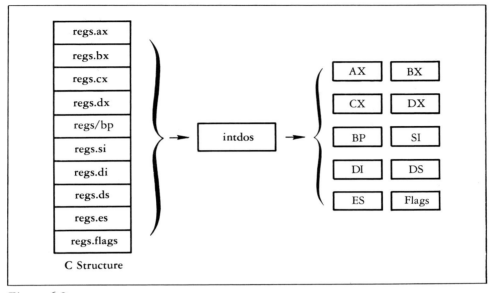

Figure 6-2.

Mapping of structure values by **intdos**

In a similar manner, Turbo Pascal provides a routine called **MsDOS**. To use this routine, your programs must declare a variable of type **REGISTERS**, as shown here:

```
Type
  REGISTERS = record
                AX, BX, CX, DX, BP, SI, DI, DS, ES, FLAGS: INTEGER
              end;

Var
  REGS: Registers;
```

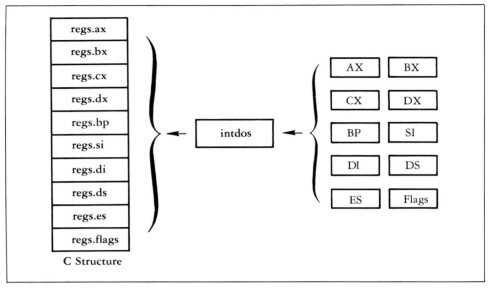

Figure 6-3.

Mapping of register values by intdos

This Turbo Pascal program again uses the DOS service 02H to display a character to the screen:

```
Program DisplayChar;

Type
  REGISTERS = record
                AX, BX, CX, DX, BP, SI, DI, DS, ES, FLAGS: INTEGER
              end;

Var
  REGS: Registers;

Begin
  WITH REGS DO
    BEGIN
      AX := $0200;
      DX := 65;
      MsDOS (REGS);
    END;
END.
```

The DOS system services are very powerful. In fact, they comprise the toolkit that the developers used to create DOS. By using these routines within your programs, you can easily and quickly develop programs of professional quality. The following section discusses each of the DOS system services. In most cases, the use of the services is shown in C, Turbo Pascal, or assembler. As you will see, many of the services are straightforward to use. They will greatly increase the capabilities of your programs.

ASCIIZ

Many of the DOS services require the use of an *ASCIIZ string*. An ASCIIZ is a string of characters terminated by a NULL or zero byte. For example, consider the following string:

"ASCIIZ strings are NULL terminated"

To make it an ASCIIZ string, you must append a NULL byte. Assuming the ASCIIZ string contains the same characters, it will appear in memory as shown in Figure 6-4. By default, C stores strings as ASCIIZ strings. If you are using Turbo Pascal, simply append null characters, as shown here:

```
ASCIIZ := str + Chr(0);
```

Service 0H Program Termination

Function   Terminate the execution of a program and return control to DOS or the parent process.

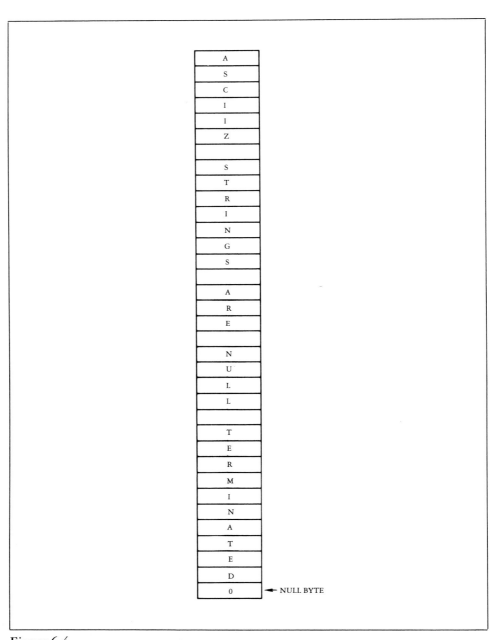

Figure 6-4.

ASCIIZ string in memory

Register	Entry Contents
AH CS	CH DOS Program Terminate Service Pointer to the program segment prefix of the terminating program
Register	Exit Contents
None	

Notes   DOS stores the terminate, CTRL-BREAK, and critical-error exit addresses in the program-segment prefix. Upon invocation of this service, DOS flushes and closes all files opened by the program and properly updates directory entries as required.

Example

```
program TERMINATE;

Procedure Terminate_Program ;

Type
  REGISTERS = record
                AX, BX, CX, DX, BP, SI, DI, DS, ES, FLAGS: INTEGER
              end;

Var
  REGS: REGISTERS;

begin
  with REGS do
    begin
      AX := 0;
      MsDOS (REGS);
    end;
end;

begin
  Terminate_Program ;
  Writeln ('This shouldn't appear');
end.
```

Service 01H Get Character
from Standard Input Device

Function   Wait for a character from standard input (unless one is present) and echo the character back to the standard output device.

Register	Entry Contents
AH	01H DOS Get Standard Input Character Service
Register	Exit Contents
AL	Byte containing the character read from the standard input device

Notes   If the character returned in AL is 0, the user pressed an extended ASCII character (such as the F10 key). In such cases, you must use a second call to this service to determine the actual key that was pressed. This service checks for a CTRL-BREAK entry.

Example

```
#include <dos.h>

int stdin_char ()
{
  union REGS inregs, outregs;

  inregs.h.ah = 0x01;
  intdos (&inregs, &outregs);
  return (outregs.h.al);
}

main ()
{
  printf ("\nCharacter in %c\n", stdin_char());
}
```

Service 02H Display Character
to Standard Output Device

Function   Output a character to the standard output device.

Register	Entry Contents
AH DL	02H Write Character to Standard Output Service Byte value of the character to display
Register	Exit Contents
None	

Note   This routine checks for a CTRL-BREAK entry.

Example

```
#include <dos.h>

int stdout_output (character)
  char character;
  {
  union REGS inregs, outregs;

  inregs.h.ah = 0xC2;
  inregs.h.dl = character;

  intdos (&inregs, &outregs);
  }

char *output = "Test string\n";

main ()
  {
  while (*output)
    stdout_output (*output++);
  }
```

Service 03H Get Character
from Standard Aux Device

Function   Wait for a character from standard auxiliary device (unless one is present).

Register	Entry Contents
AH	03H Get Character From stdaux Service
Register	Exit Contents
AL	Byte value of the character returned from standard auxiliary device

Notes   This service does not return an error-status value. By default, DOS initializes this port to 2400 baud, no parity, 1 stop bit, and 8 data bits.

Example

```
#include <dos.h>

int aux_char ()
 {
  union REGS inregs, outregs;

  inregs.h.ah = 0x03;
  intdos (&inregs, &outregs);
  return (outregs.h.al);
 }

main ()
 {
  printf ("\nCharacter in %c\n", aux_char());
 }
```

Service 04H Write Character
to Standard Aux Device

Function   Write a character to the standard auxiliary device.

Register	Entry Contents
AH	04H Write Character to stdaux Service
DL	Byte value of the character to write
Register	Exit Contents
None	

Notes   This service does not return an error-status value. By default, DOS initializes this port to 2400 baud, no parity, 1 stop bit, and 8 data bits.

Example

```
#include <dos.h>

int aux_output (character)
  char character;
 {
  union REGS inregs, outregs;

  inregs.h.ah = 0x04;
  inregs.h.dl = character;

  intdos (&inregs, &outregs);
 }

char *output = "Test string\n";

main ()
 {
  while (*output)
    aux_output (*output++);
 }
```

Service 05H Write Character
to Standard Printer Device

Function   Write a character to the standard printer device.

Register	Entry Contents
AH	05H Write Character to Printer Service
DL	Byte value of the character to write

Register	Exit Contents
None	

Note   This service does not return an error-status value.

Example

```
#include <dos.h>

int stdprn_output (character)
  char character;
  {
 .union REGS inregs, outregs;

  inregs.h.ah = 0x05;
  inregs.h.dl = character;

  intdos (&inregs, &outregs);
  }

char *output = "Test string\n";

main ()
  {
  while (*output)
    stdprn_output (*output++);
  }
```

Service 06H Direct Console I/O

Function   This service reads a character from stdin or writes a character to stdout, depending upon the value in DL.

Register	Entry Contents
AH DL	06H Get Character With Echo Service FFH for console input 0 to FEH character for console output
Register	Exit Contents
AL	None for console output. The character input for direct console input.

Notes   If DL is FFH, this service returns the next character in the keyboard buffer (if one is present). Otherwise, it returns 0. If DL is not FFH, this service outputs the character contained in DL.

Example

```
#include <dos.h>

int direct_IO (byte)
  char byte;
  {
  union REGS inregs, outregs;

  inregs.h.ah = 0x06;
  inregs.h.dl = byte;
  intdos (&inregs, &outregs);
  return (outregs.h.al);
  }

main ()
  {

  printf ("\nCharacter out %c\n", direct_IO (65));
  printf ("\nCharacter in %c\n", direct_IO (0xFF));
  }
```

Service 07H Console Input
Without Character Echo

Function   Wait for a character from the standard input device (unless one is present). This service does not echo the character.

Register	Entry Contents
AH	07H Console Input Without Echo Service
Register	Exit Contents
AL	Character input from standard input

Notes   If the character returned in AL is 0, the user has pressed an extended ASCII character (such as the F10 key). In such cases, you must use a second call to this service to determine the actual key that was pressed. This service does not perform CTRL-BREAK processing.

```
#include <dos.h>

int no_echo_read ()
  {
  union REGS inregs, outregs;

  inregs.h.ah = 0x07;
  intdos (&inregs, &outregs);
  return (outregs.h.al);
  }

main ()
  {
  printf ("\nCharacter in %c\n", no_echo_read());
  }
```

Service 08H Console Input
Without Character Echo

Function   Wait for a character from the standard input device (unless one is present). This service does not echo the character.

Register	Entry Contents
AH	08H Console Input Without Echo Service
Register	Exit Contents
AL	Character input from standard input

Notes   If the character returned in AL is 0, the user has pressed an extended ASCII character (such as the F10 key). In such cases, you must use a second call to this service to determine the actual key that was pressed. This service performs CTRL-BREAK processing.

Service 09H Display String
to the Standard Output Device

Function   Display each of the characters in a string to stdout.

Register	Entry Contents
AH	09H DOS Display String Service
DS	Segment address of the string to display
DX	Offset address of the string to display
Register	Exit Contents
None	

Note The string must be terminated with the dollar sign ($) character (decimal 36).

Example

```
Program Display;

Type
  string79 = string[79];

procedure DisplayString (str: string79);

Type
  REGISTERS = record
                AX, BX, CX, DX, BP, SI, DI, DS, ES, FLAGS: INTEGER
              end;

Var
  REGS: REGISTERS;

begin
  str := str + '$';
  with REGS do
    begin
      AX := $0900;
      DS := Seg (str);
      DX := Ofs (str[1]);
      MsDos (REGS);
    end;
end;

begin
  DisplayString ('Test string');
end.
```

Service 0AH Buffered Keyboard Input

Function Read characters from the standard input device into a user-defined buffer.

Register	Entry Contents
AH	0AH Buffered Keyboard Input Service
DS	Segment address of the user buffer
DX	Offset address of the user buffer
Register	Exit Contents
None	

Notes   The first byte of the buffer upon entry to the service contains the number of characters that the buffer can store. The second byte of the buffer upon return contains the number of characters actually read. The service places the characters into the buffer at the third byte.

Example

```
Program Buffer;

Type
  string79 = string[79];

procedure BufferedInput (var str: string79);

Type
  REGISTERS = record
                AX, BX, CX, DX, BP, SI, DI, DS, ES, FLAGS: INTEGER
              end;
Var
  REGS: REGISTERS;
  TEMP: string79;
  I: integer;
begin
  with REGS do
    begin
      AX  := $0A00;
      TEMP[1] := Chr(79);
      DS  := Seg (TEMP);
      DX  := Ofs (TEMP[1]);
      MsDos (REGS);

      for I := 3 to Ord(TEMP[2]) + 3 do
        str[I-2] := TEMP[I];

      str[0] := TEMP[2];
    end;
end;
var
  str: string79;

begin
  BufferedInput (str);
  writeln (str);
end.
```

Service 0BH Check Character Available
from Standard Input Device

Function   Examine the standard input device. Return 255 if a character is available for input; otherwise return a 0.

Register	Entry Contents
AH	0BH Check Standard Input Status Service
Register	Exit Contents
AL	255 if a character is available, 0 otherwise

Example

```
#include <dos.h>

int check_character_available ()
  {
  union REGS inregs, outregs;

  inregs.h.ah = 0x0B;
  intdos (&inregs, &outregs);
  return (outregs.h.al);
  }

main ()
  {
  int status;

  printf ("Type one or two characters\n");

  do

     status = check_character_available();

  while (status != 0xff);

  printf ("Characters available from stdin\n");
  }
```

Service 0CH Clear Keyboard Buffer and Invoke Keyboard Service

Function   Clear the DOS standard input buffer and invoke a DOS keyboard service.

Register	Entry Contents
AH	0CH Clear Keyboard Service
AL	Desired keyboard service (01H, 06H, 07H, 08H, or 0AH)
Register	Exit Contents
None	

Note By clearing the keyboard buffer, this service forces DOS to wait for another character.

Example

```
#include <dos.h>

int keyboard_service (service)
  int service;
  {
  union REGS inregs, outregs;

  inregs.h.ah = 0xCC;
  inregs.h.al = service;
  intdos (&inregs, &outregs);
  return (outregs.h.al);
  }

main ()
  {
    printf ("\nCharacter in %c\n", keyboard_service (7));
  }
```

Service 0DH Disk Buffer Flush

Function Flush all of the disk buffers.

Register	Entry Contents
AH	0DH DOS Disk Reset Service
Register	Exit Contents
None	

Note   DOS does not correctly record files that have changed in size but are not yet closed.

Example

```
#include <dos.h>

int disk_flush ()
  {
  union REGS inregs, outregs;

  inregs.h.ah = 0x0D;
  intdos (&inregs, &outregs);
  }
```

Service OEH Select Default Disk Drive

Function   Select the current default drive (A, B, C, and so on).

Register	Entry Contents
AH DL	0EH DOS Select Drive Service Disk drive desired
Register	Exit Contents
AL	Total number of disk drives present

Note   The current drive is specified as $0 = A$, $1 = B$, $2 = C$, and so on.

Example

```
#include <dos.h>

int set drive (drive)
  int drive;
  {
  union REGS inregs, outregs;

  inregs.h.ah = 0x0E;
  inregs.h.dl = drive;
  intdos (&inregs, &outregs);
  return (outregs.h.al);
  }

main ()
  {
  set_drive (1);
  }
```

Service 0FH Open a File Based
upon a File Control Block

Function   Search the current directory for the file specified in the file control block (FCB). Open the file if it exists.

Register	Entry Contents
AH	0FH DOS FCB Open Service
DS	Segment address of the file control block
DX	Offset address of the file control block
Register	Exit Contents
AL	Open status: 0 if successful, 255 if error

Note Newer applications should use DOS file handles.

Service 10H Close a File Opened
via a File Control Block

Function Close a file opened by using an FCB.

Register	Entry Contents
AH	10H DOS FCB Close File Service
DS	Segment address of the file control block
DX	Offset address of the file control block

Register	Exit Contents
AL	Close status: 0 if successful 255 if error

Note Newer applications should use DOS file handles.

Service 11H Find First Matching Directory
Entry via File Control Block

Function DOS services 11H and 12H allow your applications to perform DOS wild-card character support by using FCBs. This service examines the file specification provided in the FCB and returns the first matching file.

Register	Entry Contents
AH	11H FCB Find First Service
DS	Segment address of the file control block
DX	Offset address of the file control block

Register	Exit Contents
AL	Search status: 0 if successful 255 if error

Note   Newer applications should use DOS services 4EH and 4FH.

Service 12H Find Next Matching Directory
Entry via File Control Block

Function   DOS services 11H and 12H allow your applications to perform DOS wild-card character support by using FCBs. This service examines the file specification provided in the FCB and returns the first matching file.

Register	Entry Contents
AH	12H FCB Find Next Service
DS	Segment address of the file control block
DX	Offset address of the file control block

Register	Exit Contents
AL	Search status: 0 if successful 255 if error

Note   Newer applications should use DOS services 4EH and 4FH.

Service 13H Delete a File via
a File Control Block

Function   Examine the file name specified in an FCB, and delete it (if it exists) in the current directory.

Register	Entry Contents
AH	13H DOS FCB Deletion Service
DS	Segment address of the file control block containing the name of the file to delete
DX	Offset address of the file control block

Register	Exit Contents
AL	Deletion status: 0 if successful 255 if error

Notes   DOS supports use of the ? wild-card character. Newer applications should use DOS file handles

Service 14H Sequential File Read

Function   Read the record addressed by the current block of the current record in the FCB. The record is placed at the location specified by the disk transfer address.

Register	Entry Contents
AH	14H FCB Sequential Read Service
DS	Segment address of the file control block
DX	Offset address of the file control block

Register	Exit Contents
AL	Read status: 0 if successful
	1 if EOF and no data
	2 if disk transfer area too small
	3 if EOF and partial data

Note   Newer applications should use DOS file handles.

Service 15H Sequential File Write

Function   Write the record specified by the current block and record bytes of the FCB with the record contained at the disk transfer address.

Register	Entry Contents
AH	15H
DS	Segment address of the file control block
DX	Offset address of the file control block

Register	Exit Contents
AL	Write status: 0 if successful
	1 if disk full
	2 if disk transfer area too small

Note Newer applications should use DOS file handles.

Service 16H Create File
via a File Control Block

Function Create a file based on the name specified by the FCB.

Register	Entry Contents
AH	16H FCB File Creation Service
DS	Segment address of the file control block
DX	Offset address of the file control block
Register	Exit Contents
AL	Creation status: 0 if successful 255 if error

Notes If DOS finds a matching file, it reuses it. Otherwise, DOS creates a new file. Newer applications should use DOS file handles.

Service 17H Rename a File
via a File Control Block

Function Change the name of all files matching the specified source file in the FCB to that of the target file.

Register	Register Contents
AH	17H FCB File Rename Service
DS	Segment address of the file control block
DX	Offset address of the file control block
Register	Register Contents
AL	Rename status: 0 if successful 255 if error

Service 19H Get Current Disk Drive

Function   Obtain the current disk drive (A, B, C, and so on).

Register	Entry Contents
AH	19H DOS Get Current Drive Service
Register	Exit Contents
AL	Current drive

Note   The current disk drive is specified as $A = 0, B = 1, C = 2$, and so on.

Example

```
#include <dos.h>

int get_drive ()
  {
   union REGS inregs, outregs;

   inregs.h.ah = 0x0E;
   intdos (&inregs, &outregs);
   return (outregs.h.al);
  }

main ()
  {
   printf ("Current drive is %c\n", 65 + get_drive ();
  }
```

Service 1AH Set Disk-Transfer Address

Function   Define a new disk-transfer address (DTA).

Register	Entry Contents
AH	1AH DOS Set DTA Service
DS	Segment address of the new DTA
DX	Offset address of the new DTA

Register	Exit Contents
None	

Note   The default DTA is offset 80H of the program-segment prefix.

Example

```
Program DTA;

Type
  DTABUFFER = array [1..128] of byte;

procedure NewDta (NewDTABuffer: DTABUFFER);

Type
  REGISTERS = record
                AX, BX, CX, DX, BP, SI, DI, DS, ES, FLAGS: INTEGER
              end;

Var
  REGS: REGISTERS;

begin
  with REGS do
    begin
      AX := $1A00;
      DS := Seg (NewDTABuffer);
      DX := Ofs (NewDTABuffer);
      MsDos (REGS);
    end;
end;

var
  NewDtaBuffer: DTABUFFER;


begin
  NewDta (NewDTABuffer);
end.
```

Service 1BH Get Current Drive
Allocation Table Information

Function   Return file allocation table (FAT) information about the
current drive.

Register	Entry Contents
A H	1BH Get Allocation Table Information Service

Register	Exit Contents
A L	Number of sectors/cluster
B X	Offset address of the media descriptor byte
C X	Sector size in bytes
D S	Segment address of the media descriptor byte
D X	Number of clusters

Note   For more information on disk structure, refer to Chapter 10.

Example

```
#include <dos.h>

int default_allocation (spc, sector_size, num_clusters)
  int *spc, *sector_size, *num_clusters;
  {
  union REGS inregs, outregs;

  inregs.h.ah = 0x1B;
  intdos (&inregs, &outregs);
  *spc = outregs.h.al;           /* sectors per cluster */
  *sector_size = outregs.x.cx;
  *num_clusters = outregs.x.dx;
  }

main ()
  {
  int spc, sector_size, num_clusters;

  default_allocation (&spc, &sector_size, &num_clusters);

  printf ("Sectors per cluster %d\nSector size %d\n Cluster
          Size %d\n", spc, sector_size, num_clusters);
  }
```

Service 1CH Get Specific Drive Allocation
Table Information

Function   Return FAT information about a specific drive.

Register	Entry Contents
AH	1CH Get Allocation Table Information Service
DL	Drive number desired

Register	Exit Contents
AL	Number of sectors/cluster
BX	Offset address of the media descriptor byte
CX	Sector size in bytes
DS	Segment address of the media descriptor byte
DX	Number of clusters

Note   For more information on disk structure, refer to Chapter 10.

Example

```
#include <dos.h>

int drive_allocation (drive, spc, sector_size, num_clusters)
  int drive, *spc, *sector_size, *num_clusters;
  {
  union REGS inregs, outregs;

  inregs.h.ah = 0x1C;
  inregs.h.dl = drive;
  intdos (&inregs, &outregs);
  *spc = outregs.h.al;           /* sectors per cluster */
  *sector_size = outregs.x.cx;
  *num_clusters = outregs.x.dx;
  }

main ()
  {
  int spc, sector_size, num_clusters;

  drive_allocation (0, &spc, &sector_size, &num_clusters);

  printf ("Sectors per cluster %d\nSector size %d\n Cluster
          Size %d\n", spc, sector_size, num_clusters);
  }
```

Service 21H File Control Block
Random Access Read

Function   Read the record addressed by the current block and record numbers of an FCB into the memory location addressed by the disk-transfer address.

Register	Entry Contents
AH	21H FCB Random Read Service
DS	Segment address of the file control block
DX	Offset address of the file control block

Register	Exit Contents
AL	Read status: 0 if successful
	1 if EOF and no data
	2 if DTA too small
	3 if EOF and partial data

Note   Newer applications should use DOS file handles.

Service 22H File Control Block
Random Access Write

Function   Write the record addressed by the current block and record numbers of an FCB into the memory location addressed by the disk-transfer address.

Register	Entry Contents
AH	22H FCB Random Write Service
DS	Segment address of the file control block
DX	Offset address of the file control block

Register	Exit Contents
AL	Write status: 0 if successful
	1 if disk full
	2 if DTA too small

Note   Newer applications should use DOS file handles.

Service 23H Get File Size via
File Control Block

Function   Place the number of records contained in the file specified in the FCB into the random record number of the FCB.

Register	Entry Contents
AH	23H Get File Size Service
DS	Segment address of the file control block
DX	Offset address of the file control block
Register	Exit Contents
AL	Status 0 if the file was found 255 otherwise

Note   Newer DOS applications should use DOS file handles.

Service 24H Set Relative Record
Number Field

Function   Set the relative record number within an FCB to provide random access.

Register	Entry Contents
AH	24H Set Record Number Service
DS	Segment address of the file control block
DX	Offset address of the file control block
Register	Exit Contents
None	

Note   Newer applications should use DOS file handles.

Service 25H Set Interrupt Vector

Function   Set the segment and offset address for an interrupt service routine.

Register	Entry Contents
AH	25H Set Interrupt Vector Service
DS	Segment address of the interrupt service routine
DX	Offset address of the interrupt service routine
AL	Desired interrupt number
Register	Exit Contents
None	

Note   Always ensure that your applications reset the interrupt vectors to their original values before terminating, or you may experience unexpected results.

Example

```
procedure Set_Interrupt_Vector (INTERRUPT, SEGMENT, OFFSET:
                 integer);
Type
  REGISTERS = record
                 AX, BX, CX, DX, BP, SI, DI, DS, ES, FLAGS: INTEGER
                 end;

var
    REGS: REGISTERS;  {AX, BX, CX, DX, BP, SI, DI, DS, ES, FLAGS}

begin
    with REGS do
       begin
         AX := $2500 + interrupt;  {interrupt number is in AL}
         DS := SEGMENT;
         DX := OFFSET;
         MSDos (REGS);
       end;
end;
```

Service 26H Define New Program-Segment Prefix

Function   Define a new program-segment prefix (PSP) for the current application.

Register	Entry Contents
AH	26H DOS New PSP Service
DX	Segment address for the new PSP
Register	**Exit Contents**
None	

Note   Upon invocation, DOS copies the contents of the original PSP to the new address.

Example

```
Program PSP;

Type
  PSPBUFFER = array [1..255] of byte;

procedure NewPSP (NewPSPBuffer: PSPBUFFER);

Type
  REGISTERS = record
                AX, BX, CX, DX, BP, SI, DI, DS, ES, FLAGS: INTEGER
              end;

Var
  REGS: REGISTERS;

begin
  with REGS do
    begin
      AX := $2600;
      DS := Seg (NewPSPbuffer);
      DX := Ofs (NewPSPbuffer);
      MsDos (REGS);
    end;
end;

var
  NewPSPBuffer: PSPBUFFER;


begin
  NewPSP (NewPSPBuffer);
end.
```

Service 27H Random Block Read
via File Control Block

Function   Read the number of records specified from the file defined in the FCB into the location defined by the disk-transfer address.

Register	Entry Contents
AH	27H Random Block Read Service
CX	Number of records to read
DS	Segment address of the file control block
DX	Offset address of the file control block

Register	Exit Contents
AL	Read status: 0 if successful
	1 if EOF and no data
	2 if DTA too small
	3 if EOF and partial read
CX	Actual number of records read

Note   Newer DOS applications should use DOS file handles.

Service 28H Random Block Write
via File Control Block

Function   Write the number of records specified from the file defined in the FCB into the location defined by the disk-transfer address.

Register	Entry Contents
AH	28H Random Block Write Service
CX	Number of records to write
DS	Segment address of the file control block
DX	Offset address of the file control block

Register	Exit Contents
AL	Write status: 0 if successful
	1 if disk is full
	2 if DTA too small
CX	Actual number of records written

Note   Newer DOS applications should use DOS file handles.

Service 29H Parse File Name

Function   Parse the command line for a file name in the form DRIVE:FILENAME.EXT. If a file is found, create an FCB for it. Path names are not supported.

Register	Entry Contents
AH	29H DOS Parse File Name Service
AL	Control bit mask
DI	Offset address of unopened FCB
DS	Segment address of command line
ES	Segment address of unopened FCB
SI	Offset address of command line

Register	Exit Contents
AL	Status: 0 no wildcard characters 1 wildcard characters 255 invalid drive
DI	Offset address of formatted FCB
DS	Segment address of first character after the file name
ES	Segment address of formatted FCB
SI	Offset address of first character after the file name

Note   Control bit mask:

0	Scan past leading separators
2	Match FCB drive specifier with drive found in command line
4	Match FCB file name to file name found in command line
8	Match FCB file extension to extension found in command line

Service 2AH DOS Get Date Service

Function   Return the current system date.

Register	Entry Contents
AH	2AH DOS Get System Date Service

Register	Exit Contents
AL	Day of the week
CX	Current year
DH	Month
DL	DAY

Notes

Day is returned as (0 = Sunday, 6 = Saturday)
Year ranges from 1980 to 2099
Month ranges from 1 to 12
Day ranges from 1 to 31

Example

```
#include <dos.h>

int get_date (day, month, year, day_of_week)
  int *day, *month, *year, *day_of_week;
{
  union REGS inregs, outregs;

  inregs.h.ah = 0x2A;
  intdos (&inregs, &outregs);
  *day = outregs.h.dl;
  *day_of_week = outregs.h.al;
  *month = outregs.h.dh;
  *year = outregs.x.cx;
}

main ()
{
  int day, month, year, day_of_week;

  get_date (&day, &month, &year, &day_of_week);

  printf ("Date %d/%d/%d Day of week %d\n", month, day, year,
          day_of_week);
}
```

Service 2BH DOS Set Date Service

Function   Set the current system date.

Register	Entry Contents
AH	2BH DOS Set System Date Service
CX	Current year
DH	Month
DL	DAY

Register	Exit Contents
AL	Status 0 if valid date 255 if date invalid

Notes

Year ranges from 1980 to 2099
Month ranges from 1 to 12
Day ranges from 1 to 31

Example

```
#include <dos.h>

int set_date (day, month, year)
  int day, month, year;
  {
  union REGS inregs, outregs;

  inregs.h.ah = 0x2B;
  inregs.h.dh = month;
  inregs.h.dl = day;
  inregs.x.cx = year;

  intdos (&inregs, &outregs);

  return (outregs.h.al);
  }

main ()
  {
  set_date (31, 12, 1987);
  }
```

Service 2CH Get System Time

Function   Return the current system time.

Register	Entry Contents
AH	2CH DOS Get System Time Service

Register	Exit Contents
CL	Minutes
CH	Hours
DL	Hundredths of seconds
DH	Seconds

Example

```
#include <dos.h>

int get_time (hours, minutes, seconds, hundredths)
  int *hours, *minutes, *seconds, *hundredths;
{
  union REGS inregs, outregs;

  inregs.h.ah = 0x2C;

  intdos (&inregs, &outregs);

  *hours = outregs.h.ch;
  *minutes = outregs.h.cl;
  *hundredths = outregs.h.dl;
  *seconds = outregs.h.dh;
}

main ()
{
  int hours, minutes, seconds, hundredths;

  get_time (&hours, &minutes, &seconds, &hundredths);

  printf ("%d:%d:%d.%d\n", hours, minutes, seconds, hundredths);
}
```

Service 2DH Set System Time

Function   Set the current system time.

```
Register            Entry Contents

AH                  2DH DOS Set System Time Service
CL                  Minutes
CH                  Hours
DL                  Hundredths of seconds
DH                  Seconds

Register            Exit Contents

AL                  Status: 0 if valid time
                            255 if invalid time
```

Example

```c
#include <dos.h>

int set_time (hours, minutes, seconds, hundredths)
  int hours, minutes, seconds, hundredths;
{
  union REGS inregs, outregs;

  inregs.h.ah = 0x2D;
  inregs.h.ch = hours;
  inregs.h.cl = minutes;
  inregs.h.dl = hundredths;
  inregs.h.dh = seconds;
  intdos (&inregs, &outregs);
  return (outregs.h.al);
}

main ()
{
  printf ("%d\n", set_time (12, 0, 0, 0));
}
```

Service 2EH Set Disk Verification ON/OFF

Function   Turn disk I/O verification on or off.

Register	Entry Contents
AH	2EH DOS Disk Verification Service
AL	0 to turn verification off
	1 to turn verification on
Register	**Exit Contents**
None	

Example

```
#include <dos.h>

int set_disk_verification (status)
  int status;
  {
  union REGS inregs, outregs;

  inregs.h.ah = 0x2E;
  inregs.h.al = status;
  intdos (&inregs, &outregs);
  }

main ()
  {
  set_disk_verification (1);
  }
```

Service 2FH Get Disk-Transfer Address

Function   Many DOS services place file information at the location defined by the disk-transfer address. This service returns the memory location containing this buffer.

Register	Entry Contents
AH	2FH DOS Get DTA Service
Register	Exit Contents
ES BX	Segment address of the DTA Offset address of the DTA

Example

```
procedure Get_Disk_Transfer_Area (var SEGMENT, OFFSET: integer);

Type
  REGISTERS = record
                AX, BX, CX, DX, BP, SI, DI, DS, ES, FLAGS: INTEGER
              end;

Var
    REGS: REGISTERS;  {AX, BX, CX, DX, BP, SI, DI, DS, ES, FLAGS}

begin
    with REGS do
      begin
        AX := $2F00;
        MSDos (REGS);
        SEGMENT := ES;
        OFFSET  := BX;
      end;
end;
```

Service 30H Get DOS Version Number

Function   Returns the major and minor version numbers of DOS.

Register	Entry Contents
AH	30H Get Version Number Service
Register	Exit Contents
AL AH	Major version number Minor version number

Note Given DOS version 3.2, 3 is the major version number while 2 is the minor.

Example

```
#include <dos.h>

int DOS_version (major, minor)
  int *major, *minor;
  {
  union REGS inregs, outregs;

  inregs.h.ah = 0x30;
  intdos (&inregs, &outregs);
  *major = outregs.h.al;
  *minor = outregs.h.ah;
  }

main ()
  {
  int *major, *minor;

  DOS_version (&major, &minor);

  printf ("\nDOS Version %d.%d\n", major, minor);
  }
```

Service 31H Terminate Program
and Remain Resident

Function Terminate the current program allowing it to remain resident in memory. Chapter 15 provides several examples of this service.

Register	Entry Contents
AH	31H DOS Terminate Resident Service
AL	Exit Status Value
DX	Required memory size in 16-byte paragraphs
Register	Exit Contents
None	

Example

See Chapter 15 for complete examples.

Service 33H Get/Set State
of CTRL-BREAK Processing

Function   Sets or obtains the current state of control of break-checking.

```
Register          Entry Contents

AH                33H CTRL-BREAK Service
AL                0 Get current state
                  1 Set current state
DL                0 Set current state to off
                  1 Set current state to on

Register          Exit Contents

DL                Current State: 0 is off
                                 1 is on
```

Example

```c
#include <dos.h>

int ctrl_break_status (function, state)
  int function, state;
  {
  union REGS inregs, outregs;

  inregs.h.ah = 0x33;
  inregs.h.al = function;
  inregs.h.dl = state;

  intdos (&inregs, &outregs);

  return (outregs.h.dl);
  }

main ()
  {
  ctrl_break_status (1, 1);
  }
```

Service 35H Get Interrupt Vector

Function Return the segment and offset address of an interrupt service routine.

Register	Entry Contents
AH	35H DOS Get Interrupt Vector Address
AL	Desired interrupt number

Register	Exit Contents
ES	Segment address of the interrupt service routine
BX	Offset addresss of the interrupt service routine

Example

```
#include <dos.h>

int get_interrupt (vector, segment, offset)
  int vector, *segment, *offset;
  {
  union REGS inregs, outregs;
  struct SREGS segregs;

  inregs.h.ah = 0x35;
  inregs.h.al = vector;

  intdosx (&inregs, &outregs, &segregs);

  *segment = segregs.es;
  *offset = outregs.x.bx;
  }

main ()
  {
  int segment, offset;

  get_interrupt (5, &segment, &offset);

  printf ("Segment %x Offset %x\n", segment, offset);
  }
```

Service 36H Get Available Disk Space

Function   Return the available disk space for a specific disk drive.

Register	Entry Contents
AH	36H DOS Get Disk Space Service
DL	Desired disk drive

Register	Exit Contents
AX	FFFFH if the drive specified was invalid; otherwise, the number of sectors/cluster
BX	Available clusters
CX	Bytes/sector
DX	Clusters/disk

Note   Available__Space = AX * BX * CX

Example

```
procedure Get_Free_Disk_Space (DRIVE: byte;
                             var SPACE: real;
                             var STATUS: byte);
Type
  REGISTERS = record
                AX, BX, CX, DX, BP, SI, DI, DS, ES, FLAGS: INTEGER
              end;
var
    REGS: REGISTERS;   {AX, BX, CX, DX, BP, SI, DI, DS, ES, FLAGS}
begin
     with REGS do
        begin
          AX := $3600;
          DX := DRIVE;
          MSDos (REGS);
          if (AX = $FFFF) then    {error in operation}
            begin
              STATUS := 1;          {return error status code}
              SPACE := -1;
            end
          else
            begin                   {successful operation}
              STATUS := 0;
              SPACE := 1.0 * AX * BX * CX;   {free space}
            end;
        end;
end;
```

Service 38H Get Country-Dependent Information

Function   Return the country-dependent information for the desired function code.

Register	Entry Contents
AH	38H Get Country Information Service
AL	Country code
DS	Segment address of buffer to store country information
DX	Offset address of buffer to store country information

Register	Exit Contents
AX	Error code if the carry flag is set

Service 39H Create a DOS Subdirectory

Function   Create the subdirectory specified by the ASCIIZ string.

Register	Entry Contents
AH	39H Create Subdirectory Service
DS	Segment address of the ASCIIZ name
DX	Offset address of the ASCIIZ name

Register	Exit Contents
AX	Error codes if carry flag is set

Example

```
procedure Make_Directory (DIRECTORY: STRING79;
                          var STATUS: byte);

Type
  REGISTERS = record
                AX, BX, CX, DX, BP, SI, DI, DS, ES, FLAGS: INTEGER
              end;

var
    REGS: REGISTERS;   {AX, BX, CX, DX, BP, SI, DI, DS, ES, FLAGS}

begin
    with REGS do
      begin
        DIRECTORY := DIRECTORY + Chr(0);       {convert to asciiz}
        AX := $3900;                           {DOS function code}
        DS := Seg(DIRECTORY[1]);
        DX := Ofs(DIRECTORY[1]);
        MSDos (REGS);
        if (FLAGS and 1 = 1) then              {error in operation}
          STATUS := Lo(AX)
        else
          STATUS := 0;                         {successful operation}
      end;
end;
```

Service 3AH Remove a DOS Subdirectory

Function   Remove the subdirectory specified by the ASCIIZ string.

Register	Entry Contents
AH	3AH Remove Subdirectory Service
DS	Segment address of the ASCIIZ name
DX	Offset address of the ASCIIZ name
Register	Exit Contents
AX	Error codes if carry flag is set

Example

```
procedure Remove_Directory (DIRECTORY: STRING79;
                            var STATUS: byte);
Type
  REGISTERS = record
                 AX, BX, CX, DX, BP, SI, DI, DS, ES, FLAGS: INTEGER
              end;
var
     REGS: REGISTERS;  {AX, BX, CX, DX, BP, SI, DI, DS, ES, FLAGS}
begin
    with REGS do
      begin
        DIRECTORY := DIRECTORY + Chr(0);        {convert to asciiz}
        AX := $3A00;                            {DOS function code}
        DS := Seg(DIRECTORY[1]);
        DX := Ofs(DIRECTORY[1]);
        MSDos (REGS);
        if (FLAGS and 1 = 1) then               {error in operation}
          STATUS := Lo(AX)
        else
          STATUS := 0;                          {successful operation}
      end;
end;
```

Service 3BH Change DOS Default Subdirectory

Function   Select the default subdirectory specified by the ASCIIZ string for the current drive.

Register	Entry Contents
AH	3BH Select Subdirectory Service
DS	Segment address of the ASCIIZ name
DX	Offset address of the ASCIIZ name
Register	**Exit Contents**
AX	Error codes if carry flag is set

Example

```
procedure Change_Directory (DIRECTORY: STRING79;
                            var STATUS: byte);

Type
  REGISTERS = record
                AX, BX, CX, DX, BP, SI, DI, DS, ES, FLAGS: INTEGER
              end;

var
    REGS: REGISTERS;   (AX, BX, CX, DX, BP, SI, DI, DS, ES, FLAGS)

begin
    with REGS do
      begin
        DIRECTORY := DIRECTORY + Chr(0);      {convert to asciiz}
        AX := $3B00;                          {DOS function code}
        DS := Seg(DIRECTORY[1]);
        DX := Ofs(DIRECTORY[1]);
        MSDos (REGS);
        if (FLAGS and 1 = 1) then             {error in operation}
          STATUS := Lo(AX)
        else
          STATUS := 0;                        {successful operation}
      end;
end;
```

Service 3CH Create a File via
DOS File Handles

Function   Create a file with the name defined by the ASCIIZ string
returning a 16-bit DOS file handle.

Register	Entry Contents
AH	3CH Create File Handle Service
CX	Desired file attribute
DS	Segment address of the ASCIIZ name
DX	Offset address of the ASCIIZ name

Register	Exit Contents
AX	Error code if carry flag is set; otherwise the 16-bit file handle

Example

```
procedure Create_File (FILENAME: STRING79;
                         ATTRIBUTE: integer;
                    var FILE_HANDLE: integer;
                         var STATUS: byte);

Type
  REGISTERS = record
                AX, BX, CX, DX, BP, SI, DI, DS, ES, FLAGS: INTEGER
              end;

var
    REGS: REGISTERS;   {AX, BX, CX, DX, BP, SI, DI, DS, ES, FLAGS}

begin
    with REGS do
      begin
        FILENAME := FILENAME + Chr(0);
        AX := $3C00;
        CX := ATTRIBUTE;
        DS := Seg(FILENAME[1]);
        DX := Ofs(FILENAME[1]);
        MSDos (REGS);
        if (FLAGS and 1 = 1) then         {error in operation}
          STATUS := Lo(AX)
        else
          begin
            FILE_HANDLE := AX;            {successful operation}
            STATUS := 0;
          end;
      end;
end;
```

Service 3DH Open a File via DOS File Handles

Function   Open the specified file by using the ASCIIZ string provided, returning a 16-bit file handle.

Register	Entry Contents
AH	3DH Open File Handle Service
DS	Segment address of the ASCIIZ name
DX	Offset address of the ASCIIZ name
AL	Open access code

Register	Exit Contents
AX	Error status if the carry flag is set; otherwise, a 16-bit file handle

Notes   Open access codes:

0   Read-only file
1   Write access
2   Read/write access

Example

```
procedure    Open_File (FILENAME: STRING79;
                        MODE: byte;
                    var FILE_HANDLE: integer;
                        var STATUS: byte);

Type
  REGISTERS = record
                AX, BX, CX, DX, BP, SI, DI, DS, ES, FLAGS: INTEGER
              end;

var
    REGS: REGISTERS;   {AX, BX, CX, DX, BP, SI, DI, DS, ES, FLAGS}

begin
    with REGS do
      begin
        FILENAME := FILENAME + Chr(0);
        AX := $3D00 + MODE;                 {mode is in AL}
        DS := Seg(FILENAME[1]);
        DX := Ofs(FILENAME[1]);
        MSDos (REGS);
        if (FLAGS and 1 = 1) then           {error in operation}
          STATUS := Lo(AX)
        else
          begin
            FILE_HANDLE := AX;              {successful operation}
            STATUS := 0;
          end;
      end;
end;
```

Service 3EH Close a File via
DOS File Handles

Function   Close a file previously opened or created with a DOS file handle.

Register	Entry Contents
AH BX	3EH Close File Handle Service 16-bit file handle of the file to close
Register	Exit Contents
AX	Error value if the carry flag is set

Example

```
procedure Close_File (FILE_HANDLE: integer;
                      var STATUS: byte);

Type
  REGISTERS = record
                AX, BX, CX, DX, BP, SI, DI, DS, ES, FLAGS: INTEGER
              end;

var
    REGS: REGISTERS;  {AX, BX, CX, DX, BP, SI, DI, DS, ES, FLAGS}

begin
    with REGS do
      begin
        AX := $3E00;
        BX := FILE_HANDLE;
        MSDos (REGS);
        if (FLAGS and 1 = 1) then          {error in operation}
          STATUS := Lo(AX)
        else
          STATUS := 0;
      end;
end;
```

Service 3FH Read from DOS File Handle

Function   Read the number of bytes specified from the file or device associated with the DOS file handle provided.

Register	Entry Contents
AH	3FH Read From DOS File Handle Service
BX	File handle to read from
CX	Number of bytes to read
DS	Segment address of the buffer to read the data into
DX	Offset address of the buffer to read the data into

Register	Exit Contents
AX	Error code if carry flag is set; otherwise, the number of bytes read

Example

```
procedure Read_File (FILE_HANDLE: integer;
                     var BUFFER: DISKBUFFER;
                         NUMBYTES: integer;
                     var STATUS: byte);

Type
  REGISTERS = record
                 AX, BX, CX, DX, BP, SI, DI, DS, ES, FLAGS: INTEGER
              end;

var
    REGS: REGISTERS;    {AX, BX, CX, DX, BP, SI, DI, DS, ES, FLAGS}

begin
    with REGS do
       begin
          AX := $3F00;
          BX := FILE_HANDLE;
          CX := NUMBYTES;
          DS := Seg(BUFFER);
          DX := Ofs(BUFFER);
          MSDos (REGS);
          if (FLAGS and 1 = 1) then            {error in operation}
             STATUS := Lo(AX)
          else
             STATUS := 0;
       end;
end;
```

Service 40H Write to DOS File Handle

Function   Write the number of bytes specified to the file or the device associated with the DOS file handle provided.

Register	Entry Contents
AH	40H Write to DOS File Handle Service
BX	File handle to write to
CX	Number of bytes to write
DS	Segment address of the buffer to write the data from
DX	Offset address of the buffer to write the data from

Register	Exit Contents
AX	Error code if carry flag is set; otherwise, the number of bytes written

Example

```
procedure Write_File (FILE_HANDLE: integer;
                      BUFFER: DISKBUFFER;
                      NUMBYTES: integer;
                      var STATUS: byte);

Type
  REGISTERS = record
                AX, BX, CX, DX, BP, SI, DI, DS, ES, FLAGS: INTEGER
              end;

var
    REGS: REGISTERS;   {AX, BX, CX, DX, BP, SI, DI, DS, ES, FLAGS}

begin
    with REGS do
      begin
        AX := $4000;
        BX := FILE_HANDLE;
        CX := NUMBYTES;
        DS := Seg(BUFFER);
        DX := Ofs(BUFFER);
        MSDos (REGS);
        if (FLAGS and 1 = 1) then          {error in operation}
          STATUS := Lo(AX)
        else
          STATUS := 0;
      end;
end;
```

Service 41H Delete File

Function   Delete the file specified by the ASCIIZ string.

Register	Entry Contents
AH	41H DOS Delete File Service
DS	Segment address of ASCIIZ name
DX	Offset address of ASCIIZ name

Register	Exit Contents
AX	Error code if carry flag set

Example

```
procedure Delete_file (FILENAME: STRING79;
                       var STATUS: byte);

Type
  REGISTERS = record
                AX, BX, CX, DX, BP, SI, DI, DS, ES, FLAGS: INTEGER
              end;

var
    REGS: REGISTERS;   {AX, BX, CX, DX, BP, SI, DI, DS, ES, FLAGS}

begin
    with REGS do
      begin
        FILENAME := FILENAME + Chr(0);       {convert to asciiz}
        AX := $4100;                         {DOS function code}
        DS := Seg(FILENAME[1]);
        DX := Ofs(FILENAME[1]);
        MSDos (REGS);
        if (FLAGS and 1 = 1) then            {error in operation}
          STATUS := Lo(AX)
        else
          STATUS := 0;                       {successful operation}
      end;
end;
```

Service 42H LSEEK

Function   Move a file's read/write pointer to the byte offset specified by the CX-DX register combination.

Register	Entry Contents
AH	42H DOS LSEEK Service
AL	Move directive
BX	File handle
CX	High word of byte target offset
DX	Low word of byte target offset

Register	Exit Contents
AX	Error code if the carry flag is set; otherwise, the low-word target offset
DX	High-word target offset

Note   Move directive:

0   Offset is from the beginning of the file.
1   Offset is from the current location.
2   Offset is from the end of the file.

Example

```
procedure Lseek (FILE_HANDLE: integer;
                 DIRECTIVE: integer;
                 var BUFFER: DISKBUFFER;
                 HIOFFSET,
                 LOOFFSET: integer;
                 var STATUS: byte);

Type
  REGISTERS = record
              AX, BX, CX, DX, BP, SI, DI, DS, ES, FLAGS: INTEGER
              end;

var
    REGS: REGISTERS;  {AX, BX, CX, DX, BP, SI, DI, DS, ES, FLAGS}
```

```
begin
    with REGS do
        begin
          AX := $4200 + DIRECTIVE;
          BX := FILE_HANDLE;
          CX := HIOFFSET;
          DX := LOOFFSET;
          MSDos (REGS);
          if (FLAGS and 1 = 1) then        {error in operation}
            STATUS := Lo(AX)
          else
            STATUS := 0;
        end;
end;
```

Service 43H Change or Return File Attribute

Function   Set/Get the attribute byte of the file specified by the ASCIIZ string.

Register	Entry Contents
AH	43H Change File Attribute Service
AL	Function: 0 Get file attribute
	1 Set file attribute
CX	Desired attribute
DS	Segment address of the ASCIIZ name
DX	Offset address of the ASCIIZ name

Register	Exit Contents
AX	Error code if carry flag set
CX	File attribute byte if AL = 0

Note   File attributes:

1	Read-only
2	Hidden
4	System
8	Volume label
16	Subdirectory
32	Archive

Example

```
procedure File_Attributes (FILENAME: STRING79;
                                FUNCT: byte;
                        var ATTRIBUTES,
                             STATUS: byte);

Type
  REGISTERS = record
                AX, BX, CX, DX, BP, SI, DI, DS, ES, FLAGS: INTEGER
              end;

Var
    REGS: REGISTERS;   {AX, BX, CX, DX, BP, SI, DI, DS, ES, FLAGS}

Begin
    with REGS do
       begin
          FILENAME := FILENAME + Chr(0);      {convert to asciiz}
          AX := $4300 + FUNCT;
          DS := Seg(FILENAME[1]);
          DX := Ofs(FILENAME[1]);
          CX := ATTRIBUTES;
          MSDos (REGS);
          ATTRIBUTES := CX;

          if (FLAGS and 1 = 1) then           {error in operation}
            STATUS := Lo(AX)
          else
            STATUS := 0;                       {successful operation}
       end;
end;
```

Service 45H Duplicate a File Handle

Function Return a new file that references the same file and position as the specified file handle.

Register	Entry Contents
AX	45H Duplicate Handle Service
BX	File handle to duplicate
Register	Exit Contents
AX	Error code if carry flag is set; otherwise, 16-bit file handle

Example

```
#include <dos.h>

int duplicate_handle (handle)
  int handle
{
  union REGS inregs, outregs;

  inregs.h.ah = 0x45;
  inregs.x.bx = handle;
  intdos (&inregs, &outregs);
  return (outregs.x.ax);
}
```

Service 46H Force Handle Duplication

Function   Force DOS to duplicate the specified handle and return a second handle to the same file and position.

Register	Entry Contents
AH	46H Force Duplicate Handle Service
BX	File handle to duplicate
CX	Second file handle

Register	Exit Contents
AX	Error code if carry flag is set

Example

```
#include <dos.h>

int force_handle_duplication (source_handle, target_handle)
  int handle
{
  union REGS inregs, outregs;

  inregs.h.ah = 0x46;
  inregs.x.bx = source_handle;
  inregs.x.cx = target_handle;
  intdos (&inregs, &outregs);
  return (outregs.x.ax);
}
```

Service 47H Get Current Directory

Function   Return an ASCIIZ string containing the current directory.

Register	Entry Contents
AH	47H DOS Get Directory Service
DS	Segment address of the buffer storing the directory name
SI	Offset address of the buffer storing the directory name
DL	Drive number containing the directory desired

Register	Exit Contents
AX	Error codes if the carry flag is set

Example

```
procedure Get_Directory (DIRECTORY: STRING79;
                         var STATUS: byte);

Type
  REGISTERS = record
                 AX, BX, CX, DX, BP, SI, DI, DS, ES, FLAGS: INTEGER
              end;

var
    REGS: REGISTERS;   {AX, BX, CX, DX, BP, SI, DI, DS, ES, FLAGS}

begin
    with REGS do
       begin
          DIRECTORY := DIRECTORY + Chr(0);        {convert to asciiz}
          AX := $4700;                            {DOS function code}
          DS := Seg(DIRECTORY[1]);
          DX := Ofs(DIRECTORY[1]);
          MSDos (REGS);
          if (FLAGS and 1 = 1) then               {error in operation}
            STATUS := Lo(AX)
          else
            STATUS := 0;                          {successful operation}
       end;
end;
```

Service 48H Allocate Memory Paragraphs

Function   Allocate the specified number of paragraphs.

Register	Entry Contents
AH	48H DOS Allocate Memory Service
BX	Number of desired memory paragraphs

Register	Exit Contents
AX	Error code if carry flag is set
	Segment address of allocated memory block
BX	Size of the largest available block of memory if insufficient memory space is available

Note   A memory paragraph is a contiguous 16-byte block.

Example

```
#include <dos.h>

int allocate_memory (paragraphs, segment, size)
  int paragraphs, *segment, *size;
 {
  union REGS inregs, outregs;

  inregs.h.ah = 0x48;
  inregs.x.bx = paragraphs;
  intdos (&inregs, &outregs);
  *segment = outregs.x.ax;
  *size = outregs.x.bx;
 }
```

Service 49H Free Allocated Memory Paragraphs

Function   Release previously allocated memory.

Register	Entry Contents
AH ES	49H DOS Free Allocated Memory Service Segment address of the block to release
Register	Exit Contents
AX	Error code if the carry flag is set

Note   A memory paragraph is a contiguous 16-byte block.

Example

```
#include <dos.h>

int free_memory (segment)
  int segment;
  {
  union REGS inregs, outregs;
  struct SREGS segregs;

  inregs.h.ah = 0x49;

  segregs.es = segment;
  intdosx (&inregs, &outregs, &segregs);
  return (outregs.x.ax);
  }
```

Service 4AH Modify Previously Allocated Memory

Function   Modify the size of a previously allocated memory segment.

Register	Entry Contents
AH	4AH DOS Modify Memory Service
ES	Segment address of memory region to adjust
BX	Desired block size in paragraphs

Register	Exit Contents
AX	Error codes if carry flag is set
BX	Size of the largest available block of memory if insufficient memory space is available

Notes   A memory paragraph is a contiguous 16-byte block. This service allows previously allocated memory to grow or shrink as required.

```
#include <dos.h>

int modify_memory (segment, paragraphs, size)
  int segment, paragraphs, *size;
{
  union REGS inregs, outregs;
  struct SREGS segregs;

  inregs.h.ah = 0x4A;
  segregs.es = segment;
  inregs.x.bx = paragraphs;
  intdosx (&inregs, &outregs, &segregs);
  *size = outregs.x.bx;
  return (outregs.x.ax);
}
```

Service 4BH Load or Execute a Second Program

Function   Load or execute a secondary program for execution.

Register	Entry Contents
AH	4BH DOS Spawn Service
DS	Segment address of ASCIIZ string containing the command to load or execute.
DX	Offset address of ASCIIZ string containing the command to load or execute.
ES	Segment address of the program's parameter block
BX	Offset address of the program's parameter block
AL	Load function directive

Register	Exit Contents
AX	Error flags if the carry flag is set

Notes   Load function directive:

0   Load and execute the program.

1   Load but do not execute the program.

Example

See Chapter 7 for a complete example.

Service 4CH Program Termination with Status

Function   Terminate a program returning a status value to DOS or to the parent process.

Register	Entry Contents
AH	4CH DOS Program Termination Service
AL	Return status code

Register	Exit Contents
None	

Notes   Return status values are available to DOS batch files by using the ERRORLEVEL value command or to a program by using service 4DH.

Example

```
#include <dos.h>

int terminate_with_status (status)
  int status;
 {
  union REGS inregs, outregs;

  inregs.h.ah = 0x4C;
  inregs.h.al - status;
  intdos (&inregs, &outregs);
 }

main ()
 {
   terminate_with_status (1);

   printf ("Test: should not see\n");
 }
```

Service 4DH Get Child Process Exit Code

Function   Return the exit status value from a child process executed by using the DOS spawn system service.

Register	Entry Contents
AH	4DH DOS Get Child Exit Code Status
Register	Exit Contents
AH	Exit status code

Note   Default values are

0   Successful termination
1   CTRL-BREAK
2   Termination by using 31H

Example

```
#include <dos.h>

int get_child_status ()
  {
  union REGS inregs, outregs;

  inregs.h.ah = 0x4D;
  intdos (&inregs, &outregs);
  return (outregs.h.al);
  }

main ()
  {
  printf ("\nChild status %d\n", get_child_status());
  }
```

Service 4EH Find First Matching File

Function   Search the current directory for the first file matching the file specification contained in the ASCIIZ string.

Register	Entry Contents
AH	4EH DOS Find First File Service
CX	Desired file attribute
DS	Segment address of ASCIIZ file specification
DX	Offset address of ASCIIZ file specification

Register	Exit Content
AX	Error status code if the carry flag is set

Note   If DOS finds a matching file, it places the information shown in Figure 6-5 at the disk-transfer address.

Offset	Contents
21	Attributes
22	Creation Time
24	Creation Date
26	Low-Word File Size
28	High-Word File Size
30	File Name

Figure 6-5.

File information offset from DTA

Example

See Figure 6-6.

Service 4FH Find Next Matching File

Function   Continue the search for matching files following a call to DOS service 4EH.

Register	Entry Contents
AH	4FH
Register	Exit Contents
AX	Error status code if the carry flag is set

Note   This service is very similar to 4EH and places the same information at the disk-transfer address.

```
    Type
      DTA_INFO = record
        ATTRIBUTES   : byte;
        FILE_SIZE    : real;
        NAME         : STRING79;
      end;

    procedure Find_First (SEARCH_SPEC: STRING79;
                          ATTRIBUTES: byte;
                          var FILESPEC: DTA_INFO;
                          var STATUS: byte);

    Type
      REGISTERS = record
                    AX, BX, CX, DX, BP, SI, DI, DS, ES, FLAGS: INTEGER
                  end;
    var
        REGS    : REGISTERS;   {AX, BX, CX, DX, BP, SI,
                                DI, DS, ES, FLAGS}
        DTA_SEG,
        DTA_OFS : integer;   {address of disk transfer area}
        I       : integer;   {counter for loops}
    begin
        with REGS do
          begin
            SEARCH_SPEC := SEARCH_SPEC + Chr(0);
            AX := $4E00;                          {DOS function code}
            DS := Seg(SEARCH_SPEC[1]);
            DX := Ofs(SEARCH_SPEC[1]);
            CX := ATTRIBUTES;
            MSDos (REGS);
            if (FLAGS and 1 = 1) then
              STATUS := Lo(AX)
            else
              begin
                STATUS := 0;                      {successful operation}
                Get_DTA (DTA_SEG, DTA_OFS);

                with FILESPEC do
                  begin
                    ATTRIBUTES :=  Mem [DTA_SEG:DTA_OFS+21];

                    FILE_SIZE  := 1.0 * Mem [DTA_SEG:DTA_OFS+26] +
                                  Mem [DTA_SEG:DTA_OFS+27] * 256.0 +
                                  Mem [DTA_SEG:DTA_OFS+28] * Power
                                                         (256.0, 2) +
                                  Mem [DTA_SEG:DTA_OFS+29] * Power
                                                         (256.0, 3);

                    I := 0;
                    while ((I < 13) and (Mem[DTA_SEG:DTA_OFS+30+I] <> 0)) do
                      begin
                        name[I + 1] := Chr(Mem[DTA_SEG:DTA_OFS+30+I]);
                        I := I + 1;
                      end;

                    name[0] := Chr(I);
                  end; {with FILESPEC}
              end;
          end;          {with REGS}
    end;
```

Figure 6-6.

Example of Find First Matching File
service

Example

See Figure 6-7.

Service 54H Get Disk I/O Verification Status

Function   Return the current disk verification status.

Register	Entry Contents
AH	54H DOS Get Verfication Status Service
Register	Exit Contents
AL	Verification status 0: verify on 1: verify off

Example

```
#include <dos.h>

int get_disk_verification ()
  {
  union REGS inregs, outregs;

  inregs.h.ah = 0x54;
  intdos (&inregs, &outregs);
  return (outregs.h.al);
  }

main ()
  {
  printf ("Disk verification status %d\n", get_disk_verification());
  }
```

Service 56H Rename a File

Function   Rename the file specified by the source and target ASCIIZ names.

```
Type
  DTA_INFO = record
     ATTRIBUTES  : byte;
     FILE_SIZE   : real;
     NAME        : STRING79;
  end;
procedure Find_Next (var FILESPEC: DTA_INFO;
                     var STATUS: byte);

Type
  REGISTERS = record
                 AX, BX, CX, DX, BP, SI, DI, DS, ES, FLAGS: INTEGER
              end;
var
    REGS     : REGISTERS;  {AX, BX, CX, DX, BP, SI,
                            DI, DS, ES, FLAGS}
    DTA_SEG,
    DTA_OFS : integer;     {address of disk transfer area}
    i       : integer;     {counter for loops}

begin
    with REGS do
      begin
        AX := $4F00;
        MSDos (REGS);
        if (FLAGS and 1 = 1) then     {error in operation}
          STATUS := Lo(AX)
        else
          begin
            STATUS := 0;                 {successful operation}
            GetDTA (DTA_SEG, DTA_OFS);

            with FILESPEC do
              begin
                ATTRIBUTES :=  Mem [DTA_SEG:DTA_OFS+21];

                FILE_SIZE  := 1.0 * Mem [DTA_SEG:DTA_OFS+26] +
                              Mem [DTA_SEG:DTA_OFS+27] * 256.0 +
                              Mem [DTA_SEG:DTA_OFS+28] * Power
                                                     (256.0, 2) +
                              Mem [DTA_SEG:DTA_OFS+29] * Power
                                                     (256.0, 3);
                I := 0;
                while ((I < 13) and (Mem[DTA_SEG:DTA_OFS+30+I] <> 0))
                     do
                  begin
                    name[I + 1] := Chr(Mem[DTA_SEG:DTA_OFS+30+I]);
                    I := I + 1;
                  end;
                name[0] := Chr(I);
              end; {with FILESPEC}
          end;
      end;            {with REGS}
end;
```

Figure 6-7.

Example of Find Next Matching File
service

Register	Entry Contents
AH	56H DOS Rename File Service
DS	Segment address of ASCIIZ source name
DX	Offset address of ASCIIZ source name
ES	Segment address of ASCIIZ target name
DI	Offset address of ASCIIZ target name

Register	Exit Contents
AX	Error status code if the carry flag is set

Note   Wild-card characters are not supported.

Example

```
procedure Rename_File (OLD_NAME, NEW_NAME: STRING79;
                           var STATUS: byte);

Type
  REGISTERS = record
                AX, BX, CX, DX, BP, SI, DI, DS, ES, FLAGS: INTEGER
              end;

var
    REGS: REGISTERS;   {AX, BX, CX, DX, BP, SI, DI, DS, ES, FLAGS}

begin
    with REGS do
      begin
        OLD_NAME := OLD_NAME + Chr(0);
        NEW_NAME := NEW_NAME + Chr(0);
        AX := $5600;                      {DOS function code}
        DS := Seg(OLD_NAME[1]);
        DX := Ofs(OLD_NAME[1]);
        ES := Seg(NEW_NAME[1]);
        DI := Ofs(NEW_NAME[1]);
        MSDos (REGS);

        if (FLAGS and 1 = 1) then         {error in operation}
          STATUS := STATUS
        else
          STATUS := 0;                    {successful operation}
      end;
  end;
```

Service 57H Set or Obtain File
Date/Time Stamp

Function   Get or set a file's date and time stamp.

Register	Entry Contents
AH	57H DOS File Date/Time Stamp Service
AL	Function 0: Get stamp
	1: Set stamp
BX	File handle of file to manipulate
CX	Desired time stamp
DX	Desired date stamp
Register	**Exit Contents**
AX	Error flags if the carry flag is set
CX	Time stamp for Get File Time Stamp Service
DX	Date stamp for Get File Date Stamp Service

Example

```
procedure  File_Date_Time (FILE_HANDLE: integer;
                           OPERATION: integer;
             var DAY, MONTH, HOURS, MINUTES,
                        SECONDS, YEAR: integer;
                          var STATUS: byte);

Type
  REGISTERS = record
                 AX, BX, CX, DX, BP, SI, DI, DS, ES, FLAGS: INTEGER
              end;

var
    REGS: REGISTERS;  {AX, BX, CX, DX, BP, SI, DI, DS, ES, FLAGS}

begin
    with REGS do
       begin
          AX := $5700 + OPERATION;
          BX := FILE_HANDLE;
          DX := (YEAR - 1980) shl 9;
          DX := DX + (MONTH shl 5);
          DX := DX + DAY;
          CX := HOURS shl 11;
          CX := CX + (MINUTES shl 5);
          CX := CX + SECONDS div 2;
          MSDos (REGS);

          if (FLAGS and 1 = 1) then
            STATUS := Lo(AX)
```

```
        else
          begin
            STATUS := 0;                     {successful operation}
            YEAR   := (Hi(DX) shr 1) + 1980;
            MONTH  := (DX and $1E0) shr 5;
            DAY    := DX and $1F;
            HOURS  := Hi(CX) shr 3;
            MINUTES := (CX and $7E0) shr 5;
            SECONDS := (CX and $1F) * 2;
          end;
      end;
  end;
```

Service 59H Get Extended Error Information

Function Return the error class, locus, and recommended action for an error.

Register	Entry Contents
AH	59H DOS Get Extended Error Service

Register	Exit Contents
AX	Extended error
BH	Error class
BL	Recommended action
CH	Locus

Notes
Error:

1   Invalid function number

2   File not found

3   Path not found

4   No available handles

5   Access denied

6   Insufficient memory

Class:

1   No resources available

2   Temporary error

3	Authorization error
4	Internal software error
5	Hardware error
6	System failure
7	Application software error
8	Item not found
9	Invalid format
10	Item locked
11	Media error
12	Item already exists
13	Unknown error

Action:

1	Retry operation
2	Delay-and-retry operation
3	User retry
4	Abort processing with clean-up
5	Immediate exit, no clean-up
6	Ignore error
7	Retry with user intervention

Locus:

1	Unknown source
2	Block device error (disk)
3	Network error
4	Serial device error
5	Memory error

Example

```
#include <dos.h>

int extended_error (error, class, action, locus)
  int *error, *class, *action, *locus;
{
  union REGS inregs, outregs;

  inregs.h.ah = 0x59;
  intdos (&inregs, &outregs);
  *error = outregs.x.ax;
  *class = outregs.h.bh;
  *action = outregs.h.bl;
  *locus = outregs.h.ch;
}
```

Service 5AH Create a Unique File

Function   Create a unique file and place it in the specified directory.

Register	Entry Contents
AH	5AH DOS Create A Unique File Service
DS	Segment address of the ASCIIZ path name to place the file in
DX	Offset address of the ASCIIZ path name to place the file in
Register	Exit Contents
AX	Error codes if carry flag is set

Note   DOS appends the name of the unique file to the path name that you specify.

Example

```
procedure Create_Unique_File (PATH: STRING79;
                         ATTRIBUTES: integer;
                     var FILE_NAME: STRING79;
                     var FILE_HANDLE: integer;
                     var STATUS: byte);

Type
  REGISTERS = record
                AX, BX, CX, DX, BP, SI, DI, DS, ES, FLAGS: INTEGER
              end;

var
  REGS: REGISTERS;    {AX, BX, CX, DX, BP, SI, DI, DS, ES, FLAGS}
  I  : integer;       {counter for loops}

begin
  with REGS do
    begin
      AX := $5A00;
      PATH := PATH + Chr(0);      {asciiz}
      DS := Seg (PATH[1]);
      DX := Ofs (PATH[1]);
      CX := ATTRIBUTES;
      MSDos (REGS);
      if (FLAGS and 1 = 1) then
        STATUS := AX
      else
        begin
          STATUS := 0;            {successful operation}
          FILE_HANDLE := AX;
          i := 1;
          while Ord (PATH[I]) <> 0 do
            begin
              FILE_NAME[I] := PATH[I];
              I := I + 1;
            end;
          FILE_NAME[0] := Chr (I-1);      {length of new file name}
        end;
    end; {with REGS}
end;
```

Service 5BH Create a New File

Function   Create a new file with the specified name. If the file already exists, this service fails.

Register	Entry Contents
AH	5BH DOS Create New File Service
DS	Segment address of the file to create
DX	Offset address of the file to create
Register	Exit Contents
AX	Error code if the carry flag is set; otherwise, a 16-bit handle

Example

```
procedure Create_File (PATH: STRING79;
                       ATTRIBUTES: integer;
                   var FILE_NAME: STRING79;
                   var FILE_HANDLE: integer;
                       var STATUS: byte);

Type
  REGISTERS = record
                 AX, BX, CX, DX, BP, SI, DI, DS, ES, FLAGS: INTEGER
              end;

var
  REGS: REGISTERS;    {AX, BX, CX, DX, BP, SI, DI, DS, ES, FLAGS}

begin
  with REGS do
    begin
      AX := $5B00;
      PATH := PATH + Chr(0);        {asciiz}
      DS := Seg (PATH[1]);
      DX := Ofs (PATH[1]);
      CX := ATTRIBUTES;
      MSDos (REGS);
      if (FLAGS and 1 = 1) then
        STATUS := AX
      else
        begin
          STATUS := 0;               {successful operation}
          FILE_HANDLE := AX;
        end;
    end; {with REGS}
end;
```

Service 5CH Lock or Unlock Block
of File

Function   Lock or unlock a range of bytes in a file in support of file-sharing operations.

Register	Entry Contents
AH	5CH DOS Lock or Unlock Block Service
AL	Lock directive: 0 lock
	1 unlock
DX	File handle of the file to lock/unlock.
CX	High word of the offset address
DX	Low word of the offset address
SI	High word of the number of bytes to lock
DI	Low word of the number of bytes to lock

Register	Exit Contents
AX	Error code if the carry flag is set

OTHER HIGH-LEVEL LANGUAGES

Those using Microsoft C or Turbo Pascal can create your own interface routines if your specific compiler does not provide them. Consider Microsoft FORTRAN. The interface routines map the value from the memory locations in your register structures to the actual 8088 registers. To do this requires a simple assembly language routine. In the case of FORTRAN, you do not have records or structures. Instead, an array of integer values is defined as follows:

```
integer*2 registers(10)

integer AX,BX,CX,DX,BP,SI,DI,DS,ES,FLAGS
parameter (AX=1, BX=2, CX=3, DX=4, BP=5, SI=6,
&          DI=7, DS=8, ES=9, FLAGS=10)
```

The assembly language routine in Figure 6-8 then maps the values into the correct registers.

```
; Provide standard Microsoft FORTRAN header
;
data      segment public 'data'
          ; no data declared for this routine
data      ends

dgroup    group    data
code      segment 'code'
          assume cs:code, ds:dgroup, ss:dgroup


;
; Routine: Hi
;
; Function: Returns the high order byte of a value.
;
; Example: AH = hi (REGISTERS(AX))
;
; Notes: The result is returned in AX.
;

public    Hi
Hi        proc far

          PUSH BP          ; Save the frame pointer
          MOV  BP,SP        ; Point at system stack

; Place the value to return the High order byte of into AX
          LES BX, DWORD PTR [BP+6]
          MOV AX, [BX]

; Get the High order byte
          MOV AL, AH
          XOR AH, AH

          POP BP           ; Restore frame pointer
          RET 4            ; Values segment and offset

Hi        endp
```

Figure 6-8.

Assembly language routine to map
values into registers

```
;
; Routine: Lo
;
; Function: Returns the low order byte of a value.
;
; Example: AL = Lo (REGISTERS(AX))
;
; Notes: The result is returned in AX.
;

public  Lo
Lo      proc far

        PUSH BP         ; Save the frame pointer
        MOV  BP,SP       ; Point at system stack

; Place the value to return the Low order byte of in AX
        LES BX, DWORD PTR [BP+6]
        MOV AX, [BX]

; Return the low order byte
        XOR AH, AH

        POP BP          ; Restore frame pointer
        RET 4           ; Values segment and offset

Lo      endp


;
; Routine: DosInt
;
; Function: Provide an interface to the DOS interrupt
;           services.
;
; Example: Call DosInt (REGISTERS)
;
; Source File: TODOS.ASM
;

public  DosInt
DosInt  proc far

        PUSH BP         ; Save the frame pointer
        MOV  BP,SP       ; Point at system stack

; Get the segment and offset of the array which contains
; the values to assign to each register
        LES  BX, DWORD PTR [BP+6]

        MOV  AX, ES:[BX]       ; Load AX
        PUSH ES:[BX+2]         ; Push the value for BX
        MOV  CX, ES:[BX+4]     ; Load CX
        MOV  DX, ES:[BX+6]     ; Load DX
```

Figure 6-8.

Assembly language routine to map
values into registers (*continued*)

```
                    MOV   BP, ES:[BX+8]              ; Load BP
                    MOV   SI, ES:[BX+10]             ; Load SI
                    MOV   DI, ES:[BX+12]             ; Load DI

            ; Only load DS if it is not 0
                    CMP WORD PTR ES:[BX+14], 0
                    JE    ESLOAD
                    PUSH ES:[BX+14]                  ; Load DS
                    POP   DS
        ESLOAD:
            ; Only load ES if it is not 0
                    CMP WORD PTR ES:[BX+16], 0
                    JE    BXLOAD
                    PUSH ES:[BX+16]                  ; Load ES
                    POP   ES
        BXLOAD:
                    POP   BX                         ; Load BX

                    INT   21H

            ; Get the segment and offset of the array which will
            ; now contain the return values of each register
                    MOV   BP, SP
                    PUSH BX                          ; Save the current
                    PUSH ES                          ; contents of BX and ES
                    LES   BX, DWORD PTR [BP+6]

                    MOV   ES:[BX], AX                ; Value of AX
                    MOV   ES:[BX+4], CX              ; Value of CX
                    MOV   ES:[BX+6], DX              ; Value of DX
                    MOV   ES:[BX+10], SI             ; Value of SI
                    MOV   ES:[BX+12], DI             ; Value of DI
                    PUSH DS
                    POP   ES:[BX+14]                 ; Value of DS
                    PUSH ES
                    POP   DS
                    LAHF
                    MOV   [BX+18], AH                ; Flags register
                    POP   [BX+16]                    ; Value of ES
                    POP   [BX+2]                     ; Value of BX

                    POP BP                           ; Restore frame pointer
                    RET 4                            ; No parameters on the
                                                     ; stack

        DosInt  endp


        ;
        ; End the code segment
        ;

        code    ends
                end
```

Figure 6-8.

Assembly language routine to map
values into registers (*continued*)

From your FORTRAN programs, simply assign the elements of the array as shown in this routine, which returns the DOS version number:

```
        Program Version

        integer*2 MAJOR, MINOR

        Call DosVersion (MAJOR, MINOR)

        write (6,1) MAJOR, MINOR
1       FORMAT (1x, I1,'.',I1)

        end


        subroutine DosVersion (MAJOR, MINOR)

        implicit complex (a-z)

        integer*2 MAJOR, MINOR
        integer*2 registers(10), Hi, Lo

        integer AX,BX,CX,DX,BP,SI,DI,DS,ES,FLAGS
        parameter (AX=1, BX=2, CX=3, DX=4, BP=5, SI=6,
     &             DI=7, DS=8, ES=9, FLAGS=10)

        registers(AX) = #3000

        Call DosInt (registers)

        MAJOR = Lo (registers(AX))
        MINOR = Hi (registers(AX))

        return
        end
```

This routine maps the values from the FORTRAN array to the 8088 registers, as shown in Figure 6-9.

It is possible for you to use this strategy for any compiler from which you need to access the DOS services.

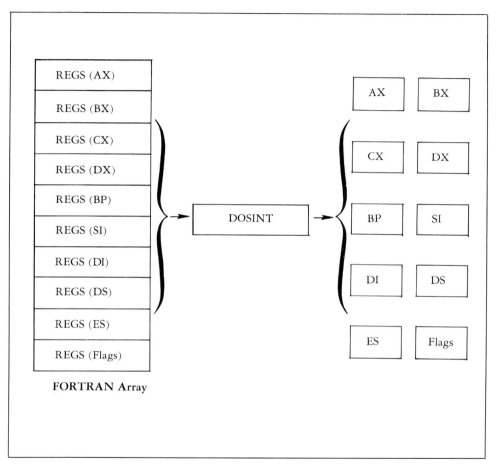

Figure 6-9.

Mapping of values from FORTRAN
array to 8088 registers

OS/2 SYSTEM SERVICES

The OS/2 developers faced the same requirements as the DOS developers:

- Provide the user interface

- Provide complete support for file-manipulation operations

- Use of each device connected to the computer

- Provide facilities for program invocation and execution

OS/2 places the additional burden of fully supporting multitasking. OS/2 developers (like the DOS developers) implemented the system services in a modular fashion, thus making each service readily available to your programs. Each of the previous DOS services is fully supported. OS/2 provides additional services for mouse, multitasking, and enhanced video support.

OS/2, however, differs drastically from DOS in that OS/2 does not use INT 21H. Instead, OS/2 provides access to each system service as a run-time library-callable routine. For example, to set the current system date and time, you would invoke

DosSetDateTime

from within your application program.

The following list provides you with an introduction to the OS/2 application program interface (API). It is not intended to teach you how to program OS/2, but rather to make you better aware of the functional capabilities required to develop a multitasking environment such as OS/2. As you examine this list of services, pay particular attention to the routines required to support multiple screens, keyboards, and threads of execution.

API Service DosAllocHuge

Function   Allocate memory greater than one segment.

API Service DosAllocSegment

Function   Allocate a segment of memory.

API Service DosAllocShrSeg

Function   Allocate a shared-memory segment. The segment returned has a name that each process can access.

API Service DosBeep

Function   Generate a sound frequency for the specified duration.

API Service DosBufReset

Function   Flush the disk buffers for the requesting process.

API Service DosCaseMap

Function   Map a binary string into an ASCII string by using a DOS code-page.

API Service DosChdir

Function   Set the current directory.

API Service DosChgFilePtr

Function   Move a file's read/write pointer (similar to LSEEK).

API Service DosCLIAccess

Function   Request CLI/STI privilege before performing low-level IN/OUT operations.

API Service DosClose

Function   Close the file associated with the specified file handle.

API Service DosCloseQueue

Function   Close the queue specified for use by the calling process.

API Service DosCloseSem

Function   Close the semaphore specified for use by the calling process.

API Service DosCreateCSAlias

Function   Create an executable alias descriptor (second name) for the data type descriptor received.

API Service DosCreateQueue

Function   Create and open the queue specified for use by the calling process.

API Service DosCreateSem

Function   Create a semaphore for use by the calling process.

API Service DosCreateThread

Function   Create an asynchronous execution thread for the calling process. Threads are the OS/2 CPU scheduling entity.

API Service DosDelete

Function   Delete the file specified by the ASCIIZ name.

API Service DosDevConfig

Function   Return device information about attached devices.

API Service DosDevIOCtl

Function   Communicate with an opened device handle.

API Service DosDupHandle

Function   Return a duplicate DOS handle for the file handle provided.

API Service DosEnterCritSec

Function   Mark the entrance of a critical section of code and prevent the execution of other threads of code in the same process for concurrent processing synchronization.

API Service DosError

Function   Allow the calling process to receive OS/2 hard-error notification as opposed to the OS/2 generation of a hard-error signal.

API Service DosErrorClass

Function   Get extended error information.

API Service DosExecPgm

Function   Spawn a secondary program as a child process.

API Service DosExit

Function   Complete the current thread of execution.

API Service DosExitCritSec

Function   Mark the end of a critical section of code and enable other threads within the current process to execute again in a concurrent fashion.

API Service DosExitList

Function   Maintain the list (add, delete, or modify) of routines that the current process is to execute upon completion.

API Service DosFileLock

Function   Lock or unlock a range of bytes within a file in support of file-sharing operations.

API Service DosFindClose

Function   Close the handle associated with the file returned by a DosFindFirst or DosFindNext API service.

API Service DosFindFirst

Function   Find the first file in a group of files matching the file specification provided.

API Service DosFindNext

Function   Find the next file in a group of files matching the file specification provided in the call to DosFindFirst.

API Service DosFlagProcess

Function   Set an external event flag that other processes can access for synchronization of concurrent processes.

API Service DosFreeModule

Function   Release the link to the dynamic link module specified by the module handle. This service decrements the usage count for the specified module.

API Service DosFreeSeg

Function   Release a previously allocated memory segment.

API Service DosGetCollate

Function   Get the current collating sequence based upon the current code-page.

API Service DosGetCP

Function   Return the code-page in use by the current application.

API Service DosGetCtryInfo

Function   Return country-dependent formatting information.

API Service DosGetDateTime

Function   Return the current system date and time.

API Service DosGetDBCSEnv

Function   Return the DBCS vector for the specified country code.

API Service DosGetEnv

Function   Return the segment and offset address of the current process command environment.

API Service DosGetHugeShift

Function   Return the shift count used by DosAllocHuge to allocate memory larger than one segment.

API Service DosGetInfoSeg

Function   Return the address of the OS/2 system variables. OS/2 places several items in read-only buffers (such as time, date, OS/2 scheduling parameters, version numbers, and trace codes).

API Service DosGetMachineMode

Function   Return the current processor mode (real or protected).

API Service DosGetMessage

Function   Obtain the text from the system message file for the specified message and place it into a user-defined buffer.

API Service DosGetModHandle

Function   Return a handle to a dynamic link module.

API Service DosGetModName

Function   Get the complete DOS path name for the dynamic link module associated with the file handle provided.

API Service DosGetProcAddr

Function   Return the far address to the procedure specified within a dynamic link library.

API Service DosGetPrty

Function   Return the priority of the current process.

API Service DosGetResource

Function   Return the segment selector for the handle to the specified resource.

API Service DosGetSeg

Function   Obtain access to the memory segment specified by the selector provided.

API Service DosGetShrSeg

Function   Obtain access to the shared memory segment specified by the name provided. The usage count of the segment is incremented.

API Service GetDosVersion

Function   Return the DOS version number.

API Service DosGiveSeg

Function   Allow the process specified by the process identification provided to access a shared-memory segment.

API Service DosHoldSignal

Function   Enable/disable signal processing for the current process.

API Service DosInsMessage

Function   Place a text string into the body of a message.

API Service DosKillProcess

Function   Terminate a process and return a termination code to the parent process or OS/2.

API Service DosLoadModule

Function   Load the dynamic link module specified and return a handle.

API Service DosLockSeg

Function   Lock a segment of memory marked as discardable.

API Service DosMakePipe

Function   Create a communications pipe for the calling process.

API Service DosMemAvail

Function   Return the size of the largest block of available memory.

API Service DosMkdir

Function   Create the specified directory.

API Service DosMonClose

Function   Close the handle to a serial device that the process has been monitoring.

API Service DosMonOpen

Function   Open a handle to a serial device for device I/O monitoring.

API Service DosMonRead

Function Wait for and return the input records to a serial device open for I/O monitoring.

API Service DosMonReg

Function Create input and output buffer structures for device I/O monitoring.

API Service DosMonWrite

Function Write a data record to the output monitor buffer of a device open for I/O monitoring.

API Service DosMove

Function Similar to RENAME. Moves a file from one location to another.

API Service DosMuxSemWait

Function Suspend the execution of the current thread until one or more semaphores has been cleared.

API Service DosNewSize

Function Change the size of the file associated with the specified file handle.

API Service DosOpen

Function   Open an existing file (if present) or create a file with name specified by the ASCIIZ string provided.

API Service DosOpenQueue

Function   Open the queue specified by the ASCIIZ string provided for use by the current process.

API Service DosOpenSem

Function   Open the semaphore specified by the ASCIIZ string provided for use by the current process.

API Service DosPeekQueue

Function   Examine, but do not remove, an element from the specified queue.

API Service DosPFSActivate

Function   Activate the code-page and font specified for the printer. This activation only affects the calling process.

API Service DosPFSCloseUser

Function   Notify the font-switching software that the process has closed its spool file. The font-switching software can release any related resources.

API Service DosPFSInit

Function   Direct the font-switching software to initialize code-page switching and font-switching for the specified printer.

API Service DosPFSQueryAct

Function   Return the current code-page and font for the specified printer.

API Service DOSPFSVerifyFont

Function   Ensure that the code-page and font desired are supported by the desired printer.

API Service DosPhysicalDisk

Function   Return partitioned disk information.

API Service DosPortAccess

Function   Request or release access to a hardware port or ports.

API Service DosPtrace

Function   Set a Ptrace buffer that is used in debugging.

API Service DosPurgeQueue

Function   Delete all of the elements contained in the queue associated with the handle provided.

API Service DosPutMessage

Function   Output the message provided to the file or device associated with a given file handle.

API Service DosQCurDir

Function   Return the current directory.

API Service DosQCurDisk

Function   Return the current disk drive.

API Service DosQFHandState

Function   Query the state of the file associated with the handle provided.

API Service DosQFileInfo

Function   Return date and time specifics about the file associated with the file handle provided.

API Service DosQFileMode

Function   Return the attribute byte for a specific file.

API Service DosQFSInfo

Function   Return information about the disk in the specified drive.

API Service DosQHandType

Function   Determine if the handle specified references a device or file.

API Service DosQueryQueue

Function   Return the number of elements in the specified queue.

API Service DosQVerify

Function   Determine whether the specified queue is active or inactive.

API Service DosRead

Function   Read the specified number of bytes from the file associated with the file handle.

API Service DosReadAsynch

Function   Read the specified number of bytes from the file associated with the file handle. The I/O operation occurs concurrently with the continued execution of the process.

API Service DosReadQueue

Function   Read and remove an element from the specified queue.

API Service DosReAllocHuge

Function   Modify the size of a previously allocated huge (larger than 1 segment) section of memory.

API Service DosReAllocSeg

Function   Modify the size of a previously allocated memory segment.

API Service DosResumeThread

Function   Restart a previously suspended thread of execution for the current process.

API Service DosRmdir

Function   Remove the directory specified by the ASCIIZ string.

API Service DosScanEnv

Function   Search a process environment segment for a specific variable and return its value if found.

API Service DosSearchPath

Function   Define a search path for data files.

API Service DosSelectDisk

Function   Set the desired current drive.

API Service DosSelectSession

Function   Select the desired foreground session.

API Service DosSemClear

Function   Clear the specified semaphore.

API Service DosSemRequest

Function   Obtain a handle to a new semaphore.

API Service DosSemSet

Function   Set the semaphore associated with the handle provided.

API Service DosSemSetWait

Function   Set the semaphore associated with the handle provided and suspend the execution of the current thread until the semaphore is cleared.

API Service DosSemWait

Function   Suspend the execution of the current thread until the semaphore associated with the handle provided is cleared.

API Service DosSendCtlC

Function   Send a CTRL-C signal to the lowest process in the tree of processes.

API Service DosSetCP

Function   Set the code-page as specified for the calling process.

API Service DosSetDateTime

Function   Set the current system date and time.

API Service DosSetFHandState

Function   Set the state of the file associated with the handle provided.

API Service DosSetFileInfo

Function   Set the date information (last read, last write, creation, and so on) for the file associated with the handle provided.

API Service DosSetFileMode

Function   Set the attribute byte for the file associated with the file handle provided.

API Service DosSetFSInfo

Function   Define the disk information for the specified drive.

API Service DosSetMaxFH

Function   Define the maximum number of file handles (up to 255) for the current process.

API Service DosSetPtry

Function   Set the priority for the current process thread.

API Service DosSetSession

Function   Set the status of a child process.

API Service DosSetSigHandler

Function   Define a signal-handling routine for a specific signal.

API Service DosSetVec

Function   Define an exception-handling routine for specific exceptions.

API Service DosSetVerify

Function   Enable or disable disk verification for the current process.

API Service DosSleep

Function   Suspend the current thread for a specific interval of time.

API Service DosStartSession

Function   Invoke a second application as an OS/2 session.

API Service DosStopSession

Function   Terminate a session previously invoked through DosStart-Session.

API Service DosSubAlloc

Function   Allocate memory from within a segment previously allocated by DosAllocSeg or DosAllocShrSeg.

API Service DosSubFree

Function   Free memory previously allocated by DosSubAlloc.

API Service DosSubSet

Function   Initialize a segment for suballocation, or change the size of a previously suballocated segment.

API Service DosSuspendThread

Function   Suspend the current thread of execution until a DosResumeThread service is invoked.

API Service DosSystemService

Function   Request OS/2 to perform a unique function (such as system-wide event notification for the specific process).

API Service DosTimerAsynch

Function   Start a timer that runs asynchronously to the thread issuing the request. Upon completion of the time interval, this service sets the specified semaphore.

API Service DosTimerStart

Function   Start a periodic interval timer that runs asynchronously to the current thread. Each time the interval completes, the service clears a specific semaphore.

API Service DosTimerStop

Function   Stop a periodic interval timer previously started by DosTimerStart or DosTimerAsynch.

API Service DosUnlockSeg

Function   Unlock a memory segment previously marked as discardable.

API Service DosWait

Function   Suspend the current process until the child process specified by the provided process identification terminates.

API Service DosWrite

Function   Write the specified number of bytes to the file associated with the file handle provided.

API Service DosWriteAsynch

Function Write the specified number of bytes to the file associated with the file handle that is provided concurrently with the thread's remaining processing.

API Service DosWriteQueue

Function Place an element in a specified queue.

API Service KbdCharIn

Function Return the character scan code from the standard input device.

API Service KbdClose

Function Close a handle associated with a logical (unique to a process) keyboard.

API Service KbdCustCP

Function Install a user-definable custom keyboard translation table. The table only affects the keyboard handle provided.

API Service KbdDeRegister

Function Remove a previously registered keyboard from the current session.

API Service KbdFlushBuffer

Function   Clear the keyboard buffer for a specific keyboard handle.

API Service KbdFreeFocus

Function   Release the logical-to-physical keyboard mapping produced by KbdGetFocus.

API Service KbdGetFocus

Function   Join a logical (process unique) keyboard to a physical keyboard.

API Service KbdGetStatus

Function   Return information about a specific logical keyboard.

API Service KbdGetXT

Function   Obtain information from the current keyboard translation table.

API Service KbdOpen

Function   Open a logical keyboard and return a keyboard handle.

API Service KbdPeek

Function   Return, but do not remove, a keyboard scan code if present in the keyboard buffer associated with the keyboard handle provided.

API Service KbdRegister

Function   Register a keyboard subsystem for a specific session.

API Service KbdSetFgnd

Function   Increase the priority of the foreground keyboard thread.

API Service KbdSetStatus

Function   Set the size characteristics for a logical keyboard.

API Service KbdSetXT

Function   Set the keyboard translation table for a logical keyboard.

API Service KbdShellInit

Function   Request the shell to identify itself to the keyboard-routing software.

API Service KbdStringIn

Function   Read a character string from a logical keyboard.

API Service KbdSynch

Function   Synchronize access to the keyboard subsystem.

API Service KbdXlate

Function   Translate a scan code into a shift state and ASCII code.

API Service MouClose

Function   Close the mouse device handle for the current screen group.

API Service MouDeRegister

Function   Remove a previously registered mouse subsystem for the current session.

API Service MouDrawPtr

Function   Notify the mouse device driver that a screen area previously restricted from access is now available.

API Service MouFlushQue

Function   Direct the mouse device driver to purge the mouse event queue for the current session.

API Service MouGetDevStatus

Function   Return the current mouse device driver settings.

API Service MouGetEventMask

Function   Return the event mask for the current mouse device driver.

API Service MouGetHotKey

Function   Return the specific mouse key used for input (left, middle, or right).

API Service MouGetNumButtons

Function   Return the number of buttons that the mouse driver supports.

API Service MouGetNumMickeys

Function   Return the number of "mickeys" per centimeter for the current mouse driver.

API Service MouGetNumQueEl

Function   Return the status of event queue for the current mouse driver.

API Service MouGetPtrPos

Function   Return the current row and column of the mouse pointer shape.

API Service MouGetPtrShape

Function   Obtain the current mouse pointer shape.

API Service MouGetScaleFact

Function   Return the current scaling factors for the mouse pointer shape.

API Service MouInitReal

Function   Initialize the mouse real-mode pointer.

API Service MouOpen

Function Open a mouse device for the current screen group. Return a device handle.

API Service MouReadEventQue

Function Read and remove an event from the current mouse driver event queue.

API Service MouRegister

Function Register a mouse subsystem for use with the current screen group.

API Service MouRemovePtr

Function Restrict a screen area from use by the mouse pointer.

API Service MouSetDevStatus

Function Set the current mouse device driver status flags.

API Service MouSetEventMask

Function Assign an event mask to the current mouse device driver.

API Service MouSetHotKey

Function Define which button (left, middle, or right) serves as the hot key for current mouse driver.

API Service MouSetPtrPos

Function   Set the mouse pointer screen coordinates.

API Service MouSetPtrShape

Function   Set the mouse pointer shape.

API Service MouSetScaleFact

Function   Set the scaling factor for the mouse pointer shape.

API Service MouShellInit

Function   Mouse shell identifies itself to the mouse router.

API Service MouSynch

Function   Direct mouse subsystems to synchronize access to the mouse device driver.

API Service VioDeRegister

Function   Remove a previously registered video subsystem from a screen group.

API Service VioEndPopUp

Function   Remove a temporary window created by VioPopUp that is no longer required.

API Service VioGetAnsi

Function   Specify whether ANSI support is on or off for the current video buffer.

API Service VioGetBuf

Function   Return the address of the logical (process unique) video buffer specified.

API Service VioGetCP

Function   Return the code-page used for display by the specified handle.

API Service VioGetConfig

Function   Return the current video display configuration.

API Service VioGetCurPos

Function   Return the current row and column cursor position for the specified logical video buffer.

API Service VioGetCurType

Function   Return the cursor type and attributes for the specified logical video buffer.

API Service VioGetFont

Function   Return the current font for the specified logical video buffer.

API Service VioGetMode

Function   Return the current video mode for the specified logical video buffer.

API Service VioGetPhysBuf

Function   Return the address of the physical video buffer.

API Service VioGetState

Function   Return the current video states, or the palette registers, the border color, or background intensity.

API Service VioModeUndo

Function   Allow one process thread to cancel a VioModeWait service issued by another thread in the same process.

API Service VioModeWait

Function   Request that a graphics-mode application be notified each time it needs to restore its video mode.

API Service VioPopUp

Function   Allocate a temporary pop-up display screen for message display.

API Service VioPrtSc

Function   Print the current screen contents.

API Service VioPrtScToggle

Function   The OS/2 session manager invokes this routine each time the user presses the SHIFT-PRTSC key combination.

API Service VioReadCellStr

Function   Read a string of characters and attributes from the screen, starting at the specified row and column location.

API Service VioReadCharStr

Function   Read a character string from the display starting at the specified row and column location.

API Service VioRegister

Function   Register a video subsystem with a specific screen group.

API Service VioSaveReDraw

Function   Request that a process be notified when it must save or redraw its contents.

API Service VioSaveReDrawUndo

Function   Allow one thread in a process to cancel a VioSavReDraw-
Wait service issued by another thread within the same process.

API Service VioScrllDn

Function   Scroll the screen contents down as specified by the row and
column numbers and number of lines to scroll.

API Service VioScrLock

Function   Lock the screen and prevent I/O operations.

API Service VioScrollLF

Function   Scroll the screen contents to the left as specified.

API Service VioScrollRt

Function   Scroll the screen contents to the right as specified.

API Service VioScrollUp

Function   Scroll the screen contents up as specified.

API Service VioScrUnLock

Function   Unlock the screen for I/O operations.

API Service VioSetAnsi

Function   Enable or disable ANSI support for the specified logical
video buffer.

API Service VioSetCP

Function   Set the code-page for the specified logical video buffer.

API Service VioSetCurPos

Function   Set the cursor position to the row and column on the
logical video buffer provided.

API Service VioSetCurType

Function   Set the cursor type (attributes) for the logical video display
provided.

API Service VioSetFont

Function   Set the font for the specified logical video display.

API Service VioSetMode

Function   Set the display mode for the logical video display provided.

API Service VioSetState

Function   Set the state for the palette registers, border color, or background intensity for the specified logical video display.

API Service VioShowBuf

Function   Update the physical display with the contents of a logical display buffer.

API Service VioWrtCellStr

Function   Write a character string (with attributes) to the specified video display location.

API Service VioWrtCharStr

Function   Write a character string to the specified video display location.

API Service VioWrtCharStrAtt

Function   Write a character string using a repeated attribute to the specified video display.

API Service VioWrtNattr

Function   Write the character attribute to the video display at the specified location. This service provides an optional repeat count.

API Service VioWrtNCell

Function   Write a character or attribute to video display the specified number of times.

API Service VioWrtNChar

Function   Write a character to the video display starting at the specified location and repeating the display *n* times.

API Service VioWrtTTY

Function   Write a character string starting at the current cursor position in TTY mode to the video display.

System services are the operating system developer's toolkit. They provide all the capabilities required to implement a fully functional operating system. Because of their tremendous capabilities and flexibility (and also because the services must reside in memory for the operating system to operate successfully), the developers make these services readily available to your applications. Under DOS, your interface to the DOS system services is through INT 21H. OS/2, however, simplifies application access to an even greater degree by presenting each system service as a callable run-time library routine.

7: DOS Programming Concerns

Most DOS power users are programmers, intent on getting the most out of their computer systems. Most have read numerous books on tips, tricks, and traps of DOS applications. Many can tell you the inner workings of undocumented DOS interrupts, the contents of machine-specific memory locations, and even the functions of various port-bit settings.

However, many power users spend so much time examining the inner workings of DOS that they neglect to write applications with adequate error checking. In many cases, their applications make assumptions about the current state of the machine, duplicate a previously developed routine, or limit the number of applications that the program can support by failing to utilize either command-line processing or the DOS I/O redirection operators.

This chapter reminds software developers about these concerns and shows how DOS can help their routines minimize the possibility of user errors. This chapter also discusses the source of the error message

```
Not ready error reading drive A
Abort, Retry, Ignore?
```

The chapter discusses how to reduce the occurrences of this message, determine the amount of free disk space, prevent the user from terminating your programs by inadvertently using CTRL-BREAK, create unique temporary files, determine the current video mode (monochrome or color graphics), set file attributes (to read-only, hidden, or read/write access), and invoke DOS commands from within your application. You will also learn about the importance of DOS volume labels, exit-status values, and several other programming utilities.

No chapter can provide a complete set of programming tools for DOS applications, but this chapter lays a foundation for you to build on.

CRITICAL ERROR HANDLING

At one time or another every user has experienced the following DOS error message:

```
Not ready error reading drive A
Abort, Retry, Ignore?
```

This message occurs most often when a user has forgotten to close the door on a disk drive or has failed to place a printer on-line. Unfortunately, depending how you respond to this prompt, your files can suffer devastating damage since they are not properly closed if the program terminates. A major goal of this chapter is to teach you techniques that your programs can incorporate to reduce the possibility of this error message. Always keep in mind that users will find ways to crash your programs; normally they will do so in the first five minutes of your demonstration.

This "not ready" DOS error message results when DOS encounters a critical error that prevents it from performing further processing without user intervention. When such an error occurs, DOS generates an interrupt 24H that, by default, displays the familiar prompt to the user. Before DOS invokes interrupt 24H, it first clears (sets to zero) the high-order bit of register AH if the error is disk-related (drive open). If the error is not disk-related, DOS sets the high-order bit of AH to 1. This allows programs to interrogate AH to determine the source of the error. Next, DOS places the address of a device-header control block in BP:SI. Offset 4 of this block contains an error status code as shown in Table 7-1.

Because DOS handles critical errors through the use of an interrupt, you can write your own routines to intercept the interrupt and gain program control over those errors. This gives your programs an added edge in handling user errors. As you can see, if you develop an interrupt 24H handler, DOS gives you considerable information about the source of the error.

Chapter 15 provides several examples of how to assign an interrupt

Table 7-1.

Error Status Codes of Offset 4

Status Code	Error
0	Write operation to write-protected disk
1	Unit unknown
2	Drive not ready
3	Command unknown
4	CRC error
5	Bad request structure length
6	Seek fault
7	Media type unknown
8	Disk sector not found
9	Printer out of paper
10	Write error
11	Read error
12	General device failure

vector to a user-developed routine. If you intend to trap interrupt 24H, follow these steps:

1. Save the current interrupt 24H vector.

2. Replace the interrupt 24H vector with a user-written routine.

3. Upon invocation, push the flag register and issue a call for instruction to the original interrupt 24H vector address.

4. Perform the desired processing.

5. Restore the original interrupt 24H vector before terminating.

Many programmers claim that a user-written critical-error handler is a "cure-all" for DOS applications. However, by making use of simple device checks, you can perform DOS handling more elegantly. If you examine the error status values associated with DOS critical errors, you will notice that critical errors are most commonly associated with the printer or with disk drives. The following Turbo Pascal procedure, **CheckDiskStatus**, returns one of the disk drive status values shown in Table 7-2. If you invoke this routine before performing disk I/O opera-

Table 7-2.

Disk Drive Status Values

Status Code	Meaning
1	Invalid command
2	Sector address not found
3	Write operation on write-protected diskette
4	Sector not found
8	DMA failure
9	DMA boundary violation
16	Invalid CRC
32	Disk controller error
64	Track seek failure
128	Device time-out error

tions, you greatly reduce the possibility of DOS critical errors caused by a disk drive.

```
Program DiskStatus;

Function CheckDiskStatus (Drive: integer): byte;

Type
  REGISTERS = record
                AX, BX, CX, DX, BP, SI, DI, DS, ES, FLAGS: INTEGER
              end;
Var
  REGS: REGISTERS;

begin
   with REGS do
      begin
        AX := $0200;
        DX := Drive;
        Intr ($13, REGS);
        CheckDiskStatus := Lo(AX);
      end;
end;

begin

  Writeln (CheckDiskStatus (0));

end.
```

Similarly, the following Turbo Pascal routine returns one of the printer status values shown in Table 7-3.

Table 7-3.

Printer Status Values

Status Code	Meaning
1	Device time-out
8	Write error
16	Printer selected
32	Printer out of paper
64	Printer acknowledgment
128	Printer not busy

```
Program PrinterStatus;

Function CheckPrinterStatus : byte;

Type
  REGISTERS = record
                 AX, BX, CX, DX, BP, SI, DI, DS, ES, FLAGS: INTEGER
              end;
Var
  REGS: REGISTERS;

begin
   with REGS do
      begin
        AX := $0200;
        Intr ($17, REGS);
        CheckPrinterStatus := Hi(AX);
      end;
end;

begin

  Writeln (CheckPrinterStatus);

end.
```

Although these routines cannot always prevent the user from corrupting files, they minimize, in an elegant fashion, the possibility of such errors occurring. If another programmer tries to sell a DOS interrupt 24H handler as a "cure-all," simply reach over and turn off the machine. If users can touch the computer, they can always find ways to corrupt files. Your job is to minimize their opportunities.

AVAILABLE DISK SPACE

Most applications that you develop for end users are likely to be database-related in one form or another. Many programs perform sophisticated I/O error-checking, but later fail to perform a simple examination of available disk space before they start writing records to disk. DOS provides a system service (36H) that allows you to determine available disk space for a drive (see Table 7-4).

The following C procedure returns the number of bytes available in the specified drive:

```
#include <dos.h>

long int diskspace (drive)
  int drive;
 {
   union REGS inregs, outregs;

   float space;

   inregs.h.ah = 0x36;
   inregs.h.dl = drive;
   intdos (&inregs, &outregs);

   space = (long int) (outregs.x.ax * outregs.x.bx) * outregs.x.cx;
   return ((outregs.x.ax == 0xFFFF) ? -1.C: space);
 }


main ()
 {
   long int diskspace();

   printf ("%ld\n", diskspace(0));
 }
```

Likewise, from Turbo Pascal the code is as follows:

```
program Space;

Type
  REGISTERS = record
                  AX, BX, CX, DX, BP, SI, DI, DS, ES, FLAGS: INTECER
              end;

function CheckDiskSpace (DRIVE: byte) :real;

var
    REGS: REGISTERS;   {AX, EX, CX, DX, BP, SI, DI, DS, ES, FLAGS}

begin
    with REGS do
      begin

        AX := $360C;
        DX := DRIVE;
        MSDos (REGS);

        if (AX = $FFFF) then   {error in operation}
            CheckDiskSpace := -1.0
        else
            CheckDiskSpace := 1.0 * AX * BX * CX;   {free space}
      end;
  end;


begin
  writeln (CheckDiskSpace (0));
end.
```

Table 7-4.

System Service 36H

Register	Entry Contents
AH	36H DOS free-space service
DL	Desired disk drive (0 = current default, 1 = A, 2 = B, 3 = C)

Register	Exit Contents
AX	FFFFH if the specified disk drive is invalid, otherwise the number of sectors per cluster
BX	Number of available clusters
CX	Number of bytes per sector
DX	Number of clusters per drive

Chapter 10 develops a simple CHKDSK command. If you include a call to **GetFreeDiskSpace** in that program, its likeness to the actual DOS CHKDSK command will be increased.

VOLUME LABELS

Issue a DOS directory command, as follows:

```
A> Dir

Volume in drive A has no label
Directory of  A:\
```

Note the following message:

Volume in drive A has no label

DOS sets aside space on every disk for a disk volume label. If you are developing end-user systems that use floppy disks, DOS volume labels should be close to your heart. Consider the following scenario.

The software system that tracks the accounts receivable for a well-known gaming establishment uses the following files:

```
Volume in drive A has no label
Directory of   A:\

JAN       REC        4    8-16-87     9:45p
FEB       REC        4    8-16-87     9:45p
MAR       REC        4    8-16-87     9:45p
APR       REC        4    8-16-87     9:45p
MAY       REC        4    8-16-87     9:45p
JUN       REC        4    8-16-87     9:45p
JUL       REC        4    8-16-87     9:45p
AUG       REC        4    8-16-87     9:45p
SEP       REC        4    8-16-87     9:45p
OCT       REC        4    8-16-87     9:45p
NOV       REC        4    8-16-87     9:45p
DEC       REC        4    8-16-87     9:45p
         12 File(s)       350208 bytes free
```

At the end of each fiscal year, you instruct the data-entry clerk to create a new floppy disk containing the same file names by using your INSTALL. BAT procedure. After three years of collections, the establishment has the floppy disks shown in Figure 7-1.

Although each disk is clearly labeled, the software has no way of knowing for sure that the data-entry clerk has placed the correct disk in the disk drive, since all three disks use identical files. DOS volume labels provide a solution to this problem. By simply using the DOS LABEL command to place the current year on the disk

```
A> LABEL 1988
A> DIR

Volume in drive A is 1988
Directory of   A:\
```

your software can perform checks of the volume label each time it performs disk I/O operations. If the volume label is incorrect, the software prompts the user to insert the correct disk. The Turbo Pascal procedure in Figure 7-2 returns the disk volume label.

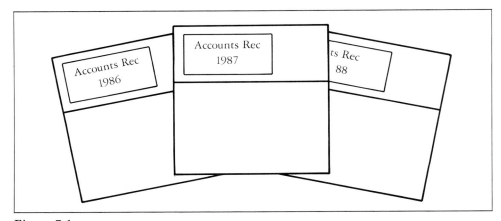

Figure 7-1.

Disks containing accounting records

EXIT-STATUS PROCESSING

Every power user has written simple utility programs such as TYPE or
COPY that manipulate files. Most of the time, users invoke these
applications from the DOS prompt. In such instances, if an error occurs,
the user has immediate feedback, as follows:

```
A> TYPE 1OFILE
File not found
```

However, if the user wants to place these routines within a DOS
batch file, the lack of exit-status values becomes restrictive. Consider the
following C program that displays the contents of the file specified by

```
type
 VOLUMENAME = string[11];

procedure Get_Volume_Label (var VOLUME_LABEL: VOLUMENAME);
   type
     REGISTERS = record
                   AX, BX, CX, DX, BP, SI, DI, DS, ES, FLAGS: INTEGER;
                 end;

   var
     REGS: REGISTERS;
     SEARCH_SPEC: VOLUMENAME;
     DTA_SEG,
     DTA_OFS : integer;  {address of disk transfer area}
     I       : integer;  {counter for loops}

   begin
     with REGS do
       begin

{convert the search specification to asciiz and set the registers
 to find the volume label}
         AX := $4E00;                           {DOS function code}
         SEARCH_SPEC := '*.*';
         DS := Seg(SEARCH_SPEC[1]);
         DX := Ofs(SEARCH_SPEC[1]);
         CX := 8;                               {attribute of label}

{invoke the DOS interrupt which finds the volume label}
         MSDos (REGS);

{set AX to request the disk transfer area}
         AX := $2F00;

{invoke the DOS interrupt which returns the disk transfer area}
         MSDos (REGS);

{return the segment and offset addresses}
         DTA_SEG := ES;
         DTA_OFS := BX;

         I := 0;
         while ((I < 11) and (Mem[DTA_SEG:DTA_OFS+30+I] <> 0)) do
           begin
             VOLUME_LABEL[I + 1] := Chr(Mem[DTA_SEG:DTA_OFS+30+I]);
             I := I + 1;
           end;

           VOLUME_LABEL[0] := Chr(I);
       end;           {with REGS}
   end;
```

Figure 7-2.

GET_VOLUME_LABEL
procedure

the first command-line argument:

```
#include <stdio.h>

#define LINE 255

main (argc, argv)
  int argc;
  char *argv[];
 {
  FILE *fp, *fopen();

  char buffer[LINE];

  if ((fp = fopen (argv[1], "r")) != NULL)
   {
    while (fgets(buffer, LINE, fp))
       fputs (buffer, stdout);
    fclose (fp);
   }
  }
```

If this program fails, a DOS BAT file has no way of knowing it. By default, DOS programs exit with a status of 0. Modifying this application to use an exit status as follows solves this restriction:

```
#include <stdio.h>

#define LINE 255

main (argc, argv)
  int argc;
  char *argv[];
 {
  FILE *fp, *fopen();

  char buffer[LINE];

  if ((fp = fopen (argv[1], "r")) != NULL)
   {
    while (fgets(buffer, LINE, fp))
       fputs (buffer, stdout);
    fclose (fp);
   }
  else
   exit (1);  /* error status */
  }
```

In this case, the following DOS BAT file can invoke the program and perform conditional processing based upon the program's exit-status value:

```
SHOW2 %1
IF ERRORLEVEL 1 GOTO ERROR
ECHO NO ERROR IN PRICESSING
GOTO DONE
:ERROR
ECHO ERROR IN PROCESSING
:DONE
```

From Turbo Pascal, the same program becomes

```
program Show ;

type
  STRING79 = string[79];

var
  LINE    : STRING79;          {line read from the file}
  IN_FILE: text;               {the input file}

begin

{make sure the user provided an input file}
  if (ParamCount = 0) then
    Writeln ('SHOW: invalid usage: SHOW filename')

{an input file was provided so read each record and
 write it stdout}
  else
    begin
      Assign (IN_FILE, ParamStr(1));
      {$I-} Reset (IN_FILE) {$I+};
      if (IOresult <> 0) then
        Halt (1)
      else
        begin
          while (not EOF (IN_FILE)) do
            begin
              Readln (IN_FILE, LINE);
              Writeln (LINE);              {write to stdout}
            end;
          Close (IN_FILE);
        end;
    end;
end.
```

Exit-status processing requires only a few extra minutes of programming. By taking these status values into account, you can increase the number of applications your programs support.

CREATING UNIQUE FILES

Many applications use temporary files throughout their processing for one reason or another. Every user has probably used a file called TEMP.DAT or something close to it to store information. Unfortunately, each time a program opens a temporary file it runs the risk of overwriting an existing file with the same name. To help you create temporary files that eliminate this concern, DOS provides the system services shown in Table 7-5.

Each time your program needs to create a temporary file, it should do so as shown in Figure 7-3. In this way, DOS ensures that the file you create is indeed unique.

```
Program Unique;

Type
  STRING79 = string[79];

procedure Create_Unique_File (PATH: STRING79;
                    ATTRIBUTES: integer;
               var FILE_NAME: STRING79;
               var FILE_HANDLE: integer;
                    var STATUS: byte);
Type
  REGISTERS = record
               AX, BX, CX, DX, BP, SI, DI, DS, ES, FLAGS: INTEGER
             end;
var
  REGS: REGISTERS;    {AX, BX, CX, DX, BP, SI, DI, DS, ES, FLAGS}
  I   : integer;      {counter for loops}
begin
  with REGS do
    begin

{set the registers to request a unique file name}
      AX := $5A00;
```

Figure 7-3.

CREATE__UNIQUE__FILE
procedure

```
        PATH := PATH + Chr(0);      {asciiz}
        DS := Seg (PATH[1]);
        DX := Ofs (PATH[1]);
        CX := ATTRIBUTES;

        MSDos (RECS);
    {if no error occurred return the file name and handle}
        if (FLAGS and 1 = 1) then
          STATUS := AX
        else
          begin
            STATUS := 0;            {successful operation}
            FILE_HANDLE := AX;
    {get the file name}
          i := 1;
          while Ord (PATH[I]) <> 0 do
            begin
              FILE_NAME[I] := PATH[I];
              I := I + 1;
            end;
          FILE_NAME[0] := Chr (I-1);       {length of new file name}
        end;
      end; {with REGS}
    end;
    var
      FILE_NAME : string79;
      FILE_HANDLE: integer;
      STATUS: byte;

    begin
      Create_Unique_File ('\', 0, FILE_NAME, FILE_HANDLE, STATUS);
    end.
```

Figure 7-3.

CREATE_UNIQUE_FILE
procedure (*continued*)

Table 7-5.

System Services for Creating
Temporary Files

Register	Entry Contents
AH	5AH DOS create-unique-file service
CX	Desired file attribute
DS	Segment address of the file name buffer
DX	Offset address of the file name buffer

Register	Exit Contents
AX	Contains the error status code if the carry flag is set

VIDEO DISPLAY

Many programs suffer from machine dependence simply because they make assumptions about the video adapter on the system.

The IBM PC and compatibles use memory location B800H for the start of the color graphics adapter video display memory (see Figure 7-4). Each time characters are displayed on a color graphics display, they are mapped to memory locations in this range. In a similar manner, monochrome systems start the video display memory at offset B000H (see Figure 7-5).

A program that performs memory-mapped output, or one that exploits character-display attributes, must determine the current video display mode (monochrome or color) if it is to execute correctly. The following C routine returns the current video display mode:

```c
#include <dos.h>

getmode ()
  {
   union REGS inregs, outregs;

   inregs.x.ax = 0x0F00;

   int86 (0x10, &inregs, &outregs);

   return (outregs.x.ax & 0xFF);
  }

main ()
  {
   printf ("Mode is %d\n", getmode());
  }
```

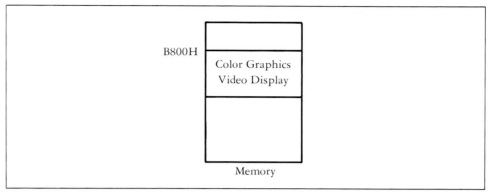

Figure 7-4.

Location in memory of color
graphics adapter video display

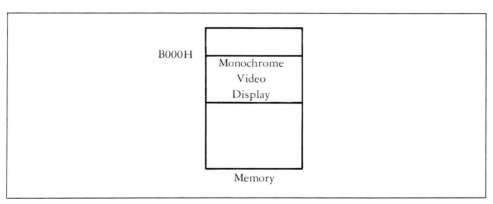

Figure 7-5.

Location in memory of monochrome
video display

The following Turbo Pascal program returns the current video display mode:

```
Function GetMode: byte ;

{     Video mode numbers
          0 - 40 column black and white text
          1 - 40 column 16 color text
          2 - 80 column black and white text
          3 - 80 column 16 color text
          4 - 4 color medium resolution graphics
          5 - 4 grey color medium resolution graphics
          6 - black and white high resolution graphics
          7 - 80 column monochrome
          8 - 15 graphics modes for the extended graphics adapter }
Type
  REGISTERS = record
                  AX, BX, CX, DX, BP, SI, DI, DS, ES, FLAGS: INTEGER
              end;
var
  REGS: REGISTERS;   {AX, BX, CX, DX, BP, SI, DI, DS, ES, FLAGS}

begin
    with REGS do
      begin

{set AH to request the current video mode}
      AX := $0F00;

      Intr ($10, REGS);

      GetMode := Lo(AX);
    end;
end;


begin
  writeln ('Mode is ', GetMode);
end.
```

FILE ATTRIBUTES

Every file on your DOS disks has a directory entry associated with it that contains the information shown in Table 7-6. DOS assigns one of the attributes shown in Table 7-7 to each file on the system.

One of the most powerful uses of file attributes is to set files to

Table 7-6.

Entry in Directory Structure

Field	Offset
File name	0
Extension	8
Attribute byte	11
Reserved for DOS	12
Time	22
Date	24
Starting cluster number	26
File size	28

Table 7-7.

File Attributes

Attributes	Meaning
0	Normal
1	Read-only
2	Hidden
4	System
8	Volume label
16	Subdirectory
32	Archive

read-only, thus preventing users from modifying or deleting them from the DOS prompt. Once a file is set to read-only, any attempt to modify or delete the file results in the following DOS error message:

```
Access denied
```

The DOS ATTRIB command allows you to set a file's attribute byte to read-only or archive as follows:

ATTRIB [+r][−r][+a][−a] *filespec*

where the following is true:

+*r* sets a file to read-only access
−*r* sets a file to read-and-write access
+*a* marks a file as requiring backup
−*a* marks a file as backed up
filespec is the complete DOS path name of the file for which to set the attributes. DOS wild-card characters are fully supported.

For example, the following command sets all files with the extension DAT to read-only:

```
A> ATTRIB +R *.DAT
```

Likewise, this command sets the files back to read/write access:

```
A> ATTRIB -R *.DAT
```

It is also convenient to modify a file's attributes from within your application programs. The following Turbo Pascal program sets a file's attributes:

```
type
  STRING79 = string[79];

procedure Set_File_Attributes (FILENAME: STRING79;
                               ATTRIBUTES: byte;
                               var STATUS: byte);
Type
  REGISTERS = record
                 AX, BX, CX, DX, BP, SI, DI, DS, ES, FLAGS: INTEGER
              end;
var
    REGS: REGISTERS;   {AX, BX, CX, DX, BP, SI, DI, DS, ES, FLAGS}

  begin
    with REGS do
      begin

         FILENAME := FILENAME + Chr(0);      {convert to asciiz}
         AX := $4301;                        {DOS function code}
         DS := Seg(FILENAME[1]);
         DX := Ofs(FILENAME[1]);
         CX := ATTRIBUTES;

         MSDos (REGS);

{return the status of the DOS operation}
         if (FLAGS and 1 = 1) then     {error in operation}
           STATUS := Lo(AX)
         else
           STATUS := 0;                     {successful operation}
      end;
  end;
```

Similarly, the following routine returns a file's attributes:

```
Type
  STRING79 = string[79];

procedure Get_File_Attributes (FILENAME: STRING79;
              var ATTRIBUTES, STATUS: byte);

Type
  REGISTERS = record
              AX, BX, CX, DX, BP, SI, DI, DS, ES, FLAGS: INTEGER
            end;

var
   REGS: REGISTERS;   {AX, BX, CX, DX, BP, SI, DI, DS, ES, FLAGS}

begin
     with REGS do
       begin

          FILENAME := FILENAME + Chr(0);     {convert to asciiz}
          AX := $4300;                       {DOS function code}
          DS := Seg(FILENAME[1]);
          DX := Ofs(FILENAME[1]);

          MSDos (REGS);

          if (FLAGS and 1 = 1) then     {error in operation}
            STATUS := Lo(AX)
          else
            begin
              STATUS := 0;                   {successful operation}
              ATTRIBUTES := Lo(CX);
            end;
       end;
  end;
```

If you are developing applications for end users, set files to read-only to prevent accidental deletion or modification. Thus, your application program must set the file to read/write access so it can later update the file contents and then restore read-only status before the program terminates.

You can also set the attribute byte on DOS subdirectories. If you place all of your files into DOS subdirectories and set a subdirectory's attribute byte to hidden, you can make that subdirectory invisible to DOS directory listings — the subdirectory name does not appear in the directory listing. However, you can still access each of the files in the directory if you know the complete DOS path name. In such instances, the only way of knowing that the subdirectory exists is by using the number of hidden files specified by the DOS CHKDSK command.

CTRL-BREAK PROCESSING

Most interactive programs should restrict the user to exiting the application at predefined points, as shown here:

```
        Enter Desired Choice

        1: Perform Payroll

        2: Print Paychecks

        3: List Tax Data

        4: Exit to DOS

            Choice:____
```

By default, DOS allows users to terminate a program by pressing the CTRL-BREAK key combination. Each time DOS encounters a CTRL-BREAK, it generates interrupt 23H. By default, interrupt 23H first examines the carry flag. If this flag is set, DOS aborts the current program. Otherwise, the program continues execution by using an IRET (interrupt return) instruction.

If you are writing Turbo Pascal programs, the compiler directive {$C—} prevents a user-entered CTRL-BREAK key combination from terminating the application. If you program in a different high-level language, Chapter 15 shows you how to redirect an interrupt vector to a user-written routine. In so doing, you ensure that the user cannot terminate your programs by unexpectedly pressing CTRL-BREAK.

AVAILABLE MEMORY

Later chapters examine memory-resident programs that, upon termination, remain in memory. Such programs allocate memory previously available for other DOS applications. It is often convenient to be able to determine the amount of memory available in the system (see Figure 7-6).

The DOS system service 48H allows you to determine the amount of available memory in the system, as shown in Table 7-8. In this case, if you request a large amount of memory for allocation, the service cannot meet the request. Instead, the service returns the largest available number of paragraphs. This value is your free space. In this way you can determine available memory, as shown here:

FREE __ SPACE = NUM __ PARAGRAPHS * 16

Note that application programs use the DOS service 49H to deallocate the memory once it determines available space. The following C program displays the available memory:

```
#include <dos.h>

main ()
 {
  union REGS inregs, outregs;
  struct SREGS segregs;

  long int freememory;

    inregs.h.ah = 0x48;
    inregs.x.bx = 65000;
    intdos (&inregs, &outregs,

    freememory = outregs.x.bx;
    freememory *= 16;

    printf ("%ld\n", freememory);

    inregs.h.ah = 0x49;
    segregs.es = outregs.x.ax;
    intdosx (&inregs, &outregs, &segregs);
 }
```

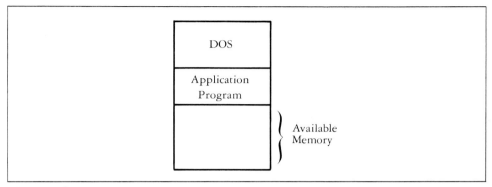

Figure 7-6.

Amount of memory available to
system

Table 7-8.

System Service 48H

Register	Entry Contents
AH	48H
BX	Number of paragraphs (16 bytes) to allocate
Register	**Exit Contents**
AX	Points to allocated memory block, or error status if the carry flag is set
BX	Size of the largest available block of memory in paragraphs

SPAWN

Programmers often wish that they could easily allow the user to execute DOS commands from within their applications. DOS provides this capability with the 4BH system service. The Turbo Pascal procedure shown in Figure 7-7 allows you to invoke a secondary DOS command

```
{
  Use the compiler options menu to set the I and A options to 400
}


Type
  COMMAND_STRING = string[128];

procedure SPAWN (command_line: COMMAND_STRING;
                 var status: integer);
const
  STACK_SEGMENT: integer = 0;
  STACK_POINTER: integer = 0;

type
  REGISTERS = record
                AX, BX, CX, DX, BP, SI, DI, DS, ES, FLAGS: INTEGER
              end;

  PARAMETER_BLOCK = record
    ENVADDR,
    COMMOFS,
    COMMSEG,
    FCB1OFS,
    FCB1SEG,
    FCB2OFS,
    FCB2SEG: integer;
    end;

  var
    REGS: REGISTERS;  {AX, BX, CX, DX, BP, SI, DI, DS, ES, FLAGS}
    PARAM: PARAMETER_BLOCK;
    COMMAND_FILE: COMMAND_STRING;

begin
  with PARAM do
    begin
      ENVADDR := 0;       {use PARENT process environment}

      if (ord(command_line[0]) <> 0) then
        command_line := '/C ' + command_line;

      command_line := command_line + chr(13);
      COMMSEG := Seg (command_line[0]);
      COMMOFS := Ofs (command_line[0]);
      FCB1SEG := -1;
      FCB1OFS := 0;
      FCB2SEG := -1;
      FCB2OFS := 0;
    end;

  with REGS do
    begin
```

Figure 7-7.

SPAWN procedure

```
        COMMAND_FILE := 'C:\COMMAND.COM' + chr(0) + chr(13);
        AX := $4B00;
        DS := Seg (command_file);
        DX := Ofs (command_file[1]);
        ES := Seg (PARAM);
        BX := Ofs (PARAM);

        STACK_SEGMENT := Sseg;
        inline ($2E/$89/$26/STACK_POINTER);

        MSDOS (REGS);

        inline ($2E/$8E/$16/STACK_SEGMENT);
        inline ($2E/$8B/$26/STACK_POINTER);

        if ((FLAGS and 1) = 1) then
          STATUS := AX
        else
          STATUS := 0;
      end;

  end;
```

Figure 7-7.

SPAWN procedure (*continued*)

processor from within your programs. To execute the DOS CHKDSK
command, invoke the routine as

```
      Spawn ('CHKDSK', STATUS);
```

Likewise, to spawn the user to the DOS prompt, use

```
      Spawn (' ', STATUS);
```

In this case, when the user later issues the DOS EXIT command, the
program that spawned the command processor regains control. To use
this routine within your Turbo Pascal programs, compile the program

with the I and A options set to 400.

For C programmers, Microsoft C provides several **spawn** procedures in the run-time library. The following program uses one of them
to invoke TEST.EXE from within an application program:

```
#include <stdio.h>
#include <process.h>

main ()
{
    spawnl (P_WAIT, "TEST.EXE", NULL);
}
```

SPOOLED PRINTING

Many application programs must generate reports of some type for the
end user. In most cases, the program simply writes its output directly to
the printer. However, it is simple to place a file in the DOS print queue
from within your applications. The user then is free to continue other
processing while the file prints in the background. The following Turbo
Pascal procedure submits the file it receives to the DOS print queue. The
routine assumes that you have previously installed the print queue. You
can install the print queue by using AUTOEXEC.BAT to ensure that the
PRINT qualifiers remain consistent.

```
type
  FILENAME = string[64];

procedure Print_File (FILE_NAME: FILENAME; var STATUS: integer);
  type
    REGISTERS = record
                  AX, BX, CX, DX, BP, SI, DI, DS, ES, FLAGS: INTEGER;
                end;

    SUBMIT_PACKET = record
                      LEVEL: Char;
                      OFFSET, SEGMENT: integer;
                    end;

  var
    REGS: REGISTERS;
    PACKET: SUBMIT_PACKET;

  begin
    FILE_NAME := FILE_NAME + Chr(0);

    with PACKET do
      begin
        LEVEL := Chr(0);
        OFFSET := Ofs (FILE_NAME[1]);
        SEGMENT := Seg (FILE_NAME);
      end;

    with REGS do
      begin
        AX := $0101;                          {DOS function code}
        DS := Seg(PACKET);
        DX := Ofs(PACKET);

        Intr ($2F, REGS);

        if ((FLAGS and 1) = 1) then
          STATUS := AX
        else
          STATUS := 0;
      end;

  end;
```

OBJECT CODE LIBRARIES

One of the most useful (yet least-used) capabilities provided with most compilers is an object code librarian. Each time you compile a source file, the compiler produces an OBJ file. The linker then combines OBJ and LIB (library) files to produce an executable EXE file. This process is illustrated in Figure 7-8.

Most programmers will develop a series of useful routines and then either retype the code into their programs or use a compiler-include directive to read the files containing the routines during compilation. The disadvantage is that the compiler spends a great deal of time recompiling files that you know are correct or, in some cases, compiling routines that are not even going to be used in your application.

Rather than requiring the compiler to process such routines repetitively, a librarian provides a useful alternative. In the following C program

```
strcpy (s1, s2)
  char *s1, s2;
{
  while (*s2++ = *s1++)
    ;
}

main ()
{
    /* main program source code */
}
```

the compiler must compile the routine **strcopy** each time you make changes to your program. Instead, you can extract the routine to the file **strcopy.c** and compile it as a stand-alone routine to produce the file **strcopy.obj**. Once you have produced this object file, a librarian allows you to place this file in a LIB file that you can later link to other programs, producing executable files.

Although the syntax and commands for each librarian may differ, consider the Microsoft librarian LIB, since its use is most common. The

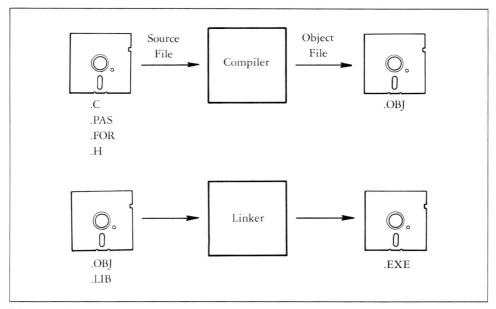

Figure 7-8.

Production of an executable file

Microsoft librarian is a software program that allows you to create, update, and utilize run-time libraries. Specifically, LIB allows you to

- Create LIB library files

- Add, delete, replace, or extract object modules to or from a file

- Produce a listing of all the routines contained in the library

For example, if the file MATH.LIB contains the object modules TRIG. OBJ, CALC.OBJ, ALG.OBJ, and HEX.OBJ, visualize the library as shown in Figure 7-9.

Each object module (OBJ file) contains the related functions, subroutines, and procedures for each mathematical subject. If you append the contents of the file OCTAL.OBJ to the library, visualize the library as

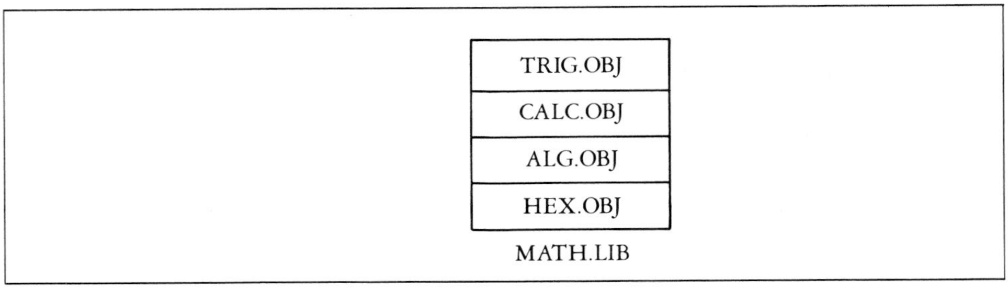

Figure 7-9.

Object modules of MATH.LIB file

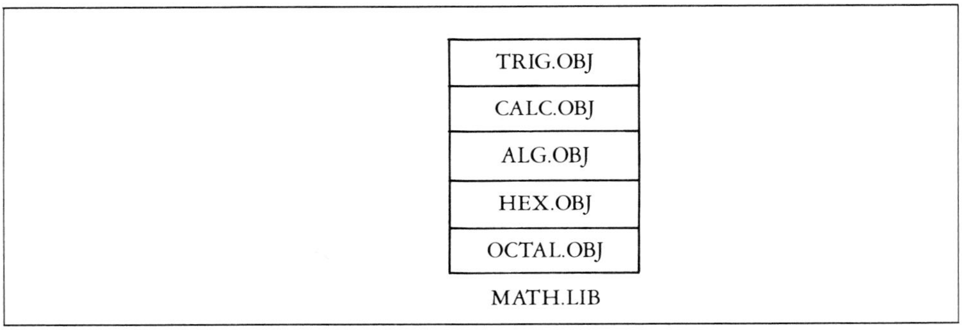

Figure 7-10.

OCTAL.OBJ file appended to library

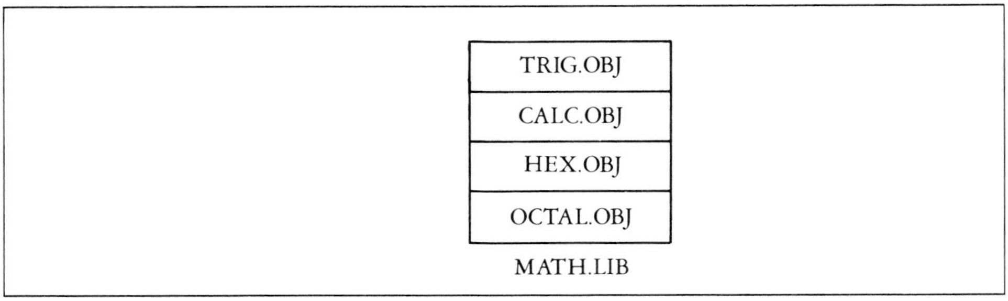

Figure 7-11.

MATH.LIB file with ALG.OBJ
deleted

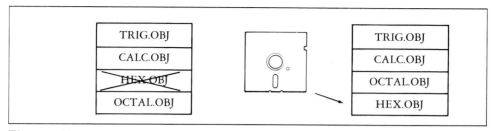

Figure 7-12.

Library-replace option

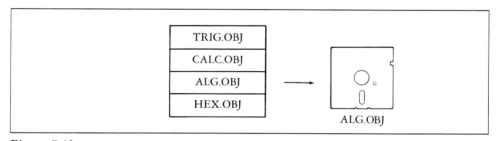

Figure 7-13.

Extract operation

containing the information shown in Figure 7-10. Likewise, if you delete the module ALG.OBJ, the library will contain the information shown in Figure 7-11. Similarly, if you replace the contents of one OBJ file with a file from disk, the operation becomes that shown in Figure 7-12. Last, the librarian allows you to extract the contents of a module to a disk file, as shown in Figure 7-13.

The easiest way to invoke the Microsoft librarian is simply to type **LIB** at the DOS prompt.

```
A> LIB
```

LIB will then prompt you for the name of the library that you want to use, as shown here:

```
Microsoft (R) Library Manager  Version 3.04
Copyright (C) Microsoft Corp 1983, 1984, 1985, 1986.

All rights reserved.


Library name:
```

Type in the name of the library and press ENTER. A library is a standard DOS file. It has an eight-character file name and a three-letter extension. By default, LIB assumes the extension LIB. In this case, create the library MATH.LIB, as follows:

```
Microsoft (R) Library Manager  Version 3.04
Copyright (C) Microsoft Corp 1983, 1984, 1985, 1986.

All rights reserved.

Library name: MATH
```

Next, LIB prompts you for the operations that you desire. The following operations are valid under LIB:

+   Append an object module to the library.
Example: + ALG.OBJ

−   Delete an object module from the library.
Example: − CALC.OBJ

−+   Replace an object module in the library.
Example: −+ OCTAL.OBJ

*   Extract an object module from the library to disk.
Example: * HEX.OBJ

−*   Extract an object module from a library to disk, deleting it from the library upon completion.
Example: −* OCTAL.OBJ

LIB allows you to combine multiple operations on the same line. Upon completion of these operations, LIB prompts you for the name of the list file.

```
Microsoft (R) Library Manager  Version 3.04
Copyright (C) Microsoft Corp 1963, 1984, 1985, 1986.

All rights reserved.

Library name: MATH
Operations: + ALU.OBJ
List file:
```

The LIB list file contains two tables. The first provides you with a list of all of the public symbols in the library. The second table shows all of the object modules in the library along with the symbols they contain.

Last, LIB prompts you for the name of the output library. If a library with the same name already exists, LIB renames the previous library to a BAK extension. This ensures that you always have a back-up copy of the library that precedes the changes you have made.

Once your library operations are complete, you can specify the library in the LINK command, as shown here:

```
A> LINK FILE, FILE, , MATH
```

LINK will examine the library for routines referenced but not found in the source code.

By using LIB files, you minimize compile time, ensure that each of your programs uses the same series of routines, and greatly reduce the possibility of duplication of effort.

This chapter has served as something of catchall for DOS programming techniques. Always keep in mind that normally a user can crash a system as long as the computer is within reach. Your job is to minimize the impact of such events. If you are not using a librarian, start doing so. You will be amazed at the convenience it provides you.

8: Addressing the PC

As discussed in previous chapters, DOS 3.x performs memory addressing in a real mode, which directly accesses physical locations in the computer's memory. This memory addressing scheme employs the concept of segments and offsets to locate objects in memory. The hardware that performs PC memory access speaks in terms of a segment-and-offset memory address combination. The segment address assigns an address to a specific 64K memory region, and the offset specifies an exact location within the 64K area.

Real mode addressing, although it has provided the foundation for addressing since the introduction of the PC, is unacceptable in a multitasking environment. Therefore, OS/2 employs a virtual addressing algorithm that allows multiple programs to coexist in the computer's memory. The OS/2 virtual memory implementation provides several advantages for memory allocation and compaction in a multitasking environment.

This chapter discusses in detail the DOS 3.x memory addressing scheme. You will learn how to access specific memory locations from C and Turbo Pascal, along with Microsoft FORTRAN. For those of you who do not program, the DOS debugger is used to illustrate several of these concepts. After fully explaining real mode addressing, this chapter examines in detail OS/2 virtual memory management.

PHYSICAL MEMORY

In 1981, when the IBM PC first hit the market, memory was one of the most expensive hardware components associated with the PC. Most systems were equipped with either 128K or 256K of memory. At that time, the cost of memory was more constraining to users and programmers than was the DOS 640K barrier. Since then, however, this trend has changed dramatically. Memory has become more affordable, and PC systems with 640K of memory are now the rule rather than the exception. In addition, memory access speed has increased tremendously over the same period, greatly improving system performance (see Figure 8-1).

Memory locations in the PC are capable of storing 1 byte (8 bits) of data. A byte of information is sufficient to store each alphabetical, numeric, and punctuation character, plus an extended character set defined by each machine. This is because 8 bits provide 256 permutations (as shown in Table 8-1). A character (the letter "A," for example) only requires 1 byte of memory. An integer value, however, can normally range from −32,768 to 32,767. This set of values requires 2 bytes of memory, as shown in Table 8-2.

Note that the PC uses the leftmost (most significant) bit of an

Table 8-1.

Permutations of Eight Bits

Binary		Decimal
0000	0000	0
0000	0001	1
0000	0010	2
0000	0011	3
.		.
.		.
.		.
1111	1110	254
1111	1111	255

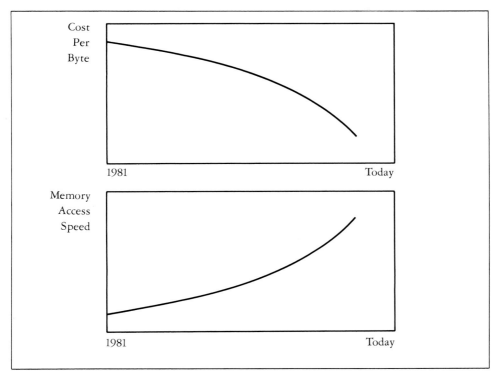

Figure 8-1.

Decrease in memory cost since 1981

Table 8-2.

Range of Integer Value

Binary				Decimal
1000	0000	0000	0000	−32,768
1000	0000	0000	0001	−32,767
1000	0000	0000	0010	−32,766
	.			.
	.			.
	.			.
0111	1111	1111	1110	32,766
0111	1111	1111	1111	32,767

integer value as the sign bit of an integer value. When this bit is 0 (clear), the value is positive. When this bit becomes 1 (set), the value is negative. This periodically results in bugs that are difficult to detect in your programs.

Consider the following Turbo Pascal program that forever adds 1 to the variable **count**.

```
Program Count;

var
    count: integer;

begin
  count := 1;
  while (true)
    begin
      writeln (count);
      count := count + 1;
    end;
end.
```

An interesting event occurs when **count** reaches 32,767. Rather than becoming 32,768, **count** becomes −32,768. This is because the increment resulted in the PC setting the sign bit, as shown in Table 8-3. Therefore, many C programs employ the concept of an unsigned variable. Unlike a variable of type **int** (which uses the most significant bit to determine the sign of a value), unsigned variables use all 16 bits for data. This means that the range of values for an unsigned variable is 0 to 65,535.

Note that an unsigned variable can only contain positive values. The following C program illustrates the use of an unsigned variable. It is similar to the previous Turbo Pascal example in that it forever increments the variable **count**:

```
main ()
  {
  unsigned count = 65001;

  while (1)
    printf ("%u\n", count++);
  }
```

Table 8-3.

Setting of Sign Bit

Binary	Decimal
0111 1111 1111 1101	32,765
0111 1111 1111 1110	32,766
0111 1111 1111 1111	32,767
1000 0000 0000 0000	−32,768
1000 0000 0000 0010	−32,767

Table 8-4.

Resetting to 0

Binary	Decimal
1111 1111 1101 1101	65,533
1111 1111 1111 1110	65,534
1111 1111 1111 1111	65,535
0000 0000 0000 0000	0
0000 0000 0000 0001	1

In this case, when **count** reaches the value 65,535, it simply resets itself to 0 and starts the processing again (see Table 8-4).

Since the computer's physical memory stores bytes of data, many objects require several memory locations to store their values. Table 8-5 illustrates common storage requirements. The following C program verifies these storage requirements:

```
main ()
{
  char str[255];

  printf ("Character requires %d bytes\n", sizeof (char));
  printf ("Integer requires %d bytes\n", sizeof (int));
  printf ("Float requires %d bytes\n", sizeof (float));
  printf ("Double requires %d bytes\n", sizeof (double));
  printf ("String[255] requires %d bytes\n", sizeof (str));
}
```

Table 8-5.

Common Storage Requirements

Data Type	Storage Requirement in Bytes
char	1
int	2
float	4
double	8
str [255]	255

Upon invocation the program displays the following:

```
Character requires 1 bytes
Integer requires 2 bytes
Float requires 4 bytes
Double requires 8 bytes
String[255] requires 255 bytes
```

The following Turbo Pascal program provides an identical function:

```
Program Size;

Type
  str255 = string[255];

begin
  writeln ('Character requires ', sizeof(char), ' bytes');
  writeln ('Integer requires ', sizeof(integer), ' bytes');
  writeln ('Real requires ', sizeof(real), ' bytes');
  writeln ('String[255] requires ', sizeof(str255), ' bytes');
end.
```

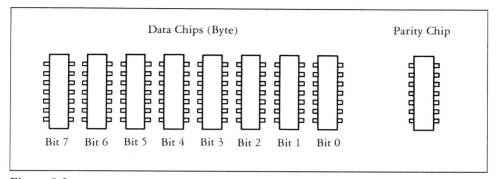

Figure 8-2.

Parity chip in set of memory chips

Take a closer look at your system memory. When you purchase memory chips for your computer, you must purchase either 64K or 256K chips. When you buy these chips, you buy them in sets of nine. This is because you are purchasing a matrix of memory. Each 64K chip stores up to 65,536 *bits* — not *bytes,* but bits. This means that to represent 65,536 bytes, you must have eight chips, each capable of storing 64K bits. You might ask, "What is the ninth chip for?" The IBM PC uses a concept called *parity* to ensure that the memory in your system is functioning correctly. The ninth chip in your set of memory chips is the parity chip (Figure 8-2). The computer manufacturer defines memory parity as either *odd* or *even.* When parity is odd, each row of bits (the nine chips) should always have an odd number of 1's. If, for example, the data stored in the eight data bits is three, an odd parity memory system will set the parity chip to 1, ensuring that an odd number (in this case three) of 1's bits exist. Table 8-6 illustrates this concept.

During each power-on sequence, your computer examines each of its memory locations to ensure that each is functioning properly. The

Table 8-6.

Parity Bits

Value	Data Bits	Parity Bit
0	0000 0000	1
1	0000 0001	0
2	0000 0010	0
.	.	.
.	.	.
254	1111 1110	0
255	1111 1111	1

system reads and writes data to each memory location. As the system accesses a row of bits (a byte in memory), it checks the parity of the row. If the parity is odd, and an odd number of bits exists, the system assumes that all is well. However, if the system parity is odd and an even number of bits exists, the system raises a *parity error.* This error informs you that you may have a bad memory chip within your system. Even parity works identically, except that the parity bit ensures that each row of bits contains an even number of 1's bits.

By now you should have a fairly good understanding of the definition of a "K" of memory. A "K" of memory, whether bits (one chip) or bytes (eight chips), refers to 1024 storage locations. Most people, for simplicity, refer to a "K" as 1000. For most applications, this simplification is close enough. Actually though, 64K is not 64,000 but rather

$$64 * 1024 = 65,536 \text{ bytes}$$

If your system has 256K of memory, it actually has

$$256 * 1024 = 262,144 \text{ bytes}$$

of storage locations. This concept is the same for 360K floppy disk drives:

$$360 * 1024 = 368,640 \text{ bytes}$$

Each memory location in the PC must be uniquely defined. This is done by assigning each memory location its own address. The IBM PC and compatibles use an addressing scheme based on a *segment* and an *offset.* Consider first the segment address.

The PC segment addresses are 16 bits long. A value of this size can uniquely reference 64K locations in memory. Unfortunately, most PC applications require more than 64K of memory. To alleviate this problem, the PC rotates the value of a segment address four places to the left (without losing the high-order bits) to create a 20-bit value. This 20-bit value allows you to address up to 1024K, or 1MB, of memory locations.

Consider the following example. Segment address 0123 when shifted left becomes 1230:

0000 0001 0010 0011   0123   original 16-bit segment address

becomes

0000 0001 0010 0011 0000   01230   left-shifted 20-bit segment address

Note that the last digit of the address is 0. With this value, the problem associated with this addressing scheme begins to surface. By always adding an additional 0 (the four 0 bits that are shifted in) to the segment value, you indeed create an address capable of referencing up to 1MB of address space. Unfortunately, since the last four bits are always 0, this scheme only allows you to access every sixteenth memory location. You should recall that four binary digits allow you to reference 16 unique values, as shown in Table 8-7.

Since the last four bits of a DOS segment address are always 0, you cannot reference a finer granularity than every sixteenth location. Since this addressing scheme restricts segment address to only accessing every sixteenth location, these locations are termed paragraph boundaries (see Figure 8-3).

To access every memory location (as opposed to every sixteenth location), the PC adds the notion of an offset address. PC memory offset addresses are in the range from 0K to 64K. For example, assuming that

Table 8-7.

Unique Values of Four Binary Digits

Binary	Decimal
0000	0
0001	1
0010	2
0011	3
0100	4
0101	5
0110	6
0111	7
1000	8
1001	9
1010	10
1011	11
1100	12
1101	13
1110	14
1111	15

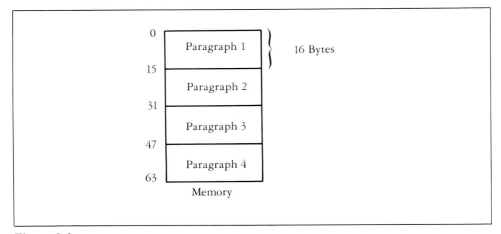

Figure 8-3.

16-byte paragraph boundaries

the segment address is FFFF, the PC adds the offsets shown in Figure 8-4 to access each highlighted memory location. By adding the offset address to the segment, the PC allows you to access up to 1024K distinct memory locations.

POINTS TO REMEMBER
ABOUT PHYSICAL MEMORY

Each memory location in the PC contains a byte (eight bits of storage).

A byte of storage requires nine memory chips (eight for data, one for parity).

The PC uses a segment and offset combination to reference each specific memory location.

By adding a 0 (four bits) to a segment value, the PC generates a 20-bit address capable of addressing more than 1024 bytes (a megabyte) of address space.

Once the PC shifts a segment address, the address refers to a paragraph boundary. Paragraph boundaries occur every 16 bytes in the PC.

The PC adds the value of the offset address to the 20-bit segment address to achieve the finer granularity required to access every memory location in the megabyte address space.

The most common notation for a segment and offset memory address is

segment:offset

You should have the BASIC programming language available on your system. To look at the value stored in a specific memory location (peeking into memory), you must specify the location of interest by using a segment-and-offset combination. In BASIC, you specify the segment address you desire by using the DEFSEG statement as follows:

DEFSEG *segment_address*

Next, you can examine the contents at a specific offset location within

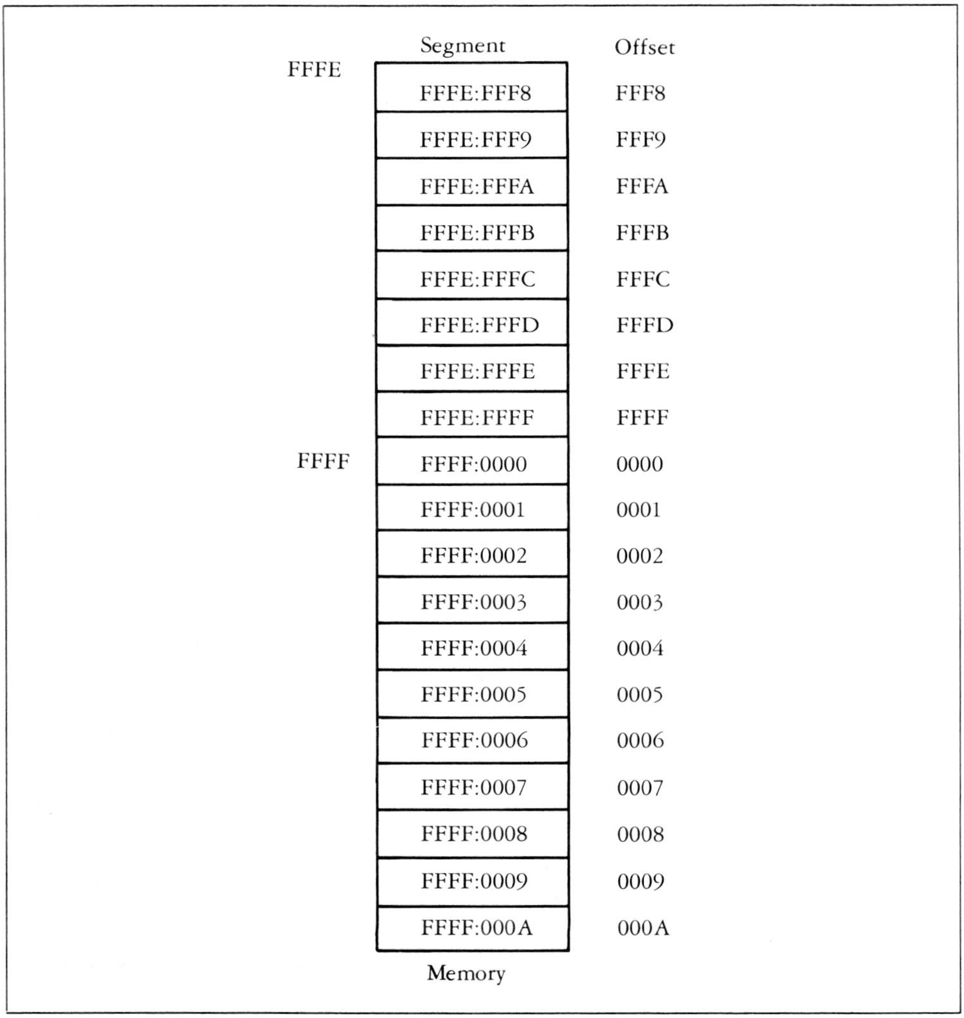

Segment	Offset
FFFE	
FFFE:FFF8	FFF8
FFFE:FFF9	FFF9
FFFE:FFFA	FFFA
FFFE:FFFB	FFFB
FFFE:FFFC	FFFC
FFFE:FFFD	FFFD
FFFE:FFFE	FFFE
FFFE:FFFF	FFFF
FFFF FFFF:0000	0000
FFFF:0001	0001
FFFF:0002	0002
FFFF:0003	0003
FFFF:0004	0004
FFFF:0005	0005
FFFF:0006	0006
FFFF:0007	0007
FFFF:0008	0008
FFFF:0009	0009
FFFF:000A	000A

Memory

Figure 8-4.

Adding offsets to access memory
locations

the segment by using the PEEK function as follows:

RESULT = PEEK (*offset__address*)

The IBM PC places the dates shown in Table 8-8 at memory locations F000:FFF5 through F000:FFFC. To examine this date from BASIC, use the following program:

```
1 DEF SEG = &HFOOO
2 FOR I = 1 TO 8
3   ROMDATE$ = ROMDATE$ +CHR$(PEEK(I+&HFFF5))
4 NEXT I
5 PRINT ROMDATE$
```

Similarly, Turbo Pascal allows you to access memory locations by using the predefined array **MEM**. Use this array to access a value contained in memory as follows:

RESULT: = **MEM**[*segment:offset*];

Table 8-8.

IBM PC ROM Dates

Date	IBM Machine
04/24/81	Original IBM PC
10/19/81	Updated PC ROM
8/16/82	Original PC XT
10/27/82	Updated PC XT ROM
11/08/82	PC Portable
06/19/83	PCjr
01/10/84	PC AT

For example, the following Turbo Pascal program displays the ROM date for the IBM PC as previously shown.

```
Program ROM_DATE;

Type
   STRING8 = string[8];

procedure Get_ROM_Date (var DATE: STRING8);

   var
     I: integer;     {counter for loop}

   begin
{assign the 8 consecutive characters in memory which specify
 the date of the ROM chip to the string DATE}
     for I := 0 to 7 do
       DATE[I + 1] := Chr(Mem[$F000:$FFF5 + I]);
     DATE[0] := Chr(8);  {date is 8 characters}
   end;

var
   ROM : string8;

begin
   Get_ROM_Date (ROM);
   writeln (ROM);
end.
```

Microsoft C provides similar functions by using pointers. Most C programmers are familiar with pointers that refer to objects within the current data segment (16-bit pointers):

int *ptr;

However, to access values in another segment, you must use far (32-bit) pointers.

int far *ptr;

The following C program displays the PC ROM date:

```
main ()
 {
   char far *ptr;
   int i;

   for (i = 0, ptr= 0xF000FFF5; i < 8; i++)
     printf ("%c", *(ptr+i));
 }
```

Likewise, to access memory locations from Microsoft FORTRAN (beginning with version 4.0), you must develop an assembly language routine called PEEK that returns the value contained at the segment: offset address you desire (see Figure 8-5).

Assemble this program as shown:

```
A> MASM PEEK.ASM;
```

The following FORTRAN program uses PEEK to display the ROM date:

```
        Program ROM

        integer peek
        integer i

        character*8 rom_date

        do 10 i = 0, 7
          rom_date(I+1:i+1) = char(peek (16#F000, 16#FFF5+i))
  10    continue

        write (6,*) rom_date
        end
```

```
; value = peek (segment, offset)
; peek into a memory location from MS FORTRAN V4.0
;
; assumes large memory model
;

TITLE PEEK

PEEK_TEXT SEGMENT BYTE PUBLIC 'CODE'
PEEK_TEXT ENDS

_DATA SEGMENT WORD PUBLIC 'DATA'
_DATA ENDS

CONST SEGMENT WORD PUBLIC 'CONST'
CONST ENDS

_BSS SEGMENT WORD PUBLIC 'BSS'
_BSS ENDS

DGROUP GROUP CONST, _BSS, _DATA
ASSUME CS:PEEK_TEXT, DS:DGROUP, SS:DGROUP, ES:DGROUP

PEEK_TEXT SEGMENT

PUBLIC PEEK
PEEK PROC FAR

   PUSH BP                          ; save the current base
                                      pointer
   MOV  BP, SP                      ; store the stack pointer

   PUSH DS                          ; save the current data
                                      segment
```

Figure 8-5.

PEEK routine for Microsoft
FORTRAN

```
        LES   BX, DWORD PTR [BP+6]   ; get the address of the
                                       offset
        MOV   DX, ES:[BX]           ; get the value of the
                                       offset

        LES   BX, DWORD PTR [BP+10] ; get the address of the
                                       segment
        PUSH  ES:[BX]              ; get the value of the
                                       segment

        POP   DS

        MOV   BX, DX
        MOV   AX, [BX]             ; get the value at the
                                       segment/offset location

        POP   DS                   ; get original data segment

        MOV   AH,0                 ; only return a byte

        MOV   [BP-2], AX           ; return value

        MOV   SP, BP
        POP   BP

      RET 8                        ; 2 arguments by reference
                                       on the stack

      PEEK ENDP

      PEEK_TEXT ENDS
      END
```

Figure 8-5.

PEEK routine for Microsoft
FORTRAN (*continued*)

Compile the program as follows:

```
A> FL ROM.FOR;
```

Next, LINK it to the assembly language application, as follows:

```
A> LINK ROM+PEEK;
```

Note the statement

MOV AH,0

within the assembly language routine PEEK shown in Figure 8-5. To simplify the processing that occurs in later chapters, this routine was modified to return only a byte value. If you would rather have the routine return an integer value, simply remove that instruction.

Lastly, invoke the DOS debugger:

```
A> DEBUG
```

The DEBUG D(UMP) command allows you to examine memory locations, as follows:

D [*address* [,] *address*]

or

D [*address* [,] [L] [,] *value*]

Using this format, the following D(UMP) command displays the ROM date:

```
C>DEBUG                                                    PC ROM Date
-D F000:FFF5,L,8
F000:FFFC              30 31 2F-31 30 2F 38 34            01/10/84
-
```

MEMORY MAPPING

One of the most commonly used applications for direct memory access is memory-mapped I/O. The IBM PC and compatibles use a specific memory region to store the values that appear on your screen. If you are using a color monitor, this range of values begins at hexadecimal segment B800. If you are using a monochrome monitor, this region begins at location B000. For 80-column text, each region requires 4000 bytes (80 * 25 characters + 80 * 25 attributes), as shown in Figure 8-6.

To place values directly into the video display memory (memory mapping), you must have a means of putting a value (poking) into any location in memory. In BASIC, you again use the DEFSEG statement to define the desired segment address. The POKE function allows you to place a value at a specific offset within the current segment, as follows:

POKE *offset,value*

In Turbo Pascal, you can still use the array **MEM**:

MEM[*segment:offset*]:=*value*;

In C, far pointers still provide the required function:

int far *ptr = 0✕B8000000;

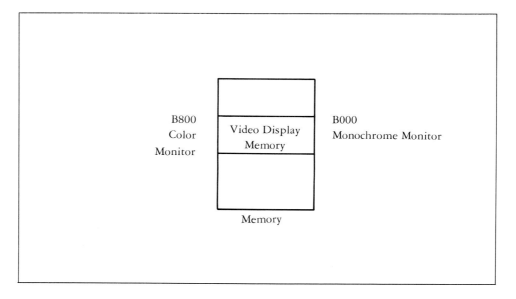

Figure 8-6.

Location of video display memory
region

Lastly, to POKE values into memory from Microsoft FORTRAN
(beginning with version 4.0), use the assembly language routine shown
in Figure 8-7.

The IBM PC stores values for display in two-byte combinations. The
first byte is the ASCII value of the character to display. The second byte
is the video attribute of this character (see Figure 8-8).

The following Turbo Pascal program places the letter "A" in the
middle of your screen. Each time you press the ENTER key, the program
increments the attribute value for the character. In this manner, you can
view all of the available character attributes.

```
Program Char_Attr;

var
  i: byte;

begin
  Clrscr;
  for i := 0 to 255 do
    begin
      Mem[$B800: 1802] := 65;
      Mem[$B800: 1803] := i;
      readln (kbd);
    end;

end.
```

In BASIC the program becomes the following:

```
1 CLS
2 DEF SEG = &HB800
3 FOR I = 1 TO 255
4   POKE 1800, 65
5   POKE 1801, I
6   DUMMY$ = INKEY$
7   IF DUMMY$ = "" THEN 6
8 NEXT I
9 END
```

In FORTRAN the program is as follows:

```
      Program Charattr

      INTEGER*2 POKE
      INTEGER*2 I
      INTEGER*2 RESULT

      do 10 I = 1, 255
        RESULT = POKE (16#B800, 1800, 65)
        RESULT = POKE (16#B800, 1801, I)
        READ (*, *)
10    continue

      end
```

```
; value = poke (segment, offset, value)
; poke a value into a memory location from MS FORTRAN V4.0
;
; assumes large memory model
;

        TITLE POKE

POKE_TEXT SEGMENT BYTE PUBLIC 'CODE'
POKE_TEXT ENDS

_DATA SEGMENT WORD PUBLIC 'DATA'
_DATA ENDS

CONST SEGMENT WORD PUBLIC 'CONST'
CONST ENDS

_BSS SEGMENT WORD PUBLIC 'BSS'
_BSS ENDS

DGROUP GROUP CONST, _BSS, _DATA
ASSUME CS:POKE_TEXT, DS:DGROUP, SS:DGROUP, ES:DGROUP

POKE_TEXT SEGMENT

PUBLIC POKE
POKE PROC FAR

    PUSH BP                      ; save the current base
                                   pointer
    MOV  BP, SP                  ; store the stack pointer

    PUSH DS                      ; save the current data
                                   segment
```

Figure 8-7.

POKE routine for Microsoft
FORTRAN

```
        LES    BX, DWORD PTR [BP+6]    ; get the address of the
                                            value to poke
        MOV    CX, ES:[BX]             ; get the value to poke

        LES    BX, DWORD PTR [BP+10]   ; get the address of the
                                            offset
        MOV    DX, ES:[BX]             ; get the value of the offset

        LES    BX, DWORD PTR [BP+14]   ; get the address of the
                                            segment
        PUSH   ES:[BX]                 ; get the value of the
                                            segment

        POP    DS

        MOV    BX, DX
        MOV    [BX], CX
        MOV    AX, [BX]                ; get the value at the
                                            segment/offset location

        POP    DS                      ; get original data segment

        MOV    AH,0                    ; only return a byte
        MOV    [BP-2], AX              ; return value

        MOV    SP, BP
        POP    BP

        RET 12                         ; 3 arguments by reference
                                            on the stack

        POKE ENDP

        POKE_TEXT ENDS
        END
```

Figure 8-7.

POKE routine for Microsoft
FORTRAN (*continued*)

ASCII Value	Character Attribute	ASCII Value	Character Attribute	...
Byte 0		Byte 1		

Figure 8-8.

Two-byte combinations for storing
display values

Again, if you are not a programmer, invoke the DOS debugger. The
DEBUG F(ILL) command allows you to place values into specific
memory locations in the format

F *range, list*

Using F(ILL), fill the screen with the letter "A" as follows:

```
C>DEBUG
-F B800:0 L 4000 "A", 7
```

For monochrome monitors use

```
C>DEBUG
-F B000:0 L 4000 "A", 7
```

Modify the Turbo Pascal program to display the following letters
continuously on the screen:

DOS-OS/2-Windows

```
Program Letters;

var
  str: string[80];
  i: byte;

begin
  ClrScr;

  str := 'DOS-OS/2-Windows';

  repeat
    for i := 1 to Length (str) do
        Mem [$B800: 1800+(i-1)*2] := Ord(str[i]);
  until (false);

end.
```

When you execute this program, your screen should become snowy. This is because your memory mapping operations are interfering with the monitor's vertical and horizontal retraces (which occur 60 and 12,000 times per second, respectively).

To avoid this problem, the program must synchronize its screen updates with the retrace. In this case, synchronize the updates to the monitor's vertical retrace. For color monitors, the PC uses port 3DA to specify the current state of the vertical retrace. When the fourth bit in this port clears (0), the vertical retrace is in progress.

The following program uses the predefined Turbo Pascal array **Port** to test the status of port 3DA. When the fourth bit is set, the program displays a character. While the fourth bit is clear, the program simply waits.

while ((*Port*[$3DA] and 8) <> 8) ;

```
Program Letters;

var
  str: string[80];
  i: byte;

begin
  ClrScr;

  str := 'DOS-OS/2-Windows';

  repeat
    for i := 1 to Length (str) do
      begin
        while ((Port[$3DA] and 8) <> 8) ;
        Mem [$B800: 1800+(i-1)*2] := Ord(str[I]);
      end;
  until (false);

end.
```

Upon invocation, the snow should disappear from the display.

Using this same concept, you can develop a Turbo Pascal routine
CLEAR_SCREEN that clears the contents of the screen from both
sides, as shown in Figures 8-9, 8-10, 8-11, and 8-12. This procedure
implements **Clear_Screen**:

```
procedure Clear_Screen;
var
   row, column: integer;
begin
   for column := 0 to 39 do
     for row := 0 to 24 do
       begin
         while ((Port[$3DA] and 8) <> 8) ;   {wait for retrace
                                               to complete}
         Mem[$B800:(row*160)+(column*2)] := 32;

         while ((Port[$3DA] and 8) <> 8) ;   {wait for retrace
                                               to complete}
         Mem[$B800:(row*160)+((79-column)*2)] := 32;
       end;
   gotoxy (1,1);
end;
```

Depending upon your system, you may be able to remove the retrace
synchronization loops.

```
LETTERS2 PAS      584   7-17-87    1:51p
LETTERS2 COM     1158^C

C>dir/w

   Volume in drive C is DOSDISK
   Directory of  C:\POWER\CHAP8

ROM       EXE    ROM       C      MEM       FOR    TEST      OBJ    TEST      EXE
PEEK      ASM    ROM       OBJ    PEEK      OBJ    C         PAS    PEEK      SAV
CHAP8     BAK    ROM       FOR    CHAP8     OUT    ART8      4      CHAP8     TXT
SIZE      C      SIZE      OBJ    SIZE      EXE    ART8      9      ART8      11
SIZE      PAS    ART8      10     ROMDATE   BAS    ART8      23     ROMDATE   PAS
ART8      27     ART8      31     ART8      30     ART8      32     ART8      33
ART8      34     ART8      35     ART8      37     CL        COM    ART8      39
POKE      ASM    POKE      OBJ    POKETEST  BAK    POKETEST  FOR    POKETEST  OBJ
POKETEST  EXE    ART8      44     CHARATTR  PAS    ART8      46     CHARATTR  BAS
CHARATTR  C      CHARATTR  OBJ    CHARATTR  EXE    CHARATTR  BAK    ART8      47
CHARATTR  FOR    ART8      48     ART8      49     CL        PAS    ART8      51
ART8      52     LETTERS   BAK    LETTERS   PAS    LETTERS   COM    ART8      53
LETTERS2  PAS    LETTERS2  COM    ART8      54
        68 File(s)   7473152 bytes free

C>
```

Figure 8-9.

First phrase of **CLEAR__SCREEN**
routine

```
M     1158^C



drive C is DOSDISK
of  C:\POWER\CHAP8

      ..          C      BAK    COUNT     PAS    COUNT
E     ROM    C      MEM       FOR    TEST      OBJ    TEST
M     ROM    OBJ    PEEK      OBJ    C         PAS    PEEK
K     ROM    FOR    CHAP8     OUT    ART8      4      CHAP8
      SIZE   OBJ    SIZE      EXE    ART8      9      ART8
S     ART8   10     ROMDATE   BAS    ART8      23     ROMDA
      ART8   31     ART8      30     ART8      32     ART8
      ART8   35     ART8      37     CL        COM    ART8
M     POKE   OBJ    POKETEST  BAK    POKETEST  FOR    POKET
E     ART8   44     CHARATTR  PAS    ART8      46     CHARA
      CHARATTR  OBJ    CHARATTR  EXE    CHARATTR  BAK    ART8
R     ART8   48     ART8      49     CL        PAS    ART8
      LETTERS   BAK    LETTERS   PAS    LETTERS   COM    ART8
S     LETTERS2  COM    ART8      54
ile(s)   7473152 bytes free
```

Figure 8-10.

Second phase of **CLEAR__SCREEN**
routine

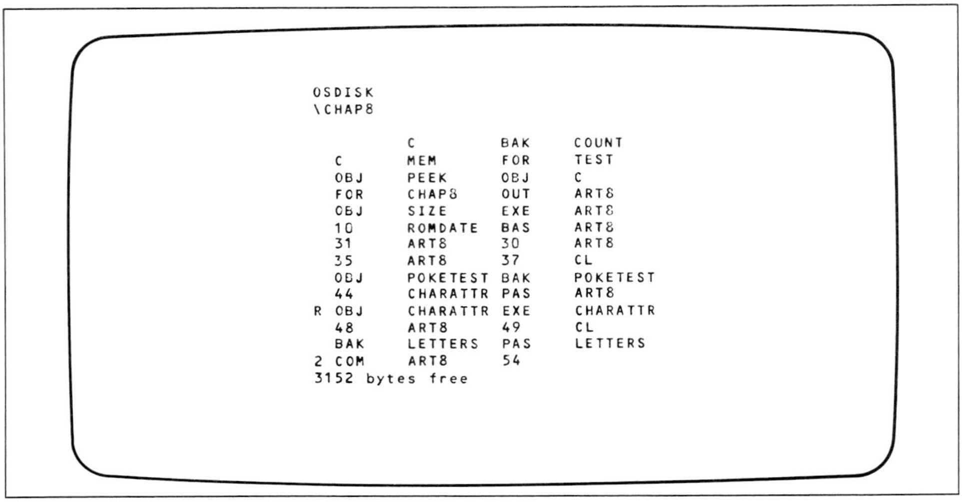

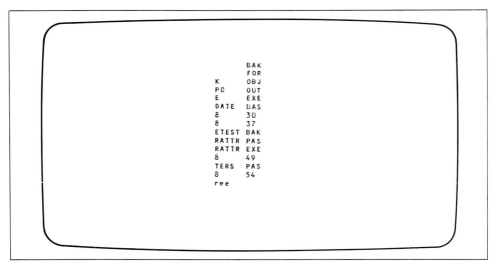

Figure 8-11.

Third phase of **CLEAR__SCREEN**
routine

Figure 8-12.

Fourth phase of **CLEAR__SCREEN**
routine

OS/2 MEMORY ADDRESSING

Previous chapters stressed that multiple programs executing in the same environment must cooperate. This prevents applications from directly accessing memory (or other hardware devices). Earlier in this chapter you saw the use of segment and offset addresses to access physical memory locations under DOS 3.x. This section examines the OS/2 virtual memory implementation in detail.

OS/2 places a level of indirection between application addresses and physical memory, as shown in Figure 8-13. This process of memory indirection is *virtual memory.* With OS/2 virtual memory, applications no longer directly access segment and offset addresses. Instead, OS/2 uses a *handle* (an index) called a *selector* into a table (called the *segment descriptor table*) that contains the attributes of specific memory locations (see Figure 8-14). Physical memory in the 80286 is divided into segments up to 64K long.

The OS/2 segment descriptor table contains an entry for each segment that specifies its attributes (which applications can access it and how). Specifically, each entry in the segment descriptor table contains

24 bits for the segment address
16 bits for the segment size
8 bits for the segment attributes

OS/2 uses the selector to determine the physical address of a segment within the computer's memory, as shown in Figure 8-15.

The 80286 combines the 24-bit segment address with the offset address to obtain the physical memory location of the desired object (see Figure 8-16). Every application executing under OS/2 has its own unique descriptor table (*local descriptor table*) that contains the locations and attributes of each of the application's code and data segments in physical memory. If OS/2 is executing multiple programs, it must keep track of multiple local descriptor tables in memory (see Figure 8-17).

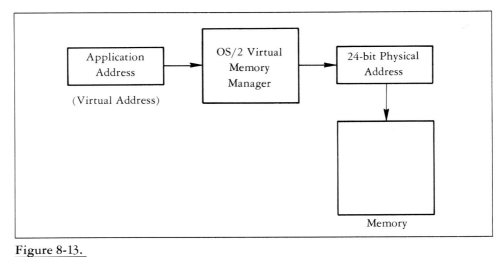

Figure 8-13.

OS/2 level of indirection between
addresses and physical memory

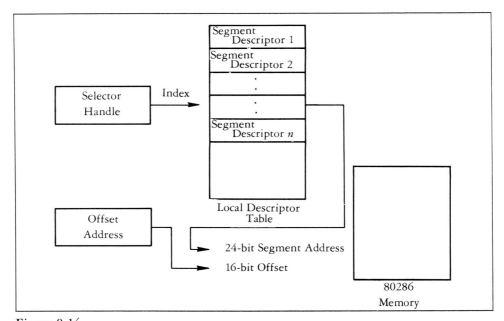

Figure 8-14.

Selector handle, index, and local
descriptor table

Figure 8-15.

Using the selector handle to determine physical address

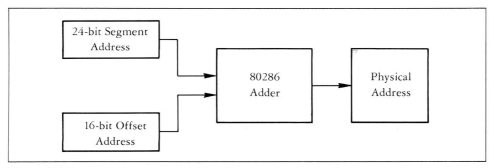

Figure 8-16.

Combining the 24-bit and 16-bit offset addresses

Since each local descriptor table is specific to an application, OS/2 shelters each program in the system from the others. This is the means by which OS/2 keeps one program from accessing the code or data of another. If a program attempts to access a memory location outside of its memory, OS/2 generates a fault and the memory access fails.

In addition to local descriptor tables, OS/2 has one *global descriptor table,* which contains entries each OS/2 application can access. The appearance and functional aspects of the global descriptor table are identical to those of a local descriptor table, except that every OS/2 application has access to it. OS/2 places its system services (called *application program interface routines*) and Kernel services within the global descriptor table. This in turn allows them to be shared by all applications running in the system.

To review what has been discussed so far, DOS 3.x uses segment and offset addresses to produce a 20-bit address (address space of 1024

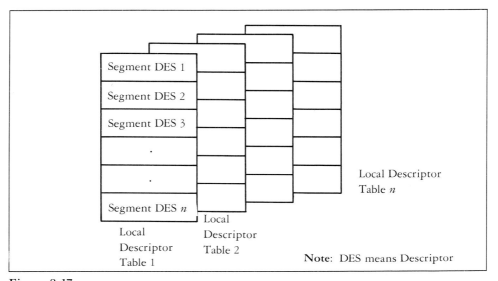

Figure 8-17.

Keeping track of multiple local
descriptor tables

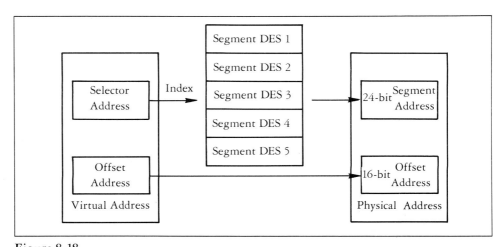

Figure 8-18.

Combining with offset address to
produce physical address

bytes). Since DOS 3.x only executes one program at a time, it is perfectly acceptable for the application to directly access physical memory. In a multitasking environment, however, the operating system must maintain strict control over memory to ensure that applications do not interfere with each other's code or data. OS/2 performs this memory management by using virtual memory.

OS/2 implements virtual memory by mapping application addresses (which are "virtual" since they do not actually point to physical memory) to physical memory addresses. Applications executing under OS/2 do not use segment and offset addresses. Instead, they use a selector (index) into a table (descriptor table) that yields a 24-bit segment address the 80286 can combine with the application's offset address to produce a physical address (see Figure 8-18).

OS/2 selectors index a descriptor that contains information about segments in physical memory. A segment is simply an area in memory that a segment descriptor defines. Segments provide OS/2 memory management with its true flexibility.

Note that the segment address is a 24-bit address. These 24 bits provide an address space of 16MB. As you saw earlier in this chapter, DOS 3.x uses a 20-bit address, which allows you to address up to 1MB. The descriptor segment size allows memory segments in the range 0 to 65,535 bytes. For example, if an application uses a segment size of 32,767 and later tries to access byte 32,768, OS/2 catches the error and raises a general-protection fault. In so doing, OS/2 forces concurrent applications to cooperate.

The OS/2 segment attribute bits define how applications can access memory segments. Consider the following attribute bits:

ACCESSED

OS/2 sets this bit each time it accesses the segment in memory. This allows OS/2 to temporarily remove segments that are not being used to disk to make room for other program segments.

CONFORM

OS/2 sets this bit for code segments that applications can call from the descriptor privilege level for the segment or higher.

DPL	This attribute defines the descriptor privilege level for the segment. The descriptor privilege level is the minimum privilege level at which an application must be executing to access this segment.
EXECUTABLE	OS/2 sets this bit to define a segment as containing code (as opposed to data). If an application attempts to access a segment in a manner inconsistent with this bit, OS/2 generates a general-protection fault.
PRESENT	OS/2 sets this bit when the segment described by the descriptor is present in physical memory (as opposed to temporarily swapped out to disk). If an application references a segment that is not present in memory, OS/2 generates a fault that results in the segment being loaded from disk into memory.
READ/WRITE/EXECUTE	OS/2 uses this field to determine in what modes an application can access a segment. If an application attempts to modify data in a segment that is read-only, OS/2 generates a general-protection fault that prevents the access. Likewise, OS/2 can prevent an application from examining code segments.

Consider what OS/2 does with a large program. Assume that your computer has 128K of memory available (see Figure 8-19). Your application program, however, requires 256K. OS/2 cannot fit the entire program into physical memory at one time. Therefore, OS/2 divides your application into four equal-sized segments, as shown in Figure 8-20. In this case, OS/2 can load segments A and B, leaving segments C and D on disk (see Figure 8-21).

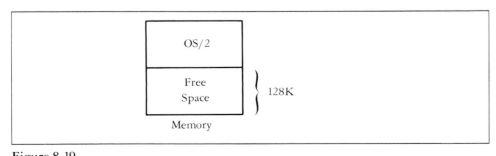

Figure 8-19.

Available memory in computer

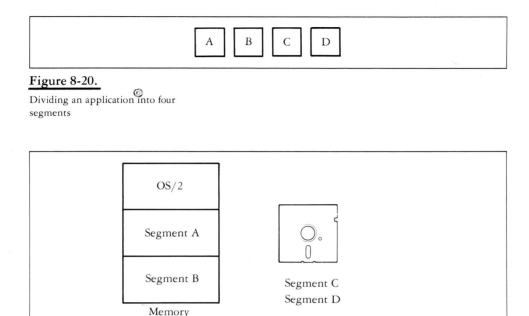

Figure 8-20.

Dividing an application into four
segments

Figure 8-21.

Loading segments A and B

If the application accesses code or data contained in segment C, OS/2 examines the PRESENT field of the segment descriptor entry for segment C. Since the segment is not present in memory, this bit is clear (0). OS/2 then generates a segment-not-present fault to load the segment from disk into memory. At this time, OS/2 must decide which segment(s) it should remove from memory to disk to make room for segment C.

In this case OS/2 examines the ACCESSED field of each segment entry for each segment present in memory to determine which segment OS/2 has used least recently. Once OS/2 locates the least recently used segment, it temporarily removes the segment from memory to disk and makes room for a new segment (see Figure 8-22). Once space is available, OS/2 loads segment C from disk into memory and sets its PRESENT attribute bit (see Figure 8-23).

This process illustrates how OS/2 applications can be larger than

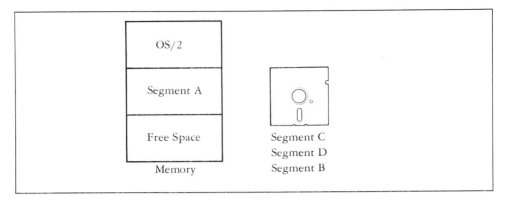

Figure 8-22.

Removing segment B from memory

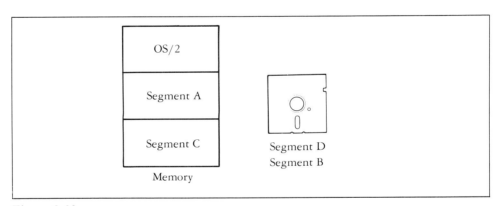

Figure 8-23.

Loading segment C

your available physical memory. You may be asking, "What's the difference between global and local descriptor tables?" As previously stated, each OS/2 application has a local descriptor table that points to its code and data. In addition, OS/2 provides one global descriptor table that all applications share. The global descriptor table maps applications to the OS/2 system services and Kernel routines. In this manner, although multiple programs are executing simultaneously, OS/2 shares a large percentage of code among applications by means of the global descriptor table.

LOCAL DESCRIPTOR TABLE

Every OS/2 application has its own unique local descriptor table that maps its virtual addresses to physical memory. If the application attempts to access memory outside of its space described in the local descriptor table, OS/2 generates a fault and the access fails.

GLOBAL DESCRIPTOR TABLE

OS/2 maintains one descriptor table that every application can access. The global descriptor table maps applications to the OS/2 system services and Kernel routines. In this way, OS/2 allows multiple programs to share the same code.

OS/2 may periodically move (compress) applications in memory to provide space for other applications. OS/2 performs this processing transparently to the application.

OS/2 applications access memory by using selectors. The value for each selector never changes during the course of the program's execution, regardless of OS/2 memory compaction operations. Instead, OS/2 changes the segment address field in the descriptor table entry pointed to by the selector. Since this field is not directly tied to the application, OS/2 can modify it transparently to the application.

This has been a quick examination of OS/2 virtual memory management. At this stage, it is more important that you understand the advantages OS/2 virtual memory provides than the details of its implementation.

DOS 3.x uses a segment and offset address to directly access locations in the computer's physical memory. The 20-bit address produced by combining the segment and offset addresses provides 1MB of address space. It is easy to peek or poke values in and out of specific memory locations.

Memory addressing in which programs can directly access physical memory locations is called real mode addressing. Although real mode addressing has provided the mainstay for the PC since its introduction, it is unacceptable for a multitasking environment. OS/2 uses virtual memory management to provide a layer of indirection between an application's address space and the computer's physical memory address space. In so doing, OS/2 allows several programs to coexist in memory, removing the threat of one application interfering with the code or data of another. In addition, OS/2 virtual memory uses a virtual address that provides a 1 gigabyte address space. Under OS/2, application size is virtually unlimited.

9: Maximizing Command-Line Processing

By now you have undoubtedly entered countless numbers of commands from the DOS prompt, and you should be intimately familiar with DOS command-line processing. If you are not, this chapter provides you with a quick review. If you already perform command-line processing within your C and Turbo Pascal programs, this chapter shows you exactly where DOS stores the command line, along with ways to enhance the command-line processing capabilities provided by C and Turbo Pascal. You will also learn how to implement command-line processing from FORTRAN. In addition, this chapter examines methods of increasing the functional aspects of your programs so that they support both command-line processing and DOS I/O redirection. In this way, your applications perform either command-line or redirected input processing based upon the user's command line.

COMMAND-LINE BASICS

Each time you enter a DOS command, the text that you enter is a *command line*. Consider the following directory command:

```
A> DIR A:
```

In this case, the command line is composed of one command (DIR) and one command-line parameter (A:). With this command line

```
A> COPY B:CONFIG.SYS A:CONFIG.SYS
```

COPY is the command, while B:CONFIG.SYS and A:CONFIG.SYS are the command-line parameters, as shown here:

```
A> COPY B:CONFIG.SYS A:CONFIG.SYS
    └─┬─┘ └──────────────┬──────────┘
   Command
                 Command-line parameters
```

Consider the following Turbo Pascal program that copies the contents of TEST.DAT to the file TEST.NEW:

```
Program File_Copy;

const
  record_size = 128;
  buffer_size = 256;

var
  input_file: file;
  output_file: file;

  data_buffer: array[1..record_size] of byte;
  num_records: integer;

begin
  Assign (input_file, 'TEST.DAT');
  Assign (output_file, 'TEST.NEW');

  Reset (input_file);
  Rewrite (output_file);

  repeat
    BlockRead (input_file, data_buffer, buffer_size, num_records);
    BlockWrite (output_file, data_buffer, num_records);
  until (num_records = 0);

  close (input_file);
  close (output_file);
end.
```

Although this program performs its required task (copying TEST.DAT to TEST.NEW), the program is severely limited in supporting future applications. Simply stated, the program is only useful if your application uses the files TEST.DAT and TEST.NEW. The ability to access command-line parameters makes it possible for this application to copy any source file to any target file, as follows:

```
A> FILECOPY SOURCE.TXT TARGET.TXT
```

Turbo Pascal and C make command-line parameters readily available to your applications. Also, by using routines that you have developed in previous chapters, command-line processing becomes readily available from FORTRAN. In this way, your FORTRAN programs quickly obtain the generic processing capabilities readily associated with C.

COMMAND-LINE PROCESSING FROM C

One of the best features of C is its ability to access command-line parameters. To access command-line parameters from within your C applications, you must declare the following parameters inside the C **main** function:

```
main (argc, argv)
   int argc;
   char *argv[];
  {

  /* program code here */

  }
```

C uses the **argc** variable to contain the number of entries present on the command line. In the same manner, **argv** is an array of pointers to character strings that contain the actual command-line parameters. Assume that the following C program is ECHOTEST.C. Examine the code for ECHOTEST, which displays each of its command-line arguments.

```
main (argc, argv)
   int argc;
   char *argv[];
  {
  while (*++argv)
    printf ("%s\n", *argv);

  }
```

You can issue the following command line:

```
A> ECHOTEST A B C
```

In this case, C assigns the variable **argc** (argument count) the value 4. Likewise, C assigns the elements of **argv** as shown here:

argv[1] points to "A"
argv[2] points to "B"
argv[3] points to "C"

The following program (REVLINE.C) displays each of its command-line parameters in reverse order:

```
main (argc, argv)
  int argc;
  char *argv[];
{
  int index;

  for (index = argc-1; index > 0; index--)
    printf ("%s\n", argv[index]);

}
```

The following program displays the contents of each line in the file specified by the first command-line parameter. Invoke the program as shown here:

```
A> SHOW FILENAME.EXT
```

This C program implements SHOW:

```
#include <stdio.h>

#define LINE 255

main (argc, argv)
  int argc;
  char *argv[];
{
  char line[LINE];

  FILE *fp, *fopen();

  if (argc > 1)
    {
      if ((fp = fopen (argv[1], "r")) == NULL)
        printf ("SHOW: Cannot open %s\n", argv[1]);
      else
        {
          while (fgets (line, LINE, fp))
            fputs (line, stdout);
          fclose (fp);
        }
    }
  else
    printf ("SHOW: File name not specified\n");
}
```

Last, this program displays the ASCII, octal, decimal, and hexadecimal representations of the decimal value you entered:

```
main (argc, argv)
  int argc;
  char *argv[];
{
  int result;

  if (argc > 1)
    {
      result = atol(argv[1]);
      printf ("ASCII %c Octal %o Decimal %d Hexadecimal %x\n",
              result, result, result, result);
    }
  else
    printf ("VALUE: No value provided\n");
}
```

Each time you compile a C program, the C compiler places header code at the front of your program. This header code is responsible for examining the command line that the user entered to invoke the program. This code assigns the values to **argc** and **argv**. When the user later executes your program, this header code executes first, building **argc** and **argv**. Next, this header code invokes **main** as a function and passes **argc** and **argv** as parameters to it.

COMMAND-LINE PROCESSING FROM TURBO PASCAL

Turbo Pascal is one of the most thoroughly designed Pascal compilers available for personal computers. The compiler provides full support for command-line processing by using the built-in functions **PARAM-COUNT** and **PARAMSTR**. The first routine, **PARAMCOUNT**, returns the number of parameters on the command line. The second, **PARAMSTR**, returns the value of a specific command-line parameter.

Consider the following command:

```
A> DISKCOPY A: B:
```

In this case, **PARAMCOUNT** returns the value 2. Likewise, the routine **PARAMSTR** returns the following:

ParamStr(1) returns A:
ParamStr(2) returns B:

Consider the program **ECHOTEST.PAS**, which displays each of its command-line arguments:

```
Program Echo_Test;

var
  PARAM: integer;

begin
  for PARAM := 1 to ParamCount do
    writeln (ParamStr(PARAM));
end.
```

Similarly, this Turbo Pascal program displays its command-line parameters in reverse order:

```
Program Rev_Line;

var
  PARAM: integer;

begin
  for PARAM := ParamCount downto 1 do
    writeln (ParamStr(PARAM));
end.
```

Next, this program copies the file specified by the first command-line parameter to the second:

```
Program F_Copy;

const
  record_size = 128;

var
  input_file: file;
  output_file: file;

  data_buffer: array[1..record_size] of byte;
  num_records: integer;
```

```
begin
   if (ParamCount >= 2) then
      begin
         {$I-}
         Assign (input_file, ParamStr(1));
         Assign (output_file, ParamStr(2));
         Reset (input_file);
         {$I+}

         If IoResult <> 0 then
            writeln ('FCOPY: Invalid file specification ', ParamStr(1))
         else
            begin
               Rewrite (output_file);

               repeat
                  BlockRead (input_file, data_buffer, record_size,
                             num_records);
                  BlockWrite (output_file, data_buffer, num_records);
               until (num_records = 0);

               close (input_file);
               close (output_file);
            end;
      end
   else
      writeln ('FCOPY: Invalid usage: FCOPY SOURCE.EXT TARGET.EXT');
end.
```

Invoke the program by entering

```
A> FCOPY SOURCE.TXT TARGET.TXT
```

The program shown in Figure 9-1 implements the DOS DATE command.

DOS places the command line into a header (program-segment prefix) that precedes every executable program. Each time you invoke **PARAMCOUNT** or **PARAMSTR**, the functions examine this header and return the appropriate values. Later in this chapter you will write a Turbo Pascal program that examines the program-segment prefix and displays the contents of the command line.

```
Program DateTest;

type
  STRING79 = string[79];

  REGISTERS = record
                AX, BX, CX, DX, BP, SI, DI, DS, ES, FLAGS: INTEGER
              end;


procedure String_to_Date (IN_DATE: STRING79;
             var DAY, MONTH, YEAR: integer;
                  var DATE_ERROR: boolean);

var
   VALCODE: integer;                       {the string convert error code}
   START_POS: integer;
begin
     DATE_ERROR := false;

{try to convert the month}
     Val(Copy (IN_DATE, 1, 2), MONTH, VALCODE);
     if VALCODE <> 0 then
       begin
         Val(Copy (IN_DATE, 1, 1), MONTH, VALCODE);
         if VALCODE <> 0 then
           DATE_ERROR := true
         else
           START_POS := 3;
       end
     else
       START_POS := 4;

{try to convert the day}
     Val(Copy (IN_DATE, START_POS, 2), DAY, VALCODE);
     if VALCODE <> 0 then
       begin
         Val(Copy (IN_DATE, START_POS, 1), DAY, VALCODE);
         if VALCODE <> 0 then
           DATE_ERROR := true
         else
           START_POS := START_POS + 2;
       end
     else
       START_POS := START_POS + 3;


{try to convert the year}
     Val(Copy (IN_DATE, START_POS, 4), YEAR, VALCODE);
     if VALCODE <> 0 then
       begin
         Val(Copy (IN_DATE, START_POS, 2), YEAR, VALCODE);
         if VALCODE <> 0 then
           DATE_ERROR := true
```

Figure 9-1.

DateTest program

```
            end;
         if YEAR < 100 then YEAR := YEAR + 1900;
end;



procedure Get_Date (var DOW, DAY, MONTH, YEAR: integer);

var
    REGS: REGISTERS;

begin
    with REGS do
      begin

{set AH to set the current date contained in the time of day clock}
        AX := $2A00;

{invoke the DOS interrupt that returns the date}
        MSDos (REGS);

{return the current date as DOW, day, month, year}
        DOW    := Lo(AX);
        DAY    := Lo(DX);
        MONTH := Hi(DX);
        YEAR   := CX;
      end;
end;



procedure Set_Date (DAY, MONTH, YEAR: integer; var status: integer);

var
    REGS: REGISTERS;   {AX, BX, CX, DX, BP, SI, DI, DS, ES, FLAGS}

begin
    with REGS do
      begin

{set the registers to set the date contained in the
 system clock}
        AX := $2B00;                {DOS function code}
        DX := (MONTH shl 8) + DAY;  {DH contains month - DL day}
        CX := YEAR;

{invoke the DOS interrupt which sets the system clock}
        MSDos (REGS);

{return the success status based upon a valid date}
        if (LO(AX) = $FF) then
          STATUS := 1
        else
          STATUS := 0;
```

Figure 9-1.

DateTest program (*continued*)

```
      end;
end;

var
  dow, day, month, year, status: integer;
  daystr, datestr: string79;
  done, error: boolean;

begin
 done := false;

 if (ParamCount >= 1) then
   datestr := ParamStr(1)
 else
   datestr := ' ';

 repeat

  Get_Date (dow, day, month, year);
  case (dow) of
   0: daystr := 'Sun';
   1: daystr := 'Mon';
   2: daystr := 'Tue';
   3: daystr := 'Wed';
   4: daystr := 'Thu';
   5: daystr := 'Fri';
   6: daystr := 'Sat';
  end;

  if (datestr = ' ') then
    begin
      writeln ('Current date is ',daystr, ' ', MONTH,'/',DAY,'/',YEAR);
      write ('Enter new date (mm-dd-yy): ');
      readln (datestr);
      if (ord(datestr[0]) = 0) then halt (0);
    end;

  String_to_Date (datestr, day, month, year, error);

  if (not error) then
    begin
      Set_Date (day, month, year, status);

      if (status = 0) then
        done := true
      else
        writeln ('Invalid date');
    end
  else
    writeln ('Invalid date');

  datestr := ' ';  { reinitialize it if an error occurred }
 until done;
end.
```

Figure 9-1.

DateTest program (*continued*)

DOS COMMAND LINE PROCESSING

As stated, each time DOS creates an executable image in memory, it places a header at the front of the executable code. This 255-byte header (called the program-segment prefix, or PSP) contains the material shown in Figure 9-2. As you can see, bytes 80H through the end of the program-segment prefix contain the command line the user entered to invoke the program.

Consider the following Turbo Pascal program. The program first uses the MSDOS routine to obtain the address in memory of its PSP. Once it has obtained the PSP address, the program displays the contents of the command used to invoke the program.

```
Program Display;

Type
  REGISTERS = record
                 AX, BX, CX, DX, BP, SI, DI, DS, ES, FLAGS: INTEGER
              end;

var
  regs: registers;
  segment: integer; { segment address of the program segment prefix }
  index: integer;   { index into the PSP of the command line }
  length: integer;  { length of the command line }

begin
  with regs do       { get the segment address of the PSP }
    begin
      regs.ax := $6200;
      MSDOS (regs);
      segment := bx;
    end;

  length := Mem[segment: $80];   { offset 80 hex has the length }

  for index := $81 to $80 + length do   { display the command line }
    write (Chr(Mem[segment:index]));

  writeln;
end.
```

To access command-line arguments from a language other than C or Turbo Pascal requires routines that return the PSP address and that can peek into memory locations to return the value they contain. The following assembly language routine returns the PSP using the Microsoft FORTRAN (beginning with version 5.0) calling convention.

Office (Hex)	Contents
0	Int20
2	Top of Memory
4	Reserved
5	OP Code
6	Number of Bytes in Segment
A	Terminate Address (Offset)
C	Terminate Address (Segment)
E	CTRL-BREAK Address (Offset)
10	CTRL-BREAK Address (Segment)
12	Critical Error Address (Offset)
14	Critical Error Address (Segment)
16	Reserved
2C	Environment Address Segment
2E	Reserved
50	DOS Call
52	Reserved
5C	File-Control Block One
6C	File-Control Block Two
80	Command-Line Length (Bytes)
81	Command-Line Parameters

Figure 9-2.

Contents of program-segment
prefix (PSP)

```
; value = GETPSP ()
;
; return the program segment prefix
;

TITLE GETPSP

PSP_TEXT SEGMENT BYTE PUBLIC 'CODE'
PSP_TEXT ENDS

_DATA SEGMENT WORD PUBLIC 'DATA'
_DATA ENDS

CONST SEGMENT WORD PUBLIC 'CONST'
CONST ENDS

_BSS SEGMENT WORD PUBLIC 'BSS'
_BSS ENDS

DGROUP GROUP CONST, _BSS, _DATA
ASSUME CS:PSP_TEXT, DS:DGROUP, SS:DGROUP, ES:DGROUP

PSP_TEXT SEGMENT

PUBLIC GETPSP
GETPSP PROC FAR

   PUSH BP             ; save the current base pointer
   MOV  BP, SP         ; store the stack pointer

   MOV  AH, 62H
   INT  21H

   MOV  AX, BX
   MOV  [BP-2], AX  ; return value

   MOV  SP, BP
   POP  BP

RET

GETPSP ENDP

PSP_TEXT ENDS
END
```

Using the peek function developed in Chapter 7, the following FOR-TRAN program displays its command line:

```
Program Display

integer peek
integer*2 getpsp
integer i, j, length
integer*2 segment
```

```
        character*128 commline

        segment = getpsp()

        length = ichar(char(peek (segment, 16#80)))

        j = 1

        do 10 i = 16#81, length + 16#81
          commline (j:j) = char(peek (segment, i))
          j = j + 1
10      continue

        write (*,*) commline (1:J)

        end
```

The routines shown in Figure 9-3 and Figure 9-4 implement
PARAMCNT and **PARAMARG** to return the number of command-
line parameters, along with the desired command-line argument.

```
        Integer*2 Function ParamCnt

        implicit complex (a-z)

        integer*2 NUMPARAMS, I, COMMLEN
        integer*2 Peek, GetPSP, PSPSEG

        integer*2 TAB, QUOTE, SPACE
        parameter (TAB=11, QUOTE=34, SPACE=32)

        NUMPARAMS = 0

        PSPSEG = GetPSP()

c Get the number of bytes in the command line

        COMMLEN = Peek (PSPSEG, #80)

c Skip leading blanks and tabs

        I = 1
```

Figure 9-3.

PARAMCNT routine

```
     10        continue
               if ((Peek(PSPSEG, #80+I) .NE. SPACE) .and.
           &       (Peek(PSPSEG, #80+I) .NE. TAB)) goto 20
                 I = I + 1
                 if (I .LE. COMMLEN) goto 10
     20        continue


     30        continue
               if (I .GT. COMMLEN) goto 80
                 if (Peek(PSPSEG, #80+I) .eq. QUOTE) then
                 I = I + 1

     40           continue
                  if ((I .GT. COMMLEN) .or.
           &          (Peek (PSPSEG, #80+I) .EQ. QUOTE)) goto 50
                    I = I + 1
                    goto 40
     50           continue
                  I = I + 1

                 else if ((Peek(PSPSEG, #80+I) .EQ. SPACE) .or.
           &        (Peek(PSPSEG, #80+I) .EQ. TAB)) then
                    NUMPARAMS = NUMPARAMS + 1
                    I = I + 1

                    if (I .LE. COMMLEN) then
     60               continue
                      if ((Peek(PSPSEG, #80+I) .NE. SPACE) .and.
           &              (Peek(PSPSEG, #80+I) .NE. TAB)) goto 70
                        I = I + 1
                        if (I .LE. COMMLEN) goto 60
     70               continue

                    endif
                 else
                    I = I + 1
                 endif

                 GOTO 30
     80        continue

               if (COMMLEN .ne. 0) then
                if (Peek(PSPSEG, #80+COMMLEN) .ne. SPACE) then
                   NUMPARAMS = NUMPARAMS + 1
                endif
               endif

               ParamCnt = NUMPARAMS
               return
               end
```

Figure 9-3.

PARAMCNT routine (*continued*)

```
            subroutine ParamArg (NUM, PARAM, LENGTH)

            implicit complex (a-z)

            integer*2 NUM, LENGTH, NUMPARAMS, I, J, COMMLEN
            character*64 PARAM, CURPARAM

            integer*2 Peek, GetPSP, PSPSEG
            integer*2 TAB, QUOTE, SPACE

            logical DONE

            parameter (TAB=11, QUOTE=34, SPACE=32)

            LENGTH = 0
            NUMPARAMS = 0
            PARAM = ' '
            DONE = .FALSE.

            PSPSEG = GetPSP()

c Skip leading blanks and tabs

            I = 1
   10       continue

            if ((Peek(PSPSEG, #80+I) .NE. SPACE) .and.
         &     (Peek(PSPSEG, #80+I) .NE. TAB)) goto 20
            I = I + 1
            goto 10
   20       continue

c Get the number of bytes in the command line

            COMMLEN = Peek (PSPSEG, #80)

            J = 1
   30       continue
            if ((DONE) .or. (I .GT. COMMLEN)) goto 80
             if (Peek(PSPSEG, #80+I) .eq. QUOTE) then
              I = I + 1

   40          continue
               if ((I .GT. COMMLEN) .or.
         &         (Peek (PSPSEG, #80+I) .EQ. QUOTE)) goto 50
                CURPARAM (J:J) = Char (Peek(PSPSEG, #80+I))
                I = I + 1
                J = J + 1
                goto 40
   50          continue
               I = I + 1
```

Figure 9-4.

PARAMARG routine

```
              else if ((Peek(PSPSEG, #80+I) .EQ. SPACE) .or.
     &          (Peek(PSPSEG, #80+I) .EQ. TAB)) then
                NUMPARAMS = NUMPARAMS + 1
                if (NUMPARAMS .eq. NUM) then
                  PARAM = CURPARAM (1:J-1)
                  LENGTH = J - 1
                  DONE = .TRUE.
                endif

                J = 1

                CURPARAM = ' '
                if (.not. DONE) then
60                continue
                  if ((Peek(PSPSEG, #80+I) .NE. SPACE) .and.
     &                (Peek(PSPSEG, #80+I) .NE. TAB)) goto 70
                    I = I + 1
                    goto 60
70                continue
                endif
              else
                CURPARAM (J:J) = Char (Peek(PSPSEG, #80+I))
                I = I + 1
                J = J + 1
              endif
              GOTO 30
80            continue

              if ((.not. DONE) .and. (CURPARAM .ne. ' ')) then
                NUMPARAMS = NUMPARAMS + 1
                if (NUMPARAMS .eq. NUM) then
                  PARAM = CURPARAM (1:J-1)
                  LENGTH = J - 1
                endif
              endif

              return
              end
```

Figure 9-4.

PARAMARG routine (*continued*)

Note that these routines enhance the functional aspects of DOS command-line processing by allowing you to group parameters within quotes to make them appear as one parameter. For example, the command

```
A> FINDWORD DOS USER'S GROUP
```

results in the following:

ParamCnt returns 3
ParamArg (1,STR,**Length**) returns DOS
ParamArg (2,STR,**Length**) returns User's
ParamArg (3,STR,**Length**) returns Group

However, the command

```
A> FINDWORD "DOS USER'S GROUP"
```

results in the following:

ParamCnt returns 1
ParamArg (1,STR,**Length**) returns DOS User's Group

This FORTRAN program uses the routines **PARAMCNT** and **PARAMARG** to implement ECHOTEST:

```
         Program EchoTest

         Integer I
         Integer ParamCnt
         Integer Length

         Character*64 STR

         DO 10 I = 1, ParamCnt()
           Call ParamArg (I, STR, LENGTH)
           write (6,*) STR(1:LENGTH)
   10    continue

         end
```

SUPPORTING COMMAND-LINE PARAMETERS AND I/O REDIRECTION

Chapter 3 discussed how to increase the generic nature of your applications by writing them to support DOS I/O redirection. It is possible, however, to develop your programs so that they support either command-line processing or I/O redirection, depending on their contexts in the command line.

Consider the program NUMLINE. If you invoke the program with

```
A> NUMLINE A.TXT
```

the program displays the contents of the file A.TXT with each line preceded by its line number. Likewise, if you invoke the program without a command-line parameter and use redirection, the program displays the redirected input in the same manner:

```
A> NUMLINE < A.TXT
```

or

```
A> DIR | NUMLINE
```

This Turbo Pascal program implements NUMLINE.PAS:

```
{$p256,g256}

Program NumLine;

type
  STRING79 = string[79];
```

```
var
   LINE    : STRING79;          {line read from the file}
   IN_FILE: text;               {the input file}
   NUM: integer;                {line number}

begin
   num := 0;

{see if the user provided an input file}
   if (ParamCount <> 0) then
      begin
         Assign (IN_FILE, ParamStr(1));
         {$I-} Reset (IN_FILE) {$I+};
         if (IOresult <> 0) then
            Writeln ('NUMLINE: error opening the file ', ParamStr(1))
         else
            begin
               while (not EOF (IN_FILE)) do
                  begin
                     NUM := NUM + 1;
                     Readln (IN_FILE, LINE);
                     Writeln (NUM, ' ', LINE);            {write to stdout}
                  end;
               Close (IN_FILE);
            end;
      end
   else
      begin
         while (not EOF) do
               begin
                  Readln (LINE);
                  NUM := NUM + 1;
                  Writeln (NUM, ' ',LINE);               {write to stdout}
               end;
      end;
end.
```

Likewise, this C program implements NUMLINE.C:

```
#include <stdio.h>

#define LINE 255

main (argc, argv)
   int argc;
   char *argv[];
   {
   char line[LINE];
   int num = 0;

   FILE *fp, *fopen();

   if (argc > 1)
      {
```

```
        if ((fp = fopen (argv[1], "r")) == NULL)
            printf ("NUMLINE: Cannot open %s\n", argv[1]
        else
          {
            while (fgets (line, LINE, fp))
              printf ("%d %s", ++num, line);

            fclose (fp);
          }
      }
   else
      while (fgets (line, LINE, stdin))
        printf ("%d %s", ++num, line);
   }
```

Last, these programs provide an enhanced version of MORE. If input is redirected to the program

```
A> DIR | IMORE
```

the program displays the input a screenful at a time. If instead, the command line contains a file

```
A> IMORE IMORE.PAS
```

the program displays the file's contents a screenful at a time. This routine implements IMORE.C:

```
#include <stdio.h>

#define LINE 255
#define SCREEN_SIZE 23

main (argc, argv)
```

```
    int argc;
    char *argv[];
{
    char line[LINE];
    int num = 0;

    FILE *fp, *fopen();

    if (argc > 1)
      {
        if ((fp = fopen (argv[1], "r")) == NULL)
            printf ("IMORE: Cannot open %s\n", argv[1]);
        else
          {
            while (fgets (line, LINE, fp))
              {
                printf ("%s", line);
                if ((++num % SCREEN_SIZE) == 0)
                  {
                    printf ("--IMORE--\n");
                    getch();
                  }
              }
            fclose (fp);
          }
      }
    else
        while (fgets (line, LINE, stdin))
          {
            printf ("%s", line);
            if (++num % SCREEN_SIZE == 0)
              {
                printf ("--IMORE--\n");
                getc(stdprn);
              }
          }
}
```

Likewise, the routine shown in Figure 9-5 implements IMORE.PAS.

DOS command-line parameters give your programs virtually unlimited application support by allowing you to use the same program in many different contexts. The C and Turbo Pascal programming languages make command-line programming easy. If you develop a few simple interface routines, languages like FORTRAN can readily support command-line processing. If you develop your programs to support command-line processing, the number of applications that each program can support will be limitless.

```
{$p256,g256}

Program Imore;

const
  screen_size = 23;

type
  STRING79 = string[79];

var
  LINE    : STRING79;         {line read from the file}
  IN_FILE: text;              {the input file}
  NUM: integer;               {line number}
  buffer: char;

begin
  num := 0;

{ see if the user provided an input file}
  if (ParamCount <> 0) then
    begin
      Assign (IN_FILE, ParamStr(1));
      {$I-} Reset (IN_FILE) {$I+};
      if (IOresult <> 0) then
        Writeln ('IMORE: error opening the file ', ParamStr(1))
      else
        begin
          while (not EOF (IN_FILE)) do
            begin
              NUM := NUM + 1;
              Readln (IN_FILE, LINE);
              Writeln (LINE);              {write to stdout}
              if (num mod screen_size) = 0 then
                begin
                  write ('--IMORE--');
                  read (kbd, buffer);
                  writeln;
                end;
            end;
          Close (IN_FILE);
        end;
    end
  else
    begin
      while (not EOF) do
        begin
```

Figure 9-5.

IMORE.PAS routine

```
                Readln (LINE);
                NUM := NUM + 1;
                Writeln (LINE);                {write to stdout}
                if (num mod screen_size) = 0 then
                  begin
                    write ('--IMORE--');
                    read (kbd, buffer);
                    writeln ;
                  end;
              end;
        end;
    end.
```

Figure 9-5.

IMORE.PAS routine (*continued*)

10: Disk Structure

One of the most fascinating (yet least understood) aspects of DOS is disk manipulation. Many of your programs perform numerous disk I/O operations. To get the most from your system, you must fully understand how DOS stores information on disk, the consequences of disk fragmentation, why DOS root directories are restricted to a limited number of files, and last, how deleted files can be retrieved.

This chapter teaches you how DOS stores data on disk; how to perform low-level disk I/O operations using both the ROM-BIOS and DOS services; how to implement the DOS CHKDSK, DISKCOPY, and DISKCOMP commands; and how to undelete previously deleted files. In addition, this chapter reviews the DOS services that relate closely to disk manipulation.

DISK STRUCTURE

Before discussing the "nitty-gritty" of DOS disk manipulation, a review
of the basics of disk structure is in order. The diagram in Figure 10-1
illustrates a standard 5 1/4-inch floppy disk.

The *write-protect notch* dictates whether DOS can modify the
contents of the disk by adding or deleting information. When this notch
is visible, DOS can modify the contents of the disk. When covered (with
a write-protect tab provided with the disk), the disk is write-protected,
which prevents its modification. Get in the habit of write-protecting all
of your disks that you know do not require modification. This simple

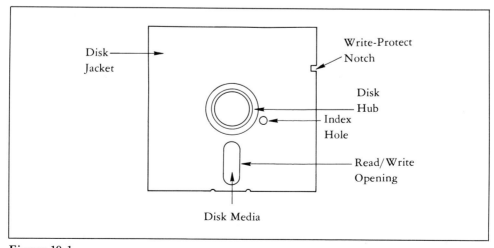

Figure 10-1.

Parts of a floppy disk

precaution will save you from frustrating, embarrassing, and possibly catastrophic data loss. As a DOS power user you are probably fully aware of disk write-protection. Use this knowledge to set an example for others.

The *disk hub* is the portion of the disk that the disk drive uses to rotate the disk past the read/write head. Once you insert a floppy disk into the drive, the disk drive rotates the floppy disk past the drive's read/write head, which retrieves and stores information. The *disk jacket* surrounds the disk and protects it from dust, fingerprints, smoke, and scratches.

The *read/write opening* provides the read/write head of the disk drive with access to the storage media. As the disk spins rapidly inside the drive, the read/write head accesses the information on the disk by way of this opening.

The *index hole* on the disk provides the floppy disk controller with a timing mechanism. As the disk spins within the disk drive, the controller waits for the index hole to pass by. Once the controller sees the index hole, it knows the orientation of the disk and simply locates the data stored on the disk as an offset from this hole.

Open up a disk and you will find that it is constructed as shown in Figure 10-2. Closely examine the plastic disk media. Turn it over. Do you notice a difference? No, you should not. For years, computer supply stores have been selling users double-sided disks at a higher cost than single-sided disks. However, if you open a double-sided disk and a single-sided disk and compare them, you will not see a difference. Never buy double-sided disks. The disk manufacturer performs the identical processing on both sides of a single-sided disk. This means that DOS can format a single-sided disk as double-sided. By purchasing only single-sided disks you gain the same functional capabilities for less cost.

More and more computers are now supporting 3 1/2-inch disks called *microfloppy disks* (see Figure 10-3). Because of their size, microfloppy disks require special disk drives. In the future, you will increasingly find software on disks of this size. Microfloppy disks are much more durable than their counterpart 5 1/4-inch floppy disks. In addition, the storage media for a microfloppy disk is must less exposed to dust, smoke, and other particles that often destroy floppy disks.

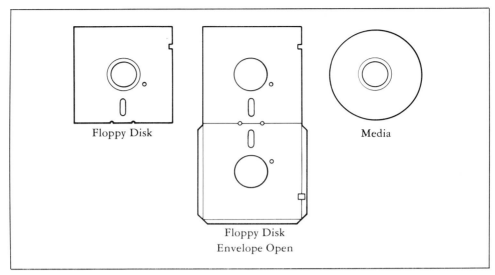

Figure 10-2.

Inner construction of floppy disks

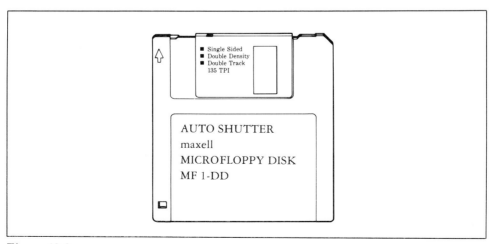

Figure 10-3.

Microfloppy disk

You should immediately notice several differences (other than size) between microfloppy disks and standard floppies. First, the microfloppy is not flimsy. Second, the microfloppy jacket is solid plastic. If you look at the top of the microfloppy disk, you will find a metal slide called a *shutter* (see Figure 10-4). Move the shutter to the left, and you will expose the microfloppy *storage media* (see Figure 10-5). Each time the computer needs to access the information stored on the microfloppy, the disk controller slides the shutter to the left to access the storage media.

Turn over the microfloppy disk and note the *write-protect switch* (see Figure 10-6). If you can see light through the switch, the microfloppy is write-protected. When the hole is sealed, DOS can access the disk in either read or write mode.

Next, notice the *disk spindle* (see Figure 10-7). The microfloppy disk drive uses this spindle to spin the disk. Unlike the standard floppy disk (which uses the index hole for timing), the microfloppy disk uses the *sector notch*. The microfloppy disk must seat itself on the spindle and the sector notch.

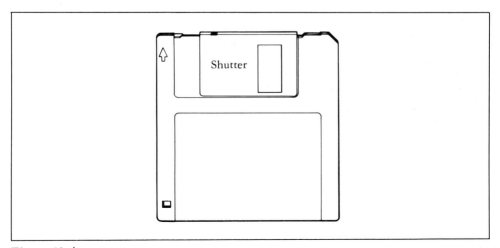

Figure 10-4.

Location of a shutter

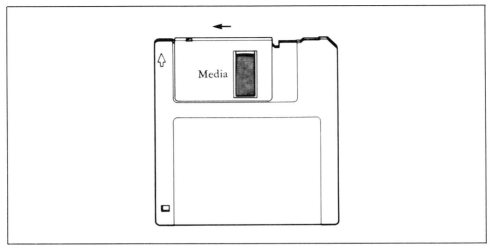

Figure 10-5.

Disk media

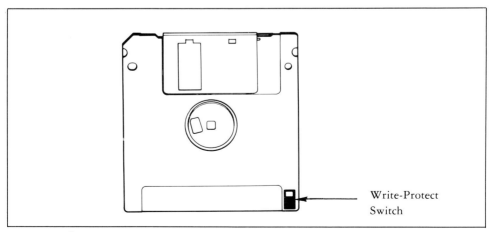

Figure 10-6.

Write-protect switch on microfloppy
disk

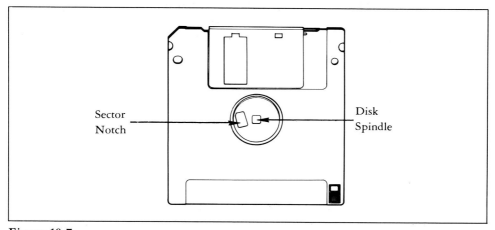

Figure 10-7.

Sector notch and disk spindle on
microfloppy disk

Microfloppy disks are on the verge of making a significant impact on the computer industry. DOS version 3.2 provides complete support for microfloppy disks. Their uses should grow for some time, especially since IBM adopted the microfloppy for use on the Model 50, 60, and 80 computers.

This chapter concentrates much of its discussion on floppy disks for two reasons. First, DOS stores data on a hard disk in the same manner it does on a floppy disk. Therefore, all of the concepts discussed will apply to both. Second, since many of the routines presented in this chapter manipulate the disk at low levels, you should feel much more comfortable trying them on a floppy disk as opposed to your critical hard disk.

SECTORS, TRACKS, AND SIDES

Visualize a disk as an album that you would play on your stereo. The disk is comprised of *tracks* that begin at the outer edge of the disk and work their way to the disk hub, as shown in Figure 10-8.

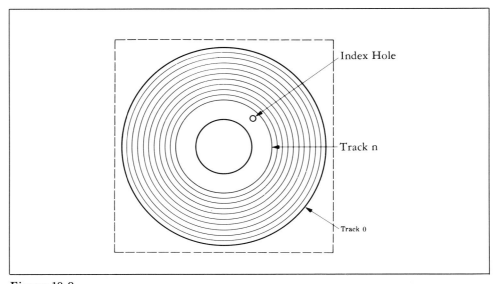

Figure 10-8.

Tracks that make up a disk

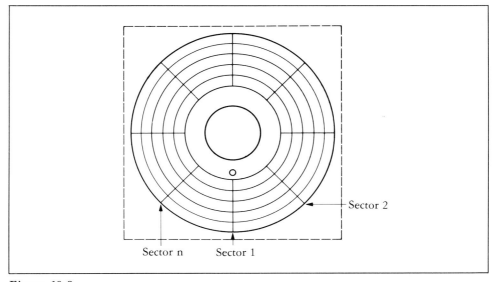

Figure 10-9.

Sectors that make up tracks

Standard floppy disks have 40 tracks; quad-density disks have 80; and fixed-disks may contain several hundred. DOS further divides each track on a disk into smaller units called *sectors* (see Figure 10-9).

The exact number of sectors on a disk depends upon the type of the disk. Common configurations include those shown in Table 10-1. DOS disk sectors contain 512 bytes (see Figure 10-10).

As previously discussed, DOS records information on both sides of a disk. Knowing the number of tracks, sectors, and bytes per sector, you can determine the storage capabilities of a disk as follows:

Storage = (number of sides) * (number of tracks) * (number
       of sectors) * (sector size)

A double-sided, double-density disk can store 368,640 bytes of information, as shown here:

Storage = (number of sides) * (number of tracks) * (number
       of sectors) * (sector size)
= (2) * (40) * (9) * (512)
= 368,640 bytes

ONCE AROUND THE TRACK

Now that you know the basics of disk layout, you can perform several powerful programs such as DISKCOPY and DISKCOMP. To develop these programs, you must have the capability to read and write specific disk sectors.

To access disk sectors, you have two choices. First, the ROM-BIOS provides you with interrupt services that perform low-level disk read-and-write operations (see Tables 10-2 and 10-3). Upon completion, the service sets the carry flag if an error occurred; otherwise, the flag is clear.

Similarly, DOS provides two services that perform disk sector read-and-write operations (for example, see Table 10-4).

Upon completion, the service sets the carry flag if an error occurred; otherwise, the flag is clear. If an error occurs, DOS places one of the

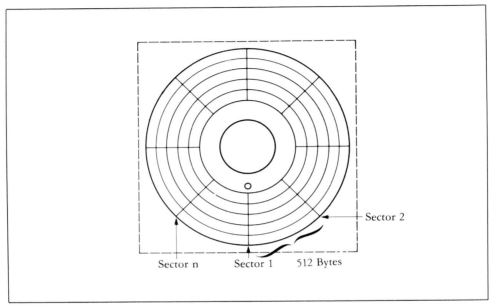

Figure 10-10.

Bytes contained in a sector

Table 10-1.

Common Disk Configurations

Disk Type	Tracks per Side	Total Sectors
Single-sided, 8 sectors per track	40	320
Single-sided, 9 sectors per track	40	360
Double-sided, 8 sectors per track	40	640
Double-sided, 9 sectors per track	40	720
Quad-density, 9 sectors per track	80	1440
Quad-density, 15 sectors per track	80	2400

Table 10-2.

Interrupt 13 Hex Service 2 Read
Disk Sector

Register	Contents
AH	The value 2 (disk read service)
AL	Number of sectors to read
CH	Track number desired (0 to 39)
CL	Starting sector number (1 to 9)
DH	Side number desired (0 to 1)
DL	Drive number desired (A=0, B=1)
ES	Segment address of the data buffer
BX	Offset address of the data buffer

error codes listed in Table 10-5 in AL.

Note that the DOS services use logical sector numbers as opposed to physical sector numbers. For example, logical sector 0 is side 0, track 0, sector 1. Likewise, logical sector 1 is side 0, track 0, sector 2.

Table 10-3.

Interrupt 13 Hex Service 3 Write
Disk Sector

Register	Contents
AH	The value 3 (disk write service)
AL	Number of sectors to read
CH	Track number desired (0 to 39)
CL	Starting sector number (1 to 9)
DH	Side number desired (0 to 1)
DL	Drive number desired (A=0, B=1)
ES	Segment address of the data buffer
BX	Offset address of the data buffer

Table 10-4.

Interrupt 25 Hex Read Disk Sector

Register	Contents
AL	Drive number desired (A=0, B=1)
CX	Number of sectors desired
DX	Starting sector number
DS	Segment address of the data buffer
BX	Offset address of the data buffer

The program **DISKCOPY** shown in Figure 10-11 provides a rudimentary form of the DOS DISKCOPY command. This program uses the ROM-BIOS services to access the disk sectors to copy each sector of the disk in drive A to the disk in drive B (see Table 10-6). This program simply reads a track from drive A and writes that track to drive B.

Similarly, you can compare the contents of two disks (similar to DISKCOMP) by displaying the track, sector, and byte locations of the first difference. In this case, the program simply compares the disk in drive A to that in drive B. However, you can increase the generic nature of this program by using command-line arguments. The code for DISKCOMP becomes that shown in Figure 10-12.

Table 10-5.

Error Codes

Value	Description
02 Hex	Unknown error
03 Hex	Write-protected disk
04 Hex	Requested sector not found
08 Hex	CRC error
40 Hex	SEEK operation failed
80 Hex	Device failed to respond to request

Table 10-6.

Interrupt 26 Hex Write Disk Sector

Register	Contents
AL	Drive number desired (A=0, B=1)
CX	Number of sectors desired
DX	Starting sector number
DS	Segment address of the data buffer
BX	Offset address of the data buffer

```
Program Diskcopy;   { copy the contents of the floppy disk
                      in drive A to the diskette in drive B }

Const
   NumSectors = 9;       { sectors per track }
   NumSides = 2;         { sides per disk }
   NumTracks = 40;       { tracks per side }
   ReadService = 2;      { BIOS disk sector read service }
   WriteService = 3;     { BIOS disk sector write service }
   SourceDisk = 0;       { drive A is the source disk }
   TargetDisk = 1;       { drive B is the target disk }
   BufferSize = 5000;    { size of the disk transfer buffer }

Type
   REGISTERS = record
                  AX, BX, CX, DX, BP, SI, DI, DS, ES, FLAGS: INTEGER
               end;

   Buffer = array [1..BufferSize] of char;   { disk transfer buffer }


Procedure ReadSectors (Var DiskBuffer: Buffer;
                       Side, Track, Drive: integer);

Var
   REGS: Registers;   { emulate the 8088 registers }
```

Figure 10-11.

DISKCOPY program

```
begin
  with REGS do
    begin
      AX := (ReadService SHL 8) + NumSectors;
      CX := (Track SHL 8) + 1;
      DX := (Side SHL 8) + Drive;
      ES := Seg (DiskBuffer[1]);
      BX := Ofs (DiskBuffer[1]);
      Intr ($13, REGS);
    end;
end;


Procedure WriteSectors (DiskBuffer: Buffer;
                        Side, Track, Drive: integer);

Var
  REGS: Registers;    { emulate the 8088 registers }

begin
  with REGS do
    begin
      AX := (WriteService SHL 8) + NumSectors;
      CX := (Track SHL 8) + 1;
      DX := (Side SHL 8) + Drive;
      ES := Seg (DiskBuffer[1]);
      BX := Ofs (DiskBuffer[1]);
      Intr ($13, REGS);
    end;
end;

Var
  DiskBuffer: Buffer;    { disk transfer buffer }
  Track, Side: integer;

begin

{ read each track from both sides writing them to drive B }

  For Side := 0 to NumSides - 1 do
    For Track := 0 to NumTracks - 1 do
        begin
          ReadSectors (DiskBuffer, Side, Track, SourceDisk);
          WriteSectors (DiskBuffer, Side, Track, TargetDisk);
        end;
end.
```

Figure 10-11.

DISKCOPY program (*continued*)

```
Program Diskcomp;   { compare the contents of the floppy disk
                       in drive A to the diskette in drive B }

Const
   NumSectors = 9;        { sectors per track }
   NumSides = 2;          { sides per disk }
   SectorSize = 512;      { bytes per sector }
   NumTracks = 40;        { tracks per side }
   ReadService = 2;       { BIOS disk sector read service }
   SourceDisk = 0;        { drive A is the source disk }
   TargetDisk = 1;        { drive B is the target disk }
   BufferSize = 5000;     { size of the disk transfer buffer }

Type
   REGISTERS = record
                  AX, BX, CX, DX, BP, SI, DI, DS, ES, FLAGS: INTEGER
               end;

   Buffer = array [1..BufferSize] of char;    { disk transfer buffer }


Procedure ReadSectors (Var DiskBuffer: Buffer;
                       Side, Track, Drive: integer);

Var
   REGS: Registers;    { emulate the 8088 registers }

begin
   with REGS do
      begin
         AX := (ReadService SHL 8) + NumSectors;
         CX := (Track SHL 8) + 1;
         DX := (Side SHL 8) + Drive;
         ES := Seg (DiskBuffer[1]);
         DX := Ofs (DiskBuffer[1]);
         Intr ($13, REGS);
      end;
end;

Var
   DiskBufferA, DiskBufferB: Buffer;      { disk transfer buffer }
   Track, Side, Index: integer;

begin

{ read each track from both sides writing them to drive B }
```

Figure 10-12.

DISKCOMP program

```
   For Side  := 0 to NumSides - 1 do
     For Track  := 0 to NumTracks - 1 do
         begin
            ReadSectors (DiskBufferA, Side, Track, SourceDisk);
            ReadSectors (DiskBufferB, Side, Track, TargetDisk);
            For Index := 1 to NumSectors * SectorSize Do
               if (DiskBufferA[Index] <> DiskBufferB[Index]) then
                 begin

                    Writeln ('Compare Error At SIDE ', SIDE);
                    Writeln ('                  TRACK ', TRACK);
                    Writeln ('                  SECTOR ', Index
                                                  DIV 512 + 1);
                    Writeln ('                  BYTE ', Index MOD 512);
                    Halt (1);
                 end;
          end;
   end.
```

Figure 10-12.

DISCOMP program (*continued*)

DISK SPACE ALLOCATION

During formatting DOS divides the disk into logical sections for storing the following:

DOS boot record
File allocation table (FAT)
Root directory entries
Data sectors

The boot record is *always* the first sector of *every* DOS disk (side 0, track 0, sector 1, as shown in Figure 10-13). The functions of the DOS boot record are to start the DOS boot process and to define the disk characteristics. Examine the layout of the DOS boot record shown in Figure 10-14.

The Turbo Pascal program **READBOOT** in Figure 10-15 reads the

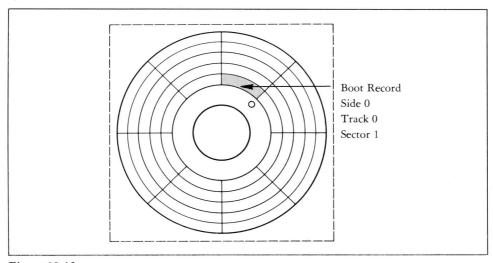

Boot Record
Side 0
Track 0
Sector 1

Figure 10-13.

Boot record in DOS

boot record and breaks up information that it contains into a more readable format. Upon invocation the program displays

```
System Id IBM  3.2
Bytes per sector 512
Sectors per cluster 2
Reserved sectors 1
Number of FAT copies 2
Maximum number of root directory files 112
Sectors per disk 720
FORMAT id 253
Sectors Per Fat 2
Sectors Per Track 9
Sides per disk 2
Number of hidden sectors 0
```

For nonprogrammers, use DEBUG to examine the boot record, as shown here:

```
C>DEBUG
-L 100 0 0 1
-D 100
36B3:0100  EB 34 90 49 42 4D 2C 2C-33 2E 32 00 02 02 01 00   k4.IBM  3.2.....
36B3:0110  02 70 00 D0 02 FD 02 00-09 00 02 00 00 00 00 00   .p.P.D..........
36B3:0120  00 00 00 00 00 00 00 00-00 00 00 00 00 00 00 0F   ................
36B3:0130  00 00 00 00 01 00 FA 33-00 8E D0 BC 00 7C 16 07   ......z3@.P<.|..
36B3:0140  BB 78 00 36 C5 37 1E 56-16 53 BF 2B 7C B9 0B 00   ;x.6E7.V.S?+|9..
36B3:0150  FC AC 26 00 5D 00 74 03-26 8A 05 AA 1A C4 E2 F1   |,&.=.t.&..*.Dbq
36B3:0160  06 1F 89 47 02 C7 07 2B-7C FB CD 13 72 67 A0 1C   ...G.G.+|<N.rg .
36B3:0170  7C 98 F7 26 16 7C 03 06-1C 7C 03 06 0E 7C A3 3F   |.k&.|...|...|#?
-
```

Many users are confused as to why DOS places a boot record on every disk. If you disk is bootable, the boot record starts the boot process. If not, the boot record is responsible for the following message:

```
Non-System disk or disk error
Replace and strike any key when ready
```

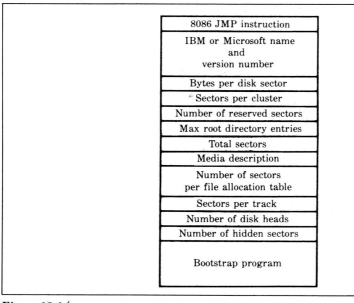

| 8086 JMP instruction |
| IBM or Microsoft name and version number |
| Bytes per disk sector |
| Sectors per cluster |
| Number of reserved sectors |
| Max root directory entries |
| Total sectors |
| Media description |
| Number of sectors per file allocation table |
| Sectors per track |
| Number of disk heads |
| Number of hidden sectors |
| Bootstrap program |

Figure 10-14.

Example boot record

```
    Program ReadBoot;   { Display the contents of the boot record from
                          the disk in drive A }

    Const
      NumSectors = 9;        { sectors per track }
      ReadService = 2;       { BIOS disk sector read service }
      SourceDisk = 0;        { drive A is the source disk }
      BufferSize = 5000;     { size of the disk transfer buffer }

    Type
      Buffer = array [1..BufferSize] of char;   { disk transfer buffer }


    Procedure ReadSectors (Var DiskBuffer: Buffer;
                           Side, Track, Drive: integer);

    Type
      REGISTERS = record
                    AX, BX, CX, DX, BP, SI, DI, DS, ES, FLAGS: INTEGER
                  end;

    Var
      REGS: Registers;    { emulate the 8088 registers }

    begin
      with REGS do
        begin
          AX := (ReadService SHL 8) + NumSectors;
          CX := (Track SHL 8) + 1;
          DX := (Side SHL 8) + Drive;
          ES := Seg (DiskBuffer[1]);
          BX := Ofs (DiskBuffer[1]);
          Intr ($13, REGS);
        end;
    end;

    Var
      DiskBuffer: Buffer;      { disk transfer buffer }
      Index: integer;
      SystemId: string[8];
      BytesPerSector, MaxRoot, SectorsPerDisk: integer;
      SectorsPerFat, SectorsPerTrack, SidesPerDisk: integer;
      HiddenSectors: integer;

    begin

     { read the Boot record from drive A }

     ReadSectors (DiskBuffer, 0, 0, SourceDisk);

     { get the system id }

     For Index := 1 to 8 do
```

Figure 10-15.

READBOOT program

```
    SystemId[Index] := DiskBuffer[Index+3];

SystemId[0] := Char(8);
writeln ('System Id ', SystemId);

{ get the number of bytes per sector }

BytesPerSector := Ord(DiskBuffer[13]) Shl 8 + Ord(DiskBuffer[12]);
writeln ('Bytes per sector ', BytesPerSector);

{ get the number of sectors per cluster }
writeln ('Sectors per cluster ', Ord(DiskBuffer[14]));

{ get the number of reserved sectors }
writeln ('Reserved sectors ', Ord(DiskBuffer[15]));

{ get the number of FAT copies }
writeln ('Number of FAT copies ', Ord(DiskBuffer[17]));

{ get the maximum number of root directory files }

MaxRoot := Ord(DiskBuffer[19]) Shl 8 + Ord(DiskBuffer[18]);
writeln ('Maximum number of root directory files ', MaxRoot);

{ get the total number of sectors per disk }

SectorsPerDisk := Ord(DiskBuffer[21]) Shl 8 + Ord(DiskBuffer[20]);
writeln ('Sectors per disk ', SectorsPerDisk);

{ get the FORMAT id }
writeln ('FORMAT id ', Ord(DiskBuffer[22]));

{ get the number of sectors used by the FAT }

SectorsPerFat := Ord(DiskBuffer[24]) Shl 8 + Ord(DiskBuffer[23]);
writeln ('Sectors Per Fat ', SectorsPerFat);

{ get the number of sectors per track }

SectorsPerTrack := Ord(DiskBuffer[26]) Shl 8 + Ord(DiskBuffer[25]);
writeln ('Sectors Per Track ', SectorsPerTrack);

{ get the number of sides per disk }

SidesPerDisk := Ord(DiskBuffer[28]) Shl 8 + Ord(DiskBuffer[27]);
writeln ('Sides per disk ', SidesPerDisk);

{ get the number of reserved sectors }

HiddenSectors := Ord(DiskBuffer[30]) Shl 8 + Ord(DiskBuffer[29]);
writeln ('Number of hidden sectors ', HiddenSectors);

end.
```

Figure 10-15.

READBOOT program (*continued*)

FILE ALLOCATION TABLE (FAT)

DOS keeps track of its used, unused, and damaged sectors by using a table called the *file allocation table* (FAT). The FAT is always the second and third sectors of a disk, as shown in Figure 10-16.

The FAT keeps track of all of the sectors on a disk. If the area of the disk containing the FAT becomes corrupted, it is possible that you will be unable to access any of the information on the disk. To prevent a single disk corruption from having such devastating impact on the system, DOS places a second copy of the FAT in sectors 4 and 5 (see Figure 10-17).

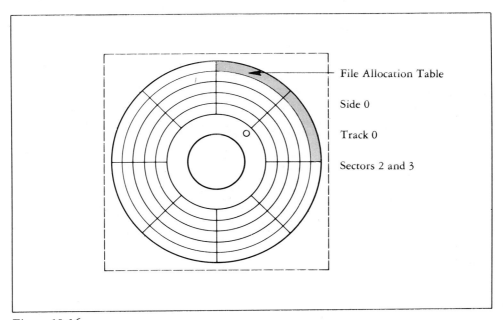

File Allocation Table

Side 0

Track 0

Sectors 2 and 3

Figure 10-16.

Location of file allocation table

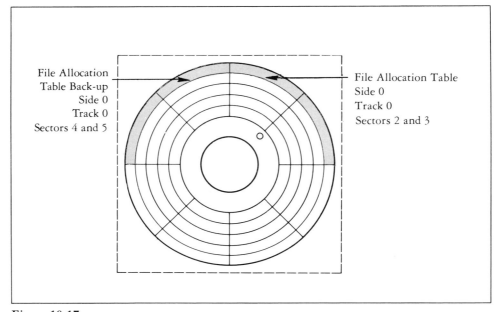

File Allocation
Table Back-up
Side 0
Track 0
Sectors 4 and 5

File Allocation Table
Side 0
Track 0
Sectors 2 and 3

Figure 10-17.

Location of file allocation table
back-up

The Turbo Pascal program in Figure 10-18, **FATCOMP**, verifies
that both copies of the FAT are consistent.

DOS groups disk sectors into collections of multiple sectors called
clusters. Each time your program allocates disk space, DOS assigns the
spaces by using clusters as opposed to individual sectors. The FAT
records clusters as opposed to sectors, as shown in Table 10-7. Table
10-8 lists the number of clusters used by each disk type. For each cluster
on the disk, DOS places one of the values shown in Table 10-9.

For example, consider the disk and FAT shown in Figure 10-19. Each
time DOS needs to allocate space for a file, it searches the FAT for
unused disk clusters (entries with a value of 0). Clusters, therefore, are
the DOS unit of disk allocation. Each time a file needs additional space,

```
Program FatComp;  { Compare both copies of the FAT from
                    the disk in drive A }

Const
  NumSectors = 9;        { sectors per track }
  ReadService = 2;       { BIOS disk sector read service }
  SourceDisk = 0;        { drive A is the source disk }
  BufferSize = 5000;     { size of the disk transfer buffer }

Type
  Buffer = array [1..BufferSize] of char;   { disk transfer buffer }


Procedure ReadSectors (Var DiskBuffer: Buffer;
                       Side, Track, Drive: integer);

Type
  REGISTERS = record
                AX, BX, CX, DX, BP, SI, DI, DS, ES, FLAGS: INTEGER
              end;

Var
  REGS: Registers;    { emulate the 8088 registers }

begin
  with REGS do
    begin
      AX := (ReadService SHL 8) + NumSectors;
      CX := (Track SHL 8) + 1;
      DX := (Side SHL 8) + Drive;
      ES := Seg (DiskBuffer[1]);
      BX := Ofs (DiskBuffer[1]);
      Intr ($13, REGS);
    end;
end;

Var
  DiskBuffer: Buffer;    { disk transfer buffer }
  Index1, Index2: integer;

begin

  { read the sector containing the FATs from drive A }

  ReadSectors (DiskBuffer, 0, 0, SourceDisk);

  Index1 := 513;    { offset to first FAT }
  Index2 := 1537;   { offset to second FAT }

  while (index1 < 1537) do
    begin
      if (DiskBuffer[index1] <> DiskBuffer[Index2]) then
        begin
```

Figure 10-18.

FATCOMP program

```
            writeln ('FATs differ at offset ', Index1 - 513);
            Halt;
         end;
      Index1 := Index1 + 1;
      Index2 := Index2 + 1;
   end;

   writeln ('FATs are identical');

   end.
```

Figure 10-18.

FATCOMP program (*continued*)

DOS allocates disk space to the file a cluster at a time. By keeping track
of which clusters a file uses, DOS in essence creates a chain of sectors
that you can follow, one right after another, to locate the contents of a
file.

Table 10-7.

FAT Clusters

Cluster	Status
2	3
3	End-of-file
4	Corrupted
.	
.	
.	
345	Available
355	Available
(Next cluster)	

Table 10-8.

Number of Clusters of Data Space
Available

Disk Type	Number of Data Clusters
Single-sided, 8 sectors per track	323
Single-sided, 9 sectors per track	630
Double-sided, 8 sectors per track	351
Double-sided, 9 sectors per track	708
Quad-density, 9 sectors per track	1422
Quad-density, 15 sectors per track	2371

The first byte of the FAT always contains a media descriptor byte that tells DOS about the disk (see Table 10-10). DOS sets the second, third, and optionally the fourth (which is set for 16-bit entries) bytes to

Table 10-9.

Cluster Values

Value	Meaning
0	Available
Numeric	
2-2371	Next cluster
FFF	End-of-file
FF7	Corrupted sector

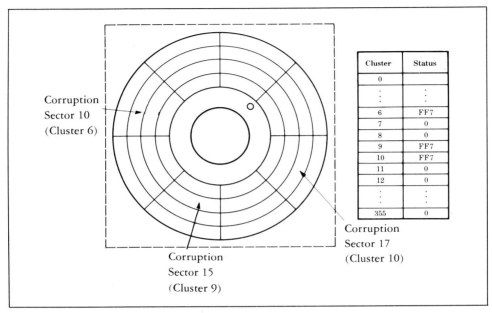

Cluster	Status
0	
:	:
6	FF7
7	0
8	0
9	FF7
10	FF7
11	0
12	0
:	:
355	0

Corruption
Sector 10
(Cluster 6)

Corruption
Sector 17
(Cluster 10)

Corruption
Sector 15
(Cluster 9)

Figure 10-19.

FAT preventing DOS from using
bad area on disk

Table 10-10.

Media Descriptor Bytes

Media Descriptor Byte (Hex)	Disk Type	Sectors/Track	Sides
F8	Fixed	Varies	Varies
F9	5 1/4	15	2
FC	5 1/4	9	1
FD	5 1/4	9	2
FE	5 1/4	8	1
FF	5 1/4	8	2

the hexadecimal value FF. Verify this by using DEBUG, as shown here:

```
C>DEBUG           Media Descriptor
-L 100 0 1 1
-D 100
36D3:01C0   FD FF FF FF 4F 00 05 60-00 C7 80 00 09 A0 00 0B    )...0..`..... .:
36D3:0110   C0 00 0D E0 00 0F C0 01-11 20 01 13 40 01 15 60    @..`..... ..@..`
36D3:0120   01 17 80 01 19 A0 01 1B-C0 01 1D E0 01 1F 00 02    ..... ..@..`....
36D3:0130   21 20 02 23 40 02 25 60-02 27 80 02 29 A0 02 2B    ! .#@.%`.'..) .+
36D3:0140   C0 02 2D E0 02 FF 0F 03-31 20 03 33 40 03 35 B0    @.-`....1 .3@.50
36D3:0150   03 F7 7F FF F7 7F FF F7-CF 03 3D E0 03 80 70 FF    .w..w..wO.=`..p.
36B3:0160   F7 7F FF F7 7F FF F7 7F-FF F7 7F FF F7 7F FF F7    w..w..w..w..w..w
36B3:0170   7F FF F7 7F FF F7 7F FF-F7 7F FF F7 7F FF F7 7F    ..w..w..w..w..w.
-
```

Depending upon your media type, FAT entries require either 12 or 16 bits. For fixed disks greater than 10 MB, DOS uses 16-bit entries. All smaller disks are 12-bit entries.

The following Turbo Pascal function returns the media descriptor byte:

```
Program Medit;   { Display the contents of the media descriptor byte
                   for the  disk in drive A }


Function GetMediaDescriptorByte: Byte;

Const
    NumSectors = 9;         { sectors per track }
    ReadService = 2;        { BIOS disk sector read service }
    SourceDisk = 0;         { drive A is the source disk }
    BufferSize = 5000;      { size of the disk transfer buffer }

Type
    REGISTERS = record
               AX, BX, CX, DX, BP, SI, DI, DS, ES, FLAGS: INTEGER
               end;

    Buffer = array [1..BufferSize] of char;   { disk transfer buffer }

Var
    REGS: Registers;   { emulate the 8088 registers }
    DiskBuffer: Buffer;

begin
    with REGS do
      begin
        AX := (ReadService ShL 8) + NumSectors;
```

```
        CX := 1;
        DX := SourceDisk;
        ES := Seg (DiskBuffer[1]);
        BX := Ofs (DiskBuffer[1]);
        Intr (S13, REGS);
      end;

  GetMediaDescriptorByte := Ord(DiskBuffer[513]);
end;

begin

  writeln ('Media descriptor byte is ', GetMediaDescriptorByte);

end.
```

Although 12-bit FAT entries conserve disk space, they require programs that access the FAT to decode each entry. Use the following algorithm to decode FAT entries to determine the next cluster in the file's data chain:

Multiply the current cluster number by 1.5. The value 1.5 is used since each 12-bit cluster entry requires 1.5 bytes.

Current_Entry : 2;

Offset := Current_Entry * 1.5; {offset becomes 3}

Use the whole number of the offset

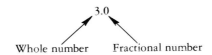

Whole number   Fractional number

as the offset to the next FAT entry.

New_Entry := Trunc (Offset); {New_Entry becomes 3}

Get the 16-bit value from the FAT location that is indexed by New_Entry. If the result of the previous multiplication (Current_Entry * 1.5) resulted in a fractional part greater than 0, shift the value 4 bits to the right.

if ((Current_Entry * 15) mod 10<> 0) then

Value := Value SHR 4;

If no fractional part exists, then AND the value with the hexadecimal value 0FFF.

else

Value := Value and $FFF;

The Turbo Pascal program in Figure 10-20 uses this algorithm to implement a simple CHKDSK command. The program starts with the first data cluster and examines each succeeding cluster for the hexadecimal value FF8, which indicates a corrupted disk sector.

```
Program ChkDsk;      { Display the number of corrupted bytes on
                       the diskette in drive A }

Const
  BufferSize = 5000;   { disk transfer size }
  Offset = 513;        { offset of FAT into disk transfer buffer }
  MaxCluster = 355;    { max number of clusters for DD DS disk }
  SourceDisk = 0;      { drive A is the source disk }

Type
  Buffer = array [1..BufferSize] of char;   { data transfer buffer }


Procedure ReadSectors (Var DiskBuffer: Buffer;
                       Side, Track, Drive: integer);
Const
  NumSectors = 9;      { sectors per track }
  ReadService = 2;     { BIOS disk sector read service }

Type

  REGISTERS = record   { emulate the 8086 registers }
                AX, BX, CX, DX, BP, SI, DI, DS, ES, FLAGS: INTEGER
              end;

Var
  REGS: Registers;

begin
  with REGS do
    begin
      AX := (ReadService SHL 8) + NumSectors;
      CX := (Track SHL 8) + 1;
      DX := (Side SHL 8) + Drive;
      ES := Seg (DiskBuffer[1]);
      BX := Ofs (DiskBuffer[1]);
      Intr ($13, REGS);
    end;

end;


Var
  DiskBuffer: Buffer;  { disk transfer buffer }

  i, cluster, entry: Integer;

  whole : boolean;  { true if multiplication has no fractional part

  ir, bad : real;   { bad is the total number of corrupted bytes }


begin
```

Figure 10-20.

CHKDSK program

```
    bad := 0;  { assume no bad sectors }

    { get the sectors containing the FAT }

    ReadSectors (DiskBuffer, 0, 0, SourceDisk);

    { examine the FAT entries for FF8 }

    for cluster := 2 to MaxCluster do
      begin
        ir := cluster * 1.5;    { get the offset }

        i := Trunc (ir);

        if ((cluster * 15) mod 10 = 0) then
          whole := true
        else
          whole := false;

        entry := Ord(DiskBuffer[Offset + i]) +
                 (Ord(DiskBuffer[Offset + i + 1]) shl 8);

        if (whole) then
          entry := entry and $FFF
        else
          entry := entry shr 4;

        if (entry = $ff7) then
          bad := bad + 1024;
      end;

    writeln ('Total bad sectors is ', bad, ' bytes');
end.
```

Figure 10-20.

CHKDSK program (*continued*)

DIRECTORY ENTRIES

Immediately following the FAT entries on each disk, DOS reserves space for directory entries of the files in the root directory. Each file DOS stores on disk requires a 32-byte entry that contains the information shown in Table 10-11.

Table 10-11.

Entry in Directory Structure

Field	Offset
File name	0
Extension	8
Attribute byte	11
Reserved for DOS	12
Time	22
Date	24
Starting cluster number	26
File size	28

Each disk type sets aside a different amount of space for root directory entries. Table 10-12 summarizes the number of files that each disk type can place in the root directory.

The Turbo Pascal program shown in Figure 10-21 reads sectors 6-9 on track 0, side 0, and then sectors 1-3 on track 0, side 1, and displays

Table 10-12.

Number of Files in Root Directory

Disk Type	Directory Sectors	Directory Entries
Single-sided	4	64
Double-sided	7	112
Quad-density	14	224
Fixed disk	32	512

```
Program ReadDirectory;  { Display the files on the disk in drive A }

Const
  NumSectors = 9;         { sectors per track }
  ReadService = 2;        { BIOS read service }
  SectorSize = 512;       { bytes per sector }
  BufferSize = 5000;      { disk transfer buffer size }
  SourceDisk = 0;         { drive A is always the source disk }

Type
  Buffer = array [1..BufferSize] of char;  { disk transfer buffer }
  DirectoryBuffer = string[32];           { 32 byte directory entry
                                                          buffer }

  DirectoryEntry = record
    filename  : string[8];  { 8 character file name }
    extension : string[3];  { 3 character file extension }
    attribute : byte;       { file attribute hidden, archive,
                                                    directory, etc }
    time,                   { time stamp }
    date,                   { date stamp }
    cluster   : integer;    { starting FAT cluster number }
    filesize  : real;       { file size in bytes }
  end;

Procedure ReadSectors (Var DiskBuffer: Buffer;
                       Side, Track, Drive: integer);
Type
  REGISTERS = record
                AX, BX, CX, DX, BP, SI, DI, DS, ES, FLAGS: INTEGER
              end;
Var
  REGS: Registers;   { emulate the 8088 registers }

begin
  with REGS do
    begin
      AX := (ReadService SHL 8) + NumSectors;
      CX := (Track SHL 8) + 1;
      DX := (Side SHL 8) + Drive;
      ES := Seg (DiskBuffer[1]);
      DX := Ofs (DiskBuffer[1]);
      Intr ($13, REGS);
    end;

end;


Procedure DecodeEntry (DirBuffer: DirectoryBuffer;
                       var Entry: DirectoryEntry);

begin
  with entry do
  begin
    filename := Copy (DirBuffer, 1, 8);   { extract the file name }
```

Figure 10-21.

READDIRECTORY program

```
       extension := Copy (DirBuffer, 9, 3);   { extract the extension }
       attribute := Ord(DirBuffer[12]);        { file attribute byte }

       time := Ord(DirBuffer[23]) Shl 8 + Ord(DirBuffer[24]);
       date := Ord(DirBuffer[25]) Shl 8 + Ord(DirBuffer[26]);
       cluster := Ord(DirBuffer[28]) Shl 8 + Ord(DirBuffer[27]);

       filesize := 1.0 * Ord(DirBuffer[29]) +
                 256.0 * Ord(DirBuffer[30]) +
                 256.0 * 256.0 * Ord(DirBuffer[31]) +
                 256.0 * 256.0 * 256.0 * Ord(DirBuffer[32]);
     end;
end;


Function IsValid (FileName: Char) : boolean;

begin
  if (Ord(FileName) <> 0) and (Filename <> Chr(229)) then
    IsValid := True
  else
    IsValid := False;
end;


Var
  DiskBuffer: Buffer;              { disk transfer buffer }
  i, j, k, Track, Side: integer;

  DirBuffer: DirectoryBuffer;      { directory entry buffer }
  Entry: DirectoryEntry;           { 32 byte directory entry }

begin
{ get the first 4 sectors of the directory from side 0, track 0,
  sectors 6-9.  Decode each entry displaying valid file names }

  ReadSectors (DiskBuffer, 0, 0, SourceDisk);

  i :=  5 * SectorSize + 1;              { start at sector 6 }
  while (i <= 9 * SectorSize) do         { end at sector 9 }
    begin
        k := 1;
        for j := i to i + 32 do
          begin
              DirBuffer[k] := DiskBuffer[j];
              k := k + 1;
          end;
        DirBuffer[0] := Chr(32);
        DecodeEntry (DirBuffer, Entry);
        i := i + 32;

        if (IsValid(Entry.filename[1])) then
          begin
```

Figure 10-21.

READDIRECTORY
program (*continued*)

```
                  write (Entry.filename, ' ', entry.extension, ' ',
                      entry.attribute:3);
                  writeln (entry.cluster:5, ' ', entry.filesize:9:0);
              end;
      end;

{ get the last 3 sectors of the directory from side 1, track 0,
  sectors 1-3.  Decode each entry displaying valid file names }

  ReadSectors (DiskBuffer, 1, 0, SourceDisk);

  i := 1;                      { start at sector 1 }
  while (i <= 3 * 512) do  { end at sector 3 }
      begin
          k := 1;
          for j := i to i + 32 do
            begin
                DirBuffer[k] := DiskBuffer[j];
                k := k + 1;
            end;
          DirBuffer[0] := Chr(32);
          DecodeEntry (DirBuffer, Entry);
          i := i + 32;

          if (IsValid(Entry.filename[1])) then
            begin
                write (Entry.filename, ' ', entry.extension, ' ',
                    entry.attribute:3);
                writeln (entry.cluster:5, ' ', entry.filesize:9:0);
            end;
      end;

end.
```

Figure 10-21.

READDIRECTORY
program (*continued*)

each of the entries in the root directory. Assuming that the disk in drive
A contains

```
    Volume in drive A has no label
    Directory of  A:\

    WIN        BAT        54    1-17-87   11:02p
    WS         COM     45056    1-01-80   12:08a
    WSMSCS     OVR     29056    1-01-80   12:26a
    WSOVLY1    OVR     41216    1-01-80   12:26a
    DCOP       PAS      2058    8-08-87    7:45p
    DCOPY      COM     11733    8-08-87    7:45p
    DCOPY      BAK      2018    8-08-87    7:44p
    X          EXE      6082    8-09-87    4:35p
              8 File(s)    117760 bytes free
```

invoking the program results in

```
WIN       BAT   32    2        54
WS        COM   32    3     45056
WSMSCS    OVR   32   47     29056
WSOVLY1   OVR   32  178     41216
DCOPY     PAS   32  219      2038
DCOPY     COM   32  221     11733
DCOPY     BAK   32  233      2018
X         EXE   32  235      6682
```

Note that the program only displays entries with valid file names.

You now have enough pieces to put the disk format puzzle together. When DOS needs to locate a file, it first searches the directory entries for an entry with a matching file name. If DOS finds a matching file, it gets the starting FAT cluster number from the directory entry. DOS then maps the starting cluster number to a sector, as shown here:

Sector = (cluster − 2) * (sectors per cluster) * DataSectorOffset
{DataSectorOffset = 1 (Boot Record) + 4 (FAT sectors) + 7 (directory sectors)}

Since clusters contain multiple sectors, DOS reads the specific number of sectors starting with the first sector number associated with the cluster. Then DOS locates the file's next cluster entry from the FAT and continues retrieving sectors and decoding FAT entries until it finds the end of the file. The flowchart in Figure 10-22 summarizes this processing.

The Turbo Pascal program shown in Figure 10-23 displays the clusters that comprise each file in the root directory of drive A.

FILE DELETION

What happens when DOS deletes a file? Each time DOS deletes a file from disk, it modifies the directory entry for the file such that the first

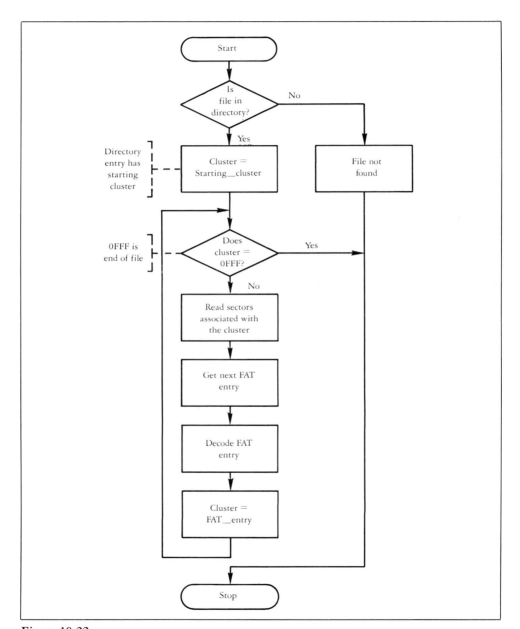

Figure 10-22.

Flowchart of file location process

```
Program ShowClusters;

Const
  NumSectors = 9;            { sectors per track }
  NumSides = 2;              { sides per disk }
  ReadService = 2;           { BIOS read disk sector service }
  SectorSize = 512;          { bytes per sector }
  BufferSize = 5000;         { disk transfer buffer size }
  DataSectorOffset = $C;     { sector offset to data section }
  SectorsPerCluster = 2;     { sectors per cluster }
  SourceDisk = 0;            { drive A is always the source disk }
  Offset = 512;              { Offset to FAT in track 0, side 0 }


Type
  DirectoryBuffer = string[32];   { 32 byte directory entry buffer }

  DirectoryEntry = record
    filename  : string[8];   { 8 character file name }
    extension : string[3];   { 3 character file extension }
    attribute : byte;        { file attribute hidden, archive,
                                                directory, etc }

    time,                    { time stamp }
    date,                    { date stamp }
    cluster   : integer;     { starting FAT cluster number }
    filesize  : real;        { file size in bytes }
  end;

  Buffer = array [1..BufferSize] of char; { disk transfer buffer }


Procedure ReadCluster (Var DiskBuffer: Buffer;
                       Side, Track, Sector, Drive: integer);

Type
  REGISTERS = record
                AX, BX, CX, DX, BP, SI, DI, DS, ES, FLAGS: INTEGER
              end;
Var
  REGS: Registers;    { emulate 8088 registers }

begin
  with REGS do
    begin
      AX := (ReadService SHL 8) + SectorsPerCluster;
      CX := (Track SHL 8) + Sector;
      DX := (Side SHL 8) + Drive;
      ES := Seg (DiskBuffer[1]);
      BX := Ofs (DiskBuffer[1]);
      Intr ($13, REGS);
    end;

end;
```

Figure 10-23.

SHOWCLUSTERS program

```
Function IsValid (FileName: char) : boolean;

begin
  if (Ord(FileName) <> 0) and (Filename <> Chr(229)) then
    IsValid := True
  else
    IsValid := False;
end;


Procedure DecodeEntry (DirBuffer: DirectoryBuffer;
                       var Entry: DirectoryEntry);


begin
  with entry do
    begin
      filename := Copy (DirBuffer, 1, 8);    { extract the file name }
      extension := Copy (DirBuffer, 9, 3);   { extract the extension }
      attribute := Ord(DirBuffer[12]);        { file attribute byte }

      time := Ord(DirBuffer[23]) Shl 8 + Ord(DirBuffer[24]);
      date := Ord(DirBuffer[25]) Shl 8 + Ord(DirBuffer[26]);
      cluster := Ord(DirBuffer[28]) Shl 8 + Ord(DirBuffer[27]);

      filesize := 1.0 * Ord(DirBuffer[29]) +
                  256.0 * Ord(DirBuffer[30]) +
                  256.0 * 256.0 * Ord(DirBuffer[31]) +
                  256.0 * 256.0 * 256.0 * Ord(DirBuffer[32]);
    end;
end;


Procedure ReadSectors (Var DiskBuffer: Buffer;
                       Side, Track, Drive: integer);
Type
  REGISTERS = record
                AX, BX, CX, DX, BP, SI, DI, DS, ES, FLAGS: INTEGER
              end;
Var
  REGS: Registers;    { emulate the 8086 registers }


begin
  with REGS do
    begin
      AX := (ReadService SHL 8) + NumSectors;
      CX := (Track SHL 8) + 1;
      DX := (Side SHL 8) + Drive;
      ES := Seg (DiskBuffer[1]);
      BX := Ofs (DiskBuffer[1]);
      Intr ($13, REGS);
    end;

end;
```

Figure 10-23.

SHOWCLUSTERS
program (*continued*)

```
Var
  DataBuffer, DiskBuffer, FATBuffer: Buffer;
  FAT_i, i, j, k: integer;

  DirBuffer: DirectoryBuffer;        { directory entry buffer }
  Entry: DirectoryEntry;             { 32 byte directory entry }

  Sector: integer;

  Cluster, ClusterEntry: Integer;

  Whole : boolean;

  Ir : real;

begin

{ get the first 4 sectors of the directory from side 0, track 0,
  sectors 6-9.  Decode each entry displaying valid file names }

   ReadSectors (DiskBuffer, 0, 0, SourceDisk);
   ReadCluster (FatBuffer, 0, 0, 1, SourceDisk);

   i :=  5 * SectorSize + 1;         { start at sector 6 }
   while (i <= 9 * SectorSize) do    { end at sector 9 }
      begin
         k := 1;
         for j := i to i + 32 do
            begin
               DirBuffer[k] := DiskBuffer[j];
               k := k + 1;
            end;

         DirBuffer[0] := Chr(32);
         DecodeEntry (DirBuffer, Entry);
         i := i + 32;

         if (IsValid(Entry.filename[1])) then
            begin
               writeln (Entry.filename, ' ', entry.extension, '  ',
                        Entry.filesize:9:0, ' bytes');
               writeln ;

               Cluster := Entry.cluster;

               repeat
                  Sector := (Cluster - 2) * SectorsPerCluster +
                            DataSectorOffset;

                  writeln ('Cluster ', Cluster:5, '  Sector ', Sector);

                  Ir := cluster * 1.5;
                  FAT_i := Trunc (ir);

                  if ((Cluster * 15) mod 10 = 0) then
```

Figure 10-23.

SHOWCLUSTERS
program (*continued*)

```
                      Whole := true
                 else
                   Whole := false;

                 ClusterEntry := Ord(FatBuffer[Offset + FAT_i]) +
                          (Ord(FatBuffer[Offset + FAT_i + 1]) Shl 8);

                 if (whole) then
                   ClusterEntry := ClusterEntry and $FFF
                 else
                   ClusterEntry := ClusterEntry shr 4;

                 Cluster := ClusterEntry;
               until (Cluster > $ff0);
               writeln ;
               writeln ;
               write ('Press Enter ');
               readln ;
               writeln ;
             end;

      end;

  { get the last 3 sectors of the directory from side 1, track 0,
    sectors 1-3.  Decode each entry displaying valid file names }

    ReadSectors (DiskBuffer, 1, 0, SourceDisk);

    i := 1;                      { start at sector 1 }
    while (i <= 3 * 512) do   { end at sector 3 }
       begin
          k := 1;
          for j := i to i + 32 do
            begin
               DirBuffer[k] := DiskBuffer[j];
               k := k + 1;
            end;
          DirBuffer[0] := Chr(32);
          DecodeEntry (DirBuffer, Entry);
          i := i + 32;

          if (IsValid(Entry.filename[1])) then
            begin
               writeln (Entry.filename, ' ', entry.extension, ' ',
                        Entry.filesize:9:0, ' bytes');
               writeln ;

               Cluster := Entry.cluster;

               repeat
                 Sector := (Cluster - 2) * SectorsPerCluster +
                           DataSectorOffset;

                 writeln ('Cluster ', Cluster:5, '  Sector ', Sector);

                 Ir := cluster * 1.5;
```

Figure 10-23.

SHOWCLUSTERS

program (*continued*)

```
              FAT_i := Trunc (ir);

              if ((Cluster * 15) mod 16 = 0) then
                Whole := true
              else
                Whole := false;

              ClusterEntry := Ord(FatBuffer[Offset + FAT_i]) +
                       (Ord(FatBuffer[Offset + FAT_i + 1]) Shl 8);

              if (Whole) then
                ClusterEntry := ClusterEntry and $FFF
              else
                ClusterEntry := ClusterEntry shr 4;

              Cluster := ClusterEntry;
            until (Cluster > $ff0);
            writeln ;
            writeln ;
            write ('Press Enter ');
            readln ;
            writeln ;
          end;
      end;
  end.
```

Figure 10-23.

SHOWCLUSTERS
program (*continued*)

character in the file name is hexadecimal E5. The remainder of the directory entry remains intact. The Turbo Pascal program shown in Figure 10 - 24 displays all of the files you have deleted from drive A. Note that when DOS deletes a file, it does not actually delete the contents of the file from disk.

Using this basic knowledge, you can develop routines to undelete files. However, several obstacles stand in the way of your file recovery. When you delete a file, DOS sets each of the file's cluster entries back to 0, signifying that they are available for use by other files. If you delete one file and then perform other file-manipulation operations, DOS will likely use the clusters just released for the deleted file. In such cases, file recovery is impossible. However, if you have just deleted the file, you can likely recover it. Text files (such as word processing documents or programs) are the easiest to recover since their contents are readily

```
Program ListDeletedFiles;    { Display all of the deleted files
                               on the disk in drive A }

Const
  NumSectors = 9;        { sectors per track }
  NumSides = 2;          { sides per disk }
  ReadService = 2;       { BIOS read disk sector service }
  SectorSize = 512;      { bytes per sector }
  BufferSize = 5000;     { disk transfer buffer size }
  SourceDisk = 0;        { disk A is the source drive }

Type
  Buffer = array [1..BufferSize] of char;   { disk transfer buffer }
  DirectoryBuffer = string[32];                 { directory entry buffer }


  DirectoryEntry = record
    filename  : string[8];   { 8 character file name }
    extension : string[3];   { 3 character file extension }
    attribute : byte;        { file attribute byte }
    time,                    { file time stamp }
    date,                    { file date stamp }
    cluster   : integer;     { starting cluster number }
    filesize  : real;        { file size in bytes }
  end;


Procedure ReadSectors (Var DiskBuffer: Buffer;
                       Side, Track, Drive: integer);

Type
  REGISTERS = record
                  AX, BX, CX, DX, BP, SI, DI, DS, ES, FLAGS: INTEGER
              end;
Var
  REGS: Registers;   { emulate the 8088 registers }


begin
  with REGS do
    begin
      AX := (ReadService SHL 8) + NumSectors;
      CX := (Track SHL 8) + 1;
      DX := (Side SHL 8) + Drive;
      ES := Seg (DiskBuffer[1]);
      BX := Ofs (DiskBuffer[1]);
      Intr ($13, REGS);
    end;

end;


Procedure DecodeEntry (DirBuffer: DirectoryBuffer;
                       var Entry: DirectoryEntry);
```

Figure 10-24.

LISTDELETEFILES program

```
begin
  with Entry do
    begin
{ decode the file name and extension }
      filename := Copy (DirBuffer, 1, 8);
      extension := Copy (DirBuffer, 9, 3);

{ get the file attribute byte }
      attribute := Ord(DirBuffer[12]);

      time := Ord(DirBuffer[23]) Shl 8 + Ord(DirBuffer[24]);
      date := Ord(DirBuffer[25]) Shl 8 + Ord(DirBuffer[26]);

{ get the starting cluster number }
      cluster := Ord(DirBuffer[28]) Shl 8 + Ord(DirBuffer[27]);

{ get the file size in bytes }
      filesize := 1.0 * Ord(DirBuffer[29]) +
                  256.0 * Ord(DirBuffer[30]) +
                  256.0 * 256.0 * Ord(DirBuffer[31]) +
                  256.0 * 256.0 * 256.0 * Ord(DirBuffer[32]);
    end;
end;

Var
  DiskBuffer: Buffer;                { disk transfer buffer }

  i, j, k, Track, Side: integer;

  DirBuffer: DirectoryBuffer;        { directory entry buffer }
  Entry: DirectoryEntry;             { 32 byte directory entry }

begin

{ read sectors 6-9 from track 0, side 0 which contain the
  first 4 sectors of directory entries }

  ReadSectors (DiskBuffer, 0, 0, SourceDisk);
  i := 5 * SectorSize + 1;             { start at sector 6 }
  while (i <= 9 * SectorSize) do        { end with sector 9 }
    begin
      k := 1;
      for j := i to i + 32 do
        begin
          DirBuffer[k] := DiskBuffer[j];
          k := k + 1;
        end;
      DirBuffer[0] := Chr(32);
      DecodeEntry (DirBuffer, Entry);
      i := i + 32;

      if (Ord(Entry.Filename[1]) = $E5) then
        begin
          Writeln (Entry.filename, '.', Entry.extension, '  ',
```

Figure 10-24.

LISTDELETEFILES program
(*continued*)

```
                        Entry.attribute, ' ',Entry.cluster, ' ',
                            Entry.filesize:9:0);
                end;
        end;

{ read sectors 1-3 from track 0, side 1 which contain the last
  3 sectors of directory entries }

    ReadSectors (DiskBuffer, 0, 0, SourceDisk);
    i := 1;                              { start at sector 1 }
    while (i <= 3 * SectorSize) do       { end with sector 3 }
        begin
            k := 1;
            for j := i to i + 32 do
                begin
                    DirBuffer[k] := DiskBuffer[j];
                    k := k + 1;
                end;
            DirBuffer[0] := Chr(32);
            DecodeEntry (DirBuffer, Entry);
            i := i + 32;

            if (Ord(Entry.Filename[1]) = $E5) then
                begin
                    Writeln (Entry.filename, '.', Entry.extension, ' ',
                         Entry.attribute, ' ',Entry.cluster, ' ',
                            Entry.filesize:9:0);
                end;
        end;

end.
```

Figure 10-24.

LISTDELETEFILES program
(*continued*)

identifiable. Also, if you only recover a portion of a text file, you can still edit its contents to replace missing text.

The Turbo Pascal program shown in Figure 10-25 provides a general-purpose file-recovery system. The program examines the disk in drive A and displays the contents of each sector on the screen,

```
Program ExamineDisk;

Const
  NumSectors = 9;
  NumSides = 2;
  ReadService = 2;
  SectorSize = 512;
  NumTracks = 40;
  BufferSize = 5000;
  Drive = 0;

Type
  REGISTERS = record
                  AX, BX, CX, DX, BP, SI, DI, DS, ES, FLAGS: INTEGER
              end;

  Buffer = array [1..BufferSize] of char;


Procedure ReadSectors (Var DiskBuffer: Buffer;
                        Side, Track, Drive: integer);

Var
  REGS: Registers;

begin
  with REGS do
    begin
      AX := (ReadService SHL 8) + NumSectors;
      CX := (Track SHL 8) + 1;
      DX := (Side SHL 8) + Drive;
      ES := Seg (DiskBuffer[1]);
      BX := Ofs (DiskBuffer[1]);
      Intr ($13, REGS);
    end;
end;


Procedure DisplaySector (SectorBuffer: Buffer;
                         Side, Track, Sector: integer;
                         var Status: char);

Var
  i, j, index: integer;
  Response: char;

begin
      ClrScr;
      gotoxy (0, 0);
      writeln ;
      writeln ('Side:', Side:2, ' Track:', Track:3, ' Sector:',
              Sector:2);
      writeln ;
```

Figure 10-25.

EXAMINEDISK program

```
      for i := 1 to 8 do
        begin
         writeln ;
         for j := 1 to 64 do
          begin
           index := (i-1) * 64 + j;
           if (Ord(SectorBuffer[index]) < 128) then
             begin
              if (Ord(SectorBuffer[index]) = 9) then
               write (SectorBuffer[index])

              else if (Ord(SectorBuffer[index]) >= 32) then
               write (SectorBuffer[index])
              else
                write ('^');
            end
           else
                write ('^');
          end;
        end;

        writeln ;
        writeln ;
        repeat
          gotoxy (1, 22);
          write ('Append to E:RECOVER.TXT (Y/N or E to Exit)? ');
          readln (Response);
        until (UpCase(Response) = 'Y') or (Upcase(Response) = 'N') or
              (UpCase(Response) = 'E') ;

        Status := UpCase(Response);
end;


Var
   SectorBuffer, DiskBuffer: Buffer;
   i, j, k, Track, Side: integer;
   Status: Char;

   RecoverFile : Text[$FFF];

begin
   { Open the file E:RECOVER.TXT }
   {$I-}
   Assign (RecoverFile, 'D:RECOVER.TXT');
   Rewrite (RecoverFile);
   If (IOResult <> 0) then
     begin
       writeln ('Unable to open RECOVER.TXT');
       Halt ;
     end;


   For Track := 0 to NumTracks - 1 do
```

Figure 10-25.

EXAMINEDISK program
(*continued*)

```
For Side := 0 to NumSides - 1 do
   begin
      ReadSectors (DiskBuffer, Side, Track, Drive);
      for i := 1 to NumSectors do
       begin
         for j := 1 to SectorSize do
            SectorBuffer[j] := DiskBuffer[(i-1) * 512 + j];

         DisplaySector (SectorBuffer, Side, Track, I, Status);

         Case Status of
          'E': begin
                 Close (RecoverFile);
                 Halt ;
               end;
          'Y': for K := 1 to SectorSize do
                 write (RecoverFile, SectorBuffer[K]);
         end;
       end;
   end;
end .
```

Figure 10-25.

EXAMINEDISK program
(*continued*)

prompting you as to whether you want the sector appended to the file RESTORE.TXT on drive B:

```
Side: 0 Track:  1 Sector: 1

gVVUTVTVUTTTTTTTSTTRRTRfTTTTSSSTTfTTTTVTVU^^^         ^^^^^^^^^
^^^^^^^^^^^^^^^<^N^^^^^^^^^^^^I^G^Y^d^X^f^j^L^y^^^^^^^^"^+^8^A^I^
W^^^o^^^^^^^^^^^^^^^^^^^^^^^^^YN ƏƏƏƏ ^ now ^^^ ^ now ^^ ^^^^ I
NTERNAL ERROR^FATAL^^^^^ NAME OF ^ TO ^FILE^MailMerge ^PRINT a f
ile  ^^^^^^^^^^^ ^^^^^^^^^^^^^^^^^^^^^^***  FATAL ERR F25: 1.0
T ENOUGH MEMORY^^$^^ File ^ not found. Menus & ^ messages will
display as ƏƏƏƏ only. ^^^  WAIT  ^^ Print\paused ^MailMerge-^pri
nting\^  \not\editing\^^^^^^^^ ^^^^^^^^^^ ^^ ^^^^ ^ ^^^^^^^^^^

Append to B:RECOVER.TXT (Y/N or E to Exit)?
```

If you enter "**N**." the program simply reads the next appropriate sector. Indeed, you may have to respond to several prompts to restore a file, but that is much less painful than losing a critical document or program.

Many file-recovery programs perform a "best guess" file recovery. In other words, given the starting cluster number and file size from a directory entry, the program repeatedly places the next available cluster into the recovery file until sufficient clusters are recovered to equal the file's original size. However, these programs are "best guess." It is very common to wind up with sectors from other files intermixed.

SURE-KILL DELETIONS

If many corporate executives were aware that DOS power users could undelete memos and documents previously deleted, they would instantly panic. To eliminate their fears, the Turbo Pascal program **KILLDISK** (shown in Figure 10-26) writes a series of zeros to each sector on the disk and overwrites the previous contents.

In a similar manner, you can use the tools provided in this chapter to write a program called **KILLFILE**, which uses FAT entries to locate a file's sectors and then overwrites them with zeros.

```
Program KillDisk;   { Overwrite the contents of the floppy disk
                      in drive A with zeros }

Const
   NumSectors = 9;        { sectors per track }
   NumSides = 2;          { sides per disk }
   NumTracks = 40;        { tracks per side }
   WriteService = 3;      { BIOS disk sector write service }
   TargetDisk = 0;        { drive A is the target disk }
   BufferSize = 5000;     { size of the disk transfer buffer }

Type
   Buffer = array [1..BufferSize] of char;    { disk transfer buffer }


Procedure WriteSectors (DiskBuffer: Buffer;
                        Side, Track, Drive: integer);
```

Figure 10-26.

KILLDISK program

```
Type
  REGISTERS = record
                AX, BX, CX, DX, BP, SI, DI, DS, ES, FLAGS: INTEGER
              end;

Var
  REGS: Registers;    { emulate the 8088 registers }

begin
  with REGS do
    begin
      AX := (WriteService SHL 8) + NumSectors;
      CX := (Track SHL 8) + 1;
      DX := (Side SHL 8) + Drive;
      ES := Seg (DiskBuffer[1]);
      BX := Ofs (DiskBuffer[1]);
      Intr ($13, REGS);
    end;
end;

Var
  DiskBuffer: Buffer;    { disk transfer buffer }
  I, Track, Side: integer;

begin

{ Create the overwrite buffer }

 For I := 1 to BufferSize do
   DiskBuffer[I] := Chr(0);

{ Overwrite each sector on drive A }

  For Side := 0 to NumSides - 1 do
    For Track := 0 to NumTracks - 1 do
         WriteSectors (DiskBuffer, Side, Track, TargetDisk);
end.
```

Figure 10-26.

KILLDISK program
(*continued*)

READING A DIRECTORY FILE

Although the limited number of sectors available for directory entries restricts the number of files that the root directory can store, DOS subdirectories have unlimited growth capabilities. They are simply DOS files that contain the 32-byte directory entry previously examined. As discussed, each directory entry contains an attribute byte. For DOS directory files, this attribute byte is 16. Knowing this, the Turbo Pascal program shown in Figure 10-27 uses the attribute byte of the directory entry to list all of the directory files in the root directory of the disk in drive A.

```
Program ShowDirectories;   { List the directories on the disk
                             in drive A }

Const
   NumSectors = 9;         { sectors per track }
   ReadService = 2;        { BIOS read service }
   SectorSize = 512;       { bytes per sector }
   BufferSize = 5000;      { disk transfer buffer size }
   SourceDisk = 0;         { drive A is always the source disk }

Type
   Buffer = array [1..BufferSize] of char;   { disk transfer buffer }
   DirectoryBuffer = string[32];             { 32 byte directory entry
                                               buffer }

   DirectoryEntry = record
      filename  : string[8];  { 8 character file name }
      extension : string[3];  { 3 character file extension }
      attribute : byte;       { file attribute hidden, archive,
                                               directory, etc }
      time,                   { time stamp }
      date,                   { date stamp }
      cluster   : integer;    { starting FAT cluster number }
      filesize  : real;       { file size in bytes }
   end;

Procedure ReadSectors (Var DiskBuffer: Buffer;
                       Side, Track, Drive: integer);
Type
   REGISTERS = record
               AX, BX, CX, DX, BP, SI, DI, DS, ES, FLAGS: INTEGER
               end;
Var
   REGS: Registers;   { emulate the 8088 registers }
```

Figure 10-27.

SHOWDIRECTORIES program

```
begin
  with REGS do
    begin
      AX := (ReadService SHL 8) + NumSectors;
      CX := (Track SHL 8) + 1;
      DX := (Side SHL 8) + Drive;
      ES := Seg (DiskBuffer[1]);
      BX := Ofs (DiskBuffer[1]);
      Intr ($13, REGS);
    end;

end;


Procedure DecodeEntry (DirBuffer: DirectoryBuffer;
                       var Entry: DirectoryEntry);

begin

  with entry do
    begin
      filename := Copy (DirBuffer, 1, 8);    { extract the file name }
      extension := Copy (DirBuffer, 9, 3);   { extract the extension }
      attribute := Ord(DirBuffer[12]);       { file attribute byte }

      time := Ord(DirBuffer[23]) Shl 8 + Ord(DirBuffer[24]);
      date := Ord(DirBuffer[25]) Shl 8 + Ord(DirBuffer[26]);
      cluster := Ord(DirBuffer[28]) Shl 8 + Ord(DirBuffer[27]);

      filesize := 1.0 * Ord(DirBuffer[29]) +
                256.0 * Ord(DirBuffer[30]) +
                256.0 * 256.0 * Ord(DirBuffer[31]) +
                256.0 * 256.0 * 256.0 * Ord(DirBuffer[32]);

    end;
end;

Function IsValid (FileName: Char) : boolean;

begin
  if (Ord(FileName) <> 0) and (FileName <> Chr(299)) then
    IsValid := True
  else
    IsValid := False;
end;


Var
  DiskBuffer: Buffer;                { disk transfer buffer }
  i, j, k, Track, Side: integer;
```

Figure 10-27.

SHOWDIRECTORIES program

(*continued*)

```
    DirBuffer: DirectoryBuffer;       { directory entry buffer }
    Entry: DirectoryEntry;            { 32 byte directory entry }

begin

{ get the first 4 sectors of the directory from side 0, track 0,
  sectors 6-9.  Decode each entry displaying valid file names }

    ReadSectors (DiskBuffer, 0, 0, SourceDisk);

    i := 5 * SectorSize + 1;              { start at sector 6 }
    while (i <= 9 * SectorSize) do        { end at sector 9 }
       begin
            k := 1;
            for j := i to i + 32 do
              begin
                  DirBuffer[k] := DiskBuffer[j];
                  k := k + 1;
              end;
            DirBuffer[0] := Chr(32);
            DecodeEntry (DirBuffer, Entry);
            i := i + 32;

            If (Entry.Attribute = 16) then

            if (IsValid(Entry.filename[1])) then
             begin
                writeln (Entry.filename, '  <DIR>  ',
                     entry.cluster:5);
               end;
       end;

{ get the last 3 sectors of the directory from side 1, track 0,
  sectors 1-3.  Decode each entry displaying valid file names }

    ReadSectors (DiskBuffer, 1, 0, SourceDisk);

    i := 1;                      { start at sector 1 }
    while (i <= 3 * 512) do  { end at sector 3 }
       begin
            k := 1;
            for j := i to i + 32 do
              begin
                  DirBuffer[k] := DiskBuffer[j];
                  k := k + 1;
              end;
            DirBuffer[0] := Chr(32);
            DecodeEntry (DirBuffer, Entry);
            i := i + 32;
```

Figure 10-27.

SHOWDIRECTORIES program
(*continued*)

```
            If (Entry.Attribute = 16) then
             if (IsValid(Entry.filename[1])) then
              begin
                writeln (Entry.filename, '  <DIR>  ',
                    entry.cluster:5);
              end;
          end;

      end.
```

Figure 10-27.

SHOWDIRECTORIES program
(*continued*)

By reading the sectors associated with a directory file, you can decode file names, as shown in Figure 10-28.

```
Program Tree;

Const
   NumSectors = 9;            { sectors per track }
   NumSides = 2;              { sides per disk }
   ReadService = 2;           { BIOS read disk sector service }
   SectorSize = 512;          { bytes per sector }
   BufferSize = 5000;         { disk transfer buffer size }
   DataSectorOffset = 5C;     { sector offset to data section }
   SectorsPerCluster = 2;     { sectors per cluster }
   SourceDisk = 0;            { drive A is always the source disk }
   Offset = 513;              { Offset to FAT in track 0, side 0 }

Type
   DirectoryBuffer = string[32];   { 32 byte directory entry buffer }
```

Figure 10-28.

TREE program

```
   DirectoryEntry = record
      filename  : string[8];   { 8 character file name }
      extension : string[3];   { 3 character file extension }
      attribute : byte;        { file attribute hidden, archive,
                                                  directory, etc }
      time,                    { time stamp }
      date,                    { date stamp }
      cluster   : integer;     { starting FAT cluster number }
      filesize  : real;        { file size in bytes }
   end;

   Buffer = array [1..BufferSize] of char; { disk transfer buffer }


Procedure ReadCluster (Var DiskBuffer: Buffer;
                       Side, Track, Sector, Drive: integer);

Type
   REGISTERS = record
                  AX, BX, CX, DX, BP, SI, DI, DS, ES, FLAGS: INTEGER
               end;
Var
   REGS: Registers;   { emulate 8088 registers }

begin
   with REGS do
      begin
         AX := (ReadService SHL 8) + SectorsPerCluster;
         CX := (Track SHL 8) + Sector;
         DX := (Side SHL 8) + Drive;
         ES := Seg (DiskBuffer[1]);
         BX := Ofs (DiskBuffer[1]);
         Intr ($13, REGS);
      end;

end;

Function IsValid (FileName: char) : boolean;

begin
   if (Ord(FileName) <> 0) and (Filename <> Chr(299)) then
      IsValid := True
   else
      IsValid := False;
end;

Procedure DecodeEntry (DirBuffer: DirectoryBuffer;
                       var Entry: DirectoryEntry);

begin
   with entry do
      begin
         filename := Copy (DirBuffer, 1, 8);    { extract the file name }
         extension := Copy (DirBuffer, 9, 3);   { extract the extension }
         attribute := Ord(DirBuffer[12]);       { file attribute byte }
```

Figure 10-28.

TREE program (*continued*)

```
           time := Ord(DirBuffer[23]) Shl 8 + Ord(DirBuffer[24]);
           date := Ord(DirBuffer[25]) Shl 8 + Ord(DirBuffer[26]);
           cluster := Ord(DirBuffer[28]) Shl 8 + Ord(DirBuffer[27]);

           filesize := 1.0 * Ord(DirBuffer[29]) +
                       256.0 * Ord(DirBuffer[30]) +
                       256.0 * 256.0 * Ord(DirBuffer[31]) +
                       256.0 * 256.0 * 256.0 * Ord(DirBuffer[32]);
      end;
end;


Procedure ReadSectors (Var DiskBuffer: Buffer;
                       Side, Track, Drive: integer);
Type
  REGISTERS = record
                AX, BX, CX, DX, BP, SI, DI, DS, ES, FLAGS: INTEGER
              end;
Var
  REGS: Registers;    { emulate the 8088 registers }

begin
  with REGS do
    begin
      AX := (ReadService SHL 8) + NumSectors;
      CX := (Track SHL 8) + 1;
      DX := (Side SHL 8) + Drive;
      ES := Seg (DiskBuffer[1]);
      BX := Ofs (DiskBuffer[1]);
      Intr ($13, REGS);
    end;

end;


Var
  DataBuffer, DiskBuffer, FATBuffer: Buffer;
  FAT_i, i, j, k, l, m: integer;

  SubDirBuffer,
  DirBuffer: DirectoryBuffer;        { directory entry buffer }
  Entry: DirectoryEntry;             { 32 byte directory entry }

  Track, Side, Sector_Offset, Sector: integer;

  Cluster, ClusterEntry: Integer;

  Whole : boolean;

  lr : real;

begin

{ get the first 4 sectors of the directory from side 0, track 0,
  sectors 6-9.  Decode each entry displaying valid file names }
```

Figure 10-28.

TREE program (*continued*)

```
ReadSectors (DiskBuffer, 0, 0, SourceDisk);
ReadCluster (FatBuffer, 0, 0, 1, SourceDisk);

i := 5 * SectorSize + 1;           { start at sector 6 }
while (i <= 9 * SectorSize) do      { end at sector 9 }
   begin
      k := 1;
      for j := i to i + 32 do
        begin
           DirBuffer[k] := DiskBuffer[j];
           k := k + 1;
        end;

      DirBuffer[0] := Chr(32);
      DecodeEntry (DirBuffer, Entry);
      i := i + 32;

      if (Entry.Attribute = 16) then
       if (IsValid(Entry.filename[1])) then
        begin
           Writeln (Entry.filename, '  <DIR>  ');
           Writeln ;

           Cluster := Entry.cluster;

           repeat
              Sector := (Cluster - 2) * SectorsPerCluster +
                        DataSectorOffset;

              writeln ('Cluster ', Cluster:5, '  Sector ', Sector);
              writeln;

              track := sector div 18;

         sector_offset := sector mod 9 + 1;

         if ((sector div 9) mod 2 = 1) then
            side := 1
         else
            side := 0;

         ReadCluster (DataBuffer, side, track,
                     sector_offset, 0);

         L := 1;
         while (L <= 2 * SectorSize) do
            begin
              for M := 1 to 32 do
                 begin
                    SubDirBuffer[M] := DataBuffer[L];
                    L := L + 1;
                 end;

              SubDirBuffer[0] := Chr(32);
```

Figure 10-28.

TREE program (*continued*)

```
                    DecodeEntry (SubDirBuffer, Entry);

              if (IsValid(Entry.filename[1])) then
                begin
                  writeln (Entry.filename, ' ',
                              entry.extension, ' ',
                      Entry.filesize:9:0, ' bytes');
                end;
            end;

        Ir := cluster * 1.5;
        FAT_i := Trunc (ir);

        if ((Cluster * 15) mod 10 = 0) then
          Whole := true
        else
          Whole := false;

        ClusterEntry := Ord(FatBuffer[Offset + FAT_i]) +
                    (Ord(FatBuffer[Offset + FAT_i + 1]) Shl 8);

        if (whole) then
          ClusterEntry := ClusterEntry and $FFF
        else
          ClusterEntry := ClusterEntry shr 4;

        Cluster := ClusterEntry;
      until (Cluster > $ff0);
      writeln ;
      writeln ;
      write ('Press Enter ');
      readln ;
      writeln ;
    end;

  end;

{ get the last 3 sectors of the directory from side 1, track 0,
  sectors 1-3.  Decode each entry displaying valid file names }

  ReadSectors (DiskBuffer, 1, 0, SourceDisk);

  i := 1;                  { start at sector 1 }
  while (i <= 3 * 512) do  { end at sector 3 }
    begin
      k := 1;
      for j := i to i + 32 do
        begin
          DirBuffer[k] := DiskBuffer[j];
          k := k + 1;
        end;

      DirBuffer[0] := Chr(32);
      DecodeEntry (DirBuffer, Entry);
      i := i + 32;
```

Figure 10-28.

TREE program (*continued*)

```
        if (Entry.Attribute = 16) then
         if (IsValid(Entry.filename[1])) then
          begin
            writeln (Entry.filename, '   <DIR>   ');
            writeln ;

            Cluster := Entry.cluster;

            repeat
              Sector := (Cluster - 2) * SectorsPerCluster +
                          DataSectorOffset;

              writeln ('Cluster ', Cluster:5, '  Sector ', Sector);
              writeln;

              track := sector div 18;

              sector_offset := sector mod 9 + 1;

              if ((sector div 9) mod 2 = 1) then
                side := 1
              else
                side := 0;

              ReadCluster (DataBuffer, side, track,
                           sector_offset, 0);

              L := 1;
              while (L <= 2 * SectorSize) do
                begin
                  for M := 1 to 32 do
                    begin
                      SubDirBuffer[M] := DataBuffer[L];
                      L := L + 1;
                    end;

                  SubDirBuffer[0] := Chr(32);

                  DecodeEntry (SubDirBuffer, Entry);

                  if (IsValid(Entry.filename[1])) then
                    begin
                      writeln (Entry.filename, ' ',
                               entry.extension, ' ',
                             Entry.filesize:9:0, ' bytes');
                    end;
                end;


            Ir := cluster * 1.5;
            FAT_i := Trunc (ir);
```

Figure 10-28.

TREE program (*continued*)

```
                    if ((Cluster * 15) mod 16 = 0) then
                       Whole := true
                    else
                       Whole := false;

                    ClusterEntry := Ord(FatBuffer[Offset + FAT_i]) +
                            (Ord(FatBuffer[Offset + FAT_i + 1]) Shl 8);

                    if (whole) then
                       ClusterEntry := ClusterEntry and $FFF
                    else
                       ClusterEntry := ClusterEntry shr 4;

                    Cluster := ClusterEntry;
                 until (Cluster > $ff0);
                 writeln ;
                 writeln ;
                 write ('Press Enter ');
                 readln ;
                 writeln ;
              end;
         end;
    end.
```

Figure 10-28.

TREE program (*continued*)

EXTRA FEATURES

Now that you fully understand DOS disk manipulation, you should be well on your way to developing routines such as TREE and RECOVER. In addition to the low-level routines that you have just been using to read and write sectors, DOS provides several system services that should prove useful in your application development. For example, the following function returns the amount of free disk space:

```
procedure Get_Free_Disk_Space (DRIVE: byte;
                           var SPACE: real;
                           var STATUS: byte);

   var
       REGS: REGISTERS;   {AX, BX, CX, DX, BP, SI, DI, DS, ES, FLAGS}
```

```
begin
      with REGS do
         begin

{set AX to request the current free disk space for the drive
 specified in DX}
         AX := $3600;
         DX := DRIVE;

{invoke the DOS interrupt which returns the free disk space}
         MSDos (REGS);

{test the status of the operation and return the amount of
 free disk space if the operation was successful}
         if (AX = $FFFF) then    {error in operation}
            begin
              STATUS := 1;          {return error status code}
              SPACE := -1;
            end
         else
            begin                   {successful operation}
              STATUS := 0;
              SPACE := 1.0 * AX * BX * CX;   {free space}
            end;
      end;
end;
```

Likewise, the following function returns the current disk drive (A=0, B=1, C=2):

```
function Get_Current_Drive: byte;

var
      REGS: REGISTERS;  {AX, BX, CX, DX, BP, SI, DI, DS, ES, FLAGS}

begin
      with REGS do
         begin

{set AX to request the current drive}
         AX := $1900;

{invoke the DOS interrupt which returns the current drive}
         MSDos (REGS);

{return the current drive}
         Get_Current_Drive := Lo(AX);
      end;
end;
```

Similarly, the following routine sets the current disk drive:

```
procedure Set_Current_Drive (DRIVE: byte);

var
    REGS: REGISTERS;   {AX, BX, CX, DX, BP, SI, DI, DS, ES, FLAGS}
begin
    with REGS do
      begin
{set the registers to select the current drive}
        AX := $E00;          {DOS function code}
        DX := DRIVE;

{invoke the DOS interrupt which selects the current drive}
        MSDos (REGS);
      end;
end;
```

The following function allows you to turn disk verification on and off from within a software program in a manner similar to the DOS VERIFY command. Each time DOS reads or writes data from disk, it manipulates sectors. For example, if you issue the command

```
A> COPY SOURCE.DAT TARGET.DAT
```

DOS will read a sector from a file SOURCE.DAT and then write the sector to the file TARGET.DAT. DOS continues this process until it has read and written all of the sectors contained in the file SOURCE.DAT. The flowchart in Figure 10-29 illustrates this processing.

Although unlikely, a serious problem can occur when the write operation that writes the contents of SOURCE.DAT to TARGET.DAT

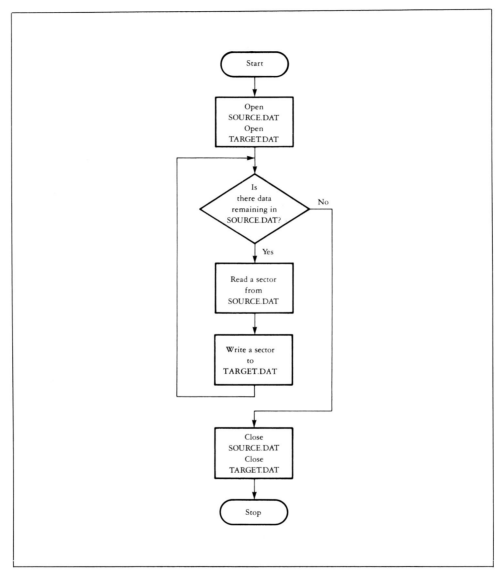

Figure 10-29.

Process of DOS reading and writing
sectors

incorrectly records the information in the target file and leaves the files different. Normally, DOS will not recognize this error unless you have disk verification turned on. The DOS VERIFY command allows you to turn on disk verification.

With disk verification enables, each time DOS reads from SOURCE. DAT and writes it to TARGET.DAT, DOS will reread the sector written to ensure that it is identical to the sector read from SOURCE.DAT. If it is, DOS continues. If it is not, DOS raises an error. This processing is summarized in the flowchart shown in Figure 10-30.

The routine becomes the following:

```
procedure Set_Verify (Status: byte);   { status = 1 on,
                                          status = 0 off }

Type
  REGISTERS = record
                 AX, EX, CX, DX, BP, SI, DI, DS, ES, FLAGS: INTEGER
                 end;
var
    REGS: REGISTERS;   {AX, BX, CX, DX, BP, SI, DI, DS, ES, FLAGS}

begin
     with REGS do
        begin
{set the registers to select the current drive}
         AX := $2E00 + STATUS;        {DOS function code}

{invoke the DOS interrupt which selects the current drive}
         MSDos (REGS);
         end;
end;
```

Likewise, this routine returns the current state of DOS disk verification:

```
Function Get_Verify : byte;   { 1 on, 0 off }

Type
  REGISTERS = record
                 AX, EX, CX, DX, BP, SI, DI, DS, ES, FLAGS: INTEGER
                 end;
var
    REGS: REGISTERS;   {AX, BX, CX, DX, BP, SI, DI, DS, ES, FLAGS}
```

```
begin
    with REGS do
        begin
{set the registers to select the current drive}
        AX := $5400;          {DOS function code}

{invoke the DOS interrupt which selects the current drive}
        MSDos (REGS);

        Get_Verify := Lo(AX);
        end;
end;
```

HOW FIXED DISKS DIFFER

Thus far, all of the information and programs presented in this chapter have centered around floppy disks. This section examines the characteristics that make fixed disks unique, and provides many answers about disk partitions.

As you have seen throughout this chapter, floppy disks store information on two sides, as shown in Figure 10-31. Fixed disks, however, are composed of multiple disks called *platters*. Most microcomputer fixed disks use two platters that give the disk four sides, as shown in Figure 10-32.

As discussed, floppy disks use tracks as a method of organizing information. Fixed disks, on the other hand, combine the tracks on multiple platters to form *cylinders* (see Figure 10-33).

One of the most distinctive features of fixed disks is that one disk can store multiple operating systems. This is accomplished by dividing the disk into up to four sections of contiguous cylinders called *partitions*. If you only have one operating system, you will allocate your entire disk as a single partition (see Figure 10-34).

The DOS FDISK command is your interface to disk partitions. *DOS: The Complete Reference*, by Kris Jamsa (Berkeley, Calif.: Osborne/McGraw-Hill, 1987), discusses FDISK in detail. If you have never used FDISK, refer to that text or to your system documentation.

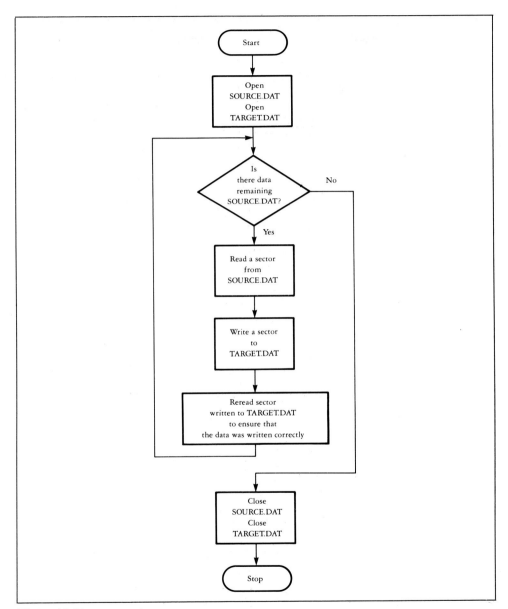

Figure 10-30.

DOS recognizes differences between
source and target sectors

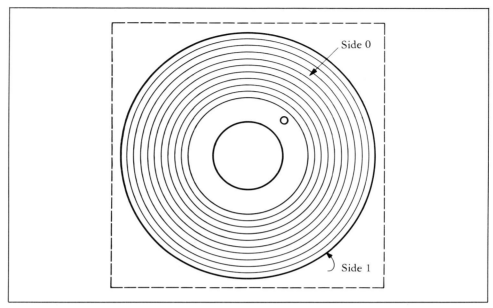

Figure 10-31.

Storage by floppy disk on two sides

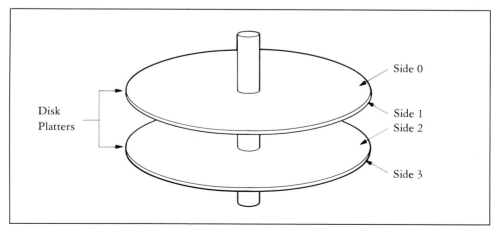

Figure 10-32.

Two platters of hard disk

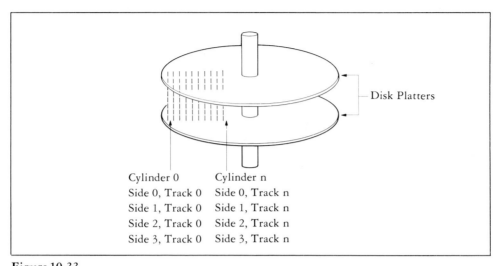

Figure 10-33.

Cylinders on hard disk

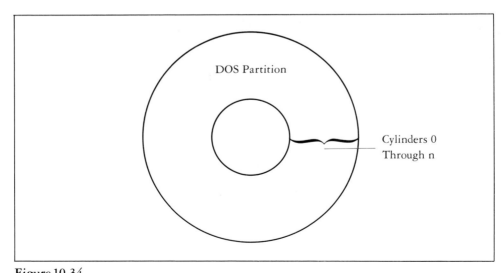

Figure 10-34.

Single partition containing DOS

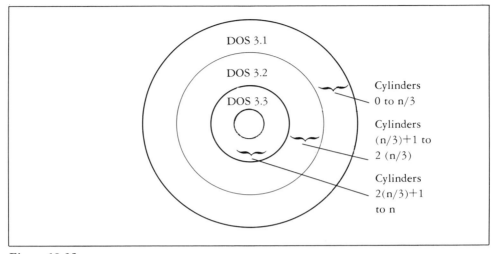

Figure 10-35.

Multiple partitions containing DOS

FIXED-DISK ARCHITECTURE

Many fixed disk users reply "it's magic" when asked how the computer knows about fixed-disk partitions. In actuality, partitions are quite straightforward. The first sector of every fixed disk contains a master boot record. You may never need to access this sector directly (FDISK is your interface). This record defines exactly where each partition begins and ends on disk, and which partition is bootable. The master boot record is shown in Figure 10-36.

As discussed, you can define up to four partitions on your fixed disk and the master boot record has entries for each. Each field of the master boot record is defined as follows:

Boot indicator	Bootable partitions are set to 80 hex while nonbootable partitions are set to 0. Only one of the four partitions can be bootable at one time. If bootable, the partition's bootstrap address immediately follows this byte in the next three bytes as follows:

Byte 1   The low-order 8 bits of a 10-bit cylinder address.

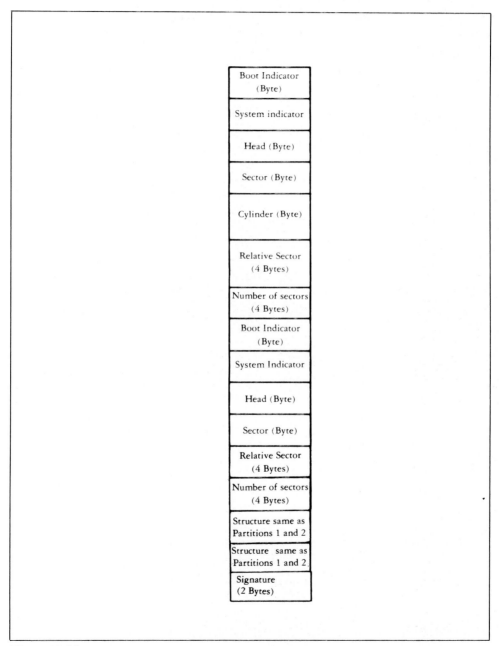

Figure 10-36.

Fixed-disk master boot record

	Byte 2	The high-order 2 bits are the high-order 2 bits for the 10-bit cylinder address. The low-order 6 bits contain the sector number.
	Byte 3	The head number.
System indicator	Specifies the partition's operation system as follows:	
	0 Unknown operating system	
	1 DOS 12-bit FAT entries	
	2 DOS 16-bit FAT entries	
Relative sector	Contains the number of sectors preceding this partition.	
Number of sectors	Contains the number of sectors this partition contains.	
Signature	The last two bytes of the master boot record must be hex 55AA for a valid boot record.	

WHAT HAPPENS AT BOOT TIME

Each time the computer boots, it first checks drive A for a valid system disk. If drive A contains a system disk, the computer uses it to boot; otherwise, the computer examines the fixed disk. If no fixed disk exists, the computer invokes ROM BASIC. If a fixed disk is present, the computer examines the master boot record in the first sector of the disk. If the master boot record is present, the computer passes control to it. The master boot record examines each partition entry for a bootable partition. If it finds one, it passes control to it. Remember, the partition bootstrap address immediately follows the bootable indicator. If none of the partitions are bootable, the master boot record invokes ROM BASIC. The flowchart shown in Figure 10-37 summarizes this processing.

This has been a very complex chapter. However, power users are expected to have a solid understanding of DOS disk manipulation. With

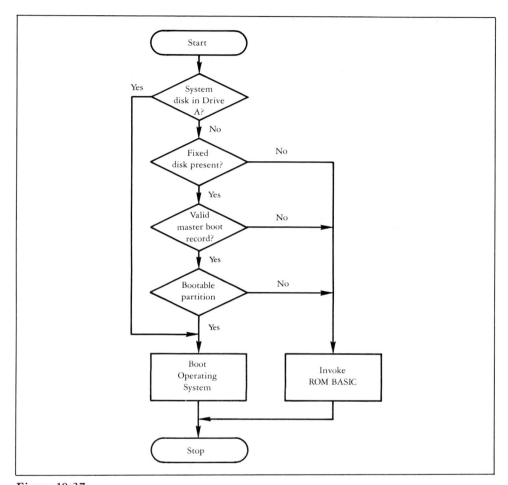

Figure 10-37.

Flowchart showing actions at boot
time

the tools presented in this chapter you should be able to develop
programs previously available only in expensive third-party software
packages. OS/2 treats disks the same way DOS does to ensure upward
compatibility. Each of the routines presented in this chapter will execute
under OS/2.

11: How the DOS FORMAT Command Really Works

By now, you should be fairly conversant with DOS disk structure and the manipulation of the FAT. As you will see, the DOS FORMAT command plays a critical role in the preparation of your fixed and floppy disks. Before discussing the inner workings of FORMAT, a review of the elements found on a DOS disk is in order (see Figure 11 - 1).

FORMAT directly influences each of the disk entries in one way or another. However, the primary function of FORMAT is to place identification marks on the storage media for every disk sector.

Each time you purchase a disk, you must FORMAT it before it is usable under DOS. This is because the disk manufacturer has no way of knowing whether you will use the disk on an IBM PC, an Apple, or a Commodore. Simply stated, FORMAT prepares a disk for use by DOS.

When you compare the processing of FORMAT to the file unerase program implemented in Chapter 10, FORMAT appears to be much simpler to implement. In general, FORMAT simply examines each disk

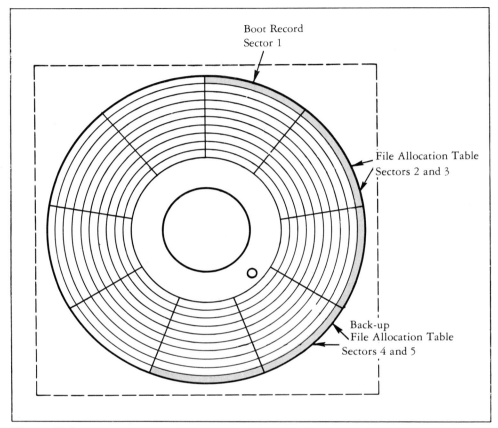

Figure 11-1.

Elements of DOS disk

sector (track by track) and places a timing mark next to each (see Figure 11-2).

FORMAT identifies each disk sector on the storage media by using a 4-byte entry containing the information shown in Figure 11-3. This 4-byte entry is often referred to as CHRN. The DOS FORMAT command places a unique CHRN value at each sector on the disk, as shown in Table 11-1.

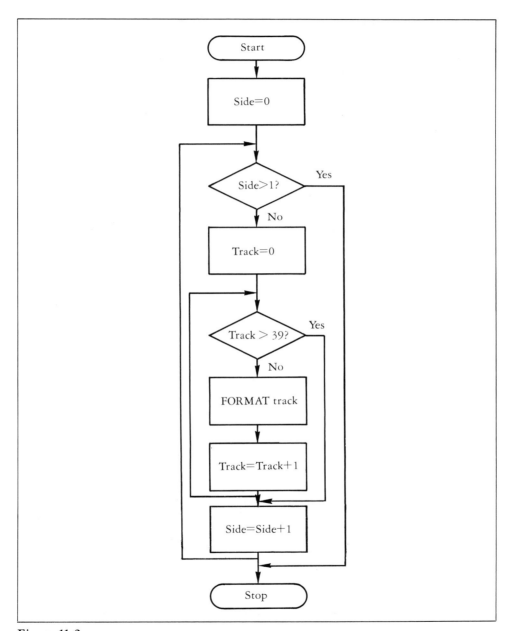

Figure 11-2.

Flowchart showing actions
of FORMAT

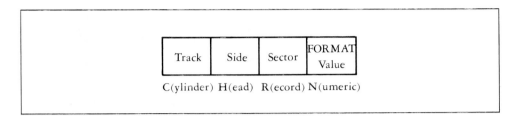

Figure 11-3.

Information of four-byte entry

For simplicity, Chapter 10 stated that the disk I/O services use the disk index hole as a timing mechanism. That statement was a partial truth. In actuality, the ROM-BIOS FORMAT service uses the index hole to determine where to place initial sector CHRN values. Once a disk FORMAT is complete, the ROM-BIOS disk I/O services use the unique CHRN values to locate specific sectors. The disk index hole has served its purpose.

The ROM-BIOS FORMAT service (INT 13H, Service 5) uses a buffer that contains a 4-byte CHRN entry for each sector on a track (see Figure 11-4). The CHRN N value specifies the disk sector size as summarized in Table 11-2.

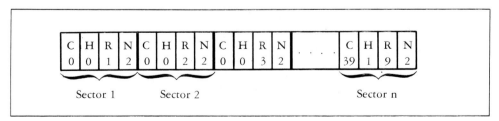

Figure 11-4.

Four-byte CHRN entry

Table 11-1.

CHRN Values

CHRN	Track	Side	Sector	Numeric
0012	0	0	1	2
0022	0	0	2	2
0032	0	0	3	2
0042	0	0	4	2
.	.	.	.	.
.	.	.	.	.
1012	1	0	1	2
1022	1	0	2	2
.	.	.	.	.
.	.	.	.	.
39192	39	1	9	2

Assume that you are formatting side 0, track 1, with 512-byte sectors. The buffer of CHRN entries for a 9-sector disk becomes that shown in Figure 11-5. Likewise, for side 1, track 2, the entries become that shown in Figure 11-6.

Table 11-2.

CHRN N Values

Numeric Value	Sector Size (Bytes)
0	128
1	256
2	512
3	1024

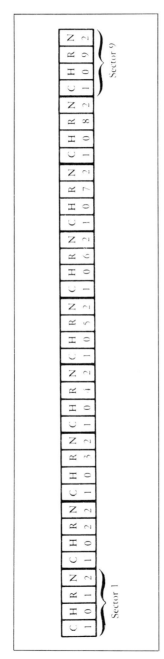

Figure 11-5.

CHRN entries for 9-sector disk

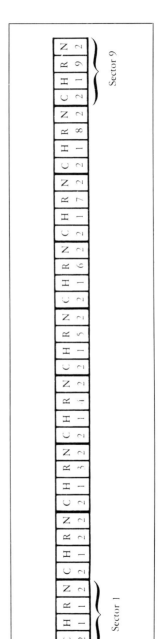

Figure 11-6.

Entries for side 1, track 2

The ROM-BIOS disk I/O interrupt uses the register values shown in Table 11-3 to FORMAT a disk. If you place a call to this service within a loop (as shown in Figure 11-7), you have completed the first step of the FORMAT process—identifying each disk sector on the storage medium. However, the ROM-BIOS FORMAT service does not create a FAT on the target disk. As shown in Chapter 10, the FAT resides in the second and third sectors of every disk (see Figure 11-8).

Think about the entries that the FAT must store, as illustrated in Table 11-4. FORMAT's most important FAT entry marks specific clusters as corrupted (unavailable to DOS disk read-and-write operations). As FORMAT identifies each sector on the disk, it must also record in the FAT whether the sector is usable by DOS (see Figure 11-9).

Recall that a hexadecimal value of FF7 in the FAT indicates that a cluster is corrupted. FORMAT is the only DOS command that logs bad sectors in the FAT. If you begin to experience disk problems, it means that the only DOS tool to record the corrupted sectors in the FAT is reformatting.

As shown in Chapter 10, each DOS disk contains a boot record in the first sector of the disk (see Figure 11-10). FORMAT is responsible for creating this record. Also, if the disk is to be bootable, FORMAT must

Table 11-3.

ROM-BIOS Interrupt Values

Register	Contents
AH	5 disk track format service
AL	Number of sectors
BX	Offset address of CHRN buffer
CH	Track number
CL	Sector number (not used)
DH	Drive number
DL	Side number
ES	Segment address of CHRN buffer

```
Program Format;  { Format the contents of a floppy disk
                   in drive A }

Const
  NumSectors = 9;         { sectors per track }
  NumSides = 2;           { sides per disk }
  NumTracks = 40;         { tracks per side }
  FormatService = 5;      { BIOS disk sector format service }
  SourceDisk = 0;         { drive A is the source disk }
  BufferSize = 512;       { size of the disk transfer buffer }

Type
  REGISTERS = record
               AX, BX, CX, DX, BP, SI, DI, DS, ES, FLAGS: INTEGER
             end;

  Buffer = array [1..BufferSize] of byte;    { disk transfer buffer }


Procedure FormatTrack (DiskBuffer: Buffer;
                       Side, Track, Drive: integer);

Var
  REGS: Registers;    { emulate the 8088 registers }

begin
  With REGS do
    begin
      AX := (FormatService SHL 8) +1;
      CX := (Track SHL 8);
      DX := (Side SHL 8) + Drive;
      ES := Seg (DiskBuffer[1]);
      BX := Ofs (DiskBuffer[1]);
      Intr ($13, REGS);
    end;
end;

Var
  DiskBuffer: Buffer;     { disk transfer buffer }
  I, Sector, Track, Side: integer;

begin

{ read each track from both sides writing them to drive B }

  For Side := 0 to NumSides - 1 do
    begin
      For Track := 0 to NumTracks - 1 do
        begin
          For I := 1 to NumSectors do
            begin
              DiskBuffer[(I-1)*4+1] := Track;
              DiskBuffer[(I-1)*4+2] := Side;
              DiskBuffer[(I-1)*4+3] := I;
              DiskBuffer[(I-1)*4+4] := 2;        { 512 byte sectors }
            end;

          FormatTrack (DiskBuffer, Side, Track, SourceDisk);
        end;
    end;
end.
```

Figure 11-7.

Format program

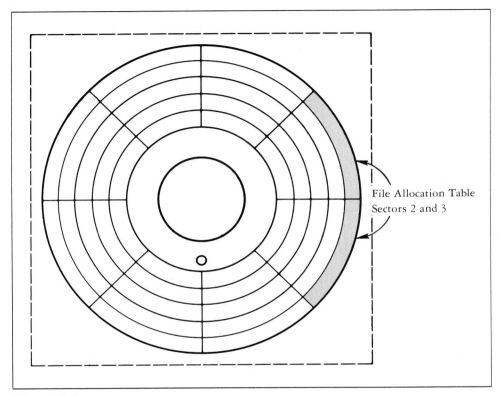

File Allocation Table
Sectors 2 and 3

Figure 11-8.

Location of file allocation table
on disk

place the system files (IBMBIO.COM and IBMDOS.COM for PC DOS; IO.SYS and MSDOS.SYS for MS-DOS) in the first two directory entries of the disk. In addition, FORMAT must ensure that the command processor (COMMAND.COM) is placed on the disk. This processing is summarized in Figure 11-11.

Most IBM PC AT computers are configured with a 1.2MB floppy disk drive. For this drive to be able to communicate with systems using a 360K floppy disk, FORMAT must be capable of producing a 360K

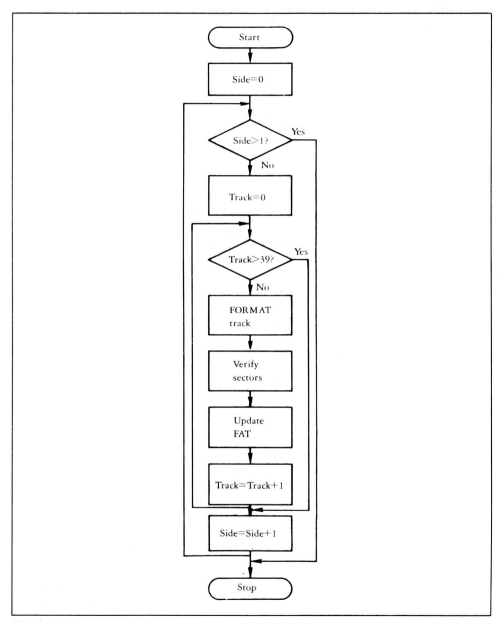

Figure 11-9.

FORMAT identifying if sector
is usable by DOS

Table 11-4.

FAT entries

Cluster	Entry
2	3 (Next entry)
3	FFF (End-of-file)
4	FF7 (Corrupted)
.	.
.	.
.	.
354	0
355	0

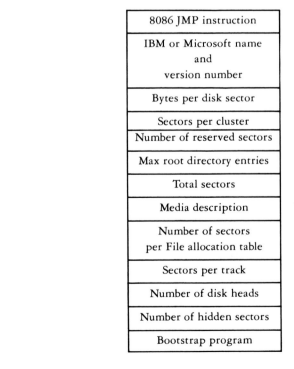

Figure 11-10.

Example boot record

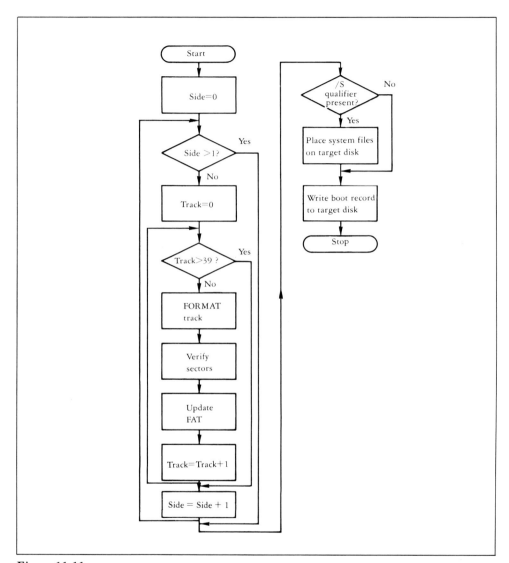

Figure 11-11.

FORMAT ensuring command
processor is present

floppy disk in the 1.2MB drive. FORMAT does this by examining the drive's disk *base table*. The disk base table contains 11 bytes, as shown in Figure 11-12. FORMAT's processing now becomes that shown in Figure 11-13. Before continuing, consider the DOS FORMAT command in detail:

FORMAT [*target__drive*:] [/B][/S][/V][/1][/4][/8]

where the following is true:

target__drive contains the disk drive identification (A, B, or C) of the drive to be formatted.

/B requests FORMAT to allocate space on the target disk for the boot files (which must reside in the first two directory entries on the disk), along with COMMAND.COM. Preallocating space this way allows the DOS SYS command to make the disk bootable later.

/S requests FORMAT to place the system boot files on the target disk, rendering it bootable.

/V requests FORMAT to prompt for the desired volume label on the target disk.

/1 requests FORMAT to format the disk as a single-sided disk (most disks are double-sided).

/4 requests FORMAT to format a double-density disk (360K disk) in a quad-density disk drive.

/8 requests FORMAT to format a disk with 8 sectors per track as opposed to the defaults of 9 or 15.

To support each of the FORMAT qualifiers, the processing becomes that shown in Figure 11-14.

Chapter 1 stated that the secret to being a power user lies in the ability to ask questions. By now, you should be taking each of your questions a few steps further and experimenting intuitively. Chapter 10 stated that DOS will successfully FORMAT a single-sided disk as double-sided. As a power user, your inquisitive nature should make you want to prove this assertion. You may ask, "How does FORMAT treat a standard

Head unload delay time
Head load delay time
Disk motor off
FORMAT numeric value yielding bytes per sector
Last sector number per track (8, 9, or 15)
Read/write Intersector gap size (2AH)
Data transfer size (FFH)
FORMAT intersector gap size (50H)
FORMAT data value (F6H)
Head settle time
Disk motor start-up time

Figure 11-12.

Disk base table

360K floppy disk in a 1.2MB floppy disk drive?" Try the following command:

```
C>FORMAT A:
Insert new diskette for drive A:
and strike ENTER when ready

Formatting...Format complete

    1213952 bytes total disk space
    1052160 bytes in bad sectors
     161792 bytes available on disk

Format another (Y/N)?
```

In this case, FORMAT gave a valiant effort, but 1.2MB high-density disks use a different technology than 360K floppies. However, by simply taking your questions a few steps further, you were able to prove this. If

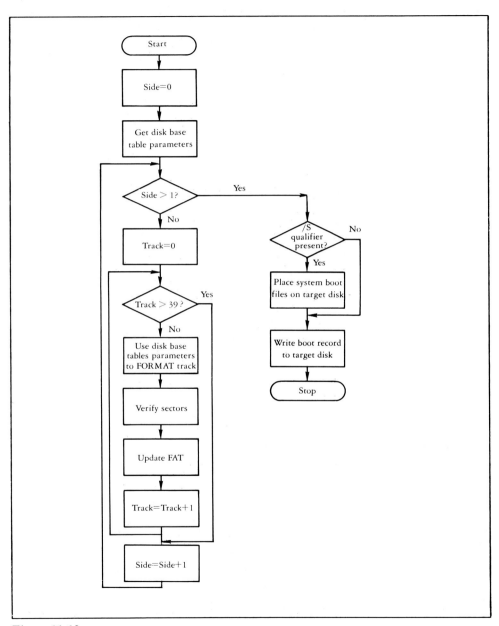

Figure 11-13.

FORMAT processing

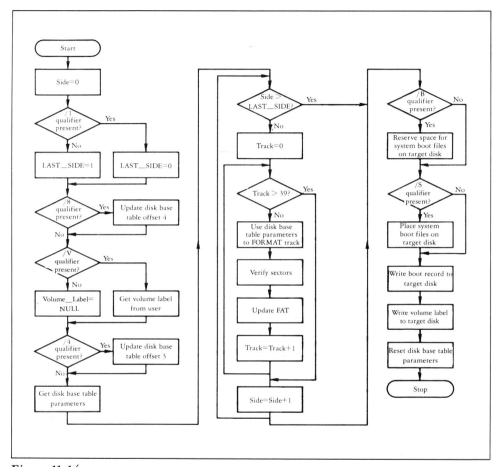

Figure 11-14.

FORMAT with qualifiers

you need to format a 360K floppy in your 1.2MB drive, use the /4
qualifier, as follows:

```
C> FORMAT A: /4
```

FORMAT will temporarily update the disk base table that specifies a 360K floppy in the 1.2MB drive.

What value does FORMAT place in the data sectors? By default, as FORMAT identifies each sector on the disk, it initializes each byte in the sector to the hexadecimal value F6. FORMAT gets this value from offset 8 of the disk base table. Verify this by using DEBUG with a newly formatted disk, as shown here:

```
C>DEBUG
-L 100 0 1C 1
-D 100
36B3:0100   00 F6 F6 F6 F6 F6 F6 F6-F6 F6 F6 F6 F6 F6 F6 F6   .vvvvvvvvvvvvvvv
36B3:0110   F6 F6 F6 F6 F6 F6 F6 F6-F6 F6 F6 F6 F6 F6 F6 F6   vvvvvvvvvvvvvvvv
36B3:0120   00 F6 F6 F6 F6 F6 F6 F6-F6 F6 F6 F6 F6 F6 F6 F6   .vvvvvvvvvvvvvvv
36B3:0130   F6 F6 F6 F6 F6 F6 F6 F6-F6 F6 F6 F6 F6 F6 F6 F6   vvvvvvvvvvvvvvvv
36B3:0140   00 F6 F6 F6 F6 F6 F6 F6-F6 F6 F6 F6 F6 F6 F6 F6   .vvvvvvvvvvvvvvv
36B3:0150   F6 F6 F6 F6 F6 F6 F6 F6-F6 F6 F6 F6 F6 F6 F6 F6   vvvvvvvvvvvvvvvv
36B3:0160   00 F6 F6 F6 F6 F6 F6 F6-F6 F6 F6 F6 F6 F6 F6 F6   .vvvvvvvvvvvvvvv
36B3:0170   F6 F6 F6 F6 F6 F6 F6 F6-F6 F6 F6 F6 F6 F6 F6 F6   vvvvvvvvvvvvvvvv
-
```

If you are writing your own formatting system, it is possible to modify the entries in the disk space table to meet your unique requirements.

HARD DISK CONCERNS

Like all DOS disk manipulation commands, FORMAT works for fixed disks just as it does for floppy disks. This explains why there is only one FORMAT command instead of an HFORMAT for hard disks or an FFORMAT for floppies. The subtle processing differences relate to the fact that for fixed disks FORMAT manipulates a partition as opposed to a complete disk. However, to the end user, this processing is transparent. Remember, once you partition your fixed disk by using FDISK, you must still specify the starting locations of each sector in the partition by using FORMAT. FDISK only sets aside a section of disk space. It does not perform any initialization.

This chapter relates as closely to the ROM-BIOS FORMAT service as it does to DOS. Keep in mind that DOS layers itself upon the I/O capabilities provided by the ROM-BIOS, in essence providing an interface for application programs. The purpose of discussing the FORMAT command in detail was to fill any gaps that may have existed in your understanding of DOS disk manipulation. If you truly want to understand disk I/O operations at the lowest level, the *IBM Technical Reference* for the PC AT contains all of the source code for the ROM-BIOS services, including the disk I/O service (INT 13H). These services provide low-level interface for all versions of DOS and OS/2. With Chapters 10 and 11 in hand, you should find these listings very readable.

12: Utilizing the DOS Environment

Each time DOS boots, it sets aside an area in memory called the *environment* for the storage of such items as the current command path, the system prompt, and other miscellaneous strings. By default, DOS allocates 127 bytes for the environment, as shown in Figure 12-1.

As long as you do not install any memory-resident programs, DOS will allocate additional memory for your environment entries as needed. Note, however, that DOS must use contiguous memory locations for the environment entries.

The DOS SET command allows you to place entries into the environment. The format of the SET command is

SET *name=value*

where the following is true:

name is a character string specifying the name of the environment entry to which you are assigning a value.

value is a character string containing the value associated with the entry.

503

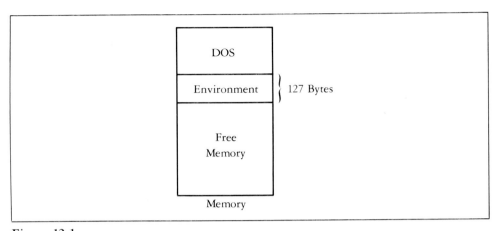

Figure 12-1.

Memory allocation for environment

For example, to set the current system prompt to DOS, enter the
following:

```
C> SET PROMPT=DOS}
```

Your current prompt should now be

```
DOS}
DOS}
```

If you invoke SET without any parameters

```
DOS} SET
```

SET will display the current contents of the environment, as follows:

```
DOS} SET
COMSPEC=C:\COMMAND.COM
PATH=
PROMPT=DOS}

DOS}
```

As mentioned, DOS allocates 127 bytes for the environment. If you exceed this space, DOS will allocate additional space transparently for your environment entries. To verify this, invoke the DOS CHKDSK command, as shown here:

```
C> CHKDSK

Volume DOSDISK       created Jan 16, 1987 7:25p

 21309440 bytes total disk space
   116736 bytes in 7 hidden files
   167936 bytes in 63 directories
 13522944 bytes in 1553 user files
    20480 bytes in bad sectors
  7481344 bytes available on disk

   655360 bytes total memory
   455248 bytes free

C>
```

Next, issue the following series of SET commands:

```
C> SET 1=1111111111111111111111111111111111111111111111
C> SET 2=2222222222222222222222222222222222222222222222
C> SET 3=3333333333333333333333333333333333333333333333
C> SET 4=4444444444444444444444444444444444444444444444
C> SET 5=5555555555555555555555555555555555555555555555
C>
```

Again invoke CHKDSK:

```
C> CHKDSK

Volume DOSDISK        created Jan 16, 1987 7:25p

 21309440 bytes total disk space
   116736 bytes in 7 hidden files
   167936 bytes in 63 directories
 13533184 bytes in 1558 user files
    20480 bytes in bad sectors
  7471104 bytes available on disk

   655360 bytes total memory
   454816 bytes free

C>
```

Note the amount of memory that DOS has allocated for additional environment entries. If, however, you load a memory-resident program, DOS cannot extend the environment space in a contiguous manner (see Figure 12-2).

In this case, a DOS SET command results in the following:

```
Out of environment space
```

To verify this, issue the DOS GRAPHICS command. This command directs DOS to load memory-resident code that aids in print screen operations using graphics.

```
C> GRAPHICS
```

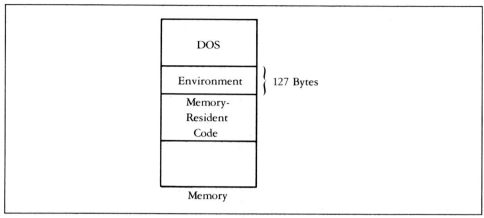

Figure 12-2.

Relationship between memory-
resident programs and environment

Once this code is loaded, DOS no longer can extend the environment.
Issuing this command

```
C> SET 6=666666666666666666666666666666666666666666
```

results in

```
Out of environment space
```

EXAMINING THE ENVIRONMENT

It is important to understand that DOS only has one environment.
Every application that executes in your system shares the same environment entries. Each time DOS executes a program, it makes a copy of
its current environment for the program. Programs do not access the
actual DOS environment, but rather a copy of it. You locate the program's copy of the environment space by examining the program-
segment prefix (PSP) as shown in Figure 12-3.

The following Turbo Pascal program displays the segment address
of its copy of the DOS environment:

```
Program Env_Address;

Type
  REGISTERS = record
                AX, BX, CX, DX, BP, SI, DI, DS, ES, FLAGS: INTEGER
              end;


Function Get_PSP: integer;
  var
    REGS: REGISTERS;  {AX, BX, CX, DX, BP, SI, DI, DS, ES, FLAGS}

  begin
    with REGS do
      begin
{set the registers to get the program segment prefix}
        AX := $6200;                        {DOS function code}

{invoke the DOS interrupt which returns the PSP}
        MSDos (REGS);

{return the address of the program segment prefix}
        Get_PSP := BX;
      end;
  end;


var
  PSP_SEG, ENVIRONMENT_SEG: integer;

begin
  PSP_SEG := Get_PSP;
  ENVIRONMENT_SEG := Memw[PSP_SEG: $2C];

  writeln ('Environment Segment Address ', ENVIRONMENT_SEG);
end.
```

Likewise, this C program performs the same function:

```
#include <dos.h>

main ()
  {
  union REGS inregs, outregs;

  long int psp_segment;
  long int env_segment;

  int far *ptr;

  char far *cptr;

  inregs.x.ax = 0x6200;
  intdos (&inregs, &outregs);
  psp_segment = outregs.x.bx;

  ptr = (int far *) ((psp_segment << 16) + 0x2C);

  printf ("Environment Segment Address (from C) %d\n", *ptr);
}
```

Executing each program sequentially results in

```
C> PASADDR
Environment Segment Address (from TURBO) 12496

C> CADDR
Environment Segment Address (from C) 12496

C>
```

Note that each program displays the same segment address, telling you that DOS is using the same memory location for storing each program's copy of the environment. If you execute the Turbo Pascal program

```
C> PASADDR
Environment Segment Address (from TURBO) 12496
```

Offset (Hex)	Contents
0	Int 20
2	Top of Memory
4	Reserved
5	OP Code
6	Number of Bytes in Segment
A	Terminate Address (Offset)
C	Terminate Address (Segment)
E	CTRL-BREAK Address (Offset)
10	CTRL-BREAK Address (Segment)
12	Critical Error Address (Offset)
14	Critical Error Address (Segment)
16	Reserved
2C	Environment Address (Segment)
2E	Reserved
50	DOS Call
52	Reserved
5C	File-Control Block One
6C	File-Control Block Two
80	Command-Line Length (Bytes)
81	Command-Line Parameters

Figure 12-3.

Environment address location in
PSP

and then invoke a memory-resident program

```
C> GRAPHICS
```

the C program's copy of the DOS environment space moves, as shown here:

```
Environment Segment Address (from C) 12569
```

This verifies that each program has a copy of the environment rather than access to the memory locations containing the actual DOS environment (see Figure 12-4).

DOS terminates the environment entries with a null (0 byte) character. Following the last environment entry is a second null character that indicates the end of the environment entries. For example, if your environment contains

```
COMSPEC=C:\COMMAND.COM
PATH=C:
```

DOS stores the environment in contiguous memory locations as shown in Figure 12-5.

The Turbo Pascal program shown in Figure 12-6 displays each entry in the DOS environment.

Likewise, from C the code becomes the following:

```c
#include <dos.h>

main ()
{
  union REGS inregs, outregs;

  long int psp_segment;
  long int env_segment;

  int far *ptr;

  char far *cptr;

  int i;

  inregs.x.ax = 0x6200;
  intdos (&inregs, &outregs);
  psp_segment = outregs.x.bx;

  ptr = (int far *) ((psp_segment << 16) + 0x2C);

  env_segment = (int far *) *ptr;

  cptr = (char far *) (env_segment << 16);

  for (i = 0; (*(cptr+i) != 0) || (*(cptr+i+1) != 0); i++)
    if (*(cptr+i) == 0)
      printf ("\n");
    else
      printf ("%c", *(cptr + i));
}
```

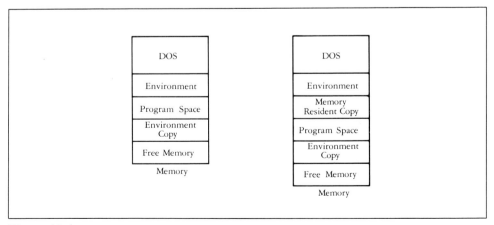

Figure 12-4.

Example of memory locations of
individual programs

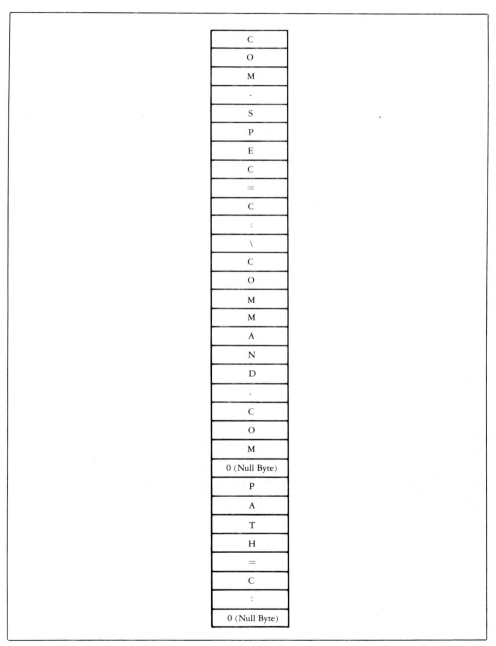

Figure 12-5.

Environment storage in contiguous
memory locations

```
    Program Display_Environment;

    Type
      REGISTERS = record
                     AX, BX, CX, DX, BP, SI, DI, DS, ES, FLAGS: INTEGER
                  end;


    Function Get_PSP: integer;
      var
         REGS: REGISTERS;   {AX, BX, CX, DX, BP, SI, DI, DS, ES, FLAGS}

      begin
        with REGS do
          begin

    {set the registers to get the program segment prefix}
           AX := $6200;                          {DOS function code}

    {invoke the DOS interrupt which returns the PSP}
           MSDos (REGS);

    {return the address of the program segment prefix}
           Get_PSP := BX;
          end;
      end;


    var
       I, J, PSP_SEC, ENVIRONMENT_SEC: integer;
       NULL: char;
       ENTRY: string[80];

    begin
       NULL := Chr(0);

       PSP_SEG := Get_PSP;
       ENVIRONMENT_SEG := Memw[PSP_SEG: $2C];

       I := 0;

       repeat
        J := 0;

        repeat
          J := J + 1;
          ENTRY[J] := Chr(Mem[ENVIRONMENT_SEG: I]);
          I := I + 1;
        until (ENTRY[J] = NULL);

        ENTRY[0] := Chr(J-1);
        writeln (ENTRY);
        until (Mem[ENVIRONMENT_SEG: I+1] = 0);
      end.
```

Figure 12-6.

DISPLAY__ENVIRONMENT

program

With this basic knowledge you can develop the Turbo Pascal procedure shown in Figure 12-7 to return the value of a specific environment entry. If the entry does not exist, the routine returns a null string. For example, determine the current command path, invoke the routine as

```
Get_Entry ('PATH=', VALUE);
```

Likewise, the following C program again verifies that each program DOS executes does receive its own copy of the environment. Upon execution, the program displays its current environment. Next, the program adds the entry LAST=ITEM and redisplays its contents.

```c
#include <dos.h>
#include <stdio.h>

main ()
 {
  union REGS inregs, outregs;

  long int psp_segment;
  long int env_segment;

  int far *ptr;

  char far *cptr;
  char *str = "LAST=ITEM";

  int i;

  inregs.x.ax = 0x6200;
  intdos (&inregs, &outregs);
  psp_segment = outregs.x.bx;

  ptr = (int far *) ((psp_segment << 16) + 0x2C);

  env_segment = (int far *) *ptr;

  cptr = (char far *) (env_segment << 16);

  for (i = 0; (*(cptr+i) != 0) || (*(cptr+i+1) != 0); i++)
    if (*(cptr+i) == 0)
      printf ("\n");
    else
      printf ("%c", *(cptr + i));
```

```
        while (*str)
          *(cptr+(++i)) = *str++;

        *(cptr+i+1) = NULL;
        *(cptr+i+2) = NULL;

        for (i = 0; (*(cptr+i) != 0) || (*(cptr+i+1) != 0); i++)
          if (*(cptr+i) == 0)
            printf ("\n");
          else
            printf ("%c", *(cptr + i));

    }
```

```
    Type
      REGISTERS = record
                    AX, BX, CX, DX, BP, SI, DI, DS, ES, FLAGS: INTEGER
                  end;


    Function Get_PSP: integer;
      var
        REGS: REGISTERS;   {AX, BX, CX, DX, BP, SI, DI, DS, ES, FLAGS}

      begin
        with REGS do
          begin

    {set the registers to get the program segment prefix}
          AX := $6200;                        {DOS function code}

    {invoke the DOS interrupt which returns the PSP}
          MSDos (REGS);

    {return the address of the program segment prefix}
          Get_PSP := BX;
          end;
      end;

    type string80 = string[80];

    procedure Get_Entry (Desired_Entry: string80;
                         var Value: string80);
```

Figure 12-7.

Turbo Pascal procedure to show
environment entry

```
var
  I, J, PSP_SEG, ENVIRONMENT_SEG: integer;
  NULL: char;
  ENTRY: string80;

begin
  NULL := Chr(0);
  VALUE[0] := Chr(0);
  PSP_SEG := Get_PSP;
  ENVIRONMENT_SEG := MemW[PSP_SEG: $2C];

  I := 0;

  repeat
   J := 0;

   repeat
     J := J + 1;
     ENTRY[J] := Chr(Mem[ENVIRONMENT_SEG: I]);
     I := I + 1;
   until (ENTRY[J] = NULL);

   ENTRY[0] := Chr(J-1);
    if (Pos(DESIRED_ENTRY, ENTRY) > 0) then
        Value := Copy (ENTRY, LENGTH (DESIRED_ENTRY) + 1,
                                      LENGTH(ENTRY));

   until (Mem[ENVIRONMENT_SEG: I+1] = 0);
  end;
```

Figure 12-7.

Turbo Pascal procedure to show
environment entry (*continued*)

Upon completion, the DOS environment remains unchanged. This is
because the program modified its copy of the environment rather than
the actual DOS environment (see Figure 12-8).

UTILIZING ENVIRONMENT ENTRIES

Now that you know how to manipulate items contained in the DOS
environment, consider how you can use the environment to enhance
your application programs. First, consider the DOS PATH command. If
DOS does not find the command that you enter for execution as you

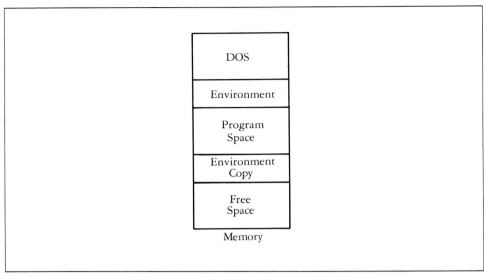

Figure 12-8.

DOS environment

specify it, DOS examines the environment for a PATH=entry.

If a command search path is defined, DOS examines each entry in the path for the file until the command is found, or until the search path is exhausted.

Similarly, many compilers require you to define an INCLUDE subdirectory, as shown here:

```
A> SET INCLUDE=C:\INCLUDE\LIB
```

If the compiler does not find a file in the current directory, it examines the environment to see if you have an INCLUDE entry. If so, it searches for files in the specified directory.

Consider the Turbo Pascal program shown in Figure 12-9, which displays the contents of the file specified by the first command-line parameter.

```
C> SHOW FILENAME
```

If the program cannot open the file as specified, it searches the environment for an entry in the following form:

```
FILENAME=
```

If it finds such an entry, the program attempts to open that file for display. For example, given the command

```
C> SHOW TEXT
```

the program first searches the current directory for a file named TEXT. If found, the program displays the contents of the file. Assume that a file named TEXT does not exist. If the user has previously issued the command

```
C> SET TEXT=SHOW.PAS
```

the program will find the TEXT= entry in the environment and attempt to open the file associated with the entry.

OS/2 ENVIRONMENT ISSUES

Chapter 2 discussed how OS/2 and DOS 3.3 support the concept of named parameters within DOS batch files. Consider the batch file on the next page.

```
        CLS
        TYPE %FILE%
```

This batch procedure types the contents of the file associated with %FILE%. If no such file exists, the procedure displays

```
        File not found
```

The way DOS 3.3 and OS/2 implement named parameters is similar to the techniques that you have been using throughout this chapter. When OS/2 encounters a named parameter, it searches the environment for an equivalent entry. If a matching entry is found, OS/2 simply uses its associated value.

```
        program Show ;

        Type
          REGISTERS = record
                          AX, BX, CX, DX, BP, SI, DI, DS, ES, FLAGS: INTEGER
                      end;


        Function Get_PSP: integer;
          var
            REGS: REGISTERS;   {AX, BX, CX, DX, BP, SI, DI, DS, ES, FLAGS}

          begin
            with REGS do
              begin

        {set the registers to get the program segment prefix}
              AX := $6200;                          {DOS function code}
```

Figure 12-9.

Turbo Pascal program to display
contents of file

```
    {invoke the DOS interrupt which returns the PSP}
        MSDos (REGS);

    {return the address of the program segment prefix}
        Get_PSP := BX;
      end;
  end;


type string80 = string[80];

procedure Get_Entry (Desired_Entry: string80;
                     var Value: string80);

var
  I, J, PSP_SEG, ENVIRONMENT_SEG: integer;
  NULL: char;
  ENTRY: string80;

begin
  NULL := Chr(0);
  VALUE[0] := Chr(0);
  PSP_SEG := Get_PSP;
  ENVIRONMENT_SEG := MemW[PSP_SEG: $2C];

  I := 0;

  repeat
   J := 0;

   repeat
     J := J + 1;
     ENTRY[J] := Chr(Mem[ENVIRONMENT_SEG: I]);
     I := I + 1;
     until (ENTRY[J] = NULL);

     ENTRY[0] := Chr(J-1);

     if (Pos(DESIRED_ENTRY, ENTRY) > 0) then
         Value := Copy (ENTRY, LENGTH (DESIRED_ENTRY) + 1,
                                       LENGTH (ENTRY));

   until (Mem[ENVIRONMENT_SEG: I+1] = 0);
  end;

  var
    LINE     : STRING80;        {line read from the file}
    LOGICAL_NAME: STRING80;     {value from environment}

    IN_FILE: text;             {the input file}

  begin
```

Figure 12-9.

Turbo Pascal program to display
contents of file (*continued*)

```
          {make sure the user provided an input file}
            if (ParamCount = 0) then
              Writeln ('SHOW: invalid useage: SHOW filename')

          {an input file was provided so read each record and
           write it stdout}
            else
            begin
              Assign (IN_FILE, ParamStr(1));
              {$I-} Reset (IN_FILE) {$I+};
              if (IOresult <> 0) then
                begin
                  Get_Entry (ParamStr(1) + '=', LOGICAL_NAME);
                  if (LENGTH (LOGICAL_NAME) > 0) then
                    begin
                      Assign (IN_FILE, LOGICAL_NAME);
                      {$I-} Reset (IN_FILE) {$I+};
                      if (IOresult <> 0) then
                        begin
                          Writeln ('SHOW: error opening the file ',
                                     LOGICAL_NAME);
                          halt (1);
                        end;
                    end
                  else
                    begin
                      writeln ('SHOW: error opening the file ',
                                 ParamStr(1));
                      halt (1);
                    end;
                end;

              while (not EOF (IN_FILE)) do
                begin
                  Readln (IN_FILE, LINE);
                  Writeln (LINE);               {write to stdout}
                end;
              Close (IN_FILE);
            end;
        end.
```

Figure 12-9.

Turbo Pascal program to display
contents of file (*continued*)

For the previous batch file to work successfully, the user must issue a
DOS SET command to assign FILE a value, as follows:

```
C> SET FILE=SHOW.PAS
```

As you have seen, each time DOS boots, it reserves space in memory for entries in a region of memory called the environment. The DOS SET command provides you with a means of adding and removing environment entries. It is easy for your applications to access values stored in the environment. With a little imagination, you can develop numerous applications that use the DOS environment.

13: Breaking Apart DOS Data Structures

This text has examined various DOS services, studied DOS memory utilization, and used several DOS data structures. This chapter fills in the remaining gaps with regard to DOS data structures, as well as the DOS and OS/2 memory maps. Each of the DOS data structures is easily manipulated from within any high-level language application.

DOS MEMORY MAP

As stated in Chapter 8, the IBM PC addresses memory by way of segment and offset combinations, as shown in Figure 13-1. The diagram in Figure 13-2 illustrates how DOS actually distributes memory.

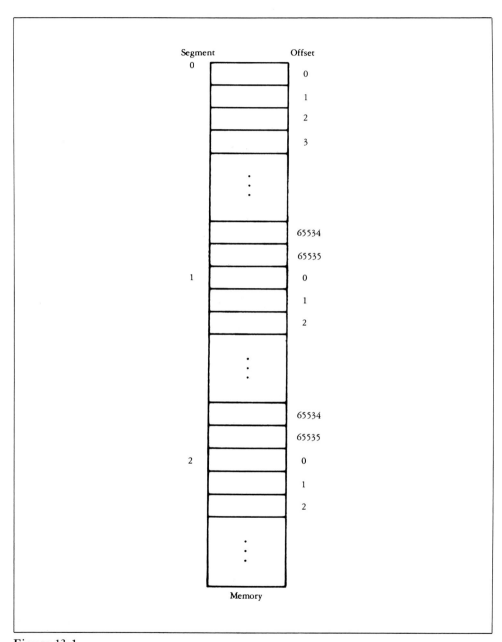

Figure 13-1.

Segment and offset combinations

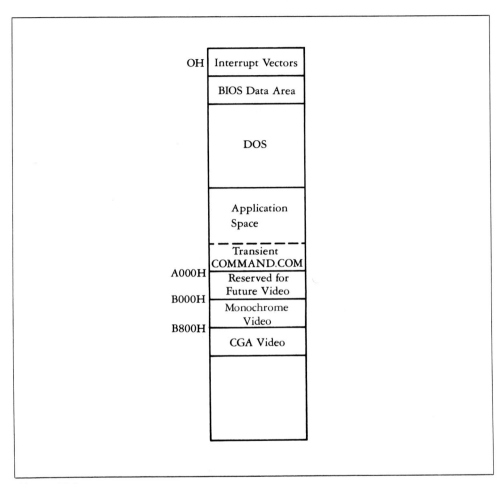

Figure 13-2.

DOS memory usage

Since DOS 20-bit addresses can reference more than 1MB of memory, many people are confused as to why DOS is restricted to 640K. As you can see in Figure 13-2, the first two entries in the DOS memory map (interrupt vectors (256 bytes) and the BIOS data area) consume approximately 1K of memory. As you also can see, video display memory for the PC and compatibles begins at location A000H. If you

Segment/Offset Address	20-Bit Address
A000H	A0000H

$$A0000H = 10 * 16^4 = 655,360$$

Figure 13-3.

Converting segment-
offset value to decimal

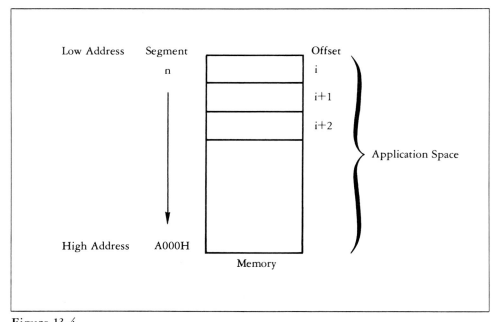

Figure 13-4.

Application address
growth

convert this value to decimal, you find that it equals 655,360 or 640K, as shown in Figure 13-3. Since DOS cannot use this memory, it becomes physically restricted to 640K.

As shown in Figure 13-4, DOS allocates memory for your programs starting at a low memory address and working toward higher memory locations. DOS allows your programs to consume memory up to the 640K limit. If your program exceeds 640K, you will most likely have to break it up by using overlays. An overlay allows one portion of your program to "overlay," or be placed in memory on top of, another section of your program that is currently not being used.

Each time a new section overlays another, the section being over-written is placed temporarily on disk (by the application program) until it is again required for execution, as shown in Figure 13-5.

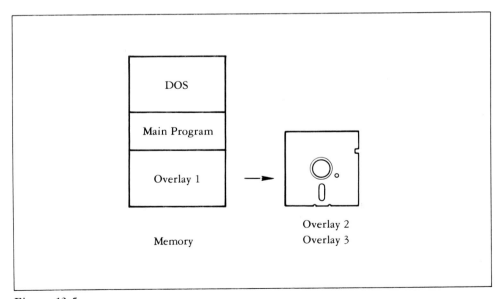

Figure 13-5.

Temporarily placing
overlay files on disk

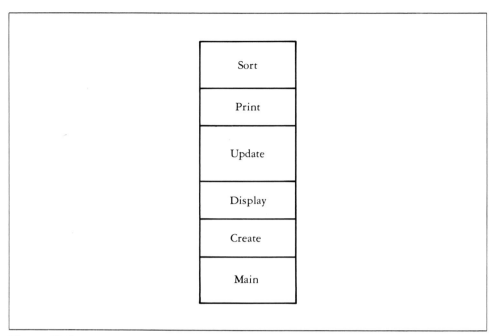

Figure 13-6.

Database functions

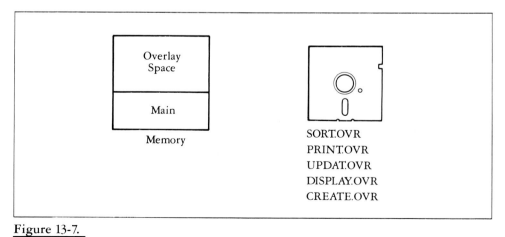

Figure 13-7.

Memory allocated for
overlay files

Consider a large data base manipulation system that performs the tasks shown in Figure 13-6. Assuming that you only have 192K of available memory, you can divide each section of code into its own overlay. In this case, your application will use memory for the main program and allocate space sufficient for the largest overlay, as shown in Figure 13-7.

If your application requires code that resides in a specific module, it checks first to see if the code is present. If the code is present, execution continues. If not, the application must save the current overlay region contents to disk, reading in the required overlay as shown in Figure 13-8.

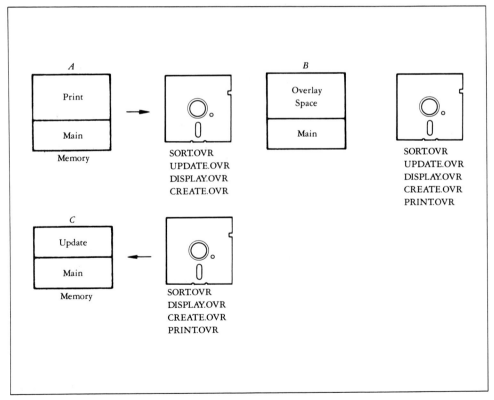

Figure 13-8.

Saving PRINT to disk and moving
UPDATE to overlay space in memory

Under DOS, overlays give your programs the ability to exceed 640K. The important point to note, however, is the responsibility of each application to manage the loading and saving of the overlay region. This processing can become quite complex. Under OS/2, however, memory management is transparent to each application. In this way, if the size of your application exceeds the physical memory in the system, or if many programs are executing concurrently, OS/2 takes care of moving portions of programs to and from disk as required. In so doing, OS/2 virtual-memory management allows you to concentrate on the details of your programs, as opposed to the complexities of memory management.

OS/2 MEMORY MAP

Figure 13-9 shows the OS/2 memory utilization. The first significant difference between DOS and OS/2 memory utilization is that OS/2 has a physical address space of 16MB. Since OS/2 is a virtual-memory operating system that appears to have more memory available for applications than is actually present, physical memory space is often overlooked because of the essentially unlimited virtual-memory address space.

However, if you are concurrently running more applications than OS/2 can fit into memory at one time, OS/2 simply swaps programs to disk temporarily so that other programs can execute (see Figure 13-10). Unfortunately, as the amount of swapping that OS/2 must perform increases, so does the amount of system overhead. This, in turn, slows down your application programs. Physical memory, therefore, becomes important when you want to reduce the amount of swapping that OS/2 must perform. A general rule for making multitasking operating systems faster is to add more memory.

Note that OS/2 is not constrained by the 640K barrier. Under OS/2, this barrier does not vanish, but is simply less of a restriction. OS/2 (to ensure compatibility) also uses the same video memory region as DOS for text and graphics output. However, as opposed to stopping the operating system at this memory region, OS/2 resides on each side of it.

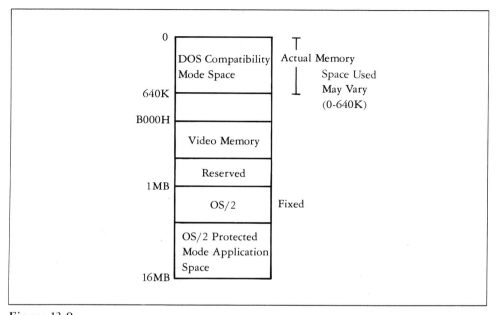

Figure 13-9.

OS/2 memory usage

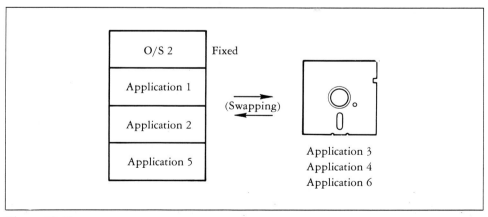

Figure 13-10.

OS/2 swapping
programs

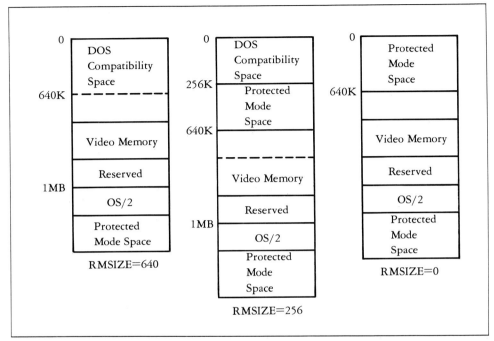

Figure 13-11.

Use of RMSIZE start-up parameter

The DOS-compatibility mode memory region is used for DOS applications that run in real mode. As shown in Figure 13-11, OS/2 real-mode applications still have the entire 640K memory region available for them. However, if you know that your DOS applications will never require this entire memory range, the OS/2 CONFIG.SYS system start-up parameter RMSIZE allows you to specify the amount of memory to retain for real-mode applications. If you reduce the amount of space OS/2 reserves for real-mode applications, OS/2 uses that space for protected-mode programs.

Note the regions of the OS/2 memory map that are marked "Fixed" (see Figure 13-9). "Fixed" means that OS/2 cannot swap these memory regions to disk to make space for other programs to execute. These regions contain the OS/2 kernel and memory-management facilities.

By marking these locations as "Fixed," OS/2 cannot swap out the code to disk that is responsible for swapping code back into memory from disk. This would render the operating system inoperative. However, this space consumes little of the available system memory.

MAPPING THE BOOT RECORD

Chapter 10 provided a detailed explanation of DOS disk manipulation by using sectors and tracks. Every DOS disk has a boot record responsible for starting DOS or for displaying the following message:

```
Non-System disk or disk error
Replace and strike any key when ready
```

The DOS boot record, which is one sector long, contains the fields shown in Figure 13-12.

Use DEBUG as shown in Figure 13-13 to note several of the fields. At first, the notion of reading and manipulating the fields of the boot record seems threatening. However, using the following Turbo Pascal record simplifies the task:

```
Type
  BootRecord = record
    JMP : integer;        { 3 bytes long.  1st byte in Id[0] }
    ID  : string[8];
    BytesPerSector: integer;
    SectorsPerCluster: byte;
    ReservedSectors: integer;
    NumberOfFats: byte;
    MaxRootEntries: integer;
    TotalSectors: integer;
    MediaDescriptor: byte;
    SectorsPerFat: integer;
    SectorsPerTrack: integer;
    DiskHeads: integer;
    HiddenSectors: integer;
    BootStrap: array [1..482] of byte;
  end;
```

8088 JMP Instruction
IBM or Microsoft name and Version Number
Bytes per Disk Sector
Sectors per Cluster
Number of Reserved Sectors
Max Root Directory Entries
Total Sectors
Media Description
Number of Sectors per File Allocation Table
Sectors per Track
Number of Disk Heads
Number of Hidden Sectors
Bootstrap Program

Figure 13-12.

Example boot record

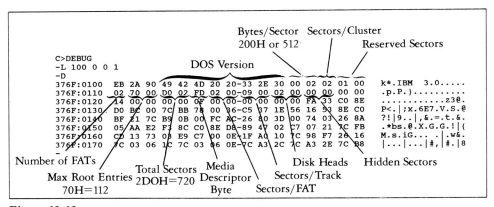

Figure 13-13.

Use of DEBUG to
show fields

Simply use the routines presented in Chapter 10 to read a disk sector, as shown here:

```
Procedure ReadSectors (Var DiskBuffer: Buffer;
                           Side, Track, Drive: integer);
Type
  REGISTERS = record
                   AX, BX, CX, DX, BP, SI, DI, DS, ES, FLAGS: INTEGER
                   end;

Var
  REGS: Registers;    { emulate the 8080 registers }

begin
   with REGS do
      begin
        AX := (ReadService SHL 8) + NumSectors;
        CX := (Track SHL 8) + 1;
        DX := (Side SHL 8) + Drive;
        ES := Seg (DiskBuffer);
        BX := Ofs (DiskBuffer);
        Intr (S13, REGS);
      end;
end;
```

In this case, when you invoke the routine to read a sector, the actual disk contents read are placed into your Pascal record. In this way, displaying the boot record contents is quite straightforward.

The Turbo Pascal program shown in Figure 13-14 displays the contents of the boot record for the disk in drive A. Upon invocation the program displays

```
Disk A Boot Record
System Id IBM  3.0
Bytes per sector 512
Sectors per cluster 2
Reserved sectors 1
Number of FAT copies 2
Maximum root entries 112
Sectors per disk 720
Media Descriptor 253
Sectors Per Fat 2
Sectors Per Track 9
Sides per disk 2
Number of hidden sectors 0

C>
```

The OS/2 boot record is identical in format.

```
Program ShowBoot;   { Display the contents of the boot record from
                      the disk in drive A }

Const
  NumSectors = 1;        { sectors per track }
  ReadService = 2;       { BIOS disk sector read service }
  SourceDisk = 0;        { drive A is the source disk }

Type
  BootRecord = record
    JMP : integer;            { 3 bytes long.  1st byte in Id[0] }
    ID  : string[8];
    BytesPerSector: integer;
    SectorsPerCluster: byte;
    ReservedSectors: integer;
    NumberOfFats: byte;
    MaxRootEntries: integer;
    TotalSectors: integer;
    MediaDescriptor: byte;
    SectorsPerFat: integer;
    SectorsPerTrack: integer;
    DiskHeads: integer;
    HiddenSectors: integer;
    BootStrap: array [1..482] of byte;
  end;

  Buffer = BootRecord;    { disk transfer buffer }


Procedure ReadSectors (Var DiskBuffer: Buffer;
                        Side, Track, Drive: integer);

Type
  REGISTERS = record
                AX, BX, CX, DX, BP, SI, DI, DS, ES, FLAGS: INTEGER
              end;

Var
  REGS: Registers;   { emulate the 8088 registers }
```

Figure 13-14.

SHOWBOOT program

```
    begin
      with REGS do
        begin
          AX := (ReadService SHL 8) + NumSectors;
          CX := (Track SHL 8) + 1;
          DX := (Side SHL 8) + Drive;
          ES := Seg (DiskBuffer);
          BX := Ofs (DiskBuffer);
          Intr ($13, REGS);
        end;
    end;

    Var

    BootSector: BootRecord;     { disk transfer buffer }
  begin
   ClrScr;

   { read the Boot record from drive A }

   ReadSectors (BootSector, 0, 0, SourceDisk);

   writeln ('Disk A Boot Record');

   with BootSector do
     begin
       Id[8] := Char(0);
       writeln ('System Id ', Id);

       writeln ('Bytes per sector ', BytesPerSector);

       writeln ('Sectors per cluster ', SectorsPerCluster);

       writeln ('Reserved sectors ', ReservedSectors);

       writeln ('Number of FAT copies ', NumberOfFats);

       writeln ('Maximum root entries ', MaxRootEntries);

       writeln ('Sectors per disk ', TotalSectors);

       writeln ('Media Descriptor ', MediaDescriptor);

       writeln ('Sectors Per Fat ', SectorsPerFat);

       writeln ('Sectors Per Track ', SectorsPerTrack);

       writeln ('Sides per disk ', DiskHeads);

       writeln ('Number of hidden sectors ', HiddenSectors);
     end;
  end.
```

Figure 13-14.

SHOWBOOT program (*continued*)

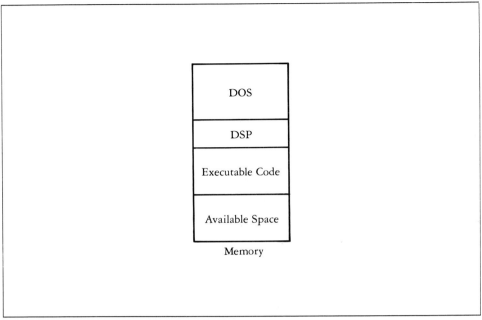

Figure 13-15.

Program-segment
prefix location in memory

PROGRAM-SEGMENT PREFIX

Each time DOS loads an executable program into memory, it places a
256-byte header at the beginning of the program. This header is called
the program-segment prefix, or PSP (see Figure 13-15). Figure 13-16
shows the fields of the PSP. The Turbo Pascal program in Figure 13-17

Offset (Hex)	Contents
0	Int 20
2	Top of Memory
4	Reserved
5	OP Code
6	Number of Bytes in Segment
A	Terminate Address (Offset)
C	Terminate Address (Segment)
E	CTRL-BREAK Address (Offset)
10	CTRL-BREAK Address (Segment)
12	Critical Error Address (Offset)
14	Critical Error Address (Segment)
16	Reserved
2C	Environment Address (Segment)
2E	Reserved
50	DOS Call
52	Reserved
5C	File-Control Block One
6C	File-Control Block Two
80	Command-Line Length (Bytes)
81	Command-Line Parameters

Figure 13-16.

Contents of program-segment prefix
(PSP)

```
    Program ShowPsp;

    function Get_PSP: integer;

    Type
      REGISTERS = record
                    AX, BX, CX, DX, BP, SI, DI, DS, ES, FLAGS: INTEGER
                  end;

    var
      REGS: REGISTERS;   {AX, BX, CX, DX, BP, SI, DI, DS, ES, FLAGS}

    begin
        with REGS do
          begin

            AX := $6200;                        {DOS function code}

            MSDos (REGS);

            Get_PSP := BX;
          end;
    end;

    var
      PSPSeg: integer;
      I: byte;

    begin
      PSPSeg := Get_PSP;
      writeln ('INT 2CH Address ', MemW[PSPSeg: 0]);
      writeln ('Terminate IP Address ', MemW[PSPSeg: $A]);
      writeln ('Terminate CS Address ', MemW[PSPSeg: $C]);
      writeln ('Ctrl-Break IP Address ', MemW[PSPSeg: $E]);
      writeln ('Ctrl-Break CS Address ', MemW[PSPSeg: $1C]);
      writeln ('Environment Segment Address ', MemW[PSPSeg: $2C]);
      writeln ('Size of Command Line ', Mem[PSPSeg: $80]);

      for I := 1 to Mem[PSPSeg: $80] do
        write (Chr(Mem[PSPSeg: $80 + I]));

      writeln ;
    end.
```

Figure 13-17.

SHOWPSP program

examines its own PSP and displays the contents, as shown here:

```
C>SHOWPSP THIS IS A TEST
INT 2CH Address 8397
Terminate IP Address 300
Terminate CS Address 12298
Ctrl-Break IP Address 313
Ctrl-Break CS Address 12298
Environment Segment Address 12872
Size of Command Line 15
 THIS IS A TEST

C>
```

Under OS/2, the PSP maintains this structure.

MEDIA DESCRIPTOR INFORMATION

Chapter 10 presented several useful disk-manipulation routines. At that time, several assumptions were made about the number of sectors per track, sectors per cluster, tracks per side, and usable sides. These assumptions were made to simplify the programming and, in turn, its readability. However, for the routines to be fully functional, they need to be more generic. The DOS service 1CH (Get File Allocation Table Information) provides the information needed (see Table 13-1).

DOS uses the media descriptor byte, as shown in Figure 13-18. The C program in Figure 13-19 uses this information to display the FAT information about the drive in the specified disk, as shown here:

```
C>FAT A
Sectors per cluster 1
Media Descriptor 6
Sector Size 512
Number of Clusters 313

C>
```

Table 13-1.

DOS Get File Allocation Table
Service

Register	Entry Contents
AH	1CH DOS Get FAT Information Service
DL	Drive number desired

Register	Exit Contents
AL	Number of sectors/cluster
BX	Offset address of media descriptor byte
CX	Sector size in bytes
DS	Segment address of media descriptor byte
DX	Number of clusters per disk

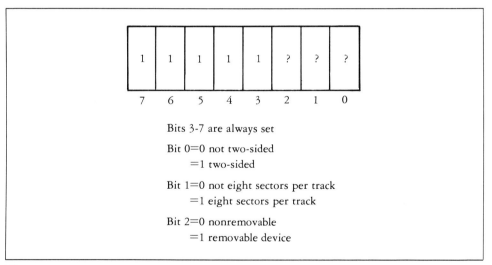

Figure 13-18.

Contents of media
descriptor byte

```
#include <dos.h>

get_FAT_info (drive, spc, media, sectorsize, clusters)
  int drive, *spc, *media, *sectorsize, *clusters;
{
  union REGS inregs, outregs;
  struct SREGS segregs;

  int long mseg;
  int far *mediaptr;

  inregs.h.ah = 0x1C;
  inregs.h.dl = drive;

  intdosx (&inregs, &outregs, &segregs);

  *spc = outregs.h.al;
  *clusters = outregs.x.dx;
  *sectorsize = outregs.x.cx;

  mseg = segregs.ds;
  mediaptr = (int far *) ((mseg << 16) + (outregs.x.bx));
  *media = (*mediaptr) & 7;
}


main (argc, argv)
  int argc;
  char *argv[];
{
  int spc, media, sectorsize, clusters, drive;
  drive = 0;  /* use default drive unless over-ridden */

  if (*argv[1] == 'A')
    drive = 1;
  else if (*argv[1] == 'B')
    drive = 2;
  else if (*argv[1] == 'C')
    drive = 3;

  get_FAT_info (drive, &spc, &media, &sectorsize, &clusters);

  printf ("Sectors per cluster %d\nMedia Descriptor %d\n", spc, media);
  printf ("Sector Size %d\nNumber of Clusters %d\n", sectorsize,
  clusters);
}
```

Figure 13-19.

Program to display
FAT information

Table 13-2.

Entry in Directory Structure

Field	Offset
File name	0
Extension	8
Attribute byte	11
Reserved for DOS	12
Time	22
Date	24
Starting cluster number	26
File size	28

FILE DATE AND TIME STAMPS

To minimize the disk-space consumption DOS requires to track every file's date and time stamps in the directory entry, as shown in Table 13-2, DOS places the stamps in 16-bit data structures as shown in Figure 13-20 and Figure 13-21. To extract the actual date and time fields, your programs must perform the following processing:

```
YEAR   := (Hi(DateBuffer) shr 1) + 1980;
MONTH  := (DateBuffer and $1E0) shr 5;
DAY    := DateBuffer and $1F;

HOURS  := Hi(TimeBuffer) shr 3;
MINUTES := (TimeBuffer and $7E0) shr 5;
SECONDS := (TimeBuffer and $1F) * 2;
```

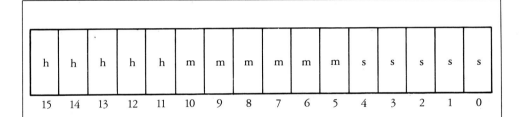

y	y	y	y	y	y	y	m	m	m	m	d	d	d	d	d

Year (0-119) or (1980-2099)
Month (1-12)
Day (1-31)

Figure 13-20.

Specifying the date

h	h	h	h	h	m	m	m	m	m	m	s	s	s	s	s
15	14	13	12	11	10	9	8	7	6	5	4	3	2	1	0

Hours (0-23)
Minutes (0-59)
Seconds (0-59)

Figure 13-21.

Specifying the time

In comparison to many of the chapters in this text, the programs and examples presented in this chapter are straightforward. However, each one helps you to better understand how DOS records data. Remember that the majority of DOS and OS/2 is written in C. Because of this, the developers had to use data structures that could be easily manipulated through high-level languages. Experiment with the DOS system services presented in Chapter 6, and you should become proficient in manipulating key data structures under DOS. Chapter 17 presents several OS/2 programmer aspects that require similar considerations.

14: DOS File
Operations

When DOS was first released in 1981, one of its major functions was to provide simple file-manipulation capabilities (such as COPY, DELETE, RENAME, and TYPE). In addition to these basic file operations, early versions of DOS provided supplemental utility programs (such as FORMAT and CHKDSK). As DOS has matured over the past few years, the requirements placed on file operations have increased. What was once simply a single-user system has expanded to multiple-user local area networks with concurrent file-access operations (see Figure 14-1).

All of the DOS file-manipulation commands are based on a simple set of DOS system services. This chapter shows you how to access each of these system services from within your application programs. Your programs will gain tremendous file-manipulation capabilities.

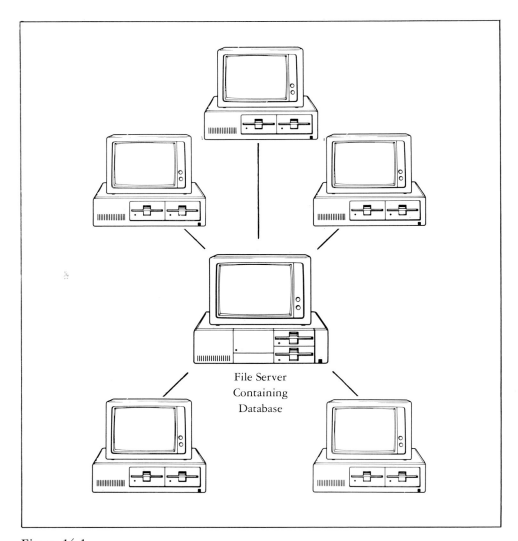

Figure 14-1.

File sharing and local area networks

FILE CONTROL BLOCKS

DOS versions before DOS 2.0 used file control blocks (FCBs) for disk I/O operations, as illustrated in Figure 14-2. To maintain compatibility with the first versions of DOS, all DOS versions since have provided full

Offset	Contents
0	Drive
1	8-character File Name
9	3-character Extension
12	Current Block Number
14	Record Size
16	File Size
20	Creation Date
22	Reserved Space
32	Current Record Number
33	Relative Record Number

Figure 14-2.

Contents of file control block (FCB)

support for FCBs. DOS versions since version 2.0 have used file handles for I/O operations, as opposed to FCBs. Because of this, you may periodically experience problems when you execute old application programs under newer versions of DOS. This is because current DOS versions provide default support for only four FCBs. In such cases, simply place the entry

FCBS=12,4

in your CONFIG.SYS file and reboot. This way your system will have adequate support for multiple FCBs.

FILE HANDLES

File control blocks give your programs direct access to many of the fields of the directory entry of a file. In many cases, programmers used FCBs to do just that. Unfortunately, many of these programs were difficult to modify, and often DOS version-dependent. Beginning with version 2.0, DOS introduced the concept of file handles for I/O operations. File handles are essentially indexes to memory locations where DOS stores data structures containing information similar to that of the FCB. This degree of indirection (indexes to data structures, as opposed to direct field manipulation), forces programmers to use the following DOS system services:

Create File Handle	3CH
Open File Handle	3DH
Close File Handle	3EH
Read File Handle	3FH
Write File Handle	40H
Move File Pointer	42H

By accessing DOS file handles, your programs gain considerable functional capabilities. The following Turbo Pascal procedures utilize all of the DOS file-manipulation services by using DOS file handles. The first procedure, **Create — File**, creates a file with the name specified by the ASCIIZ string you provide and returns a 16-bit handle to the file. If a file with the specified name does not exist, DOS creates one. If a file with the same name already exists, DOS truncates it.

```
procedure Create_File (FILENAME: STRING79;
                          ATTRIBUTE: integer;
                  var FILE_HANDLE: integer;
                       var STATUS: byte);
Type
  REGISTERS = record
                   AX, BX, CX, DX, BP, SI, DI, DS, ES, FLAGS: INTEGER
              end;

var
     REGS: REGISTERS;   {AX, BX, CX, DX, BP, SI, DI, DS, ES, FLAGS}

begin
      with REGS do
        begin
          FILENAME := FILENAME + Chr(0);
          AX := $3C00;
          CX := ATTRIBUTE;
          DS := Seg(FILENAME[1]);
          DX := Ofs(FILENAME[1]);
          MSDos (REGS);
          if (FLAGS and 1 = 1) then           {error in operation}
            STATUS := Lo(AX)
          else
            begin
              FILE_HANDLE := AX;               {successful operation}
              STATUS := 0;
            end;
        end;
end;
```

Note that the CX register contains the desired attributes for the file, as shown in Table 14-1. In a similar manner, the DOS Open File system service returns a 16-bit handle to a previously existing DOS file. If the specified file does not exist, DOS returns one of the error-status values shown in Table 14-2. Use the open-status values shown in Table 14-3 to specify the desired access mode.

The routine on the next page implements **OpenFile**.

```
procedure OpenFile (FILENAME: STRING79;
                          MODE: byte;
                 var FILE_HANDLE: integer;
                      var STATUS: byte);

Type
   REGISTERS = record
                   AX, BX, CX, DX, BP, SI, DI, DS, ES, FLAGS: INTEGER
               end;

var
     REGS: REGISTERS;   {AX, BX, CX, DX, BP, SI, DI, DS, ES, FLAGS}

begin
     with REGS do
       begin
          FILENAME := FILENAME + Chr(0);
          AX := $3D00 + MODE;                {mode is in AL}
          DS := Seg(FILENAME[1]);
          DX := Ofs(FILENAME[1]);
          MSDos (REGS);
          if (FLAGS and 1 = 1) then          {error in operation}
            STATUS := Lo(AX)
          else
            begin
               FILE_HANDLE := AX;            {successful operation}
               STATUS := 0;
            end;
       end;
   end;
```

Table 14-1.

Attributes of CX Register

Value	Attribute
0	Read/write access
1	Read-only access
2	Hidden
4	System
8	Volume
16	Subdirectory
32	Archive

Table 14-2.

Error-Status Values

Value	Error
2	File not found
3	Path not found
5	Access denied

Table 14-3.

Open-Status Values

Value	Access Mode
0	Read-only access
1	Write access
2	Read/write access

DOS service 3EH closes a file that you have previously opened through the CreateFile or OpenFile system services. Upon invocation of **Open-File**, DOS flushes all of the disk buffers associated with the file and updates the directory entries as required.

This Turbo Pascal routine implements **CloseFile**:

```
procedure CloseFile (FILE_HANDLE: integer;
                     var STATUS: byte);

Type
  REGISTERS = record
                AX, BX, CX, DX, BP, SI, DI, DS, ES, FLAGS: INTEGER
              end;
```

```
var
     REGS: REGISTERS;  {AX, BX, CX, DX, BP, SI, DI, DS, ES, FLAGS}
begin
     with REGS do
        begin
          AX := $3E00;
          DX := FILE_HANDLE;
          MSDos (REGS);
          if (FLAGS and 1 = 1) then          {error in operation}
             STATUS := Lo(AX)
          else
             STATUS := 0;
        end;
end;
```

Once your program has successfully opened a DOS file and obtained
a file handle, the DOS services 3FH and 40H allow you to perform read
and write operations to it. The first service, Read File Handle (3FH),
transfers the number of specified bytes from a file into a disk buffer
location. In this case, your program sets aside a buffer (a variable of type
array) in which DOS will store the information that it reads from disk
(see Figure 14-3).

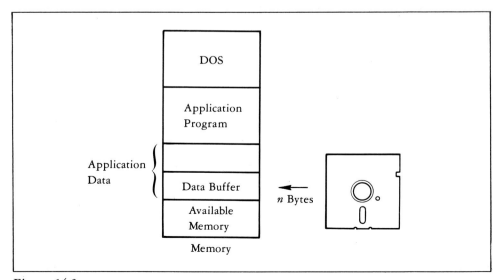

Figure 14-3.

Data buffer in memory

The following Turbo Pascal routine implements **ReadFileHandle**:

```
procedure ReadFileHandle (FILE_HANDLE: integer;
                          var BUFFER: DISKBUFFER;
                             NUMBYTES: integer;
                       var BYTESREAD: integer;
                          var STATUS: byte);
Type
  REGISTERS = record
                AX, BX, CX, DX, BP, SI, DI, DS, ES, FLAGS: INTEGER
              end;
var
    REGS: REGISTERS;   {AX, BX, CX, DX, BP, SI, DI, DS, ES, FLAGS}

begin
    with REGS do
      begin
        AX := $3F00;
        BX := FILE_HANDLE;
        CX := NUMBYTES;
        DS := Seg(BUFFER);
        DX := Ofs(BUFFER);
        MSDos (REGS);
        if (FLAGS and 1 = 1) then          {error in operation}
          STATUS := Lo(AX)
        else
          BYTESREAD := AX;
          STATUS := 0;
      end;
  end;
```

When this service encounters an end-of-file, it places the value 0 in the register AX. Similarly, the DOS service Write File Handle (40H) writes the number of a file in an application-defined buffer to the device associated with the specified file handle. The following Turbo Pascal procedure implements **WriteFileHandle**.

```
procedure WriteFileHandle (FILE_HANDLE: integer;
                              BUFFER: DISKBUFFER;
                             NUMBYTES: integer;
                          var STATUS: byte);

Type
  REGISTERS = record
                AX, BX, CX, DX, BP, SI, DI, DS, ES, FLAGS: INTEGER
              end;
var
    REGS: REGISTERS;   {AX, BX, CX, DX, BP, SI, DI, DS, ES, FLAGS}

begin
```

```
      with REGS do
        begin
          AX := $4000;
          BX := FILE_HANDLE;
          CX := NUMBYTES;
          DS := Seg(BUFFER);
          DX := Ofs(BUFFER);
          MSDos (REGS);
          if (FLAGS and 1 = 1) then          {error in operation}
            STATUS := Lo(AX)
          else
            STATUS := 0;
        end;
end;
```

The Turbo Pascal program in Figure 14-4 displays the contents of the file TEST.DAT to the screen (predefined DOS file handle stdout or handle 1). In a similar manner, **HCOPY** (shown in Figure 14-5) copies the contents of the file specified by the first command-line argument to the file specified by the second, as shown here:

```
A> HCOPY SOURCE.TXT TARGET.TXT
```

```
      Program ShowTest;

      Const
        BUFFERSIZE = 512;

      Type
        STRING79 = string[79];
        DISKBUFFER = array [1..BUFFERSIZE] of byte;


      procedure OpenFile (FILENAME: STRING79;
                                  MODE: byte;
                      var FILE_HANDLE: integer;
                           var STATUS: byte);
```

Figure 14-4.

SHOWTEST program

```
Type
  REGISTERS = record
                 AX, BX, CX, DX, BP, SI, DI, DS, ES, FLAGS: INTEGER
              end;

var
    REGS: REGISTERS;  {AX, BX, CX, DX, BP, SI, DI, DS, ES, FLAGS}

begin
    with REGS do
      begin
        FILENAME := FILENAME + Chr(0);
        AX := $3D00 + MODE;                  {mode is in AL}
        DS := Seg(FILENAME[1]);
        DX := Ofs(FILENAME[1]);
        MSDos (REGS);
        if (FLAGS and 1 = 1) then            {error in operation}
          STATUS := Lo(AX)
        else
          begin
            FILE_HANDLE := AX;               {successful operation}
            STATUS := 0;
          end;
      end;
end;

procedure CloseFile (FILE_HANDLE: integer;
                     var STATUS: byte);

Type
  REGISTERS = record
                 AX, BX, CX, DX, BP, SI, DI, DS, ES, FLAGS: INTEGER
              end;

var
    REGS: REGISTERS;  {AX, BX, CX, DX, BP, SI, DI, DS, ES, FLAGS}

begin
    with REGS do
      begin
        AX := $3E00;
        BX := FILE_HANDLE;
        MSDos (REGS);
        if (FLAGS and 1 = 1) then            {error in operation}
          STATUS := Lo(AX)
        else
          STATUS := 0;
      end;
end;


procedure ReadFileHandle (FILE_HANDLE: integer;
                          var BUFFER: DISKBUFFER;
                              NUMBYTES: integer;
                          var BYTESREAD: integer;
                          var STATUS: byte);

Type
  REGISTERS = record
                 AX, BX, CX, DX, BP, SI, DI, DS, ES, FLAGS: INTEGER
              end;

var
    REGS: REGISTERS;  {AX, BX, CX, DX, BP, SI, DI, DS, ES, FLAGS}
```

Figure 14-4.

SHOWTEST program (*continued*)

```
      begin
          with REGS do
            begin
              AX := $3F00;
              BX := FILE_HANDLE;
              CX := NUMBYTES;
              DS := Seg(BUFFER);
              DX := Ofs(BUFFER);
              MSDos (REGS);
              if (FLAGS and 1 = 1) then          {error in operation}
                STATUS := Lo(AX)
              else
                BYTESREAD := AX;
                STATUS := 0;
            end;
      end;

      procedure WriteFileHandle (FILE_HANDLE: integer;
                                     BUFFER: DISKBUFFER;
                                  NUMBYTES: integer;
                                var STATUS: byte);

      Type
        REGISTERS = record
                       AX, BX, CX, DX, BP, SI, DI, DS, ES, FLAGS: INTEGER
                    end;

      var
          REGS: REGISTERS;   {AX, BX, CX, DX, BP, SI, DI, DS, ES, FLAGS}

       begin
          with REGS do
            begin
              AX := $4000;
              BX := FILE_HANDLE;
              CX := NUMBYTES;
              DS := Seg(BUFFER);
              DX := Ofs(BUFFER);
              MSDos (REGS);
              if (FLAGS and 1 = 1) then            {error in operation}
                STATUS := Lo(AX)
              else
                STATUS := 0;
            end;
      end;

      var
        bytesread, handle: integer;
        status, readstatus, writestatus: byte;
        buffer: diskbuffer;

      begin
          OpenFile ('TEST.DAT', 0, HANDLE, STATUS);
          if (STATUS <> 0) then
            writeln ('TYPETEST: Cannot open the file TEST.DAT')
          else
            begin
              repeat
                ReadFileHandle (HANDLE, BUFFER, BUFFERSIZE, BYTESREAD,
                    READSTATUS);
                WriteFileHandle (1, BUFFER, BYTESREAD, WRITESTATUS);
              until (BYTESREAD = 0);

              CloseFile (HANDLE, STATUS);
            end;
      end.
```

Figure 14-4.

SHOWTEST program (*continued*)

```
        Program Hcopy;

        Const
          BUFFERSIZE = 512;

        Type
          STRING79 = string[79];
          DISKBUFFER = array [1..BUFFERSIZE] of byte;


        procedure OpenFile (FILENAME: STRING79;
                               MODE: byte;
                      var FILE_HANDLE: integer;
                         var STATUS: byte);

        Type
          REGISTERS = record
                        AX, BX, CX, DX, BP, SI, DI, DS, ES, FLAGS: INTEGER
                      end;

        var
            REGS: REGISTERS;   {AX, BX, CX, DX, BP, SI, DI, DS, ES, FLAGS}

        begin
            with REGS do
              begin
                FILENAME := FILENAME + Chr(0);
                AX := $3D00 + MODE;                {mode is in AL}
                DS := Seg(FILENAME[1]);
                DX := Ofs(FILENAME[1]);
                MSDos (REGS);
                if (FLAGS and 1 = 1) then          {error in operation}
                  STATUS := Lo(AX)
                  else
                    begin
                      FILE_HANDLE := AX;           {successful operation}
                      STATUS := 0;
                    end;
              end;
        end;

        procedure CloseFile (FILE_HANDLE: integer;
                               var STATUS: byte);

        Type
          REGISTERS = record
                        AX, BX, CX, DX, BP, SI, DI, DS, ES, FLAGS: INTEGER
                      end;

        var
            REGS: REGISTERS;   {AX, BX, CX, DX, BP, SI, DI, DS, ES, FLAGS}

        begin
            with REGS do
              begin
                AX := $3E00;
                BX := FILE_HANDLE;
                MSDos (REGS);
                if (FLAGS and 1 = 1) then          {error in operation}
                  STATUS := Lo(AX)
                  else
                    STATUS := 0;
              end;
        end;
```

Figure 14-5.

HCOPY program

```
        procedure   CreateFile (FILENAME: STRING79;
                              ATTRIBUTE: integer;
                          var FILE_HANDLE: integer;
                              var STATUS: byte);

        Type
          REGISTERS = record
                          AX, BX, CX, DX, BP, SI, DI, DS, ES, FLAGS: INTEGER
                      end;

        var
            REGS: REGISTERS;  {AX, BX, CX, DX, BP, SI, DI, DS, ES, FLAGS}

        begin
            with REGS do
              begin
                FILENAME := FILENAME + Chr(0);
                AX := $3C00;
                CX := ATTRIBUTE;
                DS := Seg(FILENAME[1]);
                DX := Ofs(FILENAME[1]);
                MSDos (REGS);
                if (FLAGS and 1 = 1) then          {error in operation}
                  STATUS := Lo(AX)
                else
                  begin
                    FILE_HANDLE := AX;             {successful operation}
                    STATUS := 0;
                  end;
              end;
        end;


        procedure ReadFileHandle (FILE_HANDLE: integer;
                              var BUFFER: DISKBUFFER;
                              NUMBYTES: integer;
                              var BYTESREAD: integer;
                              var STATUS: byte);

        Type
          REGISTERS = record
                          AX, BX, CX, DX, BP, SI, DI, DS, ES, FLAGS: INTEGER
                      end;

        var
            REGS: REGISTERS;  {AX, BX, CX, DX, BP, SI, DI, DS, ES, FLAGS}

        begin
            with REGS do
              begin
                AX := $3F00;
                BX := FILE_HANDLE;
                CX := NUMBYTES;
                DS := Seg(BUFFER);
                DX := Ofs(BUFFER);
                MSDos (REGS);
                if (FLAGS and 1 = 1) then          {error in operation}
                  STATUS := Lo(AX)
                else
                  BYTESREAD := AX;
                  STATUS := 0;
              end;
        end;
```

Figure 14-5.

HCOPY program (*continued*)

```
        procedure WriteFileHandle (FILE_HANDLE: integer;
                                      BUFFER: DISKBUFFER;
                                    NUMBYTES: integer;
                                var STATUS: byte);

        Type
          REGISTERS = record
                       AX, BX, CX, DX, BP, SI, DI, DS, ES, FLAGS: INTEGER
                     end;

        var
            REGS: REGISTERS;   {AX, BX, CX, DX, BP, SI, DI, DS, ES, FLAGS}

        begin
            with REGS do
              begin
                AX := $4000;
                BX := FILE_HANDLE;
                CX := NUMBYTES;
                DS := Seg(BUFFER);
                DX := Ofs(BUFFER);
                MSDos (REGS);
                if (FLAGS and 1 = 1) then          {error in operation}
                  STATUS := Lo(AX)
                else
                  STATUS := 0;
              end;
        end;


        var
          bytesread, source, target: integer;
          status, readstatus, writestatus: byte;

          buffer: diskbuffer;

        begin
          if (ParamCount < 2) then
            writeln ('HCOPY: invalid usage: HCOPY SOURCE TARGET')
          else
            begin
              OpenFile (ParamStr(1), 0, SOURCE, STATUS);
              if (STATUS <> 0) then
                begin
                  writeln ('HCOPY: Cannot open the file ', ParamStr(1));
                  CloseFile (Source, STATUS);
                end
              else
                begin
                  CreateFile (ParamStr(2), 0, TARGET, STATUS);
                  if (STATUS <> 0) then
                    writeln ('HCOPY: Cannot open the file ', ParamStr(2))
                  else
                    begin
                      repeat
                        ReadFileHandle (SOURCE, BUFFER, BUFFERSIZE,
                                         BYTESREAD, READSTATUS);
                          WriteFileHandle (TARGET, BUFFER, BYTESREAD,
                            WRITESTATUS);
                      until (BYTESREAD = 0);

                      CloseFile (SOURCE, STATUS);
                      CloseFile (TARGET, STATUS);
                    end;
                end;
            end;
        end.
```

Figure 14-5.

HCOPY program (*continued*)

Table 14-4.

DOS File Handles and Applications

File Handle	Default Device	Name	Operations
0	con:	stdin	keyboard
1	con:	stdout	screen
2	con:	stderr	screen
3	aux:	stdaux	aux:device
4	prn:	stdprn	printer

Note that DOS does not just use file handles for disk I/O operations. You can easily replace DOS file handles with any of the predefined file handles listed in Table 14-4.

Similarly, the Turbo Pascal program **HTYPE.PAS** (shown in Figure 14-6) implements the DOS TYPE command. Likewise, the program shown in Figure 14-7 implements a rudimentary version of the DOS file-comparison command, COMP.

```
Program Htype;

Const
  BUFFERSIZE = 512;

Type
  STRING79 = string[79];
  DISKBUFFER = array [1..BUFFERSIZE] of byte;


procedure OpenFile (FILENAME: STRING79;
                         MODE: byte;
               var FILE_HANDLE: integer;
                   var STATUS: byte);
```

Figure 14-6.

HTYPE program

```
Type
  REGISTERS = record
                AX, BX, CX, DX, BP  SI, DI, DS, ES, FLAGS: INTEGER
              end;

var
    REGS: REGISTERS;  {AX, BX, CX, DX, BP, SI, DI, DS, ES, FLAGS}

begin
    with REGS do
      begin
        FILENAME := FILENAME + Chr(0);
        AX := $3D00 + MODE;              {mode is in AL}
        DS := Seg(FILENAME[1]);
        DX := Ofs(FILENAME[1]);
        MSDos (REGS);
        if (FLAGS and 1 = 1) then        {error in operation}
          STATUS := Lo(AX)
        else
          begin
            FILE_HANDLE := AX;           {successful operation}
            STATUS := 0;
          end;
      end;
end;

procedure CloseFile (FILE_HANDLE: integer;
                     var STATUS: byte);

Type
  REGISTERS = record
                AX, BX, CX, DX, BP, SI, DI, DS, ES, FLAGS: INTEGER
              end;

var
    REGS: REGISTERS;  {AX, BX, CX, DX, BP, SI, DI, DS, ES, FLAGS}

begin

    with REGS do
      begin
        AX := $3E00;
        BX := FILE_HANDLE;
        MSDos (REGS);
        if (FLAGS and 1 = 1) then        {error in operation}
          STATUS := Lo(AX)
        else
          STATUS := 0;
      end;
end;


procedure ReadFileHandle (FILE_HANDLE: integer;
                          var BUFFER: DISKBUFFER;
                              NUMBYTES: integer;
                          var BYTESREAD: integer;
                              var STATUS: byte);

Type
  REGISTERS = record
                AX, BX, CX, DX, BP, SI, DI, DS, ES, FLAGS: INTEGER
              end;

var
    REGS: REGISTERS;  {AX, BX, CX, DX, BP, SI, DI, DS, ES, FLAGS}
```

Figure 14-6.

HTYPE program (*continued*)

```
    begin
        with REGS do
            begin
            AX := $3F00;
            BX := FILE_HANDLE;
            CX := NUMBYTES;
            DS := Seg(BUFFER);
            DX := Ofs(BUFFER);
            MSDos (REGS);
            if (FLAGS and 1 = 1) then          {error in operation}
                STATUS := Lo(AX)
            else
                BYTESREAD := AX;
                STATUS := 0;
            end;
    end;

    procedure WriteFileHandle (FILE_HANDLE: integer;
                                  BUFFER: DISKBUFFER;
                                  NUMBYTES: integer;
                                  var STATUS: byte);

    Type
      REGISTERS = record
                    AX, BX, CX, DX, BP, SI, DI, DS, ES, FLAGS: INTEGER
                end;

    var
        REGS: REGISTERS;   {AX, BX, CX, DX, BP, SI, DI, DS, ES, FLAGS}

    begin
        with REGS do
            begin
            AX := $4000;
            BX := FILE_HANDLE;
            CX := NUMBYTES;
            DS := Seg(BUFFER);
            DX := Ofs(BUFFER);
            MSDos (REGS);
            if (FLAGS and 1 = 1) then          {error in operation}
                STATUS := Lo(AX)
            else
                STATUS := 0;
            end;
    end;

    var
      bytesread, handle: integer;
      status, readstatus, writestatus: byte;
      buffer: diskbuffer;

    begin
      if (ParamCount < 1) then
        writeln ('HTYPE: invalid usage: HTYPE FILENAME')
      else
        begin
          OpenFile (ParamStr(1), 0, HANDLE, STATUS);
          if (STATUS <> 0) then
            writeln ('HTYPE: Cannot open the file ', ParamStr(1))
          else
            begin
              repeat
                ReadFileHandle (HANDLE, BUFFER, BUFFERSIZE, BYTESREAD,
                    READSTATUS);
                WriteFileHandle (1, BUFFER, BYTESREAD, WRITESTATUS);
              until (BYTESREAD = 0);

              CloseFile (HANDLE, STATUS);
            end;
        end;
    end.
```

Figure 14-6.

HTYPE program (*continued*)

```
Program Hcomp;

Const
  BUFFERSIZE = 512;

Type
  STRING79 = string[79];
  DISKBUFFER = array [1..BUFFERSIZE] of byte;

procedure OpenFile (FILENAME: STRING79;
                          MODE: byte;
                    var FILE_HANDLE: integer;
                        var STATUS: byte);

Type
  REGISTERS = record
                  AX, BX, CX, DX, BP, SI, DI, DS, ES, FLAGS: INTEGER
              end;

var
    REGS: REGISTERS;   {AX, BX, CX, DX, BP, SI, DI, DS, ES, FLAGS}

begin
    with REGS do
      begin
        FILENAME := FILENAME + Chr(0);
        AX := $3D00 + MODE;             {mode is in AL}
        DS := Seg(FILENAME[1]);
        DX := Ofs(FILENAME[1]);
        MSDos (REGS);
        if (FLAGS and 1 = 1) then        {error in operation}
          STATUS := Lo(AX)
        else
          begin
            FILE_HANDLE := AX;           {successful operation}
            STATUS := 0;
          end;
      end;
end;

procedure CloseFile (FILE_HANDLE: integer;
                        var STATUS: byte);

Type
  REGISTERS = record
                  AX, BX, CX, DX, BP, SI, DI, DS, ES, FLAGS: INTEGER
              end;

var
    REGS: REGISTERS;   {AX, BX, CX, DX, BP, SI, DI, DS, ES, FLAGS}

begin

    with REGS do
      begin
        AX := $3E00;
        BX := FILE_HANDLE;
        MSDos (REGS);
        if (FLAGS and 1 = 1) then        {error in operation}
          STATUS := Lo(AX)
        else
          STATUS := 0;
      end;
end;

procedure ReadFileHandle (FILE_HANDLE: integer;
                            var BUFFER: DISKBUFFER;
                              NUMBYTES: integer;
                          var BYTESREAD: integer;
```

Figure 14-7.

HCOMP program

```
                              var STATUS: byte);
        Type
          REGISTERS = record
                        AX, BX, CX, DX, BP, SI, DI, DS, ES, FLAGS: INTEGER
                      end;

        var
            REGS: REGISTERS;   {AX, BX, CX, DX, BP, SI, DI, DS, ES, FLAGS}

        begin
            with REGS do
              begin
                AX := $3F00;
                BX := FILE_HANDLE;
                CX := NUMBYTES;
                DS := Seg(BUFFER);
                DX := Ofs(BUFFER);
                MSDos (REGS);
                if (FLAGS and 1 = 1) then          {error in operation}
                  STATUS := Lo(AX)
                else
                  BYTESREAD := AX;
                  STATUS := 0;
              end;
        end;

        procedure WriteFileHandle (FILE_HANDLE: integer;
                                        BUFFER: DISKBUFFER;
                                      NUMBYTES: integer;
                                    var STATUS: byte);

        Type
          REGISTERS = record
                        AX, BX, CX, DX, BP, SI, DI, DS, ES, FLAGS: INTEGER
                      end;

        var
            REGS: REGISTERS;   {AX, BX, CX, DX, BP, SI, DI, DS, ES, FLAGS}

        begin
            with REGS do
              begin
                AX := $4000;
                BX := FILE_HANDLE;
                CX := NUMBYTES;
                DS := Seg(BUFFER);
                DX := Ofs(BUFFER);
                MSDos (REGS);
                if (FLAGS and 1 = 1) then          {error in operation}
                  STATUS := Lo(AX)
                else
                  STATUS := 0;
              end;
        end;

        var
          REC, index, bytesread1, bytesread2, source, target: integer;
          status, readstatus, writestatus: byte;
          buffer1, buffer2: diskbuffer;

        begin
          if (ParamCount < 2) then
            writeln ('HCOMP: invalid usage: HCOMP FILE1 FILE2')
```

Figure 14-7.

HCOMP program (*continued*)

```
       else
          begin
             OpenFile (ParamStr(1), 0, SOURCE, STATUS);
             if (STATUS <> 0) then
                begin
                   writeln ('HCOMP: Cannot open the file ', ParamStr(1));
                   CloseFile (Source, STATUS);
                end
             else
                begin
                   OpenFile (ParamStr(2), 0, TARGET, STATUS);
                   if (STATUS <> 0) then
                      writeln ('HCOMP: Cannot open the file ', ParamStr(2))
                   else
                      begin
                         REC := 0;
                         repeat
                            ReadFileHandle (SOURCE, BUFFER1, BUFFERSIZE,
                                            BYTESREAD1, READSTATUS);

                            ReadFileHandle (TARGET, BUFFER2, BUFFERSIZE,
                                            BYTESREAD2, READSTATUS);

                            REC := REC + 1;
                            INDEX := 1;

                            while (INDEX <= BUFFERSIZE) do
                               begin
                                  if (BUFFER2[INDEX] <> BUFFER1[INDEX]) then
                                     writeln ('HCOMP: difference at byte ',
                                              BUFFERSIZE * REC + INDEX);
                                  INDEX := INDEX + 1;
                               end;

                         until (BYTESREAD1 = 0) or (BYTESREAD2 = 0);

                         CloseFile (SOURCE, STATUS);
                         CloseFile (TARGET, STATUS);
                      end;
                end;
          end;
    end.
```

Figure 14-7.

HCOMP program (*continued*)

RANDOM-ACCESS FILES

Thus far, all of the file-manipulation programs examined have dealt with sequential-file data files. That is, each application has opened a file and begun reading files from the start of the file to the end, one record at a time, as shown in Figure 14-8. Pascal, however, supports random-access file manipulation through the use of the **Get** and **Put** run-time library routines. The DOS system service Move File Pointer (42H) lets

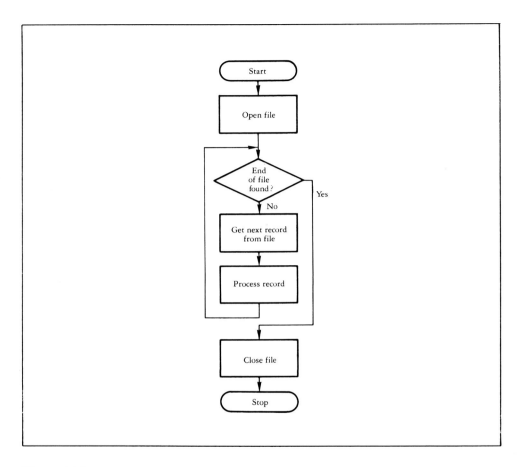

Figure 14-8.

Sequential file-manipulation process

your applications move a file's read/write pointer to access data within a file in any order (random access). Table 14-5 shows the specifications for service 42H. Figure 14-9 shows how the CX and DX registers work together to specify the byte offset within the file at which you want to place the file pointer.

Table 14-5.

DOS LSEEK Service

Register	Entry Contents
AH	42H DOS LSEEK service
AL	Method of moving file pointer
BX	File handle
CX	High-word offset value
DX	Low-word offset value

Register	Exit Contents
AX	Error code if the carry flag is set

The Turbo Pascal program in Figure 14-10 tracks the sales for a software company. Table 14-6 shows the company's sales records. Periodically, the company owner wants to know the sales amount for a specific Julian day, as shown in Figure 14-11. Since the file containing

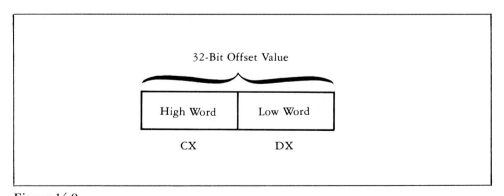

Figure 14-9.

CX-DX process of specifying byte offset

```
        Program DBase1;

        Const
          BUFFERSIZE = 2;

        Type
          STRING79 = string[79];
          DISKBUFFER = integer;

        procedure OpenFile (FILENAME: STRING79;
                               MODE: byte;
                       var FILE_HANDLE: integer;
                           var STATUS: byte);

        Type
          REGISTERS = record
                        AX, BX, CX, DX, BP, SI, DI, DS, ES, FLAGS: INTEGER
                      end;

        var
            REGS: REGISTERS;   {AX, BX, CX, DX, BP, SI, DI, DS, ES, FLAGS}

        begin
            with REGS do
              begin
                FILENAME := FILENAME + Chr(0);
                AX := $3D00 + MODE;              {mode is in AL}
                DS := Seg(FILENAME[1]);
                DX := Ofs(FILENAME[1]);
                MSDos (REGS);
                if (FLAGS and 1 = 1) then        {error in operation}
                  STATUS := Lo(AX)
                else
                  begin
                    FILE_HANDLE := AX;           {successful operation}
                    STATUS := 0;
                  end;
              end;
        end;

        procedure CloseFile (FILE_HANDLE: integer;
                             var STATUS: byte);

        Type
          REGISTERS = record
                        AX, BX, CX, DX, BP, SI, DI, DS, ES, FLAGS: INTEGER
                      end;

        var
            REGS: REGISTERS;   {AX, BX, CX, DX, BP, SI, DI, DS, ES, FLAGS}

        begin
            with REGS do
              begin
                AX := $3E00;
                BX := FILE_HANDLE;
                MSDos (REGS);
                if (FLAGS and 1 = 1) then        {error in operation}
                  STATUS := Lo(AX)
                else
                  STATUS := 0;
              end;
        end;
```

Figure 14-10.

DBASE1 program

```
           procedure ReadFileHandle (FILE_HANDLE: integer;
                               var BUFFER: DISKBUFFER;
                                   NUMBYTES: integer;
                               var BYTESREAD: integer;
                               var STATUS: byte);

       Type
         REGISTERS = record
                       AX, BX, CX, DX, BP, SI, DI, DS, ES, FLAGS: INTEGER
                     end;

       var
           REGS: REGISTERS;  {AX, BX, CX, DX, BP, SI, DI, DS, ES, FLAGS}

       begin
           with REGS do
             begin
               AX := $3F00;
               BX := FILE_HANDLE;
               CX := NUMBYTES;
               DS := Seg(BUFFER);
               DX := Ofs(BUFFER);
               MSDos (REGS);
               if (FLAGS and 1 = 1) then          {error in operation}
                  STATUS := Lo(AX)
               else
                  BYTESREAD := AX;
                  STATUS := 0;
             end;
       end;

           procedure WriteFileHandle (FILE_HANDLE: integer;
                                  BUFFER: DISKBUFFER;
                                  NUMBYTES: integer;
                              var STATUS: byte);
       Type
         REGISTERS = record
                       AX, BX, CX, DX, BP, SI, DI, DS, ES, FLAGS: INTEGER
                     end;

       var
           REGS: REGISTERS;  {AX, BX, CX, DX, BP, SI, DI, DS, ES, FLAGS}

       begin
           with REGS do
             begin
               AX := $4000;
               BX := FILE_HANDLE;
               CX := NUMBYTES;
               DS := Seg(BUFFER);
               DX := Ofs(BUFFER);
               MSDos (REGS);
               if (FLAGS and 1 = 1) then          {error in operation}
                  STATUS := Lo(AX)
               else
                  STATUS := 0;
             end;
       end;


           procedure Lseek (FILE_HANDLE: integer;
                            DIRECTIVE: integer;
                            HIOFFSET,
```

Figure 14-10.

DBASE1 program (*continued*)

```
                    LOOFFSET: integer;
                    var STATUS: byte);

    Type
      REGISTERS = record
                     AX, BX, CX, DX, BP, SI, DI, DS, ES, FLAGS: INTEGER
                  end;

    var
        REGS: REGISTERS;   {AX, BX, CX, DX, BP, SI, DI, DS, ES, FLAGS}

    begin
        with REGS do
          begin
            AX := $4200 + DIRECTIVE;
            BX := FILE_HANDLE;
            CX := HIOFFSET;
            DX := LOOFFSET;
            MSDos (REGS);
            if (FLAGS and 1 = 1) then          {error in operation}
              STATUS := Lo(AX)
            else
              STATUS := 0;
          end;
    end;


    var
      rec, offset, sales, bytesread, handle: integer;
      status, readstatus, writestatus: byte;

    begin
      repeat
      write ('Enter day number desired >');
      readln (rec);
    until (rec > 0) and (rec < 366);

    offset := (rec - 1) * 2;

    OpenFile ('SALES.DAT', 2, HANDLE, STATUS);

    Lseek (HANDLE, 0, 0, OFFSET, STATUS);

    ReadFileHandle (HANDLE, SALES, BUFFERSIZE, BYTESREAD, READSTATUS);

    CloseFile (HANDLE, STATUS);

      writeln (sales);
    end.
```

Figure 14-10.

DBASE1 program (*continued*)

Table 14-6.

Company Sales Records

Julian Day	Sales
1	$250
2	$245
3	$275
.	.
.	.
.	.
363	$400
364	$425
365	$418

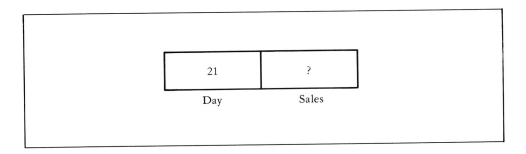

21	?
Day	Sales

Figure 14-11.

Seeking sales on a given Julian day

the records is simply a file of integer values, the sales for a specific day
are calculated as follows:

Record = (Day − 1) * 2(bytes/integer)

This Turbo Pascal routine implements **Lseek**:

```
procedure Lseek (FILE_HANDLE: integer;
                 DIRECTIVE: integer;
                 HIOFFSET,
                 LOOFFSET: integer;
                 var STATUS: byte);
Type
  REGISTERS = record
                AX, BX, CX, DX, BP, SI, DI, DS, ES, FLAGS: INTEGER
              end;
var
    REGS: REGISTERS;  {AX, BX, CX, DX, BP, SI, DI, DS, ES, FLAGS}
begin
    with REGS do
      begin
        AX := $4200 + DIRECTIVE;
        BX := FILE_HANDLE;
        CX := HIOFFSET;
        DX := LOOFFSET;
        MSDos (REGS);
        if (FLAGS and 1 = 1) then          {error in operation}
          STATUS := Lo(AX)
        else
          STATUS := 0;
      end;
end;
```

Assume that the file SALES.DAT already exists. When the user
enters the desired Julian day (1-365), the program simply looks up the
desired record by using **Lseek** and then reads it with the DOS Read File
Handle service. In this way, the program shown in Figure 14-10 performs random-access disk I/O operations.

You can further expand this application to store records of the following structure:

```
Type
  Employee_Record = record
    name: string[25];
    age: byte;
    phone: string[8];
  end;
```

In this case, each record requires 36 bytes of storage. Use the program in Figure 14-12 to place three records into the EMPLOYEE database.

```
Program DB2;

Const
  BUFFERSIZE = 2;

Type
  STRING79 = string[79];
  Employee_Record = record
    name: string[25];
    age: byte;
    phone: string[8];
    active: byte;
  end;

  DISKBUFFER = Employee_record;

procedure  CreateFile (FILENAME: STRING79;
                       ATTRIBUTE: integer;
                   var FILE_HANDLE: integer;
                       var STATUS: byte);
Type
  REGISTERS = record
                AX, BX, CX, DX, BP, SI, DI, DS, ES, FLAGS: INTEGER
              end;
```

Figure 14-12.

DB2 program

```
var
    REGS: REGISTERS;   {AX, BX, CX, DX, BP, SI, DI, DS, ES, FLAGS}

begin
    with REGS do
      begin
        FILENAME := FILENAME + Chr(0);
        AX := $3C00;
        CX := ATTRIBUTE;
        DS := Seg(FILENAME[1]);
        DX := Ofs(FILENAME[1]);
        MSDos (REGS);
        if (FLAGS and 1 = 1) then          {error in operation}
          STATUS := Lo(AX)
        else
          begin
            FILE_HANDLE := AX;             {successful operation}
            STATUS := 0;
            end;
      end;
end;

procedure CloseFile (FILE_HANDLE: integer;
                     var STATUS: byte);

Type
  REGISTERS = record
                AX, BX, CX, DX, BP, SI, DI, DS, ES, FLAGS: INTEGER
              end;

var
    REGS: REGISTERS;   {AX, BX, CX, DX, BP, SI, DI, DS, ES, FLAGS}

begin
    with REGS do
      begin
        AX := $3E00;
        BX := FILE_HANDLE;
        MSDos (REGS);
        if (FLAGS and 1 = 1) then          {error in operation}
          STATUS := Lo(AX)
        else
          STATUS := 0;
      end;
end;

procedure WriteFileHandle (FILE_HANDLE: integer;
                           BUFFER: DISKBUFFER;
                           NUMBYTES: integer;
                           var STATUS: byte);

Type
  REGISTERS = record
                AX, BX, CX, DX, BP, SI, DI, DS, ES, FLAGS: INTEGER
              end;

var
    REGS: REGISTERS;   {AX, BX, CX, DX, BP, SI, DI, DS, ES, FLAGS}

begin
    with REGS do
      begin
```

Figure 14-12.

DB2 program (*continued*)

```
            AX  := $4000;
            BX  := FILE_HANDLE;
            CX  := NUMBYTES;
            DS  := Seg(BUFFER);
            DX  := Ofs(BUFFER);
            MSDos (REGS);
            if (FLAGS and 1 = 1) then          {error in operation}
                STATUS := Lo(AX)
            else
                STATUS := 0;
        end;
end;

var
  Employee: Employee_Record;
  EMPFILE: integer;
  status, writestatus: byte;
  INDEX: integer;
  begin
    CreateFile ('EMP.DAT', 0, EMPFILE, STATUS);

    for index := 1 to 3 do
      begin
        write ('Enter Employee name >');
        readln (Employee.NAME);
        write ('Enter Employee Age >');
        readln (Employee.AGE);
        write ('Enter Employee Phone >');
        readln (Employee.PHONE);
        Employee.Active := 1;
        WriteFileHandle (EMPFILE, Employee, Sizeof(Employee),
                WRITESTATUS);
      end;

    CloseFile (EMPFILE, STATUS);
  end.
```

Figure 14-12.

DB2 program (*continued*)

Next, the program in Figure 14-13 prompts the user for the desired record number and then displays its contents. Although this program uses random access I/O, that feature is fairly useless since you must know the specific record number that you require. A more realistic approach to this application is to request the desired name from the user. Then, based on the name entered, the application displays the appropriate record. The problem becomes the way the application uses random-access files. Most programmers would simply open the database and access records sequentially until either the record or end-of-file is found. The solution to this problem lies in *indexed files*. An indexed file uses a *key* (in this case the name field) to keep track of record numbers in the file. For every file entry, the program will track the name and record number, as shown in Figure 14-14. In this case, the following

```
        Program DB3;

        Const
          BUFFERSIZE = 2;

        Type
          STRING79 = string[79];
          Employee_Record = record
            name: string[25];
            age: byte;
            phone: string[8];
            active: byte;
          end;

          DISKBUFFER = Employee_record;

        procedure OpenFile (FILENAME: STRING79;
                            MODE: byte;
                      var FILE_HANDLE: integer;
                          var STATUS: byte);

        Type
          REGISTERS = record
                      AX, BX, CX, DX, BP, SI, DI, DS, ES, FLAGS: INTEGER
                      end;

        var
            REGS: REGISTERS;   {AX, BX, CX, DX, BP, SI, DI, DS, ES, FLAGS}

        begin
            with REGS do
              begin
                FILENAME := FILENAME + Chr(0);
                AX := $3D00 + MODE;                {mode is in AL}
                DS := Seg(FILENAME[1]);
                DX := Ofs(FILENAME[1]);
                MSDos (REGS);
                if (FLAGS and 1 = 1) then          {error in operation}
                  STATUS := Lo(AX)
                else
                  begin
                    FILE_HANDLE := AX;             {successful operation}
                    STATUS := 0;
                  end;
              end;
        end;


        procedure CloseFile (FILE_HANDLE: integer;
                             var STATUS: byte);

        Type
          REGISTERS = record
                      AX, BX, CX, DX, BP, SI, DI, DS, ES, FLAGS: INTEGER
                      end;

        var
            REGS: REGISTERS;   {AX, BX, CX, DX, BP, SI, DI, DS, ES, FLAGS}

        begin
            with REGS do
              begin
                AX := $3E00;
                BX := FILE_HANDLE;
```

Figure 14-13.

DB3 program

```
                    MSDos (REGS);
                    if (FLAGS and 1 = 1) then           {error in operation}
                      STATUS := Lo(AX)
                    else
                      STATUS := 0;
                  end;
            end;

      procedure ReadFileHandle (FILE_HANDLE: integer;
                                  var BUFFER: DISKBUFFER;
                                    NUMBYTES: integer;
                                var BYTESREAD: integer;
                                    var STATUS: byte);

      Type
        REGISTERS = record
                      AX, BX, CX, DX, BP, SI, DI, DS, ES, FLAGS: INTEGER
                    end;

      var
          REGS: REGISTERS;   {AX, BX, CX, DX, BP, SI, DI, DS, ES, FLAGS}

      begin
          with REGS do
            begin
              AX := $3F00;
              BX := FILE_HANDLE;
              CX := NUMBYTES;
              DS := Seg(BUFFER);
              DX := Ofs(BUFFER);
              MSDos (REGS);
              if (FLAGS and 1 = 1) then           {error in operation}
                STATUS := Lo(AX)
              else
                BYTESREAD := AX;
                STATUS := 0;
            end;
      end;


      procedure Lseek (FILE_HANDLE: integer;
                         DIRECTIVE: integer;
                         HIOFFSET,
                         LOOFFSET: integer;
                         var STATUS: byte);

      Type
        REGISTERS = record
                      AX, BX, CX, DX, BP, SI, DI, DS, ES, FLAGS: INTEGER
                    end;

      var
          REGS: REGISTERS;   {AX, BX, CX, DX, BP, SI, DI, DS, ES, FLAGS}

      begin
          with REGS do
            begin
              AX := $4200 + DIRECTIVE;
              BX := FILE_HANDLE;
              CX := HIOFFSET;
              DX := LOOFFSET;
              MSDos (REGS);
              if (FLAGS and 1 = 1) then           {error in operation}
                STATUS := Lo(AX)
```

Figure 14-13.

DB3 program (*continued*)

```
            else
               STATUS := C;
          end;
    end;


var
   Employee: Employee_Record;
   EMPFILE, bytesread: integer;
   status, writestatus: byte;
   REC: integer;

begin
   OpenFile ('EMP.DAT', 0, EMPFILE, STATUS);

   write ('Enter employee number desired >');
   readln (rec);

   Lseek (EMPFILE, 0, 0, (REC - 1) * Sizeof(Employee), status);

   ReadFileHandle (EMPFILE, EMPLOYEE, Sizeof(EMPLOYEE), BYTESREAD,
         STATUS);

   writeln ('Employee: ', Employee.NAME);
   writeln ('Age: ', Employee.AGE);
   writeln ('Phone: ', Employee.PHONE);

   CloseFile (EMPFILE, STATUS);
end.
```

Figure 14-13.

DB3 program (*continued*)

program will use a binary tree containing records in the format shown
in Figure 14-15.

```
Record_Ptr = ^Disk_Record;
Disk_Record = record
  name: string[25];
  recordnumber: integer;
  active: byte;
  rnode,
  lnode: Record_Ptr;
end;
```

Key	Record Number		Name EMP.DAT	Age	Phone
JONES	1	1	JONES	35	363-4517
SMITH	2	2	SMITH	36	398-1231
DURAND	3	3	DURAND	45	377-4414
MATTA	4	4	MATTA	44	363-8181
BARNES	5	5	BARNES	30	672-0012
OLIVERA	6	6	OLIVERA	59	933-0911
.	.		.	.	.
.	.		.	.	.
.	.		.	.	.
EUBANK	16	16	EUBANK	27	977-2314
JACKSON	17	17	JACKSON	35	363-8111
BYRD	18	18	BYRD	35	392-4000

Figure 14-14.

Name and record numbers of employees

(If you are not fully conversant with binary trees, refer to the *Turbo Pascal Programmer's Library,* by Kris Jamsa and Steven Nameroff [Berkeley, Calif.: Borland-Osborne/McGraw-Hill, 1987].)

Each time the application begins, it calls the routine **BuildTree** with a handle to the start of the desired file. The routine reads from the file one record at a time and builds the binary tree (see Figure 14-16).

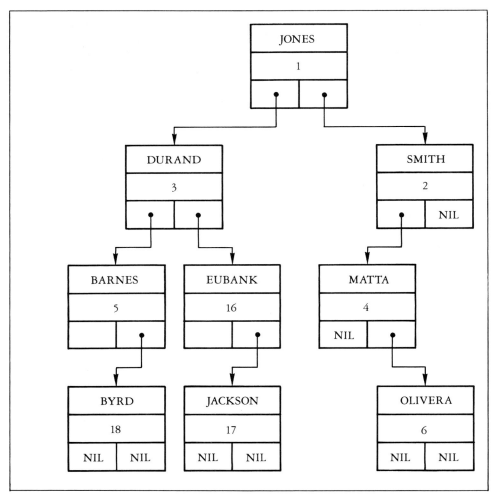

Figure 14-15.

Binary tree containing employee
records

When the user needs to display information on a specific employee,
the program passes the desired name (the key) to the routine **DisplayRecord** (see Figure 14-17). **DisplayRecord** traverses the binary
tree in search of a name matching the desired record. If it finds a

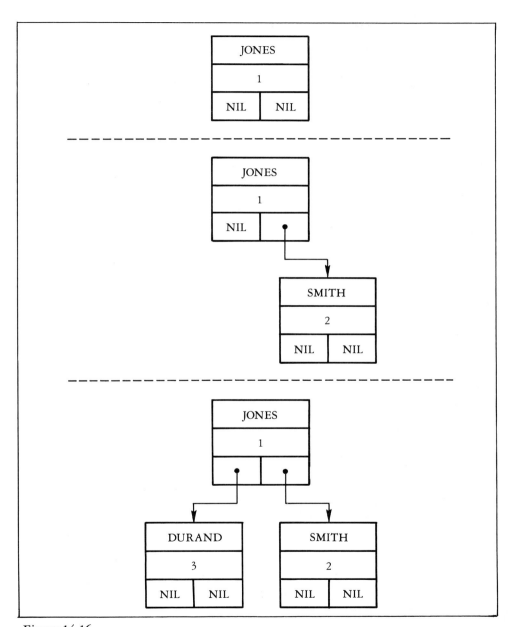

Figure 14-16.

Building of binary tree containing
employee records

```
      Procedure DisplayRecord (Root: Record_Ptr);

      var
        Node: Record_Ptr;
        RecordNumber: integer;
        Name: string25;
        BytesRead: integer;

      begin
        write ('Enter name to display >');
        readln (Name);

      { Search for the name in the index }

        Node := Root;
        RecordNumber := -1;
        while Node <> nil do
          begin
            if (Node^.Name = Name) and (Node^.Active = 1) then
              begin
                RecordNumber := Node^.RECORDNUMBER;
                Node := nil;
              end
            else if Node^.NAME < NAME then
              Node := Node^.RNODE
            else
              Node := Node^.LNODE;
          end;

        if (RecordNumber = -1) then  { record not found }
          begin
            write ('No record for ', Name, ' Press Enter');
            readln;
          end
        else
          begin
            ClrScr;
            Lseek (EMPFILE, 0, 0, (RECORDNUMBER - 1) * Sizeof(Employee),
                  status);
            ReadFileHandle (EMPFILE, EMPLOYEE, Sizeof(EMPLOYEE), BYTESREAD,
                  STATUS);
            writeln ('Employee: ', Employee.NAME);
            writeln ('Age: ', Employee.AGE);
            writeln ('Phone: ', Employee.PHONE);
            write ('Press Enter');
            readln;
          end;
      end;
```

Figure 14-17.

DISPLAYRECORD program

matching entry, it uses the record-number offset to locate the associated record within the random-access file.

Adding and deleting database entries presents additional programming concerns. Each time the user deletes an entry from the file, an

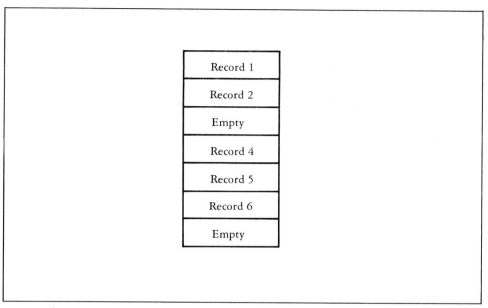

Figure 14-18.

Database file

empty space is left in the file, as shown in Figure 14-18. To utilize disk space most effectively, the program must track available records (created by a deletion) and later use this space for record additions. This application uses a second link list to track inactive records (see Figure 14-19).

If you examine the database record structure shown in Figure 14-17, you will notice a field called ACTIVE. As the routine **BuildTree** (shown in Figure 14-20) creates the binary tree of records and record numbers, it uses this field to determine whether a record from the file is currently being used. If the record is currently active (ACTIVE = 1), the routine places it in the binary tree. Otherwise, the routine places the record into the linked list of available records.

When the program **AddRecord** (shown in Figure 14-21) later needs to add a record, it first examines the available-record linked list to determine if any "holes" exist in the data file that a new record can fill. If

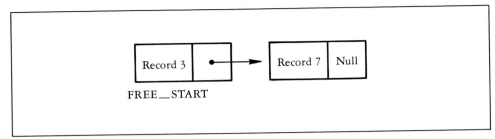

Figure 14-19.

Use of link list to track records

```
        procedure BuildTree (Var Root: Record_Ptr;
                             Var Start: Inactive_Ptr);
    var
      REC: integer;
      DISKNODE, NODE, LASTNODE: Record_Ptr;
      InactiveNode, LastInactiveNode: Inactive_Ptr;
      BytesRead: integer;

    begin
      New (Start);
      Start^.Next := Nil;

      Rec := 1;
      LastRecord := 1;

      ReadFileHandle (EMPFILE, Employee, Sizeof(Employee), BYTESREAD,
             STATUS);

      New (ROOT);
      Root^.rnode := nil;
      Root^.lnode := nil;
      Root^.Name := Employee.Name;
      Root^.RECORDNUMBER := REC;
      Root^.ACTIVE := Employee.Active;

      repeat

    { read a record and place it in the tree if it is active, or into
      the list of available records if it is an inactive record }

        ReadFileHandle (EMPFILE, Employee, Sizeof(Employee), BYTESREAD,
             STATUS);
        if (BYTESREAD <> 0) then
          begin
            REC := REC + 1;
            LastRecord := LastRecord + 1;
```

Figure 14-20.

BUILDTREE program

```
            if (Employee.Active = 1) then
          begin
            New (DiskNode);
            DiskNode^.Name := Employee.Name;
            DiskNode^.RECORDNUMBER := REC;
            DiskNode^.ACTIVE := Employee.Active;
            DiskNode^.RNODE := nil;
            DiskNode^.LNODE := nil;

    { update the index }

            Node := Root;
            while Node <> nil do
              begin
                LASTNODE := Node;
                    if Node^.NAME < DiskNode^.NAME then
                        Node := Node^.RNODE
                      else
                        Node := Node^.LNODE;
                end;
                if (LASTNODE^.NAME < DiskNode^.Name) then
                  LastNode^.RNODE := DiskNode
                else
                  LastNode^.LNODE := DiskNode;
              end
            else        { inactive record }
              begin
                New (InactiveNode);
                LastInactiveNode := Start;
                While (LastInactiveNode^.Next <> nil) do
                  LastInactiveNode := LastInactiveNode^.Next;
                InactiveNode^.RecordNumber := REC;
                LastInactiveNode^.Next := InactiveNode;
              end;
          end;

      until (BYTESREAD = 0);

    end;
```

Figure 14-20.

BUILDTREE program (*continued*)

```
        Procedure AddRecord (Root: Record_Ptr;
                      var Start: Inactive_Ptr);

    var
      NewEmp: Employee_Record;
      LastInactiveNode: Inactive_Ptr;
      LastNode: Record_Ptr;
      Node: Record_Ptr;
      RecordNumber: integer;
```

Figure 14-21.

ADDRECORD program

```
      begin
        write ('Enter employee name >');
        readln (NewEmp.Name);
        write ('Enter employee age >');
        readln (NewEmp.Age);
        write ('Enter employee phone number >');
        readln (NewEmp.Phone);
        NewEmp.Active := 1;

    { see if any unused records exist }

        LastInactiveNode := Start^.Next;
        if (LastInactiveNode <> Nil) then
         begin
          Start^.Next := LastInactiveNode^.Next;
          Lseek (EMPFILE, 0, 0, (LastInactiveNode^.RecordNumber - 1) *
                 Sizeof(Employee), status);
          RecordNumber := LastInactiveNode^.RecordNumber;
         end
        else             { no unused records so append this one }
           begin
             Lseek (EMPFILE, 0, 0, LASTRECORD * Sizeof(NewEmp), status);
             LASTRECORD := LASTRECORD + 1;
             RecordNumber := LastRecord;
           end;

        WriteFileHandle (EMPFILE, NewEmp, Sizeof (Employee), Status);

    { update the index }

        Node := Root;
        while Node <> nil do
           begin
              LASTNODE := Node;
              if Node^.NAME < NewEmp.NAME then
                Node := Node^.RNODE
              else
                Node := Node^.LNODE;
           end;

        New (NODE);
        Node^.NAME := NewEmp.Name;
        Node^.RECORDNUMBER := RecordNumber;
        Node^.RNODE := nil;
        Node^.LNODE := nil;
        Node^.Active := 1;

        if (LASTNODE^.NAME < NewEmp.Name) then
          LastNode^.RNODE := Node
        else
          LastNode^.LNODE := Node;

        write ('Employee added Press Enter');
        readln;
      end;
```

Figure 14-21.

ADDRECORD program (*continued*)

so, the new record is placed within the first available record. If no space is available, the routine appends the new record to the end of the file.

When the user later deletes a record, the routine **DeleteRecord** (shown in Figure 14-22) sets the record to inactive (**Active** = 0) in the binary tree and then updates the record space on disk to make it available to new records. In so doing, the program maximizes disk-space utilization while processing efficiently. The only routine missing from a complete database system is **UpdateRecord** shown in Figure 14-23. The complete database application becomes that shown in Figure 14-24.

```
Procedure DeleteRecord (Root: Record_Ptr;
                        var Start: Inactive_Ptr);

var
  OldEmp: Employee_Record;
  LastInactiveNode: Inactive_Ptr;
  InactiveNode: Inactive_Ptr;
  LastNode: Record_Ptr;
  Node: Record_Ptr;
  RecordNumber: integer;

begin
  write ('Enter employee name >');
  readln (OldEmp.Name);

{ search the index for the employee }

  Node := Root;
  RecordNumber := -1;
  while Node <> nil do
    begin
      if Node^.Name = OldEmp.Name then
        begin
          RecordNumber := Node^.RECORDNUMBER;
          Node^.Active := 0;
          Node := nil;
        end
      else if Node^.NAME < OldEmp.NAME then
        Node := Node^.RNODE
      else
        Node := Node^.LNODE;
    end;
```

Figure 14-22.

DELETERECORD program

```
          if (RecordNumber = -1) then   { not found }
            begin
              ClrScr;
              write ('No record for ', OldEmp.Name, ' Press Enter');
              readln;
            end
          else
            begin
              ClrScr;
              Lseek (EMPFILE, 0, 0, (RECORDNUMBER - 1) * Sizeof(OldEmp),
                     status);
              OldEmp.Active := 0;
              WriteFileHandle (EMPFILE, OldEmp, Sizeof(OldEmp), STATUS);
              Write ('Record deleted Press Enter');
              readln;

      { update the list of available records }

              LastInactiveNode := Start^.Next;

              while (LastInactiveNode <> Nil) do
                LastInactiveNode := LastInactiveNode^.Next;

              New (InactiveNode);
              LastInactiveNode^.Next := InactiveNode;
              InactiveNode^.Next := nil;
              InactiveNode^.RecordNumber := RecordNumber;
            end;
        end;
```

Figure 14-22.

DELETERECORD program
(*continued*)

```
        Procedure UpdateRecord (Root: Record_Ptr;
                       var Start: Inactive_Ptr);

        var
          Emp: Employee_Record;
          LastInactiveNode: Inactive_Ptr;
          InactiveNode: Inactive_Ptr;
          SaveNode, LastNode: Record_Ptr;
          Node: Record_Ptr;
          RecordNumber: integer;
          BytesRead: integer;

        begin
          write ('Enter employee name >');
          readln (Emp.Name);

        { search the index }

          Node := Root;
          RecordNumber := -1;
```

Figure 14-23.

UPDATERECORD program

```
        while Node <> nil do
          begin
            if Node^.Name = Emp.Name then
              begin
                RecordNumber := Node^.RECORDNUMBER;
                SaveNode := Node;
                Node := nil;
              end
            else if Node^.NAME < Emp.NAME then
              Node := Node^.RNODE
            else
              Node := Node^.LNODE;
          end;

        if (RecordNumber = -1) then
          begin
            ClrScr;
            write ('No record for ', Emp.Name, ' Press Enter');
            readln;
          end
        else
          begin
            ClrScr;
            Lseek (EMPFILE, 0, 0, (RECORDNUMBER - 1) * Sizeof(Emp),
                   status);

            write ('Enter employee name >');
            readln (Emp.Name);
            write ('Enter employee age >');
            readln (Emp.Age);
            write ('Enter employee phone number >');
            readln (Emp.Phone);
            Emp.Active := 1;
            SaveNode^.Name := Emp.Name;

            WriteFileHandle (EMPFILE, Emp, Sizeof(Emp), STATUS);
            Write ('Record updated Press Enter');
            Readln;
          end;
      end;
```

Figure 14-23.

UPDATERECORD program

(*continued*)

```
        Program DB4;

        Const
          BUFFERSIZE = 2;

        Type
          STRING79 = string[79];
```

Figure 14-24.

DB4 program

```
            STRING25 = string[25];

            Inactive_Ptr = ^Inactive_List;      { keep track of unused tables }
            Inactive_List = record
              recordnumber: integer;
              next: Inactive_Ptr;
            end;

            Record_Ptr = ^Disk_Record;          { binary tree for index entries }
            Disk_Record = record
              name: string[25];
              recordnumber: integer;
              active: byte;
              rnode,
              lnode: Record_Ptr;
            end;

            Employee_Record = record            { data record to/from disk }
              name: string[25];
              age: byte;
              phone: string[8];
              active: byte;
            end;

            DISKBUFFER = Employee_record;

            procedure OpenFile (FILENAME: STRING79;
                                      MODE: byte;
                            var FILE_HANDLE: integer;
                                  var STATUS: byte);
            Type
              REGISTERS = record
                              AX, BX, CX, DX, BP, SI, DI, DS, ES, FLAGS: INTEGER
                          end;
            var
                REGS: REGISTERS;   {AX, BX, CX, DX, BP, SI, DI, DS, ES, FLAGS}

            begin
                with REGS do
                  begin
                    FILENAME := FILENAME + Chr(0);
                    AX := $3D00 + MODE;             {mode is in AL}
                    DS := Seg(FILENAME[1]);
                    DX := Ofs(FILENAME[1]);
                    MSDos (REGS);

                    if (FLAGS and 1 = 1) then       {error in operation}
                      STATUS := Lo(AX)
                    else
                      begin
                        FILE_HANDLE := AX;          {successful operation}
                        STATUS := 0;
                      end;
                  end;
            end;


            procedure CloseFile (FILE_HANDLE: integer;
                                    var STATUS: byte);

            Type
              REGISTERS = record
                              AX, BX, CX, DX, BP, SI, DI, DS, ES, FLAGS: INTEGER
                          end;
            var
                REGS: REGISTERS;   {AX, BX, CX, DX, BP, SI, DI, DS, ES, FLAGS}
```

Figure 14-24.

DB4 program (*continued*)

```
begin
    with REGS do
        begin
        AX := $3E00;
        BX := FILE_HANDLE;
        MSDos (REGS);
        if (FLAGS and 1 = 1) then          {error in operation}
            STATUS := Lo(AX)
        else
            STATUS := 0;
        end;
end;

procedure ReadFileHandle (FILE_HANDLE: integer;
                          var BUFFER: DISKBUFFER;
                              NUMBYTES: integer;
                          var BYTESREAD: integer;
                          var STATUS: byte);
Type
  REGISTERS = record
                AX, BX, CX, DX, BP, SI, DI, DS, ES, FLAGS: INTEGER
              end;
var
    REGS: REGISTERS;   {AX, BX, CX, DX, BP, SI, DI, DS, ES, FLAGS}

begin
    with REGS do
        begin
        AX := $3F00;
        BX := FILE_HANDLE;
        CX := NUMBYTES;
        DS := Seg(BUFFER);
        DX := Ofs(BUFFER);
        MSDos (REGS);
        if (FLAGS and 1 = 1) then          {error in operation}

            STATUS := Lo(AX)
        else
            BYTESREAD := AX;
            STATUS := 0;
        end;
end;

procedure Lseek (FILE_HANDLE: integer;
                 DIRECTIVE: integer;
                 HIOFFSET,
                 LOOFFSET: integer;
                 var STATUS: byte);
Type
  REGISTERS = record
                AX, BX, CX, DX, BP, SI, DI, DS, ES, FLAGS: INTEGER
              end;
var
    REGS: REGISTERS;   {AX, BX, CX, DX, BP, SI, DI, DS, ES, FLAGS}

begin
    with REGS do
        begin
        AX := $4200 + DIRECTIVE;
        BX := FILE_HANDLE;
        CX := HIOFFSET;
        DX := LOOFFSET;
        MSDos (REGS);
        if (FLAGS and 1 = 1) then          {error in operation}
            STATUS := Lo(AX)
```

Figure 14-24.

DB4 program (*continued*)

```
                else
                    STATUS := 0;
            end;
    end;


    procedure WriteFileHandle (FILE_HANDLE: integer;
                                    BUFFER: DISKBUFFER;
                                    NUMBYTES: integer;
                                    var STATUS: byte);
    Type
        REGISTERS = record
                        AX, BX, CX, DX, BP, SI, DI, DS, ES, FLAGS: INTEGER
                    end;
    var
        REGS: REGISTERS;    {AX, BX, CX, DX, BP, SI, DI, DS, ES, FLAGS}

    begin
        with REGS do
            begin
                AX := $4000;
                BX := FILE_HANDLE;
                CX := NUMBYTES;
                DS := Seg(BUFFER);
                DX := Ofs(BUFFER);
                MSDos (REGS);
                if (FLAGS and 1 = 1) then          {error in operation}
                    STATUS := Lo(AX)
                else
                    STATUS := 0;
            end;
    end;

    var
     LASTRECORD: integer;              { last record number in the file }
     Employee: Employee_Record;        { record to/from disk }
     EMPFILE: integer;                 { handle to employee file }
     Status: byte;

    Procedure DisplayRecord (Root: Record_Ptr);

    var
      Node: Record_Ptr;
      RecordNumber: integer;
      Name: string25;
      BytesRead: integer;

    begin
      write ('Enter name to display >');
      readln (Name);

    { Search for the name in the index }

      Node := Root;
      RecordNumber := -1;
      while Node <> nil do
        begin
          if (Node^.Name = Name) and (Node^.Active = 1) then
            begin
              RecordNumber := Node^.RECORDNUMBER;
              Node := nil;
            end
          else if Node^.NAME < NAME then
            Node := Node^.RNODE
          else
            Node := Node^.LNODE;
        end;
```

Figure 14-24.

DB4 program (*continued*)

```
          if (RecordNumber = -1) then   { record not found }
            begin
              write ('No record for ', Name, ' Press Enter');
              readln;
            end
          else
            begin
              ClrScr;
              Lseek (EMPFILE, 0, 0, (RECORDNUMBER - 1) * Sizeof(Employee),
                      status);
              ReadFileHandle (EMPFILE, EMPLOYEE, Sizeof(EMPLOYEE), BYTESREAD,
                      STATUS);
              writeln ('Employee: ', Employee.NAME);
              writeln ('Age: ', Employee.AGE);
              writeln ('Phone: ', Employee.PHONE);
              write ('Press Enter');
              readln;
            end;
       end;


       Procedure AddRecord (Root: Record_Ptr;
                     var Start: Inactive_Ptr);

       var
         NewEmp: Employee_Record;
         LastInactiveNode: Inactive_Ptr;
         LastNode: Record_Ptr;
         Node: Record_Ptr;
         RecordNumber: integer;

       begin
         write ('Enter employee name >');
         readln (NewEmp.Name);
         write ('Enter employee age >');
         readln (NewEmp.Age);
         write ('Enter employee phone number >');
         readln (NewEmp.Phone);
         NewEmp.Active := 1;

       { see if any unused records exist }

         LastInactiveNode := Start^.Next;
         if (LastInactiveNode <> Nil) then
          begin
            Start^.Next := LastInactiveNode^.Next;
            Lseek (EMPFILE, 0, 0, (LastInactiveNode^.RecordNumber - 1) *
                   Sizeof(Employee), status);
            RecordNumber := LastInactiveNode^.RecordNumber;
          end
         else            { no unused records so append this one }
           begin
             Lseek (EMPFILE, 0, 0, LASTRECORD * Sizeof(NewEmp), status);
             LASTRECORD := LASTRECORD + 1;
             RecordNumber := LastRecord;
           end;

         WriteFileHandle (EMPFILE, NewEmp, Sizeof (Employee), Status);

       { update the index }

         Node := Root;
         while Node <> nil do
           begin
             LASTNODE := Node;
             if Node^.NAME < NewEmp.NAME then
               Node := Node^.RNODE
             else
```

Figure 14-24.

DB4 program (*continued*)

```
            Node := Node^.LNODE;
        end;

    New (NODE);
    Node^.NAME := NewEmp.Name;
    Node^.RECORDNUMBER := RecordNumber;
    Node^.RNODE := nil;
    Node^.LNODE := nil;
    Node^.Active := 1;

    if (LASTNODE^.NAME < NewEmp.Name) then
        LastNode^.RNODE := Node
    else
        LastNode^.LNODE := Node;

    write ('Employee added Press Enter');
    readln;
end;


Procedure DeleteRecord (Root: Record_Ptr;
                        var Start: Inactive_Ptr);

var
    OldEmp: Employee_Record;
    LastInactiveNode: Inactive_Ptr;
    InactiveNode: Inactive_Ptr;
    LastNode: Record_Ptr;
    Node: Record_Ptr;
    RecordNumber: integer;

begin
    write ('Enter employee name >');
    readln (OldEmp.Name);

{ search the index for the employee }

    Node := Root;
    RecordNumber := -1;
    while Node <> nil do
        begin
            if Node^.Name = OldEmp.Name then
                begin
                    RecordNumber := Node^.RECORDNUMBER;
                    Node^.Active := 0;
                    Node := nil;
                end
            else if Node^.NAME < OldEmp.NAME then
                Node := Node^.RNODE
            else
                Node := Node^.LNODE;
        end;

    if (RecordNumber = -1) then    { not found }
        begin
            ClrScr;
            write ('No record for ', OldEmp.Name, ' Press Enter');
            readln;
        end
    else
        begin
            ClrScr;
            Lseek (EMPFILE, 0, 0, (RECORDNUMBER - 1) * Sizeof(OldEmp),
                    status);
```

Figure 14-24.

DB4 program (*continued*)

```
            OldEmp.Active := 0;
            WriteFileHandle (EMPFILE, OldEmp, Sizeof(OldEmp), STATUS);
            Write ('Record deleted Press Enter');
            readln;

   { update the list of available records }

            LastInactiveNode := Start^.Next;
            while (LastInactiveNode <> Nil) do
              LastInactiveNode := LastInactiveNode^.Next;

            New (InactiveNode);
            LastInactiveNode^.Next := InactiveNode;
            InactiveNode^.Next := nil;
            InactiveNode^.RecordNumber := RecordNumber;
         end;
      end;

      Procedure UpdateRecord (Root: Record_Ptr;
                          var Start: Inactive_Ptr);

      var
        Emp: Employee_Record;
        LastInactiveNode: Inactive_Ptr;
        InactiveNode: Inactive_Ptr;
        SaveNode, LastNode: Record_Ptr;
        Node: Record_Ptr;
        RecordNumber: integer;
        BytesRead: integer;

      begin
        write ('Enter employee name >');
        readln (Emp.Name);

      { search the index }

        Node := Root;
        RecordNumber := -1;
        while Node <> nil do
          begin
            if Node^.Name = Emp.Name then
              begin
                RecordNumber := Node^.RECORDNUMBER;
                SaveNode := Node;
                Node := nil;
              end
          else if Node^.NAME < Emp.NAME then
            Node := Node^.RNODE
          else
            Node := Node^.LNODE;
          end;

   if (RecordNumber = -1) then
     begin
        ClrScr;
        write ('No record for ', Emp.Name, ' Press Enter');
        readln;
     end
   else
     begin
        ClrScr;
        Lseek (EMPFILE, 0, 0, (RECORDNUMBER - 1) * Sizeof(Emp),
               status);
```

Figure 14-24.

DB4 program (*continued*)

```
        write ('Enter employee name >');
        readln (Emp.Name);
        write ('Enter employee age >');
        readln (Emp.Age);
        write ('Enter employee phone number >');
        readln (Emp.Phone);
        Emp.Active := 1;
        SaveNode^.Name := Emp.Name;

        WriteFileHandle (EMPFILE, Emp, Sizeof(Emp), STATUS);
        Write ('Record updated Press Enter');
        Readln;
      end;
end;

procedure BuildTree (Var Root: Record_Ptr;
                     Var Start: Inactive_Ptr);
var
  REC: integer;
  DISKNODE, NODE, LASTNODE: Record_Ptr;
  InactiveNode, LastInactiveNode: Inactive_Ptr;
  BytesRead: integer;

begin
  New (Start);
  Start^.Next := Nil;

  Rec := 1;
  LastRecord := 1;

  ReadFileHandle (EMPFILE, Employee, Sizeof(Employee), BYTESREAD,
        STATUS);

  New (ROOT);
  Root^.rnode := nil;
  Root^.lnode := nil;
  Root^.Name := Employee.Name;
  Root^.RECORDNUMBER := REC;
  Root^.ACTIVE := Employee.Active;

  repeat

{ read a record and place it in the tree if it is active, or into
  the list of available records if it is an inactive record }

    ReadFileHandle (EMPFILE, Employee, Sizeof(Employee), BYTESREAD,
        STATUS);
    if (BYTESREAD <> 0) then
      begin
        REC := REC + 1;
        LastRecord := LastRecord + 1;

        if (Employee.Active = 1) then
          begin
            New (DiskNode);
            DiskNode^.Name := Employee.Name;
            DiskNode^.RECORDNUMBER := REC;
            DiskNode^.ACTIVE := Employee.Active;
            DiskNode^.RNODE := nil;
            DiskNode^.LNODE := nil;

    { update the index }

            Node := Root;
            while Node <> nil do
```

Figure 14-24.

DB4 program (*continued*)

```
                begin
                  LASTNODE := Node;
                  if Node^.NAME < DiskNode^.NAME then
                      Node := Node^.RNODE
                  else
                      Node := Node^.LNODE;
                end;
              if (LASTNODE^.NAME < DiskNode^.Name) then
                LastNode^.RNODE := DiskNode
              else
                LastNode^.LNODE := DiskNode;
            end
          else          { inactive record }
            begin
              New (InactiveNode);
              LastInactiveNode := Start;
              While (LastInactiveNode^.Next <> nil) do
                LastInactiveNode := LastInactiveNode^.Next;
              InactiveNode^.RecordNumber := REC;
              LastInactiveNode^.Next := InactiveNode;
            end;
        end;

    until (BYTESREAD = 0);

end;
var
  REC: integer;
  ROOT: Record_Ptr;
  START: Inactive_Ptr;
  choice: char;

begin
  OpenFile ('EMP.DAT', 2, EMPFILE, STATUS);

  BuildTree (ROOT, START);

  repeat
    ClrScr ;
    writeln ('Add employee.........A');
    writeln ('Display employee.....D');
    writeln ('Remove employee......R');
    writeln ('Update employee......U');
    writeln ('Quit.................Q');
    writeln ;
    write   ('                    >');

    readln (choice);

    ClrScr;

    case (UpCase(choice)) of
      'A': AddRecord (Root, Start);
      'D': DisplayRecord (Root);
      'R': DeleteRecord (Root, Start);
      'U': UpdateRecord (Root, Start);
    end;

  until (UpCase(Choice) = 'Q');

  CloseFile (EMPFILE, STATUS);
end.
```

Figure 14-24.

DB4 program (*continued*)

DOS file handles are powerful, yet easy to use. In a matter of minutes you have developed a complete database management system. Several of the remaining DOS file-manipulation routines use DOS file handles.

ADVANCED FILE MANIPULATION ROUTINES

The DOS Delete File system service (41H) removes the directory entry for the file specified by the ASCIIZ string that you provide, as shown here:

```
procedure Delete_File (FILENAME: STRING79;
                          var STATUS: byte);

Type
  REGISTERS = record
                  AX, BX, CX, DX, BP, SI, DI, DS, ES, FLAGS: INTEGER
              end;

var
     REGS: REGISTERS;   {AX, BX, CX, DX, BP, SI, DI, DS, ES, FLAGS}

begin
     with REGS do
        begin
           FILENAME := FILENAME + Chr(0);        {convert to asciiz}
           AX := $4100;                          {DOS function code}
           DS := Seg(FILENAME[1]);
           DX := Ofs(FILENAME[1]);
           MSDos (REGS);
           if (FLAGS and 1 = 1) then             {error in operation}
              STATUS := Lo(AX)
           else
              STATUS := 0;                        {successful operation}
        end;
end;
```

Similarly, the DOS File Rename system service (56H) uses two ASCIIZ strings for the source and target files, as shown here:

```
procedure Rename_File (OLD_NAME, NEW_NAME: STRING79;
                             var STATUS: byte);

Type
  REGISTERS = record
                 AX, BX, CX, DX, BP, SI, DI, DS, ES, FLAGS: INTEGER
              end;
var
    REGS: REGISTERS;   {AX, BX, CX, DX, BP, SI, DI, DS, ES, FLAGS}
begin
    with REGS do
       begin
          OLD_NAME := OLD_NAME + Chr(0);
          NEW_NAME := NEW_NAME + Chr(0);
          AX := $5600;                         {DOS function code}
          DS := Seg(OLD_NAME[1]);
          DX := Ofs(OLD_NAME[1]);
          ES := Seg(NEW_NAME[1]);
          DI := Ofs(NEW_NAME[1]);
          MSDos (REGS);

          if (FLAGS and 1 = 1) then            {error in operation}
            STATUS := STATUS
          else
            STATUS := 0;                        {successful operation}
       end;
   end;
```

The following routines use DOS file handles to get and set a file's date and time stamps. If the specified file does not exist, each routine returns an error status. DOS uses the date and time formats shown in Figure 14-25 and Figure 14-26 to store file date and time formats. This procedure implements **GetFileStamp**:

```
procedure GetFileStamp (FILE_HANDLE: integer;
           var DAY, MONTH, HOURS, MINUTES,
                     SECONDS, YEAR: integer;
                     var STATUS: byte);
Type
  REGISTERS = record
                 AX, BX, CX, DX, BP, SI, DI, DS, ES, FLAGS: INTEGER
              end;
```

```
var
    REGS: REGISTERS;   {AX, BX, CX, DX, BP, SI, DI, DS, ES, FLAGS}

begin
    with REGS do
      begin
        AX := $5700;
        BX := FILE_HANDLE;
        MSDos (REGS);
        if (FLAGS and 1 =1) then                 {error in operation}
          STATUS := Lo(AX)
        else
          begin
            STATUS := 0;                         {successful operation}
            YEAR   := (Hi(DX) shr 1) + 1980;
            MONTH  := (DX and $1E0) shr 5;
            DAY    := DX and $1F;
            HOURS  := Hi(CX) shr 3;
            MINUTES := (CX and $7E0) shr 5;
            SECONDS := (CX and $1F) * 2;
          end;
      end;
end;
```

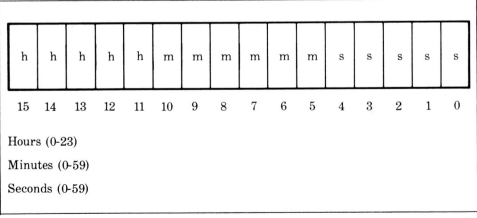

Figure 14-25.

Specifying the time

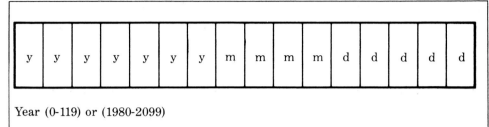

y	y	y	y	y	y	y	m	m	m	m	d	d	d	d	d

Year (0-119) or (1980-2099)

Month (1-12)

Day (1-31)

Figure 14-26.

Specifying the date

Likewise, this routine allows you to set a file's date and time stamp:

```
procedure SetFileStamp (FILE_HANDLE, DAY, MONTH,
                        HOURS, MINUTES, SECONDS, YEAR: integer;
                                        var STATUS: byte);
Type
  REGISTERS = record
                AX, BX, CX, DX, BP, SI, DI, DS, ES, FLAGS: INTEGER
              end;
var
    REGS: REGISTERS;  {AX, BX, CX, DX, BP, SI, DI, DS, ES, FLAGS}

  begin
     with REGS do
       begin
         AX := $5701;
         BX := FILE_HANDLE;
         DX := (YEAR - 1980) shl 9;
         DX := DX + (MONTH shl 5);
         DX := DX + DAY;
         CX := HOURS shl 11;
         CX := CX + (MINUTES shl 5);
         CX := CX + SECONDS div 2;
         MSDos (REGS);
         if (FLAGS and 1 = 1) then            {error in operation}
```

```
           STATUS := Lo(AX)
        else
           STATUS := 0;                        {successful operation}
        end;
   end;
```

DOS WILD-CARD CHARACTERS

By now, you should be fully conversant with the DOS wild-card characters * and ? and their uses in DOS command-line processing. Issue the
following commands:

```
A> DIR *.*
```

and

```
A> DEL *.BAK
```

By the end of this section you will be able to write programs that fully
support DOS wild-card characters. In fact, the utility programs that you
have already developed can be easily modified to support DOS wild-card
characters in the command line.

DOS provides two system services, Find First Matching File (4EH)
and Find Next Matching File (4FH), that provide the essentials for DOS
wild-card character processing. Table 14-7 shows the specifications for
the Find First Matching File service, and Table 14-8 shows the specifications for the Find Next Matching File service.

Table 14-7.

DOS Find First Matching File Service

Register	Entry Contents
AH	4EH DOS Find First service
CX	Search attribute
DS	Segment address of file specification
DX	Offset address of file specification

Register	Exit Contents
AX	Error code if carry flag is set

To fully support DOS wild-card character processing, use the Find First and Find Next services as shown in Figure 14-27.

Each DOS application has an area of memory in which all disk-transfer operations take place. To determine the address of this location, use the DOS Get Disk Transfer Address system service (2FH). Table 14-9 shows the specifications for this service.

Table 14-8.

DOS Find Next Matching File Service

Register	Entry Contents
AH	4FH DOS Find Next service

Register	Exit Contents
AX	Error code if carry flag is set

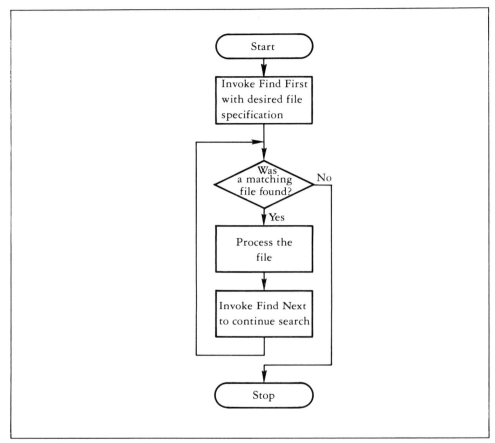

Figure 14-27.

Using the Find First and Find Next
Matching File services

The following Turbo Pascal procedure implements **GetDTA**.

```
procedure Get_DTA (var SEGMENT, OFFSET: integer);

Type
  REGISTERS = record
               AX, BX, CX, DX, BP, SI, DI, DS, ES, FLAGS: INTEGER
             end;
```

```
Var
    REGS: REGISTERS;  {AX, BX, CX, DX, BP, SI, DI, DS, ES, FLAGS}
begin
    with REGS do
       begin
          AX := $2F00;
          MSDos (REGS);
          SEGMENT := ES;
          OFFSET  := BX;
       end;
end;
```

Each time the Find First or Find Next services locate a matching file, the routines place the information shown in Figure 14-28 at the start of the application's disk-transfer address. The routine in Figure 14-29 implements Find First, and the routine in Figure 14-30 implements Find Next. Note the use of the attribute byte in the services. DOS uses this byte as follows:

- If the value of the desired attribute is 0, DOS returns all normal file entries. DOS does not return hidden, system, or subdirectory files.

- If the value is 2, 4, or 16, DOS returns each of those file types, and all DOS normal files.

- If the attribute byte is 8, DOS only returns the disk volume label.

Table 14-9.

DOS Get Disk-Transfer Address
Service

Register	Entry Contents
AH	2FH DOS Get Disk Transfer-Address service

Register	Exit Contents
ES	Segment address of DTA
BX	Offset address of DTA

Offset	Contents
21	Attributes
22	Creation Time
24	Creation Date
26	Low-Word File Size
28	High-Word File Size
30	File Name

Figure 14-28.

File information offset from DTA

```
Type
  DTA_INFO = record
    ATTRIBUTES  : byte;
    FILE_SIZE   : real;
    NAME        : STRING79;
  end;

procedure Find_First (SEARCH_SPEC: STRING79;
                      ATTRIBUTES: byte;
                      var FILESPEC: DTA_INFO;
                      var STATUS: byte);

Type
  REGISTERS = record
                AX, BX, CX, DX, BP, SI, DI, DS, ES, FLAGS: INTEGER
              end;
var
    REGS    : REGISTERS;  {AX, BX, CX, DX, BP, SI,
                           DI, DS, ES, FLAGS}
    DTA_SEG,
    DTA_OFS : integer;  {address of disk transfer area}
    I       : integer;  {counter for loops}
```

Figure 14-29.

Program to implement Find First
Matching File service

```
      begin
        with REGS do
          begin
            SEARCH_SPEC := SEARCH_SPEC + Chr(0);
            AX := $4E00;                          {DOS function code}
            DS := Seg(SEARCH_SPEC[1]);
            DX := Ofs(SEARCH_SPEC[1]);
            CX := ATTRIBUTES;
            MSDos (REGS);
            if (FLAGS and 1 = 1) then
              STATUS := Lo(AX)
            else
              begin
                STATUS := 0;                      {successful
                                                   operation}
                Get_DTA (DTA_SEG, DTA_OFS);

                with FILESPEC do
                  begin
                    ATTRIBUTES :=  Mem [DTA_SEG:DTA_OFS+21];

                    FILE_SIZE  := 1.0 * Mem [DTA_SEG:DTA_OFS+26] +
                                  Mem [DTA_SEG:DTA_OFS+27] * 256.0 +
                                  Mem [DTA_SEG:DTA_OFS+28] * Power
                                                       (256.0, 2) +
                                  Mem [DTA_SEG:DTA_OFS+29] * Power
                                                       (256.0, 3);

                    I := 0;
                    while ((I < 13) and (Mem[DTA_SEG:DTA_OFS+30+I] <> 0))
                        do
                      begin
                        name[I + 1] := Chr(Mem[DTA_SEG:DTA_OFS+30+I]);
                        I := I + 1;
                      end;

                    name[0] := Chr(I);
                  end; {with FILESPEC}
              end;
          end;          {with REGS}
      end;
```

Figure 14-29.

Program to implement Find First
Matching File service (*continued*)

```
      Type
        DTA_INFO = record
          ATTRIBUTES   : byte;
          FILE_SIZE    : real;
          NAME         : STRING79;
        end;
```

Figure 14-30.

Program to implement Find Next
Matching File service

```
         procedure Find_Next (var FILESPEC: DTA_INFO;
                              var STATUS: byte);

     Type
       REGISTERS = record
                      AX, BX, CX, DX, BP, SI, DI, DS, ES, FLAGS: INTEGER
                   end;
     var
         REGS    : REGISTERS;   {AX, BX, CX, DX, BP, SI,
                                 DI, DS, ES, FLAGS}

         DTA_SEG,
         DTA_OFS : integer;     {address of disk transfer area}
         i       : integer;     {counter for loops}

     begin
         with REGS do
           begin
             AX := $4F00;
             MSDos (REGS);
             if (FLAGS and 1 = 1) then     {error in operation}
                STATUS := Lo(AX)
             else
               begin
                 STATUS := 0;                  {successful operation}
                 GetDTA (DTA_SEG, DTA_OFS);

                 with FILESPEC do
                   begin
                     ATTRIBUTES :=  Mem [DTA_SEG:DTA_OFS+21];

                     FILE_SIZE  := 1.0 * Mem [DTA_SEG:DTA_OFS+26] +
                                   Mem [DTA_SEG:DTA_OFS+27] * 256.0 +
                                   Mem [DTA_SEG:DTA_OFS+28] * Power
                                              (256.0, 2) +
                                   Mem [DTA_SEG:DTA_OFS+29] * Power
                                              (256.0, 3);

                     I := 0;
                     while ((I < 13) and (Mem[DTA_SEG:DTA_OFS+30+I] <> 0))
                        do
                        begin
                          name[I + 1] := Chr(Mem[DTA_SEG:DTA_OFS+30+I]);
                          I := I + 1;
                        end;

                     name[0] := Chr(I);
                   end; {with FILESPEC}
               end;
           end;          {with REGS}
     end;
```

Figure 14-30.

Program to implement Find Next
Matching File service (*continued*)

Consider the program in Figure 14-31, which displays a directory listing of all the files contained in the current directory. This program slightly modifies the program in Figure 14-31:

```
    if (ParamCount >= 1) then
      Find_First (ParamStr(1), 16, FILESPEC, STATUS)
    else
      Find_First ('*.*', 16, FILESPEC, STATUS);
```

```
program Ls;

Type
 STRING79 = string[79];

 DTA_INFO = record
    ATTRIBUTES  : byte;
    FILE_SIZE   : real;
    NAME        : STRING79;
 end;


function Power (NUMBER, EXPONENT: real): real;

begin

    Power := Exp(EXPONENT * Ln(NUMBER));
end;



procedure Get_DTA (var SEGMENT, OFFSET: integer);

Type
  REGISTERS = record
                AX, BX, CX, DX, BP, SI, DI, DS, ES, FLAGS: INTEGER
              end;

Var
    REGS: REGISTERS;  {AX, BX, CX, DX, BP, SI, DI, DS, ES, FLAGS}

begin
    with REGS do
      begin
        AX := $2F00;
        MSDos (REGS);
        SEGMENT := ES;
        OFFSET  := BX;
      end;
end;
```

Figure 14-31.

LS program

```
        procedure Find_First (SEARCH_SPEC: STRING79;
                              ATTRIBUTES: byte;
                          var FILESPEC: DTA_INFO;
                              var STATUS: byte);

        Type
          REGISTERS = record
                        AX, BX, CX, DX, BP, SI, DI, DS, ES, FLAGS: INTEGER
                      end;
        var
             REGS    : REGISTERS;  {AX, BX, CX, DX, BP, SI,
                                    DI, DS, ES, FLAGS}
             DTA_SEG,
             DTA_OFS : integer;  {address of disk transfer area}
             I       : integer;  {counter for loops}

        begin
           with REGS do
             begin
               SEARCH_SPEC := SEARCH_SPEC + Chr(0);
               AX := $4E00;                           {DOS function code}
               DS := Seg(SEARCH_SPEC[1]);
               DX := Ofs(SEARCH_SPEC[1]);
               CX := ATTRIBUTES;
               MSDos (REGS);
               if (FLAGS and 1 = 1) then
                 STATUS := Lo(AX)
               else
                 begin
                   STATUS := 0;                       {successful operation}
                   Get_DTA (DTA_SEG, DTA_OFS);

                   with FILESPEC do
                     begin
                       ATTRIBUTES :=  Mem [DTA_SEG:DTA_OFS+21];

                       FILE_SIZE  := 1.0 * Mem [DTA_SEG:DTA_OFS+26] +
                                     Mem [DTA_SEG:DTA_OFS+27] * 256.0 +
                                     Mem [DTA_SEG:DTA_OFS+28] * Power
                                                    (256.0, 2) +
                                     Mem [DTA_SEG:DTA_OFS+29] * Power
                                                    (256.0, 3);

                       I := 0;
                       while ((I < 13) and (Mem[DTA_SEG:DTA_OFS+30+I] <> 0))
                          do
                            begin
                              name[I + 1] := Chr(Mem[DTA_SEG:DTA_OFS+30+I]);
                              I := I + 1;
                            end;

                       name[0] := Chr(I);
                     end; {with FILESPEC}
                 end;
             end;          {with REGS}
        end;

        procedure Find_Next (var FILESPEC: DTA_INFO;
                             var STATUS: byte);

        Type
          REGISTERS = record
                        AX, BX, CX, DX, BP, SI, DI, DS, ES, FLAGS: INTEGER
                      end;
        var
```

Figure 14-31.

LS program (*continued*)

```
          REGS    : REGISTERS;   {AX, BX, CX, DX, BP, SI,
                                   DI, DS, ES, FLAGS}
        DTA_SEG,
        DTA_OFS : integer;    {address of disk transfer area}
        i       : integer;    {counter for loops}

begin
    with REGS do
      begin
        AX := $4F00;
        MSDos (REGS);
        if (FLAGS and 1 = 1) then    {error in operation}
          STATUS := Lo(AX)
        else
          begin
            STATUS := 0;                 {successful operation}
            Get_DTA (DTA_SEG, DTA_OFS);

            with FILESPEC do
              begin
                ATTRIBUTES :=  Mem [DTA_SEG:DTA_OFS+21];

                FILE_SIZE  := 1.0 * Mem [DTA_SEG:DTA_OFS+26] +
                             Mem [DTA_SEG:DTA_OFS+27] * 256.0 +
                             Mem [DTA_SEG:DTA_OFS+28] * Power
                                                   (256.0, 2) +
                             Mem [DTA_SEG:DTA_OFS+29] * Power
                                                   (256.0, 3);

                I := 0;
                while ((I < 13) and (Mem[DTA_SEG:DTA_OFS+30+I] <> 0))
                    do
                  begin
                    name[I + 1] := Chr(Mem[DTA_SEG:DTA_OFS+30+I]);
                    I := I + 1;
                  end;

                name[0] := Chr(1);
              end; {with FILESPEC}
          end;
      end;          {with REGS}
end;

procedure OpenFile (FILENAME: STRING79;
                    MODE: byte;
                var FILE_HANDLE: integer;
                var STATUS: byte);

Type
  REGISTERS = record
                AX, BX, CX, DX, BP, SI, DI, DS, ES, FLAGS: INTEGER
              end;

var
    REGS: REGISTERS;  {AX, BX, CX, DX, BP, SI, DI, DS, ES, FLAGS}
begin
    with REGS do
      begin
        FILENAME := FILENAME + Chr(0);
        AX := $3D00 + MODE;                {mode is in AL}
        DS := Seg(FILENAME[1]);
        DX := Ofs(FILENAME[1]);
        MSDos (REGS);
        if (FLAGS and 1 = 1) then          {error in operation}
          STATUS := Lo(AX)
```

Figure 14-31.

LS program (*continued*)

```
                else
                  begin
                    FILE_HANDLE := AX;                 {successful operation}
                    STATUS := 0;
                  end;
              end;
          end;


        procedure GetFileStamp (FILE_HANDLE: integer;
                    var DAY, MONTH, HOURS, MINUTES,
                                SECONDS, YEAR: integer;
                                var STATUS: byte);
        Type
          REGISTERS = record
                        AX, BX, CX, DX, BP, SI, DI, DS, ES, FLAGS: INTEGER
                      end;

        var
            REGS: REGISTERS;    {AX, BX, CX, DX, BP, SI, DI, DS, ES, FLAGS}

        begin
            with REGS do
              begin
                AX := $5700;
                BX := FILE_HANDLE;
                MSDos (REGS);
                if (FLAGS and 1 =1) then               {error in operation}
                  STATUS := Lo(AX)
                else
                  begin
                    STATUS := 0;                       {successful operation}
                    YEAR   := (Hi(DX) shr 1) + 1980;
                    MONTH := (DX and $1E0) shr 5;
                    DAY    := DX and $1F;
                    HOURS := Hi(CX) shr 3;
                    MINUTES := (CX and $7E0) shr 5;
                    SECONDS := (CX and $1F) * 2;
                  end;
              end;
          end;


        procedure CloseFile (FILE_HANDLE: integer;

                             var STATUS: byte);

        Type
          REGISTERS = record
                        AX, BX, CX, DX, BP, SI, DI, DS, ES, FLAGS: INTEGER
                      end;

        var
            REGS: REGISTERS;    {AX, BX, CX, DX, BP, SI, DI, DS, ES, FLAGS}

        begin
            with REGS do
              begin
                AX := $3E00;
                BX := FILE_HANDLE;
                MSDos (REGS);
                if (FLAGS and 1 = 1) then               {error in operation}
                  STATUS := Lo(AX)
                else
```

Figure 14-31.

LS program (*continued*)

```
              STATUS := 0;
          end;
    end;

    Var
      FILE_DAY, FILE_MONTH, FILE_YEAR,       {file date stamp}
      HOUR, MINUTES, SECONDS,                {file time stamp}
      FILE_HANDLE: integer;

      STATUS     : byte;                     {status of file operations}
      FILESPEC   : DTA_INFO;                 {name, size, attributes}

    begin

      Find_First ('*.*', 16, FILESPEC, STATUS);

      while ((STATUS <> 18) and (STATUS <> 2) and (STATUS <> 3)) do
        begin

          OpenFile (FILESPEC.NAME, 0, FILE_HANDLE, STATUS);
          GetFileStamp (FILE_HANDLE, FILE_DAY,FILE_MONTH, HOUR,
                     MINUTES, SECONDS, FILE_YEAR, STATUS);

          CloseFile (FILE_HANDLE, STATUS);

          Write (FILESPEC.NAME, '':(15-Length(FILESPEC.NAME)));

          case FILESPEC.ATTRIBUTES of
               0: Write ('NO ATTRIBUTES':15);
               1: Write ('READONLY':15);
               2: Write ('HIDDEN':15);
               4: Write ('SYSTEM':15);
               8: Write ('VOLUME':15);
              16: Write ('SUBDIRECTORY':15);
              32: Write ('ARCHIVE':15);
          end;

          Write (FILESPEC.FILE_SIZE:10:0);

          if FILE_MONTH < 10 then
            Write (0:3, FILE_MONTH, '/')
          else
            Write (FILE_MONTH:4, '/');

          if FILE_DAY < 10 then
            Write (0, FILE_DAY:1, '/')
          else
            Write (FILE_DAY:2, '/');

          Write (FILE_YEAR:4);
          Write ((HOUR mod 12):4, ':');
          if (MINUTES < 10) then
            Write (1, MINUTES:1)
          else
            Write (MINUTES:2);

          if (HOUR div 12 = 1) then
            Writeln (' PM')
          else
            Writeln (' AM');

          FIND_NEXT (FILESPEC, STATUS);
        end;
    end.
```

Figure 14-31.

LS program (*continued*)

It performs a directory listing based upon the first command-line argument, as shown here:

```
A> LS *.TXT
```

or

```
A> LS OLD.*
```

Most DOS users have probably wished that the DOS TYPE command supported wild-card characters, as shown here:

```
A> TYPE *.*
Invalid filename or file not found
```

The program in Figure 14-32 provides the capability to display multiple files based on wild-card operators.

Now that your programs can easily incorporate support for wild-card characters, consider adding one or two command-line qualifiers. A command-line qualifier is simply a command-line argument that qualifies (modifies slightly) the execution of a command. Consider the /w qualifier on the DOS directory command, which directs it to display a file listing in short form:

```
A> LS /W
```

```
Program Htype;

Const
  BUFFERSIZE = 512;

Type
  STRING79 = string[79];
  DISKBUFFER = array [1..BUFFERSIZE] of byte;

  DTA_INFO = record
    ATTRIBUTES  : byte;
    FILE_SIZE   : real;
    NAME        : STRING79;
  end;


function Power (NUMBER, EXPONENT: real): real;

begin

    Power := Exp(EXPONENT * Ln(NUMBER));
end;


procedure Get_DTA (var SEGMENT, OFFSET: integer);

Type
  REGISTERS = record
                AX, BX, CX, DX, BP, SI, DI, DS, ES, FLAGS: INTEGER
              end;

Var
    REGS: REGISTERS;  {AX, BX, CX, DX, BP, SI, DI, DS, ES, FLAGS}

begin
    with REGS do
      begin
        AX := $2F00;
        MSDos (REGS);
        SEGMENT := ES;
        OFFSET  := BX;
      end;
end;

procedure Find_First (SEARCH_SPEC: STRING79;
                      ATTRIBUTES: byte;
                      var FILESPEC: DTA_INFO;
                      var STATUS: byte);

Type
  REGISTERS = record
                AX, BX, CX, DX, BP, SI, DI, DS, ES, FLAGS: INTEGER
              end;
var
    REGS    : REGISTERS;  {AX, BX, CX, DX, BP, SI,
                           DI, DS, ES, FLAGS}
    DTA_SEG,
    DTA_OFS : integer;  {address of disk transfer area}
    I       : integer;  {counter for loops}

begin
    with REGS do
```

Figure 14-32.

HTYPE program

```
            begin
              SEARCH_SPEC := SEARCH_SPEC + Chr(0);
              AX := $4E00;                            {DOS function code}
              DS := Seg(SEARCH_SPEC[1]);
              DX := Ofs(SEARCH_SPEC[1]);
              CX := ATTRIBUTES;
              MSDos (REGS);
              if (FLAGS and 1 = 1) then
                STATUS := Lo(AX)
              else
                begin
                  STATUS := 0;                        {successful operation}
                  Get_DTA (DTA_SEG, DTA_OFS);

                  with FILESPEC do
                    begin
                      ATTRIBUTES :=  Mem [DTA_SEG:DTA_OFS+21];

                      FILE_SIZE  := 1.0 * Mem [DTA_SEG:DTA_OFS+26] +
                                    Mem [DTA_SEG:DTA_CFS+27] * 256.0 +
                                    Mem [DTA_SEG:DTA_OFS+28] * Power
                                                     (256.0, 2) +
                                    Mem [DTA_SEG:DTA_OFS+29] * Power
                                                     (256.0, 3);

                      I := 0;
                      while ((I < 13) and (Mem[DTA_SEG:DTA_OFS+30+I] <> 0))
                          do
                        begin
                          name[I + 1] := Chr(Mem[DTA_SEG:DTA_OFS+30+I]);
                          I := I + 1;
                        end;

                      name[0] := Chr(I);
                    end; {with FILESPEC}
                end;
            end;            {with REGS}
      end;

      procedure Find_Next (var FILESPEC: DTA_INFO;
                           var STATUS: byte);
      Type
        REGISTERS = record
                     AX, BX, CX, DX, BP, SI, DI, DS, ES, FLAGS: INTEGER
                    end;
      var
          REGS    : REGISTERS;   {AX, BX, CX, DX, BP, SI,
                                  DI, DS, ES, FLAGS}
          DTA_SEG,
          DTA_OFS : integer;     {address of disk transfer area}
          i       : integer;     {counter for loops}

      begin
          with REGS do
            begin
              AX := $4F00;
              MSDos (REGS);
              if (FLAGS and 1 = 1) then    {error in operation}
                STATUS := Lo(AX)
              else
                begin
                  STATUS := 0;                        {successful operation}
                  Get_DTA (DTA_SEG, DTA_OFS);
```

Figure 14-32.

HTYPE program (*continued*)

```
                with FILESPEC do
                  begin
                    ATTRIBUTES := Mem [DTA_SEG:DTA_OFS+21];

                    FILE_SIZE  := 1.0 * Mem [DTA_SEG:DTA_OFS+26] +
                                  Mem [DTA_SEG:DTA_OFS+27] * 256.0 +
                                  Mem [DTA_SEG:DTA_OFS+28] * Power
                                                        (256.0, 2) +
                                  Mem [DTA_SEG:DTA_OFS+29] * Power
                                                        (256.0, 3);

                    I := 0;
                    while ((I < 13) and (Mem[DTA_SEG:DTA_OFS+30+I] <> 0))
                      do
                      begin
                        name[I + 1] := Chr(Mem[DTA_SEG:DTA_OFS+30+I]);
                        I := I + 1;
                      end;

                    name[0] := Chr(I);
                  end; {with FILESPEC}
              end;
          end;            {with REGS}
    end;

    procedure OpenFile (FILENAME: STRING79;
                        MODE: byte;
                    var FILE_HANDLE: integer;
                        var STATUS: byte);

    Type
      REGISTERS = record
                    AX, BX, CX, DX, BP, SI, DI, DS, ES, FLAGS: INTEGER
                  end;
    var
        REGS: REGISTERS;   {AX, BX, CX, DX, BP, SI, DI, DS, ES, FLAGS}

    begin
        with REGS do
          begin
            FILENAME := FILENAME + Chr(0);
            AX := $3D00 + MODE;                {mode is in AL}
            DS := Seg(FILENAME[1]);
            DX := Ofs(FILENAME[1]);
            MSDos (REGS);
            if (FLAGS and 1 = 1) then          {error in operation}
              STATUS := Lo(AX)
            else
              begin
                FILE_HANDLE := AX;             {successful operation}
                STATUS := 0;
              end;
          end;
    end;

    procedure CloseFile (FILE_HANDLE: integer;
                            var STATUS: byte);
    Type
      REGISTERS = record
                    AX, BX, CX, DX, BP, SI, DI, DS, ES, FLAGS: INTEGER
                  end;
        var
```

Figure 14-32.

HTYPE program (*continued*)

```
            REGS: REGISTERS;   (AX, BX, CX, DX, BP, SI, DI, DS, ES, FLAGS)

      begin
          with REGS do
             begin
               AX := $3E00;
               BX := FILE_HANDLE;
               MSDos (REGS);
               if (FLAGS and 1 = 1) then          (error in operation)
                  STATUS := Lo(AX)
               else
                  STATUS := 0;
             end;
      end;


      procedure ReadFileHandle (FILE_HANDLE: integer;
                                var BUFFER: DISKBUFFER;
                                    NUMBYTES: integer;
                                var BYTESREAD: integer;
                                var STATUS: byte);

      Type
        REGISTERS = record
                      AX, BX, CX, DX, BP, SI, DI, DS, ES, FLAGS: INTEGER
                    end;

      var
          REGS: REGISTERS;   (AX, BX, CX, DX, BP, SI, DI, DS, ES, FLAGS)

      begin
          with REGS do
             begin
               AX := $3F00;
               BX := FILE_HANDLE;
               CX := NUMBYTES;
               DS := Seg(BUFFER);
               DX := Ofs(BUFFER);
               MSDos (REGS);
               if (FLAGS and 1 = 1) then          (error in operation)
                  STATUS := Lo(AX)
               else
                  BYTESREAD := AX;
                  STATUS := 0;
             end;
      end;

      procedure WriteFileHandle (FILE_HANDLE: integer;
                                     BUFFER: DISKBUFFER;
                                     NUMBYTES: integer;
                                 var STATUS: byte);

      Type
        REGISTERS = record
                      AX, BX, CX, DX, BP, SI, DI, DS, ES, FLAGS: INTEGER
                    end;

      var
          REGS: REGISTERS;   (AX, BX, CX, DX, BP, SI, DI, DS, ES, FLAGS)

      begin
          with REGS do
             begin
               AX := $4000;
```

Figure 14-32.

HTYPE program (*continued*)

```
                  BX  := FILE_HANDLE;
                  CX  := NUMBYTES;
                  DS  := Seg(BUFFER);
                  DX  := Ofs(BUFFER);
                  MSDos (REGS);
                  if (FLAGS and 1 = 1) then            {error in operation}
                     STATUS := Lo(AX)
                  else
                     STATUS := 0;
               end;
      end;

      var
        bytesread, handle: integer;
        status, readstatus, writestatus: byte;
        buffer: diskbuffer;
        FILESPEC   : DTA_INFO;                    {name, size, attributes}
      begin
        if (ParamCount < 1) then
          writeln ('HTYPE: invalid usage: HTYPE FILENAME')
        else
          begin
            Find_First (ParamStr(1), 0, FILESPEC, STATUS);

            while ((STATUS <> 18) and (STATUS <> 2) and (STATUS <> 3)) do
              begin
                OpenFile (FILESPEC.NAME, 0, HANDLE, STATUS);

                if (STATUS <> 0) then
                  writeln ('HTYPE: Cannot open the file ', FILESPEC.NAME)
                else
                  begin
                    repeat
                      ReadFileHandle (HANDLE, BUFFER, BUFFERSIZE,
                                         BYTESREAD, READSTATUS);
                       WriteFileHandle (1, BUFFER, BYTESREAD, WRITESTATUS);
                    until (BYTESREAD = 0);

                    CloseFile (HANDLE, STATUS);
                  end;

                FIND_NEXT (FILESPEC, STATUS);
              end;
          end;
      end.
```

Figure 14-32.

HTYPE program *(continued)*

In a similar manner, the /S qualifier for the LS command directs LS to display only files that were modified or created since the specified date. Consider the command

```
A> LS /S:12/08/88
```

In this case, LS only displays files modified or created since 12/08/88.

Likewise, you can add the qualifier /D to direct LS to display only directory names:

```
A> LS /D
```

Note that you can use multiple command-line qualifiers, as shown here:

```
A> LS /S:12/08/88 /D
```

Next, the /P qualifier prompts the user as follows:

```
-- Enter --
```

after each page, along with the /W qualifier that directs LS to display a short version directory entry. Figure 14-33 shows the **LS** program modified to include these qualifiers.

DOS wild-card characters should be fully supported by all of your utility programs. Make a practice of ensuring that your routines are as generic as possible. By utilizing wild-card characters and command-line qualifiers, you can quickly develop routines of professional quality.

OS/2 DIRECTIONS

OS/2 file-manipulation capabilities remain similar to those found under DOS. Always remember that OS/2 must maintain compatibility with

```
            program Ls;

            Const
              Page = 23;

            Type
             STRING79 = string[79];

             DTA_INFO = record
                 ATTRIBUTES   : byte;
                 FILE_SIZE    : real;
                 NAME         : STRING79;
             end;


            function Power (NUMBER, EXPONENT: real): real;

            begin
                Power := Exp(EXPONENT * Ln(NUMBER));
            end;


            Function LessDate (DAY, FILE_DAY, MONTH, FILE_MONTH,
                            Year, FILE_YEAR: integer) : Boolean;
            begin
              if (FILE_YEAR < YEAR) then
                LessDate := False
              else if (FILE_YEAR = YEAR) and (FILE_MONTH < MONTH) then
                LessDate := False
              else if (File_Month = Month) and (FILE_DAY < DAY) then
                LessDate := False
              else
                LessDate := True;
            end;


            procedure Get_DTA (var SEGMENT, OFFSET: integer);

            Type
              REGISTERS = record
                            AX, BX, CX, DX, BP, SI, DI, DS, ES, FLAGS: INTEGER
                        end;

            Var
                REGS: REGISTERS;   {AX, BX, CX, DX, BP, SI, DI, DS, ES, FLAGS}

            begin
                with REGS do
                  begin
                    AX := $2F00;
                    MSDos (REGS);
                    SEGMENT := ES;
                    OFFSET  := BX;
                  end;
            end;



            procedure Find_First (SEARCH_SPEC: STRING79;
                                  ATTRIBUTES: byte;
                              var FILESPEC: DTA_INFO;
                                  var STATUS: byte);
```

Figure 14-33.

LS program with qualifiers

```
            Type
              REGISTERS = record
                             AX, BX, CX, DX, BP, SI, DI, DS, ES, FLAGS: INTEGER
                          end;
            var
                REGS     : REGISTERS;   {AX, BX, CX, DX, BP, SI,
                                         DI, DS, ES, FLAGS}
                DTA_SEG,
                DTA_OFS : integer;   {address of disk transfer area}
                I       : integer;   {counter for loops}

            begin
                with REGS do
                  begin
                    SEARCH_SPEC := SEARCH_SPEC + Chr(0);
                    AX := $4E00;                           {DOS function code}
                    DS := Seg(SEARCH_SPEC[1]);
                    DX := Ofs(SEARCH_SPEC[1]);
                    CX := ATTRIBUTES;
                    MSDos (REGS);
                    if (FLAGS and 1 = 1) then
                      STATUS := Lo(AX)
                    else
                      begin
                        STATUS := 0;                       {successful operation}
                        Get_DTA (DTA_SEG, DTA_OFS);

                        with FILESPEC do
                          begin
                            ATTRIBUTES :=  Mem [DTA_SEG:DTA_OFS+21];

                            FILE_SIZE  := 1.0 * Mem [DTA_SEG:DTA_OFS+26] +
                                          Mem [DTA_SEG:DTA_OFS+27] * 256.0 +
                                          Mem [DTA_SEG:DTA_OFS+28] * Power
                                                               (256.0, 2) +
                                          Mem [DTA_SEG:DTA_OFS+29] * Power
                                                               (256.0, 3);

                            I := 0;
                            while ((I < 13) and (Mem[DTA_SEG:DTA_OFS+30+I] <> 0))
                                do
                              begin
                                name[I + 1] := Chr(Mem[DTA_SEG:DTA_OFS+30+I]);
                                I := I + 1;
                              end;

                            name[0] := Chr(I);
                          end; {with FILESPEC}
                  end;
                end;             {with REGS}
            end;

            procedure Find_Next (var FILESPEC: DTA_INFO;
                                 var STATUS: byte);

            Type
              REGISTERS = record
                             AX, BX, CX, DX, BP, SI, DI, DS, ES, FLAGS: INTEGER
                          end;
            var
                REGS     : REGISTERS;   {AX, BX, CX, DX, BP, SI,
                                         DI, DS, ES, FLAGS}
                DTA_SEG,
                DTA_OFS : integer;      {address of disk transfer area}
                i       : integer;      {counter for loops}
```

Figure 14-33.

LS program with qualifiers
(*continued*)

```
begin
    with REGS do
        begin
          AX := $4F00;
          MSDos (REGS);
          if (FLAGS and 1 = 1) then      {error in operation}
            STATUS := Lo(AX)
          else
            begin
              STATUS := 0;                    {successful operation}
              Get_DTA (DTA_SEG, DTA_OFS);

              with FILESPEC do
                begin
                  ATTRIBUTES :=  Mem [DTA_SEG:DTA_OFS+21];

                  FILE_SIZE   := 1.0 * Mem [DTA_SEG:DTA_OFS+26] +
                                 Mem [DTA_SEG:DTA_OFS+27] * 256.0 +
                                 Mem [DTA_SEG:DTA_OFS+28] * Power
                                                         (256.0, 2) +
                                 Mem [DTA_SEG:DTA_OFS+29] * Power
                                                         (256.0, 3);

                  I := 0;
                  while ((I < 13) and (Mem[DTA_SEG:DTA_OFS+30+I] <> 0))
                      do
                    begin
                      name[I + 1] := Chr(Mem[DTA_SEG:DTA_OFS+30+I]);
                      I := I + 1;
                    end;

                  name[0] := Chr(I);

                end; {with FILESPEC}
        end;
    end;        {with REGS}
end;

procedure OpenFile (FILENAME: STRING79;
                    MODE: byte;
                var FILE_HANDLE: integer;
                    var STATUS: byte);

Type
    REGISTERS = record
                   AX, BX, CX, DX, BP, SI, DI, DS, ES, FLAGS: INTEGER
                end;

var
    REGS: REGISTERS;   {AX, BX, CX, DX, BP, SI, DI, DS, ES, FLAGS}

begin
    with REGS do
        begin
          FILENAME := FILENAME + Chr(0);
          AX := $3D00 + MODE;                 {mode is in AL}
          DS := Seg(FILENAME[1]);
          DX := Ofs(FILENAME[1]);
          MSDos (REGS);
          if (FLAGS and 1 = 1) then           {error in operation}
            STATUS := Lo(AX)
          else
            begin
              FILE_HANDLE := AX;               {successful operation}
              STATUS := 0;
            end;
```

Figure 14-33.

LS program with qualifiers
(*continued*)

```
          end;
     end;


     procedure GetFileStamp (FILE_HANDLE: integer;
               var DAY, MONTH, HOURS, MINUTES,
                         SECONDS, YEAR: integer;
                              var STATUS: byte);
     Type
       REGISTERS = record
                     AX, BX, CX, DX, BP, SI, DI, DS, ES, FLAGS: INTEGER
                   end;

     var
         REGS: REGISTERS;   {AX, BX, CX, DX, BP, SI, DI, DS, ES, FLAGS}

     begin
         with REGS do
           begin
             AX := $5700;
             BX := FILE_HANDLE;
             MSDos (REGS);
             if (FLAGS and 1 =1) then              {error in operation}
                 STATUS := Lo(AX)
             else
               begin
                 STATUS := 0;                      {successful operation}
                 YEAR   := (Hi(DX) shr 1) + 1980;
                 MONTH := (DX and $1E0) shr 5;
                 DAY    := DX and $1F;
                 HOURS := Hi(CX) shr 3;
                 MINUTES := (CX and $7E0) shr 5;
                 SECONDS := (CX and $1F) * 2;
               end;
           end;
     end;


     procedure CloseFile (FILE_HANDLE: integer;
                          var STATUS: byte);

     Type
       REGISTERS = record
                     AX, BX, CX, DX, BP, SI, DI, DS, ES, FLAGS: INTEGER
                   end;

     var
         REGS: REGISTERS;   {AX, EX, CX, DX, BP, SI, DI, DS, ES, FLAGS}

     begin
         with REGS do
           begin
             AX := $3E00;
             BX := FILE_HANDLE;
             MSDos (REGS);
             if (FLAGS and 1 = 1) then             {error in operation}
               STATUS := Lo(AX)
             else
               STATUS := 0;
           end;
     end;
```

Figure 14-33.

LS program with qualifiers
(*continued*)

```
    Var
        FILE_DAY, FILE_MONTH, FILE_YEAR,          {file date stamp}
        DAY, MONTH, YEAR, VALSTATUS,
        HOUR, MINUTES, SECONDS,                   {file time stamp}
        FILE_HANDLE: integer;
        I, LINE_COUNT, DISPLAY_COUNT : Integer;

        DIRECTORY_ONLY,
        SHORT,
        PAUSE,
        DATE: BOOLEAN;

        STATUS      : byte;                       {status of file operations}

        FILESPEC    : DTA_INFO;                   {name, size, attributes}

    begin
        DIRECTORY_ONLY := false;
        SHORT := false;
        PAUSE := false;
        DATE := false;

        For I := 1 to ParamCount do
           if ParamStr(I) = '/D' then
              DIRECTORY_ONLY := true
           else if ParamStr(I) = '/P' then
              PAUSE := true
           else if ParamStr(I) = '/W' then
              SHORT := true
           else if Copy (ParamStr(I), 1, 3) = '/S:' then
              begin
                 Date := True;
                 Val (Copy(ParamStr(I), 4, 2), MONTH, VALSTATUS);
                 Val (Copy(ParamStr(I), 7, 2), DAY, VALSTATUS);
                 Val (Copy(ParamStr(I), 10, 4), YEAR, VALSTATUS);
              end;

        LINE_COUNT := 1;
        DISPLAY_COUNT := 0;

        if (ParamCount >= 1) then
           Find_First (ParamStr(1), 16, FILESPEC, STATUS)
        else
           Find_First ('*.*', 16, FILESPEC, STATUS);

        while ((STATUS <> 18) and (STATUS <> 2) and (STATUS <> 3)) do
           begin

              OpenFile (FILESPEC.NAME, 0, FILE_HANDLE, STATUS);
              GetFileStamp (FILE_HANDLE, FILE_DAY,FILE_MONTH, HOUR,
                            MINUTES, SECONDS, FILE_YEAR, STATUS);

              CloseFile (FILE_HANDLE, STATUS);

              if (DATE) and (LessDate (DAY, FILE_DAY, MONTH, FILE_MONTH,
                            Year, FILE_YEAR)) then
              if (Not Directory_Only) or (FILESPEC.ATTRIBUTES = 16) then
              begin

                 Write (FILESPEC.NAME, '':(15-Length(FILESPEC.NAME)));
```

Figure 14-33.

LS program with qualifiers
(*continued*)

```
            if (NOT Short) then
            begin

              case FILESPEC.ATTRIBUTES of
                   0: Write ('NO ATTRIBUTES':15);
                   1: Write ('READONLY':15);
                   2: Write ('HIDDEN':15);
                   4: Write ('SYSTEM':15);
                   8: Write ('VOLUME':15);
                  16: Write ('SUBDIRECTORY':15);
                  32: Write ('ARCHIVE':15);
              end;

              Write (FILESPEC.FILE_SIZE:10:0);

              if FILE_MONTH < 10 then
                Write (0:3, FILE_MONTH, '/')
              else
                Write (FILE_MONTH:4, '/');

              if FILE_DAY < 10 then
                Write (0, FILE_DAY:1, '/')
              else
                Write (FILE_DAY:2, '/');

              Write (FILE_YEAR:4);
              Write ((HOUR mod 12):4, ':');
              if (MINUTES < 10) then
                Write (1, MINUTES:1)
              else
                Write (MINUTES:2);

              if (HOUR div 12 = 1) then
                Writeln (' PM')
              else
                Writeln (' AM');

              LINE_COUNT := LINE_COUNT + 1;
            end
            else
            begin
              Display_Count := Display_Count + 1;
              If (Display_Count mod 5 = 0) then
                begin
                  writeln;
                  LINE_COUNT := LINE_COUNT + 1;
                end;
            end;

            if (PAUSE) and (LINE_COUNT mod PAGE = 0) then
              begin
                write ('--Enter--');
                readln;
              end;
            end;

            FIND_NEXT (FILESPEC, STATUS);
          end;
      end.
```

Figure 14-33.

LS program with qualifiers
(*continued*)

DOS utilities. As such, OS/2 capabilities for the most part closely resemble DOS file-manipulation commands. The changes to OS/2 file-manipulation commands are subtle.

Consider the following TYPE command:

```
A> TYPE A.TXT B.TXT
```

In this case, TYPE will first display the contents of the file A.TXT (if it exists) and then the contents of B.TXT. Likewise, the command

```
A> DIR *.TXT *.DAT A.TXT
```

directs the DIR command first to perform a listing of files matching *.TXT, then *.DAT, and, lastly, the file A.TXT. Indeed, this capability makes your command-line processing most powerful. However, you can implement this processing within your current utility programs. Consider this abbreviated DIR command that supports the following command line:

```
A> MLS *.DAT *.TXT *.BAK
```

The program shown in Figure 14-34 loops through its command-line parameters until no more command-line arguments are present. To support multiple command-line arguments this way requires that you include this simple processing. The difficulty in this type of processing is the support of command-line qualifiers.

```
            program mls;

            Type
             STRING79 = string[79];

             DTA_INFO = record
                 ATTRIBUTES  : byte;
                 FILE_SIZE   : real;
                 NAME        : STRING79;
             end;


            function Power (NUMBER, EXPONENT: real): real;

            begin

                 Power := Exp(EXPONENT * Ln(NUMBER));
            end;


            procedure Set_DTA (SEGMENT, OFFSET: integer);

            Type
              REGISTERS = record
                          AX, BX, CX, DX, BP, SI, DI, DS, ES, FLAGS: INTEGER
                          end;

            Var
                 REGS: REGISTERS;  {AX, BX, CX, DX, BP, SI, DI, DS, ES, FLAGS}

            begin
                 with REGS do
                    begin
                      AX := $1A00;
                      DS := Segment;
                      DX := Offset;
                      MSDos (REGS);
                    end;
            end;


            procedure Get_DTA (var SEGMENT, OFFSET: integer);

            Type
              REGISTERS = record
                          AX, BX, CX, DX, BP, SI, DI, DS, ES, FLAGS: INTEGER
                          end;

            Var
                 REGS: REGISTERS;  {AX, BX, CX, DX, BP, SI, DI, DS, ES, FLAGS}

            begin
               ith REGS do
                begin
                  AX := $2F00;
                  MSDos (REGS);
                  SEGMENT := ES;
                  OFFSET  := BX;
                end;
            end;
```

Figure 14-34.

MLS program to loop through
qualifier options

```
         procedure Find_First (SEARCH_SPEC: STRING79;
                               ATTRIBUTES: byte;
                           var FILESPEC: DTA_INFO;
                           var STATUS: byte);

         Type
           REGISTERS = record
                         AX, BX, CX, DX, BP, SI, DI, DS, ES, FLAGS: INTEGER
                       end;
         var
             REGS    : REGISTERS;  {AX, BX, CX, DX, BP, SI,
                                     DI, DS, ES, FLAGS}
             DTA_SEG,
             DTA_OFS : integer;  {address of disk transfer area}
             I       : integer;  {counter for loops}

         begin
             with REGS do
               begin
                 SEARCH_SPEC := SEARCH_SPEC + Chr(0);
                 AX := $4E00;                              {DOS function code}
                 DS := Seg(SEARCH_SPEC[1]);
                 DX := Ofs(SEARCH_SPEC[1]);
                 CX := ATTRIBUTES;
                 MSDos (REGS);
                 if (FLAGS and 1 = 1) then
                   STATUS := Lo(AX)
                 else
                   begin
                     STATUS := 0;                         {successful operation}
                     Get_DTA (DTA_SEG, DTA_OFS);

                     with FILESPEC do
                       begin
                         ATTRIBUTES :=  Mem [DTA_SEG:DTA_OFS+21];

                         FILE_SIZE  := 1.0 * Mem [DTA_SEG:DTA_OFS+26] +
                                       Mem [DTA_SEG:DTA_OFS+27] * 256.0 +
                                       Mem [DTA_SEG:DTA_OFS+28] * Power
                                                         (256.0, 2) +
                                       Mem [DTA_SEG:DTA_OFS+29] * Power
                                                         (256.0, 3);

                         I := 0;

                         while ((I < 13) and (Mem[DTA_SEG:DTA_OFS+30+I] <> 0))
                             do
                           begin
                             name[I + 1] := Chr(Mem[DTA_SEG:DTA_OFS+30+I]);
                             I := I + 1;
                           end;

                         name[0] := Chr(I);
                       end; {with FILESPEC}
                   end;
               end;           {with REGS}
         end;

         procedure Find_Next (var FILESPEC: DTA_INFO;
                              var STATUS: byte);
```

Figure 14-34.

MLS program to loop through
qualifier options (*continued*)

```
Type
  REGISTERS = record
                AX, BX, CX, DX, BP, SI, DI, DS, ES, FLAGS: INTEGER
            end;
var
    REGS    : REGISTERS;   {AX, BX, CX, DX, BP, SI,
                            DI, DS, ES, FLAGS}
    DTA_SEG,
    DTA_OFS : integer;     {address of disk transfer area}
    i       : integer;     {counter for loops}

begin
    with REGS do
      begin
        AX := $4F00;
        MSDos (REGS);
        if (FLAGS and 1 = 1) then     {error in operation}
          STATUS := Lo(AX)
        else
          begin
            STATUS := 0;                    {successful operation}
            Get_DTA (DTA_SEG, DTA_OFS);

            with FILESPEC do
              begin
                ATTRIBUTES :=  Mem [DTA_SEG:DTA_OFS+21];

                FILE_SIZE  := 1.0 * Mem [DTA_SEG:DTA_OFS+26] +
                              Mem [DTA_SEG:DTA_OFS+27] * 256.0 +
                              Mem [DTA_SEG:DTA_OFS+28] * Power
                                                       (256.0, 2) +
                              Mem [DTA_SEG:DTA_OFS+29] * Power
                                                       (256.0, 3);

                I := 0;
                while ((I < 13) and (Mem[DTA_SEG:DTA_OFS+30+I] <> 0))
                     do
                  begin
                    name[I + 1] := Chr(Mem[DTA_SEG:DTA_OFS+30+I]);
                    I := I + 1;
                  end;

                name[0] := Chr(I);
              end; {with FILESPEC}
          end;
      end;          {with REGS}
end;

procedure OpenFile (FILENAME: STRING79;
                    MODE: byte;
                var FILE_HANDLE: integer;
                var STATUS: byte);

Type
  REGISTERS = record
                AX, BX, CX, DX, BP, SI, DI, DS, ES, FLAGS: INTEGER
            end;

var
    REGS: REGISTERS;   {AX, BX, CX, DX, BP, SI, DI, DS, ES, FLAGS}
```

Figure 14-34.

MLS program to loop through
qualifier options (*continued*)

```
        begin
          with REGS do
            begin
              FILENAME := FILENAME + Chr(0);
              AX := $3D00 + MODE;                  {mode is in AL}
              DS := Seg(FILENAME[1]);
              DX := Ofs(FILENAME[1]);
              MSDos (REGS);
              if (FLAGS and 1 = 1) then             {error in operation}
                STATUS := Lo(AX)
              else
                begin
                  FILE_HANDLE := AX;                {successful operation}
                  STATUS := 0;
                end;
            end;
        end;


    procedure GetFileStamp (FILE_HANDLE: integer;
              var DAY, MONTH, HOURS, MINUTES,
                        SECONDS, YEAR: integer;
                            var STATUS: byte);
    Type
      REGISTERS = record
                    AX, BX, CX, DX, BP, SI, DI, DS, ES, FLAGS: INTEGER
                  end;

    var
        REGS: REGISTERS;  {AX, BX, CX, DX, BP, SI, DI, DS, ES, FLAGS}

    begin
        with REGS do
          begin
            AX := $5700;
            BX := FILE_HANDLE;
            MSDos (REGS);
            if (FLAGS and 1 =1) then               {error in operation}
              STATUS := Lo(AX)
            else
              begin
                STATUS := 0;                        {successful operation}
                YEAR   := (Hi(DX) shr 1) + 1980;
                MONTH := (DX and $1E0) shr 5;
                DAY    := DX and $1F;
                HOURS := Hi(CX) shr 3;
                MINUTES := (CX and $7E0) shr 5;
                SECONDS := (CX and $1F) * 2;
              end;
          end;
    end;


    procedure CloseFile (FILE_HANDLE: integer;
                          var STATUS: byte);

    Type
      REGISTERS = record
                    AX, BX, CX, DX, BP, SI, DI, DS, ES, FLAGS: INTEGER
                  end;
```

Figure 14-34.

MLS program to loop through
qualifier options (*continued*)

```
var
     REGS: REGISTERS;    (AX, BX, CX, DX, BP, SI, DI, DS, ES, FLAGS)

begin
    with REGS do
        begin
          AX := $5E00;
          BX := FILE_HANDLE;
          MSDos (REGS);
          if (FLAGS and 1 = 1) then          {error in operation}
             STATUS := Lo(AX)
          else
             STATUS := 0;
        end;
end;


Var
  FILE_DAY, FILE_MONTH, FILE_YEAR,       {file date stamp}
  HOUR, MINUTES, SECONDS,                {file time stamp}
  FILE_HANDLE: integer;

  STATUS      : byte;                    {status of file operations}
  FILESPEC    : DTA_INFO;                {name, size, attributes}
  INDEX, COUNT: integer;
  TempDta: array [1..126] of byte;

begin
  INDEX := 1;
  Count := ParamCount;

{ Use a new DTA to prevent command line from being overwritten }

  Set_Dta (Seg(TempDta), Ofs(TempDta));

  repeat
   if (Count >= 1) then
     Find_First (ParamStr(INDEX), 16, FILESPEC, STATUS)
   else
     Find_First ('*.*', 16, FILESPEC, STATUS);

   while ((STATUS <> 18) and (STATUS <> 2) and (STATUS <> 3)) do
      begin
        OpenFile (FILESPEC.NAME, 0, FILE_HANDLE, STATUS);

      if (STATUS <> 0) then
        Writeln ('Error accessing date & time stamp')
      else
        begin

        GetFileStamp (FILE_HANDLE, FILE_DAY,FILE_MONTH, HOUR,
                      MINUTES, SECONDS, FILE_YEAR, STATUS);

        CloseFile (FILE_HANDLE, STATUS);

        Write (FILESPEC.NAME, '':(15-Length(FILESPEC.NAME)));

        case FILESPEC.ATTRIBUTES of
              0: Write ('NO ATTRIBUTES':15);
              1: Write ('READONLY':15);
              2: Write ('HIDDEN':15);
              4: Write ('SYSTEM':15);
              8: Write ('VOLUME':15);
             16: Write ('SUBDIRECTORY':15);
             32: Write ('ARCHIVE':15);
           end;
```

Figure 14-34.

MLS program to loop through
qualifier options (*continued*)

```
        Write (FILESPEC.FILE_SIZE:10:0);

        if FILE_MONTH < 10 then
          Write (0:3, FILE_MONTH, '/')
        else
          Write (FILE_MONTH:4, '/');

        if FILE_DAY < 10 then
          Write (0, FILE_DAY:1, '/')
        else
          Write (FILE_DAY:2, '/');

        Write (FILE_YEAR:4);
        Write ((HOUR mod 12):4, ':');
        if (MINUTES < 10) then
          Write (1, MINUTES:1)
        else
          Write (MINUTES:2);

        if (HOUR div 12 = 1) then
          Writeln (' PM')
        else
          Writeln (' AM');

        FIND_NEXT (FILESPEC, STATUS);
      end;

    INDEX := INDEX + 1;
  until (INDEX > Count);
end.
```

Figure 14-34.

MLS program to loop through
qualifier options (*continued*)

Consider the following command:

```
A> MLS *.DAT /P *.TXT /S:12/21/87
```

Here you have several possible choices of how to treat the command-line
parameters. First, you can require the user to place all the qualifiers at
the beginning of the command-line, as shown here:

```
A> MLS /P /S:12/21/87 *.DAT *.TXT
```

In this case, every qualifier is applied to all the files on the command line.

Second, you can also associate specific command-line qualifiers to command-line parameters, as shown here:

```
A> MLS *.DAT /P *.TXT /S:12/21/87
```

Last, you can allow the user to place command-line qualifiers at any location, thus applying each to all of the files on the command line.

If you decide to support the first alternative, simply loop through the command-line parameters until you find an argument that is not a valid qualifier. That becomes your first data file (see Figure 14-35). If you choose the second alternative, get a file name from the command line and then search for its qualifiers immediately after it, as shown in Figure 14-36. For the third option, make an initial pass through each of the command-line parameters and note any qualifiers (see Figure 14-37). Most DOS users are probably intimidated when they consider the development of a DOS utility program. However, as you have just seen, supporting DOS wild-card characters and command-line arguments from within your applications is straightforward.

DOS and OS/2 provide a small set of file-manipulation system services. Using these services, you can quickly develop powerful programs that support DOS wild-card characters. Always ensure that your utility programs support wild-card characters as shown in this chapter. The number of applications that they support will increase greatly.

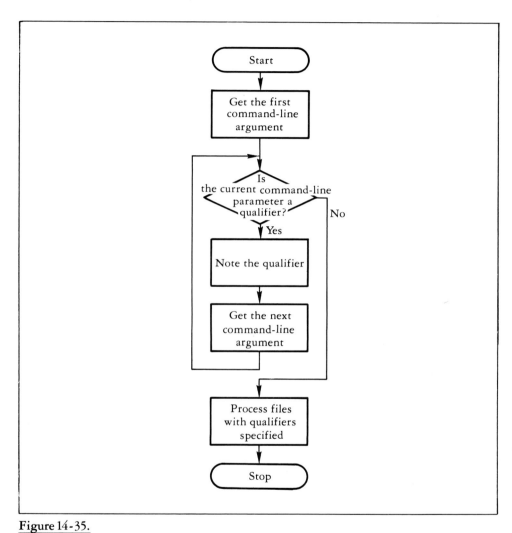

Figure 14-35.

Program loop to find qualifiers

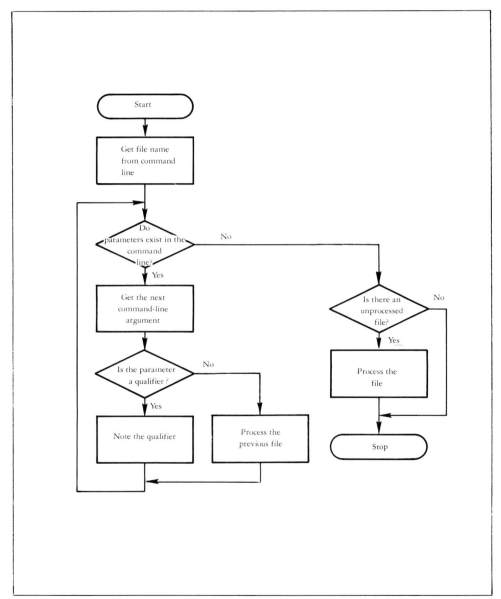

Figure 14-36.

Program flowchart showing process
of associating qualifiers to
parameters

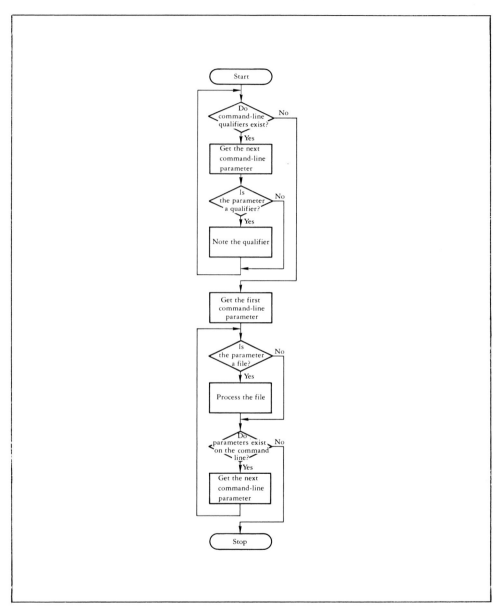

Figure 14-37.

Program flowchart showing process
of noting any qualifiers that are
present

15: Memory-Resident Programs

Over the past few years, software developers have attempted to extend the capabilities of DOS by leaving application programs resident in memory to perform special functions such as "hot key" notepads, alarm clocks, or other tasks. These applications, called *memory-resident programs,* append themselves to DOS and remain permanently installed in memory throughout your working session (see Figure 15-1).

This chapter teaches you the magic behind memory-resident programs. You will learn how to capture DOS interrupts, extend the DOS type-ahead buffer, install an alarm clock program, capture the current video display, display subliminal messages to your system's user, and how to turn off your display after five minutes of inactivity. This chapter is meant as a programming culmination to all of the details that you have tackled in the text thus far.

It is possible to make just about any DOS application memory-resident in a relatively straightforward manner. In fact, DOS provides a system service that helps you do just that, as shown in Table 15-1.

The "trick" required to utilize memory-resident programs is to determine when and how they are invoked once resident in memory. Most memory-resident programs depend on a hardware or software

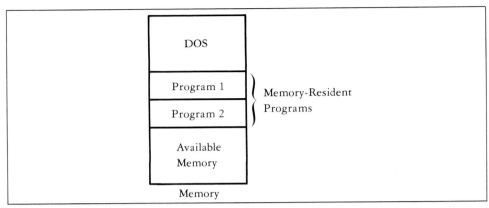

Figure 15-1.

Location of memory-resident
programs

Table 15-1.

DOS Service for Memory-Residency

Terminate Current Program

Register	Contents
AH	31H DOS terminate resident service
DX	Amount of memory required divided by 16 (in paragraphs)

interrupt as their means of invocation. An interrupt is simply a signal to the CPU from a program or hardware device directing the CPU to temporarily suspend what it is doing, in order to perform specific processing. For each interrupt, a section of code (known as an *interrupt-service routine*) is in memory. This code interrupts the processor each time its associated interrupt occurs and directs the processor to perform a specific task.

Each time an interrupt occurs, the processor locates the interrupt-service routine in memory and executes its associated code. For example, when the user presses the SHIFT and PRTSC keys, the print-screen interrupt prints the current screen contents. The CPU identifies each interrupt by way of an interrupt vector. The easiest way to view interrupt vectors is as a table with n rows and three columns (see Table 15-2).

When an interrupt occurs, the processor uses the interrupt number as an index into the interrupt vector table to locate the appropriate interrupt-service routine. The system then stores its current state (register values) and invokes the interrupt-service routine. Once the interrupt has been serviced, the system restores its state and continues processing as if it had never been interrupted. Most memory-resident programs simply redirect a specific interrupt vector to themselves. When the interrupt later occurs, the interrupt servicing results in the memory-resident program gaining control.

Most of the memory-resident programs presented in this chapter attach themselves to one of these interrupt vectors. This is done

Table 15-2.

Interrupt Vectors

Interrupt	Segment Address	Offset Address
1	0070	01ED
2	3D28	09D2
3	0070	01ED
4	3D28	0998
5	F000	FF54
.	.	.
.	.	.
.	.	.
n	xxxx	xxxx

through the DOS interrupt services 25H (Set Interrupt Vector) and 35H (Get Interrupt Vector), which are illustrated in Table 15-3.

For example, the following C program displays the interrupt vectors of the first 25 interrupts:

```
#include <dos.h>

main ()
 {
  int interrupt;

  union REGS inregs, outregs;
  struct SREGS segregs;

  for (interrupt = 1; interrupt <= 25; interrupt++)
   {
     inregs.h.ah = 0x35;
     inregs.h.al = interrupt;
     intdosx (&inregs, &outregs, &segregs);
     printf ("Interrupt %d Segment %x Offset %x\n",
             interrupt, segregs.es, outregs.x.bx);
   }
 }
```

To modify an interrupt vector, your program should perform the following steps:

1. Save the current interrupt vector address.

2. Set the interrupt vector to the desired routine.

3. Perform the desired processing.

4. Reset the interrupt vector to its original address before completing.

For example, the Turbo Pascal program shown in Figure 15-2 sets the print-screen interrupt (ROM-BIOS interrupt 5) to point at a Turbo Pascal procedure called **IgnorePrintScreen**. While this program is active, pressing the SHIFT-PRTSC key combination has no effect. Notice that the program follows the four steps previously listed. The in-line machine code within **IgnorePrintScreen** is standard for hardware interrupts. You will use it in the remainder of your interrupt-service routines.

Table 15-3.

DOS Services 25H and 35H

Set Interrupt Vector

Register	Entry Contents
AH	25H DOS interrupt service
AL	Interrupt number desired
DS	Segment address of the new interrupt handler
DX	Offset address of the new interrupt handler

No status values are returned

Get Interrupt Vector

Register	Entry Contents
AH	35H DOS interrupt service
AL	Interrupt number desired

Register	Exit Contents
BX	Offset address of the interrupt handler
ES	Segment address of the interrupt handler

```
Program PrintScreen ;  { Disable print screen operations }

Const
  DataSeg: integer = 0;

Type
  REGISTERS = record
                AX, BX, CX, DX, BP, SI, DI, DS, ES, FLAGS: INTEGER
              end;

procedure Set_Interrupt_Vector (INTERRUPT, SEGMENT, OFFSET: integer);

  var
    REGS: REGISTERS;   {AX, BX, CX, DX, BP, SI, DI, DS, ES, FLAGS}

  begin
    with REGS do
      begin

{set the registers to redefine an interrupt vector}
        AX := $2500 + interrupt;  {interrupt number is in AL}
        DS := SEGMENT;
        DX := OFFSET;

        MSDos (REGS);
      end;
  end;
```

Figure 15-2.

PRINTSCREEN program

```
procedure Get_Interrupt_Vector (INTERRUPT: integer;
                        var SEGMENT, OFFSET: integer);

   var
     REGS: REGISTERS;   {AX, BX, CX, DX, BP, SI, DI, DS, ES, FLAGS}

   begin
     with REGS do
       begin

{set the registers to redefine an interrupt vector}
       AX := $3500 + interrupt;   {interrupt number is in AL}

       MSDos (REGS);

       SEGMENT := ES;
       OFFSET := BX;
     end;
  end;


procedure IgnorePrintScreen ;

begin

  { save the current machine state }
    INLINE ($50/
            $53/
            $51/
            $52/
            $57/
            $56/
            $06/
            $1E/
            $FB/
            $2E/
            $A1/
            DataSeg/
            $8E/
            $D8);


  { restore the current machine state }
    Inline ($1F/
            $07/
            $5E/
            $5F/
            $5A/
            $59/
            $5B/
            $58/
            $8B/
            $E5/
            $5D/
            $CF);
  end;

  var
    SaveVectorSeg, SaveVectorOfs: Integer;

  begin
    DataSeg := DSeg;

    Get_Interrupt_Vector ($5, SaveVectorSeg, SaveVectorOfs);

    Set_Interrupt_Vector ($5, CSeg, Ofs(IgnorePrintScreen));

    Writeln ('Try a print screen operation.  Then press Enter');
    Readln;

    Set_Interrupt_Vector ($5, SaveVectorSeg, SaveVectorOfs);
  end.
```

Figure 15-2.

PRINTSCREEN program
(*continued*)

DOS MEMORY-RESIDENT PROGRAMS

Before examining the programming required to write memory-resident programs, consider how DOS utilizes them. Memory-resident programs are probably not new to you. You may not have realized that you have been using them all along. The DOS GRAPHICS and GRAFTABL commands both install memory-resident code that performs special processing. GRAPHICS helps with print-screen operations involving graphics displays.

To verify this, invoke CHKDSK and note the amount of available memory.

```
C> CHKDSK

Volume DOSDISK       created Jan 16, 1987 7:25p

21309440 bytes total disk space
  116736 bytes in 7 hidden files
  182272 bytes in 67 directories
14628864 bytes in 1776 user files
   20480 bytes in bad sectors
 6361088 bytes available on disk

  655360 bytes total memory
  454640 bytes free
```

Next, install the GRAPHICS memory-resident code.

```
C> GRAPHICS
```

Again invoke CHKDSK.

```
C> CHKDSK

Volume DOSDISK       created Jan 16, 1987 7:25p

21309440 bytes total disk space
  116736 bytes in 7 hidden files
  182272 bytes in 67 directories
14635008 bytes in 1778 user files
   20480 bytes in bad sectors
 6354944 bytes available on disk

  655360 bytes total memory
  453472 bytes free
```

The memory-resident code required by GRAPHICS consumed 1168 bytes of RAM. Next, consider the ANSI.SYS device driver. Install this driver (by using a CONFIG.SYS entry) as follows:

```
DEVICE=CONFIG.SYS
```

Each time your system boots, the driver attaches itself to the keyboard and screen I/O interrupts. As characters pass from the keyboard or to the screen, the ANSI driver first examines each one to see if it contains ANSI driver commands requesting additional processing (see Figure 15-3).

This is how escape sequences such as

printf ("%c[H%c[J", 27, 27);

result in the screen clearing and the cursor being placed in the home position. The ANSI driver simply recognized a command in the stream of characters heading to the screen and performed its clear-screen operation. Again, the driver does this by capturing I/O interrupts.

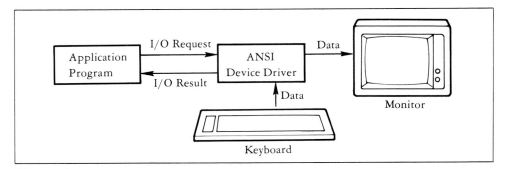

Figure 15-3.

ANSI driver examination of keyboard characters

The DOS PRINT command is one of the most powerful pieces of memory-resident code you use regularly. Each time you use this command to print a file, PRINT appears to work simultaneously with your other processing. The computer appears to be performing two tasks at once. PRINT does this by capturing clock interrupts to determine the intervals in which it should execute.

Memory-resident programs are actually quite common. Even the DOS developers have found them to be a convenient means of processing.

EXTENDING THE TYPE-AHEAD BUFFER

On the IBM PC and PC-compatibles, each keystroke you enter is placed into a circular keyboard buffer. By default, the buffer size can hold 16 characters. As you type, each keystroke causes an interrupt that results in two actions: the character is entered and its scan code is placed into the keyboard buffer (see Figure 15-4). As DOS processes keystrokes, it

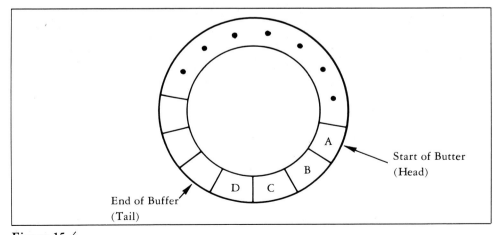

Figure 15-4.

Placement of scan code in keyboard buffer

removes them from the beginning of this buffer (see Figure 15-5).

If you enter 16 characters before DOS can process them, the keyboard buffer becomes full. If you type another character, DOS notifies you of the full buffer by sounding a bell and ignoring the character. To perform its keyboard operations, DOS must know where the keyboard buffer resides in memory, as well as the locations of the buffer's current head and tail. DOS stores these locations in a data structure beginning at memory location 480 hex, as shown in Figure 15-6.

The following Turbo Pascal program allows you to increase the size of the DOS type-ahead buffer by modifying the values in this data structure. The program defines a buffer large enough to store the desired number of characters and scan codes (in this case 512 bytes) and then modifies the keyboard buffer pointers to reference it.

```
program KeyBoard_Buffer;

const
  BUFFERSIZE = 512;        {new type ahead buffer size}
  PSP_SIZE = 256;          {program segment prefix in bytes}
  CODE_ESTIMATE = 1000;    {estimated size of resident program}

{record structure to simulate 8088 registers}
type
  REGISTERS = record
    AX, BX, CX, DX, BP, SI, DI, DS, ES, FLAGS: integer;
    end;

var
  BUFFER        : array[1..BUFFERSIZE] of byte; {new buffer}

  BUFFER_BEGIN: integer absolute $0000:$0480; {starting location}
  BUFFER_END  : integer absolute $0000:$0482; {ending location}
  BUFFER_HEAD : integer absolute $0000:$041A; {current head}
  BUFFER_TAIL : integer absolute $0000:$041C; {current tail}

  REGS          : REGISTERS;

begin
{set the offsets of the buffer relative to segment 40}
  BUFFER_BEGIN := (Seg(BUFFER[1]) - $40) * 16 + Ofs(BUFFER[1]);
  BUFFER_END   := BUFFER_BEGIN + BUFFERSIZE;
  BUFFER_HEAD  := BUFFER_BEGIN;
  BUFFER_TAIL  := BUFFER_BEGIN;

{specify the amount of memory required for resident program}
  REGS.DX := (PSP_SIZE + BUFFERSIZE + CODE_ESTIMATE) div 16 + 1;

{terminate and remain resident}
  REGS.AX := $3100;
  MsDos (REGS);
end.
```

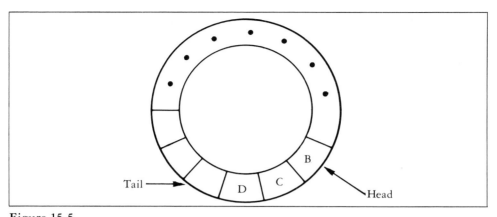

Figure 15-5.

Removing scan code from keyboard
buffer

Memory Location	Memory
$480	Start of Type-ahead Buffer Storage
$482	End of Type-ahead Buffer Storage
. . .	. . .
$41A	Current Head of Buffer
$41C	Current Tail of Buffer

Figure 15-6.

Memory location of buffer's current
head and tail

Once the DOS keyboard pointers reference this data buffer, the program must terminate residency in memory to ensure that the new keyboard buffer is contained in memory locations that other programs cannot overwrite (see Figure 15-7). If the program simply were to modify the keyboard buffer pointers to reference the array and then execute, the buffer would reside in memory marked by DOS as available. The next application you were to invoke would overwrite the keyboard buffer's contents and cause your system to hang (see Figure 15-8).

The processing in this sample Turbo Pascal program is less difficult than the memory-resident programs that follow. This provides an ideal opportunity to begin discussing the programming required for memory-resident applications. First, this example program does not modify any interrupt vectors. Instead, it simply provides a protected buffer in memory for the extended keyboard buffer. Once the program terminates itself as resident, its work is done. It never obtains CPU processing time, nor does it need to.

This explains why the program terminates with only 1K of

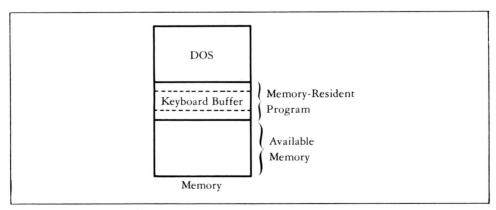

Figure 15-7.

Location of keyboard buffer in memory that other programs cannot overwrite

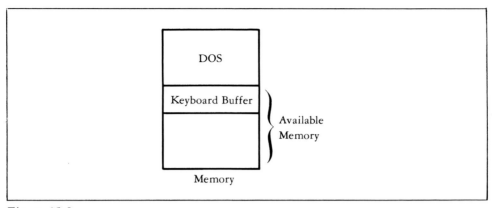

Figure 15-8.

Location of keyboard buffer in
available memory

memory-resident code, as opposed to the 10K-20K you might expect for
an entire program to reside in memory. Since the program never
executes once it is installed, its code need not be present in memory.
Instead, the program merely needs to ensure that a new keyboard buffer
resides in memory surrounded by the portion of memory-resident code.

As the memory-resident programs become more functional, they
will require the entire program to reside in memory. Although this does
not affect your programming, it does consume a larger amount of the
system's available memory.

CAPTURING THE PRINT-SCREEN INTERRUPT

Earlier in this chapter you saw how to capture the ROM-BIOS print-
screen interrupt. The Turbo Pascal program shown in Figure 15-9
modifies the code that you previously examined to copy the current
screen contents to a text file. In so doing, users can capture the screen
contents to files on disk and later print them with the DOS PRINT
command. The program in Figure 15-9 writes the current screen

```
        Program FileScreenContents ;  { file the current screen contents }

        Const
          DataSeg: integer = 0;
          CodeEstimate = 20000;
          ScrSegment = $B800;

        Type
          REGISTERS = record
                       AX, BX, CX, DX, BP, S1, DI, DS, ES, FLAGS: INTEGER
                     end;

        procedure Set_Interrupt_Vector (INTERRUPT, SEGMENT, OFFSET: integer);

           var
             REGS: REGISTERS;   {AX, BX, CX, DX, BP, S1, DI, DS, ES, FLAGS}

           begin
             with REGS do
               begin

        {set the registers to redefine an interrupt vector}
               AX := $2500 + interrupt;  {interrupt number is in AL}
               DS := SEGMENT;
               DX := OFFSET;

               MSDos (REGS);
             end;
           end;


        procedure Get_Interrupt_Vector (INTERRUPT: integer;
                          var SEGMENT, OFFSET: integer);

           var
             REGS: REGISTERS;   {AX, BX, CX, DX, BP, SI, DI, DS, ES, FLAGS}

           begin
             with REGS do
               begin

        {set the registers to redefine an interrupt vector}
               AX := $3500 + interrupt;  {interrupt number is in AL}

               MSDos (REGS);

               SEGMENT := ES;
               OFFSET := BX;
             end;
           end;

        procedure Terminate_Resident;
           var
             REGS: REGISTERS;   {AX, BX, CX, DX, BP, SI, DI, DS, ES, FLAGS}

           begin
             with REGS do
               begin

        {set the registers to terminate resident }
               AX := $3100;
               DX := (CodeEstimate div 16);

               MSDos (REGS);
             end;
           end;
```

Figure 15-9.

FILESCREENCONTENTS program

```
var
 i, j, Interrupt_Count: integer;

 fp: text;

procedure PrintScreen_Processor ;

begin
  INLINE ($50/
          $53/
          $51/
          $52/
          $57/
          $56/
          $06/
          $1E/
          $FB/
          $2E/
          $A1/
          DataSeg/
          $8E/
          $D8);

  Assign (fp, Chr(Interrupt_Count + 48));
  Rewrite (fp);

  for i := 0 to 24 do
    begin
      j := 0;
      while (j < 160) do
        begin
          write (fp, Chr(mem[ScrSegment:(i * 160) + j]));
          j := j + 2;
        end;
      writeln (fp);
    end;

  close (fp);
  Interrupt_Count := Interrupt_Count + 1;

  Inline ($1F/
          $07/
          $5E/
          $5F/
          $5A/
          $59/
          $5B/
          $58/
          $8B/
          $E5/
          $5D/
          $CF);
end;
var
  SaveVectorSeg, SaveVectorOfs: Integer;

begin
  Interrupt_Count := 1;
  DataSeg := DSeg;

  Get_Interrupt_Vector ($5, SaveVectorSeg, SaveVectorOfs);

  Set_Interrupt_Vector ($5, CSeg, Ofs(PrintScreen_Processor));

  Terminate_Resident ;
end.
```

Figure 15-9.

FILESCREENCONTENTS program
(*continued*)

contents to a file each time the user presses the SHIFT-PRTSC key combination.

Note that if your system uses a monochrome monitor, you must change the line

```
ScrSegment = $B800;
```

to

```
ScrSegment = $B000;
```

The program uses the variable **Interrupt — Count** to determine the number of print-screen operations that have been performed. The first time you invoke the interrupt, the program writes the current screen contents to a file named 1. The second time you invoke the interrupt results in a file called 2, and so on.

Although this is a fairly simple program, it provides significant functions. In fact, most of the screen images presented in this text were generated by this routine.

MEMORY-RESIDENT ALARM CLOCK

The IBM PC and PC-compatibles have a built-in real-time clock that generates an interrupt 18.2 times per second. By default, this interrupt (1CH) simply performs an IRET (interrupt return) instruction. Interrupt 1CH exists solely as your path to the system clock. By capturing this interrupt, your program gains tremendous capabilities.

In this case, the application uses the real-time clock to display a message on the screen every 15 minutes (see Figure 15-10).

Many users often become engrossed in their processing and lose track of the time. By displaying a reminder message on their screens every 15 minutes, they can greatly reduce the possibility of forgetting an important meeting.

Figure 15-11 shows a straightforward program for alarm processing. First, the program simply redirects interrupt vector 1CH to point to

Figure 15-10.

Screen message

the **Alarm__Processor** procedure. Next, the variable **Interrupt__ Count** tracks the number of times that the clock interrupt has been invoked (18.2 times per second). After 15 minutes, the program displays its message and resets its timer for the next 15-minute period.

By manipulating the system time in this fashion, your programs gain tremendous capabilities.

SUBLIMINAL-MESSAGE PROCESSING

One of the most controversial advertising ploys of the motion picture industry during the 1960s was the use of subliminal messages to sell candy, popcorn, and soda to theatergoers. At intervals of every few frames of film, a film editor would splice in a frame showing an ice-cold soda or a bucket of hot buttered popcorn. Because this frame of film was only on the screen for an instant, viewers did not consciously notice the picture.

This repetitive process was intended to subconsciously increase the viewers' desire to purchase snacks. Although that practice was ruled illegal, it raises an interesting dilemma for MIS and data processing

```
            Program Alarm_Clock ; { display a message to the user every 15 minutes }

            Const
              DataSeg: integer = 0;
              CodeEstimate = 20000;
              MessageLength = 21;
              MessageLocation = 1970;    { location on the screen }
              ScrSegment = $B800;        { cga screen }

            Type
              REGISTERS = record
                            AX, BX, CX, DX, BP, SI, DI, DS, ES, FLAGS: INTEGER
                          end;

            procedure Set_Interrupt_Vector (INTERRUPT, SEGMENT, OFFSET: integer);

              var
                REGS: REGISTERS;   {AX, BX, CX, DX, BP, SI, DI, DS, ES, FLAGS}

              begin
                with REGS do
                  begin

            {set the registers to redefine an interrupt vector}
                    AX := $2500 + interrupt;  {interrupt number is in AL}
                    DS := SEGMENT;
                    DX := OFFSET;

                    MSDos (REGS);
                  end;
              end;


            procedure Get_Interrupt_Vector (INTERRUPT: integer;
                                   var SEGMENT, OFFSET: integer);

              var
                REGS: REGISTERS;   {AX, BX, CX, DX, BP, SI, DI, DS, ES, FLAGS}

              begin
                with REGS do
                  begin

            {set the registers to redefine an interrupt vector}
                    AX := $3500 + interrupt;  {interrupt number is in AL}

                    MSDos (REGS);

                    SEGMENT := ES;
                    OFFSET := BX;
                  end;
              end;

            procedure Terminate_Resident;

              var
                REGS: REGISTERS;   {AX, BX, CX, DX, BP, SI, DI, DS, ES, FLAGS}

              begin
                with REGS do
                  begin

            {set the registers to terminate resident }
                    AX := $3100;
                    DX := (CodeEstimate div 16);

                    MSDos (REGS);
                  end;
              end;
```

Figure 15-11.

ALARM__CLOCK program

```
    var
      Interrupt_Count: integer;
      line1, line2, line3: string [MessageLength];
      i, j: integer;

    procedure Alarm_Processor ;

    begin
      INLINE ($50/
              $53/
              $51/
              $52/
              $57/
              $56/
              $06/
              $1E/
              $FB/
              $2E/
              $A1/
              DataSeg/
              $8E/
              $D8);

    Interrupt_Count := Interrupt_Count + 1;

    if (Interrupt_Count > 16380) then      { 15 minutes up? }
      begin
        Interrupt_Count := 0;              { reset the timer }
{ begin message display }
        j := MessageLocation;
        i := 1;
        while (j < MessageLocation + 2*(MessageLength)) do
          begin
            Mem[ScrSegment:J] := Ord(line1[i]);
            i := i + 1;
            j := j + 2;
          end;

        j := MessageLocation + 16380;
        i := 1;
        while (j < MessageLocation + 160 + 2*(MessageLength)) do
          begin
            Mem[ScrSegment:J] := Ord(line2[i]);
            i := i + 1;
            j := j + 2;
          end;

        j := MessageLocation + 320;
        i := 1;
        while (j < MessageLocation + 320 + 2*(MessageLength)) do
          begin
            Mem[ScrSegment:J] := Ord(line3[i]);
            i := i + 1;
            j := j + 2;
          end;

      end;

      Inline ($1F/
              $07/
              $5E/
              $5F/
              $5A/
              $59/
              $5B/
              $58/
              $8B/
              $E5/
```

Figure 15-11.

ALARM__CLOCK program

(*continued*)

```
            $5D/
            $CF);
  end;

  var
    SaveVectorSeg, SaveVectorOfs: Integer;

  begin
    Interrupt_Count := 0;
    DataSeg := DSeg;

    for i := 1 to MessageLength do
      begin
        Line1[i] := Chr(178);
        Line3[i] := Chr(178);
      end;

    Line2 := '  15 Minute Message ';
    Line2[1] := Chr(178);
    Line2[MessageLength] := Chr(178);

    Get_Interrupt_Vector ($1C, SaveVectorSeg, SaveVectorOfs);

    Set_Interrupt_Vector ($1C, CSeg, Ofs(Alarm_Processor));

    Terminate_Resident ;
  end;
```

Figure 15-11.

ALARM_CLOCK program
(*continued*)

managers: "If subliminal messages indeed have an influential effect on the target audience, why not use them to our advantage?"

For example, consider a program that displays the message

WORK FASTER!

every few seconds on the computer screen in a subliminal manner. To the end user, the message is transparent. Or the subliminal message may have been

DON'T SMOKE!
SELL, SELL, SELL!
BE CONCISE!

The Turbo Pascal program in Figure 15-12 implements subliminal-message processing. Depending on your monitor type, the message may result in snow on the screen. In such cases, simply synchronize the message display to the monitor's video retrace.

```
        Program SubLiminal_Messages ;

        Const
          DataSeg: integer = 0;
          CodeEstimate = 20000;
          MessageLength = 12;
          MessageLocation = 1970;
          ScrSegment = $B800;

        Type
          REGISTERS = record
                        AX, BX, CX, DX, BP, SI, DI, DS, ES, FLAGS: INTEGER
                      end;

        procedure Set_Interrupt_Vector (INTERRUPT, SEGMENT, OFFSET: integer);

           var
             REGS: REGISTERS;   {AX, BX, CX, DX, BP, SI, DI, DS, ES, FLAGS}

           begin
             with REGS do
               begin

        {set the registers to redefine an interrupt vector}
               AX := $2500 + interrupt;   {interrupt number is in AL}
               DS := SEGMENT;
               DX := OFFSET;

               MSDos (REGS);
             end;
           end;


        procedure Get_Interrupt_Vector (INTERRUPT: integer;
                             var SEGMENT, OFFSET: integer);

           var
             REGS: REGISTERS;   {AX, BX, CX, DX, BP, SI, DI, DS, ES, FLAGS}

           begin
             with REGS do
               begin

        {set the registers to redefine an interrupt vector}
               AX := $3500 + interrupt;   {interrupt number is in AL}

               MSDos (REGS);

               SEGMENT := ES;
               OFFSET := BX;
             end;
           end;

        procedure Terminate_Resident;

           var
             REGS: REGISTERS;   {AX, BX, CX, DX, BP, SI, DI, DS, ES, FLAGS}

           begin
             with REGS do
               begin

        {set the registers to terminate resident }
               AX := $3100;
               DX := (CodeEstimate div 16);

               MSDos (REGS);
             end;
           end;
```

Figure 15-12.

SUBLIMINAL__MESSAGES

program

```
var
  Interrupt_Count: integer;
  line, buffer: string [MessageLength];
  i, j, k: integer;

procedure Alarm_Processor ;

begin
  INLINE ($50/
          $53/
          $51/
          $52/
          $57/
          $56/
          $06/
          $1E/
          $Fb/
          $2E/
          $A1/
          DataSeg/
          $8E/
          $D8);

  Interrupt_Count := Interrupt_Count + 1;

  if (Interrupt_Count > 100) then
    begin
      Interrupt_Count := 0;
{ save the current screen contents }
      j := MessageLocation;
      i := 1;
      while (j < MessageLocation + 2*(MessageLength)) do
        begin
          Buffer[i] := Chr(Mem[ScrSegment:J]);
          i := i + 1;
          j := j + 2;
        end;


{ display the subliminal message }
      j := MessageLocation;
      i := 1;
      while (j < MessageLocation + 2*(MessageLength)) do
        begin
          Mem[ScrSegment:J] := Ord(line[i]);
          i := i + 1;
          j := j + 2;
        end;
{ delay for message display }
      for K := 1 to 250 do
        J := k;

{ redisplay the previous screen contents }
      j := MessageLocation;
      i := 1;
      while (j < MessageLocation + 2*(MessageLength)) do
        begin
          Mem[ScrSegment:J] := Ord(Buffer[i]);
          i := i + 1;
          j := j + 2;
        end;

    end;
```

Figure 15-12.

SUBLIMINAL__MESSAGES

program (*continued*)

```
        Inline ($1F/
               $07/
               $5E/
               $5F/
               $5A/
               $59/
               $5B/
               $58/
               $8B/
               $E5/
               $5D/
               $CF);
      end;

      var
        SaveVectorSeg, SaveVectorOfs: Integer;

      begin
        Interrupt_Count := 0;
        DataSeg := DSeg;

        Line := 'Work Faster!';

        Get_Interrupt_Vector ($1C, SaveVectorSeg, SaveVectorOfs);

        Set_Interrupt_Vector ($1C, CSeg, Ofs(Alarm_Processor));

        Terminate_Resident ;
      end.
```

Figure 15-12.

SUBLIMINAL__MESSAGES
program (*continued*)

SCREEN SAVE

People walk away from their screens throughout the day, and if they are gone for extended periods, it is possible for the screen to suffer "burn-in." When they turn off the monitor, its previous contents are actually burned into the display. The screen is ruined.

The Turbo Pascal program in Figure 15-13 wakes up every five minutes to examine the current contents of the screen. If the contents have not changed in the last five minutes, it blanks the display to prevent burn-in. The user can use the SHIFT and PRTSC keys to redisplay the screen's original contents.

The program captures the real-time clock (1CH) and print-screen (5) interrupts. Other than that, the processing is similar to each of the routines that you have been examining.

```
        Program ScreenSaver ;   { Blank the screen after 5 minutes of
                                  inactivity }

        Const
          DataSeg: integer = 0;
          CodeEstimate = 20000;
          ScreenSize = 4000;
          ScrSegment = $B800;   { cga adapter }

        Type
          REGISTERS = record
                        AX, BX, CX, DX, BP, SI, DI, DS, ES, FLAGS: INTEGER
                      end;

        procedure Set_Interrupt_Vector (INTERRUPT, SEGMENT, OFFSET: integer);

          var
            REGS: REGISTERS;   {AX, BX, CX, DX, BP, SI, DI, DS, ES, FLAGS}

          begin
            with REGS do
              begin

        {set the registers to redefine an interrupt vector}
              AX := $2500 + interrupt;   {interrupt number is in AL}
              DS := SEGMENT;
              DX := OFFSET;

              MSDos (REGS);
            end;
          end;


        procedure Get_Interrupt_Vector (INTERRUPT: integer;
                            var SEGMENT, OFFSET: integer);

          var
            REGS: REGISTERS;   {AX, BX, CX, DX, BP, SI, DI, DS, ES, FLAGS}

          begin
            with REGS do
              begin

        {set the registers to redefine an interrupt vector}
              AX := $3500 + interrupt;   {interrupt number is in AL}

              MSDos (REGS);

              SEGMENT := ES;
              OFFSET := BX;
            end;
          end;


        procedure Terminate_Resident;

          var
            REGS: REGISTERS;   {AX, BX, CX, DX, BP, SI, DI, DS, ES, FLAGS}

          begin
            with REGS do
              begin

        {set the registers to terminate resident }
              AX := $3100;
              DX := (CodeEstimate div 16);
```

Figure 15-13.

SCREENSAVER program

```
           MSDos (REGS);
         end;
     end;


  var
     Interrupt_Count: integer;
     i, j: integer;

     OldScreen: array [1..ScreenSize] of Byte;

  procedure Alarm_Processor ;

  begin
     INLINE ($50/
             $53/
             $51/
             $52/
             $57/
             $56/
             $06/
             $1E/
             $FB/
             $2E/
             $A1/
             DataSeg/
             $8E/
             $D8);

     Interrupt_Count := Interrupt_Count + 1;

     if (Interrupt_Count > 380) then
       begin

  { see if the screen contents have changed in the last 5 minutes }
         i := 1;
         while (i < 4000) and (OldScreen[i] = Mem[ScrSegment: i-1]) do
           i := i + 1;

  { save the current screen contents }
         for j := 1 to 4000 do
             OldScreen[j] := Mem[ScrSegment: j - 1];

  { blank the current screen }
         if (i = 4000) then
             for i := 1 to 4000 do
                 Mem[ScrSegment: i - 1] := 0;

         Interrupt_Count := 0;
       end;

     Inline ($1F/
             $07/
             $5E/
             $5F/
             $5A/
             $59/
             $5B/
             $58/
             $8B/
             $E5/
             $5D/
             $CF);
  end;
```

Figure 15-13.

SCREENSAVER program

(*continued*)

```
        { Capture print screen interrupts, restoring the screen to its
          original contents }

        procedure PrintScreen_Processor ;

        begin
          INLINE ($50/
                  $53/
                  $51/
                  $52/
                  $57/
                  $56/
                  $06/
                  $1E/
                  $FB/
                  $2E/
                  $A1/
                  DataSeg/
                  $8E/
                  $D8);

             Interrupt_Count := 0;

        { redisplay original screen contents }

             for j := 1 to 4000 do
               Mem[ScrSegment: j - 1] := OldScreen[j];

          InLine ($1F/
                  $07/
                  $5E/
                  $5F/
                  $5A/
                  $59/
                  $5B/
                  $58/
                  $8B/
                  $E5/
                  $5D/
                  $CF);
        end;

        var
          SaveVectorSeg, SaveVectorOfs: Integer;

        begin
          Interrupt_Count := 0;
          DataSeg := DSeg;

          for i := 1 to 4000 do
            OldScreen [i] := Mem[$B800: i-1];

          Get_Interrupt_Vector ($1C, SaveVectorSeg, SaveVectorOfs);

          Set_Interrupt_Vector ($1C, CSeg, Ofs(Alarm_Processor));
          Set_Interrupt_Vector ($5, CSeg, Ofs(PrintScreen_Processor));

          Terminate_Resident ;
        end.
```

Figure 15-13.

SCREENSAVER program
(*continued*)

WORD OF WARNING

Although memory-resident programs can be quite functional, they can also be devastating when they go wrong. Be ready to reboot your system several times as you experiment with the programs presented in this chapter. A "well-behaved" memory-resident program is one in which the system continues to operate as it did before the program was installed (with the exception of the program's specific processing). Installing a memory-resident program should not negatively affect the system. If so, the program has bugs that may result in devastating system errors.

OS/2 IMPACTS

DOS memory-resident programs exist to give you a tool that DOS does not provide by default — multitasking. Under OS/2, much of the "dirty work" required to terminate a program in memory is provided through standard interfaces. OS/2 is a fully functional multitasking operating system developed to support several programs in memory simultaneously. Under DOS, most memory-resident programs use system-clock or I/O interrupts to provide their means of invocation. OS/2 uses timers and device monitors that are integrated into the operating system to allow you to implement previously memory-resident DOS programs in a more elegant manner. In other words, OS/2 does not run terminate-and-stay-resident (TSR) programs.

An OS/2 device monitor is simply a software program that "watches" the characters passing through an OS/2 device driver. The most common applications for a device monitor are to monitor a stream of characters for a specific pattern (such as CTRL-ALT-DEL), or to perform character replacement or an appropriate series of operations.

Consider the OS/2 application in Figure 15-14, which requests data
from the keyboard. In this case, if you want to install an OS/2 monitor
that replaces a specific keystroke with a string of characters, press F1 to
enter the command

DIR *.*

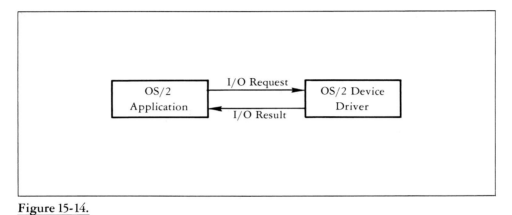

Figure 15-14.

OS/2 application requesting data
from keyboard

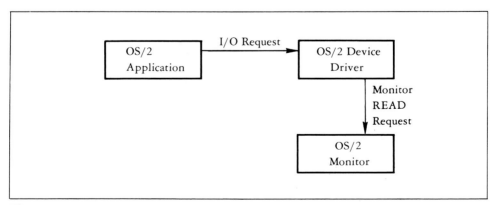

Figure 15-15.

Monitor reading request in OS/2
application

The monitor reads the data that the device driver would normally pass back to the device and checks for the F1 key (see Figure 15-15).

On completing its examination, the monitor sends either the original or modified characters back to the device driver, as shown in Figure 15-16. At this stage, the device driver can satisfy the I/O request (see Figure 15-17).

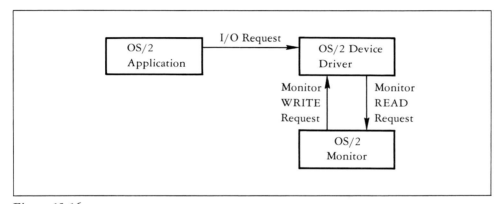

Figure 15-16.

Monitor sending back request in
OS/2 application

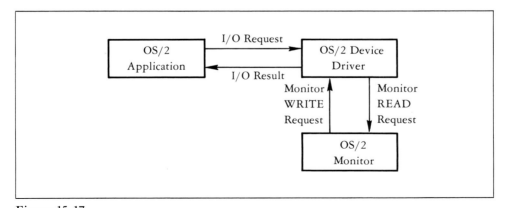

Figure 15-17.

Device driver satisfying request in
OS/2 application

OS/2 device monitors are an integrated piece of the operating system. They are simple to implement and are multifunctional.

Although the DOS **Alarm__Processing** program captures the real-time clock and provides you with extended processing capabilities, it has a major limitation. In most cases, only one DOS application can capture the clock interrupts in this way. This restriction is unsatisfactory in a multitasking environment such as OS/2.

To implement timer-dependent routines, OS/2 applications have a significant number of timer services available to them. Rather than place the system clock into the hands of an application program, OS/2 maintains strict control. OS/2 applications simply tell OS/2 to notify them when a given period has elapsed.

Although this sounds as if applications lose functionality, the opposite occurs. The simplicity with which OS/2 makes timer services available to developers takes a significant burden off the programmer. In addition, because multiple programs can utilize timer services, overall system performance is increased.

Memory-resident programs can greatly enhance your system's functional capabilities. Creating such applications is relatively straightforward. In most cases, memory-resident programs are closely related to interrupt services. If your program modifies interrupt vectors, be sure that you follow these steps to ensure that the application remains well-behaved:

1. Save the current interrupt vector address.

2. Set the interrupt vector to the desired routine.

3. Perform the desired processing.

4. Reset the interrupt vector to its original address before completing.

Your system will continue to function consistently once the program modifying the interrupt servicing completes.

16: OS/2 Overview

This text has presented bits and pieces about OS/2, its capabilities, and implementation. The next four chapters tie many OS/2 topics together to give you the foundation you require to build your OS/2 knowledge. This chapter provides you with a basic overview of OS/2. Chapter 17 presents OS/2 programmer considerations. Chapter 18 reviews each of the OS/2 commands. Finally, Chapter 19 examines the entirety of OS/2 by way of questions and answers. As DOS power users, you will most likely be at the forefront of OS/2 users.

THE NEED

Of all the software programs that have influenced our world since the advent of the computer, DOS has probably been the most influential. DOS brought the microcomputer into the office, school, and home. Today, more than 10 million people use DOS. By 1990, it is expected that more than 50 million personal computers will be in use. Each day thousands of computers are sold, and a version of DOS accompanies each one. As the interface between the user and the machine, DOS has indeed made a tremendous impact on all of us.

It is important to note, however, that the tremendous migration to personal computers has had several other impacts. First, as users become more computer literate, the complexity of their applications has increased significantly. What was once a simple inventory program that a secretary ran once a week now needs to be accessed simultaneously by several offices, which requires shared resources and support for local area networks. Second, as managers have become more conversant with software capabilities, their demand for reports and professional artwork has driven the need for integrated and desktop publishing systems. Visualize the PC's growth through the 1980s as follows:

1981   Release of the IBM PC and DOS. The PC is considered by many to be too expensive. It suffers because it does not have an "arcade game" flair. This is the era of skepticism.

1983   Personal computers exist to run spreadsheets. Small businesses are trying hard to justify applications for PCs.

1985   Word processing, spreadsheets, and small databases lead PC applications. Reduced cost is bringing the PC into more homes. Software is becoming abundant. This is the boom era for software developers.

1986   PCs are fully accepted in businesses and schools. Interest in concurrency is increasing. The key term is *integrated software*.

1987   Local area networks are growing rapidly. Microsoft Windows and Top-View give an early view of multitasking. Most applications are becoming multiuser. The PC is shedding its "personal" computer image.

1988   Desktop publishing is in full force. Small businesses can now produce professional documents in a short time. Laser printer costs drop and sales run wild. OS/2 is still on the horizon. DOS breaks the 640K barrier.

1989   DOS provides foreground and background processing. OS/2 use in business is expanding. The cost of the 80386 is down dramatically, making it readily available to the public.

1990   The 80386 and OS/2 are in general use. DOS remains fully supported. Use of optical storage media is commonplace.

Several factors may influence these predictions. However, note that DOS never disappears. Too many computers and too much software rely on DOS. Also note that OS/2 does not become fully accepted until the

80386 becomes readily available to the general public. As you will see throughout the following chapters, OS/2's tremendous functional capabilities are also responsible for considerable system overhead. The 80386 is fast enough to make this overhead transparent to the end user.

MULTITASKING

OS/2 is a multitasking operating system, which means that it can execute several programs simultaneously. For those of you who have Microsoft Windows, invoke CLOCK.EXE several times, as shown in

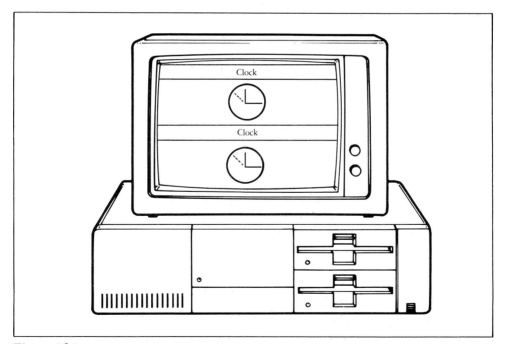

Figure 16-1.

Invoking CLOCK.EXE from Windows

Figure 16-1.In this case, each clock appears to update simultaneously on the screen. If you do not have MS Windows, invoke the DOS PRINT command. The computer prints your document while you continue to perform other commands. In either case, the computer appears to be performing two tasks at the same time; in other words, the operating system is *multitasking*.

Always keep in mind that the computer only has one CPU. Because of this, the computer can only perform one function at a time. When an operating system performs multitasking, it appears to execute several tasks simultaneously. Actually, the operating system is only executing one program for a given period and then switching to the next for a specific time interval (time slice). In the case of the DOS PRINT command, for example, the operating system gives CPU time to the user application and then to the PRINT command in a round-robin fashion. Assuming that the user is executing a word processing program, time-sharing of the CPU is visualized as shown in Figure 16-2.

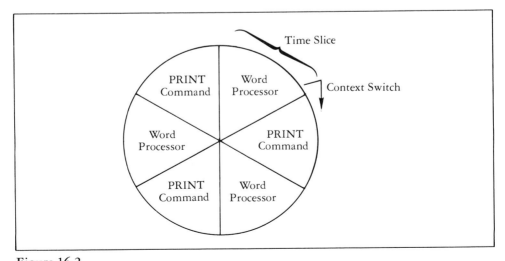

Figure 16-2.

Time-sharing on the CPU

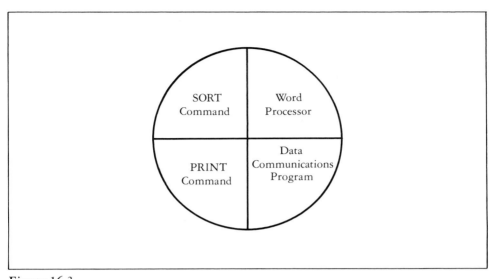

Figure 16-3.

Executing multiple programs in OS/2

OS/2 allows you to execute multiple programs this way. The user can be executing a word processor, a data communications program, the DOS PRINT command, and the DOS SORT command, as shown in Figure 16-3. OS/2 assigns the CPU to each application for a time slice and then passes control of the CPU to the next application (context switch). Each time OS/2 switches from one application to the next, it must store the state of the current application (its registers). When it later comes time for the application to receive its time slice, OS/2 can restore its registers and allow the application to proceed as if it were never interrupted. This process of saving one application's state before restoring another's is *context switching*.

Although the preceding simplifies OS/2 multitasking, it introduces the basic concepts of multitasking, time slicing, and context switching, each of which is critical to understanding the function of OS/2.

REAL VERSUS PROTECTED MODE

OS/2 runs in either real or protected mode. OS/2 real mode ensures that existing DOS programs can execute under OS/2. In this mode, programs can access specific memory locations, obtain and modify the values contained in ports, and perform low-level I/O operations. Consider the following Turbo Pascal program, which performs memory mapping to the video display memory in order to display the contents of a string.

```
Program MemoryMap;

var
  text: string[80];
  i: integer;

begin
  text := 'Test string';

  for i := 1 to Length(text) do
    Mem [$B800: (i-1) * 2] := Ord(text[i]);

  readln;
end.
```

In a single-application environment such as DOS, memory mapping in this manner is acceptable since the program cannot interfere with other applications. Under OS/2, however, several programs may be executing concurrently. Writing one application to the screen in an ad hoc manner could interfere with a second application's display. OS/2's protected mode prevents one concurrent application from affecting another.

OS/2 implements protected-mode operation by using virtual memory and I/O levels of protection, each discussed later in this chapter. The following list summarizes features of real mode versus protected-mode operation:

Real Mode

No hardware support to aid in system integrity (protection)

640K address limitation

Applications can directly access hardware devices

Low-level I/O is fully supported

DOS runs in real mode

Protected Mode

Hardware available to support system integrity

Larger physical address space

Unlimited virtual address space

I/O privilege levels

OS/2 runs in protected mode

Remember that OS/2 real-mode applications exist solely for the compatibility of existing DOS applications.

VIRTUAL MEMORY

As stated in Chapter 13, DOS applications are restricted to 640K of memory (see Figure 16-4). OS/2, however, allows your programs to be virtually any size (up to 1 gigabyte of virtual address space). OS/2 provides this essentially unlimited memory by using a memory-management scheme called virtual memory.

Under DOS, each time a program accesses memory, either for code or data, the memory reference is a physical memory address (see Figure 16-5). With OS/2, however, applications address a virtual address space, which OS/2 in turn maps to physical memory (see Figure 16-6).

Because OS/2 applications do not directly access physical memory, OS/2 can prevent one program from modifying the code or data of a

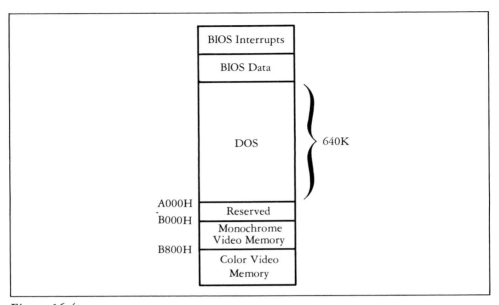

Figure 16-4.

Restriction of 640K memory in DOS

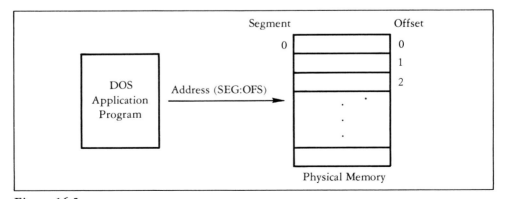

Figure 16-5.

Physical memory address

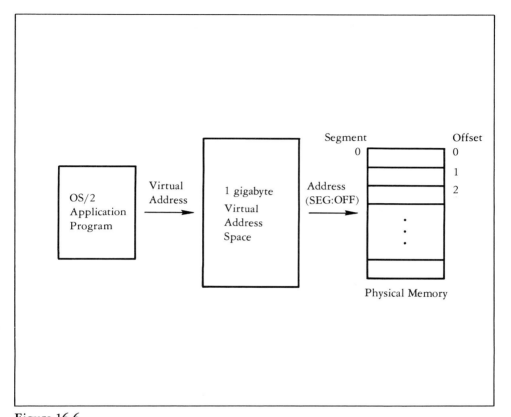

Figure 16-6.

Virtual address space

second program. This is how OS/2 applications are protected from one another. If one OS/2 application attempts to access memory outside of its own boundaries, OS/2 detects the attempt and the access fails (see Figure 16-7). Also, since OS/2 maps virtual addresses to physical memory locations, OS/2 applications can exceed the physical memory present on the system. In this way, OS/2 brings sections of code or data from disk into memory as they are needed. This process is *demand*

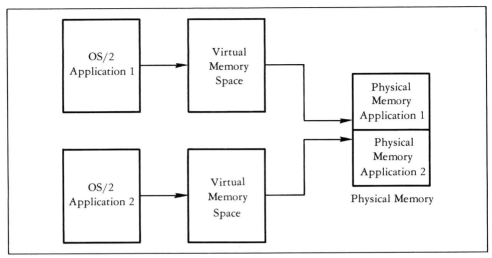

Figure 16-7.

Attempt to access memory outside of
boundary

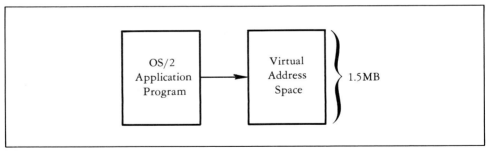

Figure 16-8.

Virtual address space of 1.5MB

paging. When OS/2 does not need a section of code or data to execute a
program, OS/2 places it back on the disk. When OS/2 later needs the
section of code or data, OS/2 loads it back into memory (on demand).

For example, assume your program maps to a virtual address space

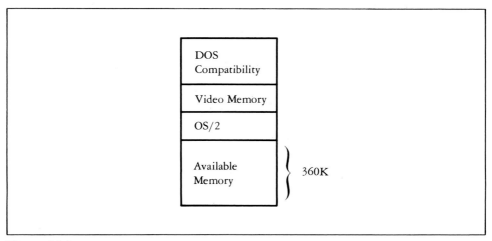

Figure 16-9.

360K of available memory in OS/2

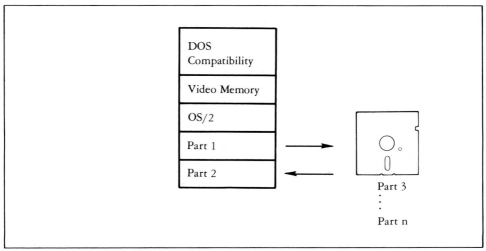

Figure 16-10.

OS/2 swapping to disk

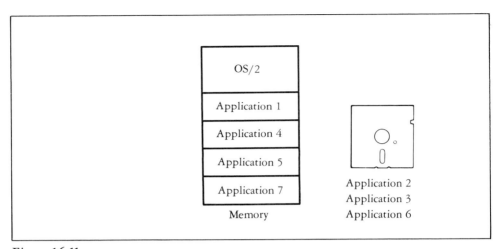

Figure 16-11.

OS/2 maximizing fairness of
resource distribution

of 1.5MB, as shown in Figure 16-8. If OS/2 only has 360K of available
memory, as shown in Figure 16-9, OS/2 must swap portions of your
program to and from disk as required (see Figure 16-10). Similarly, if
OS/2 is executing several large programs, it must bring in sections of
each, attempting to maximize fairness of resource distribution, as
shown in Figure 16-11.

In the same way that OS/2 restricts applications from accessing each
other's memory (by mapping their virtual addresses to physical
addresses), OS/2 can allow several programs to share specific memory
locations. If several programs are executing concurrently and each needs
to access the same portion of code, OS/2 can map each application to the
shared code, as shown in Figure 16-12.

In turn, the amount of memory consumed and the amount of paging
that OS/2 must perform are significantly reduced. In fact, the OS/2
Application Program Interface (API), which serves as the OS/2 system
service routines, is shared-memory code. Every time an OS/2 program
accesses an API routine, it uses the same code space available to each
program executing in the system (see Figure 16-13).

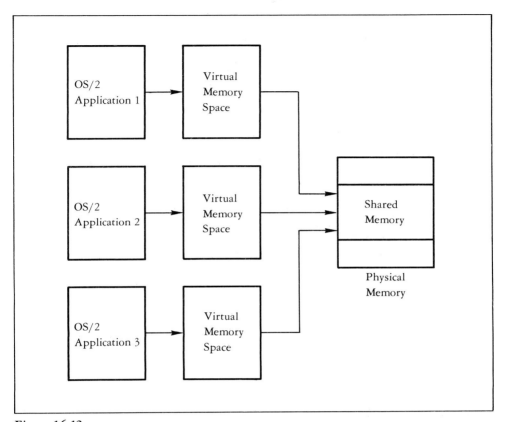

Figure 16-12.

Mapping applications to shared code

Although the actual OS/2 virtual memory implementation is complex, the concepts involved are fairly straightforward. The following list summarizes the advantages and disadvantages of OS/2 virtual memory.

Advantages

Program isolation and integrity

Multiple programs can coexist in harmony

Application address space can exceed available memory

Shared code and date is easily implemented

Disadvantage

System overhead

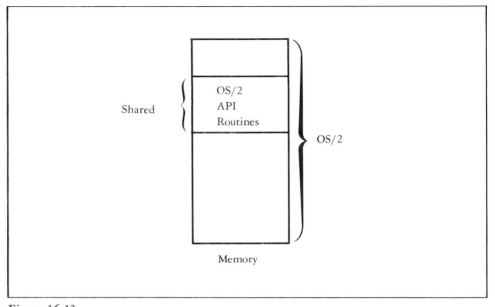

Figure 16-13.

OS/2 sharing code space

DEVICE VIRTUALIZATION

In any multitasking environment, applications must cooperate. For example, if one OS/2 application is writing to disk, a second cannot just begin low-level disk I/O operations. Or if one program is redirecting its output to the printer, a desktop publishing application should not be able to print its newly created page, interfering with the current printout. To prevent total chaos, OS/2 must maintain control over each of the devices available to the system.

If device coordination is the responsibility of each application program, the complexity of the programming required would prevent any OS/2 protected mode program from ever being completed. Rather than placing this burden on the application programmer, OS/2 accepts full responsibility for device coordination.

Essentially, OS/2 virtualizes the devices available to the system and gives each application the appearance of owning every device. OS/2 application programs access devices by using the OS/2 API routines. This gives OS/2 the ability to monitor (and intervene in, if necessary) every I/O operation occurring in the system (see Figure 16-14). By coordinating device access in this manner, OS/2 protected-mode programs maintain cooperation, complete device accessibility, and simplicity of programming.

SYSTEM REQUIREMENTS

OS/2 is an 80286-based operating system. The IBM PC AT and compatibles are based upon the 80286 processor chip. OS/2 does not work on the IBM PC (8088 processor chip) because of the system overhead and complexities of protected-mode operations. OS/2 does run on the 80386. However, early versions of OS/2 do not fully exploit the memory-management facilities of the 80386. Figure 16-15 illustrates the minimum hardware configuration required for OS/2. However, to fully exploit OS/2 capabilities, the hardware configuration shown in Figure 16-16 is recommended.

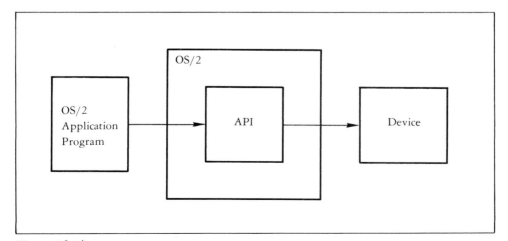

Figure 16-14.

OS/2 monitoring I/O operations

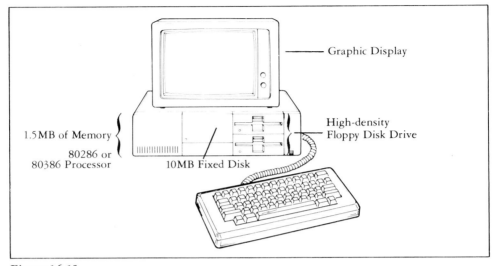

Figure 16-15.

Minimum hardware configuration
for OS/2

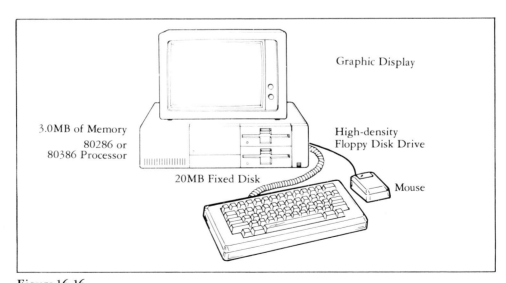

Figure 16-16.

Recommended hardware
configuration for OS/2

At first, the hardware requirements for OS/2 appear extreme. However, bear in mind the tremendous functional capabilities that OS/2 provides. OS/2 is a major operating system enhancement. For the first time, personal computers have a fully functional, protected-mode, multitasking system. OS/2 provides functions previously available only through minicomputers.

SYSTEM STRUCTURE

As stated, OS/2 executes in either real or protected mode. OS/2 real mode exists solely for the execution of existing DOS applications and can best be viewed as shown in Figure 16-17.

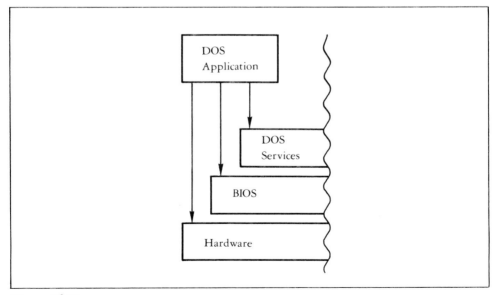

Figure 16-17.

OS/2 real mode

In real mode, OS/2 lets the application loose on the system. The program is free to access devices, ports, and memory directly. OS/2 simply does not care. A real mode program has no other programs to interfere with.

The OS/2 protected-mode structure, however, is somewhat different, as shown in Figure 16-18. In this mode, several OS/2 applications can coexist and share system resources. As you can see by this figure, OS/2 applications share memory (system services) and access devices under the strict control of OS/2.

In some instances, however, a program must be able to perform

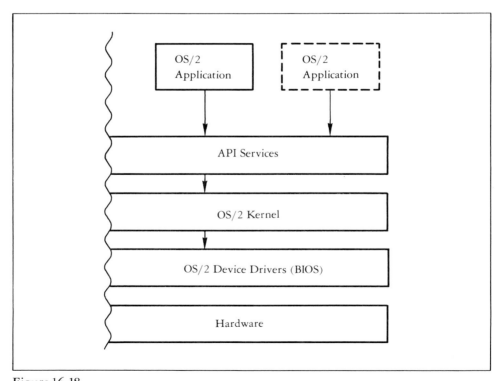

Figure 16-18.

OS/2 protected mode

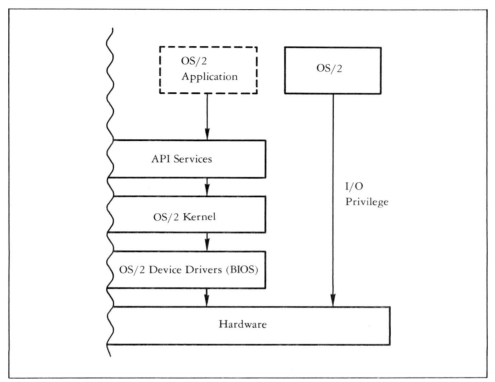

Figure 16-19.

Application directly accessing
hardware devices

low-level I/O operations. Although such applications are not common-place, OS/2 must provide a means for them to execute. So OS/2 grants the program I/O privilege levels normally unavailable to OS/2 applications. Then the application can directly access hardware devices to perform low-level I/O operations, as shown in Figure 16-19.

Note that most OS/2 programs will not require I/O privilege. If you have such an application, it must be very carefully written to ensure it is well-behaved in the OS/2 multitasking environment. Most applications of this type should be written only by very knowledgeable OS/2 system programmers.

INTERPROCESS COMMUNICATION

To fully exploit a multitasking environment, the applications that are executing concurrently must be able to share information. For example, assume that you are putting together the weekly sales and inventory report for a large software company. The report consolidates memos, graphs, and inventory records, as shown in Figure 16-20.

To produce the report, therefore, the programs shown in Table 16-1 must be active. Each program contains key information you need to produce your report. If the programs are able to exchange information conveniently, your consolidation task is greatly simplified. In this case, you use OS/2 shared memory to develop a clipboard that the applications can use to exchange information, as shown in the series of diagrams in Figure 16-21.

OS/2 provides several mechanisms to support interprocess communication:

- Shared memory

- Semaphores

- Message queues

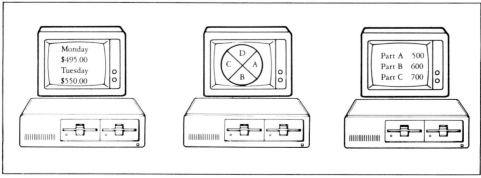

Figure 16-20.

Weekly sales and inventory report

Table 16-1.

Programs for Inventory Report

Program	Function
Word processor	Weekly memos
Spreadsheet	Sales graphs
Database	Inventory specifics
Desktop publisher	Reports

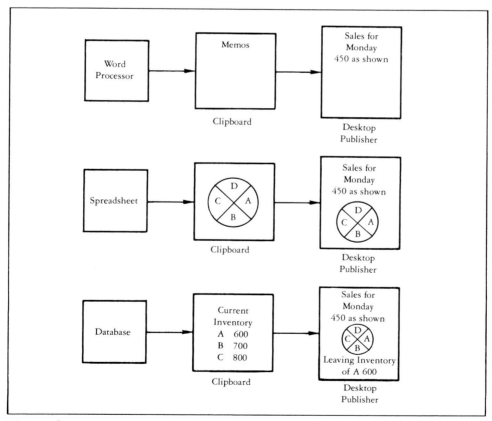

Figure 16-21.

Using OS/2 shared memory to
develop clipboard

You have just looked at a scenario in which shared memory is convenient. In this case, the shared memory takes the form of a clipboard. However, its use can be more general, allowing two or more applications to share data. For example, a data collection application at a nuclear power plant works as follows: Application A monitors the nuclear reactor, placing its current state in the shared memory regions, as shown in Figure 16-22. Application B wakes up every few seconds and examines the contents of the shared memory reactor status.

As long as the reactor's status is normal, Application B suspends itself in memory for a given time interval. However, when this status changes, Application B must initiate the reactor meltdown control processing.

Shared memory is a quick means of information exchange. However, the data residing in the shared memory region is in no way protected or coordinated among applications. To use shared memory fully, partcipating OS/2 applications must coordinate data access by using a private protocol.

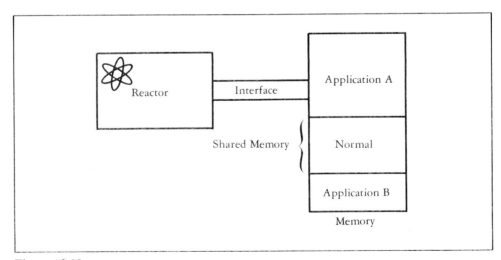

Figure 16-22.

Current state of nuclear reactor

An OS/2 *semaphore* is a flag or counter that is shared by two or more applications. The interpretation of the flag is application-specific. For example, assume that two programs need to access a data file in read/write mode. You can maintain file access coordination between the applications by using an OS/2 semaphore. In this case, if one application is about to read from the file, you do not want another program updating the file at the same time. The program issuing the read request, therefore, sets an OS/2 semaphore directing other concurrent applications that access the file not to write to it. Once the application completes its read request, it clears the semaphore and allows other applications to update the file as required (see Figure 16-23). Note, however, that for semaphores to be effective, each of the applications must follow an agreed protocol.

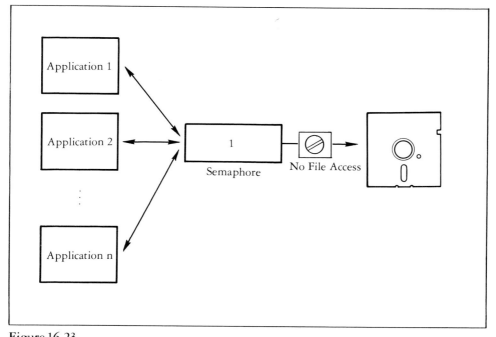

Figure 16-23.

Application clearing semaphore

A second major use of OS/2 semaphores is as usage counters. Consider a large database system that has several independent programs executing at one time. Each time a program accesses the database, the database monitor program increments a semaphore that tracks the number of programs using the database. When an application closes the database file, the monitor decrements the usage count. Once this count is zero, no applications are currently using the database, so the monitor can execute its clean-up routines.

OS/2 also supports interprocess communication by using *message queues*, which allow one OS/2 application to send a message to a second application. In this scenario, each participating OS/2 application maintains a list (or queue) in which OS/2 places messages destined for that application (see Figure 16-24).

OS/2 simply notifies the application of the message arrival and places the message into the application's message queue. The application itself is then responsible for processing the message. OS/2 message-processing is similar to message-processing under MS Windows.

Interprocess communication (IPC) is critical to the success of a multitasking environment. OS/2 provides support for multiple types of interprocess communication that you can use to meet your requirements.

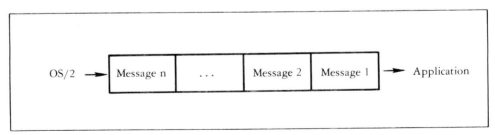

Figure 16-24.

OS/2 application queue

SCHEDULING

In a multitasking environment, significant emphasis must be placed upon the distribution of the CPU time slices to maximize fairness among the executing applications. OS/2 uses round-robin scheduling to perform most of its CPU distribution. Under this process, OS/2 rotates control of the CPU among applications, giving each a portion of the CPU (a time slice).

Periodically, however, you may have a unique application that must have control of the CPU whenever it is ready to execute. In this case, OS/2 allows you to increase the application's priority, ensuring that OS/2 gives the application to the CPU before other concurrently executing OS/2 applications.

Consider the following scenario. OS/2 executes the programs (with the indicated priorities) shown in Table 16-2. In this case, COLLECT records into the file COLLECT.DAT data received by modem. Whenever the modem has data available, COLLECT requires control of the CPU to ensure that no data is lost or overwritten. At the end of each time slice,

Table 16-2.

Programs and Priorities

Program	Priority	Function
COLLECT	1	Real-time data collection
WORDPROC	0	Word processing
SSHEET	0	Spreadsheet
DATABASE	0	Database processing

OS/2 first checks to see if COLLECT is ready to execute. If it is, OS/2 gives it control of the CPU. If COLLECT does not require the CPU, OS/2 continues its distribution of the CPU in a round-robin fashion among lower-priority applications. In this manner, OS/2 ensures that critical programs always gain control of the CPU when they require it, while maintaining fairness of CPU distribution among lower-priority programs.

It is very possible, however, that if many programs are executing at elevated priority levels, a lower-priority program may never execute. OS/2 simply continues CPU distribution among the higher-priority programs, never reaching the lower-priority tasks. This may be desirable, if, for example, you want low-priority programs to execute only when OS/2 has nothing else to do. This type of processing uses static-priority scheduling. OS/2 never modifies a program's priority by attempting to increment it in search of a fairer CPU distribution.

OS/2 also supports dynamic-priority scheduling. With this scheduling algorithm, you define a minimum time interval (by using the CONFIG.SYS MAXWAIT entry) in which OS/2 increases the priorities of applications that have not recently accessed the CPU. Eventually, because of the priority increments, each application is guaranteed a time slice. Once the time slice occurs, OS/2 restores the application's original priority, and the program once again begins its climb up the priority ladder.

As you can see, OS/2 provides tremendous scheduling flexibility. Whether you want to maximize fairness of CPU distribution in an office workstation environment or to ensure that real-time monitors always have CPU access, OS/2 scheduling facilities are flexible enough to meet your requirements.

THREADS

For simplification, each of the multitasking applications presented in this chapter has made the assumption that the OS/2 scheduler assigns time slices to programs. In actuality, however, OS/2 distributes the CPU to an entity called a *thread*. OS/2 is a multitasking operating system capable of executing several programs simultaneously. OS/2 also has the ability to execute separate portions of the same program concurrently.

Under DOS, each of your programs executes in a serial fashion, normally starting at the top and working downward sequentially through the list of instructions. Consider this C program:

```
main ()
 {
   A ();
   B ();
   C ();
 }
```

In this case, the program serially executes function A, then B, and finally function C. Expand the program slightly, as follows:

```
main ()
 {
   display_time (time);
   file_time (time);
   print_time (time);
 }
```

In this case, the program again executes the routines serially. However, assume that none of the routines are dependent upon each other. Under OS/2, the application can create a thread of execution for each function, and OS/2 will execute all three concurrently. OS/2 multitasking capabilities open up a new spectrum of programming opportunities and challenges.

An OS/2 thread, therefore, is simply a path of execution. OS/2 assigns priorities to threads, and the OS/2 scheduler distributes CPU time slices based upon them.

NETWORKING FUTURE

OS/2 also fully supports local area network software called the LAN Manager. Most applications today require support for multiple users. In fact, local area network support (shared resources) was a driving force behind many of the concepts found in OS/2. Over the past six years, DOS has accomplished an incredible feat. It has become the standard operating system for more than 10 million computers, making more than 10 million personal computers fully compatible. OS/2 is destined to have the same market impact. As such, the OS/2 LAN Manager attempts to standardize local area networks.

The OS/2 LAN Manager was fully developed to exploit the power of OS/2. It provides program-to-program communication, file sharing, and remote device access over a local area network containing OS/2, DOS, and XENIX computers, as shown in Figure 16-25.

The following list summarizes many of the LAN Manager features:

- Higher performance than MS-NET

- Increased network security through password, user, and group access

- Program-to-program communication support

- Exploitation of OS/2 functional capabilities

- Easy to program by using the API

- Remote device/server access

- Queue manipulation capabilities for job owner

- Network audit trails

- Network statistics and error logging

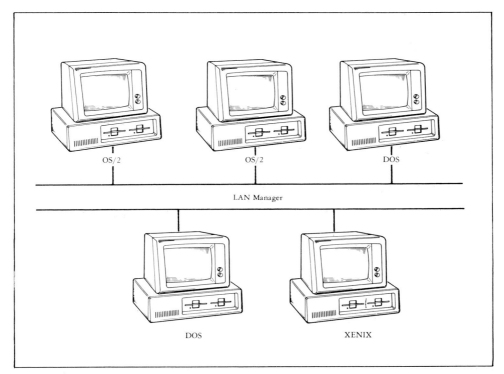

Figure 16-25.

LAN Manager

PRESENTATION MANAGER

One of the most important aspects of any successful software package is the way it presents itself to the user. If you think back on several of the more successful software packages (1-2-3, Turbo Pascal, and so on), each has a consistent, user-friendly interface. OS/2 provides you with two views of the operating system. The first is by way of the command-line prompt

```
[c:\]
```

which functions in the same manner as the DOS prompt. The second view is by way of a "MS Windows-like" interface called the Presentation Manager. This interface is so named because it manages the way in which OS/2 presents itself to the user.

To the end user, the OS/2 Presentation Manager provides the ability to view several programs on the screen simultaneously, share data between the programs, and access each application consistently. In a manner similar to MS Windows, under the Presentation Manager applications execute using a consistent user-interface with pull-down menus, dialog boxes, and full support for mouse devices. In an office environment where employees must execute several programs each day, the consistent user-interface provided by Presentation Manager applications will greatly facilitate the user's learning.

For the programmer, the OS/2 Presentation Manager has a myriad of library routines that make the development of programs that use any of the following very straightforward:

- Mouse interface

- Device-independent graphics

- Multiple windows

- Dialog boxes

- Timer routines

- Shared resources

Just as using the OS/2 Presentation Manager is similar to using MS Windows, program development for Presentation Manager applications is much the same as writing applications for Windows. Each time OS/2 starts with the Presentation Manager in use, the Presentation Manager shell appears on the screen. This shell provides the user's interface to OS/2. From this shell you can easily start one or more OS/2 applications, switch from one application to another, control OS/2 print functions, perform OS/2 file manipulation, and issue OS/2 commands.

Not all OS/2 applications are Presentation Manager applications. When the user executes or switches to an application that supports the Presentation Manager, the Presentation Manager shell remains visible and fully functional on the screen. When a non-Presentation Manager application executes, the application takes full control of the screen, independent of the Presentation Manager interface.

Many long-time command-line users do not like the concept of a Presentation Manager or shell. Instead, they like the control available to them by issuing commands on a command line. The OS/2 Presentation Manager is not necessarily for everyone. Its goal is to help new users become as productive as possible in a short time. Most users will execute the Presentation Manager. Even if you do not, as power users you should still fully understand its capabilities.

Since their introduction in 1981, the IBM PC and DOS have made a tremendous impact on the world. More than 10 million people are now using DOS and each day thousands more use it. Because of this tremendous growth, newer applications require more sophistication than is available under DOS. With the advent of the 80286 and 80386 processor chips, computer hardware capable of driving a fully functional multitasking operating system now exists. OS/2 allows users to get the most out of their computers by supporting multitasking, providing a consistent user-interface, and operating system capabilities available before only with minicomputers. OS/2 is the beginning of the future for multitasking operating systems.

17: OS/2 Programming Considerations

As a DOS power user, you will be among the first programmers to begin developing OS/2 applications. This chapter examines how to write OS/2 protected-mode programs in C, how to migrate those programs to DOS 3.x, and how to simplify your application development and modification by using the MAKE utility. Each of the programs examined in this chapter makes extensive use of the OS/2 Application Program Interface (API) that serves as your interface to the OS/2 system services.

A SIMPLE EXAMPLE

All C programmers have probably seen the C program that displays the following message:

```
Hello, world!
```

The first OS/2 example will change this output to display

```
Hello, OS/2 World!
```

Using a text editor, enter the following program:

```
main ()
 {
   printf ("Hello, OS/2 World!\n");
 }
```

To create this program, use the OS/2 Session Manager to create a real-mode session, and enter the text with a familiar word processor. Once the text has been entered, switch back to your protected-mode session to compile the program.

The Microsoft C compiler provides the CL command to compile and link the specified source file. Assuming that this program is named OS2HELLO.C, the command line to compile and link the program becomes

```
[C:\] CL /Lp OS2HELLO.C
```

The /Lp compiler option directs CL to produce a protected-mode executable. Table 17-1 summarizes many of the command-line options

Table 17-1.

CL Command-Line Options

Memory Model Options

/AS	Small model (default model)
/AC	Compact model
/AM	Medium model
/AL	Large model
/AH	Huge model

Code Optimization Directives

/O	Enable optimization
/Oa	Ignore aliasing
/Od	Disable optimizations
/Ol	Enable loop optimizations
/Op	Enable precision optimizations
/Os	Space optimization
/Ot	Speed optimization (default optimization)
/Ox	Maximize optimization (/Oalt /Gs)

Code Generation Directives

/G0	8086 instructions (default code generation)
/G1	80186 instructions
/G2	80286 instructions
/Gc	Pascal calls
/Gs	Disable stack checking
/Gt[number]	Data size threshold

Output File Generation

/Fa[assembly listing file]
/Fc[mixed source/object listing file]
/Fe<executable file>
/Fl[object listing file]
/Fm[map file]
/Fo<object file>
/Fs[source listing file]

Preprocessor Directives

/C	Leave comments
/D<name>[=text]	Define macro

Table 17-1.

CL Command-Line Options
(*continued*)

/E	Preprocess to stdout
/EP	Same as /E but no #line similar to MORE
/P	Preprocess to file
/U\<name>	Remove predefined macro
/u	Remove all predefined macros
/X	Ignore standard places

Language Extension Directives

/Za	Disable extensions
/Zd	Provide line number information
/Ze	Enable extensions (default)
/Zg	Generate declarations
/Zi	Symbolic debugging information
/Zl	Remove default library info
/Zp	Pack structures
/Zs	Syntax check only

Floating Point Options

/FPa	Calls with altmath library
/FPc	Calls with emulator
/FPc87	Calls with 8087/80287 library
/FPi	Inline with emulator (default floating-point option)
/FPi87	Inline with 8087

General Command Line Options

/c	Compile only - no link
/H\<number>	External name length
/J	Default char type is unsigned
/V\<string>	Set version string
/W\<number>	Warning level

Link Option

/F\<hex__number>	Stack size (hex. bytes)
/link [link options and libraries]	
/Lc	Link compatability mode executable
/Lp	Link protect mode executable

supported by CL. In addition, if you enter the command line

```
[C:\] CL /HELP
```

CL displays a summary of each command-line option.

At the OS/2 prompt, enter OS2HELLO, as shown here:

```
[C:\] OS2HELLO
Hello, OS/2 World!
[C:\]
```

If you switch to a real-mode session and invoke the program

```
C> OS2HELLO
Program too big to fit in memory
C>
```

the program fails. Protected-mode applications do not run in real mode.

To produce a real-mode version of this program, use the /Lc compiler option, as shown here:

```
C> CL /Lc OS2HELLO.C
```

Executing this program in real mode results in

```
C> OS2HELLO
Hello, OS/2 World!
C>
```

However, if you attempt to execute the program in protected mode

```
[C:\] OS2HELLO
DOS0191: The system has detected an unacceptable
signature in the file OS2HELLO.EXE
```

it fails. As you can see, the real- and protected-mode applications are incompatible. What you need is a simple way to migrate an application from OS/2 protected mode to DOS real mode without recompiling. Ideally, an OS/2 protected-mode program should execute in either mode transparently to the end user. As you will see, OS/2 provides this capability through the use of the BIND utility.

BIND

By default, OS/2 applications do not easily migrate from protected to real mode. However, by using the OS/2 BIND utility, the same OS/2 executable program will execute under OS/2 in protected mode and under DOS in real mode. In so doing, you can develop applications under OS/2 without regard for the target operating system (DOS or OS/2).

To migrate an OS/2 protected-mode application to compatibility mode (that is, to be able to execute under DOS or OS/2 transparently), you must follow these steps:

1. Create the source file with a text editor.

2. Compile and debug the program by using the protected-mode directive /Lp in the compiler command line.

3. Create a module-definition file for the application with a standard text editor. The file name should have the extension DEF.

4. Use BIND to build the compatibility-mode executable.

Using OS2HELLO.C, the steps become the following:

1. Create the source file with a text editor.

```
main ()
  {
    printf ("Hello OS/2 World!\n");
  }
```

2. Compile and debug the program by using the protected-mode directive /Lp in the compiler command line.

```
[C:\] CL /Lp OS2HELLO.C
```

3. Create a module-definition file for the application with a standard text editor. The file name should have the extension DEF.

```
NAME OS2HELLO
DATA MOVEABLE
CODE MOVEABLE PURE
HEAPSIZE 2048
STACKSIZE 2048
```

4. Use BIND to build the compatibility-mode executable.

```
[C:\] BIND OS2HELLO \LIB\DOSCALLS.LIB
```

Now execute the program in OS/2 protected mode, as follows:

```
[C:\] OS2HELLO
Hello, OS/2 World!

[C:\]
```

Switch to real mode and execute the program, as shown here:

```
C> OS2HELLO
Hello, OS/2 World!

C>
```

This program is now fully compatible. You can execute this program under DOS 3.2 and it will work completely. Later, this chapter examines module-definition files (DEFs) in detail. For now, it is more important that you understand the layout of the compatibility-mode executable file. Once you examine the structure of these files, you will understand how OS/2 compatibility-mode programs execute.

EXE STRUCTURE

This text has discussed the OS/2 API and dynamic-link libraries. The OS/2 API provides your interface to the OS/2 system services. Each time your program gets the system date, for example, the program invokes the OS/2 API service DosGetDateTime. A dynamic link library is a library of routines that program access during execution. Under DOS, each time you link a file, you must specify the names of the OBJ and LIB files LINK is to combine to build the EXE file. This is static linking, since all of the routines required must be present at link time (see Figure 17-1).

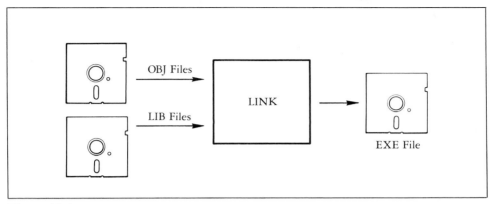

Figure 17-1.

Static linking

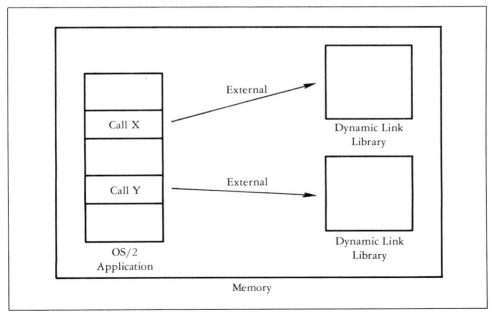

Figure 17-2.

Dynamic linking

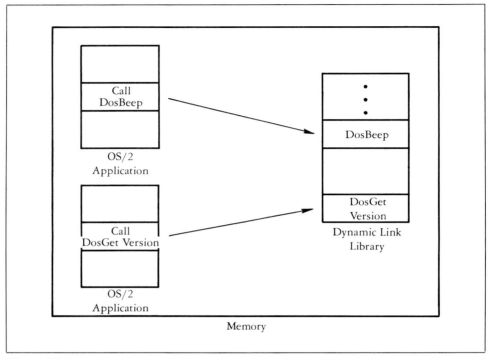

Figure 17-3.

Advantages of dynamic linking

With dynamic link libraries, the actual resolution of externals is done by the OS/2 loader when it places a program into memory. In this way, both the program and the executable code reside in memory, as shown in Figure 17-2.

The advantages of using dynamic link libraries include shared source code (since many programs can map to the same library), smaller executable files on disk (since the library code is external to the program), and easier modification of code (see Figure 17-3). In the past, each time you changed a routine in a library, you had to relink every application that accessed the routine. With dynamic link libraries, this is not required. Simply compile and reload the updated dynamic link library. Programs will map to this new code transparently. Since each program does not actually contain any code from the library, a change in the library does not affect either of them. The next time OS/2 loads a program that references the updated routine, the loader maps the program to the updated library routine transparently. In this way, every program that references the library routine is updated when the new dynamic link library is loaded.

The OS/2 API is implemented as a dynamic link library. Each time an OS/2 application requests a system service, the program does so through the OS/2 API. Consider the following C program, which uses the API routine DosGetDateTime to display the current system date and time. Using the previous four steps, the processing becomes:

1. Create the source file with a text editor.

```
#include <doscalls.h>

char *days[7] = {
    "Sunday", "Monday", "Tuesday", "Wednesday",
    "Thursday", "Friday", "Saturday" } ;

main()
  {
   struct DateTime datetime;

   DOSGETDATETIME (&datetime);

   printf ("%s %d/%d/%d %d:%d:%d\n", days[datetime.day_of_week],
       datetime.month, datetime.day, datetime.year, datetime.hour,
       datetime.minutes, datetime.seconds);
  }
```

2. Compile and debug the program by using the protected-mode directive /Lp in the compiler command line.

```
[C:\] CL /Lp DATETIME.C
```

3. Create a module-definition file for the application with a standard text editor. The file name should have the extension DEF.

```
NAME DATETIME
DATA MOVEABLE
CODE MOVEABLE PURE
HEAPSIZE 2048
STACKSIZE 2048
```

4. Use BIND to build the compatibility-mode executable.

```
[C:\] BIND DATETIME \LIB\DOSCALLS.LIB
```

This program runs in protected mode

```
[C:\] DATETIME
Sunday 9/6/1987 9:35:2

[C:\]
```

as well as real mode

```
C> DATETIME
Sunday 9/6/1987 9:35:2

C>
```

Under OS/2, this processing makes sense. Each time the program loads, OS/2 maps the DosGetDateTime call to the OS/2 API dynamic link library, as shown in Figure 17-4.

However, under DOS, the API dynamic link library does not exist. How does the program succeed? The secret lies in the compatibility mode EXE structure. OS/2 compatibility-mode EXE files have two headers. The first header appears in DOS 3.x format. The second is in

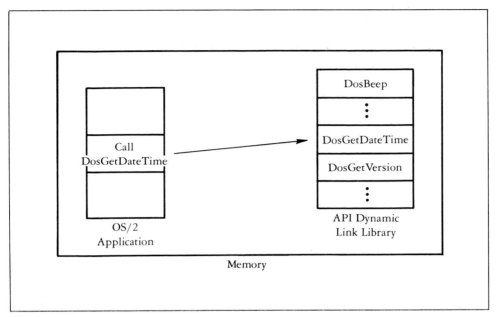

Figure 17-4.

OS/2 mapping the
DosGetDateTime call

OS/2 format. Each time your compatibility-mode program executes under OS/2 protected mode, it ignores the DOS 3.x header and maps API calls to the dynamic link library. However, when the application executes under DOS 3.x, it uses the DOS header. In this case, the program does not map to the OS/2 API dynamic link library. It cannot, because the API dynamic link library only exists under OS/2. Instead, each of the OS/2 API calls (such as DosGetDateTime) is mapped to a set of routines called the *DOS 3.x family API.* The DOS 3.x family API examines the parameters specified in the call and, in turn, invokes the corresponding INT 21H service (see Figure 17-5). In so doing, the loader actually dictates in which mode the program executes — real or protected. The BIND facility simply allows the DOS 3.x family API

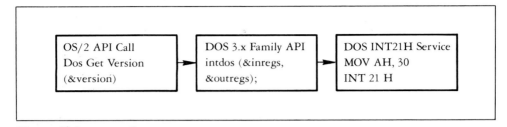

Figure 17-5.

DOS 3.x family API examining call
and invoking INT 21H service

routines to be included, thus making the program compatible with both modes.

As you might suspect, not all of the OS/2 API services are DOS 3.x compatible. This is because many of the OS/2 services exceed the capabilities of INT 21H services. The following list provides the names of the OS/2 API services that you can migrate to DOS:

DosBeep	DosChdir	DosChgFilePtr
DosClose	DosDelete	DosDevConfig
DosDevIOCtl	DosDupHandle	DosError
DosFileLock	DosFindClose	DosFindFirst
DosFindNext	DosMkdir	DosMove
DosNewSize	DosOpen	DosQCurDir
DosQCurDisk	DosQFHandState	DosQFileInfo
DosQFileMode	DosQFSInfo	DosQVerify
DosRead	DosRmdir	DosSelectDisk
DosSetFHandState	DosSetFileMode	DosSetFSInfo
DosSetVec	DosSetVerify	DosWrite
KbdCharIn	KbdFlushBuffer	KbdGetStatus
KbdPeek	KbdRegister	KbdSetStatus
KbdStringIn	VioGetBuf	VioGetCurPos
VioGetCurType	VioGetMode	VioGetPhysBuf
VioReadCellStr	VioReadCharStr	VioScrLock
VioScrUnlock	VioScrollLf	VioScrollRt
VioScrollUp	VioScrollDn	VioSetCurPos

VioSetCurType	VioSetMode	VioShowBuff
VioWrtCellStr	VioWrtCharStr	VioWrtCharStratt
VioWrtNattr	VioWrtNCell	VioWrtNChar
VioWrtTTY		

As you can see, most of these routines directly map to DOS system services.

MODULE-DEFINITION FILE (DEF)

Each time you want to build a compatibility-mode program, you must use the BIND facility. BIND uses a file called a module-definition file as part of its input, as shown in Figure 17-6. You have seen two very basic module-definition files. However, module-definition files can become

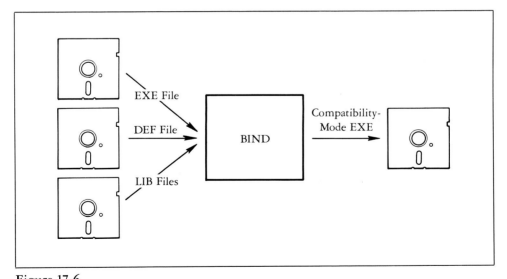

Figure 17-6.

BIND creating DOS compatibility files

quite complex. The following entries are valid in OS/2 module definition files.

This statement specifies how OS/2 treats the application code
segments:

CODE [*load_option*] [*share_option*] [*execute_option*] [*privilege*]

where the following is true:

load_option specifies when the code segments are loaded.

PRELOAD   Default — All segments are automatically loaded.
LOADONCALL   Segments loaded only when called.

share_option specifies whether the code segments can be shared by other applications.

SHARED   Segments are available to other applications.
NONSHARED   Default — segments are not shareable.

execute_option states whether a segment can only be executed, or executed and read.

EXECUTEONLY   Segments cannot be read.
EXECUTEREAD   Default — segments can be read.

privilege states whether the application has I/O privilege.

IOPL

Pure code does not contain data. For example: CODE LOADONCALL.

This statement specifies how OS/2 treats the application data
segments:

DATA [*load_option*] [*instance_option*] [*share_option*]
     [*write_option*] [*privilege*]

where the following is true:

load_option specifies when the data segments are loaded.

PRELOAD   Default — all segments are automatically loaded.
LOADONCALL   Segments loaded only when called.

instance_option specifies the manipulation of DGROUP data space, which contains
the heap and local stack space.

NONE	No automatic data segment is created.
SINGLE	All instances share same DGROUP data space.
MULTIPLE	DGROUP data space is copied for each instance.

share—option specifies whether the data segments can be shared by other applications.

| SHARED | Segments are available to other applications. |
| NONSHARED | Default — segments are not shareable. |

write—option states whether a segment can only be read, or read and written to.

| READONLY | Segments can only be read. |
| READWRITE | Default — segment can be read or written to. |

privilege states whether the application has I/O privilege.

IOPL

For example: DATA READONLY.

This statement allows you to insert comments within the module-definition file:

DESCRIPTION 'text message'

For example: DESCRIPTION 'Copyright Schaeffer Software 1987'

This statement defines the names of routines contained in this module that will be exported to other modules:

EXPORTS *entry—name*[*=internal—name*] [*@ordinal—value*]
[*RESIDENTNAME*][*NODATA*][*privilege*][...]

where the following is true:

entry—name defines the name other modules must use to reference the routine.

internal—name specifies the actual name of this routine within this module.

ordinal—value is a numeric value that serves as an index to the routine's name in the string table.

RESIDENTNAME is a keyword that specifies that the function's name must be resident at all times. It is used with ordinal values.

NODATA is a keyword that specifies that the function is not bound to a global data segment.

privilege is a numeric value that specifies the number of bytes to reserve for parameters to the function.

Example: EXPORTS
            NEWVER=NEW_DOS_VER, SETDRIVE NODATA
This statement specifies the size of the heap for the application. *num_bytes* must range from 0 to 65,536:

HEAPSIZE num_bytes

For example: HEAPSIZE 2048.
This statement defines the names of functions that the program imports from other modules:

IMPORTS [*internal_name*=[*module_name*.[*entry_name* ¦ *entry_ordinal*]]]

where the following is true:

internal_name is the name the program will use for the routine.

module_name specifies the name of the module from which the routine is imported.

entry_name is the name of the routine within the import module.

entry_ordinal is a numeric index into the string table that specifies the name of the imported function.

Example: IMPORTS
            DOSUTIL.NEW_VER=DOSUTIL.VER
This statement identifies the application as a library (as opposed to an executable) file. If no library name is given, OS/2 uses the file name minus the extension.

LIBRARY [*library_name*]

For example: LIBRARY OS2LIB.
This directive identifies the application as an executable file (as opposed to a library file). If no application name is given, OS/2 uses the

file name minus the extension.

NAME [*application__name*]

For example: NAME OS2HELLO.

This statement specifies that the application only runs in OS/2 protected mode:

PROTMODE

For example: PROTMODE.

This statement allows you to define the attributes of specific segments:

SEGMENTS [']*segment__name*['] [CLASS['*class__name*[']]]
　　　　[*minimum__bytes*] [*segment__flags*]

where the following is true:

segment__name defines the name of the segment for which you are setting the attributes.

class__name specifies the class of the specific segment (such as CODE).

minimum__bytes is the minimum number of bytes to allocate for this segment (0 to 65,536).

segment__flags defines the attributes of the segment:

EXECUTEONLY	EXECUTEREAD	IOPL
LOADONCALL	NONSHARED	PRELOAD
READONLY	READWRITE	SHARED

For example: SEGMENTS 'CODE' READONLY.

This statement specifies the size of the local stack for the application. *num__bytes* must range from 0 to 65,536:

STACKSIZE num__bytes

For example: STACKSIZE 2048.

This statement attaches the specified file to the beginning of the application. If the application is executed under DOS 3.x, the program runs first, possibly displaying a message that states the application is an OS/2 program.

STUB *file__name*

For example: STUB WARNING.EXE.

BIND PROCESSING CAPABILITIES

Previous sections of this chapter discussed BIND's function in producing compatibility mode programs. This section provides a complete overview of BIND's processing capabilities. The format for BIND is

BIND *input__file*[.ext] [*import__libraries*] [*link__libraries*]
    [−*o output__file*[.exe]] [−*n @filename*] [−*n name* [. . .]]
    [−*m map__filename*]

where the following is true:

input__file is the name of the OS/2 executable file to bind.

import__libraries specifies the names of the import libraries used to resolve external references in the *link__libraries* when the IMPORT by ORDINAL option is used in the LINK command.

link__libraries specifies the names of the libraries OS/2 binds to the application when it executes under OS/2.

−*o output__file* specifies an alternate name for the executable BIND produces.

−*n @filename* specifies a file of names of calls to map to the BADDYNLINK service.

−*n name* specifies a name of a call to map to the BADDYNLINK service.

−*m map__filename* directs BIND to produce a link map of the DOS 3.x executable file.

BIND is a critical step in your OS/2 compatibility program development. In most cases, your BIND command line will be quite straightforward, as shown here:

```
[C:\] BIND filename \LIB\DOSCALLS.LIB
```

MAKE

Although the program development stages examined thus far are straightforward, as your programs increase in complexity, maintaining them can become more of a challenge. To simplify your program maintenance, Microsoft provides a utility called MAKE that helps you update your programs when you have to change code. MAKE is an intelligent application manager that recompiles, reassembles, or links only those programs affected by a code change. It does this by analyzing the date and time stamps associated with every file used by the application.

To begin, you must create a MAKE description file (by using a text editor) that consists of one or more descriptions in the following form:

target__file: dependent__file [*,dependent__file...*]
    command
    [*command...*]

where the following is true:

target__file specifies the name of a file that may or may not need to be updated based upon a code change.

dependent__file specifies the name of a file from which the target file is built. If the date stamp on the dependent file is newer than the target file, the commands that follow are executed. If the number of dependent files exceeds one line, place a backslash at the end of the line and continue listing the names on the following line.

command specifies a DOS command to be executed when the dependent file has changed.

Think of the MAKE description file as a series of IF-THEN statements. If the dependent file is newer than the target file, or if the target file does not exist, then the series of DOS commands that follows is executed. For example:

```
OS2HELLO.EXE: OS2HELLO.C,OS2HELLO.DEF
              CL /Lp OS2HELLO.C
              BIND OS2HELLO \LIB\DOSCALLS.LIB
```

In this case, if OS2HELLO.EXE is older than either OS2HELLO.C or OS2HELLO.DEF, or if OS2HELLO.EXE does not exist, MAKE will compile, link, and bind the file. Invoke MAKE as

```
MAKE [options][macro_definitions] filename
```

where the *options* include the following:

/d directs MAKE to display the date of each file as it examines them.

/i directs MAKE to ignore error-code values returned by commands as they execute.

/n directs MAKE to display each command it would normally execute instead of actually executing the command.

/s directs MAKE to suppress the names of files as they are processed.

MAKE supports embedded macros that are later substituted during the MAKE execution. The format of a MAKE macro is

```
$(macro_name)
```

For example, consider

```
$(NAME).EXE:  $(NAME).C,$(NAME).DEF
              CL $(NAME).C
              BIND $(NAME) \LIB\DOSCALLS.LIB
```

If you later invoke MAKE with

MAKE NAME=OS2HELLO

MAKE will substitute the macro as shown here:

```
OS2HELLO.EXE:  OS2HELLO.C,OS2HELLO.DEF
               CL /Lp OS2HELLO.C
               BIND OS2HELLO \LIB\DOSCALLS.LIB
```

In addition, MAKE predefines three macros, as follows:

$*	Use target file name without the extension.
$@	Use the complete target file name.
$**	Use the complete list of dependent files.

MAKE also allows you to define inference rules that specify how MAKE should convert one file type to another. The format of an inference rule is

```
.dependent_extension.target_extension
    command
```

For example, to convert from C to EXE, you would use

```
.C.EXE
    CL $*.C
```

MAKE is a powerful and convenient programming utility. Many of you will find it useful for all applications, not just OS/2. Most OS/2 sample programs have an accompanying MAKE description file. The ability to decipher this file will greatly simplify your development tasks.

OS/2 APPLICATIONS

Most of the applications presented in this chapter are quite straightforward, and once you get a feel for it, programming OS/2 is too. Although
most of the following programs are simple, many of them illustrate
unique OS/2 features. In all cases, the code is clear-cut. Take time to
examine it.

Version

This routine uses the OS/2 API service DosGetVersion to display the
current version of the operating system.

```
#include <doscalls.h>

main()
  {
    unsigned int Version;
    int major, minor;

    DOSGETVERSION(&Version);          /* Get the version */

    major = Version >> 8;             /* High byte is major version */
    minor = Version & 0xff;           /* Low byte is minor revision */

    printf("%d.%d\n", major, minor);
  }
```

Under OS/2 protected mode, the program displayed

```
[C:\] VERSION
10.0

[C:\]
```

Likewise, under OS/2 real mode the output was

```
C> VERSION
10.0

C>
```

However, when you execute the program under DOS 3.3, the output is

```
C> VERSION
3.30

C>
```

Note the simplicity of the OS/2 API calls. Compare the readability of code to this routine, which performs the same function:

```c
#include <dos.h>

main()
 {
   union REGS inregs, outregs;

   int major, minor;

   inregs.h.ah = 0x30;
   intdos (&inregs, &outregs);

   major = outregs.x.ax >> 8;         /* High byte is major
                                          version */
   minor = outregs.x.ax & 0xff;       /* Low byte is minor
                                          revision */

   printf("%d.%d\n", major, minor);
 }
```

The module-definition file for this program contains the following:

```
NAME VERSION
DATA MOVEABLE
CODE MOVEABLE PURE
HEAPSIZE 2048
STACKSIZE 2048
```

Mode

This C program displays its current mode of execution (real or protected):

```
#include <doscalls.h>

main()
  {
    char mode;

    DOSGETMACHINEMODE(&mode);          /* Get mode */

    printf("Machine mode %s\n", (mode == 1) ? "Protected": "Real");
  }
```

In OS/2 protected mode, the output is

```
[C:\] GETMODE
Machine mode Protected

[C:\]
```

Likewise, under OS/2 real mode, the program displays

```
C> GETMODE
Machine mode Real

C>
```

Music

This program uses the OS/2 DOSBEEP API service to generate random sounds from the computer:

```
#include <doscalls.h>
#include <stdlib.h>

main()
 {
   int frequency, duration;
   int sounds = 0;

   while (sounds++ < 32000)
    {
      frequency = rand();
      duration = rand() % 255;
      DOSBEEP (frequency, duration);
    }
 }
```

Although the processing is simple, you can use this program to demonstrate multitasking. Execute the program and it will begin generating sounds. Next, using the OS/2 Session Manager, start a second OS/2 session. As you execute commands in this session, the computer continues to generate sounds. This is because OS/2 is executing both programs concurrently.

Again, the module-definition file for this program has not changed significantly, as shown here:

```
NAME MUSIC
DATA MOVEABLE
CODE MOVEABLE PURE
HEAPSIZE 2048
STACKSIZE 2048
```

Get Directory

This C program displays the current directory for the specified drive (A-C).

```
#include <doscalls.h>
#include <stdlib.h>

main (argc, argv)
  int argc;
  char *argv[];
  {
  unsigned int drive, length;

  char directory[64];

  if (argc > 1)
    {
    drive = *argv[1] - 64;
    DOSQCURDIR(drive, directory, &length);
    printf ("Current directory %s\n", directory);
    }
  }
```

To get the current directory for drive A, for example, invoke the program as

```
[C:\] GETDIR A
```

As you can see, under OS/2, command-line arguments are still fully accessible.

Setdrive

This program sets the disk drive as specified for the current program.

```
#include <doscalls.h>
#include <stdlib.h>

main (argc, argv)
  int argc;
  char *argv[];
  {
  unsigned int drive;
  unsigned int current_drive;
  long int drive_map;

  if (argc > 1)
    {
```

```
        drive = *argv[1] - 64;
        DOSSELECTDISK(drive);
        DOSQCURDISK(&current_drive, &drive_map);
        printf ("Current drive %c\n", current_drive+64);
    }
}
```

Invoke the program as

```
[C:\] SETDRIVE A
```

It is important to note that the OS/2 API routine DosSelectDisk only sets the default drive for the life of the program (current process). Once the program completes, the default drive remains unchanged. To verify that the current drive actually changes, the routine DosQCurDisk returns the current disk drive.

Wait

Chapter 15 examined DOS terminate-and-stay-resident (TSR) programs. That chapter presented many programs that captured the system clock interrupt to provide timer functions. Recall that OS/2 does not use TSR programs, but rather provides more elegant timer services. The following C program uses the OS/2 DosSleep API routine to put itself to sleep for five seconds:

```
#include <doscalls.h>

main()
{
    long int interval = 5000;

    printf ("Delaying 5 seconds\n");

    DOSSLEEP (interval);

    printf ("Awake again\n");
}
```

Upon invocation, the program displays

```
[C:\] WAIT
Delaying 5 seconds
```

After five seconds, the program wakes up and completes its processing by displaying

```
[C:\] WAIT
Delaying 5 seconds
Awake again

[C:\]
```

This simple timer routine is used to build more complex examples throughout this chapter.

Timer

Recall that an OS/2 semaphore is a flag that your applications can clear or set to indicate a specific condition or state. The following C program uses a semaphore to suspend its processing until the semaphore clears.

```
#include <doscalls.h>

main ()
 {
   unsigned long SemHandle;
   unsigned TimerHandle;

   DOSCREATESEM (1, &SemHandle, "\\SEM\\TESTSEM");

   DOSSEMSET (SemHandle);

   DOSTIMERASYNC (5000L, SemHandle, &TimerHandle);
```

```
    printf ("Waiting for asynchronous timer to clear semaphore\n");
    DOSSEMWAIT (SemHandle, (long) -1);   /* -1 no time out */
    printf ("Semaphore cleared\n");
}
```

The OS/2 API service DosCreateSem returns a handle to the semaphore specified, as follows:

DosCreateSem (1, &SemHandle, SemName);

The semaphore name must be in the form \SEM \NAME. Since C
uses the backslash (\ ) as a key character, you must use double back-
slashes, as shown here:

DosCreateSem (1, &SemHandle, " \ \SEM \ \NAME");

In this case, the program creates the semaphore by using DosCreateSem:

DosCreateSem (1, &SemHandle, " \ \SEM \ \TESTSEM");

Next, the program uses the API service DosSemSet to set the value of
the semaphore to 1:

DosSemSet (SemHandle);

The OS/2 DosTimerAsync service creates a timer for a specific
interval, which, upon completion, clears the specified semaphore and
sets its value to 0.

DosTimerAsync (5000L, SemHandle, &TimerHandle);

Finally, the DosSemWait service suspends the current application until the specified semaphore is cleared:

DosSemWait (SemHandle, (long) −1); /* −1 no time-out */

This C program, therefore, suspends itself until the asynchronous timer completes and clears the semaphore. Upon invocation, the program displays

```
[C:\] TIMER
Waiting for asynchronous timer to clear semaphore
```

After the five-second asynchronous timer elapses, the semaphore is cleared and the program displays

```
[C:\] TIMER
Waiting for asynchronous timer to clear semaphore
Semaphore cleared

[C:\]
```

Interprocess Communication

Chapter 16 stated that OS/2 uses semaphores as a means of interprocess communication. This OS/2 application uses two C programs. The first, SETSEM.C, creates a semaphore and sets its value to 1. The program then suspends itself indefinitely until the semaphore is cleared.

```
#include <doscalls.h>

main ()
  {
    unsigned long SemHandle;

    DOSCREATESEM (1, &SemHandle, "\\SEM\\TESTSEM");
```

```
    DOSSEMSET (SemHandle);

    printf ("Waiting for concurrent application to clear
            semaphore\n");

    DOSSEMWAIT (SemHandle, (long) -1);   /* -1 no time out */

    printf ("Semaphore cleared\n");
}
```

The second program, CLRSEM.C, opens the same semaphore that
SETSEM.C created. It then uses the OS/2 API service DosSemClear to
clear the semaphore, thus allowing SETSEM.C to continue its processing (see Figure 17-7).

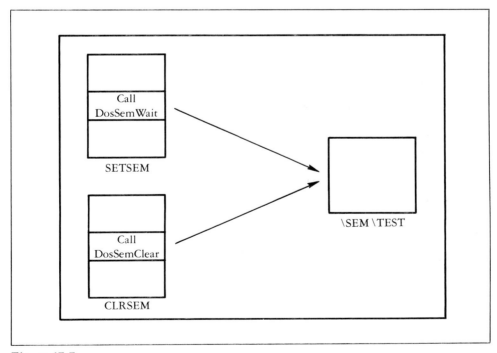

Figure 17-7.

DosSemClear clearing a semaphore

```
#include <doscalls.h>

main ()
 {
   unsigned long SemHandle;

   DOSOPENSEM (&SemHandle, "\\SEM\\TESTSEM");

   DOSSLEEP (100COL);    /* delay long enough to watch other
                            program */

   DOSSEMCLEAR (SemHandle);

   DOSCLOSESEM (SemHandle);
 }
```

The ten-second timer delay is built in to CLRSEM.C to provide you ample time to switch back to the session running SETSEM. In this way, you can watch the semaphore clear and the program display the following:

```
[C:\] SETSEM
Waiting for concurrent application to clear semaphore
Semaphore cleared

[C:\]
```

Message

Chapter 15 presented a TSR program that awoke every 15 minutes to display a message on your screen. The following OS/2 application provides similar functional capabilities:

```
#include <stdio.h>
#include <doscalls.h>
#include <subcalls.h>

main ()
```

```
{
  long int interval = 900000L;
  int flags = 1;                    /* wait for response */

  do
  {
     DOSSLEEP (interval);

     VIOPOPUP (&flags, 0);

     VIOWRTCHARSTR ("15 Minute Message", 18,  10, 25, 0);

     DOSSLEEP (10000L);

     VIOENDPOPUP (0);
  }
  while (1);                        /* forever */
}
```

Execute this program in the background by using DETACH as follows:

```
[C:\] DETACH MESSAGE
[C:\]
```

As you can see, the program loops forever. Every 15 minutes, the program wakes up. At that time, the program issues a VioPopUp service that clears the current screen and allows you to display messages to the user. In this case, your message remains on the screen for ten seconds. When the OS/2 VioEndPopUp service executes, it restores the previous screen contents and allows you to continue your previous processing as if you were never interrupted.

In this case, the program continues to execute forever in the background and displays the message every 15 minutes. This continued display may become quite annoying, but since the program is executing in the background you have no way to kill it. A more elegant implementation would be to continue the execution loop until the specified semaphore clears.

```
#include <stdio.h>
#include <doscalls.h>
#include <subcalls.h>

main ()
 {
  long int interval = 900000L;
  int flags = 1;                    /* wait for response */

  unsigned long SemHandle;

  DOSCREATESEM (1, &SemHandle, "\\SEM\\TESTSEM");

  DOSSEMSET (SemHandle);

  do
   {
     DOSSLEEP (interval);

     if (DOSSEMWAIT(SemHandle, 0L) != 0L)
       {
         VIOPOPUP (&flags, 0);

         VIOWRTCHARSTR ("15 Minute Message", 18, 10, 25, 0);

         DOSSLEEP (10000L);

         VIOENDPOPUP (0);
       }
   }
  while (DOSSEMWAIT(SemHandle, 0L) != 0L);
 }
```

In the following case, the OS/2 program ACKMSG simply sets the semaphore and terminates the background process:

```
#include <doscalls.h>

main ()
 {
   unsigned long SemHandle;

   DOSOPENSEM (&SemHandle, "\\SEM\\TESTSEM");

   DOSSEMCLEAR (SemHandle);

   DOSCLOSESEM (SemHandle);
 }
```

As you can see, OS/2 applications are quite powerful, as well as fairly easy to implement. By following these steps, you can easily migrate your OS/2 protected-mode applications to DOS 3.x:

1. Create the source file with a text editor.

2. Compile and debug the program using the protected-mode directive /Lp in the compiler command line.

3. Create a module-definition file for the application with a standard text editor. The file name should have the extension DEF.

4. Use BIND to build the compatibility mode executable.

OS/2 indeed provides the function capability previously only available to the microcomputer programmer through minicomputer operating systems such as UNIX or VMS. Welcome to a new age of computing.

18: OS/2 Command
Summary

Essentially, OS/2 is a menu-driven system that allows you to manage and select your OS/2 sessions. This chapter discribes the user's interface to OS/2. OS/2 provides support for DOS commands as well as several, new protected-mode commands. Also, OS/2 provides the Session Manager facility, which allows you to start and move quickly from one OS/2 application to the next. This chapter will make you fully conversant with the Session Manager's capabilities and each OS/2 command. This chapter also compares the OS/2 protected-mode files CMD.EXE and STARTUP.CMD to their real-mode counterparts COMMAND.COM and AUTOEXEC.BAT. In addition, the chapter discusses I/O redirection in OS/2.

OS/2 SESSIONS

Each time you execute an OS/2 application, the application executes in the context of an OS/2 session. An OS/2 session can be either protected or real mode. Each time OS/2 boots, the Session Manager becomes active and displays the following:

```
Start A Program

COMMAND.COM                              R

CMD.EXE
```

If you select the COMMAND.COM option, OS/2 starts a real-mode (DOS-compatible) session. From within this session you can execute your DOS applications as if you were running DOS instead of OS/2.

If you select the "Start A Program" option, OS/2 creates an OS/2 protected-mode session for you. From this session you can execute any OS/2 command or protected-mode application. OS/2 allows you to create multiple protected-mode sessions, and each session allows you to execute an OS/2 application. This is how you execute multiple programs concurrently under OS/2. Once you have several sessions active, you can select the desired session through the OS/2 Session Manager.

After you select either option, OS/2 displays a system prompt, as follows:

```
 [C:\]
```

This prompt is identical in function to the DOS prompt, in that you may now enter commands in this OS/2 session. If you want to start another OS/2 session or need to select an alternate session, press the CTRL-ESC key combination to activate the Session Manager.

CTRL-ESC

The CTRL-ESC key combination activates the OS/2 Session Manager.

For the real-mode session, the OS/2 Session Manager always displays COMMAND.COM, as shown in Figure 18-1. For protected-mode programs however, the Session Manager displays the name of the application currently active within each session (for an example, see Figure 18-2). If a protected-mode session is not currently executing an application, the Session Manager displays CMD.EXE, as shown in Figure 18-3.

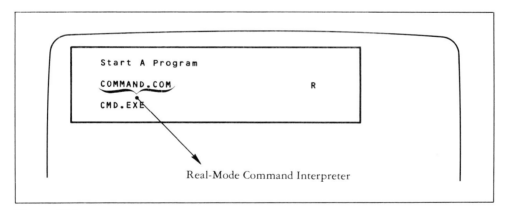

Figure 18-1.

Screen display in real-mode session

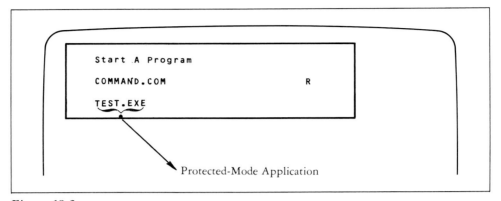

Figure 18-2.

Screen display in protected-mode
session

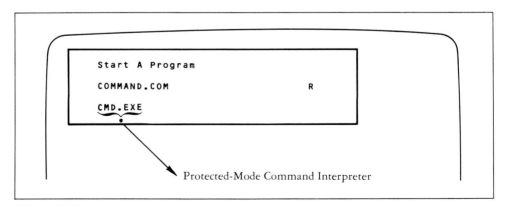

Figure 18-3.

Session Manager display in
protected mode

At first the OS/2 Session Manager and OS/2 sessions may be intimidating, but in reality the Session Manager is convenient to use. Take a step back to examine what is actually going on.

OS/2 is a multitasking operating system, which means that it can execute multiple programs simultaneously. However, you must have a mechanism for starting each program and for switching among programs as you work. To execute more than one OS/2 application concurrently, or to execute real-mode applications, you must do so through the OS/2 Session Manager. The OS/2 Session Manager allows you to start either protected- or real-mode applications.

Once you have multiple programs active, you must have a means of selecting one of them as the current program. When a session is active, OS/2 displays its current screen contents, thus allowing it to receive keyboard input.

Once you have completed your work with a specific session, OS/2 allows you to discard it and release system resources, such as memory. To do so, select the session to be discarded, and at the system prompt, type **EXIT**.

```
[C:\] EXIT
```

The OS/2 Session Manager will then delete the session from the list of available sessions.

The OS/2 Session Manager is your interface to multiple OS/2 applications. Experiment with it, and you will find it quite easy to use.

CMD.EXE VERSUS COMMAND.COM

Each time DOS boots, it loads its internal commands into memory. DOS stores its internal commands in the COMMAND.COM file. Internal commands are so named because they do not reside on disk individually

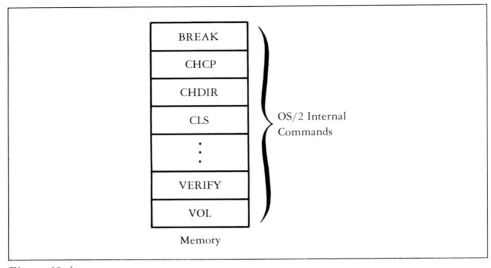

Figure 18-4.

Location of OS/2 internal
commands in memory

(such as FORMAT.COM), but rather reside in memory, as shown in
Figure 18-4.

In a similar manner, OS/2 loads a copy of its internal (protected-
mode) commands into memory each time it boots. OS/2 stores its
internal commands in the file CMD.EXE. The following is a list of the
OS/2 internal commands:

BREAK	CCHP	CHDIR
CLS	COPY	DATE
DEL	DETACH	DIR
DPATH	ECHO	EXIT
FOR	GOTO	IF
MKDIR	PATH	PAUSE
PROMPT	REM	REN
RMDIR	SET	SHIFT
TIME	TYPE	VER
VERIFY	VOL	

These commands are similar to their DOS counterparts.

The following is a list of OS/2 external commands:

ANSI	APPEND	ASSIGN
ATTRIB	BACKUP	CHKDSK
CMD	COMMAND	COMP
DISKCOMP	DISKCOPY	FDISK
FIND	FORMAT	GRAFTABL
HELPMSG	JOIN	KEYBXX
LABEL	MODE	MORE
PATCH	PRINT	RECOVER
REPLACE	RESTORE	SORT
SUBST	SYS	TREE
XCOPY		

The next section examines each of the OS/2 commands. Although many of the commands appear to be identical to their DOS counterparts (such as DIR and TYPE), carefully note the examples presented, and you will be quite surprised by their increased functional capabilities. In this discussion, the (P) denotes a command in protected mode and (R) denotes a command in real mode.

OS/2 COMMANDS

ANSI (P)

Format

ANSI [ON]

or

ANSI [OFF]

Function   Enable/disable ANSI escape sequence support for OS/2 protected-mode applications. This provides equivalent functional capability for installing ANSI.SYS in real mode. If you invoke ANSI without a parameter, ANSI displays its current setting (ON or OFF).

Example

ANSI ON   ; Enable ANSI support

APPEND (R)

Format

[drive:][path]APPEND [d:][path][;[d:][p:] . . .];

Function   Specify a search path for data files.

Each time OS/2 opens a file, it first searches the current directory or specified location for the file. If the file is not found, OS/2 will search the drives and paths in the data path defined by APPEND.

APPEND is functionally equivalent to the OS/2 PATH command. If OS/2 cannot open a file as specified, OS/2 searches each directory in the data path defined by APPEND until the file is found or the search path is exhausted.

This is a real-mode command.

Examples

APPEND ;	; Removes the current data search path specification, ; which results in OS/2 searching only the specified ; location
APPEND C: \OS2 ;A: \ ;B: \;	; If OS/2 cannot open the file as ; specified, it will search the ; subdirectory \OS2 on drive C ; and then the root directories on ; drives A and B in that order
APPEND	; APPEND without any command-line parameters ; results ; in the display of the current data path

ASSIGN (R)

Format

[drive:][path]ASSIGN [[old__drive:][=][new__drive[. . .]]

Function   Route I/O request for one disk drive to a new drive. OS/2 allows you to direct disk I/O operations from one drive to another.

Many older software packages always look for data and overlay files on drive A. The OS/2 ASSIGN command allows you to migrate such files to your fixed disk, routing all disk I/O operations from the floppy drive A to the fixed disk C.

Do not place a colon after device names.

This is a real-mode command.

Examples

ASSIGN	; Removes disk drive routing
ASSIGN A = B	; OS/2 will route all disk drive references to ; drive A to drive B
ASSIGN A = C B = C	; OS/2 will route all disk drive references ; from either drive A or B to drive C

ATTRIB (P/R)

Format

[drive:][path]ATTRIB [+R ¦ −R] [+A ¦ −A] file__specification

Function   Set or display a file's read-only archive attributes.

Setting a file to read-only prevents inadvertent deletion or modification by OS/2. A read-only file cannot be deleted, renamed, or modified.

If you are establishing a system for other end users, get in the habit of setting all of their files to read-only. This prevents the user from inadvertently deleting a file.

Examples

ATTRIB +R *.*	; Sets all files to read-only
ATTRIB −R *.TXT	; Makes all TXT files write-access
ATTRIB +A *.C	; Sets the archive status bit on all C files

BACKUP (P/R)

Format

[d:][path]BACKUP *d1:[file _spec] d2:* [/A][/D:mm-dd-yy][/M][/S][F]
[L][T:hh:mm:ss]

Function   Back up one or more files to a new disk.

d1: specifies the source disk.

file _spec is the OS/2 path name(s) for the file(s) to be backed up.

d2: specifies the target disk.

/A directs BACKUP to append source files to files on the target disk.

/D:mm-dd-yy directs BACKUP to back up files modified since the specified date.

/F tells BACKUP that the target disk is unformatted.

/L:logfile places an entry for all of the files in the specified log file. BACKUP.LOG is the
default.

/M directs BACKUP to back up files modified since the last back-up.

/S directs BACKUP to back up all subdirectory files.

/T:hh:mm:ss backs up files modified since the specified time.

BACKUP works closely with each of the system's directory entries
to select specific files for back-up. Note how OS/2 directory fields closely
relate to the BACKUP command-line qualifiers. A 10MB disk requires
approximately 25 360K floppy disks or 8 1.2MB disks for a complete
back-up.

Examples

BACKUP C: \A:/S   ; Back up disk C to drive A

BACKUP C:TEST.DAT B:/A   ; Append TEST.DAT to back up files on
                           ; drive B

BREAK (R)

Format

BREAK [ON ¦ OFF]

Function   Enable/disable OS/2 CTRL-BREAK processing.

By default, OS/2 checks only for a user-entered CTRL-BREAK upon completion of I/O operations in standard input, output, print, or auxiliary devices. BREAK ON requests OS/2 to check for a CTRL-BREAK after each OS/2 service. BREAK ON increases the amount of overhead that OS/2 must expend and is, therefore, normally used only during program development.

This command executes in real mode only.

Examples

```
BREAK OFF    ; Perform only default CTRL-BREAK checking
BREAK ON     ; Enable CTRL-BREAK checking
BREAK        ; Display current CTRL-BREAK processing status
```

CALL (P)

Format

CALL BatchFile [argument [. . .]]

Function   Invoke a nested batch procedure from within an OS/2 batch file.

This command provides similar functional capabilities as that provided by using the DOS COMMAND /C within a batch file.

Example

```
CLS
CALL MYPROC ; Invoke nested procedure
DATE
```

CHDIR (P/R)

Format

CHDIR [drive:][path]

or

CD [drive:][path]

Function   Change or display the default directory.

CHDIR changes or displays the current directory name for the specified disk drive. If you do not specify a drive, CHDIR uses the current default drive. If you do not specify a path name, CHDIR displays the current default directory name.

Examples

CHDIR   ; Display the current directory
A: \OS2
CHDIR B: \OS2 \CMDFILES   ; Set the directory on drive B to
                               ; \OS2 \CMDFILES

CCHP (P)

Format

CCHP [codepage]

Function   Select the systemwide code page for devices.

To enhance international character set support, OS/2 uses code pages, which are tables containing a character set.

Code page values include

Code Page	Character Set
437	United States
850	Multilingual
860	Portuguese
863	French-Canadian
865	Norwegian

Example

CCHP 865   ; Select the Norwegian character set

CHKDSK (P/R)

Format

CHKDSK [*drive:*][*path*][*filename*] [/F] [/V]

Function   Check a disk's current status.
   CHKDSK reports on

- The amount of free, used, and corrupted disk space

- The number of hidden files

- The amount of free and used memory (only in real mode)

drive: is the target drive that CHKDSK is to examine.

path and *filename* specify a file to be tested for contiguity.

/F directs CHKDSK to fix errors found in a directory or FAT.

/V directs CHKDSK to display the names of all files on the disk.

Examples

CHKDSK   ; Examine the current disk
CHKDSK *.*   ; Check disk fragmentation
CHKDSK A: /F   ; CHKDSK will fix errors that it encounters
                    ; on drive A. Without /F, CHKDSK only
                    ; displays information about each error.

CLS (P/R)

Format

CLS

Function   Clear the screen display.

CLS does not affect video attributes.

CLS places the cursor in the home (upper-left) position.

Example

CLS

CMD (P)

Format

CMD [/C string]

or

CMD [/K string]

Function   Start a secondary protected-mode command processor.

This command is functionally equivalent to COMMAND, which starts a real-mode command processor.

If you invoke CMD without any parameters, OS/2 will load the command processor into memory, and CMD will display its command-line prompt.

/C string directs OS/2 to load CMD long enough to execute the specified command. Once complete, OS/2 removes the secondary command processor.

/K string directs OS/2 to leave the command processor in memory upon completion of the command. This is similar to the /P option of COMMAND.

The OS/2 EXIT command allows you to terminate a secondary command processor.

Example

CMD /C DIR A:*.*

COMMAND (R)

Format

COMMAND [*drive:*][*path*][*/P*][*/C string*][*E:nnnnn*]

Function   Invoke a secondary real-mode command processor.

drive: and *path* specify the location of the command processor.

/P directs OS/2 to install the command processor in memory permanently.

/C string specifies a command for the command processor to execute. This option is used to execute nested batch files.

/E:nnnnn specifies the size of the command processor's environment. *nnnnn* must be less than or equal to 32,768. The default is 160.

The most common uses of COMMAND are to invoke nested batch procedures and to spawn an OS/2 real-mode command from within another application program.

Example

```
REM In BATCH File
:LOOP
PAYROLL
COMMAND /C PAYPROC  ; Execute a nested batch file
GOTO LOOP
```

COMP (P/R)

Format

[drive:][path]COMP *file__spec1 file__spec2*

Function   Display the first 10 differences between two files.

file__spec1 and *file__spec2* are the complete OS/2 path names of the files to be compared.

COMP displays the differences as hexadecimal offsets in the file.

If the files are identical, COMP will display the message

Files compare ok

COMP supports OS/2 wild-card characters.

Examples

COMP A.DAT B.DAT
COMP A.DAT B: ; Compare the contents of A.DAT on drives A and B

COPY (P/R)

Format

COPY *file_spec1 file_spec2* [/V][/A][/B]

or

COPY *file_spec1+file_spec2* [. . .] file_spec3

Function   Copy one or more files to a new destination.
The following examples provide simple COPY commands. COPY also supports more complex processing.

file_spec1 is the complete OS/2 path name of the source file to be copied.
file_spec2 is the complete OS/2 path name of the target file.
/V requests COPY to use disk verification to ensure that a successful copy occurred. This qualifier adds processing overhead. However, it prevents a hardware error from rendering the contents of the source and target files inconsistent.
/A informs COPY that the preceding file was an ASCII file.
/B informs COPY that the preceding file was a binary file.
COPY fully supports OS/2 wild-card characters.

WARNING: COPY overwrites target files with the same name.

Examples

COPY A:CONFIG.SYS B:CONFIG.SAV	; Copy the contents of
	; CONFIG.SYS on
	; drive A to the file
	; CONFIG.SAV on
	; drive B
COPY A:*.* B:*.*	; Copy all of the files on
	; drive A to drive B

DATE (P/R)

Format

DATE [*mm-dd-yy*]

or

DATE [*dd-mm-yy*]

or

DATE [*yy-mm-dd*]

Function   Set the OS/2 system date.

mm is the desired month (1-12).
dd is the desired day (1-31).
yy is the desired year (80-99).

The date format *mm-dd-yy* is dependent upon the COUNTRY=
specifier in CONFIG.SYS. If you do not specify a date, DATE displays
the current date. DATE does modify the AT system clock.

Examples

DATE   ; Display the current date

DATE 12/08/87   ; Set the date to Dec. 8, 1987

DATE 9/30/88   ; Set the date to Sept. 30, 1988

DEL (P/R)

Format

DEL *file_specification* [. . .]

Function   Delete a file from disk.

file_specification is the complete OS/2 path name of the file to be deleted. It can contain a drive identification and a subdirectory path. If the drive or path is not specified, DEL uses the current defaults.

> *WARNING:* Once you have deleted a file, OS/2 cannot retrieve it. DEL will not remove subdirectories. Instead, use RMDIR.
> Unless overridden with a drive or path specifier, DEL will delete only the files in the current directory.

Examples

DEL B:CONFIG.OLD   ; Delete file CONFIG.OLD from drive B

DEL \OS2 \COMMANDS \STARTUP.BAK   ; Delete file STARTUP.BAK from
                                    ; the specified subdirectory

DETACH (P)

Format

DETACH OS2_command [argument]

Function   Execute an OS/2 command in the background mode. OS/2 creates a process, displaying its process identification (pid), which executes the specified command. OS/2 returns control to the process by invoking DETACH, which allows it to continue its processing while the DETACHed command completes in the background mode.

OS/2 DETACHed processes must complete on their own. OS/2 does not provide facilities to cancel them.

Examples

DETACH CHKDSK > DISK.STS

The process identification number is 7

DETACH DIR B: > B.LIS

The process identification number is 9

DIR (P/R)

Format

DIR [*file__spec*] [*/P*] [*/W*] [...]

Function   Display a directory listing of files.

DIR lists the files specified by *file__spec* or all the files contained in the current directory if *file__spec* is omitted.

file__spec is the complete OS/2 path name of the file(s) to be listed.
/P directs DIR to pause after each screenful of information to display the prompt
Strike a key when ready...
/W directs DIR to display the files in short form (file name) with only five file names across the screen.

Examples

DIR B: ; Display a directory listing of the files on
                               ; drive B

```
DIR *.* /P              ; Display a short-form directory listing
DIR *.TXT A.DAT *.BAK   ; OS/2 issues a directory command for *.TXT, then one
                        ; for A.DAT, and then one for *.BAK in sequential fashion
```

DISKCOMP (P/R)

Format

[drive:][path]DISKCOMP [source __ drive: [target __ drive]]

Function   Compare floppy disks.

If you have a single-floppy system, DISKCOMP will perform a single-drive comparison by prompting you to enter the source and target disks at the correct time.

DISKCOMP displays the message

Compare ok

if the disks are identical. Otherwise, it displays the side and track (in hex) of the first 10 differences.

Example

```
DISKCOMP A:  B:     ; Compare the contents of the disk in
                    ; drive A to the disk in drive B
```

DISKCOPY (P/R)

Format

[drive:][path]DISKCOPY [source __ drive: [target __ drive]]

Function   Copy a source floppy disk to a target disk.

DISKCOPY copies the contents of one floppy disk to another. If you have a single-floppy system, DISKCOPY will perform a single-drive copy by prompting you to enter the source and target disks at the correct time.

DISKCOPY will FORMAT an unformatted disk during the copy. DISKCOPY does not correct disk fragmentation.

Example

```
DISKCOPY A: B:      ; Copy the contents of the disk in drive A
                    ; to the disk in drive B
```

DPATH (P)

Format

DPATH [drive:][path][;[d:][p:] . . .];

Function   Specify a search path for data files in OS/2 protected-mode.

Each time OS/2 opens a file, it first searches the current directory or location specified for the file. If the file is not found, OS/2 will search the drives and paths in the data path defined by DPATH.

DPATH is functionally equivalent to the OS/2 APPEND command. APPEND is for real mode; DPATH is for protected mode. If OS/2 cannot open a file as specified, OS/2 searches each directory in the data path defined by DPATH until the file is found or the search path is exhausted.

This is a protected-mode command.

Examples

```
DPATH ;                   ; Removes the current data search path specification,
                          ; which results in OS/2 searching only the specified
                          ; location
DPATH C: \OS2 ;A: \ ;B: \;  ; If OS/2 cannot open the file as
                          ; specified, it will search the
```

```
                             ; subdirectory  \OS2 on
                             ; drive C and then the root
                             ; directories on
                             ; drives A and B (in that order)
         DPATH               ; DPATH without any command-line parameters results
                             ; in the display of the current data path
```

ECHO (P/R)

Format

ECHO [ON ¦ OFF ¦ MESSAGE]

Function   Display or suppress batch command messages.

ECHO allows you to suppress the display of command names within an OS/2 batch file as the command executes.

ON allows command-name display.

OFF suppresses command-name display.

MESSAGE is the string of characters to be displayed.

Examples

```
ECHO ON                  ; Batch command names will be displayed as
                         ; they execute
ECHO %0                  ; Display the name of the current batch
                         ; file
ECHO THIS IS A TEST      ; Display a message to the user
ECHO OFF                 ; Suppress command name display
```

ENDLOCAL (P)

Format

ENDLOCAL

Function   Works in conjunction with SETLOCAL to preserve the current drive, directory, and environment settings within a batch file, to ensure that the batch file changes are only temporary.

Example

SETLOCAL	; Store the current settings.
CD \FILES	; Change the current directory.
C:	; Change the current drive.
PROGRAM	; Execute an application.
ENDLOCAL	; Restore original drive, directory, and environment.

EXIT (P/R)

Format

EXIT

Function   Terminate the current command-line processor (COM-MAND.COM in real mode, CMD.EXE in protected mode). OS/2 returns control to the processing that invoked the command-line processor.

EXIT allows you to terminate OS/2 sessions.

Example

EXIT

EXTPROC (P)

Format

EXTPROC [*processor__name*] [*argument* [...]]

Function   Define an external command processor to execute the commands that follow within the batch file.

processor __ name is the name of the file containing the desired command processor. *argument* is a command-line argument of the program acting as the command-line interpreter.

Example

EXTPROC SOMEPROG.EXE
CLEARSCR
DATE

FDISK (P/R)

Format

FDISK

Function   Configure partitions on a fixed disk.

OS/2 allows you to separate a fixed disk into four logical sections called *partitions*. Each partition can contain a unique operating system. FDISK allows you to specify the size of each partition as well as the active (boot) partition.

Be very careful when using FDISK. An error can result in the loss of all of the data contained on a disk.

FDISK records partition information in the master boot record, which resides in the first sector of *every* hard disk.

Example

FDISK

FIND (P/R)

Format

[drive:][path]FIND *"string"* [*file__spec*] [/C][/N][/V]

Function   Search files or piped input for a string.

string specifies the string to search for. It must be in quotation marks.

file__spec is the name of the file in which to search for the string. It can be a series of file names separated by spaces.

/C directs FIND to display a count of occurrences for the string.

/N directs FIND to precede each line containing the string with its line number.

/V directs FIND to display each line not containing the string.

If /C and /N are used together, FIND ignores /N.

Examples

DIR ¦ FIND "<DIR>"   ; Search for <DIR> from redirected input
FIND "begin" TEST.PAS   ; Examine TEST.PAS for all references of
                        ; "begin"

FOR (P/R)

Format

FOR *%%variable* IN (*set*) DO *DOS__command*

Function   Provide repetitive execution of OS/2 commands.

%%variable is the FOR loop control variable that OS/2 manipulates with each iteration.

set is a list of valid OS/2 file names. *set* can be a list of OS/2 file names separated by commas (A, B, C), or it can contain a wild-card character (*.*), or both (A, B, *.DAT).

DOS__command is the command to execute with each iteration.

FOR is used most commonly within OS/2 batch files. It can be used from the OS/2 prompt, however. The %% before the variable name is used in batch files, while % is used from the OS/2 prompt.

Examples

OS/2 PROMPT>   FOR %I IN (*.FOR) TYPE %I   ; Display all FORTRAN
                                                             ; programs
(Batch File)   FOR %%F IN (*.C) CC %%F   ; Compile all C programs

FORMAT (P/R)

Format

[*drive:*][path]FORMAT [*drive:*][/S][/V:*volume*][/4][/T:*tracks*][/N:*sectors*]

Function   Format a disk for use by OS/2.

drive: is the disk drive identification containing the disk to be formatted.

/N:*sectors* defines the numbers of sectors per track.

/S directs FORMAT to place the OS/2 system files on the disk and make the disk bootable.

/T:*tracks* defines the number of tracks per side.

/V:*volume* directs FORMAT to include the volume label.

/4 directs FORMAT to format the disk double-sided in a quad-density disk drive.

Examples

FORMAT B:/S   ; Format a bootable disk in drive B
FORMAT A:/4   ; Format a 360K disk in a 1.2MB floppy drive

GOTO (P/R)

Format

GOTO label __ name

Function   Branch to the label specified in a BAT file.

OS/2 label names contain any of the characters that are valid for OS/2 file names. If the label does not exist, OS/2 terminates execution of the batch file.

Example

```
:loop                  ; Note the colon (:) preceding the label
DIR
GOTO loop              ; No colon before label
```

This batch procedure displays a continuous directory listing until the user presses CTRL-C or CTRL-BREAK.

GRAFTABL (R)

Format

[drive:][path]GRAFTABL

Function   Load additional character-set data into memory.

The color graphics adapter in medium resolution tends to blur text in the range ASCII 120 to 255.

GRAFTABL loads additional character set data to prevent blurring. This is a real-mode command.

Example

GRAFTABL

HELPMSG (P)

Format

HELPMSG message__id

Function   Display additional text in an OS/2 error message or warning.

All OS/2 error messages and warnings have the form DOSXXXX, where XXXX is a four-digit number. Most OS/2 commands provide meaningful messages if they cannot complete. HELPMSG allows you to get additional text on a specific error.

Example

DIRB
DOS1041: The system cannot find the filename specified.
HELPMSG DOS1041
DOS1041: The system cannot find the filename specified.
EXPLANATION: One of the following errors occurred:

1. An incorrect filename was entered.

2. A filename was entered that does not contain a .BAT, .EXE, or .COM extension.

3. A ? or * character was entered in the filename.

ACTION: Retry the command using a correct filename.

IF (P/R)

Format

IF [NOT] *condition* DOS__command

Function   Provide conditional processing within OS/2 batch files.

NOT performs a Boolean NOT on the result of the condition.

condition must be one of the following:

ERRORLEVEL value   True if program exit status is greater than or equal to value

EXIST file__specification   True if the specified file exists

string1 == string2   True if both strings are identical

Examples

IF EXIST CONFIG.SYS COPY CONFIG.SYS B: ; If the file CONFIG.SYS
; exists in the current
; directory, copy it to
; drive B

IF NOT ERRORLEVEL 3 GOTO DONE   ; If the previous program
; exited with a status less than
; or equal to 3
; branch to the label
; DONE

IF'%1'=='' GOTO NULL   ; Determine if parameter %1
; exists

JOIN (R)

Format

[drive:][path]JOIN [*d1:* [*d2:path*]][/D]

Function   Join a disk drive to an OS/2 path.

JOIN makes two disks appear as one by joining a disk to an OS/2 path.

d1: specifies the disk drive to be joined to the path provided.

d2:path specifies the join directory.

If you issue a JOIN command without any parameters, JOIN will display the current joins.

OS/2 will join a disk only to an empty OS/2 directory.

This is a real-mode command.

Examples

JOIN D: C: \JOINDIR   ; References to C: \JOINDIR are the same as those to
                                        ; drive D

JOIN   ; Display current joins

KEYBXX (R)

Format

[drive:][path]KEYBxx

Function   Load foreign keyboard set.

KEYBxx loads memory-resident software to replace the standard keyboard layout supported by the ROM-BIOS.

Once a new keyboard is installed, you can toggle between it and the default keyboard by pressing CTRL-ALT-F1 for the default, and CTRL-ALT-F2 for the foreign keyboard.

This is a real-mode command.

Common keyboard layouts include

KEYBFR	France
KEYBGR	Germany
KEYBIT	Italy
KEYBSP	Spain
KEYBUK	United Kingdom
KEYBUS	United States

Example

KEYBUK   ; Select the United Kingdom keyboard

LABEL (P/R)

Format

[*drive:*][path]LABEL [drive:] [*volume __ label*]

Function   Specify a disk volume label.

drive: is the disk drive containing the disk to be labeled.
volume __ label is the 11-character volume label desired.

If you do not specify a volume label, LABEL will prompt you for one as follows:

Volume label (11 characters, ENTER for none)?

If you do not want to label the disk, simply press ENTER.

Example

LABEL B: DOSDISK

MKDIR (P/R)

Format

MKDIR [*drive:*]path [. . .]

or

MD [*drive:*]path [. . .]

Function   Create the specified subdirectory.

drive: specifies the drive on which to create the subdirectory. If a drive is not specified, MKDIR uses the current default.

The maximum path name that OS/2 can process is 63 characters.

Examples

MD \IBM   ; Create a directory called \IBM

MKDIR \IBM \NOTES   ; Create a directory called \IBM \NOTES

MKDIR B:TEST   ; Create a directory called TEST on drive B

MODE (P/R)

Format

[drive:][path]MODE n (n is 40 or 80)

or

[drive:][path]MODE [n],m,[,t] (test pattern alignment)

or

[drive:][path]MODE COM#[:] baud[,parity[,data[,stop[,P]]]]

or

[drive:][path]MODE LPT#[:] [cpl][,vli][,P]

or

[drive:][path]MODE LPT#[:]=COM#[:]

Function   Specify device characteristics.

P specifies continuous retries on timeout errors.
cpl is characters per line (80, 132).
vli is vertical lines per inch.

Examples

MODE 40	; Set the screen to 40 characters per line
MODE LPT1:=COM1:	; Route parallel data from LPT1 to the serial ; port COM1
MODE 80,R,T	; Set the screen to 80 characters per line, ; displaying a test pattern for character ; alignment

MORE (P/R)

Format

OS2 __ COMMAND ¦ MORE

or

MORE < OS2 __ COMMAND

Function   Display a command's output a screenful at a time.

The OS/2 MORE command reads data from the standard input device and displays the information to the standard output device a page at a time until the end-of-file is encountered. Each time a page of data is displayed on the screen, MORE displays the message

— MORE —

Simply press any key to continue the output, or press CTRL-C to terminate the command.

Example

SORT < DATA.DAT ¦ MORE ; Pipe the output of SORT to MORE

PATCH (P/R)

Format

PATCH file _ specification [/A]

Function   PATCH allows you to make patches to an OS/2 executable file.

Any writeable OS/2 file can be patched.

PATCH runs in one of two modes, automatic and interactive. [/A] specifies automatic.

In interactive mode, PATCH prompts you for both the patch offset and the new contents values. The values must be entered in hexadecimal. In automatic mode, PATCH uses a file containing the offsets and desired values.

Always make a back-up copy of the file you are going to patch before executing this command.

Example

PATCH TEST.EXE

PATH (P/R)

Format

PATH [[drive:][path] [[;[drive:][path]] . . .]

Function   Specify command search directories.

Each time OS/2 executes a COM, EXE, or BAT file, it searches the current working directory for the specified command. If OS/2 cannot find the file, it checks to see if you have specified a command path. If a command path is present, OS/2 will search each of the directories listed in the path until the file is found or the list is exhausted.

PATH does not validate the existence of paths. Invalid paths are not found until OS/2 attempts to search them later when looking for a command. If you invoke a path without parameters, the current command path is displayed. Likewise, if the only parameter is a semicolon, PATH will delete the current path and OS/2 will only examine the default directory for commands.

OS/2 stores the current command path as an environment entry.

Example

PATH C: \DOS; \C:UTIL;   ; Direct DOS to examine the subdirectories
                          ; \DOS and \UTIL on drive C (in that order)
                          ; for commands that do not exist as
                          ; specified in the command line

PAUSE (P/R)

Format

PAUSE [*message*]

Function   Display an optional message that delays batch file execution:

[optional message text] Strike a key when ready...
message can contain up to 123 characters.

To continue batch processing, press any key. Otherwise, press CTRL-BREAK.

Examples

PAUSE Enter a blank disk in drive B
PAUSE

PREDEFINED FUNCTION KEYS (P/R)

Function   Predefines OS/2 function keys.

OS/2 buffers each command entered in a location in memory so that you can access each function key to simplify your command entry.

F1   Copy one charater from the previous command buffer.
F2   Copy all characters in the buffer that precede the next character typed.
F3   Copy all of the characters in the command buffer.
F4   Copy all characters including and following the next character typed.
F5   Edit the current command buffer.
F6   Place a CTRL-Z (^{Z}) end-of-file marker at the end of a file.
INS   Insert characters in the current command buffer.
DEL   Delete the character that precedes the cursor.
ESC   Cancel the current command line without executing it.

PRINT (P/R)

Format

[drive:][path]PRINT [qualifiers] *file — spec*

Function   Print an OS/2 file by using the print queue.

file — spec is the complete OS/2 path name of the file to be added to or removed from the print queue.

PRINT supports wild-card characters.

Qualifers include

[/C]	(cancel a specific file)
[/D:device — name]	(specify the print device)
[/T]	(remove all files)

Examples

PRINT *.DAT	; Print *.DAT files
PRINT/T	; Abort all print jobs

PROMPT (P/R)

Format

PROMPT [*prompt __ string*]

Function   Define the OS/2 prompt.

prompt __ string is the character string that defines the OS/2 prompt. It can contain characters or the following metastrings:

$b	¦ character
$d	Date
$e	ESC
$h	Backspace
$g	> character
$l	< character
$n	Current drive
$p	Current directory
$q	= character
$t	Current time
$v	OS/2 version
$_	CR LF
$$	$ character

If no string is specified, PROMPT resets the system prompt to the current default drive.

Examples

PROMPT Real>	; Sets system prompt to "Real>"
PROMPT $t	; Sets system prompt to the current system
	; time

RECOVER (P/R)

Format

[*drive:*][path]RECOVER *file_spec*

or

[*drive:*][path]RECOVER *drive:*

Function   Recover corrupted files.

RECOVER only recovers corrupted files. RECOVER will not restore an erased file; use a third-party software package to do so.

file_spec specifies the name of the file containing bad sectors.

drive: specifies a disk drive with corrupted files. RECOVER will place files in the root directory with the name FILE*nnnn*.REC, where *nnnn* begins with 0001. These files contain the recovered files up to a bad sector.

RECOVER uses the file allocation table as shown in Chapter 10 to recover corrupted files.

Example

RECOVER B: ; Recover the entire disk contained in drive B

REM (P/R)

Format

REM [*message*]

Function   Display comments during batch file execution.

REM allows you to display messages on the standard output device during the execution of batch (BAT) files.

message is an optional command-line parameter that contains the message.

The OS/2 command ECHO OFF inhibits the display of messages by REM.

Example

:DONE
REM About to display directory listing
DIR
REM Directory listing completed
REM
GOTO DONE

RENAME (P/R)

Format

REN *file—specification filename*[.ext]

or

RENAME *file—specification filename*[.ext]

Function   Rename the file specified.

file—specification is the complete OS/2 path name of the file to be renamed. It can contain a drive and OS/2 subdirectory path.
filename cannot have a drive or OS/2 subdirectory path.

The renamed file will reside in the same directory on the same disk drive as the source file.

RENAME supports OS/2 wild-card characters.

Examples

REN B:*.BAK *.SAV	; Files remain on drive B
RENAME \DOS *.SYS *.XXX	; Path name on source files only

RESTORE (P/R)

Format

[drive:][path]RESTORE *drive:file_specification* [/P][/S]
[/B:*mm-dd-yy*][/A:*mm-dd-yy*]
[/E:*hh:mm:ss*][/L:*hh:mm:ss*]
[/M][/N]

Function   Restore files saved by BACKUP.

drive:file_specification specifies the files to be restored.

/A:*mm-dd-yy* directs RESTORE to restore only the files modified after the specified date.

/B:*mm-dd-yy* directs RESTORE to restore only the files modified on or before the specified date.

/E:*hh:mm:ss* directs RESTORE to restore only the files modified on or before the specified time.

/L:*hh:mm:ss* directs RESTORE to restore only the files modified on or before the specified time.

/M directs RESTORE to restore only the files modified since the last backup.

/N directs RESTORE to restore only the files that no longer exist on the target disk.

/P directs RESTORE to prompt the user before restoring files that have been modified or set to read-only since the back-up.

/S directs RESTORE to restore files contained in subdirectories.

To support OS/2 batch processing, RESTORE provides the following exit status values:

0   Successful restoration
1   No files found to restore
2   Shared files not restored
3   User termination via CTRL-C
4   Restoration error

Examples

RESTORE A:*.* C: /S   ; Restore files from drive A including subdirectories
RESTORE A:*.DAT C: /P   ; Prompt the user before restoring
                             ; files that have been modified since
                             ; the backup
RESTORE A:*.* B:*.* /S/P

REPLACE (P/R)

Format

*[drive:][path]*REPLACE *file__specification* *[drive:][path]* *[/A][/P][/R][/S][/W]*

file__specification is the complete OS/2 path name for the source file(s) that replace a file(s) on the target drive.

drive: contains the target drive for the file replacement.

path contains the target OS/2 subdirectory path for the file replacement.

/A directs REPLACE to replace only those files that are not already present at the target location.

/P directs REPLACE to prompt you before replacing a file:

Replace FILENAME.EXT (Y/N)?

/R directs REPLACE to replace files marked as read-only.

/S directs REPLACE to search all directories on the target disk for a matching file name.

/W directs REPLACE to prompt you before beginning execution.

Press any key to begin replacing file(s)

To support OS/2 batch processing, REPLACE uses the following exit status codes:

0	Successful replacement of all files
2	Source file not found
3	Source or target path not found
5	Access denied
8	Insufficient memory
11	Invalid command format
15	Invalid source or target drive
22	Incorrect OS/2 version

Examples

REPLACE A: *.*B:/S	; Replace all of the files on drive A to drive
	; B including subdirectories
REPLACE A:*.DAT B:/P	; Replace all of the DAT files on drive B with
	; those found on drive A

RMDIR (P/R)

Format

RMDIR [*drive:*]path [...]

or

RD [*drive:*]path [...]

Function   Remove the specified directory.

drive: specifies the drive from which to remove the subdirectory. If a drive is not specified, RMDIR uses the current default.

The maximum path name that OS/2 can process is 63 characters. A directory must be empty before it can be removed.

Examples

RD \IBM   ; Remove the directory \IBM
RMDIR \IBM \NOTES   ; Remove the directory IBM \NOTES

SET (P/R)

Format

SET [name=[value]]

Function   Place or display OS/2 environment entries.

The OS/2 SET command places or displays entries in the OS/2 environment. The OS/2 environment provides a storage location for system specifics. OS/2 commands such as PROMPT and PATH also place entries in the environment.

SET converts all entries to uppercase.

SET with no parameters displays the current environment.

Examples

```
SET                     ; Display environment entries
SET FILE=TEST.DAT       ; Place an entry in the
                        ; environment
SET FILE                ; Remove value for FILE
```

SETLOCAL (P)

Format

SETLOCAL

Function   SETLOCAL works in conjunction with ENDLOCAL to preserve the current drive, directory, and environment settings within a batch file, to ensure that the batch file changes are only temporary.

Example

```
SETLOCAL        ; Store the current settings
CD \FILES       ; Change the current directory
C:              ; Change the current drive
PROGRAM         ; Execute an application
ENDLOCAL        ; Restore original drive, directory and environment
```

SHIFT(P/R)

Format

SHIFT

Function   Shift each batch parameter left by one position.
    If more than ten parameters are passed to an OS/2 batch procedure,

you can use the SHIFT command to access each parameter past %9. If no parameter exists to the right of a parameter, SHIFT assigns the parameter a NULL string.

Example

```
ECHO OFF                    ; TEST 1 2 3 will display:
:LOOP                       ; 1
IF'%1'=="  GOTO DONE        ; 2
ECHO %                      ; 3
SHIFT
GOTO LOOP
:DONE
```

SORT (P/R)

Format

OS2__COMMAND ¦ SORT [/R][/+n]

or

SORT [/R][/+n] < file

Function   OS/2 sort filter.

The OS/2 SORT command reads data from the standard input device, sorting and then displaying the information on the standard output device until end-of-file is encountered.

/R directs SORT to sort the data in reverse order.

/+n allows you to specify the column on which to sort the data.

Examples

```
SORT < DATA.DAT ¦ MORE      ; Pipe the output of SORT to MORE
SORT /R < DATA.DAT          ; Sort DATA.DAT in reverse order
```

SPOOL (P)

Format

[*pathname*] [/*D:device*] [/*O:devicename*]

Function   Initialize the OS/2 print spooler for operations from multiple applications. The OS/2 print spooler allows programs to perform their print operations in the background.

pathname is the OS/2 name of the path into which OS/2 will place spooled files. By default, OS/2 uses the path \SWAPFILE.

/*D:device* specifies the name (LPT1, COM1) of the device OS/2 is to print to.

/*O:devicename* specifies the name of the output print device. By default, OS/2 uses the name given by /D.

Examples

```
SPOOL \MYSPOOL        ; Use \MYSPOOL for spooled files
SPOOL /D:COM1         ; Spool to serial port
```

SUBST (P/R)

Format

SUBST [*drive:*] [*path*][/*D*]

Function   Substitute a drive name for an OS/2 path name.
    Because OS/2 path names can become quite large, OS/2 allows you to substitute a drive identifier for a path name.

drive: is the disk drive identifier that will be used to reference the path.

path is the OS/2 path name to abbreviate.

/*D* directs SUBST to remove a previous disk substitution.

If you invoke SUBST without any parameters, current substitutions are displayed.

Examples

SUBST E: \DOS\HELPFILE\COMMANDS   ; Abbreviate the directory as E:
SUBST   ; Display current substitutions

SYS (P/R)

Format

[drive:][path]*SYS* drive: [/*S*]

Function   Transfer operating system files to a disk.

SYS places the required hidden files, but not the OS/2 command interpreter (CMD.EXE), on the disk contained in the specified drive.

/*S* copies the required system files to the target disk.

Example

SYS B: ; Transfer system files to the disk in
            ; drive B

TIME (P/R)

Format

TIME [*HH*:*MM*[:*SS*[.*hh*]]]

Function   Set the OS/2 system time.

HH is the desired hours (0-23).
MM is the desired minutes (1-59).
SS is the desired seconds (0-59).
hh is the desired hundredths of seconds (0-99).

If you do not specify a time, TIME displays the current time. TIME does modify the AT system clock.

Examples

TIME	; Display the current system time
TIME 12:00	; Set the time to noon
TIME 00:00:00.00	; Set the time to midnight

TREE (P/R)

Format

TREE [*drive:*][/F]

Function   Display directory structure.

TREE displays the name of each directory on a disk.

drive: is the disk drive on which the directory structure will be displayed.

/F directs TREE to display the name of each file in a directory.

Examples

TREE	; Display the directory structure
TREE B:/F	; Also display file names

TYPE (P/R)

Format

TYPE *file_specification* [. . .]

Function   Display a file's contents.

file_specification is the complete name of the file to be displayed. It can contain a path name identifying the drive. If the drive or path is not specified, TYPE uses the current defaults.

TYPE is restricted to ASCII files. Do not use COM or EXE files. These file types contain unprintable characters that will cause your system to beep and display garbled characters.

Examples

TYPE CONFIG.SYS	; Display the contents of
	; CONFIG.SYS
TYPE B:\DOS\AUTOEXEC.SAV	; Display a file on drive B
TYPE B:CONFIG.SYS AUTOEXEC.SAV	; OS/2 first TYPES the contents of the
	; CONFIG.SYS
	; file and then the contents of the
	; AUTOEXEC.SAV
	; file, in a sequential fashion

VER (P/R)

Format

VER

Function   Display the OS/2 version number.

OS/2 version numbers are composed of a major and minor version-number combination. For example, OS/2 1.0 has a major version number of 1 and a minor version number of 0.

Example

VER
MS Operating System/2 Version 10.0

VERIFY (P/R)

Format

VERIFY [ON ¦ OFF]

Function   Enable/disable disk I/O verification.

If VERIFY is ON, OS/2 will read each disk sector it writes in order to ensure that the data was correctly recorded on disk. This prevents disk corruptions that cause invalid data to be recorded.

Disk I/O verification, however, induces a significant amount of system overhead and is normally used only during system backups. If you invoke VERIFY without any parameters, the current status of disk I/O verification is displayed.

Examples

```
VERIFY         ; Display current status
VERIFY OFF     ; Disable disk I/O verification
VERIFY ON      ; Turn on verification
```

VOL (P/R)

Format

VOL [drive:]

Function   Display a disk volume label.

OS/2 volume labels are 11-character names assigned to a disk. Volume names use the same characters as OS/2 file names. If you do not specify a target drive, OS/2 uses the current default.

To assign a volume label, use the OS/2 LABEL command.

Example

```
VOL      ; Display the current volume label
Volume in drive A is OS2USER.
```

XCOPY (P/R)

Format

[drive:][path]XCOPY *file_spec1 file_spec2* [*qualifiers*]

Function   Copy files including those in subdirectories (DOS 3.2).

file—spec1 is the source file to copy.

file—spec2 is the target file to receive the copy.

qualifers include

/A	Only copy files whose archive bit is set. Do not modify the bit.
/D:*mm-dd-yy*	Copy files created or modified since the date given.
/E	Create all subdirectories on the target drive.
/M	Only copy files whose archive bit is set. Clear the bit.
/P	Before each copy, prompt.

FILENAME.EXT (Y/N)?

/S	Copy files from all subdirectories below the source.
/V	Use disk verification to ensure success.
/W	Before beginning, prompt.

Press any key to begin copying file(s).

Example

XCOPY A: *.* B: /S

BATCH PROCESSING

Just as DOS fully exploits batch processing, so does OS/2. Chapter 2 examined both OS/2 and DOS batch processing in detail. Now that you have seen each of the OS/2 commands, let's quickly review several of the OS/2 batch command features. First, remember that OS/2 batch files have the CMD extension, while DOS batch files have the BAT extension. Also, remember that each time OS/2 starts in protected mode, it executes the contents of the STARTUP.CMD file. OS/2 real mode still uses AUTOEXEC.BAT.

Consider the following STARTUP.CMD file. Many OS/2 users like to have the system date and time displayed each time they start using the computer. However, most don't like having to respond to the DATE and TIME prompts. This batch file solves the problem by using the OS/2 DETACH command.

```
ECHO OFF
DETACH TIME > TIME.DAT
DETACH DATE > DATE.DAT
TYPE TIME.DAT
TYPE_DATE.DAT
```

You will want to experiment with the OS/2 commands from within batch files.

OS/2 I/O REDIRECTION OPERATORS

As stated in Chapter 3, OS/2 supports each of the DOS I/O redirection operators and provides several new redirection operators.

REDIRECTION OPERATORS

>   Output redirection operator
Example: DIR > PRN:

<   Input redirection operator
Example: SORT < TEST.DAT

>>   Append redirection operator
Example: DIR >> DREV.LST

¦   Pipe redirection operator
Example: DIR ¦ MORE

OS/2 PROTECTED-MODE REDIRECTION
OPERATORS

&&   AND operator. OS/2 executes second command only when first is
successful.
Example: DIR TEST.DAT && TYPE TEST.DAT

‖   OR operator. OS/2 executes second command only when first is
unsuccessful.
Example: DIR TEST.DAT ‖ COPY A:TEST.DAT

&   Command separator. Allows multiple commands on the same line.
Example: DIR B:TEST & TYPE A:TEST & DIR C:TEST

I/O redirection operators are often referred to as protected-mode
redirection operators. The following OS/2 command examples illustrate their use. Consider this command that uses the OS/2 AND
operator:

```
[C:\] DIR CONFIG.SYS && TYPE CONFIG.SYS
```

In this case, OS/2 first issues the DIR CONFIG.SYS command. If
the command is successful (CONFIG.SYS exists), OS/2 executes the
command TYPE CONFIG.SYS. If the file does not exist, OS/2 does not
execute the TYPE command.

In a similar way, this command illustrates the OS/2 OR command:

```
[C:\] DIR B:CONFIG.SYS ‖ COPY A:CONFIG.SYS B:
```

If the DIR B:CONFIG.SYS command is successful (the file exists), OS/2
does not perform further processing. If the file is not found, OS/2

executes the second half of the OR command, copying the A:CONFIG.
SYS file to drive B.

OS/2 also allows you to group commands within parentheses, as
shown here:

```
[C:\] (DIR B:CONFIG.SYS && TYPE B:CONFIG.SYS) ¦¦ COPY A:CONFIG.SYS B:
```

In this case, OS/2 performs the statements contained in the parentheses
first, obtaining a result (successful or unsuccessful). If the command is
successful, OS/2 displays the contents of B:CONFIG.SYS. If unsuccessful, OS/2 does not process the second part of the statement (COPY
A:CONFIG.SYS B:). In this next example,

```
[C:\] (DIR B:CONFIG.SYS ¦¦ DIR C:CONFIG.SYS) && DIR A:CONFIG.SYS
```

OS/2 first executes the statements contained within the parentheses, looking for the CONFIG.SYS file first on drive B and then on
drive C. If OS/2 finds the file in either location, it deletes the file from
drive A. As you can see, the use of OS/2 AND and OR operators within
the command line makes your command lines essentially unlimited in
function.

In sum, OS/2 commands provide increased functional capabilities
over DOS commands while maintaining complete compatibility. More
than 10 million personal computers are currently compatible because
they use DOS. The end result is that, by the early 1990s, more than 50
million personal computers will still be fully compatible.

19: OS/2 Questions and Answers

The previous 18 chapters of this book presented detailed material for DOS power users. You have learned how DOS works at its lowest levels, and you have received a thorough overview of OS/2. By now, your foundation should be very solid. This chapter will be unique. It should expand both your knowledge of OS/2 and your learning potential. Chapter 1 stated that the power user's success lies in his or her ability to formulate and ask questions. It is hoped that this book has answered many of your questions and has generated even more questions, causing you to experiment, research, and even ponder DOS and OS/2 concepts.

This chapter looks at OS/2 through questions and answers. Some questions have simple, one-line answers, while others result in additional questions. As you read along, do not restrict your mindset. View each question as the OS/2 developer, application programmer, end user, and MIS executive. Only by seeing the entire picture first can you later appreciate its fine detail.

Have fun with this chapter. Write your own questions in the margin. Chapter 1 wished you luck as you began your journey to become a DOS power user. As you can now see, the journey never ends.

IDENTIFYING THE NEED

What were the driving forces that led to the development of OS/2?

Several key factors played significant roles in the development of OS/2. First, the IBM PC and DOS have both become readily accepted in the home, office, and school. With this acceptance has come increased knowledge, greater hardware and software processing demands, and the need for office workstations that place the items normally found on the employee's desktop onto the computer screen.

Second, businesses and schools have begun to recognize and appreciate the convenience that networking PCs and resources together

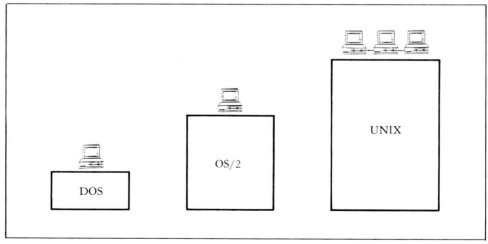

Figure 19-1.

OS/2 providing capabilities formerly
available only on minicomputers

provide. No longer are PC applications viewed as single-user programs.

Third, memory has become readily available at low costs. Memory prices are no longer a restriction. Rather, the DOS 640K barrier is a restriction.

Last, the advent of the 80286 and 80386 has given the computer industry processors fast enough to support a fully multitasking operating system.

OS/2 is the stepping stone to providing PCs with the capabilities previously available only on minicomputers (see Figure 19-1).

How long did OS/2 take to develop?

When OS/2 becomes readily available to the public, it will have been on the development table for four years. Contrast this development time with that of DOS (see Figure 19-2).

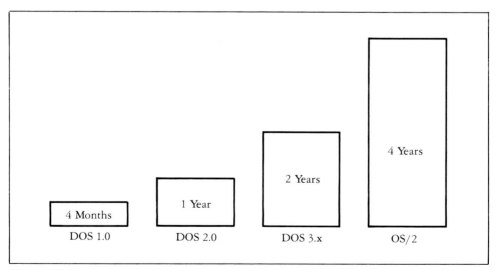

Figure 19-2.

OS/2 development time versus DOS
development time

Why did OS/2 take so long to develop?

As stated, OS/2 provides tremendous increases in functional capabilities over DOS. The OS/2 development team had to determine the functional capabilities that would be required to carry personal computers into the 1990s. These functional capabilities include

- Multitasking

- Virtual memory management

- Virtual devices

- Interprocess communication (IPC)

- Network support

- Advanced video graphics support

- A consistent user interface

- Protected-mode programming

- DOS compatibility

Next, the developers had to determine the most efficient implementation. If you can now be considered a "DOS power user," the OS/2 development team members are indeed the "masters." In four short years, this team has produced more than 350,000 lines of code. This figure becomes even more staggering when you consider that the majority of the routines broke new ground for a sophisticated multitasking operating system.

What was the most important design consideration?

That's easy — compatibility. More than 10 million users are currently using DOS. OS/2, therefore, has to ensure complete support for this incredible user base. Without compatibility for existing software products, users will not migrate to OS/2. It would not be cost-effective.

In what ways did OS/2 have to ensure compatibility with DOS?

OS/2 had to provide a means of executing existing DOS programs (using current files), while at the same time providing a familiar user interface (the command-line prompt). In some cases, the need to ensure DOS compatibility greatly restricted the creativity of the OS/2 developers. For example, many users would very much like OS/2 to maintain version numbers for their files. Because such processing would not be compatible with the DOS file structure, it could not be implemented.

GETTING STARTED

What are the OS/2 hardware requirements?

OS/2 is an 80286-based operating system. Figure 19-3 illustrates OS/2 hardware requirements.

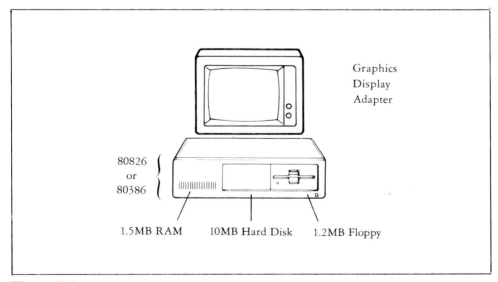

Figure 19-3.

OS/2 hardware requirements

Why does OS/2 require an 80286?

There are two reasons. First, because of OS/2's tremendous capabilities, it has a great deal of system overhead. The 80286 is fast enough to make this system overhead acceptable to the end user. Second, OS/2 is a protected-mode operating system. The 8088 does not provide protected-mode hardware support.

Does OS/2 run under the 80386?

Yes, but . . . The 80386 does provide faster processing than the 80286 along with increased memory-management capabilities. But current versions of OS/2 do not fully exploit the 80386's hardware capabilities. Many users feel that OS/2's system overhead makes it an unacceptable multitasking operating system until it fully exploits the 80386.

What is the OS/2 SDK?

Think of what made DOS fully accepted in business, schools, and the home. It was not the DOS command prompt, the DOS utilities, or the programming languages that supported DOS. Rather, it was the application software such as 1-2-3, WordStar, and dBASE. The key to OS/2's success is not necessarily its functional capabilities, but rather the number of software products that support OS/2. Microsoft offers the OS/2 Software Development Kit (SDK), which assists third-party software developers in producing OS/2 application programs. Specifically, the software development kit provides

- OS/2 Version 1.0

- OS/2 LAN Manager

- Microsoft Assembler version 4.5

- Codeview debugger

- Microsoft C Compiler version 4.5

- Attendance at an OS/2 developers conference

- Complete OS/2 documentation

- OS/2 Presentation Manager

- A year subscription to *MS Dial*

- A year subscription to *Microsoft Systems Journal*

How do I get the OS/2 Software Development Kit?

The OS/2 SDK is available through Microsoft. For more information write to

Microsoft Corporation
MS OS/2 SDK
16011 NE 36th Way
Box 97017
Redmond, WA 98073-9717

Who should order the OS/2 SDK?

If you currently develop applications marketed at a large DOS user base, the OS/2 SDK is a sound investment. If you are just starting to develop such applications, or want to do so as a hobby, consider instead acquiring the MS Windows Software Development Kit. The Windows SDK will teach you how to develop programs that execute under MS Windows, which is very similar to the OS/2 Presentation Manager. The advantage of using the Windows SDK is cost; the Windows SDK is much cheaper.

What are the best sources of OS/2 information?

By far, the most complete source of OS/2 information is the OS/2 Software Development Kit. For serious developers, Microsoft University offers a complete OS/2 curriculum. For more information, write to

Microsoft University
Box 97017
Redmond, WA 98073-9717

Also, the *Microsoft Systems Journal* provides informative articles on OS/2 in each issue. Write to

Microsoft Systems Journal
Box 1903
Marion, OH 43305

Last, the DOS User's Group provides information on OS/2 commands, system configuration, and OS/2 programming, while providing a large user base for OS/2 questions and answers. Write to

DOS User's Group
Box 26601
Las Vegas, NV 89126

PHILOSOPHY

What was the influence of MS Windows on OS/2?

Most people will probably immediately answer, "The Presentation Manager," when asked this question. Indeed, the OS/2 Presentation Manager is based upon the MS Windows user interface. However, Windows provided Microsoft with a dry run prior to the release of OS/2. Windows offers many of the features included in OS/2, such as

- Multitasking

- Interprocess communication (IPC)

- Graphics

- A consistent user interface

- Virtual devices

- DOS compatibility

More than 1 million people currently use MS Windows. Microsoft has used the feedback from these users to enhance OS/2. As you examine concepts throughout this chapter, note the lessons Microsoft learned from Windows.

What was the impact of the VGA on OS/2?

In April 1987, IBM announced its new Personal System/2 line of computers, and IBM and Microsoft announced their joint OS/2 venture. One of the most significant enhancements of the PS/2 computer line is its high-resolution video graphics adapter (VGA). With the advent of VGA, software developers now have another video monitor to add to their list of hardware-dependent modules, including

- Monochrome Graphics Adapter

- Color Graphics Adapter

- Extended Graphics Adapter

- Video Graphics Adapter

OS/2 and the Presentation Manager introduce the notion of device-independent graphics. Simply stated, you write your applications using the Presentation Manager graphics library, and the library routines handle the "dirty work" of determining the proper video display.

How will the 80386 affect OS/2?

As previously stated, OS/2 currently runs on the 80286 and 80386 processors. However, early versions of OS/2 will not fully exploit the memory-management capabilities of the 80386. But as the 1990s approach, the price of the 80386 will drop, making their use common-place. By that time, OS/2 should fully utilize the 80386's memory-management hardware capabilities to become a fast, virtual-memory operating system.

How will OS/2 affect office automation?

Office automation over the past few years has one major distinction: No other field has produced as many buzzwords. OS/2 should help unify office automation, providing a fully functional "desktop" workstation environment that allows workers to integrate their products by using an "information exchange" through interprocess communication and the OS/2 LAN Manager. For the office, OS/2 is a sound investment.

What is going to happen to DOS?

DOS still has a very bright future. More than 10 million users currently run DOS, and thousands more do each day. The 8088 is not destined to run OS/2. In light of that and its incredible market base, DOS will remain fully functional for many years to come. OS/2, therefore, will be slow to replace DOS in the home.

What is the best way to get started?

You should become fully conversant with MS Windows. If you are a software developer, start writing MS Windows applications. Once you understand multitasking, message processing, the Windows video graphics routines, and virtual devices, your transition to OS/2 will be smoother. Next, get involved in a user group. The OS/2 documentation is voluminous. Share the knowledge of your peers.

What are the keys to OS/2 success?

As did DOS, OS/2 will live or die based upon independent software vendors. If software is not readily available for OS/2, users will not migrate to it. For this reason, traning is essential. Microsoft fully recognizes the need for training and therefore offers OS/2 Developer Conferences, courses at Microsoft University, and the OS/2 Software Development Kit. In addition, Microsoft has greatly increased its support staff in preparation of OS/2. OS/2 changes the user mindset in that it offers multitasking. Users are just now comfortable with DOS. To programmers, OS/2 provides a myriad of capabilities. Unfortunately, many of these programming concepts such as IPC, and dynamic-link libraries are new. Without training, third-party software development will not take place. Without third-party software, OS/2 will fail.

Is OS/2 faster than DOS?

It depends. OS/2 is not necessarily meant to be faster than DOS. Rather, OS/2 is meant to be more functional. The goals in developing OS/2 were to give the user the ability to perform multitasking, execute protected-mode programs, surpass the 640K barrier, enhance the user interface, provide programmers with a solid set of system services, simplify program development, and provide a "virtual" view of devices and resources to software programs. In trying to meet these goals, the code also had to be very efficient. If OS/2 is slow, users will not use it (a lesson learned from Windows). Finally, while meeting these goals in the most efficient manner possible, OS/2 had to remain fully compatible with DOS.

So, is OS/2 faster than DOS? It depends. By running several programs concurrently under OS/2, sharing information among them, you can probably get your job done faster with OS/2 than with DOS. However, in a side-by-side performance test to generate 10,000 prime numbers, an identical program on an 80286 running DOS will likely outperform the same program on an 80286 running OS/2. DOS should win—it does not have the overhead associated with a multitasking operating system. However, it also does not have the same functional capabilities. So, the answer to the question on speed depends upon what you are trying to do.

SPECIFICS

What is protected mode?

OS/2 is a multitasking operating system, which means several programs can coexist in memory simultaneously. For these programs to execute in harmony, they must not be allowed to interfere with one another. For example, while one program is currently displaying its results to the screen, it is undesirable for a second program to begin randomly displaying its results to the screen. Similarly, while one program is printing its results, a second program should not be able to send characters to the printer. Likewise, if each program has complete access to the computer's physical memory, one can easily overwrite the code or data belonging to another application.

Under OS/2 protected mode, OS/2 protects concurrent applications from one another. To support protected mode fully, OS/2 uses virtual memory, virtual devices, and I/O privilege levels to maintain strict control of the state of the system. Protected mode is required for multitasking. In the past, you did not have to be concerned with protected-mode issues. DOS programs had no one to harm but themselves. DOS programs, therefore, have complete control over the computer and its devices. In this way, DOS applications execute in real mode.

What is real mode?

DOS applications execute in real mode. In this mode, programs can perform low-level I/O operations, access hardware ports, and perform memory-mapping to physical memory locations. In a multitasking environment, however, these capabilities are unacceptable. For programs to coexist in harmony within a multitasking system, each program must cooperate in terms of device and resource use. OS/2 provides support for real-mode programs to ensure compatibility for current DOS applications. However, to fully exploit OS/2, applications must run in protected mode.

Why can't the 8088 execute protected-mode programs?

The 80286 contains a hardware register not present in the 8088 called the "machine status word," or MSW. When you set the protection-enable bit of the MSW, the 80286 enters protected mode. Once in protected mode, the 80286 fully supports virtual memory and memory protection. Prior to OS/2 the hardware capabilities of the 80286 exceeded its software utilization.

What happens if I execute a protected-mode program from DOS?

If you attempt to execute OS/2 protected-mode programs under DOS 3.x, or in OS/2 real mode, the program fails, as shown here:

```
C> TEST
Program too big to fit in memory

C>
```

Protected-mode programs do not execute in real mode, nor do real-mode programs execute in protected mode.

How do I create protected-mode programs in C?

Using Microsoft C, the CL command compiles and links the source file specified. The /Lp command-line option directs CL to produce a protected-mode executable:

```
[C:\] CL /Lp PROTECT.C
```

In this case, the executable file PROTECT.EXE will only run in OS/2 protected mode.

Can I prevent real-mode execution?

Yes. Depending on your requirements, you may never want to execute real-mode programs. In such cases, you can prevent OS/2 from setting aside physical memory for DOS compatibility-mode programs (see Figure 19-4). In so doing, OS/2 will provide more space to protected-mode applications, as shown in Figure 19-5. As you will find, the more physical memory that you can provide to OS/2, the less system overhead you will experience because of paging and swapping. To eliminate real-mode processing, place the following entry in CONFIG.SYS and reboot:

```
PROTECTONLY=YES
```

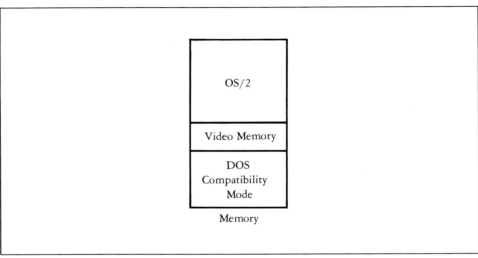

Figure 19-4.

Preventing OS/2 from setting aside
physical memory

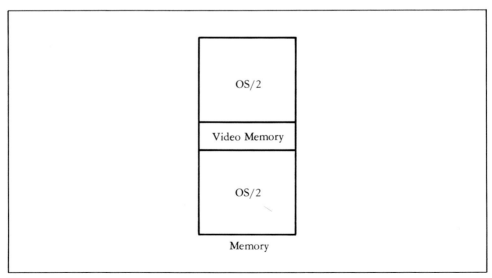

Figure 19-5.

OS/2 providing more space to
protected-mode applications

What are compatibility-mode programs?

Initially, most OS/2 software developers will be writing programs that execute under OS/2 and DOS. For example, assume that you are creating a database management system that tracks video rentals. A few of your customers have recently migrated to OS/2 while the majority still use DOS. To simplify your software development and maintenance, OS/2 allows you to migrate many OS/2 protected-mode programs to a compatibility mode that executes under both DOS and OS/2 (see Table 19-1). Many simple OS/2 programs can easily be converted to compatibility mode. In this way, the same EXE file will execute under DOS and OS/2.

How do I create compatibility-mode programs?

To create a compatibility-mode program, follow these four steps:

1. Create the source file with a text editor.

2. Compile and debug the program using the protected-mode directive /Lp in the compiler command line.

3. Create a module-definition file for the application with a standard text editor. The file name should have the extension DEF.

4. Use BIND to build the compatibility-mode executable.

Table 19-1.

Migration of Programs Across Modes

	Real Mode EXE	Protected Mode EXE	Compatibility Mode EXE
Executes in Real Mode	Yes	No	Yes
Executes in Protected Mode	No	Yes	Yes

How do compatibility-mode programs work?

OS/2 programs use a collection of routines called the Application Program Interface, or API. These routines provide your programs with access to the OS/2 system services. This collection of API routines only exists under OS/2 protected mode.

When you use BIND to convert an OS/2 protected-mode program to compatibility mode, the calls to the OS/2 API are mapped to a collection of routines called the family API. The family API services examine the parameters originally being passed to the OS/2 API services and, in turn, invoke the appropriate DOS INT 21H service. In this way, under OS/2 protected mode, the API services are used, and under DOS, the family API maps the calls to the corresponding INT 21H services.

Each OS/2 executable file, therefore, has two headers. The first is a DOS-real mode header and the second is an OS/2 protected-mode header. Depending on the mode of execution (real or protected), the compatibility-mode program uses either the API or family API services. In either case, the same executable program runs in both modes.

Are compatibility-mode programs the same size as OS/2 protected-mode programs?

No. The family API interface required for compatibility-mode programs makes them larger than protected-mode programs. However, the increase in size is normally less than 10K.

Can all OS/2 protected-mode programs be made compatible?

No. The family API routines are a subset of the OS/2 API services. Although they provide considerable functional capabilities in terms of allowing you to migrate protected-mode applications to real mode, they cannot provide support for API services that use semaphores, timers, and so forth.

What is the function of BIND?

The primary function of the OS/2 BIND utility is to create a compatibility-mode executable from a protected-mode program. BIND uses the OS/2 protected-mode executable, a module-definition file, and API library routines to build the compatibility-mode program. For most applications, your BIND command line will be

```
[C:\] BIND filename \LIB\DOSCALLS.LIB
```

What is a module-definition file?

A module-definition, or DEF, file is a text file that defines an OS/2 protected-mode program's attributes. Each time you convert a protected-mode program to compatibility mode, you must define a module-definition file for the program. The following is a sample DEF file:

```
NAME OS2HELLO
DATA MOVEABLE
CODE MOVEABLE PURE
HEAPSIZE 2048
STACKSIZE 2048
```

The OS/2 BIND utility uses the contents of the module-definition file to convert a protected-mode program to compatibility mode.

What is virtual memory?

Virtual memory is a memory-management technique in which the operating system appears to provide each application with an unlimited memory address space. Under DOS, programs are restricted to 640K.

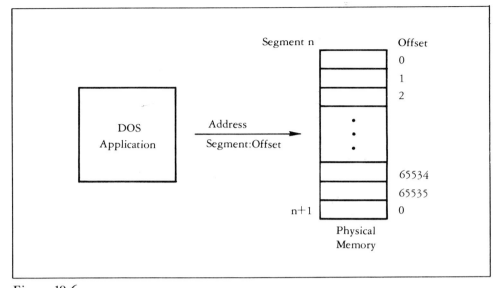

Figure 19-6.

Mapping application references to
physical memory

Each time a DOS application references a memory location, the memory
address it uses maps to an actual physical memory location, as shown in
Figure 19-6.

OS/2 protected mode, however, uses virtual memory management.
Under this technique, programs no longer address physical memory
locations. Instead, they map to an essentially unlimited (1 gigabyte)
address space that OS/2, in turn, maps to physical memory addresses, as
shown in Figure 19-7.

OS/2 implements virtual memory by breaking your large program
into a series of smaller more manageable segments (see Figure 19-8). In
this way, OS/2 can bring specific segments into memory as they are
required for execution. Whenever the code or data contained in a
segment is not required for execution, OS/2 keeps the segment on disk.

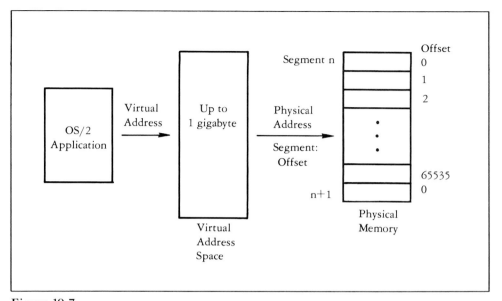

Figure 19-7.

Virtual memory management

This process of bringing segments in and out of memory as required is known as *paging*. Figure 19-9 shows the steps involved in paging.

As you can see, although OS/2 provides a very large address space, it can do so with a relatively small amount of physical memory. In addition, since all OS/2 protected-mode programs use virtual memory, OS/2 can bring portions of multiple programs into memory as required (see Figure 19-10).

If I have virtual memory, why do I need so much physical memory?

As stated, OS/2 allows programs to be very large by keeping sections of the program not currently required for execution on disk. When OS/2 needs to bring a segment containing code or data into memory from disk, first it may need to remove a segment currently residing in

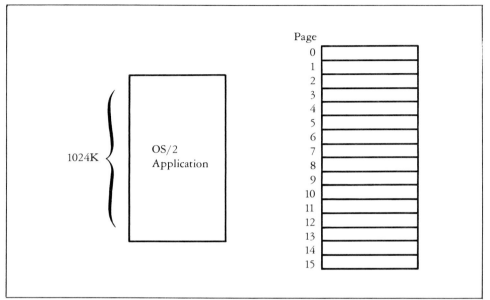

Figure 19-8.

Breaking up of large programs by
OS/2

memory to make space. As previously stated, this process is paging.
Although paging allows your programs to be virtually unlimited in size,
it places additional overhead on the system.

OS/2 multitasking capabilities allow several programs to reside in
memory simultaneously. Assume that you are currently executing the
Process A, B, and C as shown in Figure 19-10. If you later start Process D,
OS/2 must temporarily remove one of the programs from memory to
disk to make room for Process D, as shown in Figure 19-11. This process
is known as *swapping*. Although swapping allows you to execute more
programs than you physically have space for, it too increases system
overhead.

A general rule of thumb for any multitasking operating system is
that to increase performance, add physical memory. In this case, when
you add more physical memory, you reduce the amount of paging and
swapping that OS/2 must perform simply because it has more memory
to operate with. In turn, you improve your system performance.

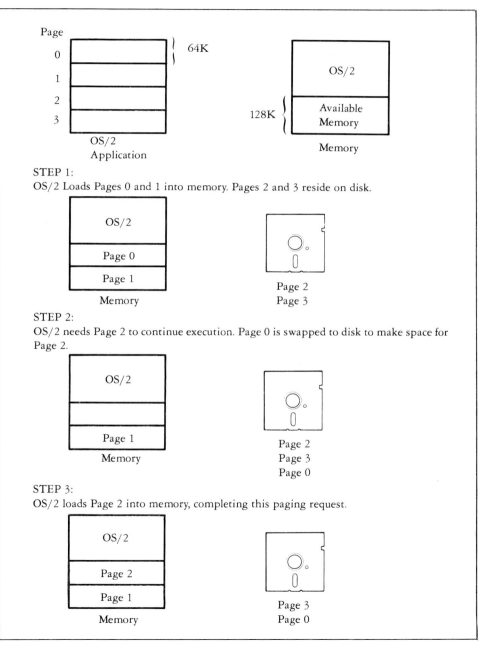

STEP 1:

OS/2 Loads Pages 0 and 1 into memory. Pages 2 and 3 reside on disk.

STEP 2:

OS/2 needs Page 2 to continue execution. Page 0 is swapped to disk to make space for Page 2.

STEP 3:

OS/2 loads Page 2 into memory, completing this paging request.

Figure 19-9.

Paging process

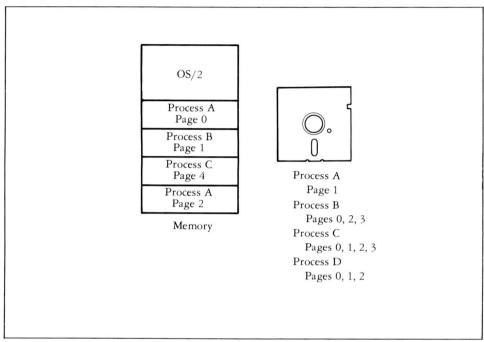

Figure 19-10.

OS/2 bringing in portions of
programs as required

What is the maximum physical memory I can have?

The 80286 allows you to place up to 16MB of physical memory in your system. Likewise, the 80386 supports up to 32MB. OS/2 requires a minimum of 1.5MB of memory.

What is the maximum virtual address space?

OS/2 currently supports a virtual address space of 1 gigabyte.

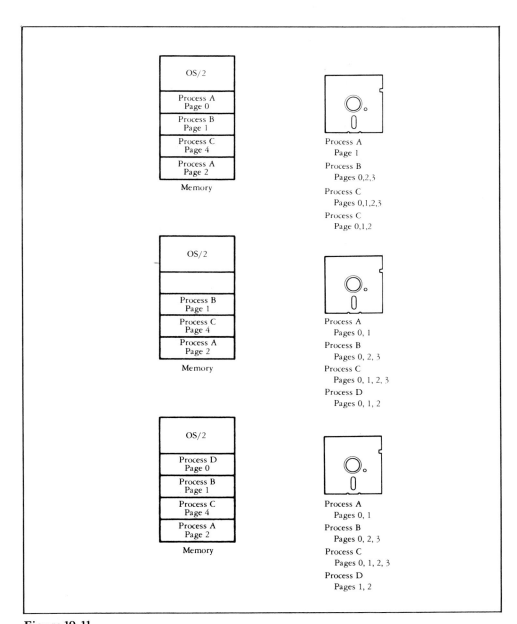

Figure 19-11.

OS/2 removing programs from
memory to disk

What are the advantages and disadvantages of virtual memory?

Advantages

- Essentially unlimited program space
- Eliminates the DOS 640K barrier
- Allows memory protection
- Allows shareable code and data
- Easier to implement multitasking
- Simplifies memory compaction

Disadvantages

- Virtual memory can place significant overhead on the operating system due to paging and swapping

How does OS/2 share code and data in protected mode?

Since OS/2 uses virtual memory management, OS/2 applications map to a virtual address space that OS/2, in turn, maps to physical memory. Since OS/2 ultimately controls the virtual-to-physical address mapping, it can easily map two or more processes to the same memory location, as shown in Figure 19-12.

What are virtual devices?

For OS/2 applications to coexist in harmony, OS/2 must maintain strict control of I/O operations. In this way, if two applications are executing simultaneously, only one can update the screen. In a similar manner, if the user enters data from the keyboard, OS/2 must ensure that the proper program receives the input. To simplify programming, OS/2 gives each application the appearance of owning all of the devices available to the system. In so doing, if five programs are executing concurrently, OS/2 gives the appearance of five screens, five keyboards, five printers, and so forth. Each program appears to have its own devices. Since these devices do not actually exist, they are virtual devices.

For output to the printer, OS/2 spools the data it receives from each application, thus ensuring that it does not intermix data. Although

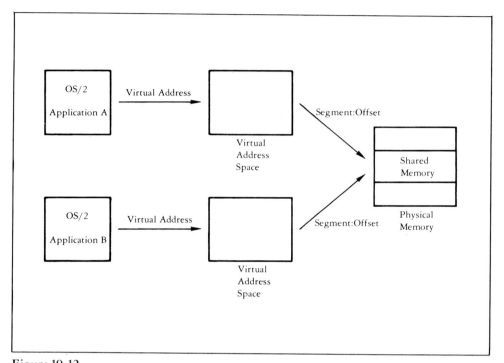

Figure 19-12.

OS/2 mapping multiple processes
to same memory location

multiple programs are writing data to the printer simultaneously, the printer only receives output from one program at a time. For disk I/O operations, the OS/2 device drivers maintain strict coordination. For keyboard input and screen output, OS/2 uses screen groups.

What is a screen group?

An OS/2 screen group is simply the virtualization of a keyboard and monitor for one or more OS/2 concurrent applications. Each time you have several programs active under OS/2 protected mode, OS/2 writes

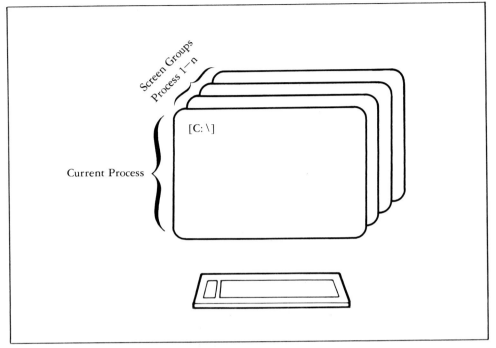

Figure 19-13.

OS/2 screen group

the output of each to a unique screen group, as shown in Figure 19-13. By switching from one session to another, you can view each program's output. Because OS/2 also associates keyboard input with a specific screen group, the data entered by the user at the keyboard is processed by the correct program.

What is an OS/2 session?

OS/2 programs run in the context of a session. OS/2 maintains a list of its active sessions and allows you to select the current session by using the OS/2 Session Manager.

What is the Session Manager?

The OS/2 Session Manager oversees your OS/2 sessions. As previously stated, OS/2 programs run in the context of a session. The OS/2 Session Manager allows you to select your desired session from its list of active sessions. To invoke the OS/2 Session Manager, use the CTRL-ESC key combination.

```
Start a Program

command.com

CMD.EXE
```

By default, OS/2 starts a real- and protected-mode session. The Start A Program option allows you to create multiple protected-mode sessions. If you select this option, OS/2 will display a protected-mode prompt.

```
[C:\]
```

From this prompt you can invoke OS/2 protected-mode programs. In this case, invoke the OS/2 LABEL command:

```
[C:\] LABEL
```

Next, again invoke the OS/2 Session Manager. As you can see, when protected-mode sessions have programs active, OS/2 displays the name of the program currently executing.

```
Start   a   Program

command.com

LABEL.COM
```

When the protected-mode program terminates, the Session Manager displays CMD.EXE to inform you that the current system is displaying the protected-mode prompt. Since OS/2 will only start one real-mode session, the Session Manager always displays COMMAND.COM.

How do I terminate an OS/2 session?

The OS/2 EXIT command terminates an OS/2 session by releasing its resources (memory) to other OS/2 sessions. If you have an active protected-mode session,

```
Start   a   Program

command.com

CMD.EXE

CMD.EXE
```

select the session to terminate and obtain a protected-mode prompt. Next, enter the EXIT command:

```
[C:\] EXIT
```

OS/2 will terminate this session and return control to the Session Manager.

```
Start a Program

command.com

CMD.EXE
```

How can I quickly change from one session to the next?

As you have just seen, OS/2 allows you to change from one session to the next by invoking the Session Manager and selecting the session you desire from the list of active sessions. In addition, if you press the ALT-ESC key combination, OS/2 will toggle from one OS/2 session to the next in a round-robin fashion.

How does an OS/2 background task differ from an OS/2 session?

OS/2 protected mode allows programs to run in one of two modes: foreground and background. Foreground commands are interactive OS/2 sessions. OS/2 foreground commands execute in the context of an OS/2 session. They have their own screen group. OS/2 allows you to select foreground programs for display by way of the Session Manager.

An OS/2 background task, however, runs in the context of an OS/2 foreground session. Background tasks are not interactive programs. They do not receive keyboard input, and, in most cases, they cannot display information to the screen. OS/2 provides two methods of issuing background commands. The first, the OS/2 DETACH command, allows you to issue background commands interactively. Consider the command on the next page.

```
[C:\] DETACH DIR > DIR.LST
```

In this case, OS/2 will execute the DIR command in the background of the current session. Since the command executes in the background mode, you are free to continue your foreground processing.

The second means of invoking an OS/2 background task is by using the RUN entry in CONFIG.SYS. In this case, each time OS/2 boots, it will invoke the command specified in the background, continuing the boot process.

In either case, OS/2 displays the background task's process identification (PID) and resumes foreground processing.

What is a PID?

PID stands for process identification. OS/2 processes are best viewed as programs. OS/2 processes its own system resources (such as files, memory, and devices). As you will see, each OS/2 process can contain one or more threads of execution (execution paths). OS/2 tracks the current system processes by way of a list of process identifications. Each time you use DETACH to create a background task, OS/2 must create a process. In the case of DETACH, OS/2 displays the process identification it creates.

```
[C:\] DETACH DIR > DIR.LST
Process Identification Number is 12
[C:\]
```

How can I stop a background task?

You can't. OS/2 background tasks cannot receive CTRL-C or CTRL-BREAK key combinations from the user. The background task, therefore, must have its own means of terminating or it will continue to execute in the background forever, or until the system resets.

For protected-mode sessions, the OS/2 Session Manager always displays CMD.EXE. What is CMD.EXE?

CMD.EXE is the OS/2 protected-mode command interpreter. CMD.EXE provides OS/2 protected mode with the same functional capabilities as COMMAND.COM does for real mode.

Does CMD.EXE provide new commands?

Yes. Using CMD.EXE, OS/2 provides support for DOS 3.x commands along with several new OS/2 commands. Like COMMAND.COM, CMD.EXE has internal and external commands.

Internal commands:

BREAK	CALL	CHCP	CHDIR	CLS	COPY
DATE	DEL	DETACH	DIR	DPATH	ECHO
ENDLOCAL	EXIT	FOR	GOTO	IF	MKDIR
PATH	PAUSE	PROMPT	REM	REN	RMDIR
SET	SETLOCAL	SHIFT	TIME	TYPE	VER
VERIFY	VOL				

External commands:

ANSI	APPEND	ASSIGN	ATTRIB	BACKUP
CHKDSK	CMD	COMMAND	COMP	DISKCOMP
DISKCOPY	FDISK	GRAFTABL	HELPMSG	JOIN
KEYBXX	LABEL	MODE	MORE	PATCH
PRINT	RECOVER	REPLACE	RESTORE	SORT
SPOOL	SUBST	SYS	TREE	XCOPY

What is the function of the new OS/2 commands?

ANSI enables ANSI support for OS/2 protected mode, as follows:

CALL	Invoke a nested batch procedure.
CHCP	Display or modify the current code page.
CMD	Start a secondary OS/2 protected-mode command processor.
DETACH	Start an OS/2 background task.
DPATH	Define a data file search path for OS/2 protected mode.
ENDLOCAL	Restore a previous environment, drive, or directory to prevent batch files from changing the current settings.

HELPMSG	Display additional text about OS/2 messages.
SETLOCAL	Save the current drive, directory, and environment for later restoration by ENDLOCAL.
SPOOL	Install the OS/2 spooler.

How does OS/2 enhance command-line processing?

Under OS/2, command-line arguments are still fully available to your programs. For C programmers, **argc** and **argv** still function in the same way they did under DOS. OS/2 does provide additional I/O redirection commands:

( )	Command grouping. OS/2 allows you to group commands to create complex logical statements using the operators described next.
&&	Logical AND. If the first OS/2 command successfully completes, OS/2 will execute the second.
	DIR A.TXT & TYPE A.TXT
||	Logical OR. If the OS/2 command fails, OS/2 will execute the second.
	DIR A:A.TXT || COPY B:A.TXT A:

Does OS/2 still support DOS batch processing?

Yes. OS/2 fully supports batch processing. The most significant change to batch processing under OS/2 is that in protected mode, batch files have the extension CMD as opposed to BAT, which is used by DOS.

Does OS/2 add new batch processing commands?

Yes. OS/2 provides CALL, SETLOCAL, and ENDLOCAL. CALL allows you to invoke nested batch procedures, as shown here:

```
CLS
CALL SOMECMD
DATE
```

The OS/2 SETLOCAL and ENDLOCAL commands work in conjunction to allow you to execute a batch procedure to prevent the current session state (drive, directory, and environment) from being changed. Consider the following batch file:

```
CLS
A:
CD \TEST
TEST
```

When this batch job completes, the current drive and directory will have changed. Using the OS/2 SETLOCAL and ENDLOCAL commands

```
SETLOCAL
CLS
A:
CD \TEST
TEST
ENDLOCAL
```

you can prevent this from happening. SETLOCAL saves the current state, and ENDLOCAL later restores it.

Does OS/2 use AUTOEXEC.BAT?

Under real mode, OS/2 uses AUTOEXEC.BAT. However, as previously stated, under protected mode, OS/2 batch files have the extension CMD. OS/2 invokes the batch procedure STARTUP.CMD for protected-mode sessions. Functionally, STARTUP.CMD and AUTOEXEC.BAT performed identical tasks. The difference is simply the mode that each is used within. STARTUP.CMD is protected mode; AUTOEXEC.BAT is real mode.

What happens at OS/2 start-up?

Each time OS/2 boots, it follows these steps:

1. The processor first checks drive A for a bootable floppy. If a system floppy is present, the processor uses it to start the boot process. If a system floppy is not found, the processor finds the bootable partition by way of the master boot record and begins booting the computer. At this time, the processor is still in real mode.

2. Next, the bootstrap performs an equipment check, loading the OS/2 Kernel to which it passes control.

3. The OS/2 Kernel then begins its initialization process, moving its components and required device drivers to their correct locations in memory. Next, the OS/2 Kernel places the processor into protected mode.

4. OS/2 concludes its configuration by examining the contents of the file CONFIG.SYS.

5. OS/2 initializes the Session Manager, creating a real- and protected-mode session.

Does OS/2 still use CONFIG.SYS?

Yes. As just shown, OS/2 still uses the contents of the file CONFIG.SYS to configure itself in memory.

What are the new configuration parameters?

In addition to the following DOS CONFIG.SYS entries

BREAK
BUFFERS
COUNTRY
DEVICE
FCBS
SHELL

OS/2 provides the following configuration parameters:

CODEPAGE	Defines the system code pages.
DEVINFO	Prepares a device for code pages.
IOPL	Enables or disables I/O privilege to a process requesting the privilege.
LIBPATH	Defines the location of OS/2 dynamic link library modules.
MAXWAIT	Establishes the minimum amount of time a process must wait before executing.
MEMMAN	Defines memory-management options.
PRIORITY	Defines the OS/2 scheduling algorithm — static or dynamic priority.
PROTECTONLY	Enables or disables real-mode processing.
RMSIZE	Specifies the amount of memory to allocate for real-mode processing.
RUN	Starts a background task at start-up.
SWAPPATH	Defines the location of the OS/2 swap file.
TIMESLICE	Defines the minimum and maximum time slice values for the OS/2 scheduler.
THREADS	Defines the maximum number of threads supported.

As you can see, most of these parameters exist to support OS/2 multitasking.

How does OS/2 perform multitasking?

The goal of any multitasking operating system is to give the appearance of executing several programs simultaneously. Always remember that the 80286 is a single-processor system. As such, it is only capable of performing one task at a time.

To give the user the appearance of several events occurring at the same time, OS/2 breaks up CPU time into segments known as *time slices*. OS/2 distributes these time slices to the list of programs awaiting execution. The process of determining which application receives control of the CPU and when is known as *scheduling*.

How does OS/2 schedule?

At the simplest level, OS/2 performs round-robin CPU distribution. Round-robin scheduling distributes CPU time slices to the list of concurrent applications one after another, as shown in Figure 19-14. In this case, when Process A's time slice completes, OS/2 passes CPU control to Process B. When Process B uses its time slice, control of CPU goes to Process C, and so on. After each available process has obtained a time slice, control of CPU returns to Process A.

As the number of concurrent processes increases, the time that each process must wait before it obtains a time slice also increases. This explains why, as the number of concurrent tasks increases, the execution performance of individual programs decreases (see Figure 19-15).

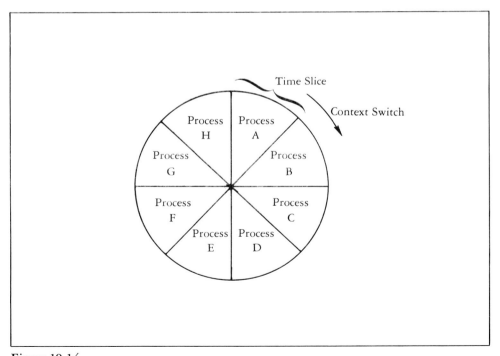

Figure 19-14.

Round-robin scheduling

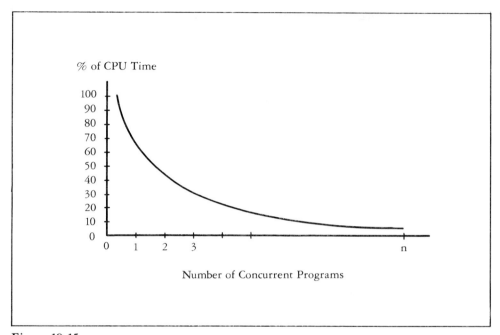

Figure 19-15.

Decrease in program
execution performance

In addition to the longer interval between time slices, programs appear to run slower because of the number of context switches OS/2 must perform. Each context switch introduces overhead on the system.

What is a context switch?

Each time OS/2 passes CPU control from one concurrent application to the next, it must first store the state of the current application (its registers). In so doing, OS/2 can later restore the registers and continue processing of this application as if it were never interrupted. This process of saving the current state of one process, while restoring that of another, is a *context switch*. Each time OS/2 passes CPU control to a new application, it must perform a context switch.

If as the number of concurrent tasks increases, the CPU time OS/2 provides to each decreases, how then does OS/2 support time-critical programs?

As stated, round-robin scheduling is the simplest way to view OS/2 scheduling. However, periodically users have a specific program (such as a data communications package or real-time event monitor) that must be able to access the CPU whenever it has data available.

To support such applications, OS/2 provides three priority levels: time-critical, standard, and idle time. Processes with time-critical priority always get first crack at the CPU. Standard-priority processes are comprised of the default OS/2 applications, while idle-time priority programs execute when OS/2 has nothing else to do. In this way, each time a time slice completes, OS/2 first checks the list of time-critical processes. If any of the processes can execute, OS/2 gives it control of the CPU. Next, if no time-critical processes require the CPU, OS/2 checks its list of standard processes. Finally, if no processes are available for execution at that level, OS/2 checks its list of idle-time processes. OS/2 follows this same processing at the end of each time slice to ensure that time-critical processes always have the CPU available to them as their processing needs require.

To increase this complexity, OS/2 allows you to prioritize applications at each priority level. In so doing, OS/2 allows you to assign a priority from 1 (low) to 32 (high) to each program at the various levels.

Given the diagram of OS/2 processes shown in Figure 19-16, OS/2 will first check its time-critical programs at the end of each time slice. In this case, Process A has the highest priority, so it gets first crack at the CPU. If A is not ready to execute, Processes B and C receive control of the CPU in a round-robin fashion since they have equal priority. As you can see, each of the standard-priority processes has the same priority. In this way, they share CPU in a round-robin fashion. Finally, note that when OS/2 passes control to the lowest-level priority tasks, Process H has first shot at the CPU.

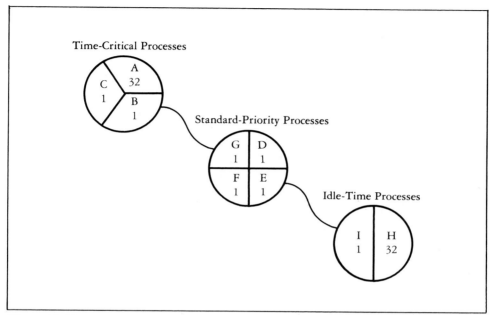

Figure 19-16.

OS/2 supporting time-critical
programs

*Given OS/2 priority scheduling, is it possible for a program to be locked
from CPU control?*

Yes. In a time-critical environment, this is desirable since you have a list
of critical programs that must gain control of the CPU whenever they
have data available to them. OS/2 provides several system configuration
parameters that affect its scheduling algorithm. Review Chapter 4 for
specifics.

What is the difference between a thread and a process?

View an OS/2 process as a program. Under OS/2, processes own system resources (such as memory and files). Each OS/2 process can have one or more paths of execution called *threads*. Each time the OS/2 scheduler must determine who is to get control of the CPU, the scheduler assigns CPU control to threads as opposed to processes. An OS/2 thread, therefore, is the OS/2 scheduling unit. Since a program (process) can be composed of multiple threads, it is possible under OS/2 for several different portions of the same program to be active concurrently. In this light, OS/2 opens the door for Ada, Modula II, and even concurrent C.

Can my programs be concurrent?

Yes. OS/2 provides a complete set of API services for creating and controlling threads of execution. In addition, OS/2 provides many asynchronous services such as timers, or even DOSWRITEASYNC, which allows your program to continue processing while OS/2 writes data to disk.

Each time your program uses one of these services, OS/2 must create a thread of execution that is capable of being scheduled and that in turn contends for CPU time slices.

What is IPC?

IPC stands for interprocess communication. A critical capability for any multitasking operating system is the ability to exchange information and status values among concurrent programs. For example, MS Windows provides a clipboard that allows you to exchange data between your word processor and spreadsheet application. In so doing, you facilitate your overall processing capabilities. OS/2 provides several tools for interprocess communication:

- Semaphores
- Pipes
- Queues
- Shared memory
- Messages and signals

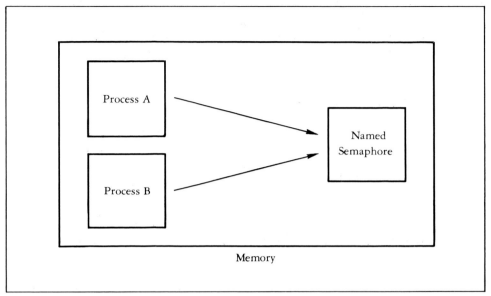

Figure 19-17.

OS/2 semaphore

As you may recall, a semaphore is a named flag that two or more concurrent applications can access to specify current processing states (see Figure 19-17). Chapter 17 provides several examples of the use of OS/2 semaphores in application programs.

An OS/2 pipe provides a direct I/O channel between two OS/2 applications (see Figure 19-18). In this case, one application writes data to the pipe, while the second reads the data. OS/2 *queues* allow multiple applications to write data into a buffer that one application can later read as shown in Figure 19-19. OS/2 *shared memory* is a region of memory that multiple OS/2 applications can map to (see Figure 19-20).

Lastly, OS/2 provides *message* and *signal* processing in a manner similar to MS Windows. OS/2 places a message into an application's message queue and notifies it of the message's arrival. The application then determines the actual message processing.

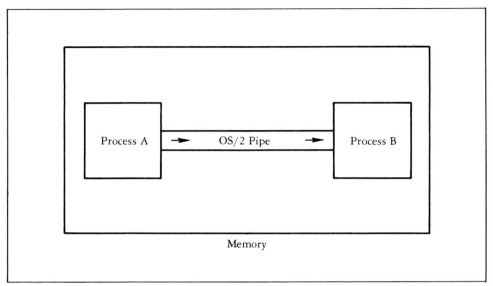

Figure 19-18.

OS/2 pipe

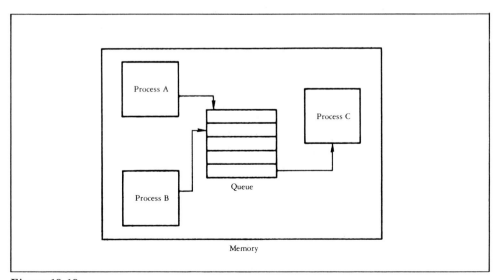

Figure 19-19.

OS/2 queue

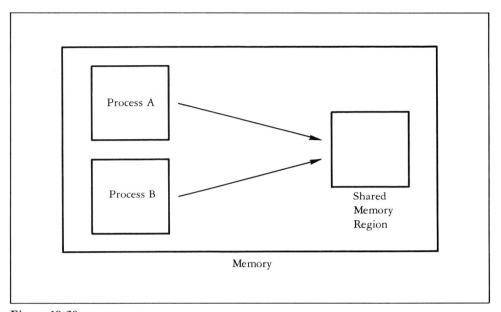

Figure 19-20.

OS/2 shared memory

What is a critical section?

Whenever concurrent applications share memory, they must have a means of coordinating access to the shared data. As the number of processes accessing shared memory increases, so too does the number of possible ways to establish deadlock or a loss of data integrity. To support the development of concurrent programs, OS/2 also allows you to specify regions of code known as *critical sections*. These are sections where processing must be allowed to complete regardless of time slicing, or where other concurrent processes cannot modify the data being used by the process in this code region. OS/2 provides several API services that programs can invoke as they enter and leave critical sections of code.

Does OS/2 use TSRs?

No. Terminate-and-stay-resident (TSR) programs give DOS a hook that it can use to simulate multitasking. Since OS/2 is already a multi-tasking operating system, TSRs are not required. Instead, OS/2 provides a complete set of timer and device monitor services.

What are timer services?

The OS/2 API services provide several routines that provide timer functions (such as delays, alarms, and so forth). Under DOS, each time you want to display a screen's contents for a brief period, you normally used a FOR loop, as shown here:

```
for (i = 1; i < time_interval; ++i)
    ;   /* do nothing but delay */
```

In this case, the CPU simply processed the FOR loop as specified, resulting in a time delay.

Since no other programs were executing, delay processing in this manner was acceptable. In a multitasking environment, however, such processing is a waste of processor time. Instead of using a loop to delay, OS/2 allows you to temporarily suspend a program's execution for the specified duration.

```
main ()
{
   /* processing */

   DOSSLEEP (interval);

   /* processing */
}
```

Once this interval expires, the program continues its processing. By suspending a program this way, the program does not waste processing time that can be used by other concurrent programs.

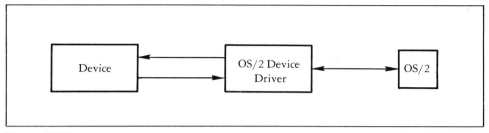

Figure 19-21.

OS/2 device monitor

What is a device monitor?

Under DOS, many users placed programs resident in memory to provide "hot key" activation of specific commands. In these cases, the memory-resident program intercepted keyboard interrupts in search of specific keystrokes. Instead of requiring your programs to capture keyboard interrupts, OS/2 uses the concept of a device monitor. An OS/2 device monitor is a software program that resides between a device and its device driver (see Figure 19-21). In this case, the monitor can use the OS/2 API service DosMonRead to read the data entered from the device, as shown in Figure 19-22. Once the monitor has processed the data, it passes to the device driver by using the routine DosMonWrite, as shown in Figure 19-23.

Where do device drivers fit into the OS/2 system map?

Device drivers play a critical role in OS/2's function. Figure 19-24 illustrates their placement in the OS/2 system structure.

OS/2's multitasking concerns have greatly increased the complexity of device drivers. Third-party hardware developers who must provide device drivers for their products, definitely have work in store for them.

What is the Presentation Manager?

The OS/2 Presentation Manager is a "Windows-like" user interface for

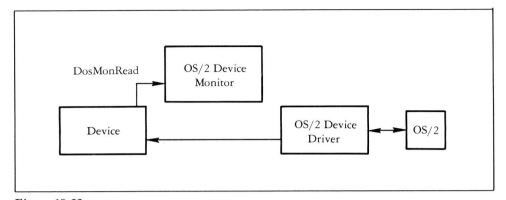

Figure 19-22.

Using DosMonRead service

OS/2. The Presentation Manager uses multiple windows, pull-down menus, and dialog boxes to provide the user with a consistent interface. By using the OS/2 Presentation Manager, users are not required to memorize OS/2 commands, which greatly increases their learning curve. In addition, since Presentation Manager applications each use the same interface, users are not intimidated when they must migrate to new applications.

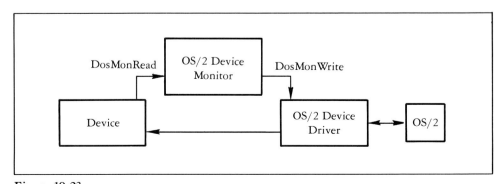

Figure 19-23.

Using DosMonWrite service

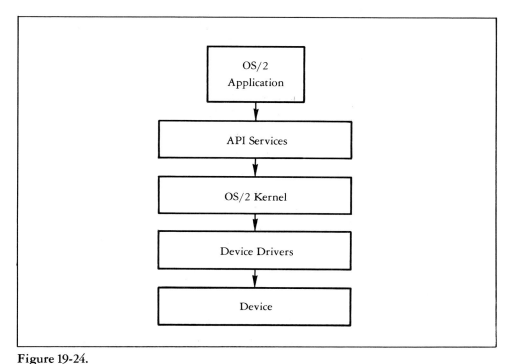

Figure 19-24.

Placement of device driver in OS/2
system structure

How does the Presentation Manager work with OS/2?

The Presentation Manager layers itself on top of OS/2 to utilize the
powerful OS/2 services. Software developers write Presentation Manager applications that use the Presentation Manager services, which in
turn invoke the OS/2 services, as in Figure 19-25.

How can I learn to write Presentation Manager programs?

The Presentation Manager is based on MS Windows. The best way to
fully understand Presentation Manager applications is either to develop
routines that utilize the Presentation Manager services, or to write MS
Windows applications. The Windows Software Development Kit is an
affordable alternative to the OS/2 SDK.

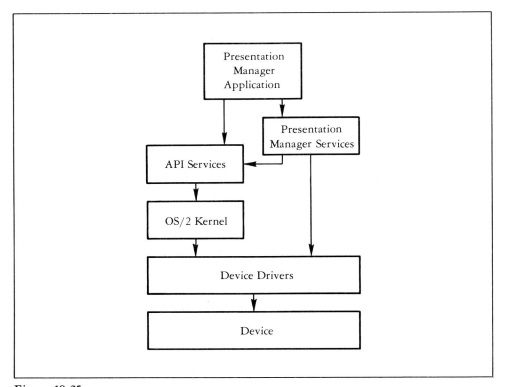

Figure 19-25.

OS/2 Presentation Manager

What is IOPL?

By default, protected-mode programs cannot perform low-level I/O operations or access hardware ports. In a multitasking environment, it is essential that programs are restricted in this manner. Periodically, however, a program must be able to issue instructions at this level. The 80286 protected mode uses three privilege levels from 0-3, where 0 is the most privileged and 3 is the least (see Figure 19-26). As you can see, OS/2 applications by default do not possess the ability to perform low-level I/O.

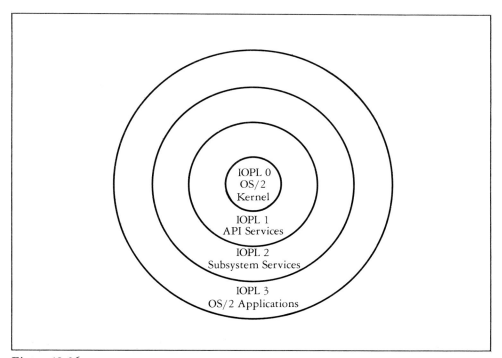

Figure 19-26.

Privilege levels

When should I enable IOPL?

Most users will never have to enable IOPL processing in this way. Remember, protected-mode processing exists to restrict programs from accessing hardware in this fashion. If you find your program requiring IOPL, take a close look at your design. Most applications should not require this capability.

What are dynamic link libraries (DLLs)?

Under DOS, each time you link an application, you must specify the OBJ and LIB files LINK is to combine to build the EXE file. Since all of the files LINK is to combine at that time must be present, the process is referred to as *static linking*. OS/2, however, also supports the notion of dynamic link libraries (DLL). With dynamic link libraries, the actual resolution of externals is done by the OS/2 loader each time it places a program into memory for execution. In this way, both the program and the dynamic link library will reside in memry simultaneously.

What are the advantages of DLLs?

Dynamic link libraries provide several advantages. First, many programs can link to the same dynamic link library in memory and allow shared code. Second, since the library routines are not contained in the executable, the program is smaller on disk. Third, and most important, dynamic link libraries simplify your program modification. In the past, each time you modified the code contained in a library file, you had to relink the programs that referenced the updated routine. Not only was this process time-consuming, the possibility of forgetting to update a program always existed. With dynamic link libraries, however, if you update a routine, you simply recompile the library and reload it into memory. The next time a program that uses the updated routine is invoked, the loader will map the call to the routine to the updated routine transparently.

GENERAL QUESTIONS

What is the LAN Manager?

As previously stated, most applications today are migrating to multiuser environments that support local area networks. The OS/2 LAN Manager is a local area network management facility that allows you to share data between systems running DOS, OS/2, or XENIX, as shown in Figure 19-27. The OS/2 LAN Manager integrates OS/2 features and functions. Microsoft has set the standard for operating systems with DOS and OS/2. The goal of the OS/2 LAN Manager is to define the standard local area network.

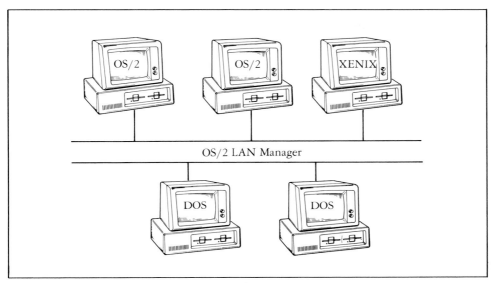

Figure 19-27.

OS/2 LAN Manager

Does OS/2 expand partition sizes?

No. The maximum disk partition size is still 32MB.

What is Codeview?

Codeview is Microsoft's new powerful, full-screen, source code debugger. Using Codeview, you can examine machine code, registers, source code, and even the comments that you embedded within your code. Codeview uses multiple windows to enhance your screen display. Codeview is provided with the OS/2 Software Development Kit. Its manual contains more than 450 pages. Codeview is indeed very functional and quite probably the most powerful debugger available today.

Can I read OS/2 disks from DOS?

Yes. OS/2 must provide full DOS compatibility. As such, OS/2 must be able to execute DOS programs and read DOS files. In this way, OS/2 and DOS disks are fully transportable.

Why does OS/2 need a print spooler?

In a multitasking environment, it is very possible that several programs may attempt to access the system printer at the same time. As stated, OS/2 provides virtual devices to each process, giving them the appearance of owning each device available to the system. In this case, OS/2 directs all printer output to the OS/2 spooler, which creates temporary files on disk. In this way, the spooler can coordinate output destined for the printer, ensuring that data is not intermixed (see Figure 19-28).

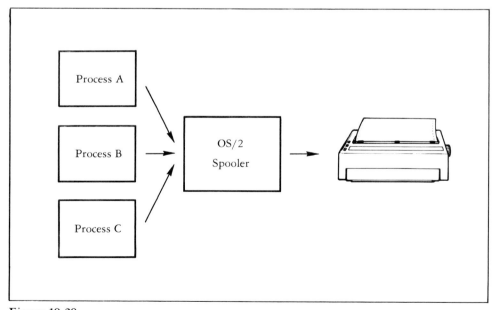

Figure 19-28.

OS/2 print spooler

This chapter has provided you with an overview of many OS/2 concepts. Because of OS/2's tremendous functional capabilities, it is impossible to cover each concept in detail. In fact, the OS/2 Software Development Kit contains eight manuals, the Presentation Manager contains three more, and if you attend an OS/2 developers conference, you get two more. OS/2 is a powerful and complex operating system. This chapter has provided you with a foundation from which you can develop the "OS/2 mindset."

A: ASCII
Codes

Table A-1 lists the ASCII codes for characters.

Table A-1.

ASCII Character Codes

DEC	OCTAL	HEX	ASCII	DEC	OCTAL	HEX	ASCII
0	000	00	NUL	10	012	0A	LF
1	001	01	SOH	11	013	0B	VT
2	002	02	STX	12	014	0C	FF
3	003	03	ETX	13	015	0D	CR
4	004	04	EOT	14	016	0E	SO
5	005	05	ENQ	15	017	0F	SI
6	006	06	ACK	16	020	10	DLE
7	007	07	BEL	17	021	11	DC1
8	010	08	BS	18	022	12	DC2
9	011	09	HT	19	023	13	DC3

Table A-1.

ASCII Character Codes (*continued*)

DEC	OCTAL	HEX	ASCII	DEC	OCTAL	HEX	ASCII
20	024	14	DC4	56	070	38	8
21	025	15	NAK	57	071	39	9
22	026	16	SYN	58	072	3A	:
23	027	17	ETB	59	073	3B	;
24	030	18	CAN	60	074	3C	<
25	031	19	EM	61	075	3D	=
26	032	1A	SUB	62	076	3E	>
27	033	1B	ESC	63	077	3F	?
28	034	1C	FS	64	100	40	@
29	035	1D	GS	65	101	41	A
30	036	1E	RS	66	102	42	B
31	037	1F	US	67	103	43	C
32	040	20	SPACE	68	104	44	D
33	041	21	!	69	105	45	E
34	042	22	"	70	106	46	F
35	043	23	#	71	107	47	G
36	044	24	$	72	110	48	H
37	045	25	%	73	111	49	I
38	046	26	&	74	112	4A	J
39	047	27	'	75	113	4B	K
40	050	28	(	76	114	4C	L
41	051	29	)	77	115	4D	M
42	052	2A	*	78	116	4E	N
43	053	2B	+	79	117	4F	O
44	054	2C	,	80	120	50	P
45	055	2D	−	81	121	51	Q
46	056	2E	.	82	122	52	R
47	057	2F	/	83	123	53	S
48	060	30	0	84	124	54	T
49	061	31	1	85	125	55	U
50	062	32	2	86	126	56	V
51	063	33	3	87	127	57	W
52	064	34	4	88	130	58	X
53	065	35	5	89	131	59	Y
54	066	36	6	90	132	5A	Z
55	067	37	7	91	133	5B	[

Table A-1.

ASCII Character Codes (*continued*)

DEC	OCTAL	HEX	ASCII	DEC	OCTAL	HEX	ASCII
92	134	5C	\	110	156	6E	n
93	135	5D	]	111	157	6F	o
94	136	5E	^	112	160	70	p
95	137	5F	_	113	161	71	q
96	140	60	`	114	162	72	r
97	141	61	a	115	163	73	s
98	142	62	b	116	164	74	t
99	143	63	c	117	165	75	u
100	144	64	d	118	166	76	v
101	145	65	e	119	167	77	w
102	146	66	f	120	170	78	x
103	147	67	g	121	171	79	y
104	150	68	h	122	172	7A	z
105	151	69	i	123	173	7B	{
106	152	6A	j	124	174	7C	|
107	153	6B	k	125	175	7D	}
108	154	6C	l	126	176	7E	~
109	155	6D	m	127	177	7F	DEL

B: DOS Commands

This appendix provides a quick overview of each of the DOS commands. For more detail on each command, refer to *DOS: The Complete Reference,* by Kris Jamsa (Berkeley, Calif.: Osborne/McGraw-Hill, 1987).

APPEND

Format

[drive:][path]APPEND [d:][path][;[d:][p:] . . .];

APPEND requires MS DOS version 3.2.

Function   Specify a search path for data files.

Each time DOS opens a file, it first searches the current directory or specified location for the file. If the file is not found, DOS searches the drives and paths defined in the data path by using APPEND. APPEND is functionally equivalent to the DOS PATH command. If DOS cannot open a file as specified, DOS searches each directory in the data path defined by APPEND until either the file is found, or the search path is exhausted (see Figure B-1).

Examples

```
APPEND ;                   ; Removes the current data search path
                           ; specification, which results in DOS only
                           ; searching the specified location
APPEND C: \DOS; A: \; B: \;   ; If DOS cannot open the file as
                           ; specified, it searches the
                           ; subdirectory \DOS on drive C
                           ; and then the root directories
                           ; on drives A and B (in that order)
APPEND                     ; APPEND without any command-line parameters
                           ; results in the display of the current data
                           ; path
```

ASSIGN

Format

[drive:][path]ASSIGN [[old__drive:][=][new__drive[...]]]

Function   Route I/O request for one disk drive to a new drive. (DOS allows you to direct disk I/O operations from one drive to another.)

Many older software packages *always* look for data and overlay files on drive A. The DOS ASSIGN command allows you to migrate such files to your fixed disk, routing all disk I/O operations from the floppy drive A to the fixed disk (drive C).

Examples

```
ASSIGN                     ; Removes disk drive routing
ASSIGN A = B               ; DOS will route all disk drive references for
                           ; drive A to drive B
ASSIGN A = C   B = C       ; DOS will route all disk drive references
                           ; for either drive A or B to drive C.
```

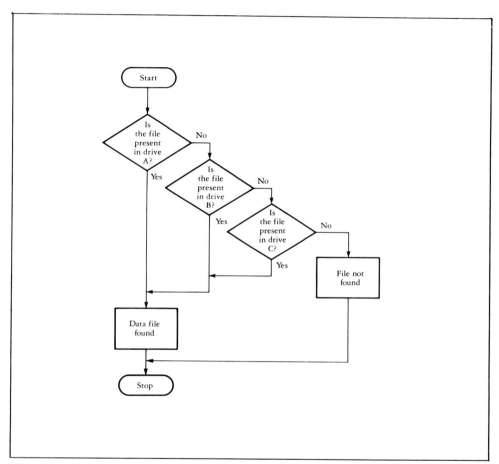

Figure B-1.

Process of searching drives for data
file

ATTRIB

Format

[drive:][path]ATTRIB [+R ¦ −R] [+A ¦ −A] file＿specification

Function   Set or display a file's read-only or archive attributes.

DOS 3.2 is required for the $[+A \mid -A]$ attribute.

Setting a file to read-only prevents inadvertent deletion or modification by DOS. A read-only file cannot be deleted, renamed, or modified.

If you are establishing a system for other end-users, set all of their files to read-only to safeguard them. Chapter 7 shows you how to change a file's attributes from within an application, which allows your programs to access files either in read or in write mode. In this way, a file only can be deleted from within your applications.

ATTRIB modifies a file's attribute byte within the directory entry shown in Table B-1.

Examples

ATTRIB +R *.*	; Sets all files to read-only
ATTRIB −R *.TXT	; Makes all TXT files write-access
ATTRIB +A *.C	; Sets the archive status bit on all
	; files in drive C

Table B-1.

Entry in Directory Structure

Field	Offset
File name	0
Extension	8
Attribute byte	11
Reserved for DOS	12
Time	22
Date	24
Starting cluster number	26
File size	28

AUTOEXEC.BAT

Function Start-up batch procedure.

Each time DOS boots, it searches the root directory for a file called AUTOEXEC.BAT. If the file is found, DOS reads its contents and executes each of the commands that the file contains. If the file is not found, DOS displays the familiar DATE and TIME prompts. (See Figure B-2.)

The OS/2 protected-mode counterpart to AUTOEXEC.BAT is STARTUP.CMD.

Example

```
DATE
TIME
DIR/P
CLS
SP
```

BACKUP

Format

[d:][path]BACKUP *d1*:[*file__spec*] *d2*:
    [/*A*][/*D:mm-dd-yy*][/*M*][/*S*]

Function Back up one or more files to a new disk.

d1: specifies the source disk.

file__spec is the DOS path name(s) for the file(s) to back up.

d2: specifies the target disk.

/*A:* directs BACKUP to append source files to files on the target disk.

/*D:mm-dd-yy* directs BACKUP to back up files modified since the date specified.

/*M directs BACKUP* to back up files modified since the last back-up.

/*S* directs BACKUP to back up all subdirectories files.

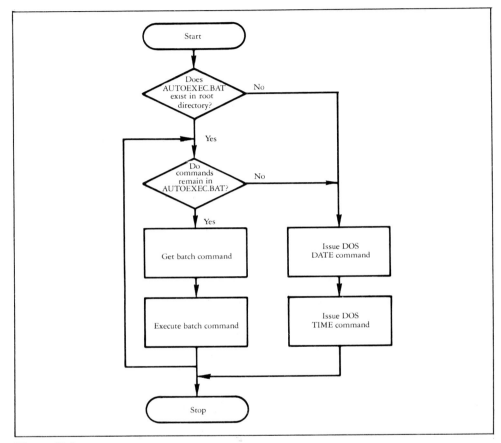

Figure B-2.

Process of displaying DATE and
TIME prompts

BACKUP works closely with each of the file's directory entries to
select specific files for back-up. Note how DOS directory fields closely
relate to the BACKUP command-line qualifiers.

A 10MB disk requires approximately twenty-five 360K floppy disks
or eight 1.2MB disks for a complete back-up.

To support batch processing fully, BACKUP supports the following exit-status values:

0   Successful back-up

1   No files found to back up

2   Shared files not backed up

3   User termination by using CTRL-C

4   Error in processing

Examples

BACKUP C: \A:/S   ; Back up disk in drive C to drive A
BACKUP C:TEST.DAT B:/A   ; Append TEST.DAT to back up files on
                           ; drive B

BATCH FILES

Function   DOS batch processing.

Most users enter DOS commands in an interactive mode at the keyboard. DOS, however, allows you to group commands into files with the BAT extension and then it opens and executes them sequentially.

Consider the following batch file procedure that executes the DOS DATE, TIME, and VER commands:

```
DATE
TIME
VER
```

DOS batch file processing can save you keystrokes by abbreviating a series of commonly used commands or can reduce the time you spend at the computer waiting for a program to complete so that you can issue subsequent commands.

Other related commands include FOR, GOTO, IF, PAUSE, REM, SHIFT, and AUTOEXEC.

BREAK

Format

BREAK [ON ¦ OFF]

Function   Enable/disable DOS CTRL-BREAK processing.

By default, DOS only checks for a user-entered CTRL-BREAK upon completion of I/O operations to standard input, output, print, or auxiliary. BREAK ON requests DOS to check for CTRL-BREAK after each DOS service. BREAK ON increases the amount of overhead DOS must perform and is normally used only during program development.

Examples

BREAK OFF	; Perform only default CTRL-BREAK checking
BREAK ON	; Enable CTRL-BREAK checking
BREAK	; Display current CTRL-BREAK processing status

CHDIR

Format

CHDIR [drive:][path]

or

CD [drive:][path]

Function   Change or display the default directory.

CHDIR changes or displays the current directory name for the specified disk drive. If you do not specify a drive, CHDIR uses the current default drive. If you do not specify a path name, CHDIR displays the current default directory name.

Examples

```
CHDIR                        ; Display the current directory
A:\DOS
CHDIR B:\DOS\BATFILES        ; Set the directory on drive B to
                             ;  \DOS\BATFILES
```

CCHP

Format

CCHP [codepage]

CCHP requires DOS 3.3.

Function   Select the system-wide code page for devices.

To enhance international character set support, DOS 3.3 uses code pages that are tables containing a character set. Before you can use a code page, you must issue the DOS 3.3 command NLSFUNC.

Code page values include

437	United States
850	Multilingual
860	Portuguese
863	French-Canadian
865	Norwegian

Example

CCHP 865   ; Select the Norwegian character set

CHKDSK

Format

CHKDSK [*drive:*][*path*][*filename*] [/F] [/V]

Function   Check a disk's current status.
CHKDSK reports on the following:

- The amount of free, used, and corrupted disk space

- The number of hidden files

- The amount of free and used memory

drive: is the target drive that CHKDSK is to examine.
path and *filename* specify a file to test for contiguity.
/F directs CHKDSK to fix errors found in a directory or FAT.
/V directs CHKDSK to display the names of all files on the disk.

Examples

```
CHKDSK              ; Examine the current disk
CHKDSK *.*          ; Check disk fragmentation
CHKDSK A: /F        ; CHKDSK fixes errors that it
                    ; encounters on drive A. Without /F,
                    ; CHKDSK only displays information
                    ; about each error.
```

CLS

Format

CLS

Function   Clear the screen display.
CLS does not affect video attributes. CLS places the cursor in the
home (upper-left) position.

Example

CLS

COMMAND

Format

COMMAND [*drive:*][*path*][/P][/C *string*][/E:*nnnnn*]

Function   Invoke a secondary command processor.

drive: and *path* specify the location of the command processor.
/P directs DOS to permanently install the command processor in memory.
/C string specifies a command for the command processor to execute. This option is used to execute nested batch files.
/E:*nnnnn* specifies the size of the command processor's environment. *nnnnn* must be less than or equal to 32,768.

The most common uses of COMMAND are to invoke nested batch procedures or to spawn a DOS command from within another application program.

Example

```
REM In BATCH File
:LOOP
PAYROLL
COMMAND /C PAYPROC        ; Execute a nested batch file
GOTO LOOP
```

COMP

Format

[drive:][path]COMP *file_spec file_spec2*

Function   Display the first ten differences between two files.

file＿spec and *file＿spec2* are the complete DOS path names of the files to compare.

COMP displays the differences as hexadecimal offsets into the file. If the files are identical, COMP will display the following message:

Files compare ok

COMP supports DOS wild-card characters.

Examples

```
COMP A.DAT B.DAT
COMP A.DAT B:                    ; Compare the contents of A.DAT on drives A and B
```

CONFIG.SYS

Function   DOS configuration file.

Each time DOS boots, it searches the root directory for the file CONFIG.SYS. If DOS finds the file, it opens it and uses the configuration parameters the file contains to build the system-specific operating system. If DOS cannot find the file, it uses its default values. (see Figure B-3).

Configuration parameters include the following:

```
BREAK= ON ¦ OFF          Default OFF
BUFFERS=n                Default for PC 2; for AT 3
COUNTRY=n                Default normally not specified
DEVICE=filename          Example:  DEVICE=ANSI.SYS
DRIVPARM drive [/checkdoor] [/f:formfactor] [/h:headnum]
              [/nonremoveable] [/s:sectors] [/t:tracks]
FCBS=max, prot           Default 4, 0
FILES=n                  Default 8, use 20
LASTDRIVE=letter         Default E
SHELL=file＿spec          Default COMMAND.COM
STACKS=frame, size       Default 9, 128
```

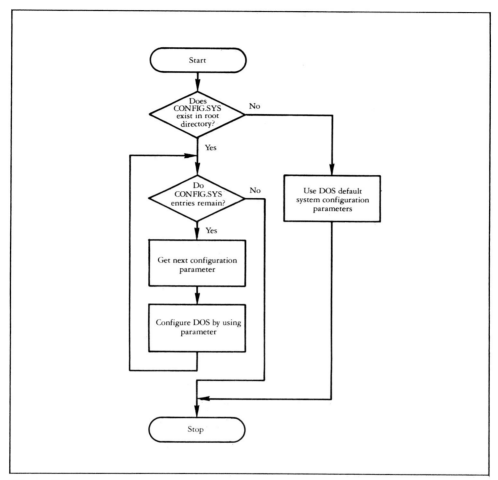

Figure B-3.

Process of searching for CONFIG.SYS
file

COPY

Format

COPY *file＿spec file＿spec2* [*/V*]

Function   Copy one or more files to a new destination.

file__spec is the complete DOS path name of the source file to copy.

file__spec2 is the complete DOS path name of the target file.

/V requests COPY to use disk verification to ensure that a successful copy occurred. This qualifier adds processing overhead. However, it prevents a hardware error from rendering the contents of the source and target files inconsistent.

COPY fully supports DOS wild-card characters.
WARNING: COPY overwrites target files that have the same name.

Examples

```
COPY A:CONFIG.SYS        ; Copy the contents of
B:CONFIG.SAV             ; CONFIG.SYS on drive A
                         ; to the file CONFIG.SAV
                         ; on drive B
COPY A:*.* B:*.*         ; Copy all of the files
                         ; on drive A to drive B
```

CTTY

Format

CTTY *device__name*

Function   Change standard I/O to an auxiliary device.

device__name is the name of the desired device for standard input.

Valid device names include AUX:, COM1:, and COM2:.
To return standard input to the console device, the command CTTY CON must be issued through the auxiliary device.

Example

```
CTTY COM1:            ; Set standard I/O to COM1:
```

DATE

Format

DATE [*mm-dd-yy*]

or

DATE [*dd-mm-yy*]

or

DATE [*yy-mm-dd*]

Function   Set the DOS system date.

mm is the desired month (1-12).
dd is the desired day (1-31).
yy is the desired year (80-99).

The date format *mm-dd-yy* is dependent upon the COUNTRY=
specifier in CONFIG.SYS. For DOS 3.3 and below, if you do not specify a
date, DATE displays the current date but DOS 3.3 does set the system
date on other systems. DATE does not modify the AT system clock. Use
the SETUP option on the diagnostic disk provided with the *AT Guide to
Operations.*

Examples

```
DATE                ; Display the current date
DATE 12/08/87       ; Set the date to Dec. 8 1987
DATE 9/30/88        ; Set the date to Sept. 30 1988
```

DEL

Format

DEL *file＿specification*

Function   Delete a file from disk.

file＿specification is the complete DOS path name of the file to delete. It can contain a drive identification and a subdirectory path. If the drive or path is not specified, DEL uses the current defaults.

> **WARNING:** Once you have deleted a file, DOS cannot retrieve it. DEL will not remove subdirectories. Instead, use RMDIR.

Unless it is overridden with a drive or path specifier, DEL only deletes files in the current directory.

Examples

```
DEL B:CONFIG.OLD                      ; Delete file CONFIG.OLD from drive B
DEL \DOS \COMMANDS \AUTOEXEC.BAT      ; Delete file AUTOEXEC.BAT
                                      ; from the specified
                                      ; subdirectory
```

DIR

Format

DIR [*file＿spec*] [*/P*] [*/W*]

Function   Display a directory listing of files.

DIR lists the files specified by *file＿spec* or all of the files contained in the current directory if *file＿spec* is omitted.

file＿spec is the complete DOS path name of the file(s) to list.

/P directs DIR to pause after each screenful of information and to

display the following prompt:

Strike a key when ready . . .

/*W* directs DIR to display the files in short form (file name only), with five file names across the screen.

Example

```
DIR B:                ; Display a directory listing of the
                      ; files on drive B
DIR *.* /W            ; Display a short-form directory listing
```

DISKCOMP

Format

[drive:][path]DISKCOMP [source—drive:
    [target—drive]][/*1*][/8]

Function   Compare floppy disks.

/*1* directs DISKCOMP to perform a single-sided disk comparison.
/*8* directs DISKCOMP to perform an eight-sector-per-track comparison.

If you have a single floppy system, DISKCOMP will perform a single-drive comparison by prompting you to enter the source and target disks at the correct time.

DISKCOMP displays the following message if the disks are identical:

Compare ok

Otherwise, the side and track (in hex) of the first 10 differences are displayed.

Example

```
DISKCOMP A:  B:        ; Compare the contents of the disk
                       ; in drive A to the disk in drive B
```

DISKCOPY

Format

[drive:][path]DISKCOPY [source__drive:
    [targetdrive]][/1]

Function   Copy a source floppy disk to a target diskette.

/1 directs DISKCOPY to perform a single-sided disk copy.

    DISKCOPY copies the contents of one floppy disk to another. If you have a single-floppy system, DISKCOPY will perform a single-drive copy by prompting you to enter the source and target disks at the correct time.
    DISKCOPY will format an unformatted disk during the copy. DISK-COPY does not correct disk fragmentation.

Example

DISKCOPY A: B: ; Copy the contents of the disk in drive A
                    ; to the disk in drive B

ECHO

Format

ECHO [ON ¦ OFF ¦ MESSAGE]

Function   Display or suppress batch command messages.

ECHO allows you to suppress the display of command names within a DOS batch file as the command executes.

ON allows command name display.

OFF suppresses command name display.

MESSAGE is the string of characters for display.

Examples

ECHO ON	; Batch command names will be
	; displayed as they execute
ECHO %0	; Display the name of the current
	; batch file
ECHO THIS IS A TEST	; Display a message to the user
ECHO OFF	; Suppress command name display

ERASE

Format

ERASE *file __ specification*

Function   Delete a file from disk.

file __ specification is the complete DOS path name of the file to delete. It can contain a drive identification and path name. If the drive or path is not specified, ERASE uses the current defaults.

WARNING: Once you have deleted a file, DOS cannot retrieve it. ERASE will not remove subdirectories. Instead, use RMDIR. Unless overridden with a drive or path specifier, ERASE only deletes files in the current directory.

Examples

ERASE B:CONFIG.OLD	; Delete the file CONFIG.OLD
	; from drive B
ERASE \DOS \COMMANDS	; Delete the file
\AUTOEXEC.BAK	; AUTOEXEC.BAK from the
	; subdirectory \DOS \COMMANDS

EXE2BIN

Format

[drive:][path]EXE2BIN *source __ file* [*target __ file*]

Function   Convert EXE files to COM files.

source—file contains the EXE file to convert.

target—file contains the desired name of the COM file. If this file specification is not provided, a file with the extension BIN is created.

Most applications should remain in EXE format. While COM files are faster-loading and more compact, they cannot be relocated. To be convertible, the COM file must be less than 64K of code and data, have no stack segment, and contain all program references in the same segment.

Example

EXE2BIN TEST.EXE TEST.COM   ; Convert TEST.EXE to a COM file

FASTOPEN

Format

[drive:][path]FASTOPEN [d:][=*numfiles*]

FASTOPEN requires DOS 3.3.

Function   Store in memory the location of recently used files and directories, to reduce the overhead of searching directory entries for files.

numfiles specifies the number of files or directory entries DOS is to store in memory. The value must be in range 10-999 (34 is the current default).

You can repeat FASTOPEN for every drive on your system.

If you make the value of *numfiles* too large, DOS may experience significant overhead searching the list of stored entries.

If you access more than *numfiles* directories or files, DOS replaces the least-recently used file with the last file accessed.

Example

FASTOPEN C:=128   ; Set space aside for 128 files

FDISK

Format

FDISK

Function   Fixed-disk partition configuration.

DOS allows you to separate a fixed disk into four logical sections called *partitions*. Each partition can contain a unique operating system. FDISK allows you to specify the size of each partition along with the active (boot) partition.

Be very careful when using FDISK. An error can result in the loss of all of the data on a disk.

FDISK records partition information in the master boot record that resides in the first sector of every hard disk (see Figure B-4).

For a complete explanation of the FDISK command, see *DOS: The Complete Reference,* by Kris Jamsa (Berkeley, Calif.: Osborne/McGraw-Hill, 1987).

Example

FDISK

FIND

Format

[drive:][path]FIND *"string"* [*file—spec*] [/C][/N][/V]

Function   Search a file(s) or piped input for a string.

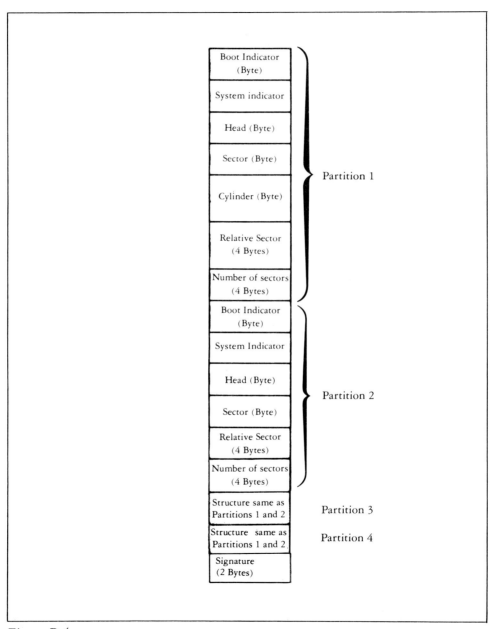

Figure B-4.

Master boot record

string specifies the string to search for (it must be in quotes).

file—spec is the file name to search for the string. It can be a series of file names separated by spaces.

/*C* directs FIND to display a count of occurrences for the string.

/*N* directs FIND to precede each line containing the string with its line number.

/*V* directs FIND to display each line not containing the string.

If /*C* and /*N* are used together, FIND ignores /*N*.

Examples

DIR ¦ FIND "<DIR>"   ; Search for <DIR> from redirected
                            ; input
FIND "begin" TEST.PAS   ; Examine TEST.PAS for all references
                            ; to begin

FOR

Format

FOR %%*variable* IN (*set*) DO *DOS—command*

Function   Provide repetitive execution of DOS commands.

%%*variable* is the FOR loop-control variable that DOS manipulates with each iteration.

set is a list of valid DOS file names. *set* can be a list of DOS file names separated by commas (A, B, C), or it can contain a wild-card character (*.*), or both (A, B, *.DAT).

DOS—command is the command to execute with each iteration.

FOR is used most commonly within DOS batch files. However, FOR can be used from the DOS prompt. The %% before the variable name are used in batch files while % is used from the DOS prompt.

Examples

(DOS PROMPT)	FOR %I IN (*.FOR) TYPE %I	; Display all ; FORTRAN programs
(Batch File)	FOR %%F IN (*.C) CC %%F	; Compile all C ; programs

FORMAT

Format

[*drive:*][path]FORMAT [drive:][/B][/S][/V][/1][/4][/8]

Function   FORMAT a disk for use by DOS.

drive: is the disk drive identification containing the disk to format.

/B directs FORMAT to allocate space on the new disk for the system files, but not to place the files on the disk. (See the SYS command.)

/S directs FORMAT to place the DOS system files on the disk, making the disk bootable.

/V directs FORMAT to prompt you for a disk volume label, as follows:

Volume label (11 characters, ENTER for none)?
/1 directs FORMAT to format the disk single-sided.
/4 directs FORMAT to format the disk double-sided in a quad-density disk drive.
/8 directs FORMAT to format the disk with 8 sectors per track. The default is either 9 or 15 sectors per track.

Examples

FORMAT B:/S	; Format a bootable disk in drive B
FORMAT A:/4	; Format a 360K disk in a 1.2MB ; floppy disk

GOTO

Format

GOTO label__name

Function Branch to the label specified in a BAT file.

DOS label names contain any of the characters valid for DOS file names. If the label does not exist, DOS terminates execution of the batch file.

Example

```
:loop              ; Note the colon (:) preceding the
                   ; label
DIR
GOTO loop          ; No colon before label
```

This batch procedure displays a continuous directory listing until the user presses CTRL-C or CTRL-BREAK.

GRAFTABL

Format

[drive:][path]GRAFTABL

Function Load additional character set data into memory.

The color graphics adapter in medium-resolution tends to blur text in the range ASCII 120 to 255. GRAFTABL loads additional character set data to prevent blurring.

Example

GRAFTABL

GRAPHICS

Format

[drive:][path]GRAPHICS [*printer__type*][/B][/R]

Function   Allow screen contents containing graphics to be printed.

printer__type specifies one of the following:

COLOR	Color printer with black ribbon
COLOR4	Color printer with red, green, and blue ribbon
COLOR8	Color printer with cyan, magenta, yellow, and black ribbon
COMPACT	Compact printer
GRAPHICS	Graphics printer

/B directs GRAPHICS to print the background color.

/R directs GRAPHICS to print white images as black, and vice versa.

Example

GRAPHICS

IF

Format

IF [*NOT*] *condition* DOS__command

Function   Provide conditional processing within DOS batch files.

NOT performs a Boolean NOT on the result of the condition.

condition must be one of the following:

ERRORLEVEL value	True if program exit status is greater than or equal to value
EXIST file__specification	True if the file specified exists
string1==string2	True if both strings are identical

Examples

IF EXIST CONFIG.SYS	; If the file
COPY CONFIG.SYS B:	; CONFIG.SYS exists in
	; the current
	; directory, copy it
	; to drive B
IF NOT ERRORLEVEL 3 GOTO DONE	; If the previous
	; program exited with
	; a status less than 3, branch
	; to the label DONE
IF'%1'=='' GOTO NULL	; Determine if
	; parameter %1 exists

I/O REDIRECTION

Format

DOS__COMMAND > OUTPUT__FILE

or

DOS__COMMAND < INPUT__FILE

or

DOS__COMMAND >> APPEND__FILE

or

DOS__COMMAND ¦ DOS__COMMAND

Function   I/O redirection.

Examples

SORT < INFILE.DAT	; Redirection of input
SORT < DATA.DAT > OUTFILE.DAT	; Redirection of input and
	; output
SORT < DATA.DAT >> OUTDATA.DAT	; Append result to
	; OUTDATA.DAT
SORT < DATA.DAT ¦ MORE	; Pipe the output of SORT to
	; MORE

JOIN

Format

[drive:][path]JOIN [*d1:* [*d2:path*]][/D]

Function   JOIN a disk drive to a DOS path.

JOIN makes two disks appear as one by joining a disk to a DOS path.

d1: specifies the disk drive to join to the path provided.

*d2:*path specifies the join directory.

If you issue a JOIN command without any parameters, JOIN displays the current joins.

DOS will only JOIN a disk to an empty DOS directory.

Examples

JOIN D: C: \JOINDIR	; References to C: \JOINDIR are the same as those
	; to drive D
JOIN	; Display current joins

KEYBxx

Format

[drive:][path]KEYBxx

Function   Load foreign keyboard set.

KEYBxx loads memory-resident software to replace the standard keyboard layout supported by the ROM-BIOS.

Once a new keyboard is installed, you can toggle between it and the default keyboard by pressing CTRL-ALT-F1 for the default and CTRL-ALT-F2 for the foreign keyboard.

Common keyboard layouts include

KEYBFR	France
KEYBGR	Germany
KEYBIT	Italy
KEYBSP	Spain
KEYBUK	United Kingdom

Example

KEYBUK   ; Select the United Kingdom keyboard

LABEL

Format

[*drive:*][path]LABEL [drive:] [*volume__label*]

Function   Specify a disk volume label.

drive: is the disk drive containing the disk to label.

volume__label is the desired 11-character volume label.

If you do not specify a volume label, LABEL will prompt you for one as follows:

Volume label (11 characters, ENTER for none)?

If you do not want to label the disk, simply press ENTER.

Example

LABEL B: DOSDISK

MKDIR

Format

MKDIR [*drive:*]path

or

MD [*drive:*]path

Function   Create the subdirectory specified.

drive: specifies the drive on which to create the subdirectory. If a drive is not specified, MKDIR uses the current default.

The maximum path name that DOS can process is 63 characters.

Examples

MD \IBM	; Create a directory called \IBM
MKDIR \IBM \NOTES	; Create a directory called IBM \NOTES
MKDIR B:TEST	; Create a directory called TEST on drive
	; B

MODE

Format

[drive:][path]MODE *n* (*n* is 40 or 80)

or

[drive:][path]MODE [n],m,[,t] (test pattern alignment)

or

[drive:][path]MODE COM#[:] baud[,parity[,data[,stop[,*P*]]]]

or

[drive:][path]MODE LPT#[:] [*cpl*][,*vli*][,*P*]

or

[drive:][path]MODELPT#[:]=COM#[:]

Function   Specify device characteristics.

P specifies continuous retries on time-out errors.

cpl is characters per line (80, 132).

vli is vertical lines per inch.

Examples

MODE 40	; Set the screen to 40 characters per ; line
MODE LPT1:=COM1:	; Route parallel data from LPT1 to the ; serial port COM1
MODE 80,R,T	; Set the screen to 80 characters per ; line, displaying a test pattern for ; character alignment

MORE

Format

DOS__COMMAND ¦ MORE

or

MORE < DOS__COMMAND

Function   Display a command's output a screenful at a time.

The DOS MORE command reads data from the standard input device, displaying the information to the standard output device a page at a time until end-of-file is encountered. Each time a page of data is displayed on the screen, MORE displays the following message:

--MORE--

Simply press any key to continue the output, or press CTRL-C to terminate the command.

Example

SORT < DATA.DAT ¦ MORE   ; Pipe the output of SORT to
                              ; MORE

NLSFUNC

Format

[drive:][path]NLSFUNC [*file＿specification*]

NLSFUNC requires DOS 3.3.

Function   Provide code-page support for the DOS CCHP command.

file＿specification is the complete DOS path name of the file containing the country information.

You must issue a NLSFUNC command before invoking CCHP.

Example

NLSFUNC COUNTRY.SYS   ; Define the code-page file as
                          ; COUNTRY.SYS

PATH

Format

PATH [[drive:][path] [[;[drive:][path]]...]

Function   Specify command search directories.

Each time DOS executes a COM, EXE, or BAT file, it searches the current working directory for the specified command. If DOS cannot find the file, it checks to see if you have a command path specified. If a command path is present, DOS searches each of the directories listed in the path until the file is found or the list is exhausted (see Figure B-5).

PATH does not validate the existence of paths. Invalid paths are not found until DOS attempts to search them later when looking for a command. If you invoke PATH without parameters, the current command path is displayed. Likewise, if the only parameter is a semicolon, PATH deletes the current path and DOS examines only the default directory for commands.

DOS stores the current command path as an environment entry.

Example

PATH C: \DOS; \C:UTIL;   ; Direct DOS to examine the
                            ; subdirectories \DOS and \UTIL on
                            ; drive C (in that order) for commands
                            ; that do not exist as specified in the
                            ; command line

PAUSE

Format

PAUSE [*message*]

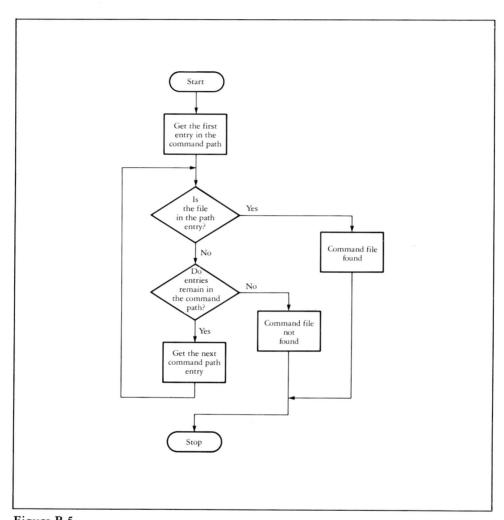

Figure B-5.

Flowchart to determine if file is in
command path

Function   Pause batch file execution and display an optional message as follows:

[optional message text]
Strike a key when ready . . .

message can contain up to 123 characters.

To continue batch processing, press any key. Otherwise, press CTRL-BREAK.

Examples

PAUSE Enter a blank disk in drive B
PAUSE

PREDEFINED FUNCTION KEYS

Function   DOS Function keys.

DOS buffers each command entered in a location in memory that you can access to simplify your command entry. The following are the assignments for function keys:

F1	Copy one character from the previous command buffer
F2	Copy all characters in the buffer that precede the next character typed
F3	Copy all of the characters in the command buffer
F4	Copy all characters including and following the next character typed
F5	Edit the current command buffer
F6	Place a CTRL-Z ($^\wedge$Z) end-of-file marker at the end of a file
INS	Insert characters in the current command buffer
DEL	Delete the character that precedes the cursor
ESC	Cancel the current command line without executing it

PRINT

Format

[drive:][path]PRINT [qualifiers] *file _ spec*

Function   Print a DOS file by using the print queue.

file _ spec is the complete DOS path name of the file to add or remove
to or from the print queue.

PRINT supports wild-card characters.
    Qualifers include the following:

[/B:buffer _ size]
[/C] (cancel a specific file)
[/D:device _ name]
[/M:max _ ticks]
[/P] (add file(s))
[/Q:queue _ size]
[/S:time _ slice]
[/T] (remove all files)
[/U:busy _ ticks]

    Many of the print qualifiers can only be issued with the first PRINT
command. PRINT uses these parameters to configure its data structures
in memory.

Examples

PRINT/Q:32 *.DAT	; Create queue for 32 entries, print *.DAT
	; files
PRINT/T	; Abort all print jobs
PRINT	; Display all files in the print queue

PROMPT

Format

PROMPT [*prompt — string*]

Function   Define the DOS prompt.

prompt — string is the character string that defines the DOS prompt. It can contain characters or the following metastrings:

$b	¦ character
$d	date
$e	ESC
$h	backspace
$g >	character
$l <	character
$n	current drive
$p	current dir
$q	= character
$t	current time
$v	DOS version
$_	CR LF
$$	$ character

If no string is specified, PROMPT resets the system prompt to the current default drive.

Examples

PROMPT WHAT?	; Sets system prompt to "WHAT?"
PROMPT $t	; Sets system prompt to the current
	; system time

RECOVER

Format

[drive:][path]RECOVER *file__spec*

or

[drive:][path]RECOVER *drive:*

Function   Recover corrupted files.

RECOVER only recovers corrupted files. RECOVER will not unerase a file. Use a third-party software package to do so.

file__spec specifies the name of the file containing bad sectors.

drive: specifies a disk drive with corrupted files. RECOVER will place files in the root directory with the name FILE*nnnn*.REC where *nnnn* begins with 0001. These files contain the recovered files up to a bad sector.

RECOVER uses the FAT as shown in Chapter 10 to recover corrupted files.

Example

RECOVER B: ; Recover the entire disk contained in drive B

REM

Format

REM [*message*]

Function   Display comments during batch file execution.

REM allows you to display messages to the standard output device during the execution of batch (BAT) files. *message* is an optional command-line parameter that contains the message. The DOS command ECHO OFF inhibits the display of messages by REM.

Example

```
:DONE
REM About to display directory listing
DIR
REM Directory listing completed
REM
GOTO DONE
```

RENAME

Format

REN *file _ specification filename*[.ext]

or

RENAME *file _ specification filename*[.ext]

Function   Rename the specified file.

file _ specification is the complete DOS path name of the file to rename. It can contain a drive and a DOS subdirectory path.

filename cannot have a drive or a DOS subdirectory path.

The renamed file resides in the same directory on the same disk drive as the source file.

RENAME supports DOS wild-card characters.

Examples

REN B:*.BAK *.SAV   ; Files remain on drive B
RENAME \DOS*.SYS *.XXX   ; Path name on source files only

RESTORE

Format

[drive:][path]RESTORE *drive:file__specification* [/P][/S]

Function   Restore files saved by BACKUP.

drive:file__specification specifies the files to restore.

/P directs RESTORE prompt to the user before restoring files that have been modified or set to read-only since the back-up.

/S directs RESTORE to restore files contained in subdirectories.

     To support DOS batch processing, RESTORE provides the following exit-status values:

0   Successful restoration
1   No files found to restore
2   Shared files not restored
3   User termination via CTRL-C
4   Restoration error

Examples

RESTORE A:*.* C: /S   ; Restore files from drive A,
                           ; including subdirectories
RESTORE A:*.DAT C:/P   ; Prompt the user before restoring
                           ; files that have been modified
                           ; since the back-up
RESTORE A:*.* B:*.* /S/P

RMDIR

Format

RMDIR [*drive:*] path

or

RD [*drive:*] path

Function   Remove the specified directory.

drive: specifies the drive from which to remove the subdirectory. If a drive is not specified, RMDIR uses the current default.

The maximum path name that DOS can process is 63 characters. A directory must be empty before it can be removed.

Examples

RD \IBM	; Remove the directory \IBM
RMDIR \IBM \NOTES	; Remove the directory \IBM \NOTES

ROOT DIRECTORY

Function   Every DOS disk has a root directory from which all subdirectories grow. The back slash (\ ) represents the root directory.

Each root directory is restricted to a fixed number of files as follows:

Disk Type	File Limit
Single-sided disk	64 file entries
Double-sided disk	112 file entries
Quad-density disk	224 file entries
Hard-disk	512 file entries

Use DOS subdirectories to improve your disk organization. If you are using a hard disk, attempt to restrict your root directory to the files CONFIG.SYS, COMMAND.COM, and AUTOEXEC.BAT.

REPLACE

Format

[drive:][path]REPLACE *file—specification* [*drive:*][*path*] [/A][/P][/R][/S][/W]

Function   Replace all files on the target disk with files found on source disk.

file—specification is the complete DOS path name for the source file(s) that are to replace a file(s) on the target drive.

drive: contains the target drive for the file replacement.

path contains the target DOS subdirectory path for the file replacement.

/A directs REPLACE to only replace those files not already contained in the target location.

/P directs REPLACE to prompt you before replacing a file, as follows:

Replace FILENAME.EXT (Y/N)?

/R directs REPLACE to replace files marked as read-only.

/S directs REPLACE to search all directories on the target disk for a matching file name.

/W directs REPLACE to prompt you before beginning, as follows:

Press any key to begin replacing file(s)

To support DOS batch processing, REPLACE uses the following exit-status codes:

0   Successful replacement of all files
2   Source file not found
3   Source or target path not found
5   Access denied
8   Insufficient memory
11 Invalid command format
15 Invalid source or target drive
22 Incorrect DOS version

Examples

REPLACE A: *.* B:/S	; Replace all of the files on drive A to
	; drive B, including subdirectories
REPLACE A:*.DAT B:/P	; Replace all of the DAT files on drive B
	; with those found on drive A

SELECT

Format

[drive:][path]SELECT [[*A:* | *B:*] *d:*[*path*]] *ccode kcode*

Function   Select international country support.

A: and *B:* specify source drive for the keyboard commands.

d:[*path*] specifies the target location of the country files.

ccode is the country code.

kcode is the keyboard code.

Country	kcode	ccode
France	KEYBFR.COM	33
Germany	KEYBGR.COM	49
Italy	KEYBIT.COM	39
Spain	KEYBSP.COM	34
U.K.	KEYBUK.COM	44

Example

SELECT 033 KEYBFR.COM   ; Select FRENCH support

SET

Format

SET [name=[value]]

Function   Place or display DOS environment entries.

The DOS SET command sets or displays entries in the DOS environment. The DOS environment provides a storage location for system specifics. DOS commands such as PROMPT and PATH place entries in the environment.

SET converts all entries to UPPERCASE.

SET with no parameters displays the current environment.

Examples

SET	; Display environment entries
SET FILE=TEST.DAT	; Place an entry in the
	; environment
SET FILE	; Remove value for FILE

SHARE

Format

SHARE [/*F:nnnnn*] [/*L:nnn*]

Function   Enable file-sharing support.

/*F:nnnnn* specifies the number of bytes to allocate for file space. Each open file requires 74 bytes. The default is 2048 bytes.

/*L:nnn* specifies the number of locks required. The default is 20.

DOS 3.0 and greater support file- and record-locking. Each time a file is opened when file-sharing is enabled, DOS checks to see if the file is locked. Likewise, on each record read or write, DOS first checks to see if the record is currently locked.

Examples

```
SHARE                  ; Enable file-sharing with defaults
SHARE /F:4096 /L:30    ; Enable file-sharing with space for
                       ; 148 files and 30 locks
```

SHIFT

Format

SHIFT

Function   Shift each batch parameter left one position.

If more than 10 parameters are passed to a DOS batch procedure, you can use the SHIFT command to access each parameter past %9. If no parameter exists to the right of a parameter, SHIFT assigns the parameter a NULL string.

Example

```
ECHO OFF                          ; TEST 1 2 3 will
                                  ; display:
:LOOP                             ; 1
IF'%1'=="  GOTO DONE              ; 2
ECHO %                            ; 3
SHIFT
GOTO
LOOP
:DONE
```

SORT

Format

DOS__COMMAND ¦ SORT [/R][/+n]

or

SORT [/R][/+n] < file

Function   DOS sort filter.

The DOS SORT command reads data from the standard input device, sorting and displaying the information to the standard output device until end-of-file is encountered.

/R directs SORT to sort the data in reverse order.

/+n allows you to specify the column on which to sort the data.

Examples

```
SORT < DATA.DAT ¦ MORE           ; Pipe the output of SORT to
                                 ; MORE
SORT /R < DATA.DAT               ; Sort DATA.DAT in reverse
                                 ; order
```

SUBST

Format

SUBST [*drive:*] [*path*][/*D*]

Function   Substitute a drive name for a DOS path name.

Because DOS path names can become quite large, DOS allows you to substitute a drive identifier for a path name.

drive: is the disk drive identification that will be used to reference the path.

path is the DOS path name to abbreviate.

/*D* directs SUBST to remove a previous disk substitution.

If you invoke SUBST without any parameters, current substitutions are displayed.

Examples

```
SUBST E: \DOS \HELPFILE \COMMANDS    ; Abbreviate the directory as
                                     ; E:
SUBST                                ; Display current
                                     ; substitutions
```

SYS

Format

[drive:][path]SYS drive:

Function   Transfer operating system files to a disk.

SYS places the required hidden files and DOS command interpreter (COMMAND.COM) to the disk contained in the specified drive to make the disk fully bootable.

The target disk must be empty, previously formatted with /B, or previously formatted with /S.

If these attributes do not exist, the system cannot be transferred. Hidden files include IBMDOS.COM, IBMBIOS.COM (PC DOS); MSDOS.SYS, IO.SYS (MS DOS).

Example

```
SYS B:                    ; Transfer system files to the disk in
                          ; drive B
```

TIME

Format

TIME [*HH:MM*[*:SS*[.*hh*]]]

Function   Set the DOS system time.

HH is the desired hours (0-23).

MM is the desired minutes (1-59).

SS is the desired seconds (0-59).

hh is the desired hundredths of seconds (0-99).

If you do not specify a time, TIME displays the current time for DOS 3.3 and below. TIME does not modify the AT system clock. DOS 3.3 does set the system clock. Use the SETUP option provided with the *AT Guide to Operations.*

Examples

```
TIME                      ; Display the current system time
TIME 12:00                ; Set the time to noon
TIME 00:00:00.00          ; Set the time to midnight
```

TREE

Format

TREE [*drive:*][/F]

Function   Display directory structure.

TREE displays the name of each directory on a disk.

drive: is the disk drive of which to display the directory structure.

/F directs TREE to also display the name of each file in a directory.

Examples

```
TREE                        ; Display the directory structure
TREE B:/F                   ; Also display file names
```

TYPE

Format

TYPE *file __ specification*

Function   Display a file's contents.

file __ specification is the complete name of the file to display. It can contain a drive identification path name. If the drive or path is not specified, TYPE uses the current defaults.

TYPE is restricted to ASCII files. Do not TYPE COM or EXE files. These file types contain unprintable characters that will cause your screen to beep and display garbled characters.

Examples

```
TYPE CONFIG.SYS              ; Display the contents of CONFIG.SYS
TYPE B: \DOS \AUTOEXEC.SAV   ; Display a file on drive B
```

VER

Format

VER

Function   Display the DOS version number.

DOS version numbers are comprised of a major and minor version number combination. For example, DOS 3.2 has a major version number of 3 and a minor version number of 2.

Example

VER
IBM Personal Computer DOS Version 3.0

VERIFY

Format

VERIFY [ON ¦ OFF]

Function   Enable or disable disk I/O verification.

If VERIFY is ON, DOS will read each disk sector it writes to ensure that the data was correctly recorded on disk. This prevents disk corruptions from causing invalid data to be recorded. Assume that the user enters the following command with disk verification enabled:

COPY SOURCE.DAT TARGET.DAT

Visualize the processing as shown in Figure B-6.

Disk I/O verification, however, induces a significant amount of system overhead and is normally only used during system back-ups. If you invoke VERIFY without any parameters, the current status of disk I/O verification is displayed.

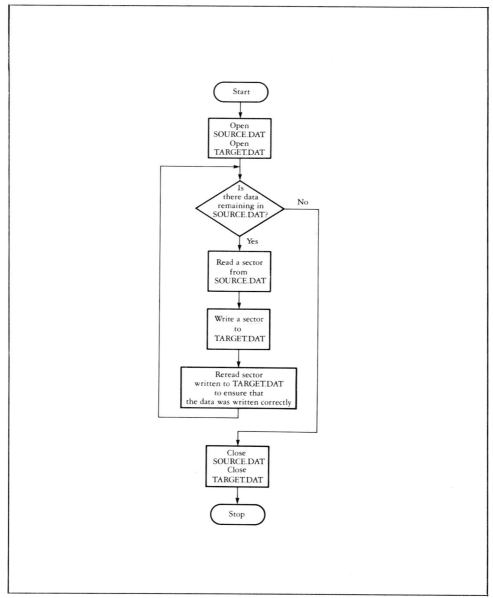

Figure B-6.

DOS recognizes differences between
source and target sectors

Examples

VERIFY	; Display current status
VERIFY OFF	; Disable disk I/O verification
VERIFY ON	; Turn on verification

VOL

Format

VOL [drive:]

Function   Display a disk volume label.

DOS volume labels are 11-character names assigned to a disk. Volume names use the same characters as DOS file names. If you do not specify a target drive, DOS uses the current default.

To assign a volume label, use the DOS LABEL command.

Example

VOL	; Display the current volume
	; label Volume in drive A is DOSUSER

XCOPY

Format

[drive:][path]XCOPY *file＿spec file＿spec2* [*qualifiers*]

Function   Copy files including those in subdirectories (DOS 3.2).

file＿spec is the source file to copy.

file＿spec2 is the target file to receive the copy.

qualifiers include the following:

/A copy only files whose archive bit is set. Do not modify the bit.
/D:mm-dd-yy copy files created or modified since the date given.
/E create all subdirectories on the target drive.
/M copy only files whose archive bit is set. Clear the bit.
/P prompt before each copy, as follows:

FILENAME.EXT (Y/N)?

/S copy files from all subdirectories below the source file.
/V use disk verification to ensure success.
/W prompt before beginning, as follows:

Press any key to begin copying file(s)

Example

XCOPY A: *.* B: /S

Trademarks

Apple®	Apple Computer, Inc.
AT™	International Business Machines Corporation
CodeView™	Microsoft Corporation
Color/Graphics Adapter™	International Business Machines Corporation
CP/M®	Digital Research, Inc.
dBASE®	Ashton-Tate
Extended Graphics Adapter™	International Business Machines Corporation
IBM®	International Business Machines Corporation
Lotus®	Lotus Development Corporation
Microsoft®	Microsoft Corporation
MS-DOS®	Microsoft Corporation
1-2-3®	Lotus Development Corporation
OS/2™	International Business Machines Corporation
PS/2™	International Business Machines Corporation
Topview™	International Business Machines Corporation
Turbo Pascal®	Borland International, Inc.
UNIX®	AT&T
WordStar®	MicroPro International Corporation
XENIX®	Microsoft Corporation
XT™	International Business Machines Corporation

Index

80286, Intel, 802
80386, Intel, 802, 805
8088, Intel, 808

A
Address space, virtual, 679, 818
Addressing the PC, 349-386
Allocate memory paragraphs, 255
ANSI (OS/2), 749
ANSI.SYS, 117-121, 650
API services (OS/2), 278-312, 379, 712-719, 812
   list of, 718
APPEND, 180-182, 855
APPEND (OS/2), 750
Application Program Interface (API), 278-312, 379, 712-719, 812
Applications, OS/2, 728-741
ASCII codes, 851-853
ASCIIZ strings, 199
Assembly language, mapping values with, 273
ASSIGN, 856
ASSIGN (OS/2), 750
ATTRIB, 332, 857
ATTRIB (OS/2), 751
Attribute byte, get/set, 251
Attributes, file, 330-335
AUTOEXEC.BAT, 67-68, 829, 859
Available disk space, 318-320
Available memory, checking, 336-337

B
Background tasks, OS/2, 825

BACKUP, 859
BACKUP (OS/2), 752
Base table, disk, 497
Batch commands, 37-63
   background, 73
   conditional, 47-54
   iterative, 55-58
Batch file diskette, removing, 64
Batch files, 861
   creating with EDLIN, 32
Batch parameters, 58-63
Batch procedures, nested, 65-66
Batch processing, 25-76
   OS/2, 68-76, 792, 828
Binary trees, 583
BIND utility, OS/2, 710-712, 724, 813
Block devices, 122-123
Boot record, 430
   example, 495
   fixed disk, 480
   mapping the, 535-540
   master, 876
BREAK, 107-109, 862
BREAK (OS/2), 752
Buffered keyboard input, 210
BUFFERS, 109-114
Byte, 350

C
C, command-line processing from, 390-393.
   (*See also* Microsoft C)
CALL (OS/2), 69, 753
CCHP, 863

CCHP (OS/2), 754

Central processing unit. (*See* CPU)

Change DOS default subdirectory, service, 242

Character codes, ANSI, 119

Character devices, 122-123

CHDIR, 167-170, 862

CHDIR (OS/2), 754

Check character available from std. input device, 211

Child process exit code, get, 259

Child subdirectories, 158

Chips, memory, 355

CHKDSK, 440, 505, 863

CHKDSK (OS/2), 755

CHRN values, 486-490

CL command-line options (Microsoft C), 707

Clear keyboard buffer, 212

Clear screen routine, Turbo Pascal, 375

Clipboard, 693

Close a file opened via a FCB, 216

Close a file via DOS file handles, 245

CLS, 864

CLS (OS/2), 755

Clusters, 434-437
using to delete files, 453

CMD (OS/2), 756
file extensions (OS/2), 72

CMD.EXE, 827
versus COMMAND.COM, 747-749

CODE (OS/2), 720

Code segments, OS/2 attribute bits, 381

Code space, sharing, 686, 820

Code-page switching, 131
specifying, 136

CODEPAGE (OS/2), 135

Codeview, 847

COMMAND, 65, 865

COMMAND (OS/2), 757

Command line operator, OS/2, 101

Command summary
DOS, 855-906
OS/2, 743-795

Command-line processing, 387-412
C, 390-393
DOS, 399-406
OS/2, 828
Turbo Pascal, 393-398

COMMAND.COM versus CMD.EXE, 747-749

Commands,
background, 73
batch, 29, 37-63
entering, 388
functions of new OS/2, 827
internal and external, 747-749

COMP, 865

COMP (OS/2), 757

Compatibility, DOS and OS/2, 801

Compatibility mode, OS/2, 710, 811

Compiler, 342-347

COMSPEC, 511

Conditional processing, 27

Conditional processing based on exit-status, 325

CONFIG.SYS, 91, 105-126, 830, 866

Configuration parameters, OS/2, 830

Console device, copying from, 30

Console input without character echo, 208

Context switching, 677, 833

COPY, 867

COPY (OS/2), 758

Copying from the console device, 30

COUNTRY, 114-116

Country-dependent information, get, 240

CPU
time-sharing on the, 676
utilization of, 7-15

Create a file via DOS file handles, 243

Create a file via FCB, 219

Create a new file, service, 270

Create DOS subdirectory, service, 240

Creating unique files, 327

Critical sections, 839

CTRL-BREAK interrupt, capturing, 108

CTRL-BREAK processing, 335
get/set state of, 237

CTRL-C or CTRL-BREAK, 35
CTRL-Z, 30
CTTY, 868
Current directory, 162
    get, 254
Cylinders, 476

D
DATA (OS/2), 720
Data, sharing, 820
Database programs, 579
DATE, 869
DATE (OS/2), 759
Date and time, specifying, 604-605
    get DOS, 229
    set DOS, 231
Date/time stamp, get/set, 266
DEF (OS/2), 719-724
Default disk drive, select, 214
Define new program-segment prefix, 227
DEFSEG (BASIC) __, 359
DEL, 870
DEL (OS/2), 760
Delete a file via FCB, 217
Delete file system service, 249, 602
Deleting files, 447-460
Deletions, sure-kill, 460-461
Demand paging, 682
Descendants, root directory, 159
DESCRIPTION (OS/2), 721
Descriptor tables, OS/2, 380
Design considerations, OS/2, 800
DETACH (OS/2), 73-76, 760, 826
DEVICE, 116-122
Device
    drivers, 116-122
    monitors, 841
    virtualization, 686
Devices, virtual, 820
DEVINFO (OS/2), 136
DIR, 870
DIR (OS/2), 761
Direct console I/O, 207
Direct memory access, 367

Directories
    changing, 167
    changing in batch files, 64
    creating, 166
    current, 162
    managing DOS, 155-190
    manipulating within applications, 188
    naming, 187
    removing, 170
    using in OS/2, 189-190
Directory, displaying in OS/2, 731
Directory entries, 442-447
Directory files, reading, 461-471
Disk buffer flush, 213
Disk drive
    get current, 220
    setting in OS/2, 732
Disk drive status values, 316
Disk hub, 415
Disk I/O verification status, get, 263
Disk layout, basics of, 421
Disk space
    checking available, 318-320, 471
    get available, 239
Disk space allocation, 428-432
Disk spindle, 417
Disk structure, 413-483
Disk verification, 473
    set, 234
Disk-transfer address
    get, 234, 609
    set, 220
DISKCOMP, 427, 871
DISKCOMP (OS/2), 762
DISKCOPY, 424-425, 872
DISKCOPY (OS/2), 762
Disks. (*See also* Fixed, Floppy)
    elements of DOS, 486
    exchanging DOS and OS/2, 847
Display character to standard output device, 203
Display string to the standard output device, 209
DISPLAY.SYS (DOS 3.3), 131-133

DLL. (*See* Dynamic link libraries)
DOS 3.3 parameters, 126-134
DOS get date service, 229
DOS set date service, 231
DOS version number, 235
DOS, future of, 806
DPATH (OS/2), 763
Drive allocation table information, 222
Drive names, substituting for path names, 183-185
DRIVER.SYS (DOS 3.3), 134
Drives, joining to a directory structure, 185
DRIVPARM, 122-123
Duplicate a file handle, 252
Dynamic link libraries, 137-140, 845
Dynamic linking, 713
Dynamic priority, 148

E
ECHO, 44-46, 872
ECHO (OS/2), 764
EDLIN, 32
EGA, code-page switching with, 131
End-of-file marker, 30
ENDLOCAL (OS/2), 71, 764
Environment entries, utilizing, 517
Environment
    DOS, 503-523
    DOS 3.3, 520
    OS/2, 519-523
    segment address, 509
ERASE, 873
Error
    handling, 314-318
    information, extended, 267
    messages, bypassing I/O redirection, 98
    status codes, 315, 555
ERRORLEVEL, 47
Errors, parity, 356
Escape symbol, OS/2, 103
EXE structure, OS/2, 712-719
EXE2BIN, 873
Execution path, defining, 177-180
EXIST, 47
EXIT (OS/2), 765

Exit-status processing, 322-326
EXPORTS (OS/2), 721
Extended error information, get, 267
EXTPROC (OS/2), 70, 765

F
FASTOPEN, 874
FAT, 433-442, 491. (*See also* File Allocation Table)
FCBS, 123-124. (*See also* File Control Blocks)
FDISK, 875
FDISK (OS/2), 766
File allocation table, 433-442
File attributes, 251, 330-335
File comparison routine, 564
File control block random access read, 224
File control block random access write, 224
File control blocks, 3, 123-124
    contents of, 551-552
    services involving, 215-219
File deletion, 447-460
File handles, 3, 91-92, 124-125, 552-569
    predefined, 564
    service for closing files via, 245
    service for creating files via, 243
    service for duplicating, 252
    service for opening files via, 244
    service for reading from, 246
    service for writing to, 248
File manipulation, OS/2, 624-641
File manipulation routines, advanced, 602-606
File matching, 607. (*See also* System services)
File name, parse, 229
File operations, 549-641
File pointers, 570
File size, get via FCB, 225
FILES, 91, 124-125
Files
    accessing subdirectory, 172-174
    batch, 25-76, 861
    creating temporary, 327
    creating unique, 326-327
    database, 587
    date and time stamping, 546-548

Files, *continued*
    indexed, 579
    OBJ and LIB, 342-347
    overlay, 529-532
    random-access, 569-602
FIND, 875
FIND (OS/2), 767
Find first matching directory entry via FCB, 216
Find first matching file, 260, 608-612
Find next matching directory entry via FCB, 217
Find next matching file, 261, 608-612
Fixed disk architecture, 480
Fixed disks, 476-483
    formatting, 501
Floppy disks, design of, 414
Flush disk buffers, 555. (*See* also Disk buffers)
FOR, 55-58, 877
FOR (OS/2), 767
Force handle duplication, 253
FORMAT, 485-501, 878
FORMAT (OS/2), 768
Free allocated memory paragraphs, 255
Free disk space, determining, 471
Function keys,
    predefined, 889
    predefined (OS/2), 777

G
Get character from standard aux device, 204
Get character from standard input device, 202
Get current directory, 254
Get current disk drive, 220
Get current drive allocation table information, 222
Get disk-transfer address, 234
Get file size via FCB, 225
Get specific drive allocation table information, 223
Get system time, 232
Global descriptor table (OS/2), 379
GOTO, 51, 879
GOTO (OS/2), 768

GRAFTABL, 879
GRAFTABL (OS/2), 769
GRAPHICS, 506, 649, 880
Graphics adapters, OS/2 and, 805

H
Handle, OS/2, 377
Handles, file, 552-569. (*See also* File handles)
Hard disks, 476-483
    formatting, 501
Hardware requirements, OS/2, 801
HEAPSIZE (OS/2), 722
HELPMSG (OS/2), 769
High-level language interface routines, 272-277
History of DOS, 3-4

I
I/O operations, disk, 551-602
I/O protection level, 136
I/O redirection, 77-85, 881
    command-line parameters and, 402-412
    operators, OS/2, 793-795
    programming, 92-100
IBM PC, ROM dates, 361
IBM Proprinter, device drivers for, 127-131
IBM PS/2 display screens, 131
IBMBIO.COM, 493
IBMDOS.COM, 493
IF, 47, 880
IF (OS/2), 770
IMPORTS (OS/2), 722
Indexed files, 579
Input device, standard, 78
INT 13H, 488
INT 21H, 194-199
INT 23H, 335
INT 24H, 315-316
Integer values, range of, 351
Interactive processing, 26
Interface routines, high-level language, 272-277
International country characteristics, 114-116
Interprocess communication, 692-696, 836
    example of, 736

Interrupt services, ROM-BIOS, 423
Interrupt values, ROM-BIOS, 491
Interrupt vector, 527, 645
   get, 238
   set, 226
Interrupts, 194
   invoking memory resident programs,
     644
   machine code for hardware, 646
Interrupt-service routines, 644
Invalid command message, 35
Invoke keyboard service, 212
IOPL (OS/2), 136, 844
IO.SYS, 493
IPC, 836. (*See also* Interprocess
  communication)
Iterative processing, 55-58

J
JOIN, 185-186, 882
JOIN (OS/2), 771

K
K, meaning of, 356
Keyboard scan codes, 651
KEYBxx, 882
KEYBxx (OS/2), 772

L
LABEL, 883
LABEL (OS/2), 772
LAN Manager, 700, 846
LASTDRIVE, 125
LIBPATH (OS/2), 137-140
Libraries
   dynamic link, 713
   object code, 342-347
LIBRARY (OS/2), 722
Link list, 588
Linker, 342-347
Linking, static and dynamic, 713
Load or execute a second program, 257
Local descriptor table (OS/2), 377
Lock or unlock block of file, 272
Looping, batch commands for, 51
LSEEK, 250, 571

M
Machine status word, 808
MAKE (OS/2), 725-727
Matching files, finding, 260
MAXWAIT (OS/2), 140-143
Media descriptor byte, 437
   contents of, 544
Media descriptors, information, 543-546
MEMMAN (OS/2), 143-147
Memory addressing, 349-386
   OS/2, 377-386
   segmented and offset, 357-367
Memory buffers, 109-114
Memory management, 16-22
   OS/2, 143-147
Memory map
   DOS, 525-532
   OS/2, 532-535
Memory mapping, 367-376
Memory paragraphs, 255
Memory resident programs, 643-671
   DOS environment and, 507
   OS/2 and, 669-671
Memory. (*See also* Virtual memory)
   checking available, 336-337
   cost of, 351
   paging, 817
   physical, 350-367, 818
   shared, 692, 836
   virtual, 377
Message processing, 836
   OS/2, 738
   subliminal, 659
Message queues, 692
Microfloppy disks, 415
Microsoft C
   creating protected mode programs in,
     809
   interface routines, 272-277
   using in OS/2, 706
Microsoft FORTRAN, 363-365
   interface routines, 272-277
Microsoft Windows, 6
   influence of, 804

MKDIR, 166, 884
MKDIR (OS/2), 773
MODE, 884
MODE (OS/2), 774
Mode of execution, displaying in OS/2, 730
Modify previously allocated memory, 256
Module-definition file (DEF), 719-724, 813
Monitor program, 11
MORE, 885
MORE (OS/2), 775
Mouse interface, 701-703
Move file pointer, 569
MSDOS.SYS, 493
Multiprogramming operating system, 7
Multitasking, 675-677
Music, generating in OS/2, 730

N
NAME (OS/2), 723
Networking, OS/2, 700
NLSFUNC, 886
NOMOVE (OS/2), 145
NOSWAP (OS/2), 145
Not ready error, handling, 314-318
NULL, 62

O
Object code libraries, 342-347
Office automation, OS/2 and, 805
Offset address, 349, 357-367
Open a file based upon a FCB, 215
Open a file via DOS file handles, 244
Open file system service, 553
Open-status values, 555
Operating system attributes, specifying, 107
Operating system, multiprogramming, 7
Operators, redirection, 104
OS/2
    batch processing under, 68-76
    command summary, 743-795
    comparing performance to DOS, 807
    compatibility with DOS, 801
    design considerations, 800
    environment issues, 519-523
    example applications, 728-741

OS/2, *continued*
    factors in development of, 798
    file manipulation in, 624-641
    functions of new commands, 827
    I/O redirection in, 100-104
    memory addressing in, 377-386
    memory resident programs and,
        669-671
    overview of, 673-703
    programming considerations, 705-741
    questions and answers, 797-849
    Software Development Kit, 802
    sources of information on, 803
    starting up, 830
    structure of, 689-691
    swapping process in, 19
    system requirements of, 687
    time to develop, 799
    utilization of time slices in, 15
Output device, standard, 78
Overlays, 529-532

P
Paging, 815-817
Parameters
    command, 388
    command-line, 402
    DOS 3.3, 126-134
    OS/2, 72, 831
    passing to batch procedures, 58-63
    system configuration, 105-153, 831
Parity errors, 356
Parity, memory, 355
Parse file name, 229
Partitions, 476
PATCH (OS/2), 776
PATH, 177-180, 517, 887
PATH (OS/2), 776
Path names, 163
Paths
    defining, 177-180
    effect on system performance, 182
PAUSE, 40-43, 887
PAUSE (OS/2), 777

PC convertible LCD screen, 131
PEEK function, BASIC, 361
PEEK routine for Microsoft FORTRAN,
    363-365
Personal computers, trends in usage of, 674
Physical memory, 818
PID, 826
Pipe operator, 78, 85-89, 836
Platters, disk, 476
POKE function, BASIC, 367
POKE routine for Microsoft FORTRAN,
    369-371
Predefined function keys, 889
    OS/2, 777
Presentation Manager, 701-703, 841-843
PRINT, 340, 890
PRINT (OS/2), 778
Print-screen operations, disabling, 647
Print-screen interrupt, capturing, 655-658
Print spooler, 848
Printer status values, 317
PRINTER.SYS (DOS 3.3), 127-131
Printing, spooled, 340-341
PRIORITY (OS/2), 147-148
Priority assignment, OS/2, 15
Priority scheduling (OS/2), 140, 697-698,
    834
Procedures, batch, 25-76
Process identification, 826
Program, load or execute a second, 257
Program-segment prefix (PSP), 399-400,
    540-543
    define new, 227
Program termination, 199-201
    with status, 258
Programming considerations
    DOS, 313-347
    OS/2, 705-741
Programs
    compatibility-mode, 811
    concurrent, 836
    memory-resident, 643-671
    migrating across modes, 811
    well-behaved, 669

PROMPT, 891
PROMPT (OS/2), 779
Prompt, setting the system, 504
Protected mode, 148, 678
    definition of, 807
    session, 744
Protected versus real mode, 22-23
PROTECTONLY (OS/2), 148
PROTMODE (OS/2), 723

Q
Queues, 836

R
RAM disk, 118
Random block read via FCB, 228
Random block write via FCB, 228
Random-access files, 569-602
Read file handle, 556
Read from DOS file handle, 246
Read/write opening, 415
Read/write pointer, 570
Real mode, 148
    addressing, 349
    definition of, 808
    preventing execution in, 809
    session in OS/2, 744
    switching from, 709
Real versus protected mode, 22-23, 678
Records, adding and deleting database, 591
RECOVER, 892
RECOVER (OS/2), 780
Recursive batch functions, 66-67
Redirection operators, 78-85
    OS/2, 793-795
    table of, 104
Redirection suppression operator, OS/2, 103
Redirection, I/O, 77-85, 881
    OS/2, 100-104
    programming, 92-100
Registers, 8088, 192-194
Relative record number field, set, 225
REM, 37-40, 892
REM (OS/2), 780
Remove DOS subdirectory, service, 241

RENAME, 893
RENAME (OS/2), 781
Rename a file via FCB, 219
Rename file system service, 263, 602
REPLACE, 896
REPLACE (OS/2), 783
Resource management, 9-10
RESTORE, 894
RESTORE (OS/2), 782
RMDIR, 170, 895
RMDIR (OS/2), 784
RMSIZE (OS/2), 149, 534
ROM dates, IBM PC, 361
ROM-BIOS, 421
    FORMAT service, 488
    interrupt values, 491
Root directory, 158, 895
    number of files in, 443
RUN (OS/2), 149
Run-time library-callable routine, 278

S
Scan codes, keyboard, 651
Scheduler, OS/2, 140, 697-698, 832
Screen group, 821
Screen save program, 665-668
Sector notch, 417
Sector size, 109
Sectors, 419
Segment address, 349, 357-367
    DOS environment, 508
Segment attribute bits, OS/2, 381
Segment descriptor table (OS/2), 377
SEGMENTS (OS/2), 723
SELECT, 897
Select default disk drive, 214
Selector, OS/2, 377
Semaphores, 692, 836
    example of using, 736
Sequential file
    manipulation, 570
    read, 218
    write, 218

Services, system, 191-312
    DOS, 191-277
    OS/2, 278-312
Session
    definition of OS/2, 822
    terminating OS/2, 824
Session Manager, OS/2, 706, 745, 823
Sessions
    changing, 825
    OS/2, 743-747
SET, 503-523, 898
SET (OS/2), 72, 784
Set disk-transfer address, 220
Set disk verification, 234
Set interrupt vector, 226
Set relative record number field, 225
Set system time, 233
SETLOCAL (OS/2), 71, 785
SHARE, 899
Shared memory, 692, 836
SHELL, 125-126
SHIFT, 61, 899
SHIFT (OS/2), 785
Shutter, microfloppy, 417
Sides, disk, 419
Sign bit, integer, 352
Signal processing, 836
Software Development Kit, OS/2, 802
SORT, 81, 900
SORT (OS/2), 786
Spawn, 337-340
SPOOL (OS/2), 787
Spooled printing, 340-341
STACKS (DOS 3.3), 126-127
Standard aux device, 204
Standard input device, 202
Standard output device, 203
STARTUP.CMD (OS/2), 71, 829
Static linking, 713
Static modules, 137
Status values, 315-317
stderr, 99
stdin, 78

stdout, 78
Storage requirements, data type, 354
STRING1, 47
Subdirectories, 155-190
    maximum number of, 157
    service for changing, 242
    service for creating, 240
    service for removing, 241
SUBST, 183-185, 901
SUBST (OS/2), 787
SWAPPATH (OS/2), 150
Swapping, memory, 17, 816
SYS, 901
SYS (OS/2), 788
System configuration, 105-126
    OS/2, 134-153
System requirements, OS/2, 687
System service 36H, 320
System service 48H, 337
System services, 191-312
    DOS, 191-277
    file manipulation, 552
    OS/2, 278-312
    OS/2 API, 718
System time, get/set, 232-233

T
Terminate and stay resident programs, 236.
    (*See also* Memory resident)
    OS/2 and, 839
Terminating batch procedures, 35-37
Terminating programs, 199-201
THREADS (OS/2), 151
Threads, OS/2, 698-699
TIME, 902
TIME (OS/2), 788
Time slices, 8-15, 676
Time-critical programs, 834
Time-sharing, CPU, 10-15, 676
Timer function, OS/2, 733-736
Timer services, 840
TIMESLICE (OS/2), 152
Tracks, 419
TREE, 175-176, 465, 903
TREE (OS/2), 789
Trees, binary, 583

Turbo Pascal
    command-line processing from, 393-398
    interface routines, 272-277
TYPE, 903
TYPE (OS/2), 789
    program for using wildcards with, 619
    redirecting output of, 85
Type-ahead buffer, extending the, 651-655

U
Unique file, create, 269
User interface, improving with I/O redirection, 89-90

V
VDISK.SYS, 117-121
VER, 904
VER (OS/2), 790
VERIFY, 473, 904
VERIFY (OS/2), 790
Version, displaying in OS/2, 728
Version number, get DOS, 235
Versions, review of DOS, 3
VGA, impact on OS/2, 805
Video display mode, checking the current, 328-330
Virtual address space, 679, 818
Virtual addressing algorithm, 349
Virtual devices, 820
Virtual disk, 118
Virtual memory, 377, 679-685
    address space, 18
    advantages and disadvantages of, 685
    definition, 813
    management, 349
VOL, 906
VOL (OS/2), 791
Volume labels, checking, 320-321

W
Well-behaved programs, 669
Wild-card characters, DOS, 606-624
Windows, 701-703
    influence of Microsoft, 804
Write character to standard aux device, 205
Write character to standard printer device, 206

Write file handle, 557
Write to DOS file handle, 248
Write-protect notch, 414
Write-protect switch, 417

X
XCOPY, 906
XCOPY (OS/2), 791

The manuscript for this book was prepared and submitted to Osborne **McGraw-Hill** in electronic form. The acquisitions editor for this project was Jeffrey Pepper, the technical reviewers were Bill Murray and Chris Pappas, and the project editor was Fran Haselsteiner.

Text design by Judy Wohlfrom, using Garamond for both text body and display.

Cover art by Bay Graphics Design Associates. Cover supplier, Phoenix Color Corp. Book printed and bound by R.R. Donnelley & Sons Company, Crawfordsville, Indiana.

MAXIT™ increases your DOS addressable conventional memory beyond 640K for only $195.

- Add up to 256K above 640K for programs like FOXBASE+ and PC/FOCUS.

- Short card works in the IBM PC, XT, AT, and compatibles.

- Top off a 512 IBM AT's memory to 640K and add another 128K beyond that.

- Run resident programs like Sidekick above 640K.

- Add up to 96K above 640K to all programs, including PARADOX and 1-2-3.

- Compatible with EGA, Network, and other memory cards.

Break through the 640 barrier.
MAXIT increases your PC's available memory by making use of the vacant unused address space between 640K and 1 megabyte. (See illustrations)

Big gain—no pain.
Extend the productive life of your, IBM PC, XT, AT or compatible. Build more complex spreadsheets and databases without upgrading your present software.

Installation is a snap.
The MAXIT 256K memory card and software works automatically. You don't have to learn a single new command.

If you have questions, our customer support people will answer them, fast. MAXIT is backed by a one-year warranty and a 30-day money-back guarantee.

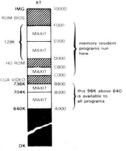

XT class machine (8088, 8086) w/640K and a CGA Color Monitor or a Compaq Type Dual Mode Display

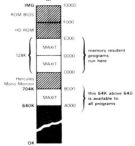

AT class machine (80286) w/640K and a Mono HERC Monitor

Order toll free 1-800-227-0900. MAXIT is just $195 plus $4 shipping, and applicable state sales tax. Buy MAXIT today and solve your PC's memory crisis. Call Toll free 1-800-227-0900 (In California 800-772-2531). Outside the U.S.A. call 1-415-548-2805. We accept VISA, MC.

DOS Command Card

[drive:][path]APPEND [drive:][path][;[drive:][path]...] or APPEND ;	Define or display the data file search path. MS-DOS version 3.2
[drive:][path]ASSIGN [drive1 [=] drive2 [...]]	Route disk I/O request for drive 1 to drive 2
[drive:][path]ATTRIB [+R¦-R][+A¦−A] [drive:][path]filename[.ext]	Set the file's read-only and archive- attribute bits
[drive:][path]BACKUP [drive:[path][filename[.ext]] d: [/S][/M][/A][/D:mm-dd-yy]	Back up one or more files to another disk
BREAK [ON¦OFF]	Allow or inhibit DOS CTRL-BREAK checking when DOS functions finish
CHCP [codepage] DOS 3.3.	Change code page.
CHDIR [drive:][path] or CD [drive:[path]	Change or display the current directory on the specified drive
[drive:][path]CHKDSK [drive:][path][filename[.ext]] [/F][/V]	Analyze and (optionally) repair directories, files, and the FAT
CLS	Clear the screen display
[drive:][path]COMMAND [drive:][path][/P][/C string][/E:nnnnn]	Invoke a secondary command processor
[drive:][path]COMP [drive:][path][filename[.ext]] [drive:][path][filename[.ext]]	Compare the contents of the files specified
COPY [/A][/B] [drive:][path]filename[.ext] [/A][/B] [+[[,,]drive:][path]filename[.ext][/A][/B]...] [drive:][path][filename[.ext]][/A][/B][/V]	Copy the contents of the source file(s) to the target file(s)
CTTY device_name	Modify standard input (stdin) to point to an alternate device
DATE [mm-dd-yy] ¦ [dd-mm-yy] ¦ [yy-mm-dd]	Set or display the current system date
DEL [drive:][path]filename[.ext]	Delete the specified file names from disk
DIR [drive:][path][filename[.ext]][/P][/W]	List the files as specified
[drive:][path]DISKCOMP [drive1: [drive2:]] [/1][/8]	Compare the contents of the disks in drive 1 and in drive 2
[drive:][path]DISKCOPY [drive1: [drive2:]][/1]	Copy the contents of the disk in drive 1 to the disk in drive 2
ECHO [ON¦OFF¦message]	Allow or suppress the screen display of DOS command names as the command executes within a BAT file
ERASE [drive:][path]filename[.ext]	Delete the specified file names from disk
[drive:][path]EXE2BIN [drive:][path]filename[.ext] [drive:][path][filename[.ext]]	Convert an EXE file specified by the first file name to a COM file
[drive:][path]FASTOPEN drive:[numfiles]	Directs DOS to set aside memory to remember the location of recently used files and directo- ries. numfiles must be in range 10-9999. Default 34. DOS 3.3

[drive:][path]FDISK	Define fixed-disk partitions
[drive:][path]FIND [/V][/C][/N] "string" [[drive:][path][filename[.ext]]	Display all of the lines that contain the specified string
FOR %%variable IN (set) DO command	Allow iterative processing of DOS commands
[drive:][path]FORMAT drive:[/S][/1][/V][/B][/4]	Format the disk in the specified drive
GOTO label_name	Allow branching within BAT files
[drive:][path]GRAFTABL	Load software to support the display of extended ASCII characters for the color/graphics adapter
[drive:][path]GRAPHICS [printer_type][/R][/B]	Load software to print graphics
IF [NOT] condition command	Allow conditional batch processing condition is one of the following: ERRORLEVEL number string1==string2 EXIST [drive:][path]filename[.ext]
[drive:][path]JOIN [drive: /D] ¦ [drive: path]	Connect a disk drive to a directory
[drive:][path]KEYBxx	Load software for a foreign keyboard
[drive:][path]LABEL [drive:] [volume_label]	Create or modify an 11-character volume label
MKDIR [drive:][path] or MD [drive:][path]	Create the specified subdirectory
[drive:][path]MODE LPT#[:][n][,[m][,P]] or [drive:][path]MODE n or [drive:][path]MODE [n],m[,T] or [drive:][path]MODE COM#[:]baud[,[parity][,[databits] [,[stopbits][,P]]]] or [drive][path]MODE LPT#[:]=COM#	Set the characteristics of the system printer, monitor, or asynchronous communications adapter
[drive:][path]MORE	Display data obtained from standard input to standard output a screen at a time
[drive:][path]NLSFUNC[[drive:][path]filename[.ext]]	Must be invoked before CCHP to specify the location of a COUNTRY.SYS file containing code-page support. DOS 3.3.
PATH [[drive:]path[;[drive:]path]...]] or	Define the optional command search path

DOS Command Card

PATH ;

[drive:][path]PRINT
[/B:buffersize][/C][/D:device_name]
[/M:maxticks][/P][/Q:maxentries]
[/S:timeslice][T]
[/U:busyticks]
[[drive:][path]filename[.ext]...]

Install the DOS print queue and print the
specified file(s)

PAUSE [remark]

Suspend BAT processing and display a
prompt for the user to
Strike a key when ready...

PROMPT [prompt-string]

Set the system prompt as specified. The
following metastrings can be used:

    $$ Dollar-sign character
    $_ carriage return linefeed
    $B ¦ character
    $D System date
    $E ESCape character
    $G > character
    $H Delete previous character
    $L < character
    $N Default-drive letter
    $P Current directory
    $Q = character
    $T System time
    $V DOS version number

[drive:][path]RECOVER
[drive:][path]filename[.ext] ¦ [drive:]

Recover the specified file(s) or disk drive

REM [remark]

Display remarks from within a BAT file

REN[AME] [drive:][path]filename[.ext]
filename[.ext]

Rename the file provided as specified

[drive:][path]REPLACE
[drive:][path]filename[.ext]
[drive:][path][/A][/P][/R][/S][/W]

Allow selective replacement/addition of
files from the source to the target location

[drive:][path]RESTORE drive:
[drive:][path]filename[.ext][/S][/P]

Restore the specified file(s) from the
back-up device

RMDIR [drive:]path ¦ RD [drive:]path

Remove the specified subdirectory

[drive:][path]SELECT [[A: ¦ [B:]
drive:[path]] country keyboard

Create a DOS disk with the specified foreign-country
support

SET [name=[string]]

Define an item in the command environment

[drive:][path]SHARE
[/F:filespace][/L:numlocks]

Install file-sharing software

SHIFT

Shift the command line parameters %0-%n
left one parameter

[drive:][path]SORT [/R][/+ column]

Sort and display data received from
standard input

[drive:][path]SUBST [drive: drive:path] ¦
[drive: /D]

Substitute a DOS path name with a disk-
drive specifier

[drive:][path]SYS drive:	Copy the system files to the specified disk, making it bootable
TIME [hh:mm[:ss[.nn]]]	Set or display the system time
[drive:][path]TREE [drive:][/F]	Display all of the directory paths on a disk and (optionally) the files that they contain
TYPE [drive:][path]filename[.ext]	Display the contents of the specified file
VER	Display the DOS version number
VERIFY [ON ¦ OFF]	Enable or disable disk-write verification
VOL [drive:]	Display the 11-character volume label of the specified drive

[drive:][path]XCOPY
[drive:][path]filename[.ext]
[drive:][path][filename[.ext]][/A][/D:mm-
dd-yy][/E][/M]
[/P][/S][/V][/W]

or

[drive:][path]XCOPY
[drive:]path[filename[.ext]]
[drive:][path][filename[.ext]][/A][/D:mm-
dd-yy][/E][/M]
[P][/S][/V][/W]

or

[drive:][path]XCOPY
drive:[path][filename[.ext]]
[drive:][path][filename[.ext]][/A][/D:mm-
dd-yy][/E][/M]
[/P][/S][/V][/W]

Provide selective copies of the specified file(s) to the target destination. DOS version 3.2

CONFIG.SYS Entries

BREAK=[ON¦OFF] default OFF
BUFFERS=n default 2 for PC 3 for AT
COUNTRY=nnn
DEVICE=[drive:][path]filename[.ext]
FCBS=n,n default 4,1
FILES=n default 8
LASTDRIVE=letter default E
SHELL=[drive:][path]filename[.ext]
STACKS=frames, size default 9,128